MW01707909

Hands-On Microsoft Windows Server 2003 Administration

Dan DiNicolo

THOMSON
COURSE TECHNOLOGY

Australia • Canada • Mexico • Singapore • Spain • United Kingdom • United States

THOMSON
COURSE TECHNOLOGY

Hands-On Microsoft Windows Server 2003 Administration
is published by Course Technology

Senior Editor:
William Pitkin III

Product Manager:
Charles G. Blum

Production Editor:
Tim Wood

Developmental Editor:
Ralph Moore

Manufacturing Coordinator:
Trevor Kallop

MQA Technical Leader:
Nicole Ashton

Product Marketing Manager:
Jason Sakos

Associate Product Manager:
Tim Gleeson

Editorial Assistant:
Nick Lombardi

Cover Design:
Julie Malone

Text Designer:
GEX Publishing Services

Compositor:
GEX Publishing Services

COPYRIGHT © 2003 Course Technology, a division of Thomson Learning, Inc. Thomson Learning™ is a trademark used herein under license.

Printed in the United States of America

2 3 4 5 6 7 8 9 GLOB 04

For more information, contact Course Technology, 25 Thomson Place, Boston, Massachusetts, 02210.

Or find us on the World Wide Web at: www.course.com

ALL RIGHTS RESERVED. No part of this work covered by the copyright hereon may be reproduced or used in any form or by any means—graphic, electronic, or mechanical, including photocopying, recording, taping, Web distribution, or information storage and retrieval systems—without the written permission of the publisher.

For permission to use material from this text or product, contact us by
Tel (800) 730-2214
Fax (800) 730-2215
www.thomsonrights.com

Disclaimer
Course Technology reserves the right to revise this publication and make changes from time to time in its content without notice.

ISBN 0-619-18611-9

BRIEF

Contents

CHAPTER ONE
Windows Server 2003 Network Administration 1

CHAPTER TWO
Managing Windows Server 2003 Hardware and Software 31

CHAPTER THREE
Administering Active Directory 55

CHAPTER FOUR
Managing Group Policy 93

CHAPTER FIVE
Administering File Resources 139

CHAPTER SIX
Managing Printers, Publishing, Auditing, and Disk Resources 169

CHAPTER SEVEN
Administering Web Resources in Windows Server 2003 215

CHAPTER EIGHT
Administering TCP/IP 259

CHAPTER NINE
Administering DNS 303

CHAPTER TEN
Monitoring and Troubleshooting Windows Server 2003 347

CHAPTER ELEVEN
Administering Remote Access Services 391

GLOSSARY 445

INDEX 455

TABLE OF

Contents

INTRODUCTION

CHAPTER ONE
Windows Server 2003 Network Administration **1**
Network Administration Overview 2
Installing and Maintaining the Operating System 2
Administering Active Directory 2
Administering File and Print Resources 3
Administering Internet Resources 3
Administering the Network Infrastructure 3
Monitoring and Troubleshooting Windows Server 2003 4
Administering Routing and Remote Access Services 4
Network Administration Procedures 4
Network Troubleshooting Process 4
Windows Server 2003 Management Tools 5
The Secondary Logon Feature 13
Additional Administrator Utilities 15
Introduction to Windows Server 2003 Active Directory 16
Active Directory Objects 16
The Active Directory Schema 17
Active Directory Components 17
Active Directory Communication Standards 21
The Active Directory Physical Structure 22
Chapter Summary 23
Key Terms 24
Review Questions 25
Case Projects 29

CHAPTER TWO
Managing Windows Server 2003 Hardware and Software **31**
Planning the Installation 32
Assessing the Hardware and Software Needs 32
Accessing the BIOS Configuration 33
Verifying Hardware and Software Compatibility 34
Installing and Configuring Hardware Devices 36
Configuring Driver Signing Options 42
Installing and Managing Windows Server 2003 Updates Using Service Packs and Hot Fixes 48
Slipstreaming Windows Server 2003 Service Packs 50
Chapter Summary 50
Key Terms 51
Review Questions 51
Case Projects 53

CHAPTER THREE
Administering Active Directory **55**
Administering Active Directory Objects 56
Exploring Active Directory Users and Computers 56
Creating Organizational Units 59
Creating New User Accounts 62
Creating Computer Accounts 67
Moving Active Directory Objects 68
Creating Group Objects 69

Group Types 70
Group Scopes 70
Creating Group Objects 72
Modifying Group Memberships 73
Understanding the Built-in Local Groups 75
Managing Security Groups 78
Administering Permissions in Active Directory 80
Active Directory Object Permissions 81
Permission Inheritance 83
Delegating Authority Over Active Directory Objects 84
Managing Active Directory Replication 85
Replication Components and Processes 86
Identifying Replication Problems 86
Chapter Summary 87
Key Terms 87
Review Questions 89
Case Projects 91

CHAPTER FOUR
Managing Group Policy 93
Introduction to Group Policy 94
Creating a Group Policy Object 94
Application of Group Policy 98
Controlling User Desktop Settings 98
Managing Security with Group Policy 100
Using the Security Configuration Manager Tools with Group Policy 107
Analyzing the Preconfigured Security Templates 109
Security Configuration and Analysis 112
Assigning Scripts and Redirecting Folders 115
Managing Group Policy Inheritance 119
Configuring Block Policy Inheritance, No Override, and Filtering 122
Troubleshooting Group Policy Settings 125
Deploying Software Using Group Policy 128
Software Preparation 128
Deployment 129
Software Maintenance 131
Software Removal 132
Chapter Summary 133
Key Terms 133
Review Questions 134
Case Projects 137

CHAPTER FIVE
Administering File Resources 139
Creating and Managing Shared Folders 140
Using Windows Explorer To Create a Shared Folder 140
Using Computer Management to Create a Shared Folder 143
Managing Shared Folder Permissions 146
Integrating Shared Folders with NTFS Permissions 149
NTFS File and Directory Permissions Concepts and Rules 149
Special NTFS Permissions 151
Combining Share and NTFS Permissions 155
Configuring File Encryption 156
Monitoring Access to Shared Folders 158
Configuring and Managing a Distributed File System 160
DFS Models 161
Managing DFS 162
Chapter Summary 163
Key Terms 164
Review Questions 164
Case Projects 167

CHAPTER SIX
Managing Printers, Publishing, Auditing, and Disk Resources 169
Creating and Modifying Shared Printer Resources 170
Adding a Printer as a Local Print Device 170
Adding a Printer as a Network Print Device 173
Configuring an Existing Printer 174
Setting Up and Updating Client Computers 179
Troubleshooting Printers 180
Publishing Resources in Active Directory 181
Publishing Shared Folders into Active Directory 182
Publishing Printers into Active Directory 184
Searching for Objects in Active Directory 187
Auditing Access to Shared Resources 189
Configuring Auditing 190
Analyzing Security Logs 194
Configuring the Event Viewer 197
Managing Data Storage 199
Basic versus Dynamic Disks 199
Configuring Volumes 200
Disk Quotas 204
Managing File and Folder Compression 206
Chapter Summary 208
Key Terms 208
Review Questions 209
Case Projects 212

CHAPTER SEVEN
Administering Web Resources in Windows Server 2003 215
Installing and Configuring Internet Information Services 216
Installing Internet Information Services 216
Architectural Changes in IIS 6.0 221
Configuring Web Server Properties 222
Creating and Configuring Web-Site Virtual Servers 226
Modifying Web-Site Properties 229
Creating Virtual Directories 232
Configuring Authentication for Web Sites 234
Anonymous Access 235
Basic Authentication 235
Digest Authentication 235
Integrated Windows Authentication 235
.NET Passport Authentication 236
Configuring Server Certificates and Secure Sockets Layer 237
Configuring FTP Virtual Servers 238
File Transfer Protocol 239
Configuring FTP Properties 239
Creating an FTP Site Virtual Server 241
Updating and Maintaining Security for an IIS Server 243
Resource Permissions 244
IP Address and Domain Name Security 245
Starting and Stopping Services 246
Backing Up the IIS Configuration 246
Creating and Modifying Web Folders 248
Installing and Using Remote Administration (HTML) tools 251
Troubleshooting Web Client Connectivity Problems 253
Client Access Problems 253
Chapter Summary 254
Key Terms 254
Review Questions 255
Case Projects 258

CHAPTER EIGHT
Administering TCP/IP **259**
Understanding TCP/IP 260
TCP/IP Architecture 260
The TCP/IP Protocol Stack 260
Installing TCP/IP 263
Configuring TCP/IP on Windows Server 2003 Computers 265
Configuring Static IP Addresses 266
Configuring IP Addresses Dynamically 267
Automatic Private IP Addressing 267
Troubleshooting TCP/IP and Network Connectivity 269
Verifying TCP/IP Configurations 269
Verifying Network Connectivity 271
Administering DHCP in Windows Server 2003 280
Installing a DHCP Server 281
Configuring DHCP Scopes 282
Authorizing a DHCP Server 289
Using DHCP Options 291
Configuring DHCP in a Routed Network 293
DHCP and DNS Integration 296
Maintaining DHCP Services 297
Chapter Summary 297
Key Terms 297
Review Questions 298
Case Projects 301

CHAPTER NINE
Administering DNS **303**
DNS Fundamentals 304
Basics of DNS 304
The Name Resolution Process 306
Installing DNS 306
Creating and Configuring DNS Zones 311
Standard DNS Zones 311
Active Directory–Integrated DNS Zones 318
DNS Resource Records 320
DNS Forwarders 324
Configuring Dynamic DNS Updates 326
Configuring DNS Client Settings 327
Testing the DNS Server 330
Name Resolution Files 332
The HOSTS File 332
The LMHOSTS File 334
Troubleshooting Name Resolution Problems 335
DNS Troubleshooting Utilities 337
Chapter Summary 340
Key Terms 341
Review Questions 342
Case Projects 344

CHAPTER TEN
Monitoring and Troubleshooting Windows Server 2003 **347**
Monitoring Windows Server 2003 Health and Performance 348
System Monitor 348
Performance Logs and Alerts 355
Event Viewer 359
Task Manager 362
Identify and Disable Unnecessary Services 366
Troubleshooting Windows Server 2003 Startup Procedures 369
The Windows Server 2003 Startup Process 370

Advanced Startup Options 373
Last Known Good Configuration 375
Recovery Console 376
Installing the Recovery Console 377
The Automated System Recovery Feature 378
The Windows Server 2003 Backup Utility 379
Backing Up and Restoring Files and Folders 379
Backing Up the System State 382
Chapter Summary 384
Key Terms 385
Review Questions 386
Case Projects 388

CHAPTER ELEVEN
Administering Remote Access Services 391
Configuring Remote Access and Virtual Private Network Connections 392
Configuring Dial-up Connections 396
Implementing Virtual Private Network Access 403
Configuring Remote Access Authentication 411
Configuring Encryption Protocols 414
Troubleshooting Remote Access 416
Implementing and Troubleshooting Remote Access Policies 416
Elements of a Remote Access Policy 416
Creating a Remote Access Policy 418
Troubleshooting Remote Access Policies 422
Configuring and Troubleshooting Network Address Translation 422
Installing NAT 423
Troubleshooting NAT 426
Configuring Internet Connection Sharing 426
Enabling ICS 427
Troubleshooting ICS 429
Configuring Terminal Services and Remote Desktop for Administration 430
Enabling Remote Desktop for Administration 430
Installing Terminal Services 432
Managing Terminal Services 433
Terminal Services Client Software 437
Chapter Summary 440
Key Terms 440
Review Questions 441
Case Projects 443

GLOSSARY 445

INDEX 455

Introduction

Welcome to *Hands-on Microsoft Windows Server 2003 Administration*. This book offers you real-world examples, interactive activities, and hundreds of hands-on projects that reinforce key concepts and help you prepare for a career in Microsoft network management. This book provides in-depth study of configuring, administering, and troubleshooting the services available within a network infrastructure. Throughout the book, we provide pointed review questions to reinforce the concepts introduced in each chapter. In addition to review questions, we provide detailed hands-on projects that let you experience firsthand the processes involved in Windows Server 2003 configuration and management. Finally, to put a real-world slant on the concepts introduced in each chapter, we provide case studies to prepare you for situations that must be managed in a live networking environment.

Intended Audience

Hands-On Microsoft Windows Server 2003 Administration is intended for people who have some experience administering and supporting Windows Server 2003 network and directory services. To best understand the material in this book, you should have a background in basic computer concepts and have worked with the material presented in Course Technology's *Hands-On Microsoft Windows XP Professional* and *Hands-On Microsoft Windows Server 2003*.

Chapter Descriptions

Chapter 1, "Windows Server 2003 Network Administration" provides an overview network administration and procedures, and introduces Windows Server 2003 Active Directory.

Chapter 2, "Managing Windows Server 2003 Hardware and Software" emphasizes the importance of planning an installation and assessing hardware and software needs in advance. It shows how to install and configure hardware devices, as well as how to install and manage Windows Server 2003 updates.

Chapter 3, "Administering Active Directory" outlines how to administer Active Directory Objects and group types. Various permissions in Active Directory are described and information is provided about how to manage Active Directory replication.

Chapter 4, "Managing Group Policy" introduces Group Policy and explains how to manage Group Policy inheritance and how to deploy software using Group Policy.

Chapter 5, "Administering File Resources", focuses on creating and managing shared folders and monitoring access to them. This chapter also teaches how to configure both shared folder and NTFS permissions, along with file encryption settings. In addition, configuring and organizing shared resources using the Distributed File System (DFS) is also explored.

Chapter 6, "Managing Printers, Publishing, Auditing, and Disk Resources" describes how to install and configure both local and network printers, as well as how to publish resources like shared folders and printers in Active Directory. It also focuses on how audit settings can be used to monitor access to network resources, and how to manage disk resources like volumes and quota settings on a Windows Server 2003 system.

Chapter 7, "Administering Web Resources in Windows Server 2003" outlines the new features of Internet Information Services (IIS) 6.0, and explains how to configure Windows Server 2003 as a Web or FTP server.

This chapter also outlines the various authentication and security settings that can be configured to make an IIS server or site more secure.

Chapter 8, "Administering TCP/IP" explains the functions of the TCP/IP protocol and how to configure TCP/IP on Windows Server 2003 computers, as well as how to use various utilities to troubleshoot TCP/IP and network connectivity.

Chapter 9, "Administering DNS" explains the purpose of the Domain Name System, as well as how the DNS service is installed and configured on Windows Server 2003. The chapter also takes a look at the utilities and methods that can be used to troubleshoot network name resolutions issues.

Chapter 10, "Monitoring and Troubleshooting Windows Server 2003" outlines issues involving monitoring Windows Server 2003 health and performance. It also discusses troubleshooting Windows Server 2003 startup procedures, advanced startup options, and troubleshooting methods.

Chapter 11, "Administering Remote Access Services" explains how to configure remote access and Virtual Private Network connections and how to implement and troubleshoot remote access policies. This chapter also outlines how to configure Network Address Translation (NAT), Internet Connection Sharing (ICS), along with Remote Desktop for Administration and Terminal Services for remote access.

Features and Approach

Hands-On Microsoft Windows Server 2003 Administration differs from other networking books in its unique hands-on approach and its orientation to real-world situations and problem solving. To help you comprehend how Microsoft Windows network management concepts and techniques are applied in real-world organizations, this book incorporates the following features:

- **Chapter Objectives**—Each chapter begins with a detailed list of the concepts to be mastered. This list gives you a quick reference to the chapter's contents and is a useful study aid.
- **Hands-on Activities**—Hands-on activities are incorporated throughout the text, giving you practice in setting up, managing, and troubleshooting a network system. The activities give you a strong foundation for carrying out network administration tasks in the real world. Because of the book's progressive nature, completing the hands-on activities in each chapter is essential before moving on to the end-of-chapter projects and subsequent chapters.
- **Chapter Summary**—Each chapter's text is followed by a summary of the concepts introduced in that chapter. These summaries provide a helpful way to recap and revisit the ideas covered in each chapter.
- **Key Terms** — All of the terms within the chapter that were introduced with boldfaced text are gathered together in the Key Terms list at the end of the chapter. This provides you with a method of checking your understanding of all the terms introduced.
- **Review Questions** — The end-of-chapter assessment begins with a set of review questions that reinforce the ideas introduced in each chapter. Answering these questions will ensure that you have mastered the important concepts.
- **Case Projects** — Finally, each chapter closes with a section that proposes certain situations. You are asked to evaluate the situations and decide upon the course of action to be taken to remedy the problems described. This valuable tool will help you sharpen your decision-making and troubleshooting skills, which are important aspects of network administration.
- **On the CD ROM** — On the CD-ROM you will find a free 180-day evaluation copy of Windows Server 2003 Enterprise Edition.

Text and Graphic Conventions

Additional information and exercises have been added to this book to help you better understand what's being discussed in the chapter. Icons throughout the text alert you to these additional materials. The icons used in this book are described below.

Tips offer extra information on resources, how to attack problems, and time-saving shortcuts.

Notes present additional helpful material related to the subject being discussed.

The Caution icon identifies important information about potential mistakes or hazards.

Each Hands-on Activity in this book is preceded by the hands-on icon.

Case project icons mark the end-of-chapter case projects, which are scenario-based assignments that ask you to independently apply what you have learned in the chapter.

Instructor's Resources

The following supplemental materials are available when this book is used in a classroom setting. All of the supplements available with this book are provided to the instructor on a single CD-ROM.

Electronic Instructor's Manual. The Instructor's Manual that accompanies this textbook includes Additional instructional material to assist in class preparation, including suggestions for classroom activities, discussion topics, and additional projects.

Solutions to all end-of-chapter material, including the Review Questions, and where applicable, Hands-on Projects and Discovery Exercises.

ExamView®. This textbook is accompanied by ExamView, a powerful testing software package that allows instructors to create and administer printed, computer (LAN-based), and Internet exams. ExamView includes hundreds of questions that correspond to the topics covered in this text, enabling students to generate detailed study guides that include page references for further review. The computer-based and Internet testing components allow students to take exams at their computers and also save the instructor time by grading each exam automatically.

PowerPoint presentations. This book comes with Microsoft PowerPoint slides for each chapter. These are included as a teaching aid for classroom presentation, to make available to students on the network for chapter review, or to be printed for classroom distribution. Instructors, please feel at liberty to add your own slides for additional topics you introduce to the class.

Figure files. All of the figures and tables in the book are reproduced on the Instructor's Resource CD, in bitmap format. Similar to the PowerPoint presentations, these are included as a teaching aid for classroom presentation, to make available to students for review, or to be printed for classroom distribution.

Minimum Lab Requirements

- **Hardware:**

Hardware Component	Windows Server 2003 Standard Edition
CPU	Pentium III 550 or higher
Memory	256 MB RAM
Disk Space	Minimum of two 4 GB partitions (C and D), with at least 500 MB of free space left on the drive
Drives	CD-ROM Floppy Disk
Networking	All lab computers should be networked and placed within groups of two. If you are completing the labs as a single user, two computers are recommended. Connect computers via a hub, switch, or crossover cable. Make sure to have Windows Server 2003-compatible network adapters. A connection to the Internet via some sort of NAT or Proxy server is assumed.

- **Software:**
  - **Windows Server 2003 Standard or Enterprise Edition**
- **Set Up Instructions:**

To successfully complete the lab exercises, set up classroom computers as listed below:

1. Install Windows Server 2003 onto drive C: of the instructor and student servers. The following specific parameters should be configured on individual servers during the installation process:

Parameter	Settings
Disk Partitioning	Create two 4 GB NTFS partitions during the installation process, C and D. Ensure that at least 500 MB of free space is left on the hard disk for student exercises. If the decision is made to install Windows XP Professional in a dual boot configuration, create an additional 2 GB NTFS partition for this purpose.
Computer Names	Instructor (first server), ServerXX (subsequent student servers)
Administrator Password	Password01
Components	Default Settings
Network Adapter	IP Address: 192.168.1.X. The instructor computer should be allocated a unique IP address on the same subnet as client computers. The suggested IP address for the Instructor machine is 192.168.1.100. Subnet Mask: 255.255.255.0 DNS: The IP address of the Instructor computer Default Gateway: The IP address for the classroom default gateway. If the Instructor computer will be used to provide Internet access via ICS or NAT, it will require a second network adapter card or modem.
Workgroup Name	workgroup

In the table above, "X" or "XX" should represent a unique number to be assigned to each student. For example, student "1" would be assigned a computer name of Server01 and an IP address of 192.168.1.1.

2. Once the installation process is complete, use Device Manager to ensure that all devices are functioning correctly. In some cases, it may be necessary to download and install additional drivers for devices listed with a yellow question mark icon.
3. Create a new folder named Source on drive D of all classroom servers. Copy the entire contents of the Windows Server 2003 CD to this folder on all servers.
4. Create a new folder named Shared on drive D of the Instructor computer only. Share this folder using the shared folder name Shared, and ensure that the Everyone group is granted the Full Control shared folder permission.
5. Copy the files SUPTOOLS.MSI and SUPPORT.CAB from the D:\Source\SUPPORT\TOOLS directory into the D:\Shared directory on the Instructor server.
6. Run dcpromo.exe on the Instructor computer to install Active Directory and DNS. Name the new domain (the first in a new forest) Dovercorp.net, ensure that both nonsecure and secure dynamic updates are allowed, and accept all other default options.
7. On the Instructor server, open Active Directory Users and Computers. Right-click the Dovercorp.net domain and click Raise Domain Functional Level. Change the domain functional level of the Instructor server only to Windows Server 2003. Students will change the functional levels of their own domains as part of a hands-on exercise.
8. After the previous steps are completed and theDovercorp.net domain is completely installed on the Instructor server, run dcpromo.exe on each student server to install Active Directory, making each a child domain of Dovercorp.net. Name the student domains DomainXX.Dovercorp.net, where XX is the student number assigned to each student. Once the process is completed on all classroom servers, all DNS zones should be switched to Primary Standard Zones (with nonsecure and secure dynamic updates still allowed) from the Active Directory integrated type that dcpromo.exe will create automatically. The Active Directory structure in the classroom once this is complete is illustrated in the figure below.

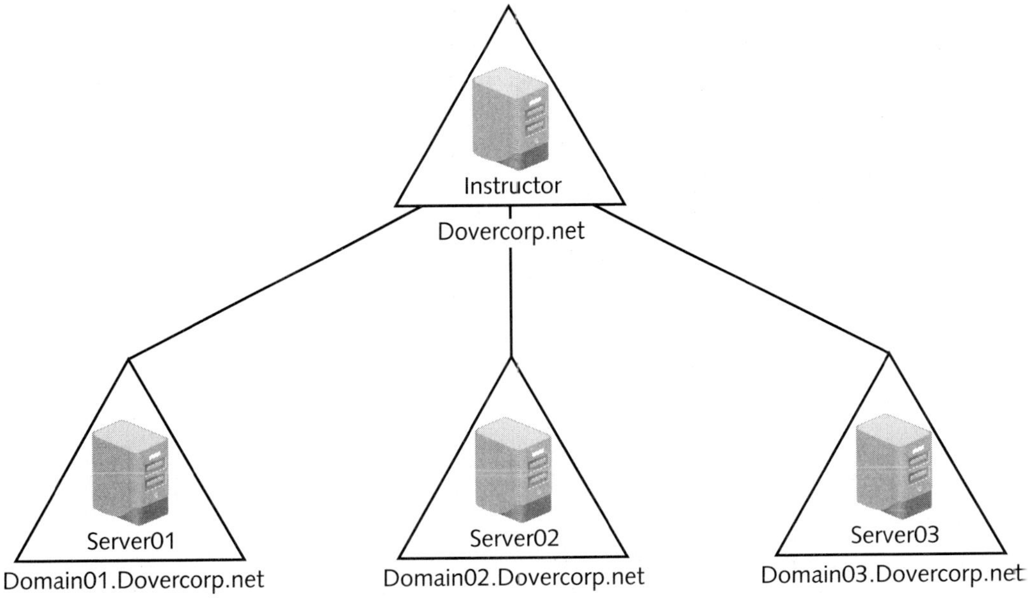

The Active Directory structure

9. In each child domain, use Active Directory Users and Computers to create a user account named AdminXX in the Users container, where XX corresponds to the student number assigned to each student. The password associated with this account should be Password01. This account should be added to the Domain Admins group in the same domain, as well as the Enterprise Admins group in the Dovercorp.net domain. Note that to add the user to the Enterprise Admins group, you will need to be logged on using the Administrator account from the Dovercorp.net domain.

10. On each server, edit the Default Domain Controllers Group Policy object to grant the Domain Users group the right to log on locally. This is accomplished by opening Active Directory Users and Computers, right-clicking the Domain Controllers OU, and clicking Properties. Click the Group Policy tab, click the Default Domain Controllers Policy, and then click Edit. In the Group Policy Object Editor window, browse to the Computer Configuration\Windows Settings\Security Settings\Local Policies\User Rights Assignment node. Double-click the Allow log on locally right, and then add the Domain Users group to the list.

CHAPTER

1

WINDOWS SERVER 2003 NETWORK ADMINISTRATION

After reading this chapter and completing the exercises, you will be able to:

- List the various tasks of a Windows Server 2003 Network administrator
- Understand general troubleshooting techniques
- Ease network management with the help of various Windows Server 2003 Administration Tools
- Explain Windows Server 2003 Active Directory concepts

Windows Server 2003 Network Administration consists of two major goals. The first goal is to ensure availability of network resources, such as files, folders, e-mail, and printers, to users whenever they need access. The second goal is to secure the network so that available resources are only accessible to users that have been granted the proper permissions. Most day-to-day network administration tasks focus on achieving these two goals to ensure an efficient and secure computer network infrastructure.

To acquire the skills needed to meet your network administration goals, you need to understand a number of basic concepts, from the account creation process to server and resource management. A Windows Server 2003 network administrator requires an understanding of **Active Directory (AD)** concepts and management, along with troubleshooting techniques. These objectives are covered in three parts throughout the chapter.

The first section of this chapter outlines the tasks network administrators are expected to understand and carry out to successfully manage a Windows Server 2003 network. This section provides a basic outline of the concepts and procedures covered in the subsequent chapters of this book.

It is very important for you to be able to quickly troubleshoot problems and resolve any issues that may interfere with your network resource availability and security goals. The second section of this chapter outlines a network troubleshooting process that can assist you. This section also introduces you to common Windows Server 2003 management tools for routine administration activities, such as creating **Microsoft Management Consoles (MMCs)** and using the secondary logon feature.

Because most network management tasks take place within a **domain** environment, it is also essential to understand the basic concepts of Windows Server 2003 Active Directory and how Active Directory influences your network management procedures. The final section of this chapter discusses basic Active Directory concepts to give you a solid foundation on which to build the rest of your network administration skills.

To become a successful Microsoft Certified Systems Administrator (MCSA) or Microsoft Certified Systems Engineer (MCSE), you need practical, hands-on experience with products like Microsoft Windows Server 2003. This text includes numerous hands-on activities and case studies to help ensure that you not only understand the theory behind the concepts covered but also that you feel comfortable carrying out common system administration tasks. To help simulate a real-world network environment, all of the activities in the text relate to a fictitious multinational organization called Dover Leasing Corporation, a property management company with a head office based in Boston. For the purpose of the activities and case projects, you have been hired by Dover Leasing Corporation as a junior network administrator, responsible for looking after the day-to-day administration of an Active Directory domain within their Windows Server 2003 network. The scenarios presented are designed to help you relate the concepts that you learn to tasks typically carried out by a system administrator in a corporate Windows Server 2003 environment.

Network Administration Overview

As a Windows Server 2003 Network administrator, you are expected to possess a wide range of networking knowledge. This knowledge can help you successfully complete the tasks needed to provide efficient and reliable network operations. Some of these tasks include:

- Installing and maintaining the operating system
- Administering Active Directory
- Administering file and print resources
- Administering Internet resources
- Administering the network infrastructure
- Monitoring and troubleshooting Windows Server 2003
- Administering **Routing and Remote Access Services (RRAS)**

Installing and Maintaining the Operating System

The first skill required to become a successful network administrator is installing the operating systems that your environment uses. You need to be able to install the client workstation operating systems, as well as install and configure the server environment. In the event that an installation fails, you have to be able to troubleshoot and resolve the cause of the failure. As security and software updates become available, you must also be able to efficiently install and manage the required service packs and hot fixes.

Note: Chapter 2 covers issues related to planning and installing Windows Server 2003. You also learn how to troubleshoot common installation problems and install and maintain software updates for computers running Windows Server 2003.

Administering Active Directory

One of the most important responsibilities related to Windows Server 2003 network management is administering Active Directory. This involves such tasks as creating or modifying user, computer, and group objects. In addition, you must also be able to manage Active Directory container and object permissions to make sure that only authorized users can access or manage the objects stored within Active Directory.

Active Directory enables you to easily enforce desktop restrictions and security or to deploy software through the use of **Group Policy**. This is a Windows Server 2003 feature that enables you to create policies that affect domain users and computers. Being able to create and troubleshoot group policies adds much to your value as a Windows Server 2003 network administrator.

Note

Chapters 3 and 4 cover managing users, groups, computers, and Group Policy objects within Active Directory. An Active Directory overview is offered later in this chapter to benefit those who do not have previous Active Directory knowledge.

Administering File and Print Resources

Many daily operations involve troubleshooting user access to files and printers. This can easily consume a large portion of your administrative duties as users contact you about printing problems or an inability to gain access to files that are needed on the network. It will be your job to plan and maintain the most efficient and secure way for users to work with the file and print resources available on the network.

Note

Chapters 5 and 6 cover configuring shared folders and printers for both a local network and for Web access.

Administering Internet Resources

The Internet has become one of the most important business tools available to an organization. Business-to-business (B2B) and business-to-consumer (B2C) online commerce opportunities require that network administrators not only understand local network management but also understand Internet administration as well. The first step in this task is to master the configuration options within the Windows Server 2003 Internet Information Services (IIS). Important concepts to understand include providing secure access to Internet-accessible resources, as well as troubleshooting client connectivity problems.

Note

Chapter 7 covers configuring and maintaining IIS.

Administering the Network Infrastructure

The network infrastructure consists of a number of network services and protocols that may require regular maintenance and periodic troubleshooting. Windows Server 2003 primarily uses the TCP/IP protocol for network communications throughout the infrastructure and the Internet. To properly administer and troubleshoot connectivity problems, a solid understanding of TCP/IP is required.

The most important service on a Windows Server 2003 network is the **Domain Name System (DNS)**, which provides name resolution and network service location capabilities to other Windows Server 2003 network servers and clients. Other services or hardware that may be present in your network include routers, Dynamic Host Configuration Protocol (DHCP) servers, and WINS servers. Each of these requires the administrator to be able to configure, monitor, and troubleshoot problems as they arise.

Note

Chapters 8 and 9 cover configuring and troubleshooting TCP/IP connectivity and related services.

Monitoring and Troubleshooting Windows Server 2003

Routine maintenance includes monitoring server health and system performance. This can be accomplished by using management tools such as System Monitor or Event Viewer. To assist in troubleshooting any problems that occur when you start a system, Windows Server 2003 also provides advanced troubleshooting tools such as Recovery Console and Safe Mode. Network administrators can become proactive and decrease disaster recovery time by learning how to use these tools to assist in management and recovery procedures.

> **Note** Chapter 10 covers the use of such tools as System Monitor, Event Viewer, and Task Manager. The Recovery Console and Safe Mode are also covered.

Administering Routing and Remote Access Services

Windows Server 2003 Routing and Remote Access Services (RRAS) includes a wide variety of features. Basic RRAS allow access to the company network using dial-up modems. For example, if users need to access the company network from home, they might use a modem to dial into the network to access the desired resources. Windows Server 2003 also includes such remote access features as **virtual private networking (VPN)**, **Internet connection sharing (ICS)**, **network address translation (NAT)**, and even a basic firewall. Windows Server 2003 also includes a feature called Remote Desktop for Administration, which was formerly known as Terminal Services in Remote Administration Mode. Remote Desktop for Administration enables administrators to network servers remotely, as if sitting in front of that server. Application Mode Terminal Services still exists to provide access to applications on network servers.

> **Note** Chapter 11 covers configuring various remote access connections such as dial-up and VPN connections.

Network Administration Procedures

Once the network is operational, you will inevitably run into connectivity or availability issues. There may be various reasons for network problems, including hardware failures, security or virus attacks, and file corruption. Being able to quickly solve these problems is a valuable asset.

Network Troubleshooting Process

A major task for you, as a network administrator, is troubleshooting computer and network problems. A systematic approach to troubleshooting helps to define the exact problem and quickly solve it.

A successful troubleshooting process involves the following steps:

1. Define the problem.
2. Gather detailed information about what has changed.
3. Devise a plan to solve the problem.
4. Implement the plan and observe the results.
5. Document all changes and results.

Define the Problem

Problems are often indicated by some cryptic error message or a general complaint from a user. The first step is to ask questions of the user having the problem. Be specific in your questioning; you want answers from the user on exactly what the problem is and how long the problem has been evident. If possible, you should also try to recreate the problem in a test lab so you can attempt various solutions.

Note: Windows Server 2003 provides the net utility to assist you in identifying specific error messages. At a command prompt, type "net helpmsg *number*" (where *number* is the number associated with the error message) to retrieve additional information about a specific error message. In addition, Windows Server 2003 includes a new and improved Help & Support Center that you can access directly from the Start menu. You can also access the Microsoft Help and Support Web site at *support.microsoft.com* to learn the specifics on various error messages.

Gather Detailed Information About What Has Changed

Once the problem is identified, it is important to find out what has changed recently to cause the issue. Important factors to consider include whether any new components have been installed on the computer, who has access to the computer and might have changed previous settings, and whether any software or service patches that were installed recently might be causing conflicts. Knowing about any changes that have occurred makes it easier for you to devise a plan to solve the problem, which is the next step in the troubleshooting process.

Devise a Plan To Solve the Problem

Before making any additional changes to the system, you should devise a plan to ensure that no additional problems are created. A rollback strategy should also be in place in case the proposed fix does not work.

When devising the plan to solve the problem, you should consider the following:

- Interruptions to the network or its components (e.g., restarting the server)
- Possible changes to the network security policy (e.g., permission or group membership changes, firewall adjustments, etc.)
- The need to document all changes and troubleshooting steps

Implement the Plan and Observe Results

Once you have devised a plan, be sure to notify all users on the network if network availability will be interrupted. As you implement your plan, do not make too many configuration changes at one time. It can be difficult to roll back or test a specific step if too many changes have taken place.

Once you implement your plan, if the problem still occurs, you must document what was tested or adjusted up to this point and start the troubleshooting process all over again.

Document All Changes and Results

It is essential that you document all troubleshooting steps, results, and configuration changes to keep track of what has changed on the network. If the problem occurs again, the documentation helps explain the possible cause and provide the solution that was discovered during the previous troubleshooting phase.

Windows Server 2003 Management Tools

As you read through all of the tasks that a network administrator performs, it becomes clear that any tool that can assist in making network management more efficient is valuable. Windows Server 2003 provides a number of features and utilities to assist in your daily management tasks. Some of these features include:

- The **Microsoft Management Console (MMC)**
- The secondary logon feature
- Additional management utilities, such as the Task Scheduler or the netdiag command

Before undertaking any administrative tasks on Windows Server 2003, the network administrator is required to log on to the server. Although the logon process is very similar to previous Windows versions, the steps involved in shutting down or restarting a server have changed. Windows Server 2003 includes a feature known as the Shutdown Event Tracker that logs each time a server is shut down or restarted, allowing you to include comments on why the action took place. This information is logged as event 1074 in the Event Viewer system log. In Activity 1-1, you will log on to Windows Server 2003 for the first time and change your password. In Activity 1-2, you will restart the server to generate a 1074 event, and in Activity 1-3, you will view that event in the Event Viewer system log.

Activity 1-1: Logging on to Windows Server 2003 and Changing Your Password

Time Required: 10 minutes

Objective: Perform the Windows Server 2003 logon procedure.

Description: To gain access to the Windows Server 2003 domain environment, all users must be authenticated. By default, the ability to log on to a domain controller is restricted to members of the Administrators, Account Operators, Backup Operators, Print Operators, and Server Operators groups. As a new network administrator at Dover Leasing, your user account has been made a member of the Domain Admins group, which is by default a member of the Administrators group. To log on successfully, you are required to provide a valid user name and password and must specify the domain in which your account exists. In this activity, you will first log on to Windows Server 2003 and then choose a new password to make your account more secure.

1. At the Welcome to Windows logon screen, press **Ctrl+Alt+Del**.
2. In the User name text box, type **Admin*XX***, where *XX* is your assigned student number.
3. In the Password text box, type **Password01**.
4. If the Log on to drop-down box is not visible, click the **Options** button to view it.
5. In the Log on to drop-down box, ensure that **DOMAIN*XX*** is selected, where *XX* is your assigned student number.
6. Click **OK** to log on to Windows Server 2003.
7. Click **Start**, point to **Administrative Tools**, and click **Active Directory Users and Computers**.
8. Click the **plus sign (+)** next to your domain name to expand the contents.
9. Click the **Users** folder to view its contents.
10. Right-click the **Admin*XX*** account, and click **Reset Password**.
11. In the Reset Password dialog box, type **PasswordXX**, where XX is your assigned student number, in the New password text box, and then type it again in the Confirm password text box. Ensure that the **User must change password at next logon** check box is not selected, and click **OK**.
12. Click **OK** to close the dialog box confirming that the password was changed.
13. Exit Active Directory Users and Computers.

Activity 1-2: Restarting Windows Server 2003

Time Required: 10 minutes

Objective: Restart Windows Server 2003.

Description: A server running Windows Server 2003 will sometimes need to be restarted after installing new software or services, or to perform hardware upgrades and maintenance, or because of security issues. Because the Shutdown Event Tracker feature has been implemented in Windows Server 2003, the IT manager at Dover Leasing has decided to implement a new policy where all administrators must provide an appropriate comment explaining the reasons why a server was shut down or restarted. In this activity, you are asked to restart the server to gain a better understanding of this new process.

1. Click **Start** and then click **Shut Down**.
2. In the Shut Down Windows dialog box, click **Restart** in the What do you want the computer to do? drop-down box. The Shut Down Windows dialog box is illustrated in Figure 1-1.

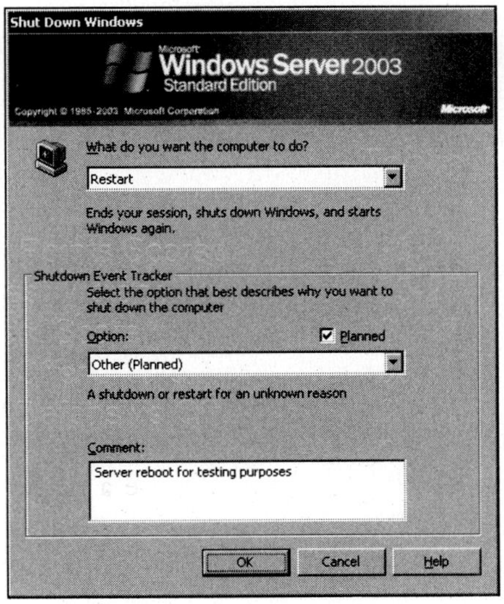

Figure 1-1 The Shut Down Windows dialog box

3. In the Shutdown Event Tracker section, ensure that the **Planned** check box is checked.
4. On the Option drop-down list, ensure that **Other (Planned)** is selected.
5. In the Comment field, type **Server reboot for testing purposes**.
6. Click **OK** to restart the server.

Activity 1-3: Viewing Shutdown Events in the Event Viewer System Log

Time Required: 10 minutes

Objective: Use Event Viewer to view server shutdown events.

Description: All server shutdown events in Windows Server 2003 are recorded as event 1074 in the Event Viewer system log. The IT manager at Dover Leasing wants you to be familiar with the process of checking the system log on a daily basis to determine and document all of the reasons why a server was shut down or restarted. In this activity, you will log on to your server and use Event Viewer to locate event 1074 in the system log.

1. Log on to your server using the **AdminXX** user name and your new password. Review Activity 1-1 if necessary.
2. Click **Start**, point to **Administrative Tools**, and click **Event Viewer**.
3. Click **System**. The contents of the system log appear in the details pane of Event Viewer.
4. Use the Event column to find the most recent Information event with identification number 1074. Double-click the event to view its details.
5. Read the event description data. Notice that both the shutdown type and comment from the last shutdown event are documented.

6. Close the Event Properties window.
7. With the most recent 1074 event still selected, click the **Event** column header to group all events with the same identification number together.
8. Double-click on a different 1074 event to view its contents.
9. Close the Event Properties window, and exit Event Viewer.

The Microsoft Management Console

The MMC is a customizable management framework that can host a number of management tools, thus providing a single, unified application for network administration. The management tools that are added to the interface are called **snap-ins** and can be obtained from Microsoft or a variety of third-party companies. For example, if you need to create a console to administer your DNS and DHCP servers, you might add the DNS and DHCP snap-ins to an MMC interface. This would provide you with an administration tool to manage both DNS and DHCP.

The advantage of using the MMC is that you can add or remove management tools as necessary and save custom tools for use by authorized administrators. The console is saved as a **Management Saved Console (MSC)** file with the .msc extension.

The supplied Windows Server 2003 Administration Tools, such as Computer Management or Active Directory Users and Computers, are actually prebuilt MMCs with various snap-ins added. In Activity 1-4, you will create and save a customized MMC that includes both the Event Viewer and Device Manager snap-ins.

Note: Perform a search for *.msc to view all of the prebuilt consoles available in Windows Server 2003.

Activity 1-4: Creating a Customized MMC

Time Required: 10 minutes

Objective: Create a customized MMC.

Description: The MMC is the common environment in which all of the Windows Server 2003 administrative tools run. Although these tools are individually available from the Administrative Tools section of the Start menu, administrative tasks can be simplified by grouping commonly used tools into a single customized MMC. The IT manager at Dover Leasing has asked you to create and save a custom MMC to be used to access both Event Viewer and Device Manager. In this activity, you will create a custom MMC and save it to your desktop for more convenient access.

1. Click **Start**, click **Run**, and then type **mmc** in the Open text box. Click **OK**. Figure 1-2 shows an empty MMC window.

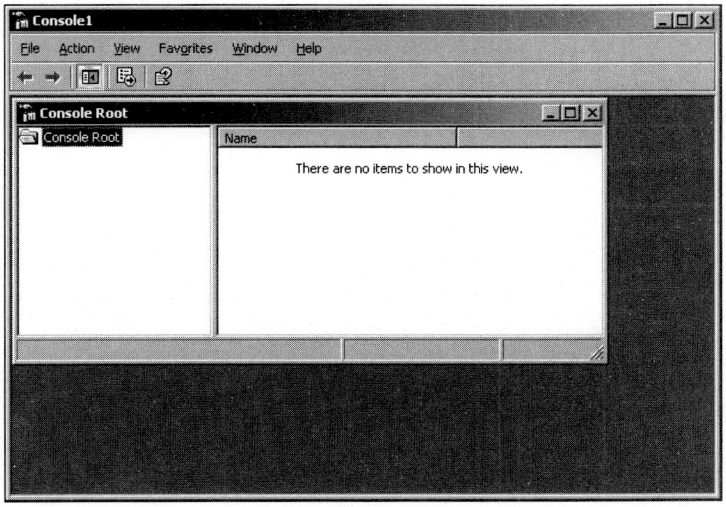

Figure 1-2 An empty MMC

2. Click the **File** menu, and click **Add/Remove Snap-in**. Figure 1-3 shows ar open Add/Remove Snap-in dialog box.

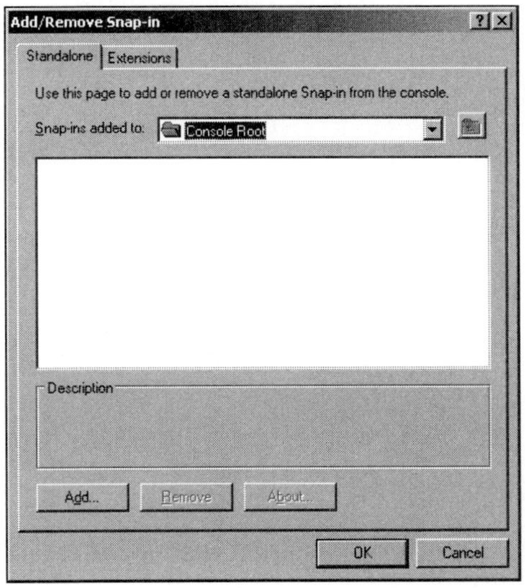

Figure 1-3 The Add/Remove Snap-in dialog box

3. Click the **Add** button to open the Add Standalone Snap-in dialog box listing the available snap-ins, as shown in Figure 1-4.

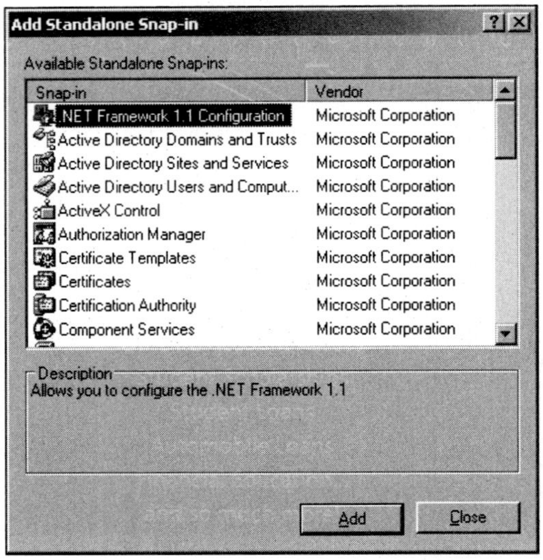

Figure 1-4 The Add Standalone Snap-in dialog box

4. From the list of available snap-ins, click **Event Viewer** and click **Add**. When the Select Computer dialog box opens, make sure that the **Local computer** radio button is selected, as shown in Figure 1-5, and click **Finish**.

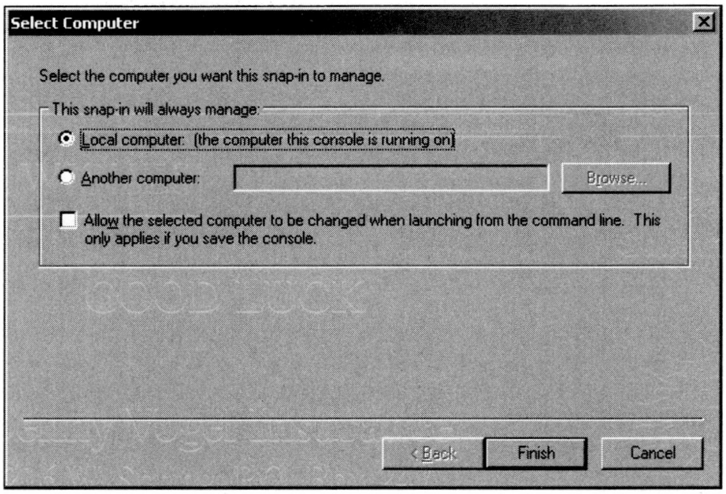

Figure 1-5 Selecting the snap-in focus

5. Click **Device Manager** on the list of available snap-ins and click **Add**. In the Device Manager dialog box, ensure that the **Local computer** radio button is selected and click **Finish**.
6. Click **Close** in the Add Standalone Snap-in dialog box.
7. Click **OK** in the Add/Remove Snap-in dialog box.
8. To save the console, click the **File** menu, and click **Save As**. In the **Save in** drop-down box, select your desktop, type the file name **My Console**, and click **Save**. A finished console is shown in Figure 1-6.
9. Close the My Console window. If prompted to save changes, click **Yes**.

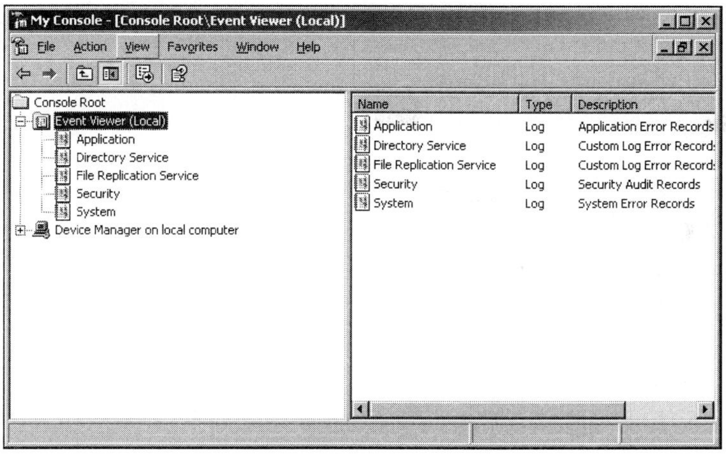

Figure 1-6 A customized MMC

One of the most useful features of the MMC is that it enables you to manage both local and remote computers. By default, most MMC snap-ins will be focused on the computer on which the console is running. However, the focus of many snap-ins can be changed to point to remote clients or servers. For example, an administrator in a domain environment could easily view the Event Viewer system logs on a remote Windows Server 2003 by changing the focus of the Event Viewer snap-in to point to that server. The remote administration capabilities supported by the MMC provide network administrators with a single point of management for common monitoring, configuration, and troubleshooting tasks. In Activity 1-5, you will use remote management capabilities of the MMC to view information stored on a remote computer.

Activity 1-5: Using the MMC To View Information on a Remote Computer

Time Required: 10 minutes

Objective: Use the remote administration capabilities of the MMC.

Description: Because your domain at Dover Leasing includes many Windows Server 2003 servers, the IT manager wants you to be familiar with the procedure for switching the focus of MMC snap-ins to other computers. This will allow you to gather information and carry out administrative tasks on remote computers using a single management utility. In this activity, you will use the remote management capabilities of the MMC to view Event Viewer system logs on another computer.

1. Double-click the **My Console.msc** file you created in Activity 1-4 to open it. Right-click the **Event Viewer** icon and click **Connect to another computer**.
2. In the Select Computer dialog box, ensure that the **Another computer** radio button is selected and type the name of your partner's computer in the Another computer text box. This should be in the format SERVER*XX*, where *XX* is your partner's student number. Click **OK** to continue.
3. With the focus of Event Viewer now changed to your partner's computer, expand Event Viewer by clicking the **plus sign (+)** to the left. Browse through the system and application logs on the remote computer.
4. Right-click the **Event Viewer** icon and click **Connect to another computer**. In the Select Computer dialog box, ensure that the **Local computer** radio button is selected, and click **OK**. Close the MMC console without saving any changes.

Some of the MMC snap-in tools may be confusing to an inexperienced administrator. To better understand these tools, you can create a **taskpad** view of the console. Taskpad views simplify administrative procedures by providing you with a graphical representation of the tasks that can be performed in an MMC.

See Figure 1-7 for an example of a taskpad view of the Services snap-in. In Activity 1-6, you will create a taskpad that provides access to the Event Viewer system log.

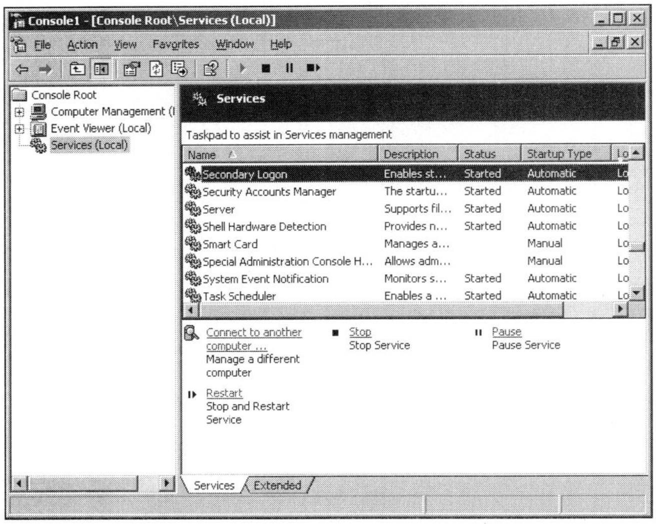

Figure 1-7 A taskpad view of the Services snap-in

Activity 1-6: Creating a Taskpad

Time Required: 15 minutes

Objective: Create a taskpad to simplify administrative tasks.

Description: Although the MMC provides access to all of the Windows Server 2003 administrative tools, situations may arise where users not familiar with the various snap-ins may be asked to carry out a task. Taskpads enable you to define a simplified environment from which shortcuts to common tasks can be created. The IT manager at Dover Leasing has asked you to begin creating a taskpad that will ultimately be used by the network help desk staff for the purpose of checking the Event Viewer system log. In this activity, you will create a new MMC and define a taskpad that creates a shortcut to the system log on the local computer.

1. Click **Start**, click **Run**, and then type **mmc** in the Open text box. Click **OK**.
2. Click the **File** menu, and click **Add/Remove Snap-in**.
3. Click **Add** to view the list of available snap-ins. On the list, click **Event Viewer** and click **Add**. Ensure that the **Local computer** radio button is selected, and click **Finish**. Click **Close**, and then click **OK** to close the Add/Remove Snap-in dialog box and return to the console.
4. Right-click **Console Root** and click **New Taskpad View**. Click **Next** at the Welcome screen.
5. In the Taskpad Display dialog box, click **No list**, and click **Next**.
6. In the Taskpad Target dialog box, accept the defaults, and click **Next**.
7. In the Name text box, type **Network Helpdesk Taskpad**. In the description text box, type **Network Help Desk Management Utility**. Click **Next**.
8. At the Completing the New Taskpad View Wizard, click the **Start New Task wizard** check box if it is not already selected. Click **Finish**.
9. Click **Next** at the Welcome screen.
10. Verify that **Menu command** is selected, and then click **Next**.

11. At the Shortcut Menu Command screen, click **Tree item task** on the Command source drop-down menu.
12. In the lower left column, expand **Event Viewer**. Click **System**, and then click **Open** in the Available commands column. Click **Next**.
13. In the Task name text box, type **Shortcut to System log**, type an appropriate description, and click **Next**.
14. Choose an icon for the task, and click **Next**.
15. At Completing the New Task Wizard, click **Finish**.
16. From the Network Helpdesk Taskpad, click the **Shortcut to System log** icon to open the system log.
17. Right-click **Console Root** and click **Edit Taskpad View**.
18. In the Network Helpdesk Taskpad Properties dialog box, click the **Tasks** tab. Note that you can add additional tasks to this taskpad by clicking the **New** button.
19. Click **Cancel** to close the Network Helpdesk Taskpad Properties dialog box.
20. Save this new MMC to your desktop using the filename **Help Desk.msc**.
21. Close the console window.

The Secondary Logon Feature

It is a recommended best practice for network administrators to have two logon accounts. One account is granted administrative rights and is only used for network management. A second account has normal user rights and is used for any nonadministrative tasks. The problem with this recommendation is that you may have to log on and off many times throughout the day to gain the rights needed to complete your tasks.

To save the time required to log on and off, Windows Server 2003 provides the secondary logon feature. This feature allows you to log on with your regular user account and then open administrative tools as an administrator. In Activity 1-7, you will use the secondary logon feature to open Event Viewer using the built-in administrator account.

Tip: You can disable this feature by stopping the Secondary Logon service found in the Services administrative console.

Activity 1-7: Using the Windows Server 2003 Secondary Logon Feature

Time Required: 5 minutes

Objective: Use the Run as command to open a program using alternate credentials.

Description: In most network environments, administrative staff are provided with both a normal user account and one used to carry out administrative tasks. The Run as command provides a simplified way of allowing an administrator to carry out normal network functions as a regular user, while accessing administrative tools with appropriate credentials. The IT manager has decided that administrators at Dover Leasing should follow this model beginning next month. He has asked you to test the Run as command in Windows Server 2003 to see whether it will meet Dover's requirements. In this activity, you will use the graphical version of the Run as command to open Event Viewer using the credentials of the domain administrator account.

1. Click **Start**, point to **Administrative Tools**, and then right-click **Event Viewer**.

2. Click **Run as**. The Run As dialog box opens. Select the **The following user** radio button on the lower half of the screen, as shown in Figure 1-8. Type **Password01** in the Password text box, and then click **OK**.
3. Close Event Viewer.

Note: If Run as does not appear, hold down the Shift key and right-click the shortcut icon.

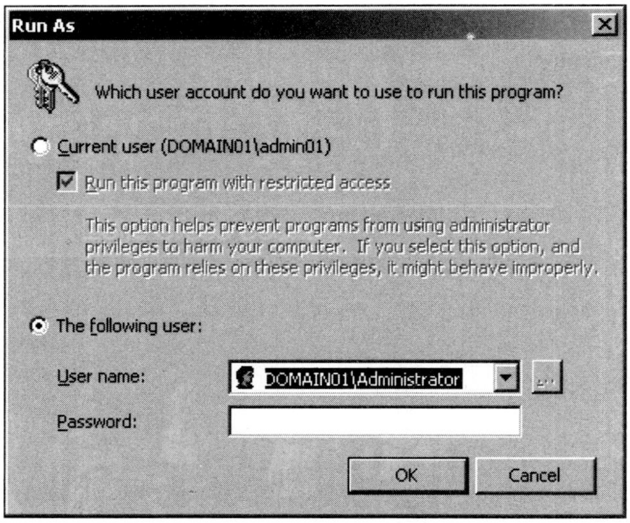

Figure 1-8 The Run As dialog box

You can also use a command prompt to start applications under the administrator account. The command to do so is runas /user:<*domain\username*> *cmd*. The *domain\username* is the domain and user account in which you want to start the application, and *cmd* is the command used to start the application. In Activity 1-8, you will use the secondary logon feature to open Event Viewer from the command line.

Activity 1-8: Using the Secondary Logon Feature from the Command Line

Time Required: 5 minutes

Objective: Log on using alternate credentials from the command line.

Description: Although the graphical version of the Run as command is useful for Windows Server 2003 administrators who primarily work from the graphical environment, a command-line version also exists in the form of the "runas" command. This command allows an administrator to open programs from the command line with alternate credentials. In this activity, you will start Event Viewer from the command line, again using the credentials of the domain administrator account.

1. Click **Start**, and then click **Run**.
2. In the Open text box, type **cmd** and then press **Enter** to open a command prompt.
3. At the command prompt, type **runas /user:<*domain*>\administrator eventvwr** where <*domain*> is the name of your domain in the format DOMAINXX. Press **Enter**.
4. Type **Password01** at the password prompt, and press **Enter**.
5. Event Viewer opens. Browse the various logs in Event Viewer.
6. Close all open windows.

Additional Administrator Utilities

There are many additional utilities available with Windows Server 2003 or the Windows Server 2003 Resource Kit that can assist you in troubleshooting or general network management. Following are a few interesting utilities that you may want to investigate further:

- *The Windows Server 2003 Task Scheduler*—Use this utility to schedule various tasks to run at certain times and intervals. The task scheduler service starts when you switch on your machine and it runs in the background. To use the task scheduler, open Control Panel, and access the Scheduled Tasks icon.
- *netdiag*—This troubleshooting tool reports on a number of functions such as WINS, trust relationships, IP configuration, DHCP, routing, running tests on DNS, and more. This tool is available from Windows Server 2003 Support Tools, which can be installed from the Support\Tools folder of the Windows Server 2003 CD-ROM. To run the utility, open a command prompt and type netdiag. Use the /l switch to send results to a file called NetDiag.log stored in the directory from which the command was run. The /v switch provides extensive verbose output. You will install the Windows Server 2003 Support Tools in Activity 1-9.
- *The net command*—Use the net command to perform a variety of management tasks such as starting and stopping services, viewing shares on the computer, and viewing the system time. For a list of the options you can use with the net command, open a command prompt, and type net ?.

Activity 1-9: Installing the Windows Server 2003 Support Tools

Time Required: 10 minutes

Objective: Install the Windows Server 2003 Support Tools.

Description: The Windows Server 2003 Support Tools consist of additional tools, scripts, and diagnostic utilities not included as part of the original server installation process. The IT manager at Dover Leasing has asked you to install the Support Tools on one server to evaluate whether any of the utilities will be useful for troubleshooting purposes and ultimately wider deployment. In this activity, you will install the Support Tools from a copy of the Windows Server 2003 CD-ROM stored in the Source folder on your server's D drive and then attempt to run the netdiag troubleshooting tool.

1. Click **Start**, right-click **My Computer**, and click **Explore**.
2. Click drive **D:** to view its contents.
3. Double-click the **Source** folder, and browse to the **Support\Tools** folder.
4. Double-click **SUPTOOLS.MSI**.
5. Click **Next** in the Welcome dialog box.
6. Click the **I Agree** radio button and click **Next**.
7. Click **Next** at the User Information screen.
8. At the Destination Directory screen, accept the default path and click **Install Now**.
9. Once the installation process is completed, click **Finish**.
10. To test a specific support tool, click **Start**, and then click **Run**. Type **cmd** in the Open text box and press **Enter**.
11. At the command prompt, type **netdiag** and press **Enter** to perform diagnostic tests on your computer.
12. Close all windows and log off.

Introduction to Windows Server 2003 Active Directory

Active Directory is a directory service database provided with Windows Server 2003 server-based operating systems. Active Directory provides the following services and features to the network environment:

- A central point for storing, organizing, managing, and controlling network objects, such as users, computers, and groups
- A single point of administration of objects, such as users, groups, computers, and Active Directory-published resources, such as printers or shared folders
- Logon and authentication services for users
- Delegation of administration to allow for decentralized administration of Active Directory objects, such as users and groups

The Active Directory database is stored on any Windows Server 2003 server that has been promoted to a domain controller. Each domain controller throughout the network has a writeable copy of the directory database. This means that you can make Active Directory changes to any domain controller within your network, and those changes are replicated to all of the other domain controllers. This process is called **multi-master replication**, which also provides a form of fault-tolerance because every domain controller has a writeable copy of the directory database. If a single server fails, Active Directory does not fail because replicated copies of the database are available from other servers within the network.

Active Directory uses the DNS to maintain domain-naming structures and locate network resources. What this means to a network designer is that all Active Directory names must follow standard DNS naming conventions. An example of a standard DNS naming convention would be *Dovercorp.net.* A child domain of *Dovercorp.net* would add its name as a prefix, such as *Europe.Dovercorp.net.*

Active Directory Objects

Active Directory stores a variety of objects within the database. An **object** represents network resources such as users, groups, computers, and printers. When an object is created in Active Directory, various attributes are assigned to it to provide information about the object. For example, Figure 1-9 illustrates creating a new user object and the ability to add various attributes, such as First name, Last name, and User logon name.

If you need to locate information about an object from Active Directory, you can perform a search on specific attributes relating to the object. For example, Figure 1-10 shows how you can find the e-mail address of a user object by searching for the specific user name in Active Directory and then viewing the attributes for the object.

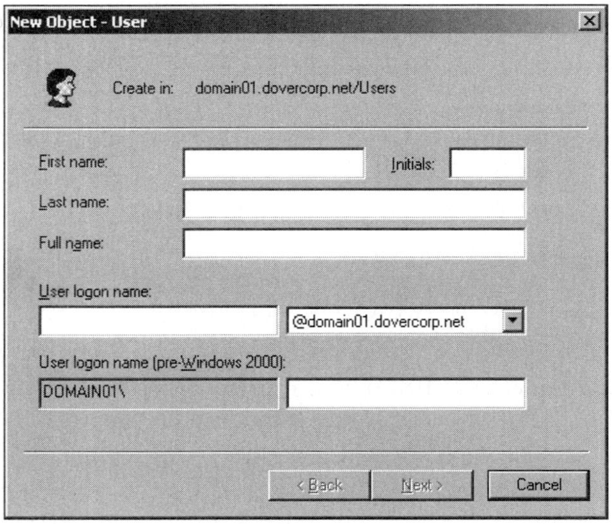

Figure 1-9 Creating a new user object

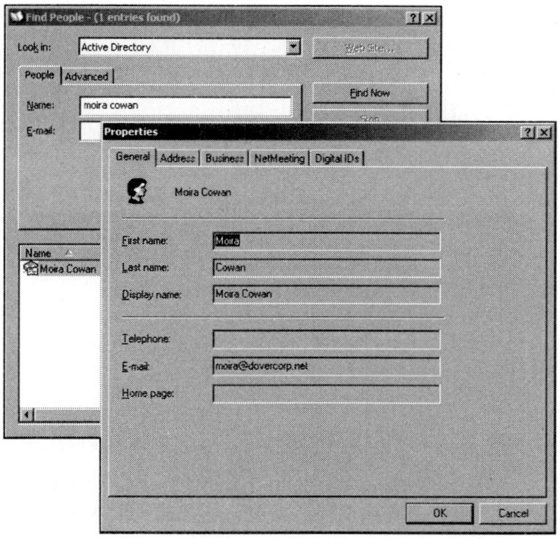

Figure 1-10 Searching for the e-mail address of a user object

The Active Directory Schema

All of the objects and attributes that are available in Active Directory are defined in the **Active Directory schema**. In Windows Server 2003, the schema defines the objects for the entire Active Directory structure. This means that there is only one schema for the entire Active Directory, and this schema is replicated among all domain controllers within the network.

The Active Directory schema consists of two main definitions: **object classes** and **attributes**. Object classes define which types of objects can be created within Active Directory, such as user objects and printer objects. All object classes consist of various attributes that describe the object itself. For example, the user and printer object classes may both have an attribute called description, which is used to describe the use of the object. Attributes are created and stored separately in the schema and can be used with multiple object classes to maintain consistency.

The Active Directory database stores and replicates the schema partition to all domain controllers in an Active Directory environment. Storing the schema within the Active Directory database provides the ability to dynamically update and extend the schema, as well as provides instant access to information for user applications that need to read the schema properties.

Active Directory Components

Active Directory is made of several components that provide a way to design and administer the hierarchical, logical structure of the network. The logical components that make up an Active Directory structure include:

- Domains and organizational units
- Trees and forests
- A global catalog

To ensure efficient maintenance and troubleshooting within Active Directory, it is essential that you understand these logical components. The next few sections discuss each component in greater detail.

Domains and Organizational Units

A Windows Server 2003 domain is a logically structured organization of objects, such as users, computers, groups, and printers, that are part of a network and share a common directory database. Each domain has a unique name and is organized in levels and administered as a unit with common rules and procedures. On the Internet, domains are defined by an IP address. Windows Server 2003 domains provide a number of administrative benefits including the ability to configure unique security settings, decentralize administration, and control replication traffic. This means that objects, such as user accounts, and security settings, such as password policies, are assigned at the domain level and do not replicate to other domains. By default, members of the Administrators group are only allowed to manage the objects within their own domain. As mentioned earlier, all the domain controllers within a single domain store a copy of the Active Directory database, and domain-specific information is only replicated between the domain controllers of the same domain.

An **organizational unit (OU)** is an Active Directory logical container used to organize objects within a single domain. Objects such as users, groups, computers, and other OUs, can be stored in an OU container. For example, you may want to organize your users based upon the department in which they work. You might create a Sales OU to store all of your sales department users and objects. You might also create a Marketing OU to store all of your marketing department users and objects. Not only does this make it easier to locate and manage the Active Directory objects, you can then apply a Group Policy to define more advanced features such as software deployment or desktop restrictions based upon department. Figure 1-11 illustrates a domain with several OUs.

Another main advantage of using an OU structure is the ability to delegate administrative control over OUs. For example, you may want to give a set of users the right to add or remove new users within the Sales OU. You do not have to provide the group with full administrative rights to accomplish this task because Active Directory allows you to delegate very specific tasks, if necessary.

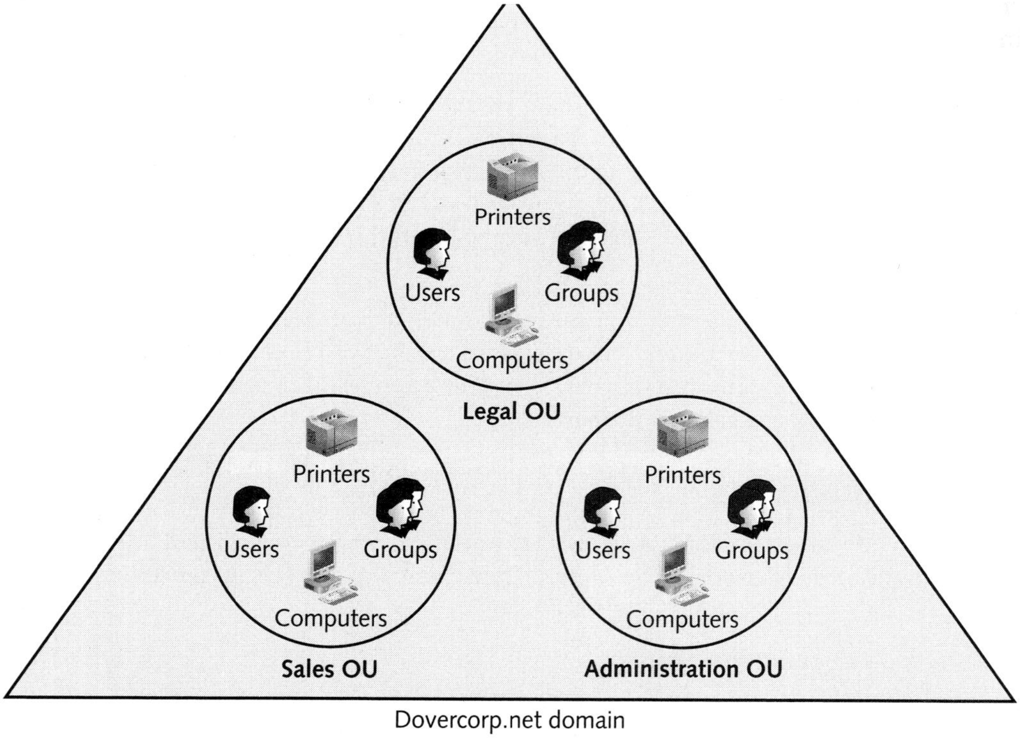

Figure 1-11 An Active Directory Domain and OU structure

Trees and Forests

When designing a Windows Server 2003 network infrastructure, there might be times when you are required to create multiple domains within an organization. Reasons for doing this include the following:

- Divisions within the company may be administered on a geographic basis. To make administration easier, a separate domain is created for each division.
- Different password policies are needed between divisions within an organization.
- An extraordinarily large number of objects need to be defined.
- Replication performance needs to be improved.

Note: Although domains are replication boundaries, there is another way to control replication by using site objects. Site objects are discussed later in the chapter.

The first Active Directory domain created in an organization is called the **forest root domain**. When multiple domains are needed, they are connected to the forest root to form either a single **tree** or multiple trees, depending upon the design of the domain name structure. A tree is a hierarchical collection of domains that share a contiguous DNS namespace. For example, Dovercorp Leasing has its head office in Boston with a forest root domain called *Dovercorp.net*. Dovercorp has two divisions, one located in London and the other located in Hong Kong. Because of geographic and administrative differences, you might decide to create a distinct domain for each division. Two child domains can be created off of the forest root domain. The London domain can be named *Europe.Dovercorp.net*, which follows the contiguous DNS namespace design. Similarly, the Hong Kong domain can be called *Asia.Dovercorp.net*. See Figure 1-12 for an example of this structure.

Whenever a child domain is created, a two-way, transitive trust relationship is automatically created between the child and parent domains. A **transitive trust** means that all other trusted domains implicitly trust one another. For example, because *Europe.Dovercorp.net* trusts the *Dovercorp.net* forest root domain, Europe also implicitly trusts the *Asia.Dovercorp.net* domain via the *Dovercorp.net* domain. These two-way, transitive trusts allow for resource access anywhere throughout the Active Directory structure.

A **forest** is a collection of trees that do not share a contiguous DNS naming structure. For example, Dover Leasing purchases a large international company called Seven Acres Property Management. It may not make sense to make the Seven Acres domain a child of *Dovercorp.net* because of the renaming required to maintain a contiguous naming convention based on *Dovercorp.net*. Instead, you could create a new tree and allow Seven Acres to start its own contiguous naming hierarchy. Both trees make up an Active Directory forest. See Figure 1-13 for an illustration.

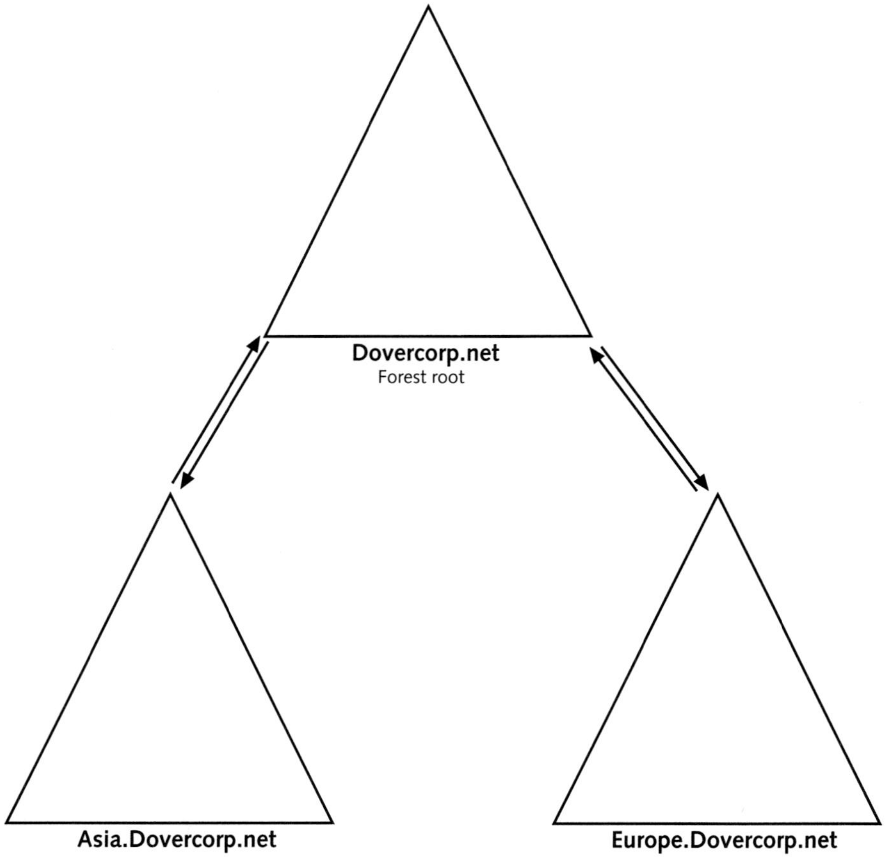

Figure 1-12 The *Dovercorp.net* domain tree

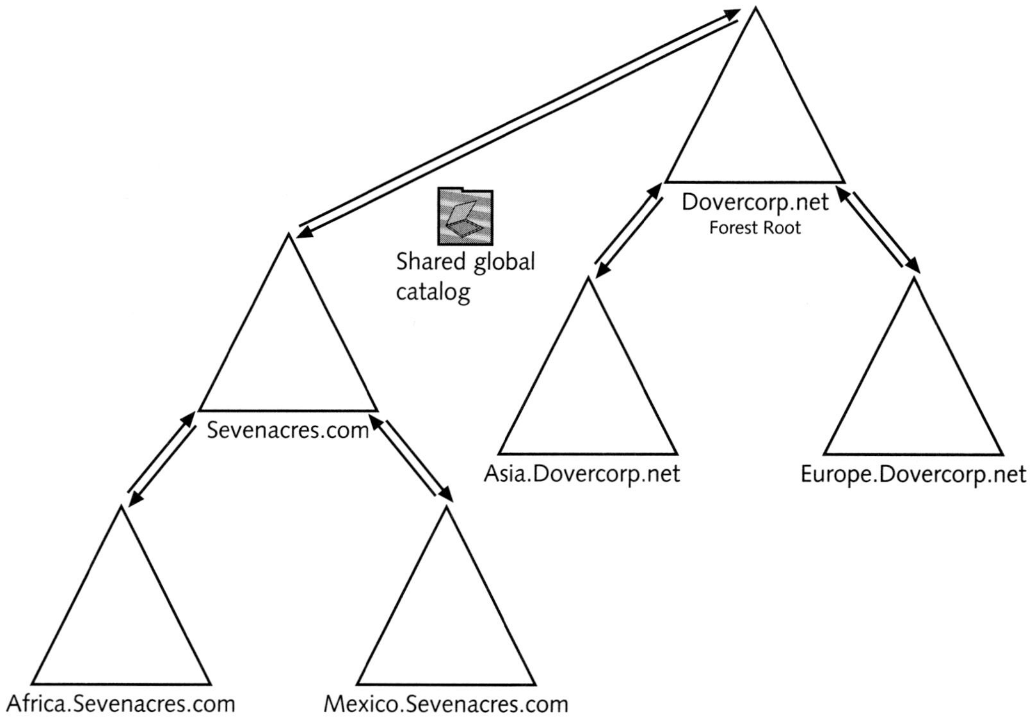

Figure 1-13 Example of an Active Directory forest

Even though the trees within a forest do not share a common namespace, they do share a single Active Directory schema, which ensures that all object classes and attributes are consistent throughout the entire structure. A special user group called Enterprise Admins is also created, which allows members to manage objects throughout the entire forest. The Enterprise Admins group is created within the initial forest root domain and has a scope throughout the entire forest. Another component that is shared throughout the forest is a **global catalog**.

Global Catalog

A global catalog is an index and partial replica of the objects and attributes most frequently used throughout the entire Active Directory structure. Some of the common attributes that are stored in a global catalog include a user's first and last names, logon name, or e-mail address. A global catalog is replicated to any server within the forest that is configured to be a global catalog server.

A global catalog is used primarily for four main functions:

- Enables users to find Active Directory information from anywhere in the forest.
- Provides universal group membership information to facilitate logging on to the network.
- Supplies authentication services when a user from another domain logs on using a **user principal name (UPN)** (A UPN is a representation of a user's logon credentials in the form user@domain.com. When a UPN is used, a domain name does not need to be explicitly specified in the Log on to drop-down box.)
- Responds to directory lookup requests from Exchange 2000 and other applications.

The first domain controller in Active Directory automatically becomes a global catalog server. To provide redundancy, additional domain controllers can easily be configured to also be global catalog servers. Multiple global catalogs can improve user query and logon authentication performance, especially in Active Directory environments that include geographically distant sites connected by WAN links. Microsoft recommends that each Active Directory site be configured with at least one domain controller acting as a global catalog server.

Active Directory Communication Standards

As mentioned previously, Active Directory uses the DNS naming standard for IP name resolution and for providing information on the location of network services and resources. For example, if you need to locate a server called *database.Dovercorp.net*, your workstation first queries a DNS server to resolve the IP address of the database server. Once the IP address is known, then a direct communication session can take place.

The same process occurs when you need to log on to the domain. Your workstation queries DNS to find a domain controller that can perform the authentication. Once the location of a domain controller is known, then the authentication process can take place, thus allowing access to the network resources.

When users need to access Active Directory, the **Lightweight Directory Access Protocol (LDAP)** is used to query or update the Active Directory database directly. Just as a DNS name contains a specific naming convention (e.g., *Dovercorp.net*), LDAP also follows a specific naming convention. LDAP naming paths are used when referring to objects stored within the Active Directory. Two main components of the naming paths include:

- *Distinguished name* — Every object in Active Directory has a unique **distinguished name (DN)**. For example, the *Dovercorp.net* domain component (DC) has a user object with a common name (CN) of Moira Cowan that is stored within the Marketing OU. The distinguished name for the object would be CN=Moira Cowan, OU=Marketing, DC=Dovercorp, DC=Net.

- *Relative distinguished name* — A portion of the distinguished name that uniquely identifies the object within the container is referred to as the **relative distinguished name**. For example, the distinguished name OU=Marketing, DC=Dovercorp, DC=Net would have a relative distinguished name of OU=Marketing. For the distinguished name CN=Moira Cowan, OU=Marketing, DC=Dovercorp, DC=Net, the relative distinguished name would be CN=Moira Cowan.

The Active Directory Physical Structure

The Active Directory physical structure relates to the actual connectivity of the physical network itself. Because the Active Directory database is stored on multiple servers, you need to make sure that any modification to the database is replicated as quickly as possible between domain controllers. You must also design your topology so that replication does not saturate the available network bandwidth. One replication problem that you may encounter is when domain controllers are separated over a slow WAN connection. In this scenario, you likely want to control the frequency and the time that replication takes place.

In addition to replication, you may also want to control logon traffic. Referring back to the previous scenario, you do not want any users to have to cross the slow WAN link when obtaining authentication to log on to the network. Users should have to authenticate to a domain controller on their side of the WAN connection.

Note

Keep in mind that the physical structure of Active Directory is totally separate from the logical structure. The logical structure is used to organize your network resources, whereas the physical structure is used to control network traffic.

You can control Active Directory replication traffic and network logon traffic by configuring sites and site links. An Active Directory **site** is a combination of one or more Internet Protocol (IP) subnets connected by a high-speed connection. It is assumed that domain controllers that belong to the same site all have a common network connection. It is also assumed that any connection between sites that are not reliable at all times must have replication controlled through replication schedules and frequency intervals.

A **site link** is a configurable object that represents a low-bandwidth or unreliable/occasional connection between sites. Site links created using the Active Directory Sites and Services snap-in are the core of Active Directory replication. The site links can be adjusted for replication availability, bandwidth costs, and replication frequency. Windows Server 2003 uses this information to generate the replication topology for the sites, including the schedule for replication. Figure 1-14 shows an example of a site structure within a domain. Each site contains domain controllers that share a high-speed connection. Because of a slower WAN connection between Boston, Hong Kong, and London, sites and site links have been created to enable control over replication and logon traffic.

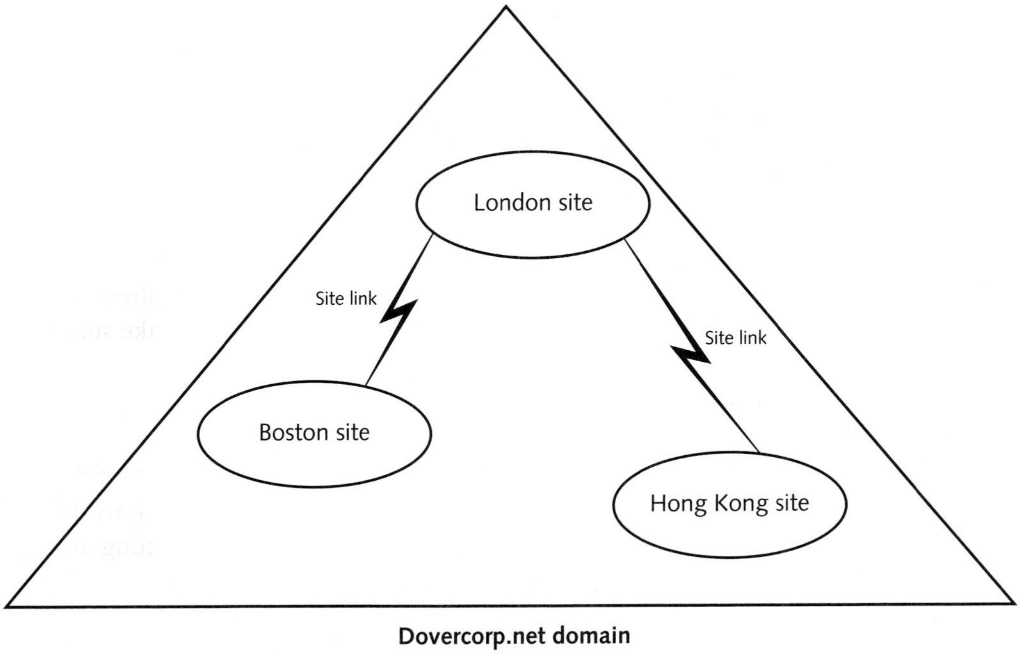

Figure 1-14 The site structure of *Dovercorp.net*

Replication within a site takes place based on a change notification process. If any change is made within Active Directory, the server waits 15 seconds and then announces the changes to another domain controller. In cases where a domain controller has multiple replication partners within a site changes are sent out to additional domain controllers at three-second intervals. If no changes have been made, replication takes place within an hour. Replication between sites is initially set at every three hours but can easily be changed by editing the properties of the site link object.

Chapter Summary

- There are many tasks and procedures that a network administrator is expected to be able to perform on a daily basis. Some of these tasks include software installation, Active Directory (AD) administration, file and print administration, Internet and remote access administration, network performance monitoring, and troubleshooting.
- A network administrator needs to follow a systematic approach to troubleshooting network problems. This requires defining the problem, gathering detailed information on what has changed, devising a plan to solve the problem, implementing the plan, observing what happens, and documenting all changes and results.
- Some of the tools that a network administrator can use to help with routine network management include the Microsoft Management Console (MMC), the secondary logon service, and various command-line utilities such as netdiag.exe and the net command.
- Active Directory is a directory service database provided with Windows Server 2003 Operating Systems. Active Directory provides the following services to the network environment:
  - A central point for storing, organizing, managing, and controlling network objects such as users, computers, and groups
  - A single point of administration of objects such as users, groups, computers, and Active Directory-published resources such as printers or shared folders
  - Logon and authentication services for users
  - Delegation of administration to allow for decentralized administration of Active Directory objects such as users and groups

- The logical components that make up an Active Directory structure include:
  - Domains and organizational units
  - Trees and forests
  - A global catalog
- Active Directory uses the DNS naming standard for IP name resolution and provides information on the location of network services. When users need to access Active Directory, the Lightweight Directory Access Protocol (LDAP) is used to query or update the Active Directory database directly.
- Active Directory replication traffic and network logon traffic can be controlled by configuring sites and site links. An Active Directory site is a combination of one or more Internet Protocol (IP) subnets connected with a high-speed connection. A site link is a low-bandwidth or unreliable/occasional connection between sites. The site links can be adjusted for replication availability, bandwidth costs, and replication frequency. They enable control over replication and logon traffic.

Key Terms

Active Directory (AD) — A directory service included with Windows Server 2003 that provides a single point of administration, authentication, and storage for user, group, and computer objects.

Active Directory schema — Contains the definition of all object classes and attributes used in the Active Directory database.

attributes — Used to define the characteristics of an object class within Active Directory.

distinguished name (DN) — An LDAP component used to uniquely identify an object throughout the entire LDAP hierarchy by referring to the relative distinguished name, domain name, and the container holding the object.

domain — A logically structured organization of objects, such as users, computers, groups, and printers, that are part of a network and share a common directory database. Domains are defined by an administrator and administered as a unit with common rules and procedures.

Domain Name System (DNS) — A hierarchical name resolution system that resolves host names and fully qualified domain names (FQDNs) into IP addresses and vice versa. It is a method for maintaining domain naming structure and locating network resources.

forest — A collection of Active Directory trees that do not necessarily share a contiguous DNS naming convention but do share a common global catalog and schema.

forest root domain — The first domain created within the Active Directory structure.

global catalog — An index of the objects and attributes used throughout the Active Directory structure. It contains a partial replica of every Windows Server 2003 domain within Active Directory, enabling users to find any object in the directory.

Group Policy — The Windows Server 2003 feature that allows for policy creation that affects domain users and computers. Policies can be anything from desktop settings to application assignment to security settings and more.

Internet connection sharing (ICS) — A Windows Server 2003 service that allows the use of a single, live Internet IP address to be shared among multiple clients. DHCP and DNS cannot be configured.

Lightweight Directory Access Protocol (LDAP) — An access protocol that defines how users can access or update directory service objects.

Management Saved Console (MSC) — The filename extension of a console saved using the MMC.

Microsoft Management Console (MMC) — A customizable management interface that can contain a number of management tools to provide a single, unified application for network administration.

multi-master replication — A replication model in which any domain controller accepts and replicates directory changes to any other domain controller. This differs from other replication models in which one computer stores the single modifiable copy of the directory and other computers store back-up copies.

network address translation (NAT) — The process of converting between IP addresses used within an intranet or other private network (called a stub domain) and Internet IP addresses. This approach makes it possible to use a large number of addresses within the stub domain without depleting the limited number of available numeric Internet IP addresses. Also, the network is protected when NAT replaces the source internal address and ports of all outgoing packets with a single public IP address.

object — A collection of attributes that represent items within Active Directory, such as users, groups, computers, and printers.

object classes — Define which types of objects can be created within Active Directory, such as users, groups, and printers.

organizational unit (OU) — An Active Directory logical container used to organize objects within a single domain. Objects such as users, groups, computers, and other OUs can be stored in an OU container.

relative distinguished name (RDN) — An LDAP component used to identify an object within the object's container.

Routing and Remote Access Services (RRAS) — A Windows Server 2003 service that allows users to access a company network or access the Internet through a variety of ways such as dial-up, VPN, or NAT services.

site — A combination of one or more Internet Protocol (IP) subnets connected by a high-speed connection.

site link — A low-bandwidth or unreliable/occasional connection between sites. The site links can be adjusted for replication availability, bandwidth costs, and replication frequency. They enable control over replication and logon traffic.

snap-ins — The management tools that are added to an MMC interface.

taskpad — Allows you to simplify administrative procedures by providing a graphical representation of the tasks that can be performed in an MMC.

transitive trust — The ability for domains or forests to trust one another, even though they do not have a direct explicit trust between them.

tree — A hierarchical collection of domains that share a contiguous DNS namespace.

user principal name — A user-account naming convention that includes both the user name and domain name in the format user@domain.com.

virtual private networking (VPN) — A Windows Server 2003 service that allows a private and secure connection with a company network over the Internet.

Review Questions

1. What service does Active Directory use for name resolution and locating network resources?
   a. DHCP
   b. DNS
   c. WINS
   d. none of the above
2. What is the name of the first domain installed within the Active Directory database?
   a. master root domain
   b. principal root domain
   c. primary root domain
   d. forest root domain

3. Assuming a user name of John Doe with a user account located in the Sales OU of the domain *Dovercorp.net*, what would be the object's distinguished name?
   a. OU=Sales, CN=John Doe
   b. CN=John Doe
   c. CN=John Doe, OU=Sales, DC=Dovercorp, DC=Net
   d. DC=Net, DC=Dovercorp, OU=Sales, CN=John Doe
4. In Windows Server 2003, a two-way, transitive trust relationship is maintained between which of the following?
   a. child and parent forests
   b. child and parent groups
   c. child and parent domains
   d. none of the above
5. Assuming a user name of John Doe with a user account located in the Sales OU of the domain *Dovercorp.net*, what would be the object's relative distinguished name?
   a. OU=Sales, CN=John Doe
   b. CN=John Doe
   c. CN=John Doe, OU=Sales, DC=Dovercorp, DC=Net
   d. DC=Net, DC=Dovercorp, OU=Sales, CN=John Doe
6. Which of the following logical components make up an Active Directory structure? (Choose all that apply.)
   a. domain
   b. global catalog
   c. forest
   d. tree
   e. all of the above
7. How often does replication between Active Directory sites take place by default?
   a. every three hours
   b. every hour
   c. every 30 minutes
   d. every 10 minutes
8. Which of the following describe advantages of the secondary logon feature? (Choose all that apply.)
   a. Two users can access a group at the same time.
   b. The administrator can log on with a user account and then as an administrator.
   c. A user can access more than one group at a time.
   d. It saves the administrator having to log off and then log back on to perform administrative tasks.
9. Which of the following are administrative utilities available with Windows Server 2003? (Choose all that apply.)
   a. the Windows Server 2003 task scheduler
   b. netdiag
   c. the NET command
   d. all of the above

10. Replication between domain controllers within a site is triggered by a change notification process initiated how many seconds after the change occurs?
    a. 5 seconds
    b. 10 seconds
    c. 15 seconds
    d. 30 seconds
11. Which step of the troubleshooting process is associated with the task of investigating whether software has been installed recently on the workstation?
    a. define the problem
    b. gather detailed information on what has changed
    c. devise a plan to solve the problem
    d. implement the plan and observe results
12. You need to search for all custom MMCs on your server. What extension should you search for?
    a. .mcs
    b. .mmc
    c. .msc
    d. .mcm
13. Which of the following is the management tool that can be added to customize an MMC?
    a. snap-let
    b. snap-in
    c. plug-in
    d. none of the above
14. Which of the following is where you would find the global address list for Exchange 2000 e-mail systems?
    a. the universal group
    b. a transitive trust
    c. the global catalog
    d. a global group
15. Which group exists within the forest root domain only but has administrative privleges in all forest domains by default?
    a. Administrators
    b. Power Users
    c. Enterprise Admins
    d. Domain Admins
16. The Active Directory schema primarily consists of which two of the following?
    a. object classes
    b. groups
    c. archives
    d. attributes
    e. domains

17. An organizational unit structure is useful because it allows the administrator to do which of the following?
    a. administer one large corporation at a time
    b. delegate specific tasks
    c. dictate the maximum number of trees in a forest
    d. none of the above
18. You are currently logged in with your regular user account. At a command prompt, which command would you type to start the Event Viewer console under the context of the administrator?
    a. runas /user:<*domain\username*> eventvwr
    b. runas /console:<*domain\username*> eventvwr
    c. start /user:<*domain\username*> eventvwr
    d. start/console:<*domain\username*> eventvwr
19. Which protocol is used to query and update the Active Directory database?
    a. LDAP
    b. SMTP
    c. SNMP
    d. RPC
20. Which of the following are valid reasons for creating more than one domain for an organization? (Choose all that apply.)
    a. replication issues
    b. large number of objects to be defined
    c. different password policies
    d. all of the above
21. What type of replication model is used by Active Directory?
    a. single master
    b. multi-master
    c. multi-homed
    d. master-slave
22. Which of the following objects can be stored within an organizational unit? (Choose all that apply.)
    a. Active Directory
    b. printer objects
    c. user objects
    d. a and c
23. Which domain controllers will become global catalog servers by default?
    a. the first domain controller in every domain
    b. the first domain controller in the forest
    c. all domain controllers
    d. none
24. How many Active Directory domains must be created before a forest exists?
    a. one
    b. two
    c. at least two domains with different DNS namespaces
    d. none

25. In Windows Server 2003, the Active Directory schema defines which of the following?
    a. how to access System Monitor
    b. the rules for accessing e-mail through Exchange 2000
    c. the objects for the entire Active Directory structure
    d. none of the above

CASE PROJECTS

Case Project 1-1: Assessing Dover Leasing's Active Directory Implementation

Dover Leasing Corporation has recently implemented Windows Server 2003 and Active Directory. Dover's network consists of three main locations with offices in Boston, Hong Kong, and London. The Boston location is the head office and connects to London via a dedicated T1 WAN link, whereas the Hong Kong location connects to London via a 256-Kbps Frame Relay link. Dover had recently considered opening a new office in San Francisco, which would connect via WAN links to both the Boston and Hong Kong offices. Different password policies need to be implemented in the Boston, Hong Kong, and London locations. Ultimately, the San Francisco office will become the administrative responsibility of IT staff in Boston. Based on what you know of Windows Server 2003 thus far and the information provided above, the IT manager has asked you to assess Dover Leasing's Active Directory design by answering the following questions.

1. Of the factors listed in the scenario, which would influence the logical design of Dover Leasing's Active Directory implementation?
2. What type of domain structure would you suggest for Dover Leasing?
3. Based on Dover Leasing's current and future locations, what would be the best naming strategy for their Active Directory domain structure?
4. How many sites would likely be configured as part of Dover Leasing's Active Directory implementation once the San Francisco office opens, and how many site links would be required?
5. Once the San Francisco office is opened, how many global catalog servers should be implemented on the network to ensure adequate performance?

Case Project 1-2: Troubleshooting a User Logon Problem

A user in the legal department of Dover Leasing phones you on Monday morning and states that she cannot log on to the network using her laptop, even though everything was working perfectly when she left work on Friday. Using the troubleshooting procedures discussed in this chapter, list each step and state what questions you would ask or what procedures you would follow for each of the steps to attempt to solve the problem.

Case Project 1-3: Creating a Custom Taskpad for Network Help Desk Staff

The IT manager at Dover Leasing has decided that using a custom taskpad is the best administrative strategy for network help desk staff until complete training on the various administrative tools can be provided later in the quarter. Using the Help Desk.msc taskpad originally developed in Activity 1-6, you have been asked to add additional shortcuts to tasks and tools that the network help desk staff will be responsible for using. In particular, the IT manager has asked you edit the existing taskpad to include the following:

- A shortcut to the application log
- A shortcut to the command prompt
- A shortcut to connect to another computer
- Shortcuts to save both the application and system logs

Each of these tasks should include both a description and an appropriate icon. After you have added all of the new tasks, save the console file and have the instructor check your work.

CHAPTER

2

MANAGING WINDOWS SERVER 2003 HARDWARE AND SOFTWARE

After reading this chapter and completing the exercises, you will be able to:

- Plan your operating system installation to ensure Windows Server 2003 hardware and software compatibility
- Assess your hardware and software needs by using the Windows Server 2003 qualifier tools
- Install and configure computer hardware devices and drivers
- Configure driver signing options and verify digital signatures on existing drivers
- Install and manage Windows Server 2003 updates using service packs and hot fixes

A Windows Server 2003 installation and deployment is not always a straightforward process. Many companies have complex networking needs and diverse environments that can present challenges for the administrator. However, with the proper installation and maintenance plan, you can proactively discover any potential problem areas that may interfere with a successful server or workstation deployment.

As you deploy Windows Server 2003 throughout your network, you need to be sure that all existing hardware and software are compatible with the new operating system. This chapter introduces you to the Microsoft qualifier tools that help you determine if your current hardware is compatible with Windows Server 2003. These tools can also help assess any hardware you are considering purchasing and verify its compatibility with Windows Server 2003.

After installing the operating system, there may be a number of additional tasks you need to perform before the server is ready for the production environment. For example, there may be hardware or components that were not automatically detected during the installation. You may need to obtain and update device drivers to ensure the functionality expected under the new operating system. To ensure that a Windows Server 2003-compatible driver is installed, you can configure driver code-signing options to only allow tested and verified device drivers to be incorporated into the installation. This chapter describes how to install and troubleshoot hardware devices, as well as how to configure and verify driver signatures and signing options.

Microsoft periodically releases service pack updates and **hot fixes** to correct potential security or software problems with Windows Server 2003. You should be aware of how to obtain these updates and how slipstreaming works to incorporate **service packs** into the Windows Server 2003 source files to make sure that all future installations incorporate the updates. The final portion of this chapter discusses how to manage Windows Server 2003 updates, such as service packs and hot fixes.

PLANNING THE INSTALLATION

To be sure that a deployment of Windows Server 2003 goes as smoothly as possible, it is important that you plan your installation. Planning helps ensure that all aspects of the installation are thought out before the start of the setup process and that all problem areas can be identified and minimized.

As you analyze your environment, you need to collect and document a variety of information to prepare for your Windows Server 2003 deployment. This information includes:

- *Computer hardware configurations*—It is vital to know exactly what computer hardware configurations are deployed throughout the organization. As discussed in the next section, Windows Server 2003 installations must meet the minimum hardware requirements for a successful and reliable installation.
- *Network infrastructure configuration*—It is very helpful to understand the physical layout of servers, workstations, routers, and hubs. All LAN and WAN speeds, bandwidth, and latency issues should also be documented. In addition, you should also create or obtain a diagram and listing of the IP subnets and network addresses. This information can assist you when configuring TCP/IP settings on the machines.
- *Organizational unit illustration*—A diagram illustrating each organizational unit (OU) is also helpful. This can assist you in network configurations such as domain and OU memberships.
- *Network interoperability issues*—It is important to understand which network operating systems are integrated within your organization. Specific configurations are needed when incorporating Windows Server 2003 with Novell NetWare, UNIX, or a Macintosh environment.
- *Existing applications*—All applications should be analyzed to ensure that they work within a Windows Server 2003 environment. Custom applications may need to be rewritten to function correctly within the Windows Server 2003 environment.

In addition to analyzing the network for Windows Server 2003 compatibility and functionality issues, keep in mind the risks associated with deploying a new network system. A proactive approach to risk management means that you are able to predict and possibly prevent trouble before it happens. A reactive approach is when you fix the problem after it has happened. A reactive approach to problem solving causes user frustration, network downtime, company expenditures, and possibly the loss of your job. Therefore, a thoroughly planned Windows Server 2003 installation or deployment plan is part of a proactive approach that allows you to know exactly what can go wrong and how to prevent or minimize disruption if something does go wrong.

ASSESSING THE HARDWARE AND SOFTWARE NEEDS

Your Windows Server 2003 infrastructure is only as reliable as the hardware upon which it is based. This is why it is vital that you understand the system requirements of Windows Server 2003. Before you install Windows Server 2003, make sure that your hardware meets and, if possible, exceeds the minimum requirements set forth by Microsoft. It is also wise to buy hardware that is listed in the **Microsoft Hardware Compatibility List (HCL)**. Although you may find that most hardware devices perform well with Windows Server 2003, Microsoft may not provide troubleshooting support if the hardware has not been specifically tested and registered with the HCL.

Note: As a rule, only buy servers that have hardware listed on the HCL. You can check the HCL on the Microsoft Web site at *www.microsoft.com/hcl*.

Windows Server 2003 minimum system requirements on new servers may not matter as much as they did in the past because most computers sold today exceed the minimum requirements. However, in the event that you need to upgrade an older server to Windows Server 2003, make sure that the minimum requirements are met to ensure constant reliability and performance. Meeting the minimum hardware requirements also helps to ensure that Windows Server 2003 functions as expected.

Table 2-1 lists hardware specifications for both Windows Server 2003 Standard Edition and Enterprise Edition.

Table 2-1 Hardware specifications for Windows Server 2003

Requirement	Standard Edition	Enterprise Edition
Minimum CPU Speed	133 MHz	■ 133 MHz for x86-based computers ■ 733 MHz for Itanium-based computers
Recommended CPU Speed	550 MHz	733 MHz
Minimum RAM	128 MB	128 MB
Recommended Minimum RAM	256 MB	256 MB
Maximum RAM	4 GB	■ 32 GB for x86-based computers ■ 64 GB for Itanium-based computers
Multi-Processor Support	Up to 4	Up to 8
Disk Space for Setup	1.5 GB	■ 1.5 GB for x86-based computers ■ 2.0 GB for Itanium-based computers

Accessing the BIOS Configuration

Another aspect that is often overlooked is whether or not the computer's **Basic Input/Output System (BIOS)** is compatible and configured to work properly with Windows Server 2003. The BIOS is a program stored on a flash memory chip attached to the motherboard. This program establishes the initial communication between the components of the computer, such as the hard drive, CD-ROM, floppy disk, video, and memory. A sample BIOS configuration screen is shown in Figure 2-1.

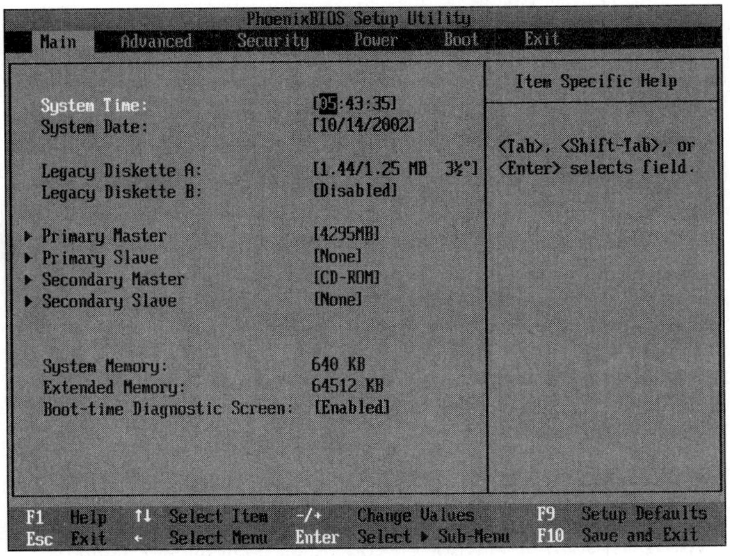

Figure 2-1 Sample computer BIOS configuration screen

You can usually access the BIOS by pressing the Delete key or F2 on the keyboard during the initial startup of the computer before the operating system loads. Some obvious settings that you may need to adjust in the BIOS include the order in which devices start when you start your system from CD-ROM during setup. If you have a legacy component in your computer that is not compatible with Plug and Play, you may also have to reserve a specific **interrupt request (IRQ)**, which will ensure that conflicts do not take place. For example, you may have an old ISA-based sound card that requires interrupt 5. When your Plug and Play components come online, there may be one that prefers and attempts to use interrupt 5 and causes a conflict with the sound card. If you reserve the interrupt in the BIOS for devices that are not Plug and Play compatible, the Plug and Play component must choose an alternate configuration and give first priority to the ISA card to use interrupt 5.

Note: In addition to configuration settings, you may also need to download a BIOS flash update from your computer motherboard manufacturer to ensure that all Windows Server 2003 settings, such as device configuration features, are supported.

Verifying Hardware and Software Compatibility

Beyond verifying that your computer meets the minimum hardware requirements of Windows Server 2003, it is important to ensure that all of your individual components, such as your video card and network adapter, are also supported. You also need to ensure that your current software supports Windows Server 2003. There are two ways in which you can evaluate the compatibility of your existing components and software: by utilizing the Windows Server 2003 Readiness Analyzer or by accessing the Microsoft Windows Catalog Web site.

The Microsoft Windows Upgrade Advisor

The **Microsoft Windows Upgrade Advisor** utility launches the first part of Windows Server 2003 setup but only checks for hardware and software compatibility and does not actually install Windows Server 2003. Run this check by inserting the Windows Server 2003 CD-ROM or accessing the i386 installation directory and typing "winnt32.exe /checkupgradeonly" at a command prompt. Once the check is complete, the utility will display a list of incompatible items in the window shown in Figure 2-2. This information can also be saved as a text file for future reference.

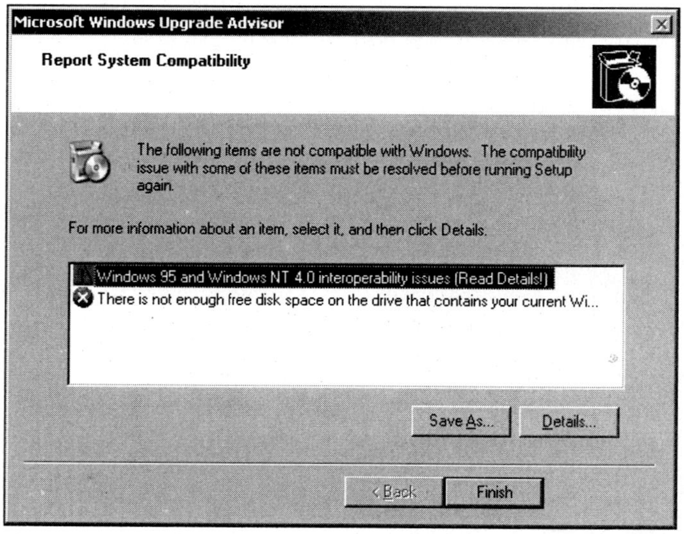

Figure 2-2 Running the Microsoft Windows Upgrade Advisor

Note: Be sure to run the Microsoft Windows Upgrade Advisor on compatible systems. For example, you cannot run the Windows .NET Standard Server 2003 version on a Windows 2000 Advanced Server machine. Windows 2000 Advanced Server only allows you to upgrade to Windows Server 2003, Enterprise Edition, and so you must use the Windows .NET Advanced Server 2003 version of the utility. In Activity 2-1, you will use the Microsoft Windows Upgrade Advisor to identify whether any of your server hardware or software is incapable of running Windows Server 2003.

Activity 2-1: Using the Microsoft Windows Update Advisor

Time Required: 10 minutes

Objective: Identify whether server software and hardware are capable of running Windows Server 2003.

Description: Although Dover Leasing has already upgraded most of their Windows 2000 servers to Windows Server 2003, a few existing Windows 2000 servers still need to be upgraded. Because these servers consist of different hardware and software configurations, Dover's IT manager has asked you to identify any issues that may arise as part of the upgrade process. In this activity, you will run the **Microsoft Windows Upgrade Advisor** on an existing server to get a better feel for how the utility works and the information that it provides.

1. Log in using your **AdminXX** account, click **Start**, and then click **Run**.
2. In the Open text box, type **d:\source** and click **OK**.
3. After the SOURCE folder opens, double-click the file **setup.exe**.
4. On the Welcome to Microsoft Windows Server 2003 Family screen, click the last option, **Check system compatibility**.
5. Click **Check my system automatically**. The Microsoft Windows Upgrade Advisor window opens.
6. On the Report System Compatibility screen, click one of the items listed and click **Details**. After reading the item, close the Details window.
7. On the Report System Compatibility screen, click **Save As**. Save the file to your desktop using the default filename of **upgrade.txt**.
8. Click **Finish** to close the Microsoft Windows Upgrade Advisor, and close all other open windows.
9. Double-click the newly created **upgrade.txt** file on your desktop. Note whether any system compatibilities exist.
10. Close the **update.txt** file and then drag it to the Recycle Bin to delete it.

The Hardware and Software Compatibility Web Site

As shown in Figure 2-3, Microsoft provides a Web page that you can query to evaluate current or future hardware and software compatibility. The Web page can be accessed at *www.microsoft.com/windows/catalog/*.

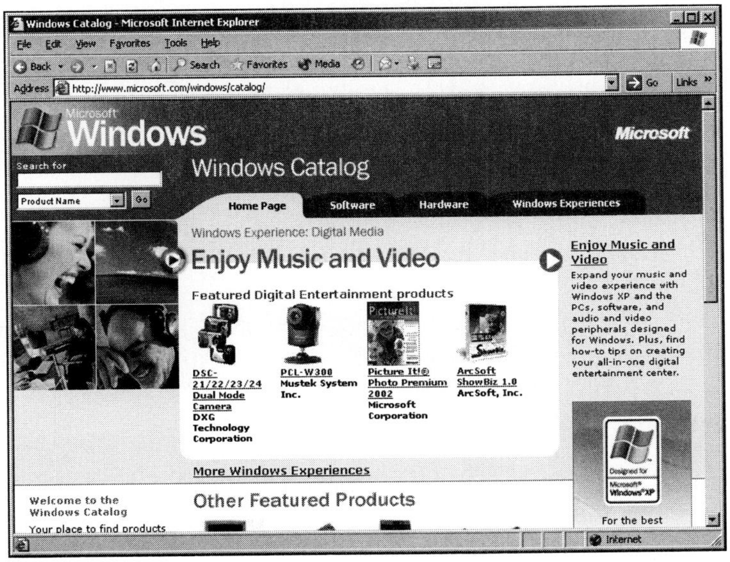

Figure 2-3 Accessing the Windows Server 2003 compatibility Web site

This online utility allows you to type in a specific manufacturer or model of a hardware or software component, and then it indicates whether the component is compatible with Windows Server 2003 and where to find updated drivers, if necessary.

INSTALLING AND CONFIGURING HARDWARE DEVICES

After a successful installation, there are still a few tasks that you might need to complete before assigning the server to the production environment. Some of these tasks include verifying hardware detection and updating device drivers. You also need to install the latest service packs and hot fixes.

Your first step is to verify that all hardware devices have been detected properly by Windows Server 2003. To accomplish this task, open the **Device Manager** to view all of the installed devices. Use the Device Manager to view and modify hardware device properties, update device drivers, and uninstall unneeded hardware. The Device Manager program is shown in Figure 2-4.

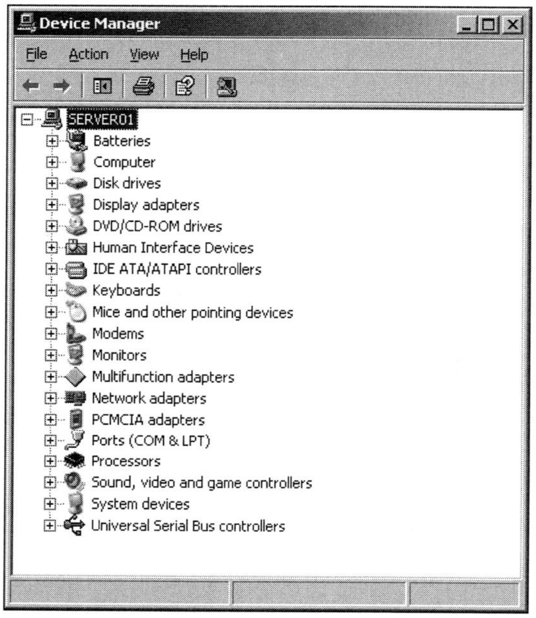

Figure 2-4 Viewing hardware devices using the Device Manager

As shown in Figure 2-5, any device that is not functioning is indicated with a yellow exclamation point, while manually disabled hardware is indicated with a small red "x" over the device icon.

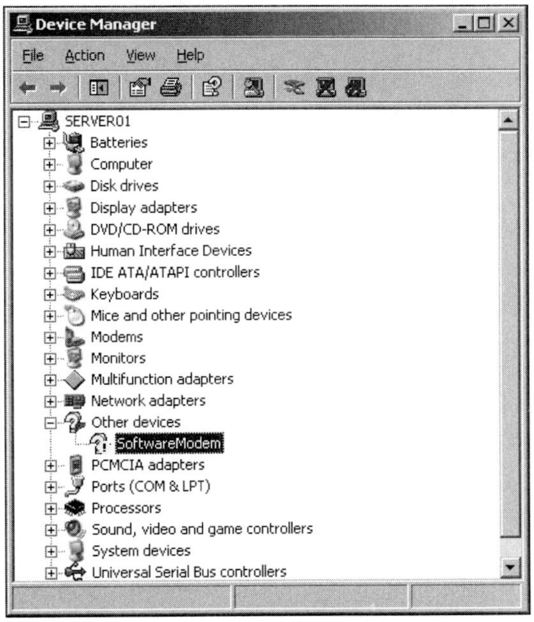

Figure 2-5 Viewing devices that are disabled or have a problem

If a specific device is missing or is not functioning, Windows Server 2003 provides two ways to troubleshoot or repair the problem. The first method is to obtain a new driver from the manufacturer's Web site and then install the new driver from within the Device Manager. The Driver tab in the properties of a device is used to view current driver details and access the Update Driver button, as shown in Figure 2-6.

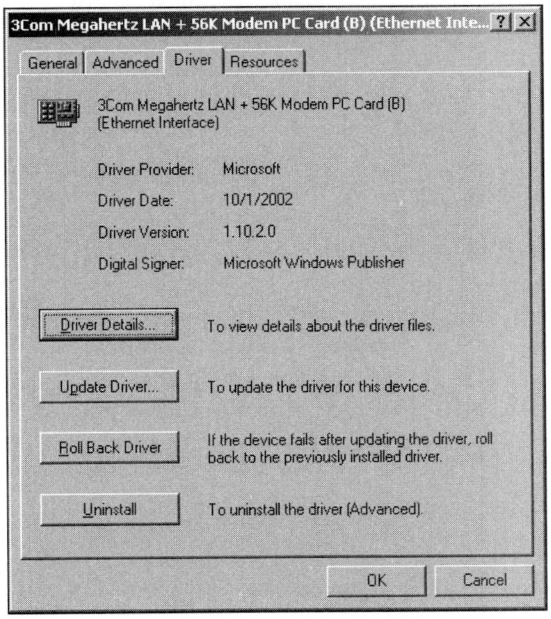

Figure 2-6 Installing an updated device driver

Windows Server 2003 allows you to update drivers from Device Manager by using the Hardware Update Wizard, as shown in Figure 2-7. This wizard steps you through the task of selecting and installing the updated device driver. In Activity 2-2, you will explore both hardware and configuration settings for your server using Device Manager.

Figure 2-7 Starting the Hardware Update Wizard

Activity 2-2: Exploring Device Manager

Time Required: 10 minutes

Objective: Use Device Manager to gather information about existing hardware and ways of viewing information.

Description: The IT manager at Dover Leasing plans to give all network help desk staff access to the Device Manager utility to enable them to gather information about the hardware status of existing servers. In this activity, you will use Device Manager to view the properties of existing hardware devices, including driver options and settings, resource usage, hardware status icons, and the different ways in which information can be displayed with the tool.

1. Click **Start**, right-click **My Computer**, and click **Properties**.
2. On the System Properties screen, click the **Hardware** tab.
3. In the Device Manager section, click the **Device Manager** button. Maximize Device Manager once it opens.
4. Click the **plus sign (+)** next to Network adapters to expand it, if necessary. A list of network adapters installed on your system will appear.
5. Right-click the first network adapter listed and review the shortcut menu options.
6. On the shortcut menu, click **Properties**.
7. On the General tab, notice that the Device type, manufacturer, and location are listed. Review all messages in the Device status box to ensure that the network adapter is functioning correctly.
8. In the Device usage list box (see Figure 2-8), click **Do not use this device (disable)**. Click **OK**.

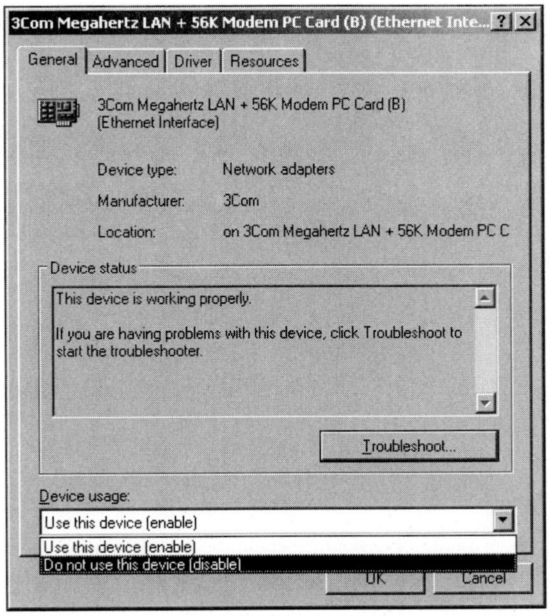

Figure 2-8 Disabling a network adapter

9. Notice that the icon associated with this specific network adapter has changed to signify that it has been disabled. Double-click the network adapter again to access its properties. On the General tab, click **Use this device (enable)** in the Device usage list box. Click **OK** to enable the device.

10. Double-click the network adapter icon again to access its properties. Click the **Advanced** tab, and notice both the Property and Value settings (see Figure 2-9). Note that different network adapter cards and drivers will support different advanced features. Make no changes on this screen, and click the **Driver** tab.

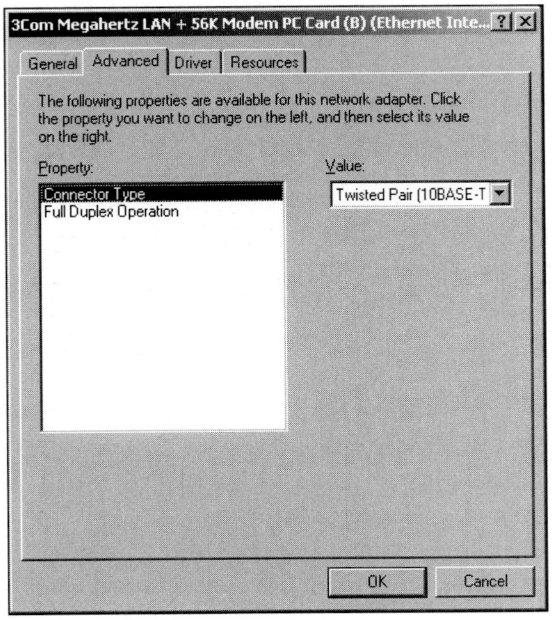

Figure 2-9 Advanced properties of a network adapter

11. Note the driver provider, date, version, and digital signer information. Click the **Driver Details** button to view more information about the driver, including its filename and location.
12. Click **OK** to close the Driver File Details window.
13. Do not click any additional buttons, but note the purpose of the Roll Back Driver button, as shown in Figure 2-10.
14. Click the **Resources** tab, and note both the IRQ and I/O Range associated with the network adapter card. Click **OK** to close the network adapter's properties and return to Device Manager.
15. Click **View** on the menu bar. Notice that Devices by type is selected as the Device Manager view in use. Click **Devices by connection** to switch the view of Device Manager.
16. In the PCI bus section, expand the various items (if necessary) until you find your network adapter listed.
17. Click **View** on the menu bar and click **Resources by type**. Click the **plus sign (+)** next to Interrupt request (IRQ) to expand it. Note that all IRQs assigned by the system and their associated devices are listed.
18. Click **View** on the menu bar. Click **Devices by type** to switch the Device Manager view back and close Device Manager. Close all open windows.

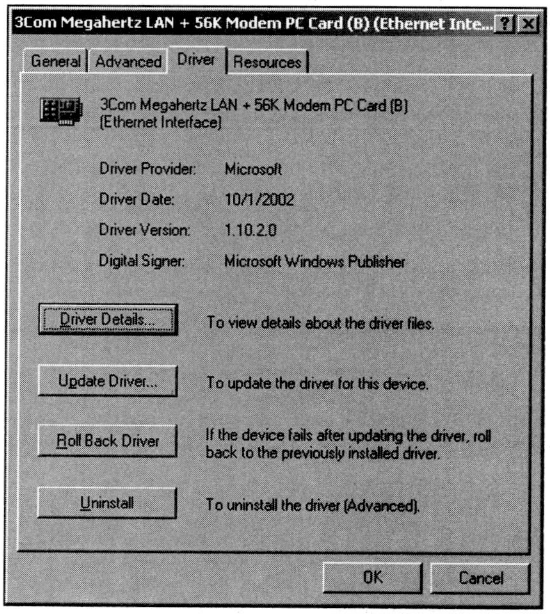

Figure 2-10 Driver properties of a network adapter

The second method of installing or repairing a hardware device is to use the **Add Hardware Wizard** found in Control Panel. By default, the Add Hardware Wizard will attempt to automatically detect any new hardware devices via Plug and Play. If the wizard does not detect a new device, it will give you the option to add a new hardware device manually, as shown in Figure 2-11.

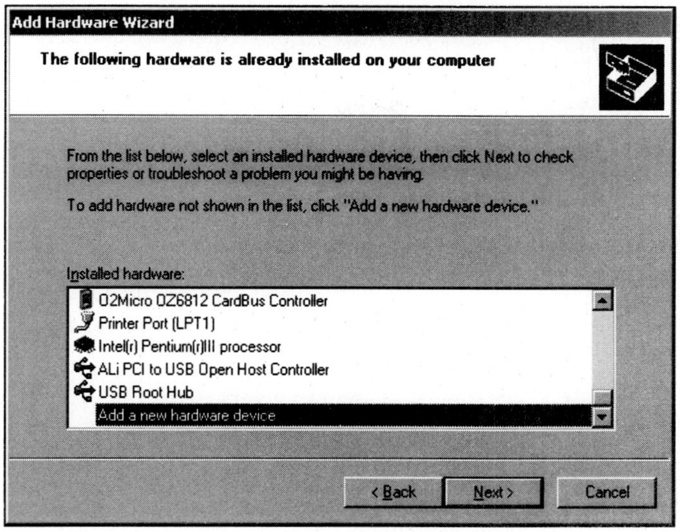

Figure 2-11 Adding hardware with the Add Hardware Wizard

Once the Add Hardware Wizard completes the process of adding or changing the driver associated with a hardware device, it lists the functional status of the device, as shown in Figure 2-12. In Activity 2-3 you will use both Device Manager and the Add Hardware Wizard to first uninstall and then reinstall the DVD or CD-ROM drive on your server.

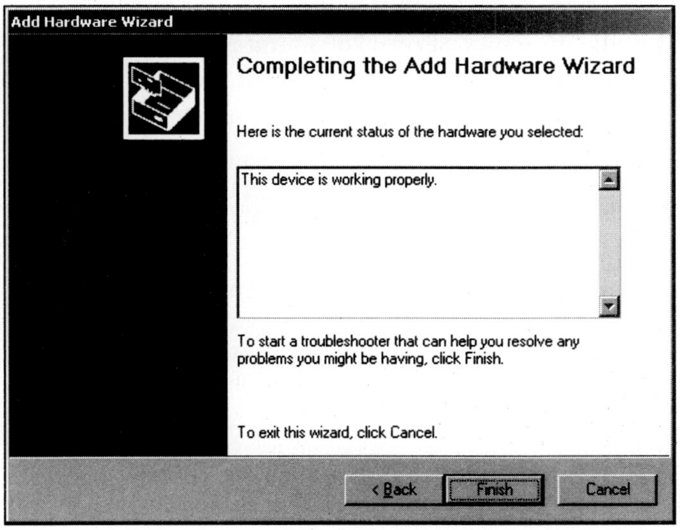

Figure 2-12 The current status of a hardware device

Activity 2-3: Using the Add Hardware Wizard

Time Required: 5 minutes

Objective: Use Device Manager and the Add Hardware Wizard to uninstall and then reinstall a device.

Description: While exploring Device Manager in Activity 2-2, you noticed that one of the options available was the ability to uninstall a device. In this activity, you have decided to test what happens when a device is uninstalled using Device Manager, and you will then attempt to reinstall the device using the Add Hardware Wizard from Control Panel.

1. Click **Start**, and then click **Run**.

2. In the Open text box, type **devmgmt.msc** and click **OK**.
3. Click the **plus sign (+)** next to DVD/CD-ROM drives to expand it. Right-click the DVD or CD-ROM device associated with your computer and click **Uninstall**.
4. Click **OK** on the Confirm Device Removal screen.
5. Close Device Manager.
6. Click **Start**, and then click **My Computer**. Confirm that your DVD or CD-ROM drive is unavailable. Close My Computer.
7. Click **Start**, select **Control Panel**, and then click **Add Hardware**. On the Add Hardware Wizard welcome screen, click **Next**.
8. The wizard should search for, find, and configure your DVD or CD-ROM drive automatically.
9. Click **Finish** to close the Add Hardware Wizard.
10. In the System Settings Change dialog box, click **No** if prompted to restart your computer. Click **Start**, and then click **My Computer** and verify that your DVD or CD-ROM drive is present.
11. Close My Computer.

Configuring Driver Signing Options

Every Windows Server 2003 operating system file and built-in driver has been digitally signed by Microsoft to ensure compatibility and quality. **Driver signing** ensures that a driver for a specific device has been verified by Microsoft to work with Windows Server 2003, and a unique digital signature has been incorporated into the driver. This digital signature assures you that it has met a certain quality test standard and that the file has not been altered or overwritten by another program's installation process.

When you configure driver signing options, you are presented with three choices:

- *Ignore*—This option effectively turns off driver and file verification. If this option is selected, driver signing is ignored.
- *Warn*—If this option is selected, a message appears when you attempt to install an unsigned driver, as shown in Figure 2-13. This alerts you that a digital signature was not found on the driver and there is no guarantee that the driver is going to work with Windows.

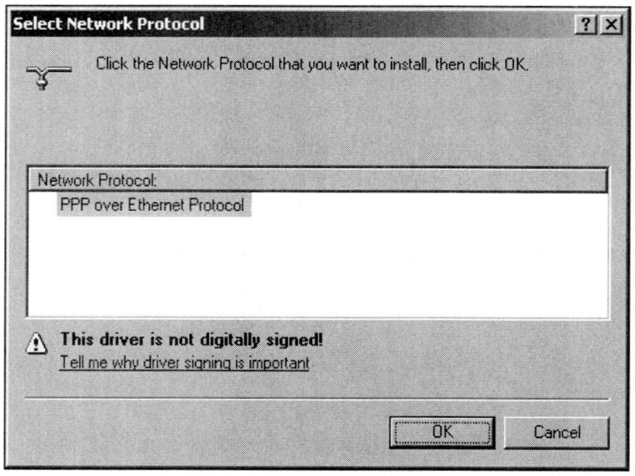

Figure 2-13 Verifying digital signatures

- *Block*—This option prevents the installation of any driver that is not signed.

In Activity 2-4, you will configure driver signing options on your server to block the installation of unsigned drivers.

Note: After a Windows Server 2003 installation, the Warn driver signing option is selected by default.

Activity 2-4: Configuring Driver Signing Options

Time Required: 10 minutes

Objective: Configure Windows Server 2003 to block the installation of all driver files that are not digitally signed.

Description: For Dover Leasing's original Windows Server 2003 deployment, the IT manager made a decision that only driver files digitally signed by Microsoft should be installed on corporate servers. In this activity, you have been asked to configure the driver signing options on your server so that it will block the installation of any unsigned driver files.

1. Click **Start**, and then right-click **My Computer**. Click **Properties** to access the System Properties tool.
2. Click the **Hardware** tab. In the Device Manager section, click the **Driver Signing** button. This will open the Driver Signing Options dialog box, as shown in Figure 2-14.

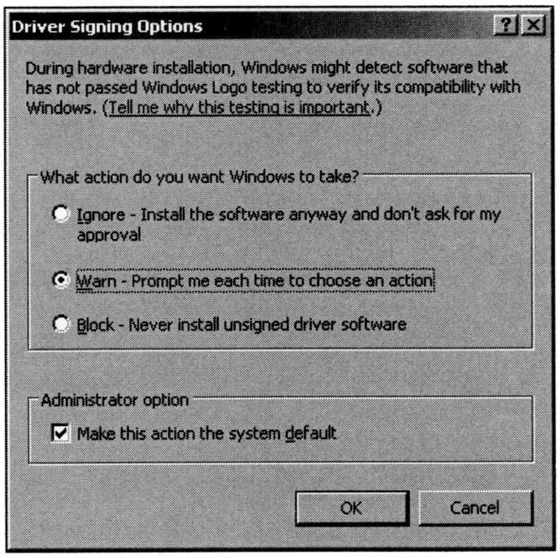

Figure 2-14 Configuring driver signing

3. Click the **Tell me why this testing is important** hyperlink. The Help and Support Center opens automatically.
4. In the Hardware section to the left of the Help and Support Center window, click the **Driver signing for Windows** hyperlink. Read the Driver signing for Windows help topic displayed on the right. Close the Help and Support Center window.
5. Note each of the three options listed in the **What action do you want Windows to take?** section. Click the **Block** radio button.
6. In the Administrator option section, ensure that the **Make this action the system default** check box is selected, and click **OK**.
7. Click **OK** to close the System Properties dialog box.

If you decide to leave the driver signing option set to Warn, it is possible that unsigned or incompatible device drivers can inadvertently be installed. If you are having problems with operating system instability, you can run a verification check to see which existing drivers on your computer are not digitally signed. Windows Server 2003 includes a utility called the **File Signature Verification.** This utility can identify unsigned files and give you information such as the file name, location, modification date, and version number, as shown in Figure 2-15.

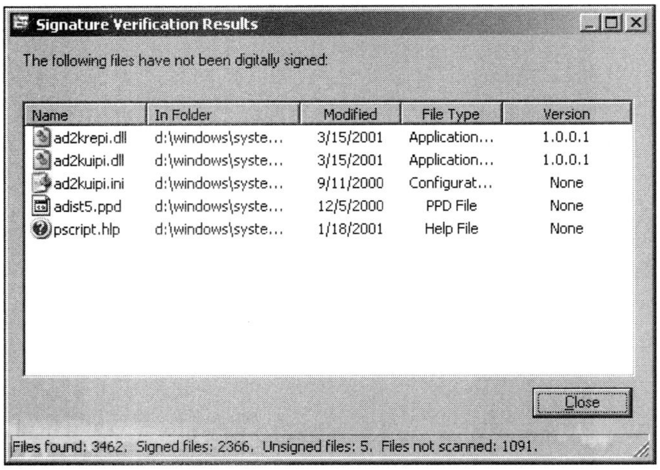

Figure 2-15 The results of the File Signature Verification scan

By default, the File Signature Verification utility only checks Windows Server 2003 system files. If you want to check other files to see if they are digitally signed, you must configure this in the program's advanced settings, as shown in Figure 2-16. In Activity 2-5, you will use the File Signature Verification utility to scan your server for unsigned system files.

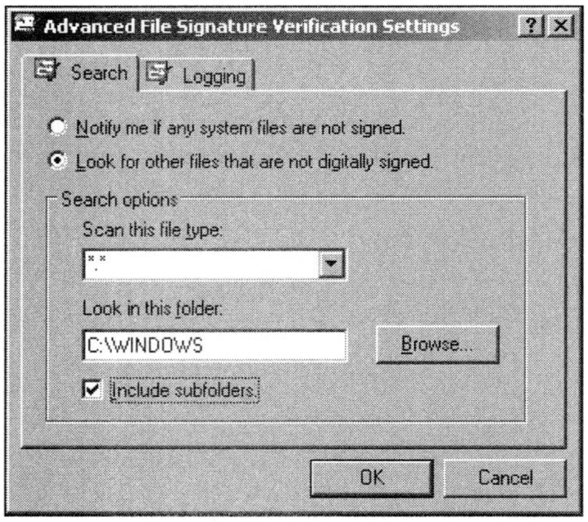

Figure 2-16 Scanning other files for digital signatures

Activity 2-5: Using the File Signature Verification Utility

Time Required: 10 minutes

Objective: Use the File Signature Verification utility to verify that Microsoft has digitally signed all installed system files.

Description: Dover Leasing still uses a number of older software packages on their servers for which Windows Server 2003 upgrades are not yet available. One of the concerns of the IT manager at Dover is that some of these older applications are overwriting system files with their own versions as part of their installation process. In this activity, you have been asked to use the File Signature Verification utility to scan your server to identify any system files that may not be digitally signed.

1. Click **Start**, and then click **Run**.
2. In the Open text box, type **sigverif.exe**, and then click **OK**. The File Signature Verification utility opens, as shown in Figure 2-17.

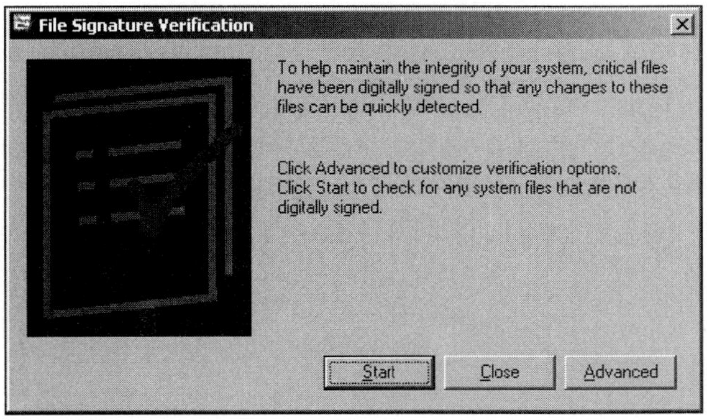

Figure 2-17 Starting the File Signature Verification utility

3. Click the **Advanced** button.
4. In the Advanced File Signature Verification Settings window, click the **Logging** tab. Ensure that the **Save the file signature verification results to a log file** check box is selected, and click **OK**.
5. Click the **Start** button to begin the file signature verification scanning process. Note that this process may take several minutes to complete.
6. Once scanning is complete, click the **Close** button.
7. Click the **Advanced** button and then click the **Logging** tab.
8. Click the **View Log** button to open the **SIGVERIF.TXT** file in Notepad.
9. Scroll through the contents of the log file being sure to note the number of files scanned and signed, as well as the Status column for individual files. Close the SIGVERIF.TXT file.
10. Click **Cancel** to close the Advanced File Signature Verification Settings window.
11. Click **Close** to close the File Signature Verification utility.

Windows Server 2003 also includes protection for any system files that may be overwritten by installing software. **Windows File Protection** helps to prevent the replacement of protected files such as .sys, .dll, .ocx, .ttf, .fon, and .exe files. When you install an application that attempts to replace a protected file, Windows File Protection checks the file's digital signature to determine if it is a correct Microsoft version. If the file is not the correct version, Windows File Protection replaces the file from a backup of the original file, which is stored in the hidden Windows\system32\dllcache folder. This feature is enabled by default and only allows the replacement of protected files from signed Windows Server 2003 service packs, hot fixes, OS upgrades, or the **Windows Update** Web site.

If you want to be sure that all of your Windows system files are the correct versions, Microsoft provides a utility called the **System File Checker**. The System File Checker is a command-line utility that scans and verifies all of the protected system files on your computer. If it discovers that a protected file has been overwritten, it replaces the file with an original backup from the dllcache folder.

In Activity 2-6, you will change the Windows Server 2003 folder options to make system files visible. In Activity 2-7, you will use the System File Checker to scan and verify protected system files.

Activity 2-6: Viewing Windows Server 2003 System Files

Time Required: 10 minutes

Objective: Make system files visible by changing Windows Server 2003 folder options.

Description: Having been told that Windows Server 2003 automatically caches copies of protected system files in a folder named dllcache, you have decided to open and view the contents of this folder to ensure that this is the case. However, because the dllcache folder has both its system and hidden attributes set, it is not visible in the Windows Server 2003 interface by default. In this activity, you will access Folder Options and change settings such that Windows Explorer will display both hidden and system files and folders.

1. Click **Start**, and then click **Run**. In the Open text box, type **explorer.exe** and click **OK**.
2. Click **Tools** on the menu bar, and then click **Folder Options**.
3. Click the **View** tab, as shown in Figure 2-18.

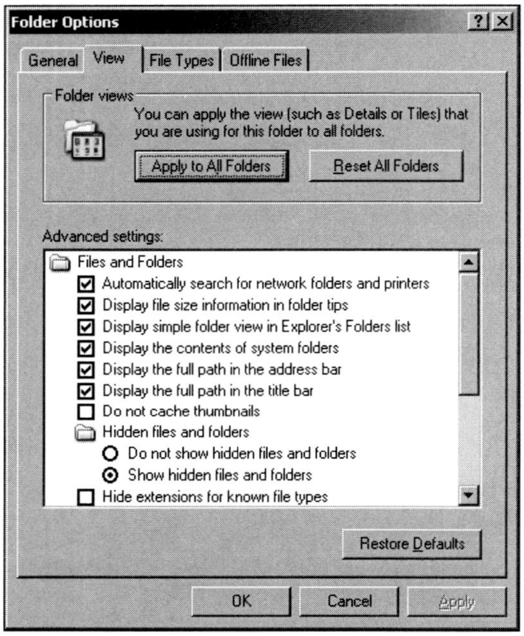

Figure 2-18 Revealing hidden files and folders

4. In the Advanced settings section, ensure that the **Show hidden files and folders** radio button is selected.
5. Uncheck the **Hide protected operating system files (Recommended)** check box. When the Warning window opens, click **Yes**.
6. Click **OK** to close the Folder Options window. Close Windows Explorer.
7. Click **Start**, and then click **Run**.
8. In the Open text box, type **%systemroot%** and click **OK**. The C:\WINDOWS directory on your server should appear.
9. Double-click the **system32** directory.
10. Scroll down until you find the dllcache directory. Notice that the directory name is listed in blue, meaning the folder is compressed. Because the folder has the hidden attribute set, its icon should appear transparent.

11. Notice that the attribute column for the dllcache folder contains the four letters RHSC. These represent the read-only, hidden, system, and compressed attributes of the folder respectively.
12. Double-click the **dllcache** folder to view its contents. These are backup copies of protected files that Windows File Protection will replace should the correct version not be present on the system.
13. Close the C:\WINDOWSsystem32\dllcache window.

Activity 2-7: Testing and Verifying Windows File Protection

Time Required: 20 minutes

Objective: Test the Windows File Protection feature and verify that system files are correct using the System File Checker utility.

Description: The IT manager at Dover Leasing has asked you to verify that the Windows File Protection feature in Windows Server 2003 works correctly. However, he has also let you know that when the system needs to replace a file and doesn't find it in the dllcache folder, it will attempt to access the original version of the file from the Windows Server 2003 source files. Because Windows Server 2003 was originally installed from a CD-ROM to which you currently do not have access, you have been provided with instructions as to how to edit the Registry to change the directory in which Windows File Protection and sfc.exe will attempt to gather the files. In this activity, you will change the source path directory to point to your D:\source folder, test Windows File Protection, and then configure sfc.exe to run once when your server is restarted.

1. Click **Start**, and then click **Run**.
2. In the Open text box, type **Regedit** and click **OK**.
3. Click the **plus sign (+)** next to HKEY_LOCAL_MACHINE to expand it.
4. Click the **plus sign (+)** next to SOFTWARE to expand it.
5. Click the **plus sign (+)** next to Windows to expand it.
6. Click the **plus sign (+)** next to CurrentVersion to expand it.
7. Click on the **Setup** folder.
8. Double-click the **SourcePath** value in the right-hand pane.
9. In the Edit String window, change the Value data to read **D:\source** and click **OK**. This changes the location from which Windows Server 2003 looks for its source files when required.
10. Close the Registry Editor.
11. Click **Start**, and then click **Run**. In the Open text box, type **C:\WINDOWS\system32** and click **OK**.
12. Scroll down the list of files until you find Notepad.exe. Right-click on **Notepad.exe** and click **Delete**.
13. When the Confirm File Delete window appears, click **Yes**.
14. Scroll to the bottom of the C:\WINDOWS\system32 window. Notice that after a few seconds, Notepad.exe again appears at the end of the list, because Windows File Protection has replaced the protected Notepad.exe file. Close the C:\WINDOWS\system32 window.
15. Click **Start**, and then click **Run**. In the Open text box, type **cmd** and click **OK**.
16. At the command line, type **sfc /?** and press **Enter**. Notice the switches available with the sfc command and their purposes.

17. Type **sfc /scanonce** and press **Enter**. This will force the System File Checker to scan for changes to system files when the server next reboots.
18. Close the command prompt window, and restart your computer. Log on using your **AdminXX** account, note the scanning process that takes place, as well as its duration.

INSTALLING AND MANAGING WINDOWS SERVER 2003 UPDATES USING SERVICE PACKS AND HOT FIXES

As problems and bugs are discovered with the Windows Server 2003 operating system, Microsoft provides updates known as service packs that can be applied to the current operating system to fix the reported problems. As service packs are released, a version sequence number identifies them. For example, as each service pack is released, it may be called Service Pack 1, Service Pack 2, and so on. By their nature, service packs are also cumulative, meaning that Service Pack 3 would include new updates, as well as those originally released in Service Packs 1 and 2. The latest service pack can be downloaded from the Microsoft Web site at *www.microsoft.com*, or you can order a CD-ROM for a small fee.

Between service pack releases, there may be bugs or security alerts discovered that require immediate updates. These interim updates are called Quick Fix Engineering (QFE) updates, or, more commonly, **hot fixes** for short. Windows Server 2003 hot fixes are usually deployed to fix specific problems or security issues with the operating system. When the next service pack is released, it incorporates all of the service packs and hot fixes previously released. Depending upon the type of hot fix available, you usually access a Microsoft Web site to download the patch. You can install the patch by double-clicking the downloaded file.

You can also use the **Windows Update** feature from the Help and Support tool or the Program Files section of the Start menu to install service packs and hot fixes, as shown in Figure 2-19.

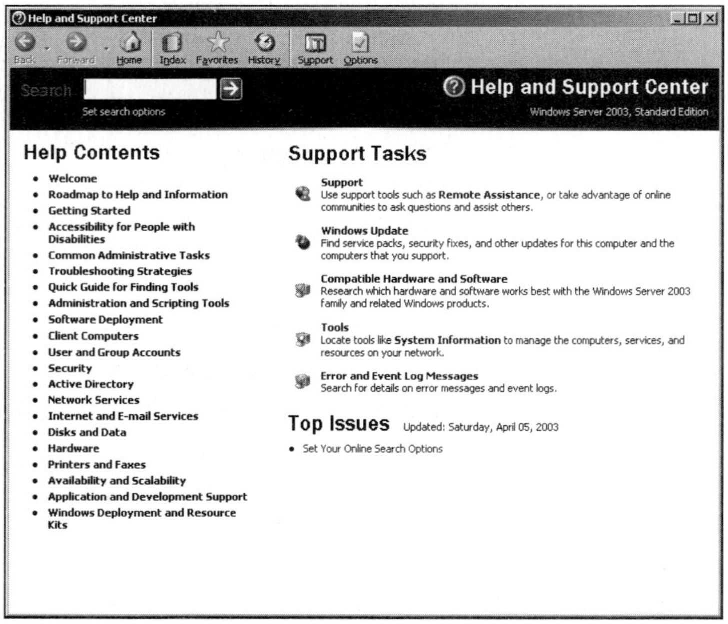

Figure 2-19 The installation of a Windows .NET Server 2003 service pack

When you click the Windows Update hyperlink, you will have the option of scanning the operating system to determine which service packs and updates are required on your computer, as shown in Figure 2-20. A list of critical updates and service packs is then listed according to what is currently available. In Activity 2-8, you will access the Windows Update tool to install an available update.

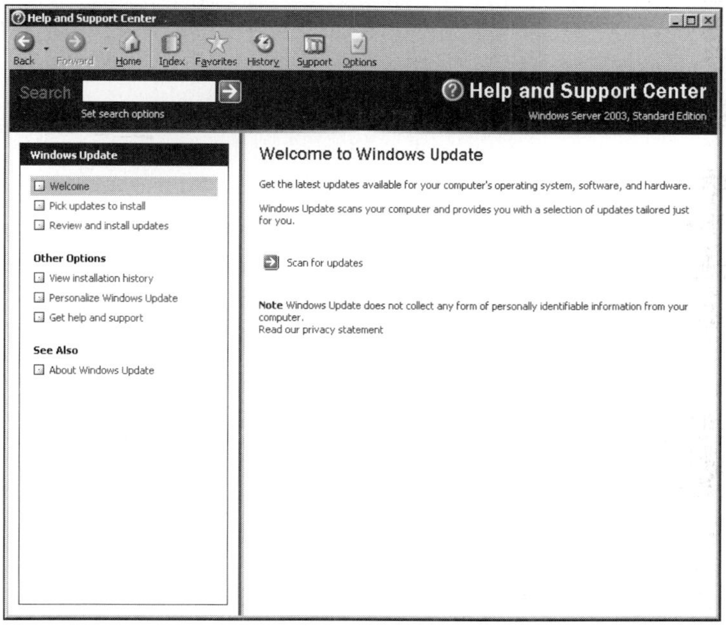

Figure 2-20 Accessing the Windows Update utility

Activity 2-8: Using Microsoft Windows Update

Time Required: 10 minutes

Objective: Find and install hot fixes and product updates using the Windows Update utility.

Description: Dover Leasing has always manually downloaded and installed any necessary hot fixes or product updates as Microsoft has released them. Noting that this process can be cumbersome, prone to error, and difficult to document, you have suggested that the Windows Update feature of Windows Server 2003 be considered as an alternative. Having used this feature in the past, the IT manager found that it often included unnecessary updates that later caused problems. In this activity, you will demonstrate the features and functionality of the Windows Update tool, install an update, and visit the Windows Update Web site.

1. Click **Start**, and then click **Help and Support**.
2. Under the Support Tasks heading, click the **Windows Update** hyperlink.
3. At the Welcome to Windows Update screen, click the **Scan for updates** hyperlink.
4. Once the scanning process is complete, click the **Windows Server 2003 Family** hyperlink in the left-hand navigation menu.
5. From the list of Recommended Updates, choose a smaller-sized update and click the **Add** button. Note that it is possible that there may not be any updates available.
6. In the left-hand navigation menu, click the **Review and install updates** hyperlink.
7. At the Total Selected Updates screen, click the **Install Now** button.
8. When the licensing screen appears, click **Accept**.
9. Once the download and installation processes are complete, you will be prompted to restart your computer. Click **OK** to restart. After the computer restarts, login with your ***AdminXX*** user account.
10. Open Internet Explorer and type the URL **http://windowsupdate.microsoft.com** in the Address bar. Press **Enter**.

11. Notice that the format of the Windows Update Web site is similar to the interface found on Windows Server 2003.
12. Close all open windows.

Windows Update downloads and automatically installs all updates that you had indicated on the main page. If you have the need to uninstall any of the hot fixes or service packs, you can uninstall them via the Help and Support tool or by accessing the Add/Remove Programs applet in Control Panel.

To verify which hot fixes and service packs have been installed, you can download a utility called the **Microsoft Baseline Security Analyzer (MBSA)**. This utility can be downloaded from: *www.microsoft.com/technet/treeview/default.asp?url=/technet/security/tools/Tools/MBSAhome.asp.*

Slipstreaming Windows Server 2003 Service Packs

Slipstreaming is a process that integrates a Windows Server 2003 service pack with the original Windows Server 2003 installation files. The advantage of this is that you no longer need to perform separate installations of the operating system and the individual service packs. When you perform a new installation, the service pack is automatically installed with the original setup files. Furthermore, when new services are added to the server, service packs do not need to be reapplied because the most recent versions exist within the slipstreamed source files.

After the files have been extracted, browse to the \i386\update folder found in the extraction directory, and type "update -s <*install point name and path*>".

For example, if you have extracted the service pack to a folder called C:\SP and you want to integrate this service pack with an installation point on drive D: called SOURCE, you would type "C:\SP\i386\update\update.exe -s:d:\SOURCE" at the command prompt.

The Windows Server 2003 Service Pack Setup dialog box opens and starts to integrate the service pack files into the installation point.

Chapter Summary

- Before installing Windows Server 2003, you must consider a number of pre-installation tasks that can potentially affect both your organizational and hardware needs. Some of these tasks include understanding the network infrastructure, domain configuration, interoperability issues, existing applications, and current hardware configurations.
- When assessing the organization's current and future hardware needs, check the Microsoft Hardware Compatibility List to verify that Windows Server 2003 has been tested with the hardware that is to be upgraded or installed. You can also use the Microsoft Windows Update Advisor and the Microsoft Windows Catalog Web site.
- Verify that your system BIOS has been updated and is compatible with Windows Server 2003 Advanced Configuration and Power Interface (ACPI). ACPI can cause an installation failure if your BIOS does not support ACPI.
- Some post-installation tasks that you might need to perform include checking the Device Manager for device failures, updating device drivers, and installing the latest service pack or hot fix.
- To assist in maintaining computer stability, you can configure driver signing to only allow drivers and system files to be installed if they contain authorized digital signatures.
- A Windows Server 2003 installation point can be easily integrated with the latest service pack to prevent you from having to perform a separate service pack installation after the operating system installation.

Key Terms

Add Hardware Wizard — Enables you to add hardware and troubleshoot any hardware-related problems.

Basic Input/Output System (BIOS) — A program stored on a flash memory chip attached to the motherboard that establishes the initial communication between the components of the computer, such as the hard drive, CD-ROM, floppy disk, video, and memory.

Device Manager — Used to view and modify hardware device properties, update device drivers, and uninstall unneeded hardware.

driver signing — Ensures that a driver for a specific device has been verified by Microsoft and a unique digital signature has been incorporated into the driver.

File Signature Verification — This utility can identify unsigned files and give you information such as the file name, location, modification date, and version number.

hot fixes — Interim updates to Windows Server 2003 that are released between major service pack releases. These are used to fix operating system bugs and security issues.

interrupt request (IRQ) — A signal sent by a device to notify the processor when the device is ready to accept or send information. Each device typically has a unique IRQ number.

Microsoft Baseline Security Analyzer — Analyzes the security of your server, including information about any vulnerabilities it finds.

Microsoft Hardware Compatibility List (HCL) — A list of hardware devices that have been tested by Microsoft to determine whether they can work with Windows Server 2003.

Microsoft Windows Upgrade Advisor — A Windows Server 2003 utility used to check for hardware and software compatibility.

service packs — Periodic updates to the Windows Server 2003 operating system to fix reported bugs and security issues.

slipstreaming — A process that integrates a Windows Server 2003 service pack with the original Windows Server 2003 installation files.

System File Checker — A command-line utility that scans and verifies all of the protected system files on your computer.

Windows File Protection — Helps to prevent the replacement of protected Windows Server 2003 files such as .sys, .dll, .ocx, .ttf, .fon, and .exe files.

Windows Update — A Microsoft Web site used to automatically download and install Windows Server 2003 service packs, hot fixes, and updates.

Review Questions

1. What is the first step that should be completed when installing Windows Server 2003 on a new computer?
   a. typing winnt32 at the command prompt
   b. typing winnt at the command prompt
   c. typing ERD at the command prompt
   d. verifying that your hardware is listed in the Hardware Compatibility List
2. The /runonce switch should be used in conjunction with the System File Checker utility to perform a system scan once a server reboots. True or False?
3. After installing Windows Server 2003 on an older computer, you notice that some features such as Advanced Power Management do not work. You are logged in as the administrator. What might be wrong?
   a. You do not have permissions to run any Advanced Power Management features.
   b. The computer BIOS needs to be updated.
   c. Windows Server 2003 does not support Advanced Power Management.
   d. Advanced Power Management only functions on Pentium III processors.

4. Which command can be used to start the Microsoft Windows Upgrade Advisor?
   a. winnt /checkupgradeonly
   b. winnt /s
   c. winnt32 /checkupgradeonly
   d. winnt32 /s
5. You want to check the hardware and software of a Windows 2000 Advanced Server computer for Windows Server 2003 compatibility. You insert the Windows Standard Server 2003 CD-ROM into the drive and attempt to start the Microsoft Windows Upgrade Advisor, but it fails. What is wrong?
   a. Windows 2000 cannot run the Microsoft Windows Upgrade Advisor.
   b. Windows 2000 Advanced Server cannot be upgraded to Windows Standard Server 2003. Run the Microsoft Windows Upgrade Advisor from a Windows Server 2003 Enterprise Edition CD-ROM.
   c. You do not have the proper permissions to run the Microsoft Windows Upgrade Advisor.
   d. You can only run the Microsoft Windows Upgrade Advisor after the installation is complete.
6. Which of the following items are included in the recommended minimum hardware requirements for Windows Server 2003 Server? (Choose all that apply.)
   a. 128 MB of RAM
   b. Intel Pentium 550
   c. 1 GB of space for setup
   d. all of the above
7. Which of the following is used to view and modify hardware device properties, update device drivers, and uninstall unneeded hardware?
   a. File Signature Verification
   b. Add/Remove Programs
   c. Device Manager
   d. b and c
8. Windows Server 2003 stores cached copies of protected system files in the %systemroot%\system32\backupcache folder. True or False?
9. Service pack files are not slipstreamed automatically during the installation process. True or False?
10. What icon is used to represent a disabled device in Device Manager?
    a. exclamation point
    b. red "x"
    c. red arrow
    d. blue circle
11. Which of the following choices are available driver signing options? (Choose three.)
    a. Block
    b. Disable
    c. Warn
    d. Ignore
12. Which Windows Server 2003 tool(s) can assist you in troubleshooting hardware problems? (Choose all that apply.)
    a. Device Manager
    b. Add/Remove Programs
    c. Add Hardware
    d. Windows Update

13. Which command is used to start the File Signature Verification utility?
    a. sigupdate
    b. verifsig
    c. sfc /verify
    d. sigverif
14. Which switch is used to integrate a service pack into a Windows Server 2003 installation point?
    a. update -a
    b. update -x
    c. update -s
    d. update -u
15. Windows Server 2003 requires an absolute minimum of 64 MB of RAM to function. True or False?
16. Which tool can be used to verify which hot fixes and service packs have been installed on your computer?
    a. MBSA
    b. sigverif
    c. winnt32 /verify
    d. scandisk
17. In Windows Server 2003, the Windows Update utility is accessed via the Device Manager tool. True or False?

18 The Block option effectively turns off the driver-signing requirement in Windows Server 2003. True or False?

19 When a service pack is slipstreamed, the files that it contains are integrated with existing Windows Server 2003 source files. True or False?

CASE PROJECTS

Case Project 2-1

As a junior network administrator at Dover Leasing, you have been asked to document the processes that administrators should follow as part of upgrading servers to Windows Server 2003. What information would you want to collect and document before starting the upgrade process? List and explain at least five main points.

Case Project 2-2

A few of the older servers at Dover Leasing are Pentium 200 models running Windows 2000 Server. The IT manager has asked you to verify whether these servers will be capable of running Windows Server 2003. What additional information do you need before you can answer this question? What can you do to verify whether Windows Server 2003 Professional works with these computers?

Case Project 2-3

The IT Manager at Dover Leasing has asked you confirm that the main hardware components installed in your server are listed on the Microsoft Hardware Compatibility list. Use Device Manager to find manufacturer and model information for the display adapter, network adapter, and DVD/CD-ROM installed in your server. Use this information to search the online Hardware Compatibility List found at *www.microsoft.com/hwdq/hcl/search.asp* to verify whether the compatibility level of each of these devices with Windows Server 2003.

Case Project 2-4

As part of a new server security strategy at Dover Leasing, the IT manager has mandated that all servers should have their floppy disk and CD-ROM drives disabled by default. You have been asked to disable each of these devices for testing purposes and then restart your server to ensure that they are not accessible once logged on. Once verified, be sure to return each drive to an enabled state.

CHAPTER

3

ADMINISTERING ACTIVE DIRECTORY

After reading this chapter and completing the exercises, you will be able to:

- Create and modify Active Directory objects such as organizational units, users, computers, and groups
- Identify and troubleshoot Active Directory group types and scopes
- Administer Active Directory object permissions
- Manage and troubleshoot Active Directory replication

In the previous chapters, you learned the basics of network administration, Active Directory, and installing Windows Server 2003. Your next step is to understand how to access hardware and software needs for the Active Directory containers, users, groups, and other objects stored within the directory service. The **Active Directory Users and Computers** console provides you with an administrative tool to help you perform the tasks needed to create and manage these objects. The first part of this chapter discusses how to use this tool to manage your Active Directory domain.

Managing Active Directory also requires a thorough knowledge of how object permissions are inherited and delegated throughout the domain. For example, you may want to allow a specific group of users full control over a particular **organizational unit (OU)**. You can apply these permissions manually or use the Delegation of Control Wizard to assist you in assigning these rights to the group. More information is presented on administering permissions and delegation later in the chapter.

As a Windows Server 2003 administrator, you also need to have a good understanding of how Active Directory replicates throughout the infrastructure. Because Windows Server 2003 uses a multi-master domain controller concept, you need to understand the implications of an object being modified by two different administrators at the same time. The final section of this chapter discusses the concept of managing and troubleshooting Active Directory replication concepts.

Administering Active Directory Objects

In reality, administering a Windows Server 2003 domain means administering Active Directory objects. Objects stored in the Active Directory database can be either **container** objects or **leaf** objects. A container is an object that is used to contain and organize related objects within the Active Directory hierarchy. Container objects can consist of other child containers or leaf objects. An example of a container object is the OU, which can consist of objects such as users, groups, and other OUs.

A leaf is an object that represents resources within a selected domain. Leaf objects are stored within a container and cannot contain other objects. An example of a leaf object is a user or computer object.

After Active Directory is installed on a Windows Server 2003 server, management tools are automatically installed to assist you in the administration of the directory objects. Look at the Administrative Tools menu to discover a number of new entries such as **Active Directory Users and Computers**, **Active Directory Sites and Services**, and **Active Directory Domains and Trusts**, as shown in Figure 3-1.

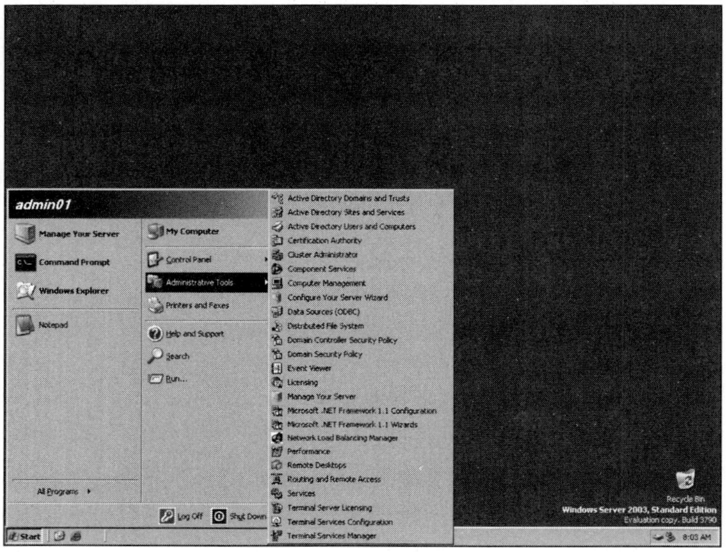

Figure 3-1 Viewing the Administrative Tools menu

Each of these tools assists in configuring and managing specific areas of Active Directory. By default, these tools are only installed on Windows Server 2003 servers. Because each of these tools is a Microsoft Management Console (MMC) application, they can also be installed on systems running Windows XP Professional. The easiest way to make these tools available to Windows XP machines is to install the Windows Server 2003 Administrative Tools Pack, which is named Adminpak.msi and is found in the \I386 folder of the Windows Server 2003 CD-ROM. You can install this installation file locally or make it available via Group Policy. More information on deploying applications with Group Policy is presented in Chapter 4.

Most of your time will likely be spent using the Active Directory Users and Computers console because this is where all OU, user, group, computer, and published information is created and maintained. The next section explores this management console in more detail.

Exploring Active Directory Users and Computers

Active Directory Users and Computers is the primary administration tool used to manage users, groups, OUs, and published information within an Active Directory domain. It is also one of the tools that can be used to create and manage Group Policy objects, which control such elements as user desktop settings, security, logon/logoff **scripts** (computer programs that automate routine operations), and software deployment. This tool is an MMC application with the filename of Dsa.msc.

To open the Active Directory Users and Computers console, you can either type "dsa.msc" at the Run command or open it from the Administrative Tools shortcut on the Start menu. The Active Directory Users and Computers console is shown in Figure 3-2. In Activity 3-1, you will explore the Active Directory Users and Computers interface.

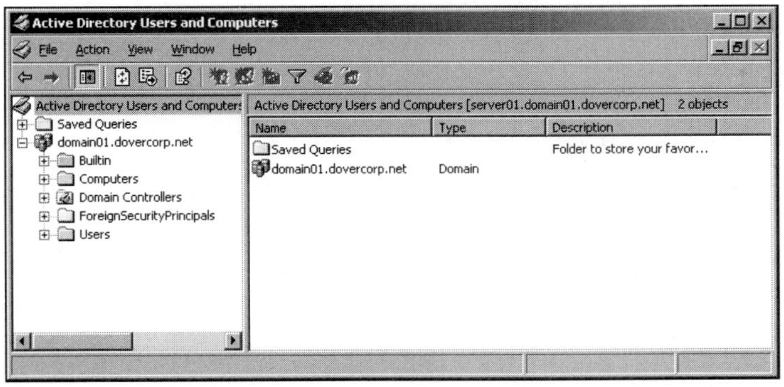

Figure 3-2 Viewing the Active Directory Users and Computers console

Activity 3-1: Using Active Directory Users and Computers

Time Required: 10 minutes

Objective: Open and explore the Active Directory Users and Computers interface.

Description: The IT Manager at Dover Leasing has informed you that you will be responsible for training all newly hired administrators on how to use Active Directory Users and Computers to create user and computer accounts, as well as to manage group and OU membership. As such, he has asked you to familiarize yourself with the tool and document the steps required to carry out these tasks. In this activity, you will explore Active Directory Users and Computers to familiarize yourself with the tool's interface and capabilities.

1. Click **Start**, point to **Administrative Tools**, and click **Active Directory Users and Computers**.
2. Right-click **Active Directory Users and Computers** at the top of the left navigation menu and click **Connect to Domain Controller**. Note the current domain controller on which Active Directory Users and Computers is focused, as well as the ability to connect to other domain controllers. Click **OK**.
3. Right-click the **Domain*XX*.Dovercorp.net** icon and click **Properties**. On the General tab, type the words **Windows 2003 domain** in the description text box.
4. Click the **Managed By** tab, and then click the **Change** button. In the Enter the object name to select text box, type **Admin*XX***, where *XX* is your preassigned student number. Click **OK**. Click **OK** again to close the Domain*XX*.Dovercorp.net Properties dialog box.
5. Click the **plus sign (+)** next to the Domain*XX*.Dovercorp.net icon to expand it, if necessary.
6. Click the **Builtin** container to view its contents. Then click the **Computers**, **Domain Controllers**, **ForeignSecurityPrincipals**, and **Users** containers to view their contents as well.
7. Right-click the **Users** container and select **New**. Note the options that exist for creating new objects within the Users container, as shown in Figure 3-3. In the Users container, right-click the **Administrator** user account to view the options provided by the shortcut menu.

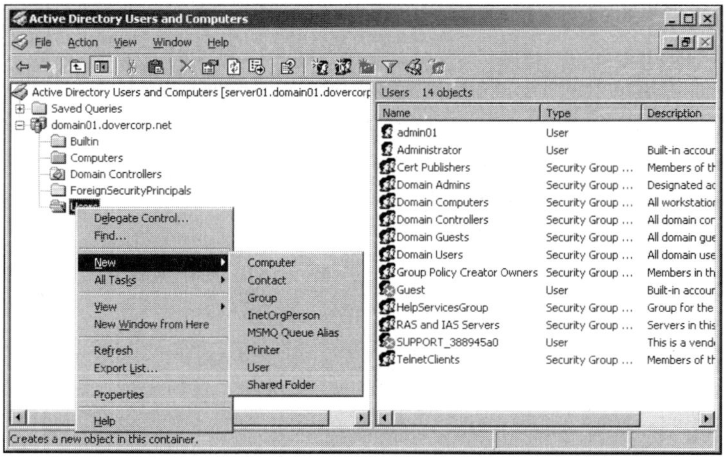

Figure 3-3 Creating new objects within the Users container

8. Right-click the **DomainXX.Dovercorp.net** icon and click **Find**. Click the **Find** list arrow to display a list of the different object types that can be searched for using this tool.
9. On the Users, Contacts, and Groups tab, type **admin** in the Name text box. Click the **Find Now** button.
10. In the Search results section, right-click the account **Admin*XX*** and note the various options that are provided. Right-click the **Administrators** group and note the associated options.
11. Double-click the **Admin*XX*** account. Notice that the properties of the Admin*XX* account appear. Click **Cancel** to close the properties of the Admin*XX* account.
12. To clear the search results, click the **Clear All** button. When prompted, click **OK** to confirm that search results should be cleared. Close the Find window.
13. Move your cursor over each of the icon buttons found under the menu items. Note the purpose of each button according to the tool tips that appear.
14. Close Active Directory Users and Computers.

When a Windows Server 2003 server is promoted to domain controller, several container objects are created automatically. Table 3-1 lists and explains the purpose of each of the default containers created when Active Directory is installed.

The **security accounts manager (SAM) database** is the local database that stores user and group information for stand-alone Windows .NET Server computers. When a member server is promoted to a domain controller, all information in the SAM database is transferred to the Active Directory database. Even though it may seem that you will never use the SAM database again, do not forget the administrator account and password that are stored in the SAM database. This is the account that is used to boot the computer into the recovery console and directory services restore mode. More information about the recovery console is discussed in Chapter 10.

Even though the default containers are used initially to store various Active Directory objects, you are free to modify, create, and move objects to any container desired, including the root container. The only objects that cannot be moved are the local security groups stored within the Builtin container.

It is recommended to keep all domain controller objects together within the Domain Controllers OU. Moving domain controllers out of this container may cause replication problems between the individual replicas of the Active Directory database.

3

Table 3-1 Purpose of the default container objects in Active Directory

Container Object	Purpose of Container
Builtin	This container holds local **security group** objects for the domain. During an upgrade, this is where the local groups of the member server are placed.
Computers	This container holds all member server and workstation account objects that belong to the domain.
Domain Controllers	This OU holds the computer accounts for each Active Directory domain controller within the domain.
ForeignSecurityPrincipals	This container is used to store objects that represent security principals such as users from trusted Windows Server 2003 or Windows 2000/NT domains outside of the forest.
Users	This container holds all user accounts and global groups for the domain. During an upgrade from Windows NT, all user accounts are placed into this container.

Active Directory Users and Computers enables you to create new containers and objects easily via a shortcut menu. Figure 3-4 displays this shortcut menu being used to create a new OU within the *Dovercorp.net* domain.

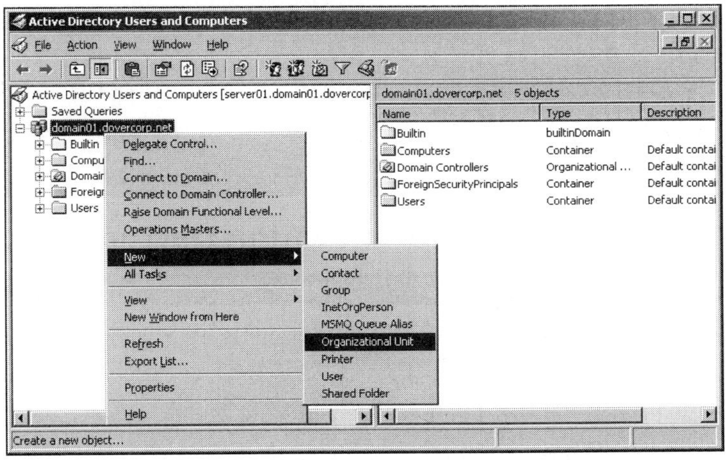

Figure 3-4 Creating a new object in Active Directory

As stated previously, there are a number of objects that you can create within the domain. Table 3-2 lists the objects that can be created with Active Directory Users and Computers.

The following sections discuss creating and managing the most common objects that you encounter: OUs, user accounts, groups, and computer objects.

Creating Organizational Units

An OU is a logical container that contains other objects such as users, groups, computers, published resources, or other OUs. OUs can only consist of objects from their home domain. The main reason to create an OU is to organize and partition a single domain into logical administrative units. For example, a company may have three departments within its organization: Marketing, Sales, and Accounting. You could place the objects from different departments into the root container of Active Directory, as shown in Figure 3-5, but you would most likely have some administrative problems with this structure.

Table 3-2 Objects available in Active Directory Users and Computers

Object Type	Description
Computer	An object that represents a computer account that is a member of the domain
Contact	An object that represents an account that does not have any logon or security rights within the domain; typically used for e-mail or informational purposes
Group	An object that represents a collection of users, computers, contacts, or other groups; Windows Server 2003 groups can be used as security groups or e-mail distribution lists
InetOrgPerson	An object class used in many Lightweight Directory Access Protocol (LDAP) and X.500 directory services to represent a person; this object class is provided to ease migrations from other directory services to Active Directory
MSMQ queue alias	An object class used to define a message queue for public or private queues that are not natively stored within Active Directory
Organizational unit	A logical container object that can contain and organize users, groups, computers, and other OUs within a single domain
Printer	An object that represents a shared printer available on the network
User	An object that contains all of the information that defines a user that has access permissions to the network; this includes the user name, password, and group memberships
Shared folder	An object that represents a shared folder available on the network and that has been published into Active Directory

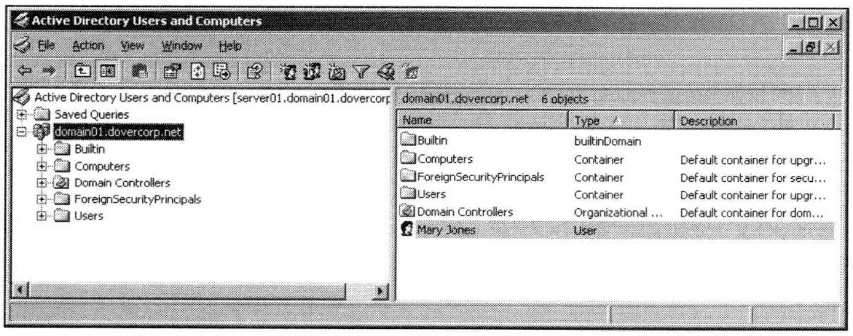

Figure 3-5 Placing objects into the root container

Note OU objects can be distinguished from built-in containers by their associated icons in Active Directory Users and Computers. Built-in containers use a traditional folder icon, whereas a folder icon that includes a book symbol signifies an OU.

How would you delegate permissions to allow a specific user to only manage the Sales Department objects? How would you control the desktop environment of only the Accounting Department? If you wanted to deploy a specific application to only the Marketing Department, how would you accomplish this task? As you can see, if you organize the objects into specific OUs, administration becomes easier. Figure 3-6 illustrates creating various OUs and the placement of related objects within a specific OU.

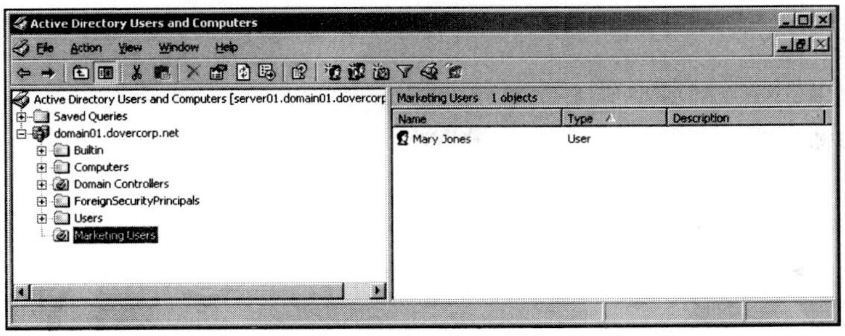

Figure 3-6 Organizing objects within an OU structure

OUs can be useful for a number of management tasks. Administrators can use OUs to create and apply Group Policies to either the entire domain or specific OUs within a domain. Administration can also be delegated in a very granular fashion to allow specific individuals or groups to have various levels of control over OUs, without necessarily requiring full administrative permissions. For example, you may want to allow the office manager to unlock or reset user passwords within a specific department. By delegating this task to another individual, you free up your time to do other tasks, as well as allow the OU to have local control over its own resources.

When designing an OU structure, try to design with administrative delegation and Group Policy in mind. Your goal is to design a domain that is logically organized, easy to administer, and easy to control.

Activity 3-2: Creating OU Objects

Time Required: 10 minutes

Objective: Use Active Directory Users and Computers to create OU objects.

Description: Based on the flexibility that OUs provide in terms of administration and deploying policy settings for users and computers, the IT manager has decided that you should create an OU structure based on Dover Leasing's functional areas. In this activity, you will create an OU structure that will be used throughout the remaining activities in this chapter.

1. Click **Start**, and then click **Run**.
2. In the Open text box, type **dsa.msc** and click **OK**. Active Directory Users and Computers opens.
3. Click the **plus sign (+)** next to Domain*XX*.Dovercorp.net to expand it if necessary. Right-click **Domain*XX*.Dovercorp.net**, select **New**, and then click **Organizational Unit**.
4. In the **New Object – Organizational Unit** window, type **Marketing** in the Name text box and click **OK**. Notice that a new OU appears listed under the Domain*XX*.Dovercorp.net domain.
5. Repeat Steps 3 and 4 to create four additional OUs named **Sales**, **Finance**, **Executives**, and **Information Technology**. Creating the Sales OU is illustrated in Figure 3-7.
6. Right-click the **Information Technology** OU, select **New**, and then click **Organizational Unit**. In the New Object – Organizational Unit window, type **Help Desk** in the Name text box and click **OK**. Notice that a new OU appears listed under the Information Technology OU.
7. Repeat Step 6 to create an additional OU named **Network Support** within the Information Technology OU.

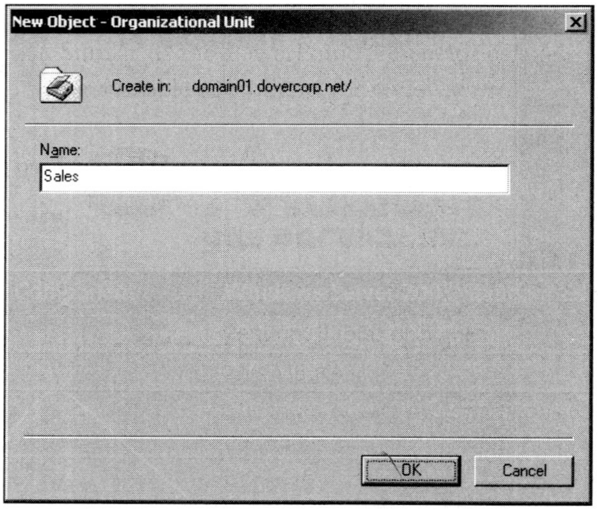

Figure 3-7 Creating a new organizational unit

8. Expand all OUs so that all of the newly created OUs are visible from the left navigation menu in Active Directory Users and Computers if they are not already visible.
9. Close Active Directory Users and Computers.

Tip: Most organizations create an OU structure that is static and does not change for the first level. For example, an international company with a single domain might have the first level of the OU structure based upon geographic locations. For a smaller company with a single domain, the first level may be based according to department. Again, the main goal is to create a granular structure that meets the Group Policy and delegation needs of the organization.

Creating New User Accounts

A **user account** is an object that is stored in Active Directory that represents all of the information that defines a physical user with access permissions to the network. The information that defines a physical user may include attributes such as first and last name, password, and group memberships, as well as a number of other options.

Any person who needs access to resources available on the network requires a user account. User accounts can assist in the administration and security of the network by making it possible to:

- Require authentication of anyone connecting to the network
- Control access to network resources such as shared folders or printers
- Monitor access to resources by auditing actions performed by a user logged on with a specific account

When creating a new user account, it is important that an organization set standards on the various elements of a user object. Some of these standards might include:

- *Establishing a naming convention*—Each user account name within the domain should follow a consistent naming convention. Common examples include:
  - *First name and last initial*: The account name for Kirk Jefferies would be *KirkJ*
  - *First initial and last name*: The account name for Karen Armstrong would be *Karmstrong*.
  - *Last name and first initial*: The account name for Mike Smith would be *Smithm*. Adding additional initials such as the first letter of a user's middle name can accommodate users with the same name.

- *Controlling password ownership*—You need to decide whether you control the password for each user or allow users to maintain their own passwords. A password policy that requires a password at least six characters long, containing a variety of alphanumeric characters, and that has a password expiration setting is considered a best practice by many organizations.
- *Including additional required attributes*—You need to decide which additional attributes you should include when creating the user account. For example, will you require that all phone numbers and e-mail addresses be included with the account information? Keep in mind that every additional attribute requires additional replication bandwidth and storage space within Active Directory.

Tip: The user logon name is also called the **user principal name (UPN)** when combined with the domain suffix listed next to the User logon name text box (e.g., *@dovercorp.net*). The UPN allows users to log on from any trusted domain within the forest by simply providing the UPN name and password in the logon screen. This is a convenient feature because administrators can configure the UPN to look like a user's e-mail address and allow users to log on to the network using this convention.

The process of creating new user accounts also allows you to configure a number of initial account settings, such as whether a user's password ever expires or if the account should initially be disabled. The initial account policy options are listed in Table 3-3.

Table 3-3 Initial account policy options for a new user account

Option	Description
User must change password at next logon	Requires a new user to change their password upon initial logon; this option will be turned off when the password change takes place
User cannot change password	Prevents the user from being able to change the password
Password never expires	Prevents the account from expiring as configured in the password expiration policy of the domain
Account is disabled	If checked, the account cannot be used to log on to the domain

Activity 3-3: Creating Domain User Accounts

Time Required: 20 minutes

Objective: Use Active Directory Users and Computers to create user accounts.

Description: In the past, Dover Leasing hasn't had a set naming convention for user accounts. Some accounts were created using first names only, while other variations were created as the company grew larger. Hoping to address some of the scalability issues previously encountered, Dover's IT manager has decided that all corporate user names should follow a convention of first initial and last name. For cases where two users have the same name, the solution will be to use the first initial of subsequent users' middle names to ensure uniqueness. In this activity, you will create a number of new user accounts within your dedicated child domain.

1. Open **Active Directory Users and Computers**.
2. Right-click the **Users** container, select **New**, and click **User**.
3. In the New Object – User dialog box, type **John** in the First name text box, as shown in Figure 3-8.

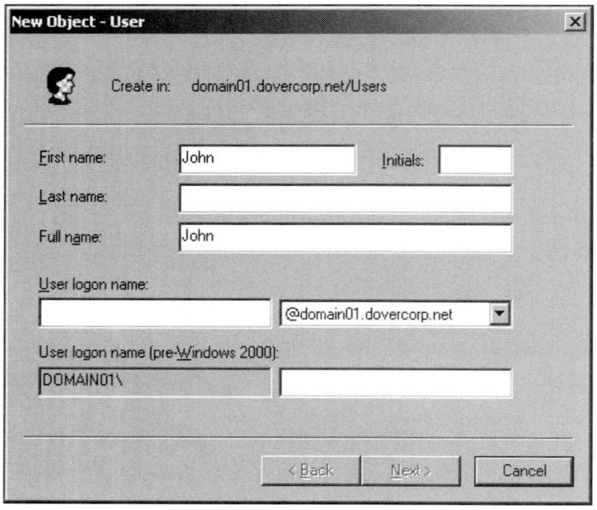

Figure 3-8 Creating a new user object

4. Press the **Tab** key twice to reach the Last name text box and type **Smith**. Notice that the Full name text box is populated automatically.
5. Press the **Tab** key twice to reach the User logon name field. Type **jsmith** and press the **Tab** key.
6. In the list box, ensure that your domain name in the form **Domain*XX*.Dovercorp.net** is selected rather than the Dovercorp.net domain. Click the **Next** button.
7. In the Password text box, shown in Figure 3-9, type **Password01** and press the **Tab** key. In the **Confirm password** text box, type **Password01** again.

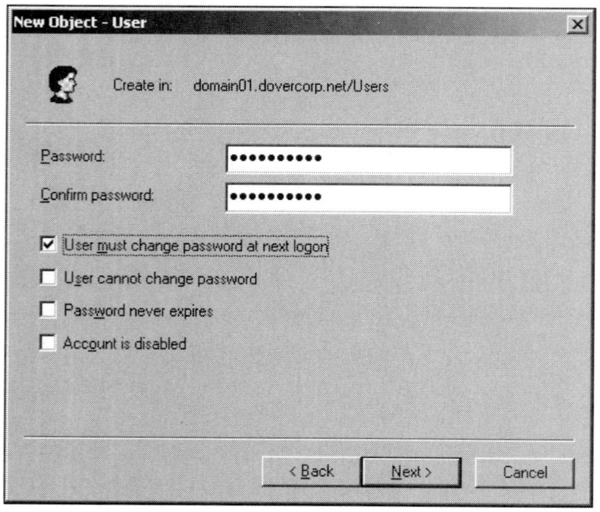

Figure 3-9 Configuring password and initial password policies for a new user object

8. Uncheck the **User must change password at next logon** check box and click **Next**. Click **Finish**.

9. Repeat Steps 2 through 8 to create user accounts for **Mark Manore**, **Frank Adili**, **Christy Jackson**, **John Harold Smith**, **Chris Medved**, **Moira Cowan**, **Mike Aubert**, and **Jason Zandri**. Remember to use the user account naming convention originally specified in the description for this activity.
10. When finished, leave Active Directory Users and Computers open.

Modifying User Account Attributes

When you create a new user account, the initial attribute options are very basic. After you create the account, there are a number of additional tasks and attributes that you can apply to the user account. Some of the more popular tasks include:

- *Copy*—Used to copy and create a new account based on some of the attributes, such as group memberships
- *Add to a Group*—Used to quickly add selected users to a specific group
- *Disable Account*—Used to disable the selected account, thus denying access to secured domain resources
- *Reset Password*—Used to reset the password of the selected user account; you do not need to know the previous password to complete this task
- *Move*—Used to move the selected object to another container within the domain
- *Open Home Page*—Used to open the home page configured in the properties of the user account
- *Send Mail*—Used to send an e-mail message to the e-mail address specified in the properties of a user account, group, or contact
- *Properties*—Used to access the various attributes of the selected user object

To view the additional tasks, right-click the user account, as shown in Figure 3-10.

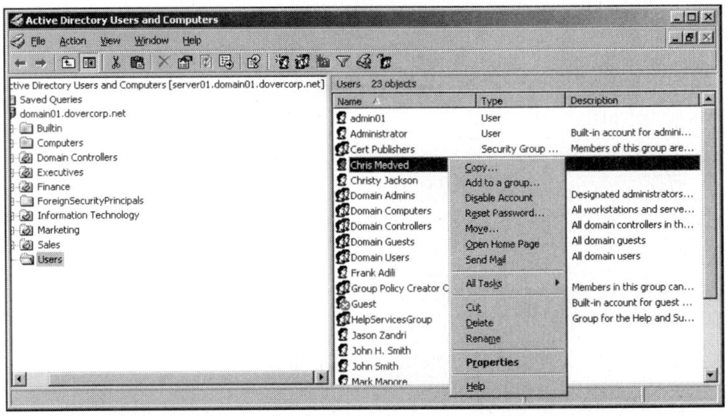

Figure 3-10 Viewing the additional tasks associated with a user object

To view and modify user account attributes, right-click the user account and then click Properties. As shown in Figure 3-11, a user account has a number of tabs that allow you to add specific information or enable specific functionality for the user account.

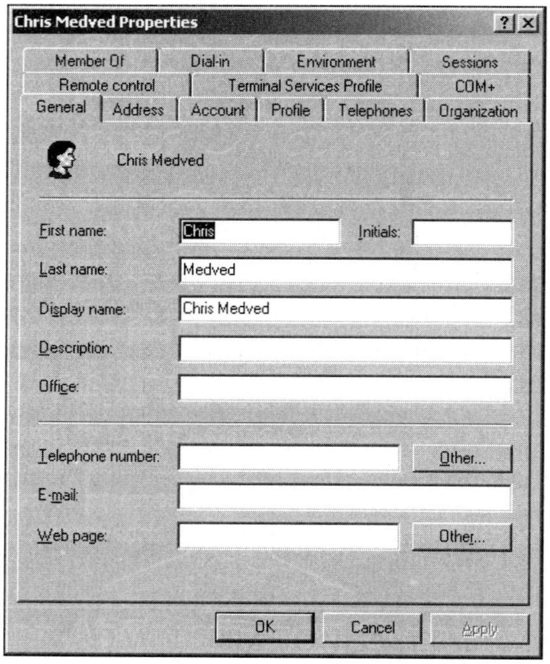

Figure 3-11 Viewing user object attributes

You can use most of the attributes listed in the properties dialog box of a user account as search criteria within Active Directory. For example, if you wanted to find the address of a specific user, a search for the username would reveal any attributes that the administrator has allowed to be viewed from the user object. For more information on searching Active Directory, refer to Chapter 5. Table 3-4 describes the tabs that are available for the properties of a user account object.

Table 3-4 Properties of a user account object

Tab	Description of Attributes
General	Displays user name, Description, Office, Telephone number, E-mail, and Web page information
Address	Displays fields for the full physical address of the user account
Account	Displays account information, such as logon name, logon restrictions, password options, and expiration date options. Also accessed to unlock user accounts
Profile	Displays the User Profile and Logon script paths as well as the User's Home folder location
Telephones	Displays fields for various types of telephone numbers, such as Home, Pager, Mobile, Fax, and IP Phone
Organization	Displays information related to the organization, such as Title, Department, and the Manager's name
Member Of	Displays all of the user's group memberships
Dial-in	Displays the user's dial-in permissions and configurations
COM+	Allows a user to be associated with a COM+ partition set, giving them access to a COM+ application throughout a domain
Remote control, Terminal Services Profile, Environment, Sessions	These tabs relate to the user's terminal services permissions and configurations

Activity 3-4: Modifying User Account Attributes

Time Required: 15 minutes

Objective: Use Active Directory Users and Computers to modify user account attributes.

Description: After creating all of the necessary user accounts in the previous activity, the IT manager at Dover Leasing has asked you to begin populating the accounts with additional information, such as phone numbers, addresses, descriptions, and so forth. Ultimately, executives at the company have requested the ability to search for employee information using Active Directory if possible. Dover currently has this information stored in a variety of distributed sources that have become unmanageable. In this activity, you will modify the attributes of one user account for testing purposes.

1. In Active Directory Users and Computers, click the **Users** container if it is not already selected.
2. Double-click the user account for **Moira Cowan** to access the account's properties.
3. On the General tab, type **Marketing Executive** in the Description text box.
4. Type **Toronto** in the Office text box.
5. In the Telephone number text box, type **416-555-0155**.
6. In the E-mail text box, type **mcowan@dovercorp.net**.
7. In the Web page text box, type **http://www.microsoft.com**.
8. Click the **Address** tab. In the Street text box, type **123 Alphabet Avenue**. In the City text box, type **Toronto**, and in the State/province text box, type **Ontario**. In the Country/region list box, click **Canada**.
9. Click the **Account** tab. Click the **Logon Hours** button. Select the entire **Sunday** row and then click the **Logon Denied** radio button. Click **OK**.
10. In the Account options section, check the **User cannot change password** check box.
11. Click the **Organization** tab. In the Title text box, type **VP of Marketing**. In the Department text box, type **Marketing**. In the Company text box, type **Dover Leasing**.
12. In the Manager section, click the **Change** button. In the Enter the object name to select text box, type **John H. Smith** and click **OK**.
13. Click **OK** to close and save the user account properties for Moira Cowan.
14. Right-click the **Users** container and click **Find**. In the Find Users, Contacts, and Groups dialog box, click the **Advanced** tab.
15. Click the **Field** button, select **User**, and then click **Job Title**. In the value text box, type **vp**. Click the **Add** button, and then click **Find Now**. The account for Moira Cowan should appear in the Search results field.
16. Close the Find Users, Contacts, and Groups dialog box, but leave Active Directory Users and Computers open.

Creating Computer Accounts

A **computer account** is an Active Directory object. There are two primary ways to create a computer account in Active Directory:

- You can create the computer account automatically during the initial installation of the client operating system. The computer object is placed in the Computers container within Active Directory.
- The computer account can be preconfigured in Active Directory before the client installation. The advantage of this method is that you can designate a specific container in which to place the computer object.

Activity 3-5: Creating Computer Account Objects

Time Required: 5 minutes

Objective: Use Active Directory Users and Computers to create computer account objects.

Description: In the past, Dover Leasing has never had the need to create computer accounts because all client computers ran versions of Windows 95 or 98. Having upgraded all desktop PCs to Windows XP Professional, the IT manager has recognized that computer accounts must be created for all XP workstations in the domain. In this activity, you have been asked to evaluate how difficult this will be by creating three computer accounts using Active Directory Users and Computers.

1. Right-click the **Computers** container object in Active Directory Users and Computers, select **New**, and then click **Computer**.
2. In the New Object – Computer dialog box, type **Workstation1** in the Computer name text box. Notice that the Computer name (pre-Windows 2000) text box is populated automatically, as shown in Figure 3-12. Click **Next.** Click **Next** again, and then click **Finish**.

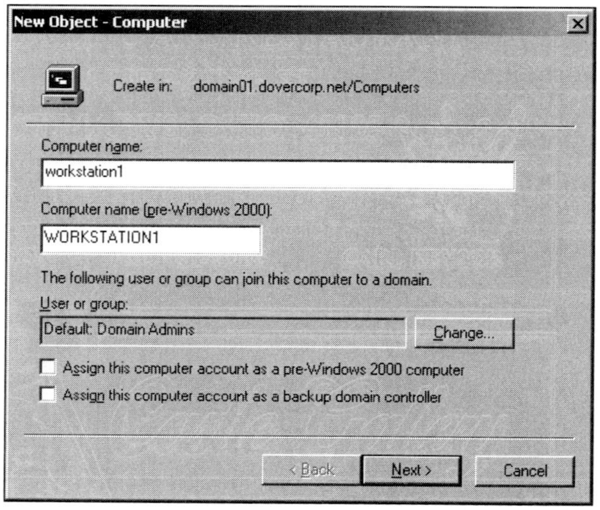

Figure 3-12 Creating a new computer object

3. Repeats Steps 1 and 2 to create two additional computer objects in the Computers container using the names **Workstation2** and **Fileserver**.
4. Leave Active Directory Users and Computers open.

Moving Active Directory Objects

You can move objects created within the Active Directory Users and Computers console between any containers within the same domain. The only containers you cannot move are the Builtin, Computers, Domain Controllers, ForeignSecurityPrincipals, and Users containers. You also cannot move the default local groups found in the Builtin container because these groups are local and they provide rights to the specific computer itself.

Activity 3-6: Moving Active Directory Objects

Time Required: 10 minutes

Objective: Use Active Directory Users and Computers to move Active Directory objects within a domain.

Description: After speaking with the IT manager, you recognize that you made an error in Activity 3-3 by creating all user accounts within the Users container instead of within the OUs associated with the user accounts. In this activity, you will move the user accounts created in Activity 3-3 to a more suitable OU based on users' job functions.

1. Click the **Users** container in Active Directory Users and Computers to view its contents.
2. Right-click the user account for **Moira Cowan** and click **Move**. The Move dialog box opens, as illustrated in Figure 3-13.

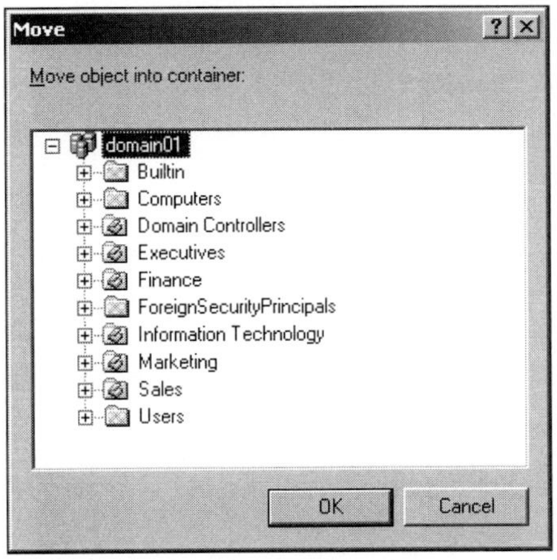

Figure 3-13 Moving an object within the domain

3. In the Move object into container section, click the **Marketing** OU and then click **OK**.
4. Click the **Marketing** OU to view its contents and to verify that the Moira Cowan user account now resides in the Marketing OU.
5. Click the **Users** container again to view its contents. Click the **Mike Aubert** user account. Hold down the **Ctrl** key and click the **Jason Zandri** account. Both accounts should now be selected. Right-click the **Jason Zandri** account and click **Move**.
6. In the Move object into container section of the Move dialog box, click the **plus sign (+)** next to Information Technology to expand it, and then click **Network Support**. Click **OK** to move both user accounts to the Network Support OU.
7. In the left navigation menu, click the **plus sign (+)** next to the Information Technology OU to expand it if necessary, and then click the **Network Support** OU to verify that both the Mike Aubert and Jason Zandri user accounts now reside in the correct OU.
8. Use the techniques learned in the previous steps to move the Chris Medved user account to the Finance OU, the Frank Adili and Christy Jackson accounts to the Sales OU, the Mark Manore account to the Information Technology OU, the John Smith account to the Help Desk OU, and the John Harold Smith account to the Marketing OU.
9. Leave Active Directory Users and Computers open.

Note

Windows Server 2003 also provides drag-and-drop functionality to move objects in Active Directory Users and Computers, as well as the ability to select and edit many objects simultaneously. These features were not available in the version supplied with Windows 2000.

Creating Group Objects

A Windows Server 2003 **group** is a container object that is used to organize a collection of users, computers, contacts, or other groups into a single security principal. You would use a group object to simplify administration by assigning rights and resource permissions to a group rather than to individual users.

Groups sound similar to OUs in that both organize other objects into logical containers. The main differences between an OU and a group are as follows:

- OUs are not security principals and as such cannot be used to define permissions on resources or be assigned rights. Active Directory security groups are security principals that can be assigned both permissions and rights.
- OUs can only contain objects from their parent domain. Some groups can contain objects from any domain within the forest.
- The next few sections introduce you to the different group types and group scopes available in Windows Server 2003.

Group Types

Windows Server 2003 allows you to create two group types:

- *Security group*—A group defined by a Security Identifier (SID) that can be listed in **discretionary access control lists (DACLs)** used to define permissions on resources and objects. A security group can also be used as an e-mail entity. Sending an e-mail message to the group sends the message to all the members of the group.
- *Distribution group*—A group that is used solely for e-mail distribution and that does not have an associated SID. Distribution groups cannot be listed in DACLs used to define permissions on resources and objects. Distribution groups can be used only with e-mail applications (such as Microsoft Exchange Server 2000) to send e-mail to collections of users. If you do not need a group for security purposes, create a distribution group instead of a security group.

Group Scopes

The group scope refers to the logical boundary within which a group can be assigned permissions to a specific resource within the domain or forest. Security and distribution groups in Active Directory can be assigned one of three possible scopes: global, domain local, and universal. The following sections define each scope option.

Global

A **global group** can be assigned permissions to any resource in any domain within the forest. The main limitation of a global group is that it can only contain members of the same domain in which it is created. Global groups are mainly used to organize user objects into logical groupings according to function. For example, if sales managers from Domain A need access to a shared file stored in Domain B, you can create a global group in Domain A called sales managers, place all individual sales manager user accounts from Domain A into this group, and then grant this sales managers global group permission to access the resource located in Domain B.

Domain Local

A **domain local group** is created on a domain controller and can only be assigned permissions to a resource available in the local domain in which it is created. However, group membership can come from any domain within the forest. Domain local groups are mainly used to assign access permissions to a resource. For example, you may want to add users, global groups, or universal groups to a domain local group and then assign the domain local group the actual permissions to a resource within the domain. This technique allows you to assign permissions once rather than many times for individuals or multiple groups.

Note

Groups created on Windows Server 2003 member servers or Windows XP Professional clients are called **local groups**. Local groups can only be assigned permissions to a resource available on the local machine on which it is created.

Universal

A **universal group** can be assigned permissions to any resource in any domain within the forest. This seems very similar to a global group, but it actually has two main differences. First of all, a universal group can consist of user objects from any domain in the forest; global groups can only consist of user objects from the same domain. Second, universal groups are only available when a domain is configured in **Windows 2000 native mode** or the Windows Server 2003 functional level. If your domain is in the default **Windows 2000 mixed mode**, this group scope is disabled.

Unlike Windows 2000, Windows Server 2003 consists of three functional domain modes. When a new Windows Server 2003 domain is implemented, it will be configured in Windows 2000 mixed mode by default. This functional level provides support for Windows NT, Windows 2000, and Windows Server 2003 domain controllers. When configured in Windows 2000 native mode, both Windows 2000 and Windows Server 2003 domain controllers are supported, along with support for universal groups. A third functional level, known as Windows Server 2003, supports Windows Server 2003 domain controllers only and is required to take advantage of new features such as the ability to rename domain controllers and create two-way transitive trusts between Active Directory forests.

To change a domain to Windows 2000 native mode or the Windows Server 2003 functional level, open Active Directory Users and Computers, right-click the domain name, click Raise Domain Functional Level, select the appropriate level from the list, and then click Raise.

Note

Be sure to only switch to Windows 2000 native mode when there is no longer any need for NT 4.0 Backup Domain Controllers (BDCs) or the Windows Server 2003 functional level once Windows 2000 domain controllers are no longer required. Once the functional level of a domain has been raised, it can never be dropped to a lower level.

Caution

Use universal groups with caution. All universal groups along with their memberships are listed in the global catalog. When there is any change to any member of a universal group, this change must be replicated to every global catalog in the forest. Global and domain local groups are also listed in the global catalog but do not have their memberships listed. A best practice is to place individual members within the global groups and then place the global groups within universal groups.

Table 3-5 provides a summary of each group type, its use, and its membership options

Table 3-5 Windows Server 2003 group summary

Group Type	General Use	Windows 2000 Mixed Mode Membership Options	Windows 2000 Native Mode or Windows Server 2003 Membership Options
Local	Assigned to resources on local computer	User accounts from any domain, global groups from any domain	User accounts from any domain, global groups from any domain
Domain local	Assigned to resources within local domain	User accounts from any domain, global groups from any domain	User accounts, global, and universal groups from any domain;other domain local groups from the same domain
Global	Used to organize individual objects such as user accounts into administrative units	User accounts only from the domain in which the group is created	User accounts and other global groups from the same domain in which the group is created
Universal	Used to organize various objects into administrative units	N/A	User accounts, global, and universal groups from any domain

Creating Group Objects

Creating group objects in Active Directory is very similar to creating user and group objects. The first step involves deciding in which container object, such as a built-in container or OU, the group should be created. The second step involves choosing an appropriate group name, scope, and type, based on your needs. In Activity 3-7, you will create both domain local and global groups that will later be populated with both user and other group accounts.

Activity 3-7: Creating Domain Local and Global Groups

Time Required: 15 minutes

Objective: Use Active Directory Users and Computers to create domain local and global groups.

Description: Having read about the different group types and scopes in Windows 2003 .NET Server, you have decided to try and take advantage of some of the time savings associated with using groups to manage resource access in an Active Directory environment. In this activity, you will create a series of global and domain local groups that will be associated with different job functions and associated resource access at Dover Leasing.

1. Right-click the **Marketing** OU, select **New**, and then click **Group**.
2. In the New Object – Group dialog box, type **Marketing Users** in the Group name text box, as shown in Figure 3-14.

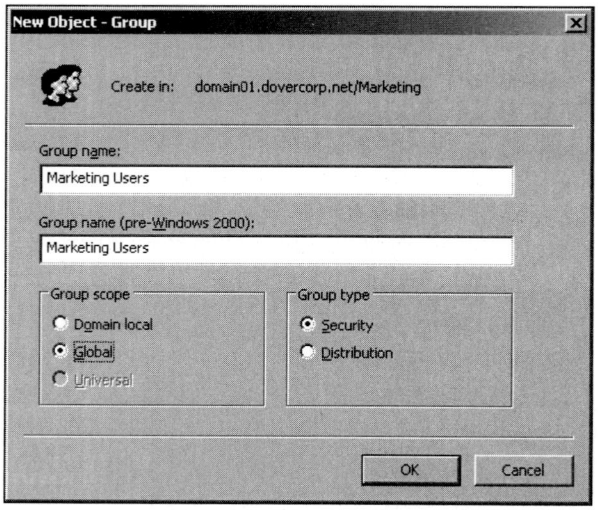

Figure 3-14 Creating a new group object

3. Under Group scope, ensure that the **Global** radio button is selected.
4. Under Group type, ensure that the **Security** radio button is selected. Click **OK** to create the group.
5. Repeat Steps 1 through 4 to create global groups named **Help Desk Users**, **Finance Users**, **IT Users**, **Network Support Users**, and **Sales Users** within their associated OUs.
6. Right-click the **Marketing** OU, select **New**, and then click **Group**.
7. In the New Object – Group dialog box, type **Marketing Resources** in the Group name text box.
8. Under Group scope, click the **Domain local** radio button.
9. Under Group type, ensure that the **Security** radio button is selected. Click **OK** to create the group. Notice that a group's scope and type can be distinguished via the Type header when viewing the contents of a container.

10. Repeat Steps 6 through 9 to create domain local groups named **Help Desk Resources**, **Finance Resources**, **IT Resources**, **Network Support Resources**, and **Sales Resources** within their associated OUs.
11. Leave Active Directory Users and Computers open.

To create universal groups, a domain must be switched to native mode. In Activity 3-8, you will switch your domain to native mode and then create universal groups.

Activity 3-8: Switching a Domain to the Windows Server 2003 Functional Level

Time Required: 5 minutes

Objective: Switch a domain to the Windows Server 2003 **domain functional level**.

Description: After creating both global and domain local groups in the previous activity, you notice that you were not given the option to create universal security groups. After doing some research, you have found that the domain functional level of your domain does not permit universal groups to be created. In this activity, you will change the domain functional level such that support for universal groups will be possible.

1. In Active Directory Users and Computers, right-click the **Domain*XX*.Dovercorp.net** domain and click **Raise Domain Functional Level**.
2. In the Raise Domain Functional Level dialog box, click **Windows Server 2003** in the **Select an available domain functional level** list box. Note the warning message that appears below the list box.
3. Click the **Raise** button.
4. Click **OK** to confirm that this action will affect the entire domain.
5. Click **OK** when prompted that the function level was raised successfully, being sure to read the associated message that appears.
6. Leave Active Directory Users and Computers open.

Modifying Group Memberships

Once a group object is created, you can then add the membership required. Depending upon which type of group is created, Windows Server 2003 groups can possibly contain users, contacts, other groups, and computers.

Activity 3-9: Modifying Group Memberships

Time Required: 15 minutes

Objective: Modify group membership using Active Directory Users and Computers.

Description: Although you created a number of global groups in a previous activity, these groups haven't yet been populated with any members. The IT manager at Dover Leasing has asked you to evaluate some of the different ways of adding users to groups to see which method will ultimately be most efficient and the easiest to teach to new staff. In this activity, you will add both single and multiple users to a group at once using two different techniques.

1. In Active Directory Users and Computers, click the **Information Technology** OU to view its contents.
2. Double-click the **IT Users** global group to view its properties, as shown in Figure 3-15.
3. Click the **Members** tab.
4. Click the **Add** button. In the Select Users, Contacts, Computers, or Groups dialog box, type **Mark Manore** in the Enter the object names to select text box and click **OK**. The Mark Manore user account should be listed as a member of the group.

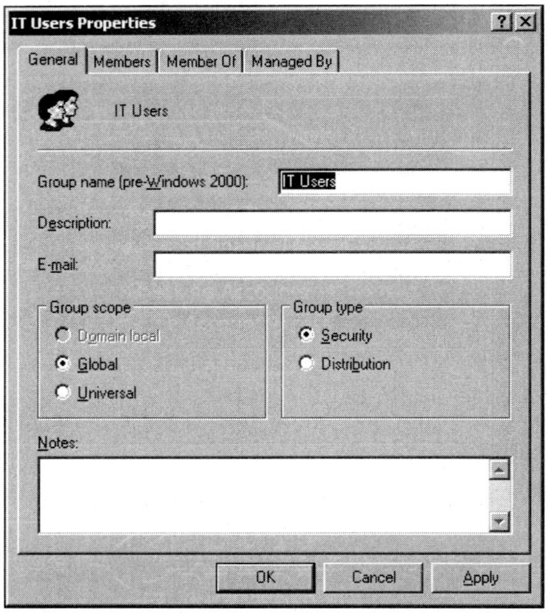

Figure 3-15 Adding or modifying group memberships

5. Click **OK** to close the properties of the IT Users global group.
6. Click the **Marketing** OU to view its contents.
7. Click the **Moira Cowan** user account to select it. Hold down the **Ctrl** key and click the **John H. Smith** user account. Both accounts should now be selected.
8. Right-click the **John H. Smith** account and click **Add to a group**.
9. In the Select Group dialog box, type **marketing** in the Enter the object name to select text box and click **OK**.
10. In the Multiple Names Found dialog box, click the **Marketing Users** global group and click **OK**. Click **OK** again at the message telling you that the operation was successful.
11. Using any combination of the steps outlined here, add the **Chris Medved** account to the Finance Users group, the **Mike Aubert** and **Jason Zandri** accounts to the Network Support Users group, the **Frank Adili** and **Christy Jackson** accounts to the Sales Users group, and the **John Smith** account to the Help Desk Users group.
12. Leave Active Directory Users and Computers open.

Changing a Group Scope

Windows Server 2003 enables you to change a group scope, if the need arises. For example, you may want to change a global group to a universal group if you need to add user accounts from another domain. You can change the group scope by accessing the properties of the group and selecting the appropriate group scope that is needed. However, there are a few rules that you must follow:

- You can only change a global group to a universal group as long as it is not a member of another global group.
- You can only change a domain local group to a universal group as long as it does not contain any other domain local groups as a member.
- To summarize, a group can change its scope as long as the group's membership rules, as stated in Table 3-5, are not violated.

Activity 3-10: Changing Group Scopes

Time Required: 5 minutes

Objective: Use Active Directory Users and Computers to change the scope of groups.

Description: After reading through the Windows Server 2003 documentation, you have learned that there are a few key rules that can affect whether or not you can change the scope of an Active Directory group. In this activity, you will attempt to change the scope of groups that contain different users and groups as members.

1. In Active Directory Users and Computers, click the **Marketing** OU to view its contents.
2. Double-click the **Marketing Users** global group to access its properties.
3. From the General tab, click the **Universal** radio button in the Group scope section. Click **OK** to change the scope of the group. Note that the group now appears as the type Security Group – Universal when the contents of the Marketing OU are displayed.
4. Double-click the **Marketing Resources** domain local group to access its properties. On the General tab, notice that the scope of the group can be changed to Universal.
5. Click the **Members** tab, and then click **Add**.
6. In the Select Users, Contacts, Computers, or Groups dialog box, type **Marketing Users** in the Enter the object names to select text box and click **OK**. The Marketing Users universal group is added to the Marketing Resources domain local group. Click **OK** to close the properties of the Marketing Resources local group.
7. Double-click the **Marketing Resources** domain local group again. On the General tab, notice that the option to change the scope of this group to Global is not available. Changing the group to a global group would violate the rule that a global group cannot have a universal group as a member. Close the Marketing Resources Properties dialog box.
8. Leave Active Directory Users and Computers open.

Understanding the Built-in Local Groups

There are a number of built-in local security groups with various preassigned rights, which you may want to use to allow users to perform certain network tasks. Whenever possible, you should use one of the built-in local groups to assign rights because this eases the implementation of delegation and security rights throughout the network. For example, rather than creating a special group with rights to back up and restore servers, you can use the built-in backup operators group.

Windows Server 2003 domain controllers have built-in local groups that provide certain rights within the domain. These groups can be found in the Active Directory Users and Computers console in the Builtin container, as shown in Figure 3-16.

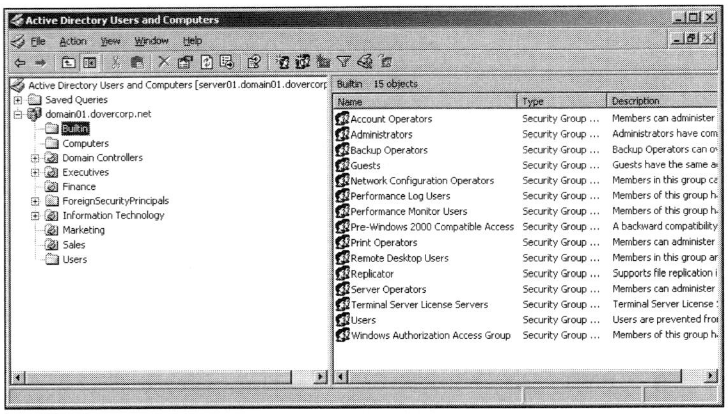

Figure 3-16 Viewing the built-in local groups

Table 3-6 lists some of the built-in local groups available in Active Directory and the abilities associated with each.

Table 3-6 Local groups and their rights

Group Type	Rights
Account Operators	Able to create, delete, and modify user accounts and groups within the domain; they cannot place themselves or anyone else in the administrators group.
Administrators	Assigned complete unrestricted access to the local computer and possibly the domain.
Backup Operators	Able to override security restrictions for the purpose of backing up or restoring files.
Network Configuration Operators	Able to change TCP/IP settings on domain controllers within the domain.
Performance Log Users	Able to remotely access servers to schedule logging of performance counters.
Performance Monitor Users	Able to remotely access servers to monitor performance.
Guests	Have no default permissions or rights (Note: The guests group is a member of the special group Everyone. This means that any access permissions to the Everyone group gives permission to the Guests group.)
Pre-Windows 2000 Compatible Access	This group is created to support applications that work with Windows NT 4.0, but may have problems with Windows Server 2003 security. This group has read access on all users and groups within the domain. This is used primarily for Windows NT RAS servers that require access to Active Directory.
Print Operators	Have all print administration rights.
Remote Desktop Users	Able to log on to domain controllers within the domain remotely.
Replicator	Used by the File Replication Service.
Server Operators	Able to share disk resources, back-up and restore files, and shut down or restart the server.
Users	Have no default permissions, except for permissions assigned by the administrator.

The Users container in Active Directory Users and Computers also contains various global groups that can be used throughout the domain, as shown in Figure 3-17.

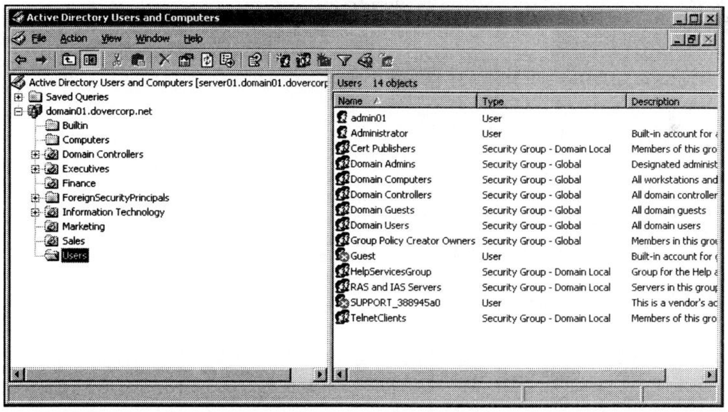

Figure 3-17 Viewing built-in global groups

Activity 3-11: Modifying the Membership of Built-in Local Groups

Time Required: 5 minutes

Objective: Use Active Directory Users and Computers to change the membership of built-in local groups.

Description: Because of problems allocating user rights in their old Windows NT 4.0 domain, the IT manager at Dover Leasing has asked you to evaluate the degree of difficulty in assigning user rights through the use of the Active Directory built-in local groups. In particular, he is interested in determining whether there is an easy way to ensure that all information technology staff are able to manage printing issues. In this activity, you will add three global groups to the Print Operators built-in local group.

1. In Active Directory Users and Computers, click the **Builtin** container to view its contents.
2. Double-click the **Print Operators** built-in local group to access its properties.
3. Click the **Members** tab, and then click the **Add** button.
4. In the Select Users, Contacts, Computers, or Groups dialog box, type **IT Users** in the Enter the objects to select text box and click **OK**. The IT Users global group is added to the Print Operators built-in local group.
5. Click the **Add** button again. In the Select Users, Contacts, Computers, or Groups dialog box, type **Network Support Users;Help Desk Users** in the Enter the object names to select text box and click **OK**. Both the Network Support Users and Help Desk Users global groups are added to the members list.
6. Click **OK** to close the properties of the Print Operators built-in local group.
7. Click the **Information Technology** OU to view its contents.
8. Double-click the **IT Users** global group to view its properties.
9. Click the **Member Of** tab. Notice that the IT Users group is now listed as a member of the Print Operators built-in local group. Close the IT Users Properties dialog box.
10. Close Active Directory Users and Computers.

Managing Security Groups

As you start to implement the use of security groups, a general strategy is to use the acronym A G U DL P. This refers to the following:

1. Create user **A**ccounts, and organize them within **G**lobal groups. Often users are grouped in global groups based on departments in the organization.
2. Optional: Create **U**niversal groups and place global groups from any domain within the universal groups.
3. Create **D**omain **L**ocal groups that represent the resources in which you want to control access, and add the global or universal groups to the domain local groups.
4. Assign **P**ermissions to the domain local groups.

For example, Dover Leasing has a shared file called Reports. All users in all domains that work in the Marketing Department must have access to the Reports Share. Following the steps previously discussed, this is how you could organize access:

1. In each domain, create a global group called **Marketing Users**, and add any appropriate user account to the group.
2. Optional: Create a universal group called **Dovercorp Marketing**, and add all global groups created in Step 1, from all domains to the universal group.
3. Create a domain local group called **Reports Share**, and add the Dover Marketing universal group to the local group. (If you skipped Step 2, you can add the Marketing Users global group instead.)
4. Assign the Reports Share local group to the access control list of the actual share on the network, and specify the appropriate permissions.

If your domain is running in Windows 2000 native mode or the Windows Server 2003 functional level, you can use the option of nesting groups to simplify administrative tasks. For example, Dover Leasing may have three global groups called Help Desk, IT Managers, and Network Support. Together, these three groups of users may represent the Information Technology department of Dover Leasing. You could create the Information Technology global group and put the Help Desk, IT Managers, and Network Support groups into this one group, thus simplifying the assignment of permissions for resources to which all three groups should have access. You do not need to add individuals to the Information Technology group. When you are assigning permissions to resources, assign the permissions to domain local groups.

If you are working in a single domain, you can use global groups or universal groups interchangeably. Choose one of these options to group your users, and then add these groups to the local domain groups.

Activity 3-12: Nesting Active Directory Groups and Testing Folder Permissions

Time Required: 20 minutes

Objective: Use Active Directory Users and Computers to nest groups and then test folder permissions.

Description: Having seen the power of nesting groups as per your previous activities, the IT manager at Dover has asked you to test and evaluate whether the recommended nesting procedures work well in resource access situations. In this activity, you will attempt to determine this by securing a resource and then attempting to access it as a user whose account has been placed in a group nested within one that has access to the resource.

1. Click **Start**, and then click **My Computer**.
2. Double-click drive **D:** to view its contents.
3. Right-click a blank area, select **New**, and then click **Folder**. Name the new folder **HelpDesk**.

4. Right-click the **HelpDesk** folder and then click **Properties**.
5. Click the **Security** tab, and then click the **Advanced** button, as shown in Figure 3-18.

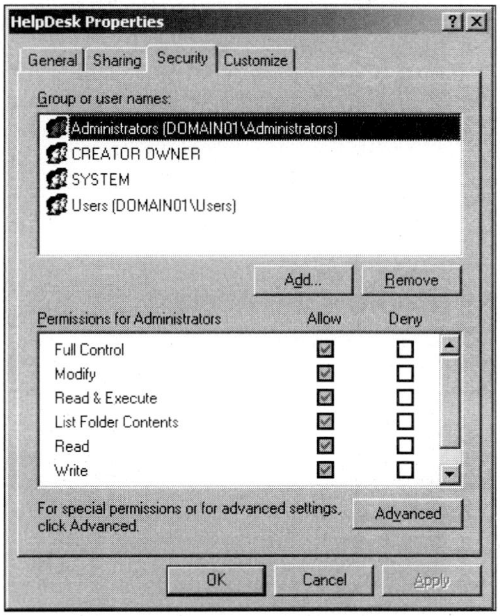

Figure 3-18 Viewing the Security options

6. Click the **Allow inheritable permissions from the parent to propagate to this object and all child objects** check box to deselect it, as illustrated in Figure 3-19.

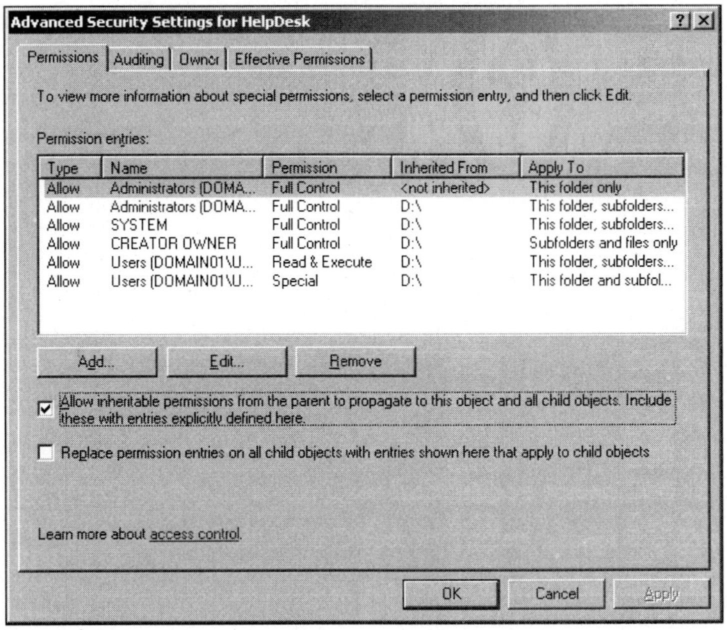

Figure 3-19 Configuring permissions options

7. When prompted with the **Security** dialog box, click **Remove**. Click **OK**.
8. On the **Security** tab, click on the **Administrators group** entry, and click **Remove**.
9. On the **Security** tab, click the **Add** button. The Select Users, Computers, or Groups dialog box will open.

10. In the Enter the object names to select text box, type **Help Desk Resources** and click **OK**.
11. In the Permissions for Help Desk Resources section, click the **Full Control** check box in the **Allow** column to select it, as illustrated in Figure 3-20, and then click **OK**. This grants members of the Help Desk Resources domain local group complete control over the HelpDesk folder.

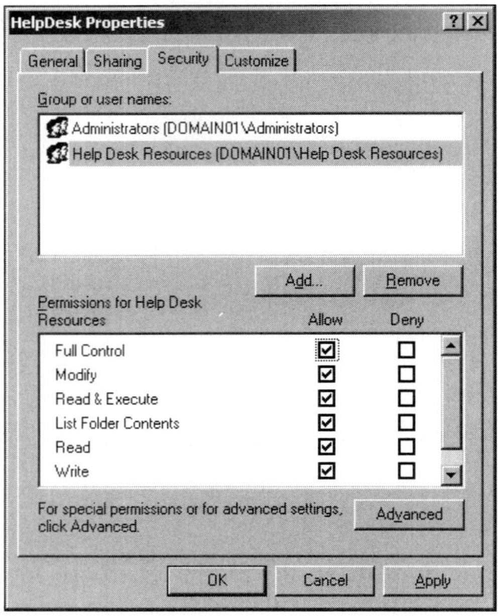

Figure 3-20 Granting members control of the local group

12. Double-click the **HelpDesk** folder to attempt to access it. Access will be denied because your Admin*XX* account is not a member of the Help Desk Resources group.
13. Open **Active Directory Users and Computers**. Click the **plus sign (+)** next to the Information Technology OU to expand it. Click the **Help Desk** OU to view its contents.
14. Double-click the **Help Desk Resources** group to view its properties. Click the **Members** tab and click **Add**. Type **domain admins** in the text box and click **OK**. Click **OK** to close the Help Desk Resources Properties dialog box.
15. Close Active Directory Users and Computers, log off, and then log back on using your Admin*XX* account.
16. Open My Computer and attempt to access the **D:\HelpDesk** folder. Access should now be allowed. Your Admin*XX* account is a member of the Domain Admins group, which is nested within the HelpDesk group.
17. Close My Computer.

Administering Permissions in Active Directory

Active Directory is a database that must be protected like any other network resource. Active Directory uses permissions much like regular NTFS file permissions to protect the creation, deletion, or viewing of objects within the database. By default, administrators have full access to all objects within the domain. Users are given the initial permission to read most attributes of the objects stored in the database. You, as an administrator, can easily edit the object permissions within the database, although care must be taken not to assign permissions that might make an object inaccessible by everyone including yourself.

Active Directory Object Permissions

Active Directory objects can be assigned permissions at two levels:

- **Object-level permissions** define which types of objects a user or group can view, create, delete, or modify within Active Directory.
- **Attribute-level permissions** define which attributes of a certain object a user or group can view or modify within Active Directory.

Object-level permissions must be granted for a user to have the right to create or modify an object such as an OU, user, or group account. Attribute-level permissions are administered to control which attributes a user or group can view or modify. For example, if you want the address information of user accounts to be viewed only by the Human Resources Department, you would modify the attribute-level permissions to apply this restriction.

Object-level permissions can be applied according to a preconfigured set of standard permissions. Table 3-7 lists some common standard permissions available for most objects in Windows Server 2003.

Table 3-7 Common standard permissions available in Windows Server 2003 Active Directory

Permission	Gives the Ability To...
Full Control	Perform all standard permissions plus change permissions and take ownership of an Active Directory object
Read	View Active Directory objects and their attributes
Write	Make changes to an Active Directory object's attributes
Create All Child Objects	Add child objects to an OU
Delete All Child Objects	Remove child objects from an OU

For each permission listed in Table 3-7, you can allow, deny, or not specify the permission. If you do not explicitly select the Allow or Deny check boxes to specify a permission, you allow the object to inherit the permission settings from its parent container.

Activity 3-13: Exploring Active Directory Object Permissions

Time Required: 10 minutes

Objective: Use Active Directory Users and Computers to explore Active Directory object permission settings.

Description: The ability to administer resources in a granular fashion is one of the main reasons that Dover Leasing originally decided to implement Windows Server 2003 and Active Directory. The IT manager at Dover has asked you to evaluate the ability to configure permissions on both objects and their properties to see whether this is a reasonable way to attempt to control administration capabilities throughout the forest. In this activity, you will explore the various permission settings for Active Directory objects.

1. Open **Active Directory Users and Computers**.
2. Click **View** on the menu bar, and click **Advanced Features**. Notice a number of additional containers and objects appear in the Active Directory Users and Computers interface.
3. Right-click the **Marketing** OU and click **Properties**.
4. Click the **Security** tab, as illustrated in Figure 3-21.

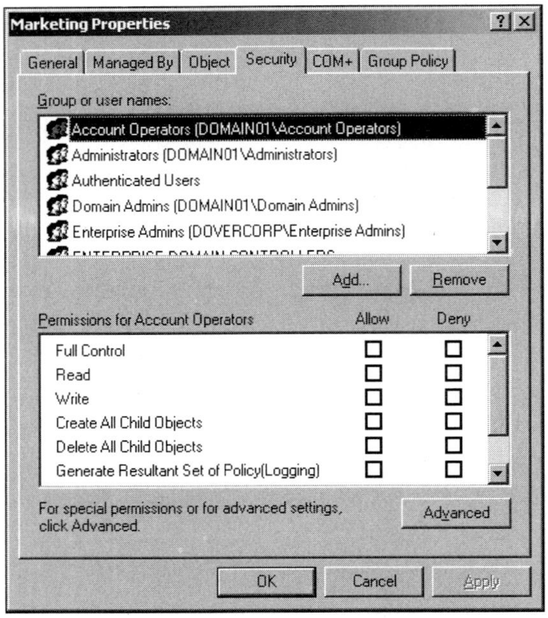

Figure 3-21 Viewing the Security tab of an Active Directory object

5. Click some of the different group names found in the Group or user names list. As different groups are selected, the corresponding permissions found at the bottom of the screen are shown for that group. Note the difference in permissions available for the **Domain Admins** group versus the **Account Operators** group. Note also that some permissions are inherited, whereas others are configured directly on the object.
6. Click the **Advanced** button. On the Permissions tab, there is a list of all permissions assigned to the object, as shown in Figure 3-22. In the Permission entries section, double-click the first entry for the **Account Operators** group. This shows the details of the permission entry.

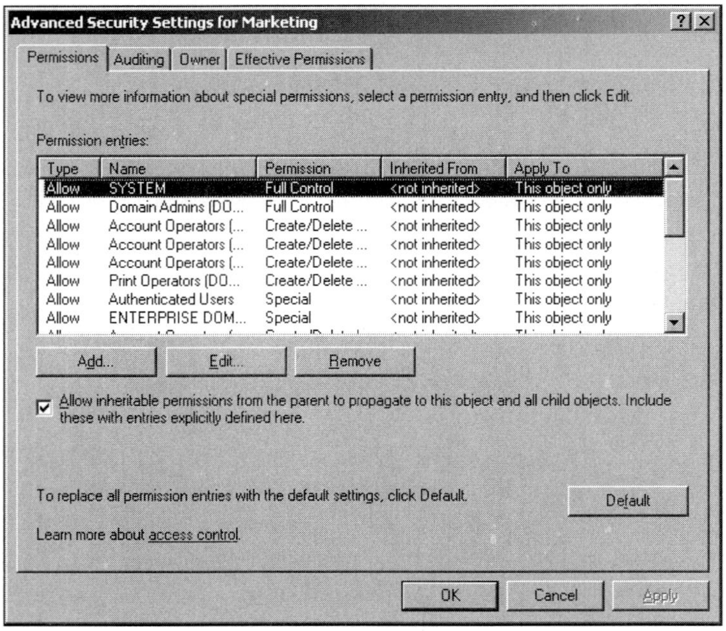

Figure 3-22 Viewing Advanced permissions

7. Use the scroll bar to view the individual object permissions included in this permission entry, as illustrated in Figure 3-23.

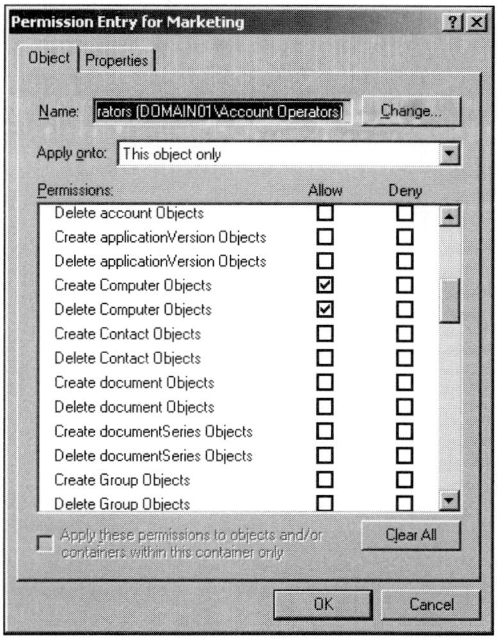

Figure 3-23 Viewing the attribute level permissions

8. Click the **Properties** tab and use the scroll bar to view the permissions associated with individual account properties.
9. Click the **Apply onto** list arrow to view all of the different ways in which permissions can be applied to objects and their properties.
10. Click **Cancel** to close the Permission Entry for Marketing dialog box, click **Cancel** to close the Advanced Security Settings for the Marketing OU, and then click **Cancel** again to close the Marketing OU properties.
11. Leave Active Directory Users and Computers open.

Note: The Advanced Features mode must be turned on for you to view the Security tab on each object in Active Directory. To turn on the Advanced Features setting, click View on the menu bar in Active Directory Users and Computers and click Advanced Features.

Permission Inheritance

By default, all child objects inside a container object inherit permissions from parent objects. By using this inheritance and planning carefully, you can eliminate the need to assign permissions to every container object or to every object inside a container. The permissions are inherited from the parent container when the object is created. If the permissions to the parent container are changed after the child object has been created, the permissions can be forced to the child container by making sure that all child objects inherit any change in permissions. You can do this by making sure that "This object and all child objects" is selected in permission entries for the Active Directory parent container.

You can modify the default inheritance of permissions by blocking the inheritance at a container or object level. For example, you may want to have all of the permissions that are set at an upper-level OU inherited by all child OUs except for one particular child OU. You may want to give the Help Desk personnel the right to reset the passwords for all of the users at the corporate head office OU except for the executives. In this case, you could put all of the executives in an Executives OU, and then accept the default inheritance for all child OUs but block the inheritance for the Executives OU. Figure 3-24 illustrates the choices available when you choose not to have an object inherit permission settings from its parent object.

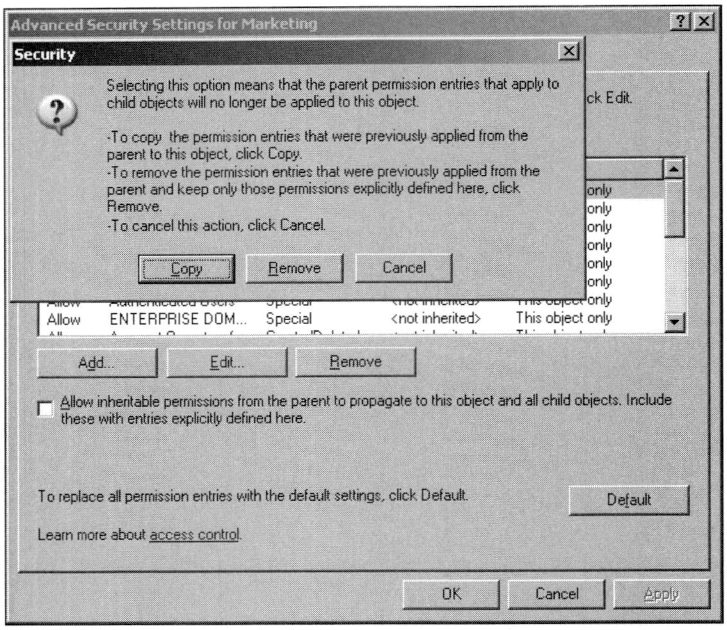

Figure 3-24 Overriding inherited permissions

Delegating Authority Over Active Directory Objects

The delegation of administration allows you to distribute and decentralize the process of administering Active Directory. To accomplish this goal, the first step is to design the OU structure so that the administration work can be distributed. For example, you may want to assign the task of managing one small part of the network to a junior administrator or an administrator in a remote location. Creating an OU and then delegating the administrative control to that person is an ideal solution to accomplish this step.

The second step in delegating the administrative control is to configure the appropriate level of administrative permissions for each administrator. You may want to give another administrator full control of one particular OU, but you may not want that person to have any administrative permissions anywhere else. Again, assigning permissions to specific OUs allows you to achieve this goal.

Implementing Delegation

You can manage the permissions on every Active Directory object by directly viewing and modifying the Security tab on the object. However, this can be a very complicated task, especially if you are delegating a variety of tasks in a complex OU structure.

To make the delegation quicker and easier, Windows Server 2003 provides the **Delegation of Control Wizard**. This wizard guides you through the process of determining the permissions that you want to delegate and then configures the permissions for the object and child objects.

Activity 3-14: Using the Delegation of Control Wizard

Time Required: 10 minutes

Objective: Use the Active Directory Users and Computers Delegation of Control Wizard to delegate control of an OU.

Description: After you walked the IT manager through the permission settings in the previous exercises, he decided that, although the level of granularity was useful, it would also be difficult to track any mistakes that might be made. Instead, he has asked you to evaluate the Delegation of Control Wizard to see whether it represents a feasible alternative. In this activity, you will use the wizard to attempt to grant help desk staff the ability to reset passwords for users in the marketing OU.

1. In Active Directory Users and Computers, right-click the **Marketing** OU and click **Delegate Control**. The Delegation of Control Wizard starts.
2. Click **Next** at the welcome screen.
3. At the Users or Groups screen, click **Add**. In the Enter the object names to select text box, type **Help Desk Users**, click **OK**, and click **Next**.
4. At the Tasks to Delegate screen illustrated in Figure 3-25, click the **Reset user passwords and force password change at next logon** check box under Delegate the following common tasks. Click **Next**.

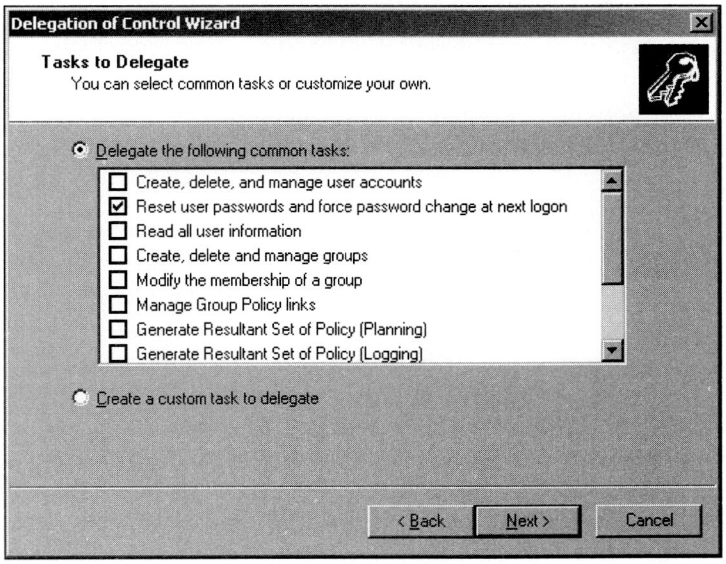

Figure 3-25 Delegating an administrative task in Active Directory

5. Click **Finish** to complete the Delegation of Control Wizard.
6. Click the **Marketing** OU to display its contents, if necessary.
7. Double-click the **Moira Cowan** user account to access its properties. Click the **Security** tab, and then click the **Advanced** button.
8. Scroll through the Permission Entries until you find the **Reset Password** entry for the Help Desk Users group. Double-click this entry to view it.
9. Scroll through the Permissions list on the Object tab until you find the Reset Password permission. Notice that this permission is allowed for the Help Desk Users group and has been inherited from the Marketing OU.
10. Close all open windows and exit Active Directory Users and Computers.

If you decide to change the permissions you have granted to a user, you can run the Delegation of Control Wizard again and assign new permissions to the user. The new permissions overwrite or add to all previous permissions.

MANAGING ACTIVE DIRECTORY REPLICATION

Active Directory replication refers to the process of directory data being synchronized and maintained between domain controllers throughout the domain. As stated previously, Windows Server 2003 uses a multi-master replication model, which means that multiple domain controllers have the authority to update and replicate database changes to each domain controller. Multi-master replication also provides a level of fault tolerance because if one domain controller fails, the other domain controllers within the domain can provide the services needed.

Because changes can potentially be made at two domain controllers at the same time, a mechanism must be in place to ensure that all changes are updated correctly and any conflicting changes can be resolved. For example, if two administrators were to change the telephone number of the same user object at the same time, Active Directory must be able to resolve which change to accept.

Replication Components and Processes

When an object is created, deleted, or modified, replication has to take place among all domain controllers within the domain. The initial modification to the database on a specific domain controller is called the **originating update**. This originating update then needs to be replicated to all other domain controllers. All synchronized copies sent to the other domain controllers are called **replicated updates**. The time that it takes to replicate an update to another domain controller is called **replication latency**.

Each time an originating or replicated update takes place within a site, the domain controller where the change occurred waits 15 seconds to enable an accumulation of changes. After 15 seconds, a change notification message is sent to its first replication partner notifying the other domain controller about the change. After a three-second interval, it then notifies its other replication partners. The replication partners then pull the changed information into their own copies of the database. If no changes occur, replication takes place automatically every hour to ensure that all database information is converged.

Note: Any changes that are considered security sensitive, such as an account lockout, are immediately replicated to all replication partners and do not wait the 15-second interval. This process is called **urgent replication**.

To optimize replication traffic, Active Directory sites can be configured between areas connected by slow network connections. For more information on sites, refer to Chapter 1.

Identifying Replication Problems

Replication problems can easily arise in multi-master scenarios such as Windows Server 2003 Active Directory. There are three main areas that can cause potential conflict within the database:

- *Attribute value errors*—These can occur when the same attribute of an object is edited at the same time on two different domain controllers.
- *Placing objects within containers marked for deletion*—This error occurs in a situation where one administrator may delete a container, while another administrator creates an object or moves an object into the deleted container before replication takes place.
- *Sibling name error*—This error can occur if two administrators concurrently create an object with the same relative distinguished name on two different domain controllers.

To help resolve possible conflicts, Active Directory applies unique stamps to every attribute that is replicated. The stamp includes a version number that is increased by one for each originating update. The stamp also includes a time stamp and an indication of the server where the replicated attribute originated.

To resolve attribute value errors, Active Directory uses the highest stamp value as the value to be written to the attribute. Before replication has taken place, if an object has been created or moved into a deleted container, the object is automatically moved into the LostAndFound container within Active Directory after replication takes place. To resolve sibling name errors, the object with the higher time stamp retains the relative distinguished name and the object with the lower time stamp is renamed with its Globally Unique Identifier (GUID) appended to the name.

There are three tools that can assist you in viewing replication information or diagnosing replication problems:

- *Event Viewer*—If replication problems occur, Windows Server 2003 will generate errors that you can view in the directory service, file replication service, and system logs of a domain controller.
- *DCDIAG*—Use this command-line utility to view a variety of information including replication status. To use the utility, type "dcdiag" at the command prompt.
- *Replication Monitor*—This utility is part of the Windows Server 2003 Support Tools available on the Windows Server 2003 Server CD in the \Support\Tools folder. This utility can check for replication errors, illustrate the replication topology, and generate replication status reports, as well as other useful information.

Chapter Summary

- After installing Active Directory on a Windows Server 2003 server, management tools are automatically installed to assist in the administration of the directory objects. Some of these management tools include Active Directory Users and Computers, Active Directory Sites and Services, and Active Directory Domains and Trusts.
- Active Directory Users and Computers is the primary administration tool used to manage users, groups, OUs, and published information within an Active Directory domain. It is also one of the tools that can be used to create and manage Group Policy objects, which control such elements as user desktop settings, security, logon/logoff scripts, and software deployment.
- When designing an OU structure, the main goal is to create a granular structure that meets the group policy and delegation needs of the organization.
- Some standards that should be considered when creating user accounts include establishing a naming convention, determining password ownership, and determining which attributes are required to be added for each user.
- A computer account can be created automatically during the initial client installation of the operating system, or it can be preconfigured in Active Directory before the initial installation.
- There are two types of groups that can be created in Windows Server 2003—security groups and distribution groups. Security groups are used for defining permissions on resources. Distribution groups are used only for e-mail distribution lists.
- Groups can be assigned one of three types of scopes: domain local, global, or universal.
- As you start to implement the use of security groups, a general strategy is to use the acronym A G U DL P. This refers to placing user accounts into global groups, global groups into universal groups, universal groups are then assigned to domain local groups, and domain local groups are assigned permissions to a resource.
- Active Directory permissions can be assigned at the object level or attribute level.
- The Delegation of Control Wizard can be used to simplify applying and delegating Active Directory object permissions to departmental network administrators.
- There are three main replication problems that may occur within Active Directory: attribute-level conflicts, sibling name conflicts, and creating or moving objects to deleted containers.

Key Terms

Active Directory Domains and Trusts — An Active Directory MMC tool that allows you to configure trust relationships between domains as well as the UPN suffix for the forest.

Active Directory Sites and Services — An Active Directory MMC tool that allows you to configure site objects and site links, and configure replication costs and times between sites.

Active Directory Users and Computers — An Active Directory MMC tool that allows you to create various objects such as OUs, user accounts, groups, computers, and contacts.

attribute-level permissions — Define which attributes of a certain object a user or group can view or modify within Active Directory.

computer account — An Active Directory object that represents a physical computer that is a member of the domain.

container — An object that is used to organize related objects within the Active Directory hierarchy. Container objects can consist of other child containers or leaf objects, such as OUs or users.

Delegation of Control Wizard — An Active Directory MMC tool that guides you through the process of determining the permissions that you want to delegate and then configures the permissions for the object and child objects.

discretionary access control list (DACL) — A part of the security descriptor of an object that contains a list of user or group references that have been allowed or denied permissions to the resource.

distribution group — A group that is only used for an e-mail distribution list.

domain functional level — The level at which a Windows Server 2003 domain is configured, such as Windows 2000 mixed mode, Windows 2000 native mode, or Windows Server 2003.

domain local group — Can only be assigned permissions to a resource available in the domain in which it is created. However, group membership can come from any domain within the forest. Created on domain controllers within the domain.

global group — A group that is mainly used for organizing other objects into administrative units. A global group can be assigned permissions to any resource in any domain within the forest. The main limitation of a global group is that it can only contain members of the same domain in which it is created.

group — A container object that is used to organize a collection of users, computers, contacts, or other groups into a single object reference.

leaf — An object that represents resources within a selected domain. Leaf objects are stored within a container and cannot contain other objects (e.g., user or group objects).

local group — Can only be assigned permissions to a resource available on the local machine in which it is created.

object-level permissions — Define which types of objects a user or group can view, create, delete, or modify within Active Directory.

originating update — The initial change to the Active Directory database performed on a specific domain controller (e.g., creating a user).

organizational unit (OU) — A logical container that can contain other objects such as users, groups, computers, published resources, or other OUs.

replicated update — An update to the Active Directory database that has been copied from another domain controller.

replication latency — The time that it takes to replicate an Active Directory update to another domain controller.

script — A file that includes various commands to automate routine operations.

security accounts manager (SAM) database — The local database that stores user and group information for standalone Windows NT, Windows 2000, and Windows Server 2003 computers.

security group — A group that can be used to define permissions on a resource object.

universal group — Can be assigned permissions to any resource in any domain within the forest. Universal groups can consist of any user or group object except for local groups.

urgent replication — The immediate replication that takes place when any changes that are made to the Active Directory database are considered security-sensitive, such as account lockouts.

user account — An object that is stored in Active Directory that represents all of the information that defines a physical user who has access permissions to the network.

user principal name (UPN) — Consists of the user logon name and a domain name that can be used for logon purposes.

Windows 2000 mixed mode — The default domain functional level consisting of Windows Server 2003 domain controllers and/or Windows NT back-up domain controllers (BDCs) and Windows 2000 domain controllers.

Windows 2000 native mode — The domain functional level consisting of Windows Server 2003 and Windows 2000 domain controllers only. No Windows NT BDCs exist in the domain.

Review Questions

1. Which type of security group has its entire membership stored in the global catalog?
   a. domain local groups
   b. universal groups
   c. local computer groups
   d. global groups
   e. all of the above
2. Which of the following can be considered a container object in Active Directory?
   a. user
   b. contact
   c. OU
   d. none of the above
3. Which MMC is the primary administration tool used to create user, group, and computer objects?
   a. Active Directory Domains and Trusts
   b. Active Directory Sites and Services
   c. Active Directory Users and Computers
   d. none of the above
4. Distribution groups are not security principals and as such cannot be allocated permissions in an access control list. True or False?
5. You would like to allow access to a shared file in your domain to a trusted domain. To what type of group should the users belong for you to assign the permission to the group?
   a. global group
   b. domain local group
   c. local computer group
   d. domain local or global group
   e. any of the above
6. Your company is opening an office in a city where you do not currently have a location. You would like to be able to have one of the users in the new office perform some simple user administration tasks and reset passwords, but the user should not be able to do anything else on your network. What would be the most appropriate configuration option in Active Directory for the users and computers in the new office?
   a. Create an OU inside of an existing domain.
   b. Create a new domain that is not part of an existing domain tree.
   c. Create a new child domain inside an existing domain tree.
   d. Create a new domain tree inside an existing forest of domain trees.

7. You want to give the help desk personnel the right to reset passwords for all user accounts in your office except for the user accounts for the executives and managers. Which of the following is the easiest way to do this?
   a. Give the help desk personnel the right to reset user accounts at the domain level.
   b. Put all the help desk personnel into an OU, and assign the OU the right to reset passwords.
   c. Put the executive and manager accounts into an OU, and assign the help desk personnel the reset password permission at the domain level.
   d. Put all the nonexecutive and nonmanager user accounts into an OU, and give the help desk personnel the right to reset passwords for the OU.
8. You have created a new group in your domain called Managers, and you put all of the appropriate users into the group. You have also just installed a new file and print server on your network and configured a new Managers share on the server. However, when you try to add the Managers group to the NTFS permission on the folder, you cannot locate the group through the interface. What happened? (Choose all that apply.)
   a. The new server has not been added to your domain.
   b. You created a distribution group rather than a security group.
   c. You created a global group rather than a domain local group.
   d. You did not enable the group.
9. Members of the Incoming Forest Trust Builders built-in local group have the ability to create one-way incoming trusts for a domain. True or False?
10. When a domain is at the Windows 2000 mixed-mode domain functional level, universal groups can be created. True or False?
11. *jsmith@dovercorp.net* would be the user principal name (UPN) associated with a user account named jsmith in the *Dovercorp.net* domain. True or False?
12. An administrator attempts to create a universal group, but the selection is grayed out. What could be the problem?
    a. He must create a global group first and then convert it to a universal group.
    b. Universal groups can only be created on the first domain controller in the forest.
    c. The domain needs to be converted to the Windows Server 2003 domain functional mode.
    d. The domain needs to be converted to the Windows 2000 mixed mode.
13. Members of the Account Operators built-in local group have the ability to change TCP/IP settings on domain controllers. True or False?
14. A global group can only be converted to a universal group if it is not a member of any other global groups. True or False?
15. Which built-in local group has the ability to create, delete, and modify user accounts and groups within the domain but cannot place themselves or anyone else in the Administrators group?
    a. back-up operators
    b. guests
    c. account operators
    d. print operators
16. The Write permission grants a user the ability to change the attributes of an Active Directory object. True or False?

17. You try to modify permissions to various objects using Active Directory Users and Computers, but you notice that the Security tab is missing. You are an administrator of the domain. What is the problem?
    a. You cannot modify Active Directory object permissions using Active Directory Users and Computers.
    b. Advanced features is not selected in the View menu of the console.
    c. Active Directory only allows changes on one domain controller at a time.
    d. none of the above
18. You create a new OU, and then view the access control list. You notice that some of the entries have gray-shaded boxes under Permissions. What does this mean?
    a. Permissions are not applied to the specific user or group.
    b. Permissions are not inherited from a parent container.
    c. Permissions are inherited from a parent container.
    d. Permissions are suggested as indicated by the gray-shaded boxes.
19. A new user account created on a specific domain controller is known as a replicated update. True or False?
20. An administrator changes the telephone number attribute on a user object. One minute later, a second administrator changes the e-mail address of the same user object from a different domain controller. What will happen when replication occurs?
    a. Only the changes from the last administrator take effect because replication takes place at the object level.
    b. Both changes merge, because replication takes place at the attribute level.
    c. Only the changes from the first administrator take effect.
    d. An error will occur and result in no changes taking effect.

CASE PROJECTS

Case Project 3-1

Dover Leasing consists of five main departments: Marketing, Legal, Finance, Sales, and Information Technology. The company currently has locations in Boston, London, and Hong Kong, with a new office planned for San Francisco. The link between the Boston and San Francisco offices is planned to be a 100-Mbps ATM link. Assuming that each geographic location will have its own IT group responsible for administration function and that the company has decided to use a single domain model, answer the following questions:

1. Design a possible OU structure for *Dovercorp.net*. What are the main decision goals in your design?
2. If the connection between Boston and San Francisco is much slower than initially thought, what can be done to optimize replication traffic?
3. Replication problems are occurring. Which tools can help you troubleshoot the problems?

Case Project 3-2

Dover Leasing has a folder on a file server that stores all of the human resources information for the entire company. You need to give access to this folder to all members of the Human Resources Department within the Active Directory forest. Explain how you would complete this task. Do you need universal groups?

Case Project 3-3

The IT Manager at Dover Leasing has asked you to implement a new OU design for their Active Directory implementation that will first divide the domain along geographic boundaries and then according to function. He has asked that you create this OU structure for both the London and Hong Kong offices on your domain controller. The Hong Kong office includes Sales, Marketing, and Information Technology departments, while the London office includes Human Resources, Sales, and Information Technology departments. Beyond the OU structure, you have also been asked to ensure that a new universal group called International IT has full control over all London departments. Using the information provided here, implement the new OUs and permissions in the most efficient manner possible.

Case Project 3-4

In many companies, user account templates are created to help ease the administrative burden of creating many similar accounts. Create an account template called "MktgTemplate" in the Marketing OU that is made a member of the Marketing Users global group and has logon denied on Sundays. After completing the template, right-click it and click Copy. Name the new account "Mary Walsh", and ensure that the properties configured on the template apply to the new user account.

CHAPTER

4

MANAGING GROUP POLICY

After reading this chapter and completing the exercises, you will be able to:

- Create and manage Group Policy objects to control user desktop settings, security, scripts, and folder redirection
- Manage and troubleshoot Group Policy inheritance
- Deploy and manage software using Group Policy

An important part of your Windows Server 2003 management skills is the ability to effectively incorporate Group Policy into your Active Directory structure. **Group Policy** allows you to easily manage and control various configurations, such as user desktop settings and desktop and domain security, as well as deploy and manage software.

Another important aspect of Group Policy involves understanding how to control the inheritance and application of Group Policies throughout the Active Directory hierarchy. The following sections discuss these concepts as well as basic Group Policy troubleshooting techniques.

Introduction to Group Policy

Group Policy enables the centralized management of user and computer configuration settings throughout your network. A **Group Policy object (GPO)** is an Active Directory object that is used to configure and apply policy settings for user and computer objects and perform a variety of administrative tasks, including:

- Configure desktop settings using administrative templates
- Control security settings for users and computers
- Assign **scripts** to run when a user logs on or off, or when a computer is started up or shut down
- Redirect folders, such as the My Documents folder, out of a user's local profile to a different network location
- Automate software distribution and maintenance to computers throughout the network

To implement Group Policy, you must first create a GPO or modify one of the default GPOs to meet the company requirements.

Note: There are two default GPOs created when Active Directory is installed. The first GPO is linked to the domain container and is called the **default domain policy**. The second is linked to the domain controllers organizational unit (OU) and is called the **default domain controllers policy**.

Once a GPO is created, you can then link it to a site, domain, or OU. When you link a GPO to one of these container objects, its policy settings are applied to all users and computers in the container, including those within child OUs.

Note: Group Policy can only be applied to computers running Windows Server 2003, Windows 2000, and Windows XP. If you still have down-level clients, such as those running Windows NT or Windows 9x, you must use system policies to control environment settings.

Creating a Group Policy Object

You can create a GPO in two different ways: use the Group Policy standalone Microsoft Management Console (MMC) snap-in (as shown in Activity 4-1) or use the Group Policy extension in Active Directory Users and Computers (Activity 4-2).

Activity 4-1: Creating a Group Policy Object Using the MMC

Hands-on Project

Time Required: 10 minutes

Objective: Use the Group Policy Object Editor MMC snap-in to create GPOs.

Description: The IT manager at Dover Leasing has decided that the company will use GPOs for the purpose of configuring a standard user desktop environment, as well as the deployment of software applications and updates. You have been asked to explore some of the different ways in which GPOs can be created from a Windows Server 2003 system. In this activity, you will create a new GPO using the Group Policy Object Editor MMC snap-in.

1. Click **Start**, and then click **Run**. In the Open text box, type **mmc** and press **Enter**.
2. Click **File** on the menu bar, and click **Add/Remove Snap-in**.
3. Click **Add**. In the Add Standalone Snap-in dialog box, click **Group Policy Object Editor** as shown in Figure 4-1 and click **Add**.
4. In the Select Group Policy Object dialog box, click **Browse**.
5. In the Browse for a Group Policy Object dialog box, click the **All** tab to display a list of all GPOs that currently exist.

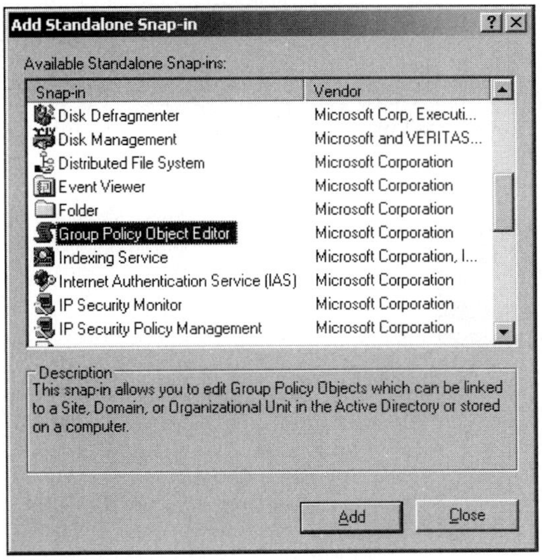

Figure 4-1 Adding a standalone snap-in

6. In the All Group Policy Objects stored in this domain section, right-click a blank area and click **New**.
7. Rename the new GPO using the name **Test Policy** and press the **Enter** key. Click **OK**, and then click **Finish**.
8. Click **Close** at the Add Standalone Snap-in window, and click **OK** at the Add/Remove Snap-in window.
9. Close the MMC window without saving your changes.

Activity 4-2: Creating a Group Policy Object and Browsing Settings Using Active Directory Users and Computers

Time Required: 20 minutes

Objective: Use Active Directory Users and Computers to create GPOs.

Description: While the Group Policy Object Editor MMC snap-in provides one method used to create new or edit existing GPOs, you have learned that another alternative is to create and edit these objects from within the Active Directory Users and Computers tool. Because this tool is the primary administrative application in use at Dover Leasing, you have decided to explore its integrated GPO management features. In this activity, you will create a new GPO and explore some of the settings that can be configured through the use of Group Policy.

1. Click **Start**, point to **Administrative Tools**, and click **Active Directory Users and Computers**.
2. Click the **plus sign (+)** next to the Domain*XX*.Dovercorp.net domain object to view its contents, if necessary.
3. Right-click the **Marketing** OU and click **Properties**.
4. Click the **Group Policy** tab.
5. Click **Add**. The Add a Group Policy Object Link window opens. Click the **All** tab.
6. In the All Group Policy Objects stored in this domain section, click **Test Policy** and click **OK**. Notice that the GPO named Test Policy now appears in the list of Current Group Policy Object Links for Marketing.

7. Click the **New** button to create a new GPO named **Marketing Policy**. This new GPO is now linked to the Marketing OU.
8. Ensure that **Marketing Policy** is selected and click **Edit**. The Group Policy Object Editor will open to allow the configuration settings of the Marketing Policy to be viewed and configured, as shown in Figure 4-2.

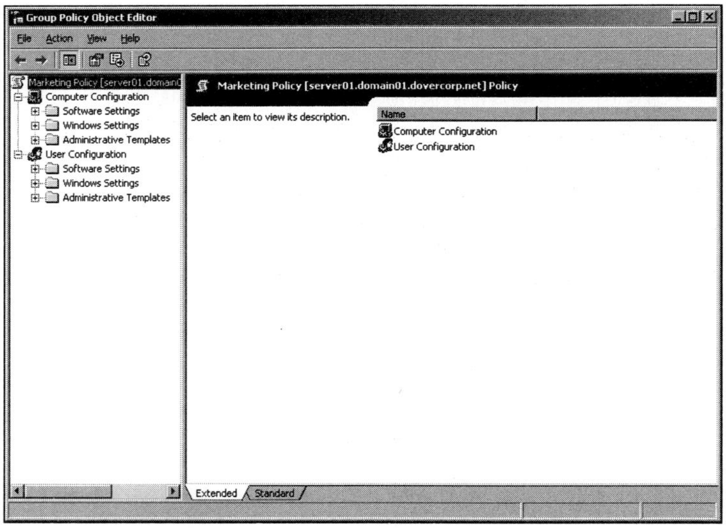

Figure 4-2 Creating a Group Policy object

9. In the User Configuration section, click the **plus sign (+)** next to Administrative Templates to expand its contents, and then click the **Start Menu and Taskbar** icon.
10. Double-click **Remove My Documents icon from Start Menu**. Notice that the configuration settings include Not Configured, Enabled, and Disabled. Do not change any configuration settings at this point.
11. Click the **Explain** tab, and read the purpose and notes associated with this setting. Click **OK** to close the window.
12. As time permits, browse through additional Group Policy settings in both the User Configuration and Computer Configuration sections. Do not configure any settings during this exercise.
13. Close the Group Policy Object Editor window when you are finished, along with the properties of the Marketing OU. Leave Active Directory Users and Computers open.

After a GPO has been created, it needs to be edited to control specific user or computer settings that should be applied. Table 4-1 lists the configuration categories available in both the Computer Configuration and User Configuration sections of a GPO.

Table 4-1 Configuration categories available for GPOs

Configuration Categories	Explanation
Software Settings	Used to centralize the management of software installation and maintenance; the installation, upgrading, and removal of applications can be controlled from one central location
Windows Settings	Used to manage the deployment and management of scripts, security settings, Internet Explorer settings, and features such as Remote Installation Services and folder redirection
Administrative Templates	Used to set registry-based settings to configure application and user desktop settings; this includes access to the operating system components, access to Control Panel settings, and configuration of offline files

As you are creating or editing a GPO, if you want to enable a particular setting, choose the appropriate configuration category in the left console pane of the MMC snap-in and then, in the details pane, right-click the specific configuration setting, and click Properties.

Figure 4-3 shows the User Configuration\Administrative Templates\Control Panel category selected and the properties of the option to hide specified control panel applets. The Setting tab allows you to enable or disable the setting, as well as set any parameters that may be needed. The Explain tab provides information on what the effect of applying that setting is.

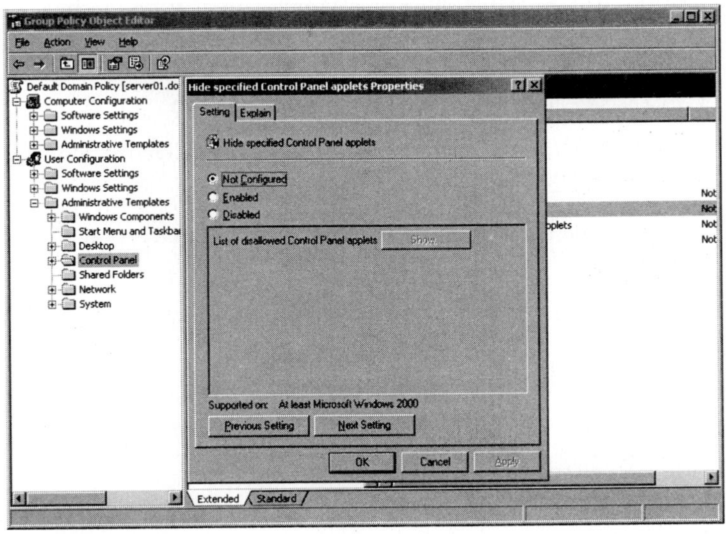

Figure 4-3 Configuring a Group Policy setting

When a GPO is created, the GPO content is stored in two different locations on the server:

- *Group Policy container (GPC)*—An Active Directory container that stores information about the GPO and includes a version number that is used by other domain controllers to ensure that they have the latest information. The version number is also used to make sure that the Group Policy template is synchronized. The GPC is located in Active Directory Users and Computers\System\Policies.

Note: The Advanced Features view must be enabled to view the GPC.

- *Group Policy template (GPT)*—The GPT contains the data that makes up the Group Policy. The template includes all the settings, administrative templates, security settings, software installation settings, scripts, and so forth. The registry changes are stored in a configuration file named Registry.pol. A configuration file is stored for both the user settings and computer settings. The GPT is stored in the %systemroot%\\Sysvol\<Domain Name>\Policies folder.

Both the GPC and the GPT are identified by a **globally unique identifier (GUID)**, which is a unique 128-bit number assigned to the object when it is created. GUIDs are guaranteed to be unique for the entire forest. When a computer accesses the GPO, it uses the GUID to distinguish between GPOs.

In Activity 4-3, you will permanently delete an existing GPO.

Activity 4-3: Deleting Group Policy Objects

Time Required: 5 minutes

Objective: Use Active Directory Users and Computers to permanently delete a GPO.

Description: Having learned how to create new GPOs, you are interested in learning about what happens if you attempt to delete one of these objects when it has been linked to one or more containers. In this activity, you will attempt to delete a linked GPO to learn more about the options presented to you.

1. In Active Directory Users and Computers, right-click the **Marketing** OU and click **Properties**.
2. Click the **Group Policy** tab.
3. Ensure that the Test Policy GPO is selected and press the **Delete** button.
4. In the Delete dialog box, click the **Remove the link and delete the Group Policy Object permanently** radio button and click **OK**.
5. When the Delete Group Policy Object dialog box opens, click **Yes**. Notice that the Test Policy GPO is removed from the list.
6. Click **Add** and click the **All** tab to confirm that the Test Policy GPO has been deleted. Then click **Cancel**.
7. Click the **Close** button to close the Marketing Properties window, leaving Active Directory Users and Computers open.

Application of Group Policy

GPOs can apply a variety of configuration options to the local computer, site, domain, and OU. There are two main categories to a Group Policy:

- *Computer Configuration*—Any configuration settings set within this category affect computers located in the container to which the GPO is linked.
- *User Configuration*—Any configuration settings set within this category apply to any user objects located in the container to which the GPO is linked.

When a computer is started and a user logs on, the following process takes place:

1. A Windows 2000, Windows XP, or Windows Server 2003 computer in a domain starts up. The client computer queries the domain controller for a list of GPOs that it needs to apply. The domain controller examines all of the GPOs to see which policies apply to the computer. Policies that are executed on the computer include the computer settings and startup scripts.
2. The domain controller presents the client with the list of GPOs that apply to it in the order that the GPOs need to be processed. The computer contacts the domain controller and extracts the Group Policy templates from the Sysvol share and applies the settings and runs the scripts.
3. When the user logs on, the same process happens again, except this time the user settings, logon scripts, software policies, and so forth are applied.

Controlling User Desktop Settings

Companies spend a lot of time and money designing standard computer installation configurations only to have users change settings, thus resulting in nonstandard configurations and increased calls to the help desk. Group Policy helps reduce administrative costs by allowing you to enforce standard computer configurations, limit user access to various areas of the operating system, and ensure that users have their own personal desktop and application settings. Administrative templates consist of a number of administrative configurations, which you can use to apply these settings.

Administrative templates are basically registry settings that you can configure to manage computer and user desktop settings. There are seven main categories of configuration settings that you can apply to either the computer or user section of a GPO.

Table 4-2 explains each of the main categories of configuration settings for administrative templates and the section of the GPO to which each can be applied.

Table 4-2 Configuration categories of administrative templates

Configuration Category	Explanation	Configuration
Windows components	Configures settings for applications such as Internet Explorer, NetMeeting, Task Scheduler, and the Microsoft Management Console	User and computer
System	Configures settings related to Group Policy, disk quotas, logons, and code signing	User and computer
Network	Configures offline files and network and dial-up connections	User and computer
Printers	Configures settings related to installing, publishing, and maintaining printers	Computer
Start menu and taskbar	Configures settings related to options available on the Start menu and taskbar	User
Desktop	Configures user desktop settings such as wallpaper, display of icons, and Active Desktop	User
Control Panel	Restrict various icons and applets within Windows Control Panel	User
Shared Folders	Configures shared folder and DFS root publishing settings	User

In Activity 4-4, you will create a new GPO that will assign desktop settings to users in the Marketing OU.

Hands-on Project

Activity 4-4: Configuring Group Policy Object User Desktop Settings

Time Required: 15 minutes

Objective: Configure and test the application of Group Policy settings.

Description: The IT manager at Dover Leasing has asked you to test the use of GPO settings for the purpose of controlling the user desktop environment. In this activity, you attempt to remove the Recycle Bin icon, as well as restrict access to Control Panel for users whose accounts exist within the Marketing OU.

1. Using Active Directory Users and Computers, access the configuration settings of the **Marketing Policy** GPO.
2. Under the User Configuration settings section, click the **plus sign (+)** next to Administrative Templates to view its contents.
3. Click the **Desktop** folder to view its contents. Double-click the **Remove Recycle Bin icon from Desktop** item to view its properties.
4. Click the **Enabled** radio button and click **OK**.
5. Click the **Start Menu and Taskbar** folder to view its contents. Double-click the **Remove Run menu from Start Menu** item to view its properties.
6. Click the **Enabled** radio button and click **OK**.
7. Click the **Control Panel** folder to view its contents. Double-click the **Prohibit access to the Control Panel** item to view its properties.
8. Click the **Enabled** radio button and click **OK**.
9. Close the Group Policy Object Editor window, close the properties window of the Marketing OU, and then close Active Directory Users and Computers.

10. Log off and then log on as the Marketing OU user **mcowan**, using the **password Password01**.
11. Confirm that the Recycle bin does not appear on the user desktop. Click **Start** to confirm that both the Run command and access to Control Panel are unavailable.
12. Log off and log back on using your **Admin*XX*** account.

Managing Security with Group Policy

Group Policy can be used to modify and maintain a number of domain-based security configurations to comply with organizational security standards. Windows Server 2003 enables you to create security templates based on current security standards. These templates can then be used to continually ensure that standards are being met.

The most common security settings that you are likely to configure are those in the Account Policies section. Items found here allow you to configure settings that are used to control user password, account lockout, and Kerberos configurations.

Configuring Account Policies

One security category that deserves special attention is the Account Policies node. This node includes configuration settings that may be the initial step to securing the computer network. The Account Policies node, as shown in Figure 4-4, can be found under the computer configuration category of a GPO and includes three subcategories: Password Policy, Account Lockout Policy, and Kerberos Policy.

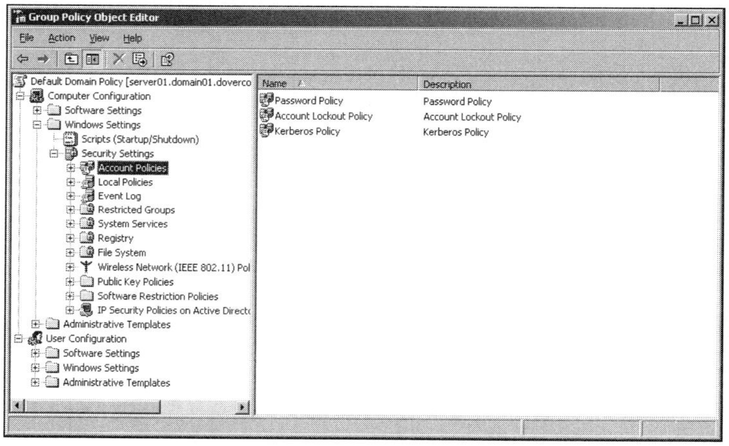

Figure 4-4 Viewing the account policies node in a Group Policy object

Password Policy The Password Policy node contains configuration settings that refer to the password's history, length, and complexity. Table 4-3 describes each setting:

Table 4-3 Password policies in Windows Server 2003

Configuration Setting	Description
Enforce password history	Defines the number of passwords that have to be unique before a user can reuse an old password
Maximum password age	Defines the number of days that a password can be used before the user is required to change it; if you never want the passwords to expire, set the number of days to 0
Minimum password age	Defines the number of days that a password must be used before a user is allowed to change it

Table 4-3 Password policies in Windows Server 2003 (continued)

Configuration Setting	Description
Minimum password length	Defines the least number of characters required in a password (values can be from 1 to 14 characters); if no password is required, set the value to 0
Password must meet complexity requirements	Increases password complexity by enforcing rules that passwords must follow (see the list of complexity requirements after this table)
Store password using reversible encryption for all users in the domain	This setting is the same as storing passwords in clear text; this policy provides support for applications using protocols that need the passwords in clear text for authentication purposes

If you configure the Password Policy node, passwords must meet the following complexity requirements:

- They cannot contain any part of the user's account name.
- They must be at least six characters in length.
- They must contain characters from three of the four categories below:
  - English uppercase letters
  - English lowercase letters
  - Numbers
  - Non-alphanumeric (e.g., !, $, #)

Activity 4-5: Configuring Password Policy Settings in the Default Domain Policy

Hands-on Project

Time Required: 15 minutes

Objective: Use Group Policy settings at the domain level to configure password policies.

Description: In the past, Dover Leasing has not enforced any password requirements on domain users because previous attempts to do so have resulted in increased calls to the help desk owing to users forgetting their passwords. As a result, many users have configured very simple passwords, and in some cases even use blank passwords. Concerned about the potential security risk that this represents, the IT manager at Dover Leasing has asked you to evaluate the use of password policies to control elements such as minimum password length, the number of passwords remembered by the system, and so forth. In this activity, you will configure and test a new password policy for the *DomainXX.Dovercorp.net* domain.

1. Open **Active Directory Users and Computers**.
2. Right-click the **Domain*XX*.Dovercorp.net** domain object and click **Properties**.
3. Click the **Group Policy** tab, ensure that the Default Domain Policy is selected, and then click **Edit**.
4. In the Computer Configuration section, click the **plus signs (+)** next to Windows Settings, Security Settings, and Account Policies to expand them.
5. Click **Password Policy** to view its contents.
6. Double-click **Enforce password history** to view its properties, as shown in Figure 4-5. In the passwords remembered spin box, change the number of passwords remembered to **8**, and click **OK**.
7. Double-click **Minimum password length** to view its properties. In the characters spin box, change the required password length to **5** characters, and click **OK**.
8. Close the Group Policy Object Editor window, and close the properties of the Domain*XX*.Dovercorp.net domain.
9. Click the **Marketing** OU to view its contents. Right-click the **Moira Cowan** user account and click **Reset Password**.

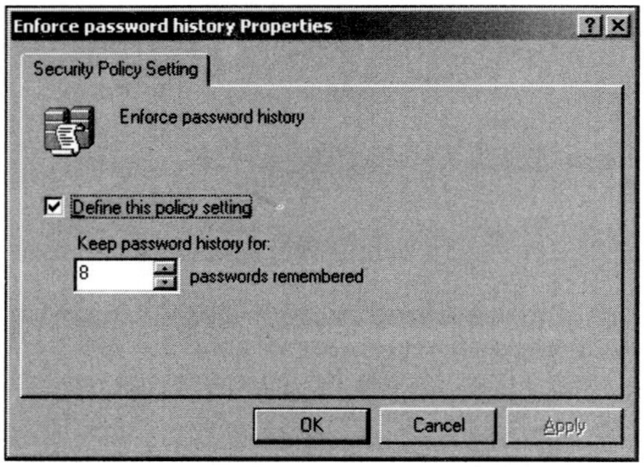

Figure 4-5 Viewing the Enforce password history properties

10. In the **Reset Password** dialog box, type **art** as the password in both the New password and Confirm password text boxes and click **OK**.
11. Read the message that appears as a result of attempting to change the password length to one that does not meet the new password length complexity requirements, as illustrated in Figure 4-6. Click **OK**.
12. Leave Active Directory Users and Computers open.

Figure 4-6 Attempting to change a password without meeting password policy requirements

Account Lockout Policy The Account Lockout Policy node contains configuration settings that refer to the password lockout threshold and duration, as well as reset options. Table 4-4 describes each setting.

Table 4-4 Account Lockout Policies

Configuration Setting	Description
Account lockout threshold	Determines the number of failed logon attempts that results in the user account being locked
Account lockout duration	Determines the number of minutes that a locked account remains locked; after the specified number of minutes, the account automatically becomes unlocked. You can specify that an administrator must unlock the account by setting the value to 0
Reset account lockout counter after	Determines the number of minutes that must elapse after a single failed logon attempt before the bad logon counter is reset to 0

Activity 4-6: Configuring Account Lockout Policy Settings

Time Required: 15 minutes

Objective: Use Group Policy settings to configure domain account lockout policies.

Description: Even though the IT manager at Dover Leasing has recognized the importance of a better password policy, you feel that an equal security risk exists in the fact that user accounts are not locked out after incorrect logon attempts. This leaves corporate user accounts vulnerable to hackers because an account will not be temporarily disabled in the event that an unauthorized user attempts to gain access to the network by repeatedly trying different passwords with another user's account. In this activity, you will configure and test account lockout settings for the *DomainXX.Dovercorp.net* domain.

1. Open the **Default Domain Policy** to view its settings. In the Computer Configuration section, browse to the **Account Policies** section.
2. Click **Account Lockout Policy** to view its settings.
3. Double-click **Account lockout duration** to view its properties. Click the **Define this policy setting** check box and specify **5** minutes in the Account is locked out for section. Click **OK**.
4. The Suggested Value Changes dialog box opens. Read the suggested changes and then click **OK**.
5. Double-click **Account lockout threshold** to view its properties, as illustrated in Figure 4-7. Specify **2** in the invalid logon attempts check box and click **OK**.

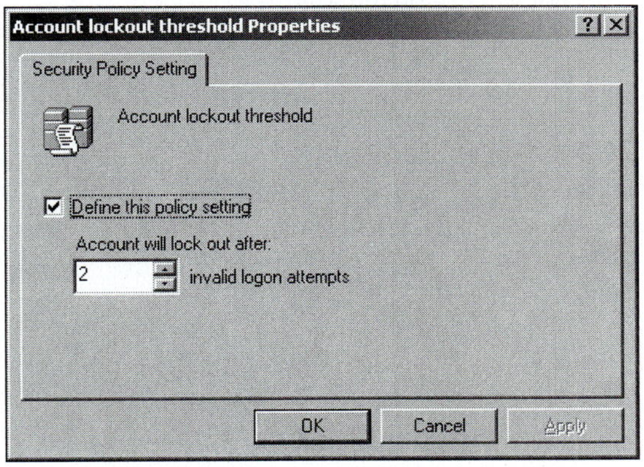

Figure 4-7 Viewing the Account lockout threshold properties

6. Close the Group Policy Object Editor window and the properties of the Domain*XX*.Dovercorp.net domain.
7. Close Active Directory Users and Computers and log off.
8. Attempt to log on with the user account **mcowan** twice, using an incorrect password in both attempts.
9. Attempt to log on as the user **mcowan** one additional time, using an incorrect password. Note the account lockout message that appears.
10. After 5 to 6 minutes, attempt to log on as the user **mcowan** using the correct password of **password**. Because the account lockout duration has passed, logon should now be possible.
11. Log off and then log on using your **Admin*XX*** account.

Kerberos Policy The Kerberos Policy node contains configuration settings that refer to the Kerberos **ticket-granting ticket (TGT)** and session ticket lifetimes and time stamp settings. Table 4-5 describes each setting.

Table 4-5 Kerberos policy node configuration

Configuration Setting	Description
Enforce user logon restrictions	Requires the **Key Distribution Center (KDC)**, a service of Kerberos V5, to validate every request for a session ticket against the user rights policy of the target computer; if enforced, there may be performance degradation on network access
Maximum lifetime for service ticket	Determines the maximum amount of time, in minutes, that a service ticket is valid to access a resource; the default is 600 minutes (10 hours)

Table 4-5 Kerberos policy node configuration (continued)

Configuration Setting	Description
Maximum lifetime for user ticket	Determines the maximum amount of time, in hours, that a (TGT) may be used; the default is 10 hours
Maximum lifetime for user ticket renewal	Determines the amount of time, in days, that a user's TGT may be renewed; the default is seven days
Maximum tolerance for computer clock synchronization	Determines the amount of time difference, in minutes, clock synchronization that Kerberos tolerates between the client machine's clock and the time on the server's clock; the default is five minutes (used to prevent "replay attacks")

Note

To configure an account policy for the domain, the GPO must be linked at the domain level of Active Directory. Account policy configurations applied at an OU level only affect the local SAM database of the computers within the OU and do not affect domain logons.

The other nodes under the security settings category can be applied to both the domain and OU levels. Here is a summary of the functions of each node:

- *Local Policies*—This category applies security settings to the local account database of the workstation or server. These may be overwritten at the site, domain, or OU level but remain in effect if there are no other policies at those levels. There are three subcategories that can be configured:
  - *Audit Policy*—Defines various successful or unsuccessful events that can be audited and recorded in the event logs
  - *User Rights Assignment*—Controls local computer rights that may be assigned to users or groups (e.g., the right to log on locally or to shut down the computer)
  - *Security Options*—Defines a wide variety of configuration settings that adjust the registry (e.g., logon banner configurations, restricting floppy or CD-ROM access, and removing the last logged-on user name from the logon screen)
- *Event Log*—This category defines configuration settings in relation to event log size, retention period, and access restrictions.
- *Restricted Groups*—This category gives the administrator the ability to control who is a member of any security group. Each time that the policy is refreshed, any users that have been added to the group by any means other than the security template are removed automatically. This category can also control the other groups to which a particular security group belongs.
- *System Services*—This category allows an administrator control over service startup mode, disabling of a service, permissions to edit the service mode, and auditing of the service.
- *Registry*—This category defines security and auditing access control list (ACL) settings for Registry keys and subkeys. This allows an administrator to control who has the ability to change or overwrite various registry settings.
- *File System*—This category defines and maintains NTFS security permissions and auditing permissions for any folder or file listed in the policy. Files or folders must reside on an NTFS partition.
- *Wireless Network (IEEE 802.11) Policies*—This category defines security settings for wireless networks, including the wireless networks to which a client can connect, whether access points should be used, and data encryption settings.
- *Public Key Policies*—This category defines configuration settings relating to the use of different public key-based applications like the Encrypting File System (EFS), certificate auto-enrollment settings, and Certificate Authority (CA) trusts.

- *Software Restriction Policies*—This category defines security settings related to the deployment of software, such as the ability to manually define which file extensions are considered executable, control security settings of software-related Registry paths, and override software settings from other GPOs.
- *IP Security Policies on Active Directory*—This category is used to define different IP Security settings based on the role of a server or workstation. Three default policies exist, but none are applied by default.

Activity 4-7: Configuring Group Policy Object Security Settings

Time Required: 10 minutes

Objective: Use Group Policy settings to configure a logon banner for domain users.

Description: Windows Server 2003 enables you to configure a variety of different security settings using GPOs. The IT manager at Dover Leasing is concerned about legal issues relating to the fact that the user authentication process does not include any type of warning message about which users are authorized to access Dover's computers. In this activity, you will configure and test Group Policy settings to require that users accept the parameters of a warning message before logging on.

1. Using Active Directory Users and Computers, access the configuration settings of the **Default Domain Policy** GPO.
2. In the Computer Configuration section, click the **plus signs (+)** next to Windows Settings, Security Settings, and Local Policies to expand them.
3. Click **Security Options** to view its settings.
4. Double-click **Interactive logon: Message text for users attempting to log on** to view its properties.
5. Click the **Define this policy setting in the template** check box. In the text box, type **Only Authorized Users of Dover Leasing are permitted to log on** and click **OK**.
6. Double-click **Interactive logon: Message title for users attempting to log on** to view its properties.
7. Click the **Define this policy setting** check box. In the text box, type **Dover Corporate Security Policy** and click **OK**.
8. Close the Group Policy Object Editor window, as well as the properties of Domain*XX*.Dovercorp.net.
9. Close Active Directory Users and Computers and restart your server.
10. Press **Ctrl+Alt+Delete** to begin the logon process. The Dover Corporate Security Policy window opens. Click **OK**.
11. Log on using your **Admin*XX*** account.

Activity 4-8: Configuring File System Security Using Group Policy Settings

Time Required: 15 minutes

Objective: Use Group Policy settings to configure security permissions on a file or folder.

Description: Users in the Marketing Department at Dover Leasing use a custom application requiring that a folder named Reports be present on their D: drive. The security requirements of this application dictate that only users in the Marketing Department should have access to the folder. The IT manager at Dover Leasing has asked you to attempt to find a way to use Group Policy settings to configure the necessary folder security, to avoid the need to manually configure each and every computer. In this activity, you will test the ability to control file and folder permissions through the use of Group Policy file system settings.

1. Open **My Computer** and then double-click your **D:** drive to view its contents.
2. Right-click in a blank area, select **New**, and click **Folder**.
3. Name the new folder **Reports**, and then close My Computer.
4. Open **Active Directory Users and Computers** and access the configuration settings of the **Marketing Policy** GPO.
5. In the Computer Configuration section, click the **plus sign (+)** next to Windows Settings and Security Settings to expand it.
6. Right-click **File System** and click **Add File**, as shown in Figure 4-8.

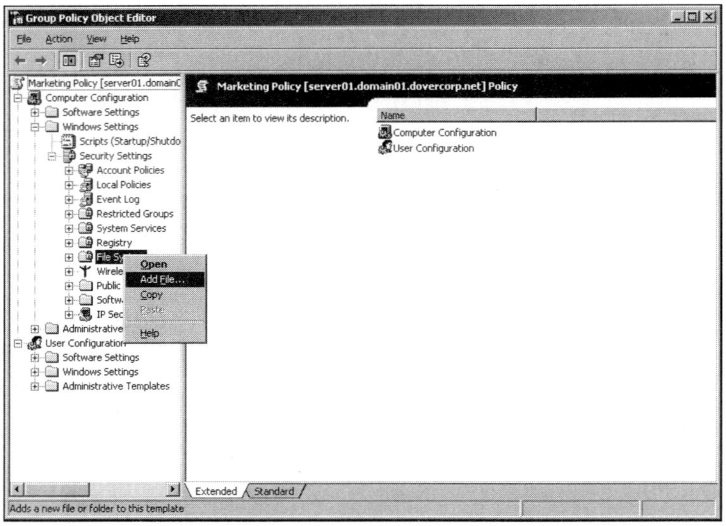

Figure 4-8 Adding a security file to the file system

7. In the add a file or folder dialog box, browse to the **Reports** folder on drive D: and click **OK**. The Database Security for %SystemDrive%\Reports window opens.
8. Click **Add**. In the Enter the object names to select text box, type **Moira** and click **OK**.
9. In the Permissions for Moira Cowan section, click the **Allow** check box next to the Full Control permission and click **OK**. When the Add Object dialog box opens, read the available options and then click **OK**.
10. Close the Group Policy Object Editor window, as well as the properties of the Marketing OU.
11. Open **My Computer** and browse to the **D:\Reports** folder. Right-click the folder and click **Properties**. Click the **Security** tab, making note of the fact that no permissions for the Moira Cowan user account are explicitly defined. Close the Reports Properties window, then close My Computer.
12. Close Active Directory Users and Computers and restart your server.
13. Log on as the user **mcowan** using the password **Password01**.

14. Open **My Computer** and browse to the **D:\Reports** folder. Right-click the folder and click **Properties**. Click the **Security** tab, making note of the fact that permissions for the Moira Cowan user account are now explicitly defined, as per the GPO linked to the Marketing OU.
15. Log off and log back on using your **Admin*XX*** account.

Using the Security Configuration Manager Tools with Group Policy

In the past, as network systems increased in size and complexity, administering security across the enterprise also became increasingly complex. Windows NT did not provide adequate tools or utilities to implement and manage an effective network security policy. For example, if administrators wanted to implement security auditing on a particular group of workstations, either they would have to visit each machine individually or try to find adequate third-party tools to assist in the configuration.

Another common problem with managing security policies in Windows NT involves maintaining the configuration. If a company or department has more than one administrator in charge of applying and maintaining the security settings, it can be difficult to keep track of configuration changes to the policy. Without proper documentation and good communication between the administrators, a great deal of time may be spent figuring out which auditing and security settings each administrator has changed.

Windows Server 2003 makes significant changes to how security configurations can be maintained. Tools included for this purpose are collectively referred to as the **Security Configuration Manager tools**. This tool set, together with Windows Server 2003 Group Policies, allows an administrator to configure a specific group of security settings to form a **Security Policy template**. This template can then be administered centrally and applied throughout Active Directory.

To assist with security policy changes, the Security Configuration Manager tools can also be used to analyze and implement security settings on a computer system. In the analysis, a comparison can be made between a computer system's security settings and a previously defined security template file. Differences between the computer system and the policy template can then be viewed and reported, and action can then be taken to change the settings on the computer to the desired settings.

For example, your security plan may provide detailed information on the security settings for the company's computers. Creating the design is only the first step, however. You also need to implement the design, which could mean making changes to every computer on the network. The Security Configuration Manager tools are designed to make the implementation of the security policy much easier. When the security policy has been designed and approved, the settings can then be defined in a security template. This template can then be compared to the current settings on the network by using the Security Configuration and Analysis tool. This will show which current settings match the security policy and which do not. You can then apply and implement the new settings with a simple command.

The Security Configuration Manager tools are also useful in maintaining security settings. It is also easy to check the security settings for the network on a regular basis and reapply any settings that may have been changed.

The Security Configuration Manager tools consist of the following core components:

- Security templates
- Security settings in Group Policy objects
- Security Configuration and Analysis tool
- Secedit command-line tool

Security Templates

An administrator uses a security template to define, edit, and save baseline security settings to be applied to computers with common security requirements to meet organizational security standards. Templates help ensure that a consistent setting can be applied to multiple machines and be easily maintained.

The templates are text-based files that can be read but should not be changed or edited using any text editor. Be sure to use the Security Templates snap-in to create and edit the templates. The Security Templates snap-in is illustrated in Figure 4-9.

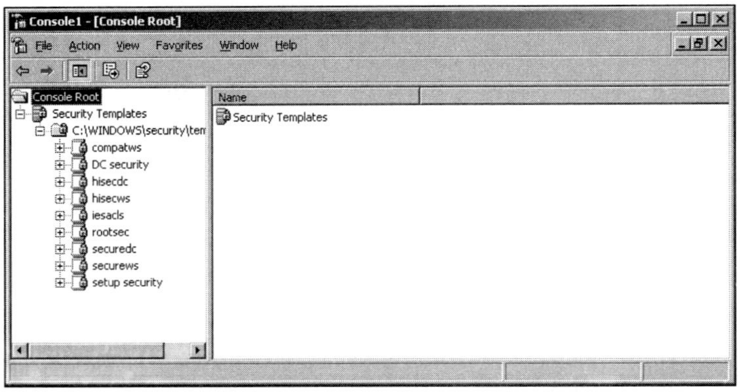

Figure 4-9 Viewing the Security Templates console

Security templates include the same categories as discussed earlier in Tables 4-3, 4-4, and 4-5. You can configure settings such as audit or security policies and then save them as a template to be applied to any number of computers in the domain.

Hands-on Project

Activity 4-9: Browsing Security Templates

Time Required: 10 minutes

Objective: Exploring settings associated with built-in security templates.

Description: Windows Server 2003 includes a number of predefined templates that can be used to configure security settings on domain workstations and servers. The IT manager at Dover Leasing is interested in evaluating the potential impact of using these settings but wants to be sure that increasing the overall level of security will not render certain systems unable to communicate. In this activity, you will browse through some of the default security templates included with Windows Server 2003 to evaluate their configuration settings.

1. Open a new **MMC**.
2. Click **File** on the menu bar, click **Add/Remove Snap-in**, and then click **Add**.
3. On the Available Standalone Snap-in window, click **Security Templates** and click **Add**.
4. Click **Close** to close the window, and then click **OK**.
5. Click the **plus sign (+)** next to Security Templates to expand it, and then click the **plus sign (+)** next to C:\WINDOWS\Security\Templates to view the available templates.
6. Click the **plus sign (+)** next to hisecdc to view its contents.
7. Click the **plus sign (+)** next to Account Policies, and then click **Password Policy**. Browse through the password settings associated with the hisecdc security template.

8. Click **Account Lockout Policy** to view the template's associated settings.
9. Click the **plus sign (+)** next to the securedc template to expand it, and then click the **plus sign (+)** next to Account Policies.
10. Click **Account Lockout Policy** to view its settings, as shown in Figure 4-10. Compare the account lockout settings configured in the hisecdc template to those found in the securedc template.

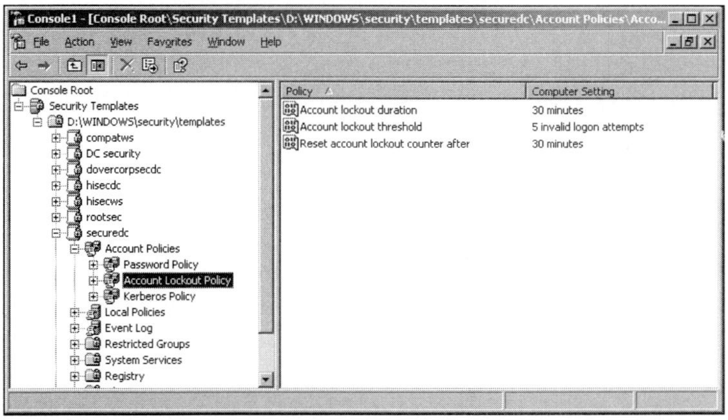

Figure 4-10 Viewing the Account Lockout Policy settings

11. As time permits, browse through some additional security templates to compare differences between settings configured in the various security templates.
12. Leave the MMC open.

Analyzing the Preconfigured Security Templates

The first step in configuring and implementing security templates is to categorize the network computers into three main categories: workstations, servers, and domain controllers. These three categories relate to the default security templates included with Windows Server 2003, although an administrator can also design custom templates. Keep in mind that only computers running Windows Server 2003, Windows XP, and Windows 2000 can take advantage of security template configurations and deployments.

The Default Template

When Windows Server 2003 is installed, the default security settings applied to the computer are stored in a template called Setup Security.inf. The contents of this template will be different depending upon the original configuration of the computer, such as whether the operating system was freshly installed or upgraded from a previous version of Windows. The purpose of this template is to provide a single file in which all of the original computer security settings are stored. If the security settings of a computer are ever changed and an administrator wishes to easily return the system to its original settings, the Setup Security.inf template could simply be reapplied.

Note

The Setup Security.inf template should never be applied using Group Policy because it contains a large number of settings that can seriously degrade Group Policy processing performance.

Incremental Templates

If the basic security settings do not meet your security needs, you can apply various additional security configurations using **incremental templates**. These templates modify security settings incrementally. However, these templates should only be applied to machines already running the default security settings because they do not include any of the initial configurations that the template created during the initial installation.

- *Compatws.inf*—This template can be applied to workstations or servers. Windows Server 2003 has increased the default security considerably over previous versions like Windows NT. In some cases, this increased security brings application compatibility problems, especially for noncertified applications that require user access to the registry. One way to run these applications is to make the user a member of the **Power Users group**, which has a higher level of rights and permissions than a normal user. Another option is for the administrator to increase the security permissions for the Users group. The Compatws.inf template provides a third alternative by weakening the default security to allow legacy applications to run under Windows Server 2003.
- *Securews.inf* and *Securedc.inf*—These templates provide increased security for areas such as account policy, auditing, and registry permissions. The securews template is for any workstation or server, whereas the securedc template should only be applied to domain controllers.
- *Hisecws.inf* and *Hisecdc.inf*—These templates can be incrementally applied after the secure templates have been applied. Security is increased in the areas that affect network communication protocols through the use of such features as packet signing. These templates should only be applied to client computers running Windows 2000 or higher, and all domain controllers must be running Windows 2000 or Windows Server 2003. These templates should only be applied to all machines to ensure proper connectivity. The hisecws template is for workstations or servers, whereas the hisecdc template should only be applied to domain controllers.
- *DC Security.inf*—This template is applied automatically whenever a Windows 2000 or Windows Server 2003 member server is promoted to a domain controller. This is available to give the administrator the option to reapply the initial domain controller security settings if the need arises.
- *Rootsec.inf*—This template specifies the original permissions assigned to the root of the system drive. The main purpose of this template is for use in reapplying security permissions to resources on the system drive that have been changed, whether on purpose or by accident.

The security templates included in Windows Server 2003 provide the administrator with acceptable security configurations for a variety of situations. If there is a unique situation where a preconfigured template is not suitable, you can also create custom templates to meet your needs.

> Note: You can also use a preconfigured template as a baseline and save any changes to a new template. To do this, right-click a preconfigured template, and then choose Save As.

Applying Security Templates

Security templates can be applied to either the local machine or the domain via GPOs. To apply a security template to a local machine, open the Local Security Settings MMC snap-in by running secpol.msc. Right-click Security Settings in the console pane, and choose Import Policy. You can then select the template file to be imported, as shown in Figure 4-11.

Security settings that are applied using Group Policy will always override local settings. Group Policy security settings are refreshed any time the machine is rebooted, at 90-minute intervals for servers and workstations, and every 5 minutes on domain controllers. Even if there have been no changes, the security settings are refreshed every 16 hours.

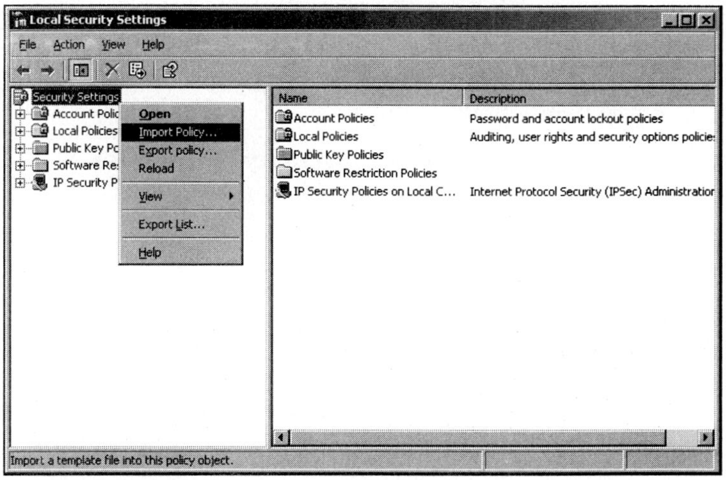

Figure 4-11 Importing a policy into Local Security Settings

Activity 4-10: Creating a Security Template

Time Required: 10 minutes

Objective: Define a new security template to meet custom requirements.

Description: Although the default security templates include a variety of different settings that can be used to increase the security level of Dover Leasing's servers and workstations, the IT manager has decided to explore the possibility of defining a custom template containing settings specific to Dover's requirements. Ultimately, a custom template will be defined that can be distributed to other Dover business units to standardize the security process if necessary. In this activity, you will explore the process of defining a custom security template based on some of Dover's specific requirements.

1. In the MMC with the Security Templates snap-in added, right-click **C:\WINDOWS\Security\Templates** and click **New Template**.
2. In the Template name text box, type **dovercorptest**. In the Description text box, type **Test security template for the Domain*XX*.Dovercorp.net domain**. Click **OK**.
3. Browse through the configuration settings of the new dovercorptest security template. Notice that because the template is new, no settings have yet been configured.
4. Click the **plus sign (+)** next to the dovercorptest template to expand it, browse to the **Password Policy** section, and configure the following settings:

Enforce password history	5 passwords remembered
Maximum password age	20 days
Minimum password age	19 days
Minimum password length	6 characters
Password must meet complexity requirements	Enabled

5. Click on **Account Lockout Policy** and then configure the following settings:

Account lockout duration	5 minutes
Account lockout threshold	3 invalid logon attempts
Reset account lockout counter after	5 minutes

6. Right-click the **dovercorptest** security template and click **Save**. Close the MMC. Click **No** in the Microsoft Management Console dialog box.
7. Open **My Computer** and browse to **C:\WINDOWS\Security\Templates**. Double-click the **dovercorptest.inf** file to open it in a text editor. Notice that the settings originally configured in the Security Templates tool now appear in the text file.
8. Close the dovercorptest.inf file, then close My Computer.

Activity 4-11: Applying Security Template Settings to Group Policy Objects

Hands-on Project

Time Required: 10 minutes

Objective: Deploy security template settings using Group Policy.

Description: Although security templates allow you to configure security settings directly on a local computer, their settings can also be imported into GPOs to facilitate easier deployment. The IT manager at Dover Leasing has asked you to explore the possibility of using Group Policy to deploy settings configured in the template defined as part of the previous activity. In this activity, you will import the security settings of a security template into an existing GPO.

1. Open **Active Directory Users and Computers**.
2. Right-click **Domain*XX*.Dovercorp.net** and click **Properties**.
3. Click the **Group Policy** tab, ensure that Default Domain Policy is selected, and then click **Edit** to view its settings.
4. In the Computer Configuration section, click the **plus sign (+)** next to Windows Settings to expand it.
5. Right-click **Security Settings** and click **Import Policy**.
6. In the Import Policy From window, click **dovercorptest.inf** and click **Open**.
7. After importing the security template settings to the Default Domain Policy, browse through the Password Policy and Account Lockout Policy sections. Verify that the settings from the dovercorptest security template have been imported into the GPO.
8. Close the Group Policy Object Editor window, as well as the properties of the *DomainXX.Dovercorp.net* domain. Close Active Directory Users and Computers.

Security Configuration and Analysis

The Security Configuration and Analysis utility illustrated in Figure 4-12 allows administrators to compare current system settings to a previously configured security template. The comparison identifies any changes to the original security configurations and any possible security weaknesses that may be evident when compared to a stronger security baseline template.

The Security Configuration and Analysis tool uses a container, also referred to as a database, to store the imported templates that will be compared to the current system. The administrator imports a template into the database and then compares the template settings to the actual computer settings. If desired, the administrator can import more than one template to compare the effects of combining templates on the current settings. Once a combined template has been created, it can be saved and exported for future analysis, or it can be used to configure working computer systems.

After the analysis process is complete, the security categories will appear. As each node is expanded, you can see the comparison between the database (imported templates) and the computer's current configuration. A green check mark indicates that the two settings match; a red "x" indicates a mismatch. You can make changes by double-clicking any configuration entry and selecting the desired configuration.

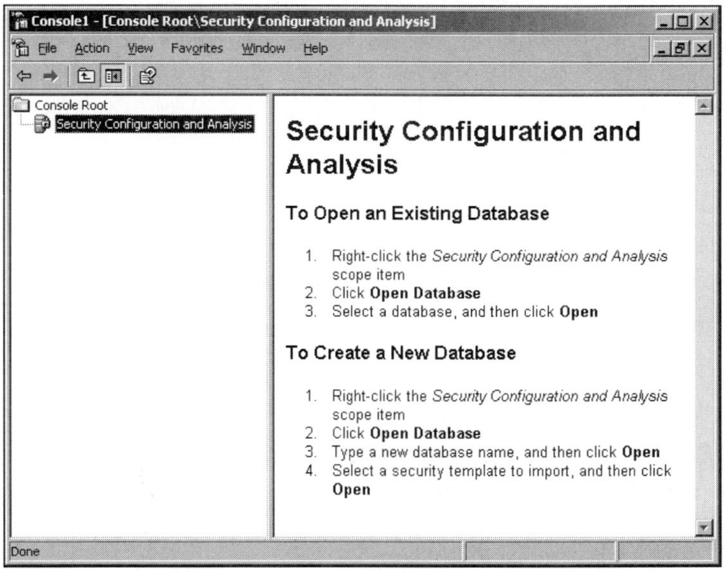

Figure 4-12 Viewing the Security Configuration and Analysis tool

Activity 4-12: Analyzing Security Settings Using Security Configuration and Analysis

Time Required: 15 minutes

Objective: Use the Security Configuration and Analysis tool to compare Group Policy and security template settings.

Description: As part of a new security initiative, the IT manager at Dover Leasing has decided that a mechanism must exist to allow systems to be periodically evaluated to ensure that they meet Dover's defined security-setting requirements. You have been asked to evaluate the Security Configuration and Analysis tool to determine whether or not this application will meet the stated requirements. In this activity, you will compare the current configuration of your domain controller with the settings found in the built-in hisecdc.inf security template.

1. Open a new **MMC** and add the **Security Configuration and Analysis** snap-in.
2. Right-click the **Security Configuration and Analysis** icon and click **Open Database**.
3. In the Open database window, type **SecurityTest** in the File name text box, as illustrated in Figure 4-13, and then click **Open**.

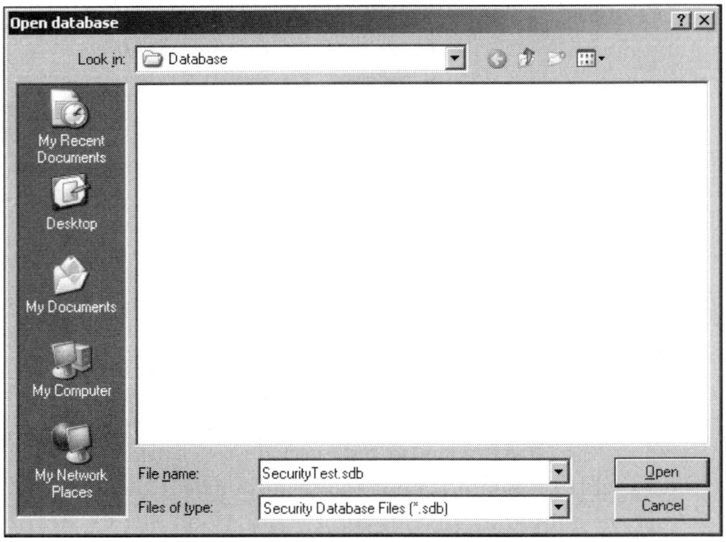

Figure 4-13 Importing a security template

4. In the Import Template window, click **hisecdc.inf** and click **Open**.
5. Right-click the **Security Configuration and Analysis** icon and click **Analyze Computer Now**.
6. In the Perform Analysis dialog box, click **OK** to accept the default log file location. The Analyzing System Security dialog box opens, as shown in Figure 4-14.

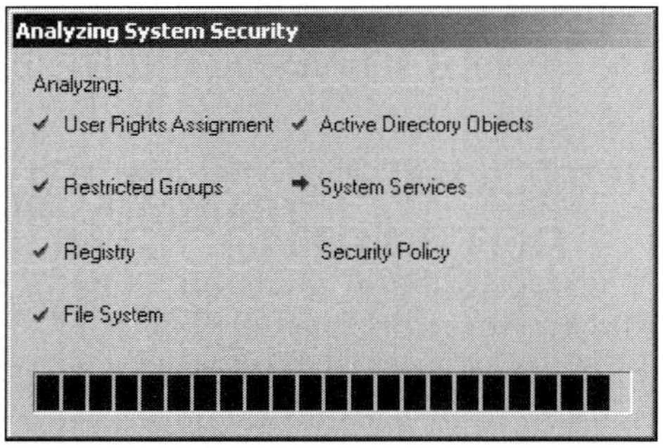

Figure 4-14 Analyzing security on a computer

7. Click the **plus sign (+)** next to Security Configuration and Analysis and Account Policies to expand them, and then click **Password Policy**, as shown in Figure 4-15.
8. Review both the Database Setting column and the Computer Setting column. The first column outlines the settings found in the database that relate to the template, whereas the second column outlines the settings currently configured on your server. Note that the icons displayed as part of each setting outline whether or not your server's current configuration meets or exceeds the settings outlined in the security database.
9. As time permits, browse through additional settings such as those found in the Account Lockout Policy, User Rights Assignment, and Security Options sections.
10. Close the MMC without saving any changes.

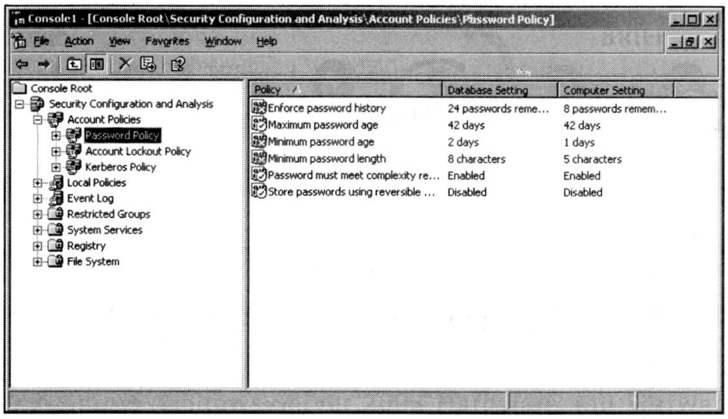

Figure 4-15 Viewing the results of the security analysis

Secedit Command-Line Tool

Secedit.exe is a command-line tool used to create and apply security templates, as well as analyze security settings. This tool can be used in situations where Group Policy cannot be applied, such as in workgroup configurations. Secedit.exe, along with the Task Scheduler, can ensure that every computer in the workgroup maintains consistent security-policy settings. The secedit.exe command uses six main switches:

- */analyze*—Analyzes database settings and compares them to a computer configuration
- */configure*—Configures a system with database and template settings
- */export*—Exports database information to a template file
- */import*—Imports template information into a database file for analysis purposes
- */validate*—Verifies the syntax of a template
- */GenerateRollback*—Generates a template that saves the current security settings of a system; this template can be used to return to previous security settings in the event that settings are changed

Note: The Windows Server 2003 version of secedit.exe no longer includes the /refreshpolicy switch that was used to manually refresh computer and user Group Policy settings in Windows 2000. Refreshing Group Policy settings is now accomplished using the command-line tool gpupdate.exe.

Assigning Scripts and Redirecting Folders

Most administrators are familiar with the application of various types of scripts or files that incorporate a number of commands used to automate routine operations. Logon scripts have been most popular in the past and were used to automate such tasks as drive mapping or application updates.

Windows Server 2003 can use scripts to perform tasks at various times during the logon or logoff process. Group Policy allows you to configure computer startup and shutdown scripts, which are configured in the computer section of a GPO, as shown in Figure 4-16. User logon and logoff scripts can also be configured by accessing the user section of a GPO.

If you assign multiple logon/logoff or startup/shutdown scripts to the configuration containers, each script is run synchronously in order from top to bottom. You can modify the order by selecting the script and clicking the Up or Down buttons in the Properties dialog box. In addition to modifying the order, other policy settings for groups allow you to specify script time-outs, change the running of the scripts to asynchronous, and specify whether scripts are hidden when they are executed.

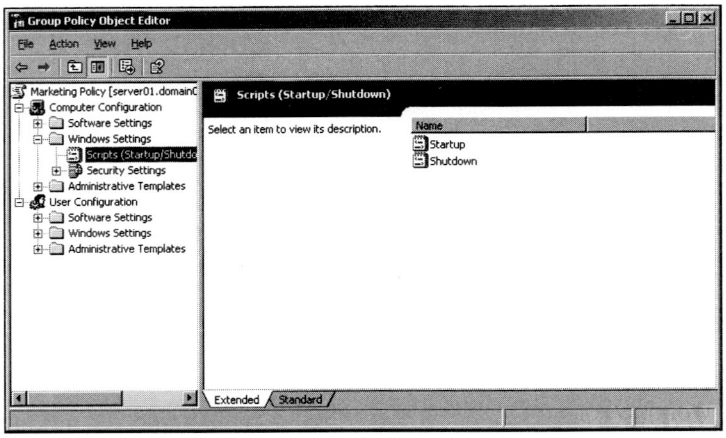

Figure 4-16 Viewing the startup and shutdown script configuration icons

Activity 4-13: Assigning Login Scripts to Users Using Group Policy

Time Required: 15 minutes

Objective: Use GPOs to assign logon scripts to domain users.

Description: Dover Leasing has traditionally used logon scripts to easily define user environment settings, such as mapped network drives, printers, and so forth. Although the logon scripts in use at Dover currently meet all requirements, they have become very long and difficult to manage based on the specific requirements of users from different departments. Because of this, the IT manager at Dover Leasing has asked you to evaluate the ability to deploy logon scripts using GPO settings. In this activity, you will deploy a logon script that maps a drive for Marketing users only through the use of a GPO.

1. Open **My Computer**, click **Tools** on the menu bar, and then click **Folder Options**.
2. Click the **View** tab. In the Advanced settings section, ensure that the Hide extensions for known file types check box is unchecked, and click **OK**.
3. Open drive **D:** and create a new folder called **Scripts**.
4. Open the **Scripts** folder. Right-click an area of free space, select **New**, and then click **Text Document**.
5. Double-click **New Text Document.txt** to open it.
6. In the first line of the file, type **net use x: \\instructor\shared**. Save the file and then close it.
7. Right-click **New Text Document.txt** and click **Rename**. Rename the file to **logon.bat** and press **Enter**. When prompted, click **Yes** to confirm the change.
8. Right-click the **logon.bat** file and click **Copy**. Close My Computer.
9. Open **Active Directory Users and Computers** and access the configuration settings of the Marketing Policy GPO.
10. Under User Configuration, click the **plus sign (+)** next to Windows Settings to expand it and then click **Scripts (Logon/Logoff)**.
11. Double-click **Logon** to access its properties. Click the **Show Files** button.
12. In the new window that opens, right-click an area of free space, click **Paste**, and then close the window.

13. In the Logon Properties window, click **Add**. In the Add a Script window, click **Browse** and then double-click **logon.bat**. Click **OK** to close the window, and then click **OK** again to close the Logon Properties window shown in Figure 4-17.

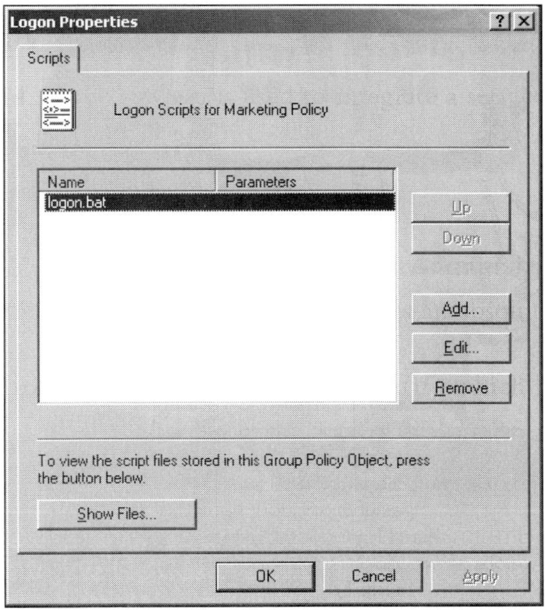

Figure 4-17 Assigning a startup script in Group Policy

14. Close the Group Policy Object Editor window, close the properties of the Marketing OU, and then close Active Directory Users and Computers.
15. Log off and then log back on as the user **mcowan** using the password **password**.
16. Open **My Computer** and verify that drive X has been mapped to the \\instructor\shared folder. Close My Computer.
17. Log off and then log back on using your **Admin*XX*** account. Open **My Computer** to verify that drive X has not been mapped because the Admin*XX* account does not fall under the scope of the Marketing Policy GPO.
18. Close My Computer.

Folder redirection is a Group Policy feature that enables you to redirect the following contents of a user's profile to a network location:

- Application data
- Desktop
- My Documents
- Start menu

Some of the reasons why you would want to redirect the folders out of a user's profile include the following:

- Storing the folders on the network ensures that user information is backed up at all times, as opposed to being stored on the local workstation.
- User logon time is reduced because the contents of the folder do not have to be copied from the workstation to the server each time the user logs on or off.
- Folder redirection allows you to create a standard desktop for multiple users.

The Settings tab has a number of options that control the behavior of folder redirection. Table 4-6 describes each setting.

Table 4-6 Folder redirection settings

Configuration Setting	Description
Grant the user exclusive rights to <folder name>	This setting makes sure that only the individual user that owns the folder has access; this is enabled by default.
Move the contents of <folder name> to the new location	This setting moves the contents of the folder to the new location specified; if this check box is cleared, the contents of the folder, before the redirection, are not moved to the new location (this is enabled by default).
Policy removal	When a folder redirection policy is removed, by default the redirected folder remains in the redirected location; you can choose to redirect the folder back to the user's profile if the policy is removed.

Activity 4-14: Configuring Folder Redirection Settings Using Group Policy

Time Required: 15 minutes

Objective: Redirect users' My Documents folder to a network location.

Description: Although users at Dover Leasing have been trained to save all of their documents to their home folder on a local server, many users continue to save documents to the My Documents folder on their local workstation. Understanding that this represents a potential risk should a user's local hard drive fail, you have decided to explore the possibility of redirecting a user's My Documents folder to a network location, making the change transparent to the user. In this activity, you will use the Folder Redirection feature of Group Policy to redirect users' My Documents folders to a network location.

1. Open **My Computer**.
2. Open drive **D:**, and create a new folder called **Shared**.
3. Right-click the **Shared** folder and click **Properties**. Click the **Sharing** tab, click the **Share this folder** radio button, and then click **OK**. Close **My Computer**.
4. Open **Active Directory Users and Computers** and then access the configuration settings of the **Marketing Policy** GPO.
5. Under User Configuration, click the **plus signs (+)** next to Windows Settings and then Folder Redirection to expand them, as shown in Figure 4-18.

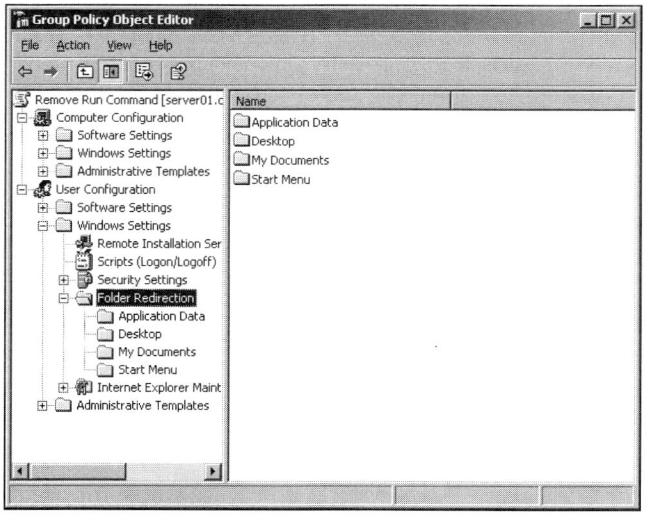

Figure 4-18 Redirecting a folder in Group Policy

6. Right-click **My Documents** and click **Properties**.
7. In the Setting list box, click **Basic – Redirect everyone's folder to the same location**, as shown in Figure 4-19.

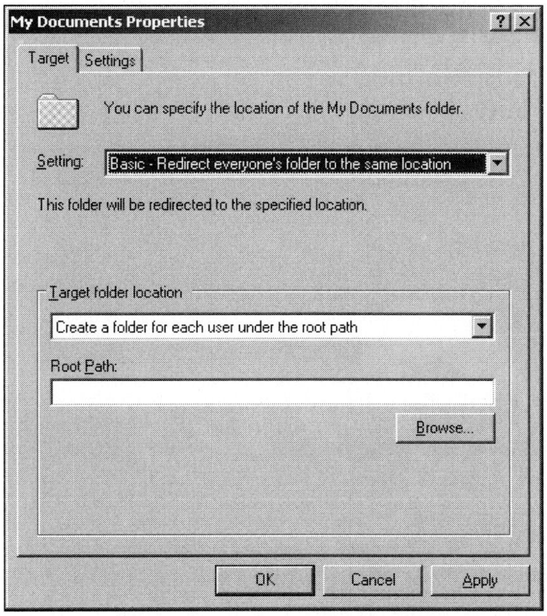

Figure 4-19 Configuring basic folder redirection

8. In the Root Path text box, type **\\server*XX*\shared**. Note the full path to which user folders will be redirected at the bottom of the window and click **OK**.
9. Close the Group Policy Object Editor, as well as the properties of the Marketing OU.
10. Close Active Directory Users and Computers and then reboot.
11. Log on as user **mcowan** using the password **Password01**.
12. Click **Start**, select **All Programs**, select **Accessories**, and then click **Windows Explorer**.
13. Right-click the **My Documents** folder and then click **Properties**. Verify that the Target folder location for the user mcowan now points to \\server*XX*\shared\mcowan\My Documents.
14. Close all open windows. Log off and then log back on using your **Admin*XX*** account.

MANAGING GROUP POLICY INHERITANCE

As a Windows 2000, Windows XP, or Windows Server 2003 computer starts, GPOs are applied in the following order:

1. Local computer
2. Site
3. Domain
4. Parent OU
5. Child OU

All of the individual GPO settings are inherited by default. For example, a Group Policy setting on a parent container is also applied to child containers and, therefore, to all the users and computers in the child containers. One computer or user could be processing many policies during startup and logon.

At each level, more than one GPO can be applied. If there is more than one GPO per container, the policies are applied in the order that they appear on the Group Policy tab for the container, starting with the bottom GPO first.

Note: Be careful about the number of GPOs that are to be applied. Computer startup and logon performance may be affected if a large number of GPOs need to be applied to the user or workstation.

Because of the multiple policies that can be applied to a user or computer, there is the chance that there could be a conflict in the settings between policies. The computer uses the following steps to determine which policy to apply:

1. If there is no conflict, then both policies are applied. For example, if a policy at a domain level enables a certain setting and the policy at an OU level has that setting set as "Not Configured," then the domain policy is applied.
2. If there is a conflict, later settings overwrite earlier settings. If both a domain-level policy and an OU-level policy configure the same setting differently, then the OU-level policy is applied.
3. Computer policies usually overwrite user policies.

After a user has logged on, the computer refreshes its policies every 90 minutes plus a random number of minutes (no more than 30) so that all the computers don't contact the DC to refresh at the same time. If a user does not shut down his computer, or a setting has changed in the Group Policy, then refreshing the policy makes sure that the computer and user settings are up to date. Domain controllers refresh their policy settings for groups every five minutes.

Note: You can refresh Group Policy settings manually by running gpupdate.exe from the command prompt.

As mentioned previously, GPOs can be linked to site, domain, or OU containers in Active Directory. This allows the administrator maximum flexibility when applying Group Policies in the domain. There are a number of possibilities:

- If you have a certain policy that applies to everyone in a physical location, then apply the policy at the site level. You can also configure other settings at a domain level. Some policy settings, such as account policy, can only be set at the domain level. You can then set very specific policies based on OUs.
- You can have multiple Group Policies assigned to one container. You may want to create several GPOs that define different settings and then link all of them to a specific container. For example, you might want to create a policy that defines security settings and another that defines user desktop settings, and then link both of them to the same container.
- You can use the same Group Policy and link it to multiple containers. This allows you to create a policy once and then use that policy for different containers. For example, you may create a policy for software distribution and then link that policy to the OUs where the policy should be applied.

Activity 4-15: Linking a Group Policy Object to Multiple Containers

Time Required: 10 minutes

Objective: Link a single GPO to multiple containers.

Description: As part of planning the deployment of GPOs for the *DomainXX.Dovercorp.net* domain, you have recognized that there are some cases where users in different departments (but not the entire domain) require the same configuration settings. Instead of configuring multiple GPOs that contain identical settings, you have decided that a smaller number of more generic policies linked to multiple containers might better meet your needs. In this activity, you will create a new GPO that will remove the Run command from user desktops and then link that policy to multiple containers.

1. Open **Active Directory Users and Computers**, if it is not already opened.
2. Expand the **DomainXX.Dovercorp.net** domain if necessary, right-click on the **Information Technology** OU, and click **Properties**.
3. Click the **Group Policy** tab and then click **New**. Name the new GPO **Remove Run Command**.
4. Click **Edit** to access the properties of the Remove Run Command GPO.
5. Under User Configuration, click the **plus sign (+)** next to Administrative Templates to expand it, and then click **Start Menu and Taskbar** to view its settings.
6. Double-click the **Remove Run menu from Start Menu** icon to access its properties, as shown in Figure 4-20. Click the **Enabled** radio button, and then click **OK**.

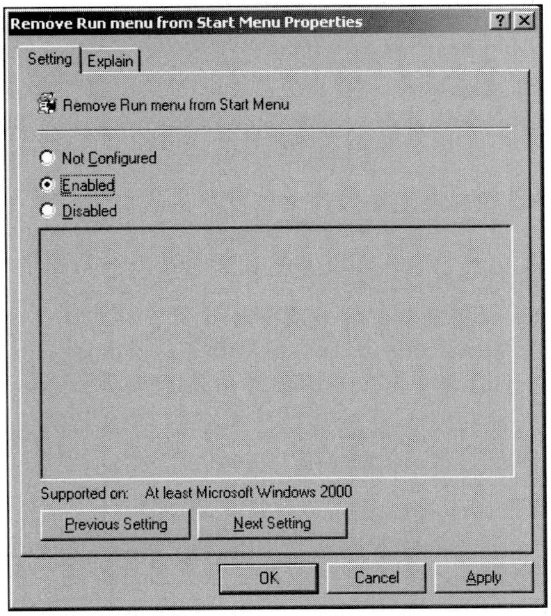

Figure 4-20 Viewing the Remove Run menu from Start Menu properties

7. Close the Group Policy Object Editor window and then close the properties of the Information Technology OU.
8. Right-click the **Sales** OU and then click **Properties**.
9. Click the **Group Policy** tab and then click **Add**.

10. In the Add a Group Policy Object Link window, click the **All** tab. Click the **Remove Run Command** GPO and then click **OK**. The Remove Run Command GPO is now linked to both the Information Technology OU as well as the Sales OU.
11. Close the properties of the Sales OU, but leave Active Directory Users and Computers open.

Configuring Block Policy Inheritance, No Override, and Filtering

By default, all policy settings for groups are inherited from parent containers. However, there are several ways to change this default behavior:

- *Blocking Group Policy inheritance*—If you do not want any of the higher-level settings to be applied to a particular child container, then check the Block Policy inheritance check box on the Group Policy tab for the container properties. Figure 4-21 shows the interface.

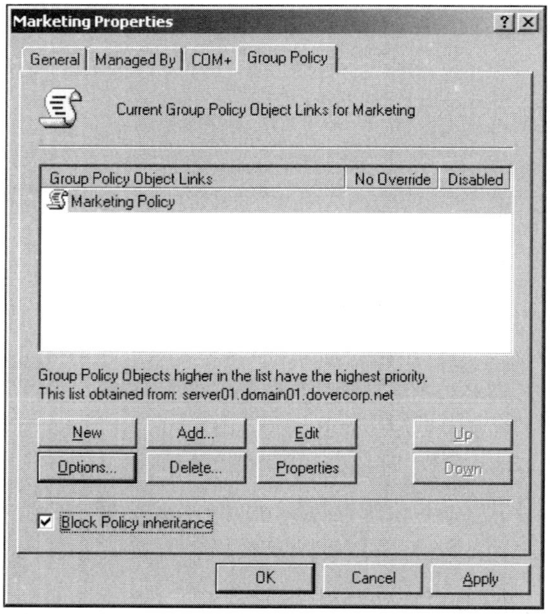

Figure 4-21 Blocking Group Policy inheritance

Checking this option means that all higher-level policies for other containers are blocked. For example, if the properties of the Marketing OU were set to block Group Policy inheritance, then GPOs from the site or domain levels would not be applied. Blocking Group Policies can be very useful if you have one OU that has very different policy requirements than all of the other OUs, or if the OU must be separately managed.

- *Configuring No Override*—If you want a particular GPO's settings to always be enforced, you can configure the policy using the No Override option, as shown in Figure 4-22.

  This results in the policy being enforced even if a lower-level policy that is processed later tries to change a setting. The No Override setting also enforces a policy on a container that has Block Policy inheritance set. Use this option if there is a particular group of settings that must be enforced in your entire network and then link this policy to the domain or site level so that it applies to all containers.

- *Filtering policy settings for groups*—Another way of affecting the inheritance of Group Policies is to prevent policy settings for groups from applying to a particular user, group, or computer within a container. For example, the Marketing OU may have a GPO linked to it, but you don't want the settings from the GPO to apply to the Marketing Vice President. To filter the Marketing Vice President so that she does not have the GPO applied, you could access the security settings associated with the GPO and deny the Read and Apply Group Policy permissions for the Marketing

Vice President user account only. This would prevent the Group Policy from being applied to the Marketing Vice President, with the settings still affecting all other users within the OU.

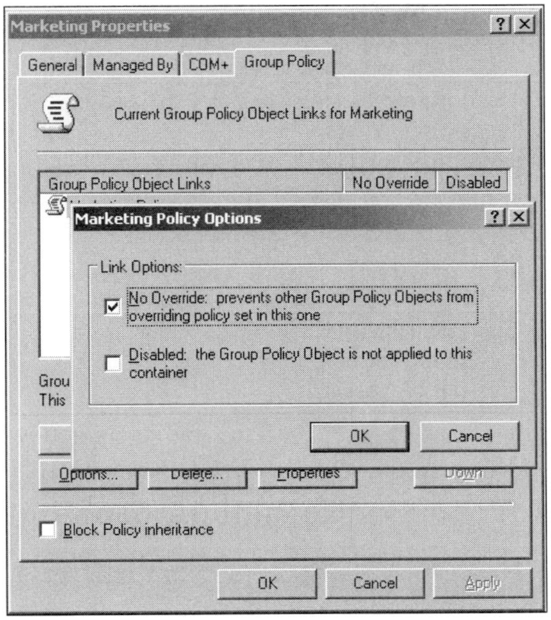

Figure 4-22 Configuring No Override on a Group Policy object

Activity 4-16: Configuring Group Policy Object Inheritance Settings

Time Required: 20 minutes

Objective: Configure Group Policy inheritance settings.

Description: As part of his decision to deploy configuration settings using GPOs, the IT manager at Dover Leasing has identified a number of potential issues about how GPOs are processed in Active Directory environments. In particular, the IT manager is concerned that if administration is ultimately decentralized, administrators responsible for a particular OU might configure policy settings that override those configured at the domain level. You have been asked to configure and test Group Policy inheritance settings that will ensure that settings configured at the domain level will not be overwritten by OU-level configurations. In this activity, you will configure and test the Group Policy No Override setting.

1. Open **Active Directory Users and Computers** and then access the configuration settings of the Default Domain Policy GPO.

2. Under the User Configuration settings section, click the **plus sign (+)** next to Administrative Templates to expand it, and then click **Start Menu and Taskbar** to view its settings.
3. Double-click **Remove Run menu from Start Menu**, click the **Enabled** radio button, and then click **OK**. This will disable the Run command for all domain users.
4. Close the Group Policy Object Editor window, and close the properties of the Domain*XX*.Dovercorp.net domain.
5. Access the configuration settings of the Marketing Policy GPO.
6. Under the User Configuration settings section, click the **plus sign (+)** next to Administrative Templates to expand it, and then click **Start Menu and Taskbar** to view its settings.
7. Double-click **Remove Run menu from Start Menu**, click the **Disabled** radio button, and then click **OK**. This will stop the removal of the Run command for all users in the Marketing OU.
8. Close all open windows and log off.
9. Log on using your **Admin*XX*** account, noting that the Run command is no longer available. Log off.
10. Log on using the **mcowan** account with the password **Password01**. Note that the Run command is now available because OU-level policies are applied after domain-level policies.
11. Log off and then log on using your **Admin*XX*** account.
12. Open **Active Directory Users and Computers** and then access the properties of the Domain*XX*.Dovercorp.net domain.
13. Click the **Group Policy** tab and ensure that the **Default Domain Policy** is selected. Click the **Options** button. Under **Link Options**, check the **No Override** check box and then click **OK**. Notice the checkmark next to the Default Domain Policy in the No Override column. This will prevent settings in the Default Domain Policy from being overridden by policy settings applied at the OU level.
14. Close all open windows and log off.
15. Log on as user **mcowan** using the password **Password01**.
16. Click **Start** to verify that the Run command no longer appears.
17. Log off and then log back on using your **Admin*XX*** account. Remove the **No Override** setting from the Default Domain Policy GPO. Close all open windows.

Activity 4-17: Filtering Group Policy Objects Using Security Permissions

Time Required: 10 minutes

Objective: Use security permissions to filter and control the application of Group Policy settings.

Description: Although the OU structure in place in the *DomainXX.Dovercorp.net* domain was designed with network administration issues in mind, the IT manager is concerned about the fact that in some cases he does not want Group Policy settings to apply to all users. For example, in some departments he would rather not restrict the desktop settings of managers, many of whom find it intrusive. In this activity, you will configure and test the ability to filter the application of Group Policy settings through the use of security permissions.

1. In Active Directory Users and Computers, access the properties of the Marketing OU.
2. Click the **Group Policy** tab, ensure that the Marketing Policy is selected, and then click **Properties**.

3. Click the **Security** tab, and review the permissions associated with the Authenticated Users group. Note that this group has both the Read and Apply Group Policy permissions set to allow.
4. Click **Add**. In the Enter the object names to select text box, type **Moira** and then click **OK**.
5. Ensure that the **Moira Cowan** user account is selected and then note the permissions associated with the account. Check the **Deny** check box for the Apply Group Policy permission. This will stop settings in the Marketing Policy GPO from applying to Moira Cowan. Click **OK**. Click **Yes** in the Security dialog box.
6. Close all open windows and log off.
7. Log on as the user **jhsmith** with the password **Password01**. Click the **Start** menu to confirm that the Run command is available for jhsmith as per the Marketing Policy GPO setting. Log off.
8. Log on as the user **mcowan** with the password **Password01**. Click the **Start** menu to confirm that the Run command is not available for mcowan because the Marketing Policy GPO does not apply due to permission filtering. As such, the policy settings applied by the Default Domain Policy are applied to the mcowan user account.
9. Log off and then log back on using your **Admin*XX*** user account.

Troubleshooting Group Policy Settings

There may be times when a GPO does not work as expected. Restrictions may not be enforced as configured, or may be too restrictive and thus interfere with user productivity.

A careful inspection of the Active Directory hierarchy could possibly uncover the reasons for a Group Policy not working the way it should. Do not forget the order of Group Policy processing: local computer, site, domain, and OU. Be sure to inspect all containers above and below the OU that is causing the problem. In some cases, improper use of No Override or Block Policy inheritance settings can cause problems. Another area to be aware of is the Group Policy's Security tab. Make sure that the user or group has been assigned the Read and Apply Group Policy permissions.

Windows Server 2003 also includes two main utilities that allow you to view the effective Group Policy settings that have been applied to a particular user or computer in the form of the command-line gpresult.exe tool and the graphical **Resultant Set of Policy (RSoP)** tool. These utilities are useful because they can be used to discover Group Policy-related problems and to illustrate which GPOs were applied to a user or computer. **Gpresult** also lists all group memberships of the user or computer being analyzed, along with information about any GPOs that may have been filtered using security permissions.

If you are experiencing performance problems that you can relate to the processing of GPOs, you may want to disable the unused portion of the computer or user section of the policy. For example, if a particular GPO is only used to apply computer-related settings, then disabling the user configuration section of the policy would improve group policy processing performance. To disable processing of the computer or user configuration section of a policy, access the policy's properties and choose the appropriate setting, as shown in Figure 4-23.

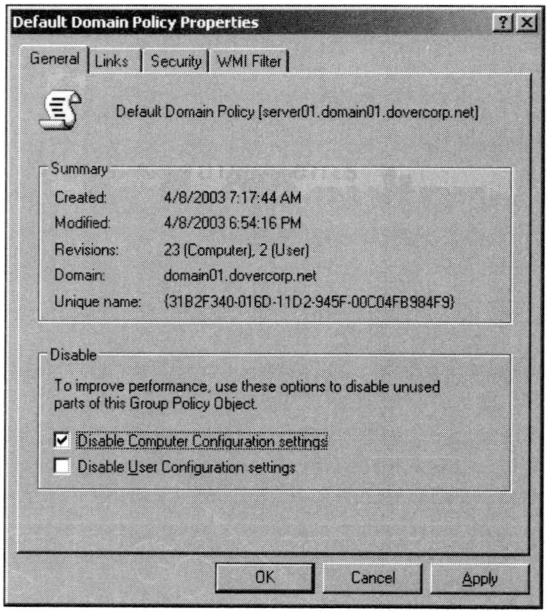

Figure 4-23 Disabling a section of a Group Policy object

Activity 4-18: Determining Group Policy Settings Using Gpresult.exe

Time Required: 5 minutes

Objective: Use Gpresult.exe to determine effective Group Policy settings.

Description: Although the ability to configure Group Policy settings at many different levels within Active Directory provides a great deal of flexibility, it can also be difficult to troubleshoot Group Policy issues, especially in cases where multiple levels of policies with conflicting settings may apply. The IT manager at Dover Leasing has asked you to evaluate the Gpresult.exe tool as a method of determining the effective Group Policy settings that apply to a particular user. In this activity, you will use Gpresult.exe to determine the effective Group Policy settings for a particular domain user.

1. Click **Start**, select **Administrative Tools**, and then click **Active Directory Users and Computers**.
2. Right-click on the **Domain*XX*.Dovercorp.net** icon and click **Properties**. Click the **Group Policy** tab. Ensure that the Default Domain Policy is selected, and then click **Edit**.
3. Click the **plus sign (+)** next to Administrative Templates in the User Configuration section, and then click on **Start Menu and Taskbar**. Double-click on **Remove Run menu from Start Menu**. Click the **Not configured** radio button, and then click **OK**. This will allow the Admin*XX* user account to access the Run command. Close all open windows.
4. Log off, and then log back on using the Admin*XX* user account.
5. Click **Start** and then click **Run**. In the Open text box, type **cmd** and click **OK**.
6. At the command prompt, type **gpresult /?**. Review the switches associated with the gpresult command and their purposes.
7. To view the Group Policy settings applied to Moira Cowan's user account, type **gpresult /user mcowan** and press **Enter**.
8. Scroll through the output provided by the gpresult tool, as illustrated in Figure 4-24. Review the information provided by the gpresult command, including which policies are applied to the mcowan user account and those filtered out through the use of permissions.

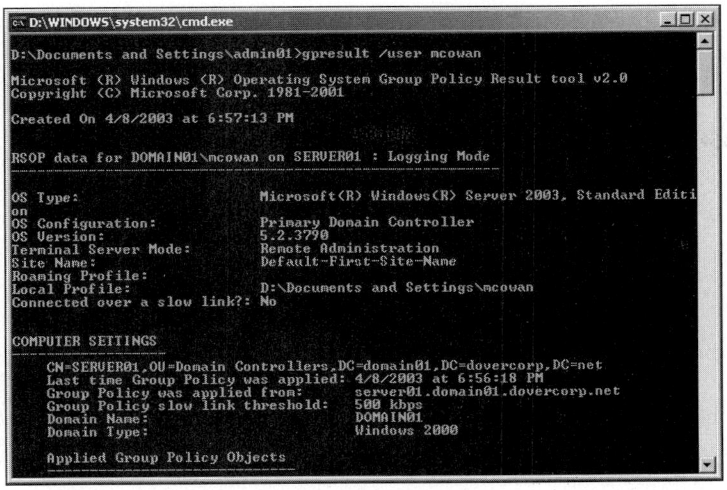

Figure 4-24 Using the Gpresult tool

9. Close the command prompt.

Activity 4-19: Determining Group Policy Settings Using the Resultant Set of Policy Tool

Hands-on Project

Time Required: 10 minutes

Objective: Use Resultant Set of Policy to determine effective Group Policy settings.

Description: Although Gpresult.exe provides all of the information necessary to troubleshoot effective Group Policy settings, you have decided that the data it provides can be overwhelming from the command line. As an alternative, you have decided to try the graphical Resultant Set of Policy tool. In this activity, you will again evaluate the effect of Group Policy settings for a domain user but this time using the Resultant Set of Policy tool.

1. Open a new **MMC** and add the **Resultant Set of Policy** snap-in.
2. Right-click the **Resultant Set of Policy** icon and click **Generate RSoP Data**, as shown in Figure 4-25.
3. At the Resultant Set of Policy Wizard welcome screen, click **Next**.

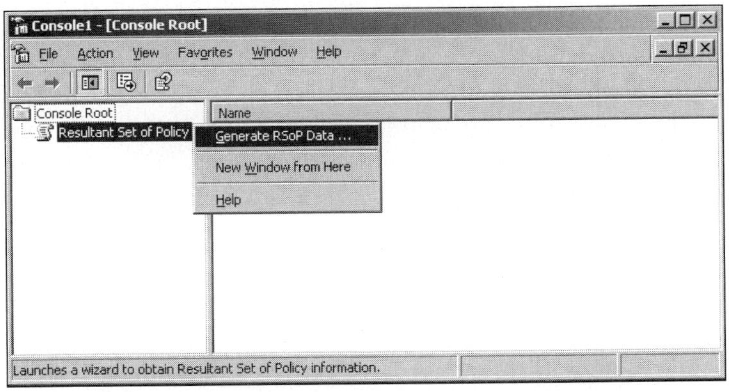

Figure 4-25 Generating RSoP data

4. At the Mode Selection window, ensure that the **Logging mode** radio button is selected and click **Next**.
5. At the Computer Selection window, ensure that the **This computer** radio button is selected, and click **Next**.
6. At the User Selection window, click the **Select a specific user** radio button. Click the **DOMAIN*XX*\mcowan** user account and then click **Next**.
7. At the Summary of Selections window, click **Next** to begin the analysis process.
8. Click **Finish** to complete the Resultant Set of Policy Wizard.
9. Click the **plus sign (+)** next to mcowan on ServerXX – RSOP. Under the Computer Configuration section, click the **plus sign (+)** next to Windows Settings, Security Settings, and Local Policies to expand it. Click **Security Options** to view its settings.
10. Scroll through the list to view the Security Options that are applied to the Moira Cowan user account as a result of Group Policy settings.
11. If time permits, browse through additional sections to view other policies that have been applied to the Moira Cowan user account via GPO settings.
12. Close the MMC without saving changes.

Deploying Software Using Group Policy

In addition to managing user desktops, maintaining security, applying scripts, and redirecting folders, Group Policy can also help you deploy and maintain software installations throughout the domain. There are a variety of applications that can be deployed using Group Policy, including business applications such as Microsoft Office, utilities such as anti-virus software, and software updates such as service packs.

When a company rolls out a new software application, there are four main phases that are addressed:

- Software preparation
- Deployment
- Software maintenance
- Software removal

Software Preparation

The first phase of software deployment is to prepare the software for distribution. Windows Server 2003 Group Policy uses a special installation file called a **Microsoft Windows installer package (MSI)**. An MSI file contains all of the information needed to install an application in a variety of configurations. Many software vendors are starting to include preconfigured MSI packages with their applications to enable administrators to take advantage of the features provided by Windows Server 2003 Group Policy. For older applications, you can create your own MSI packages using third-party utilities, such as a program called WinINSTALL from VERITAS.

After you obtain or create an MSI package file, place the file, along with any related software installation files, in a shared folder on the network. You configure Group Policy to access this shared folder so that a successful installation is ensured.

If an MSI package is not available for an application, and you cannot repackage the application using an application like WinINSTALL, you have an option to use another file type called a **ZAP file**. A ZAP file is a text file that can be used by Group Policy to deploy an application. However, the following limitations apply to applications deployed using the ZAP file:

- Can only be published and not assigned
- Are not resilient and do not repair themselves automatically
- Usually require user intervention and require the user to have the proper permissions to install applications on their local computer

Note: For more information on creating a ZAP file, consult KB article Q231747 on the Microsoft Web site.

Deployment

Using Windows Server 2003 Group Policy, applications can be deployed in one of two ways:

- Assigning applications
- Publishing applications

Assigning Applications

When you create a policy to assign an application, any user to which the policy applies has a shortcut to the application advertised on the Start menu. The application is installed when a user clicks the shortcut for the first time or double-clicks a document that is associated with the application. If the user does not click the shortcut, the application is not installed, which saves space on the hard drive.

If the policy was configured in the computer section of the Group Policy, any computer to which the policy applies has the application automatically installed the next time that the computer is started.

One other advantage to assigned applications is that these applications are resilient, meaning that if files were to become corrupted, the application would automatically reinstall itself.

Publishing Applications

When a policy is created to publish an application, the application is not advertised on the Start menu. Users can install published applications by accessing the Add/Remove Programs applet in Control Panel or by double-clicking a document associated with the application. Applications can only be published to users and not to computers.

One other caution about publishing applications is that if a user deletes an application, or if the application becomes corrupt, it does not reinstall itself. Only assigned applications are resilient.

Configuring the Deployment

Configuring the deployment of the software package involves creating or editing a GPO and then specifying application deployment options. For example, an administrator might choose to assign a certain application to all computers at the domain level, which would automatically install the application the next time individual computers were started. Similarly, a different application might be published to members of the Marketing OU only, allowing users to whom this policy applies to install the application, if necessary, at their own discretion.

Activity 4-20: Publishing an Application to Users Using Group Policy

Hands-on Project

Time Required: 15 minutes

Objective: Publish an application using Group Policy settings.

Description: Dover Leasing has traditionally used Microsoft's System Management Server to deploy software packages and updates to domain users. Although the system is effective, the IT manager at Dover has found it both difficult and expensive to train system administrators in the use of this product. Understanding that Windows Server 2003 Group Policy includes features associated with software deployment, the IT manager has asked you to evaluate the ability to make software available for installation by users without administrative privileges. In this activity, you will publish an application to users in the Information Technology OU.

1. Open **My Computer**, and then double-click the **D:\software** folder to open it. Copy the files named **suptools.msi** and **support.cab** to the **D:\shared** folder.

2. Open **Active Directory Users and Computers** and create a new GPO named **Support Tools Publishing** linked to the Information Technology OU.
3. Click **Edit** to access the configuration settings of the Support Tools Publishing Group Policy Object.
4. Under User Configuration, click the **plus sign (+)** next to Software Settings to expand it.
5. Right-click **Software installation**, click **New**, and then click **Package**, as shown in Figure 4-26.

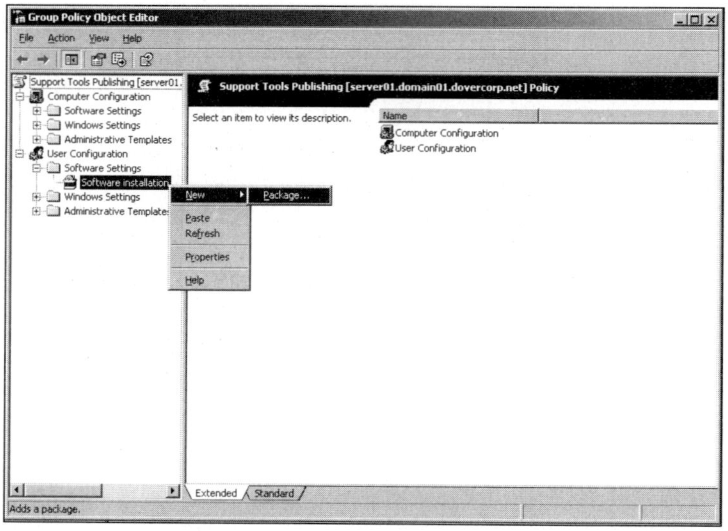

Figure 4-26 Configuring software deployment using Group Policy

6. In the Open dialog box, type **\\server*XX*\shared\suptools.msi** in the File name text box and click **Open**.
7. In the Deploy Software dialog box, ensure that the **Published** radio button is selected and click **OK**. Click on the **Software installation** icon. Notice that the Support Tools application, source folder, and deployment option information is now listed, as illustrated in Figure 4-27. Close all open windows.

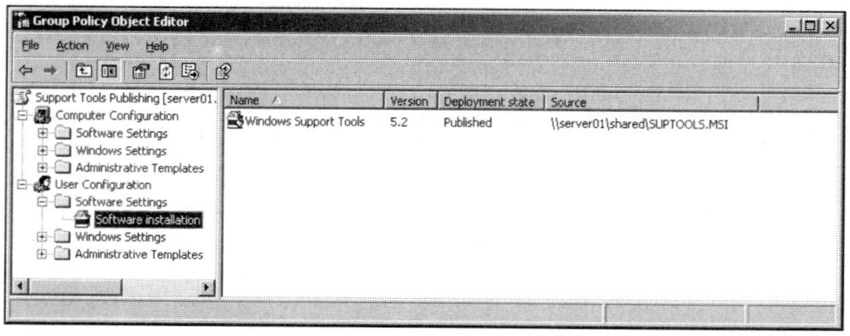

Figure 4-27 Viewing a published application

8. Log off and then log back on as **mmanore** using the password **password**.
9. Click **Start**, click **Control Panel**, and then click **Add or Remove Programs**. Notice that the Windows Support Tools are now available for installation by the mmanore user account.

10. Close all open windows, log off, and then log back on using your **Admin*XX*** account.
11. Open **Active Directory Users and Computers** and delete the **Support Tools Publishing** GPO from the properties of the **Information Technology** OU. Close the properties of the Information Technology OU, but leave Active Directory Users and Computers open.

Activity 4-21: Assigning an Application to Users Using Group Policy

Time Required: 10 minutes

Objective: Assign an application using Group Policy settings.

Description: Having now seen the results of publishing applications to users, the IT manager at Dover Leasing has asked you to evaluate whether it is possible to ensure that the Windows Support Tools are always available for all users in the Information Technology OU without the need for them to manually install the application. In this activity, you will configure and test a GPO designed to assign the Windows Support Tools to users in the Information Technology OU.

1. In Active Directory Users and Computers, create a new GPO named **Support Tools Assignment** linked to the Information Technology OU.
2. Click **Edit** to access the configuration settings of the Support Tools Assignment Group Policy Object.
3. Under User Configuration, click the **plus sign (+)** next to Software Settings to expand it.
4. Right-click **Software installation**, click **New**, and then click **Package**.
5. In the Open dialog box, type **\\server*XX*\shared\suptools.msi** in the File name text box and click **Open**.
6. In the Deploy Software dialog box, ensure that the **Assigned** radio button is selected and click **OK**. Click on the **Software installation** icon. Notice that the Support Tools application, source folder, and deployment option information is now listed. Close all open windows.
7. Log off and then log back on as **mmanore** using the password **password**.
8. Click **Start**, select **All Programs**, select **Windows Support Tools**, and then click **Command Prompt**. The Windows Support Tools will install, and the Command Prompt will open.
9. Close all open windows, log off, and then log on using your **Admin*XX*** account.

Software Maintenance

After an application has been deployed, there are various types of maintenance tasks that usually need to be performed. Most vendors provide periodic updates and service patches to fix reported problems with their applications. You have the task of keeping the deployed software updated with the latest service releases. If vendors release new versions of the software, your users may want to transition slowly to the new version. You may want to allow the users to use both the old and new versions of the software.

When deploying application patches or upgrades, you have three choices for how the deployment is performed:

- A mandatory upgrade
- An optional upgrade
- Redeploying an application

A mandatory upgrade automatically replaces the old version of the software with the new version that is being deployed. Figure 4-28 shows the Upgrades tab found in the properties of a deployed application.

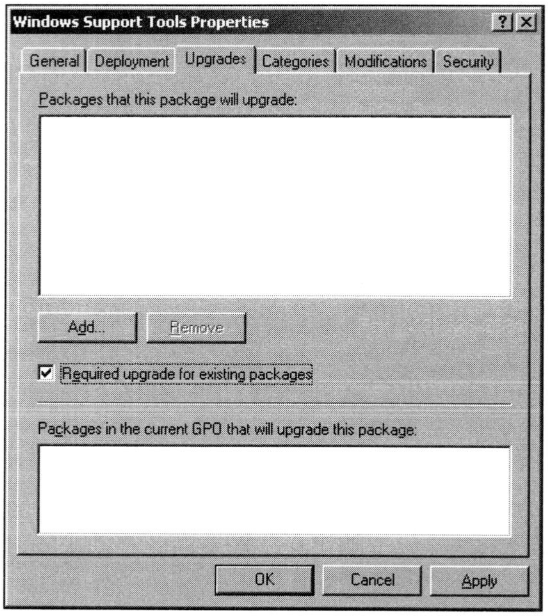

Figure 4-28 Configuring a mandatory upgrade

Note: If the original package and the updated package are both native Windows installer files, the update automatically knows that it is to replace the original package; you just have to configure the mandatory selection box.

To perform an optional upgrade, do not check the Required upgrade for existing packages option. If the user has installed the original application, all shortcuts still open the first version of the program. To install the upgrade, the user has to access Add or Remove Programs from Control Panel and choose to install the upgrade. If the original version was never installed, clicking the advertised icons invokes an installation of the updated version.

Redeployment of a package means to force an application to reinstall itself everywhere that it is already installed. You may have to do this if you need to deploy an application service pack or hot fix. The main requirement for redeployment is that the patch has to come with an MSI file. To configure redeployment, place the update in the same installation folder as the original application. Open the original GPO that deployed the package, right-click the application, and click All Tasks, Redeploy application.

Software Removal

The final phase of an application life cycle is the removal process. When you need to remove an application that you no longer want to deploy in the organization, Group Policy can save a great amount of time and money. The only caution is that the application must have been originally installed using a Windows installer package.

When you remove an application, you are given two choices about how the removal process takes place:

- A forced removal
- An optional removal

A forced removal automatically uninstalls the application from all computers and prevents the software from being reinstalled. The removal takes place either the next time the computer restarts (for computer-based policies) or when the user logs on (for user-based policies).

An optional removal does not remove any of the installed copies of the software, but it does prevent any future installations from taking place. If users remove the application, they are not able to reinstall it.

Activity 4-22: Configuring Group Policy Software Removal

Time Required: 10 minutes

Objective: Remove software using Group Policy.

Description: After testing the assignment of software to users using Group Policy, you are concerned about the ability to remove this software in the case of necessary changes or deployment errors. You understand that Group Policy provides different options for software removal but decide to test this feature to ensure that it functions correctly. In this activity, you will remove the Windows Support Tools assigned to users in the Information Technology OU in the previous activity.

1. Open **Active Directory Users and Computers**, and access the configuration settings of the Support Tools Assignment GPO.
2. Under User Configuration, click the **plus sign (+)** next to Software Settings to expand it, and click **Software installation** to view deployed packages.
3. Right-click **Windows Support Tools**, select **All Tasks**, and then click **Remove**.
4. In the Remove Software dialog box, ensure that the **Immediately uninstall the software from users and computers** radio button is selected and click **OK**.
5. Close all open windows and log off.
6. Log on as the user **mmanore** using the password **password**. During the logon process, watch for the message stating that the Windows Support Tools software is being removed.
7. To confirm that the Windows Support Tools have been uninstalled, click **Start**, click **Control Panel**, and then click **Add or Remove Programs**. Note that the Windows Support Tools are no longer installed.
8. Close all open windows.

Chapter Summary

- Group Policy enables the centralized management of user and computer settings throughout your network. GPOs can be used to perform a variety of administrative tasks, including configuration of desktop settings, control of security settings for users and computers, assignment of scripts, the redirection of folders, and the automation of software distribution on computers throughout the network.
- Group Policy is applied in the following order: local computer, site, domain, OU, child OU.
- The Security Configuration and Analysis tool can be used to analyze, modify, and apply security templates to objects within Active Directory.
- Group Policy is automatically inherited from parent containers to child containers. This can be modified by applying Block Policy inheritance, No Override, or by filtering the policy for specific users.
- When deploying software, Group Policy uses an MSI file to determine the installation options.
- Applications can either be assigned or published within a GPO. Assigned applications are advertised for users and automatically installed for computers. Published applications appear in the Add/Remove Programs applet for users. Computers cannot have applications published.

Key Terms

default domain controllers policy — The name of the default GPO that is linked to the domain controllers OU. Used primarily for configuration of policy settings that are only to be applied to the domain controllers in the domain (i.e., auditing).

default domain policy — The name of the GPO that is linked to the domain container in Active Directory; used primarily for configuration of domain-wide password policies.

folder redirection — A Group Policy feature that enables you to redirect the contents of the Application Data, Desktop, My Documents, My Pictures, and Start menu folders from a user's profile to a network location.

globally unique identifier (GUID) — A unique 128-bit number assigned to the object when it is created.

Gpresult — This utility can be used to discover Group Policy-related problems and to illustrate which GPOs were applied to a user or computer. Gpresult also lists all group memberships of the user or computer being analyzed.

Group Policy — Enables the centralized management of user desktop settings, desktop and domain security, and the deployment and management of software throughout your network.

Group Policy object (GPO) — An Active Directory object that is configured to apply Group Policy and linked to either the site, domain, or OU level.

incremental templates — A set of text-based security template files that you can use to apply uniform security settings on computers within an enterprise. The templates modify security settings incrementally and do not include the default security settings.

Key Distribution Center (KDC) — A Kerberos version service that runs on a domain controller. It issues TGTs and service tickets for obtaining network authentication in a domain.

Power Users group — Power Users have less system access than administrators, but more than users. By default, members of this group have Read/Write permissions to other parts of the system in addition to their own profile. Power Users can perform many system-wide operations, such as changing system time and display settings, and creating user accounts and shares.

Resultant Set of Policy (RSoP) — A graphical utility included with Windows Server 2003 that enables you to review the aggregated Group Policy settings that apply to a domain user or computer.

script — A file that includes various commands to automate routine operations.

secedit.exe — A command-line tool that allows you to perform security configuration and analysis.

Security Configuration Manager tools — A security toolset consisting of security templates and utilities that can be used to analyze and apply security configurations.

Security Policy template — A template used to apply various security settings to an Active Directory container or object.

ticket-granting ticket (TGT) — A ticket issued by the Kerberos version Key Distribution Center (KDC) for purposes of obtaining a service ticket from the ticket-granting service (TGS).

Windows installer package (MSI) — A file that contains all of the information needed to install an application in a variety of configurations.

ZAP file — A text file that can be used by Group Policy to deploy an application; it has a number of limitations compared to an MSI file.

Review Questions

1. Joe attempts to publish an application to a computer, but the publish setting is disabled. What is wrong?
    a. Joe has wrong permissions on the installation share.
    b. The computer is turned off.
    c. The GPO has not replicated to all domain controllers.
    d. You cannot publish applications to computers.

2. What is the order in which GPOs are applied?
   a. OU, domain, site, local computer
   b. local computer, site, domain, OU
   c. site, local computer, domain, OU
   d. domain, site, local computer, OU
3. You configure a GPO to apply a password policy to a particular OU, but you notice that the GPO has not been applied. What is wrong?
   a. The GPO has not replicated correctly.
   b. It takes 90 minutes to update the GPO settings.
   c. You have to click the Save button in the policy window.
   d. Password policies must be configured at the domain level.
4. You need to configure two user accounts in a certain OU to not have any GPO applied to them, while ensuring that the other users still get the restrictions. What can be done to accomplish this?
   a. Configure a block inheritance
   b. Configure GPO filtering using security permissions
   c. Configure No Override
   d. none of the above
5. Published applications are resilient in that they reinstall automatically if any files become corrupt. True or False?
6. Assigned applications are added to Add/Remove Programs, allowing them to be installed by a user if necessary. True or False?
7. What type of file is used to deploy applications with Windows Server 2003 Group Policy?
   a. .msc
   b. .mcs
   c. .msi
   d. .csi
8. When a GPO is created, its content is actually stored in which two locations on the server? (Choose two.)
   a. the Group Policy container within the Active Directory database
   b. the Group Policy container in the Sysvol folder
   c. the Group Policy template within the Active Directory database
   d. the Group Policy template in the Sysvol folder
9. You have created a GPO that removes the Run command and have linked it to the domain level. At the OU level, you have created a GPO to enable the Run command. Which GPO takes effect?
   a. the OU level
   b. the domain level
   c. The GPO settings cancel each other out and have no effect.
10. Account policy settings must be defined in a GPO linked to which container within the domain to take effect?
    a. the domain controllers OU
    b. a departmental OU
    c. a site object
    d. the domain container

4

11. A security template named Setup Security.inf is automatically defined during the Windows Server 2003 installation process, allowing you to return to the computer's original security settings if necessary. True or False?
12. You have just made a change to the computer portion of a Windows Server 2003 GPO and want to manually refresh the policy settings. Which command accomplishes this?
    a. secedit /refreshpolicy
    b. gpresult
    c. gpupdate
    d. all of the above
13. A ZAP file can be used by a GPO to publish an application for which an MSI file is not available. True or False?
14. If an application has been assigned to a computer using Group Policy, when is the application installed?
    a. when a user accesses Add/Remove Programs and starts the installation
    b. when a user logs on to the computer
    c. when the computer is restarted
    d. when the computer is about to shut down
15. A user has accidentally deleted a required file on his local machine for an application that you had previously assigned to the domain using an MSI file and Group Policy. What must you do to make sure that the application continues to function?
    a. Redeploy the application using the original GPO and MSI file.
    b. Do nothing; the application automatically fixes itself.
    c. Publish the application to the domain.
    d. Reinstall the application locally on the user's machine using a CD-ROM or the installation point.
16. Which removal option allows users to continue to work with an installed application but prevents any new installations?
    a. forced removal
    b. optional removal
    c. installation removal
    d. none of the above
17. In which folder do scripts have to be stored to ensure proper functioning and replication to all DCs?
    a. the temp folder
    b. the sysvol folder
    c. the replication folder
    d. the system32 folder
18. For Group Policy settings to apply to a user, that user must be a member of a group with both the Read and Apply Group Policy permissions set to Allow. True or False?
19. You need to redirect the My Documents folder to a server location based upon security group memberships. Which setting do you choose?
    a. basic
    b. advanced
    c. none of the above
20. Both the gpresult and Resultant Set of Policy tools can be used to view the aggregated Group Policy settings that apply to a user. True or False?

Case Projects

Case Project 4-1

One of the Dover Leasing user accounts is located in the Help Desk OU. The Help Desk OU is a child OU of the Information Technology OU. The Information Technology OU is in the *DomainXX.Dovercorp.net* domain, which is in the Default-First-Site-Name site. The following table lists the GPO settings for the domain.

Container	GPO Setting
Default-First-Site-Name	Restricts the user from using author mode when using customized MMCs
Dovercorp.net	Password length must be at least eight characters; removes the Run command from the Start menu
Help Desk OU	Disables Control Panel; adds the Run command to the Start menu
Information Technology OU	Allows the user to use author mode in MMC; password length must be at least 10 characters

What effective settings are applied to the user account located in the Help Desk OU?

Case Project 4-2

A fellow administrator is having problems with GPOs not being applied as expected. List five troubleshooting methods that you would use to diagnose problems with GPOs.

Case Project 4-3

Dover Leasing has decided to implement GPOs to configure different settings for all users within the Information Technology OU and its child OUs. All Information Technology users should have the Windows .NET Server Administrative Tools appear to be installed regardless of the workstation that they log on to and have the Run command enabled. Users in the Network Support OU only should have the ability to install the Windows Support Tools if necessary. Finally, all users in the Help Desk OU should have access to the Microsoft Management Console in user mode only. Given these requirements, what OUs should be created and which settings should they contain to deploy Group Policy in the most efficient manner possible?

Case Project 4-4

Dover Leasing has decided to deploy GPOs for the purpose of controlling desktop settings for users in the Marketing OU of the *DomainXX.Dovercorp.net* domain. Although these settings should apply to almost all marketing staff, the IT manager has decided that the new settings should not apply to three marketing executives. Given these requirements, how should Group Policy settings be applied so that only the required marketing users are affected by the new settings?

CHAPTER

5

ADMINISTERING FILE RESOURCES

After reading this chapter and completing the exercises, you will be able to:

- Create and manage shared folders using Windows Explorer and the Microsoft Management Console
- Manage shared folder permissions
- Integrate shared folder and NTFS permissions
- Configure EFS encryption
- Monitor access to shared folders
- Configure and manage DFS

One of the most common functions of a computer network is to provide client access to shared-file storage locations. Windows Server 2003 includes a variety of methods to create, configure, and manage shared-file resources. For example, features such as traditional file sharing and the **distributed file system (DFS)** can be used to simplify sharing information in an organization. This chapter discusses some of the various options available and how they are used to share files throughout a networking environment.

Windows Server 2003 supports two main types of permissions in order to secure file and folder resources. NTFS permissions can be applied to resources that are stored on partitions formatted with the NTFS file system, while shared folder permissions can be applied to any folder that has been shared to allow access from network workstations. The combination of NTFS and shared folder permissions has often been the basis of intensive troubleshooting tasks for administrators. It is important to understand how permissions are applied to ensure that clients obtain appropriate access to resources. To ensure an understanding of this concept, the integration of NTFS and **shared folder** permissions is discussed later in this chapter, as is monitoring access to folders that are shared on the network. You are also introduced to file encryption, which provides another level of security in addition to the regular permissions used to protect folders and files.

Once you have created and shared the file resources, your users may need a simple and effective way to search for these objects throughout the network. Publishing resources into Active Directory allows any Active Directory-aware client to perform a simple search of the directory for network resources. This chapter also illustrates how to configure resource publishing and perform Active Directory searches.

Creating and Managing Shared Folders

To permit general user access to data on a network system, you are often required to configure shared folders with the proper access-control permissions. A shared folder is a data resource that has been made available over the network to authorized network clients. These clients can then view or modify the contents of the folder, depending upon the level of permissions granted to either the user or group of which the user is a member.

To create shared folders, users are required to have appropriate rights. A member of the Administrators or Server Operator groups has the right to create shared folders within a domain. There are several ways to create shared folders; two of the more popular methods include using the Windows Explorer interface and the Computer Management console.

Using Windows Explorer To Create a Shared Folder

Windows Explorer is the standard method used to create and share folders for all versions of Windows since Windows 95. It can be used to create, maintain, and share folders on any drive connected to the computer. There are many ways to open Windows Explorer. For example, you can click the Windows Explorer icon on the Accessories menu, or you can right-click almost any drive-related object, and click the Explore command on the shortcut menu. Figure 5-1 illustrates the Windows Explorer window.

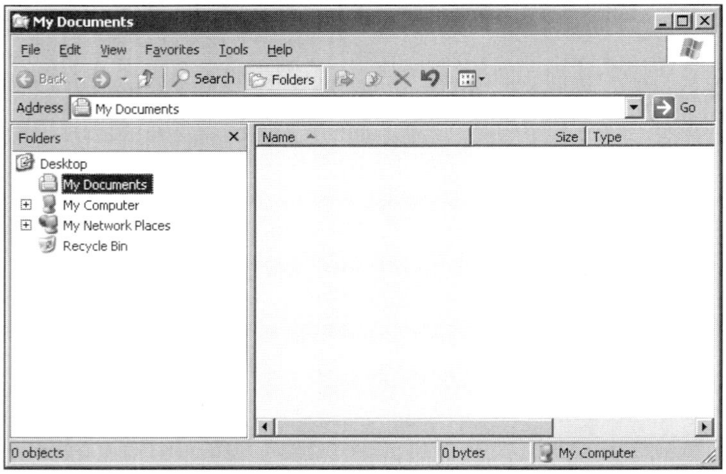

Figure 5-1 Viewing the Windows Explorer

If you do not have an existing folder that you want to share, the first step in sharing a folder is to select a drive and create a new folder. In Activity 5-1 you will first create a new folder and then share it using Windows Explorer.

Folders are shared in Windows Server 2003 by accessing the Sharing tab of a folder's properties, as illustrated in Figure 5-2.

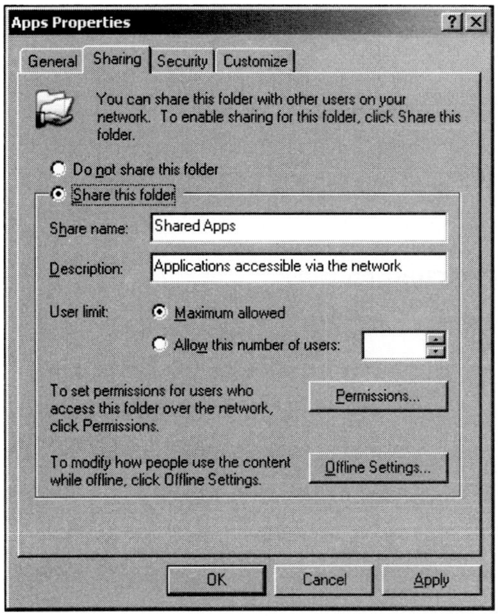

Figure 5-2 Sharing a folder using Windows Explorer

> **Tip** By default, the shared name of a folder will be the same as the actual folder name, but this is not a requirement. It is important to provide a meaningful share name because this is how your users will find the share. Be careful of any share names that are longer than eight characters in cases where you have any legacy clients such as Windows 3.1 or DOS that cannot handle long file names.

Windows Explorer indicates a shared folder by placing a hand icon under the folder, as shown in Figure 5-3.

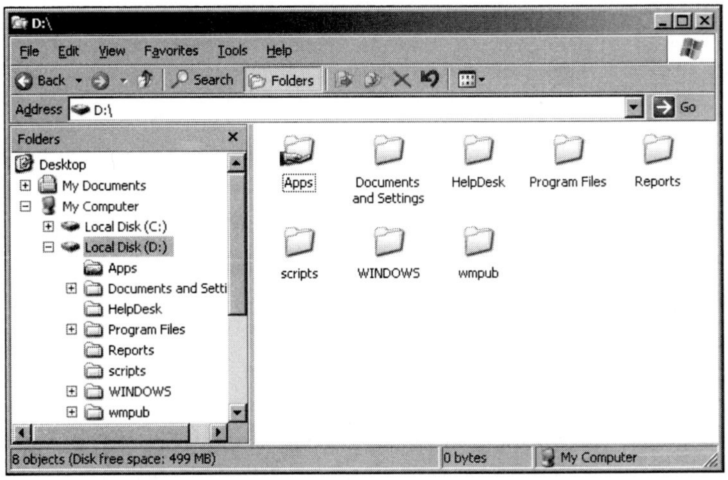

Figure 5-3 Viewing shared folders in Windows Explorer

Activity 5-1: Creating a Shared Folder Using Windows Explorer

Time Required: 5 minutes

Objective: Create a shared folder using Windows Explorer.

Description: The IT manager at Dover Leasing has asked you to create a shared folder on a new Windows Server 2003 system that will ultimately be used to store network-accessible applications for users in the Marketing Department. In this activity, you create a new folder called Apps and then share it over the network using Windows Explorer.

1. Click **Start**, select **All Programs**, select **Accessories**, and then click **Windows Explorer**.
2. Click the **plus sign (+)** next to My Computer to expand it, then click drive **D:**.Click **File** on the menu bar, select **New**, and then click **Folder**. Name the new folder **Apps**.
3. Right-click the **Apps** folder and then click **Sharing and Security**.
4. On the Sharing tab, click the **Share this folder** radio button.
5. In the Share name text box, type **Applications**.
6. In the Description text box, type **Applications for Marketing Users**.
7. Click **OK** to share the folder and close the Apps Properties dialog box.
8. To verify that the new shared folder called Applications is available over the network, open a command prompt, and at the command line type **net view \\server*XX***, where *XX* is your assigned student number. Press **Enter**.
9. All of the shared folders available on your server should be visible, including the new Applications folder just created. Close all open windows once complete.

There may be times when you would like to create a shared folder but not have it listed in My Network Places or Network Neighborhood. To hide a shared folder, place a dollar sign ($) after its name. For example, if you create a shared folder called "Salary," you can hide it by giving it the share name "Salary$." To map or connect to a hidden share, a user needs to manually type the share name, including the dollar sign. Windows Server 2003 creates a number of hidden administrative shares by default during the installation process. For example, the Admin$ share allows an administrator to easily connect to the Windows folder on a server or workstation across the network, whereas shares like C$ provide an administrator with easy access to the root of the C drive on a computer. In Activity 5-2, you create and test a hidden shared folder using Windows Explorer.

Activity 5-2: Creating Hidden Shared Folders

Time Required: 5 minutes

Objective: Create a hidden shared folder.

Description: The IT manager at Dover Leasing is concerned that some of the more curious users may waste time during the day browsing the network and attempting to access resources unnecessarily. To help circumvent this potential issue, he has asked you to create a hidden shared folder to ensure that it isn't visible to users browsing the network. In this activity, you create a new folder called "Payroll" and then share it so that it is hidden from browsing but still accessible. At the beginning of the exercise, you will make changes to the Default Domain Policy to ensure that the Run command is once again available for all users.

1. Click **Start**, point to **Administrative Tools**, and click **Active Directory Users and Computers**. Right-click on **Domain*XX*.Dovercorp.net** and click **Properties**. Click the **Group Policy** tab, and then click **Edit**.
2. Click the **plus sign (+)** next to User Configuration to expand it. Click the **plus sign (+)** next to Administrative Templates to expand it. Click on **Start Menu and Taskbar** to view its contents.
3. Double-click **Remove Run menu** from Start menu. Click the **Disabled** radio button, and then click **OK**. Close the Group Policy Object Editor window.
4. Click the **Options** button. Check the **No Override** checkbox, click **OK**, and then click **OK** again. Close all open windows and log off. Log on again using your **Admin*XX*** account.
5. Open **My Computer**.

6. Create a new folder on drive **D:** called **Payroll** and access its **Sharing** tab.
7. Share the folder using the share name **Payroll$**.
8. Click **Start**, and then click **Run**. In the Open text box type **\\server*XX*\payroll$** and click **OK**. The Payroll$ folder should open in a new window.
9. To confirm that the Payroll$ folder is not visible to clients browsing the network, open a command prompt and at the command line type **net view \\server*XX*** and press **Enter**. While other shared folders should be visible, the Payroll$ folder should not.
10. Close all open windows.

The final step in creating a shared folder is to secure the share by modifying user and group permissions on the resource. By default, Windows Server 2003 will initially allow the Read permission to the Everyone group for the new shared folder. Because the Everyone group also consists of unauthenticated users, it is usually a good idea to change this permission such that only a more secure group such as Authenticated Users is granted access. If the shared folder is located on an NTFS-formatted partition, NTFS permissions can also be used to further control user access. NTFS permissions are covered later in this chapter.

Using Computer Management to Create a Shared Folder

Another popular method for creating and managing shared folders in Windows Server 2003 is through the use of the **Computer Management console**. Computer Management is a predefined Microsoft Management Console (MMC) application that allows you to perform a variety of administrative tasks, such as sharing and monitoring folders for both local and remote computers.

Shared folders are created in the Shared Folders section of Computer Management using the Share a Folder Wizard. Beyond simply allowing you to create new shared folders, this wizard also allows you to configure shared folder permissions. Three of the choices are preconfigured, whereas the fourth allows custom permissions to be specified. Permission options found in the wizard include:

- *All users have read-only access*—Grants the Read permission to the Everyone group
- *Administrators have full access; other users have read-only access*—Grants Full Control to the local Administrators group and Read to the Everyone group
- *Administrators have full access; other users have read and write access*—Grants Full Control to the local Administrators group and both Read and Change access to the Everyone group
- *Use custom share and folder permissions*—Allows you to define both share and NTFS permissions manually; manually assigning permissions is dealt with later in the chapter

Tip

If you want to stop sharing a folder, the easiest way to do this is via the Shares node in the Computer Management console. The list of shares appears in the details pane of the console. To stop sharing a particular folder, you simply right-click the share that is to be discontinued and click Stop Sharing on the shortcut menu.

In Activity 5-3, you create and view shared folders using the Computer Management tool.

Hands-on Project

Activity 5-3: Creating and Viewing Shared Folders Using Computer Management

Time Required: 10 minutes

Objective: Create and view shared folders using Computer Management.

Description: To streamline the training process for new help desk staff at Dover Leasing, the IT manager has asked you to document the process for using the Computer Management tool to create and view shared folders on network servers. In this activity, you use the Computer Management tool to both view the existing visible and hidden shares, as well as create a new shared folder.

1. Click **Start**, right-click **My Computer**, and click **Manage**. The Computer Management tool opens, as illustrated in Figure 5-4. If necessary, click the **plus sign (+)** next to System Tools to expand it.

2. Click the **plus sign (+)** next to the Shared Folders node to expand it. The Shares, Sessions, and Open Files node appear.

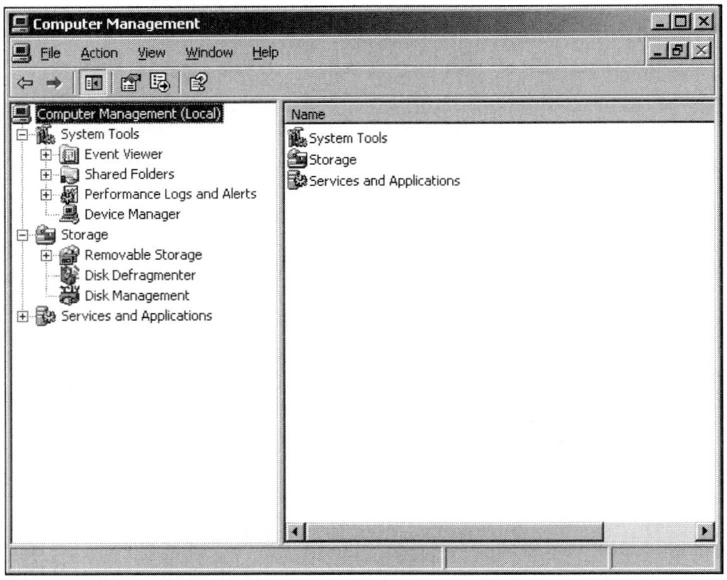

Figure 5-4 Viewing the Computer Management console

3. Click the **Shares** folder to view its contents, as illustrated in Figure 5-5. Notice that the list includes folders that have been manually created (such as Apps), administrative shares (such as C$), and shared folders used by operating system communication processes (such as IPC$). The Shares node also provides the complete filesystem path to the shared folder.

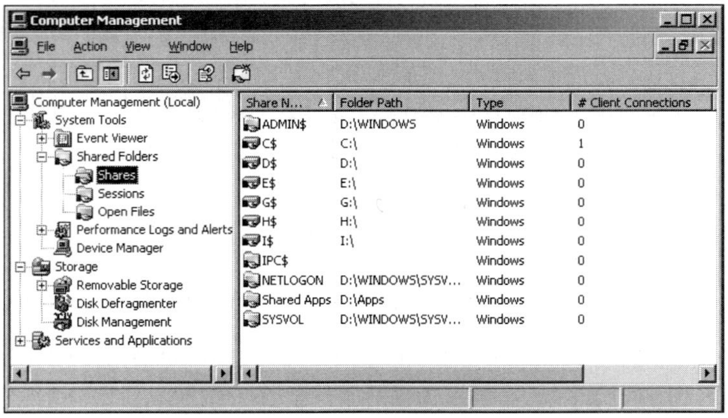

Figure 5-5 Viewing shared folders on the local computer

4. Right-click the **Shares** folder and click **New Share**. The Share a Folder Wizard appears. At the welcome screen, click **Next**.

5. At the Folder Path screen, type **D:\mktgdocs** in the Folder path text box, as illustrated in Figure 5-6. Click **Next**.

6. When prompted with the dialog box specifying that the folder doesn't exist and asking whether you want to create it, click **Yes**.

7. At the Name, Description, and Settings screen, type **Marketingdocs** in the Share name text box and **All Marketing Documentation** in the Description text box. Click **Next**.

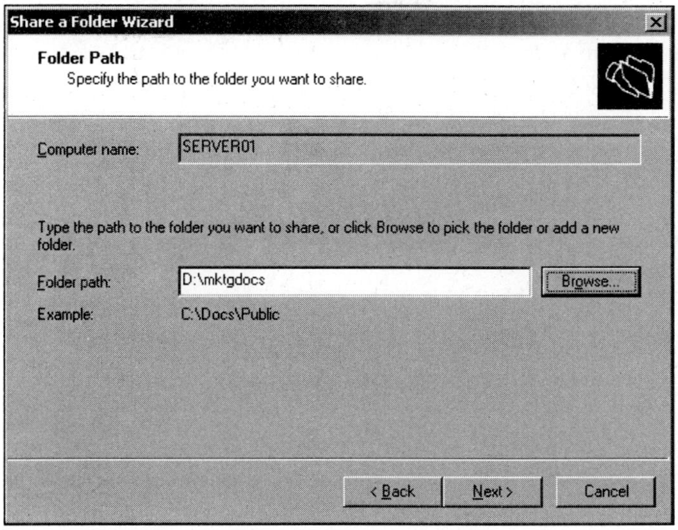

Figure 5-6 Creating a new shared folder using the Computer Management console

8. At the Permissions screen, select the **Administrators have full access; other users have read-only access** radio button, as shown in Figure 5-7. Click **Finish**.

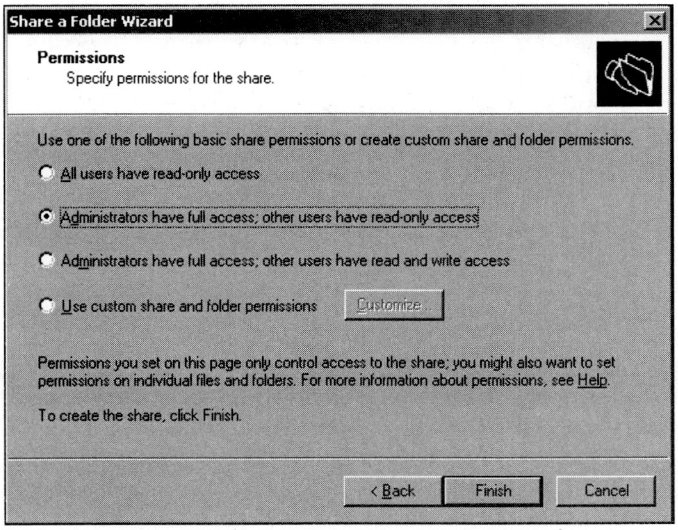

Figure 5-7 Configuring permissions on a shared folder using the Share a Folder Wizard

9. At the Sharing was Successful screen, review the Summary information and then click **Close**.
10. Verify that the new Marketingdocs shared folder is visible in the details pane of the Shares node in Computer Management.
11. To verify that the Marketingdocs folder is accessible over the network, open the **Run** command and type **\\server*XX*\marketingdocs** in the Open text box and click **OK**. The Marketingdocs folder should open in a new window.
12. Close all open windows.

Managing Shared Folder Permissions

Each folder that is shared has a **discretionary access control list (DACL)** associated with it. A DACL is a part of an object's security descriptor that contains a list of user or group references that have been allowed or denied permissions to the resource. Each user or group name listed in the DACL is referred to as an **access control entry (ACE).** To access the DACL, click the Permissions button on the Sharing tab of a folder's properties. You can also access it by clicking the Custom button when using the Share a Folder Wizard. Figure 5-8 illustrates the DACL for a shared folder called Apps.

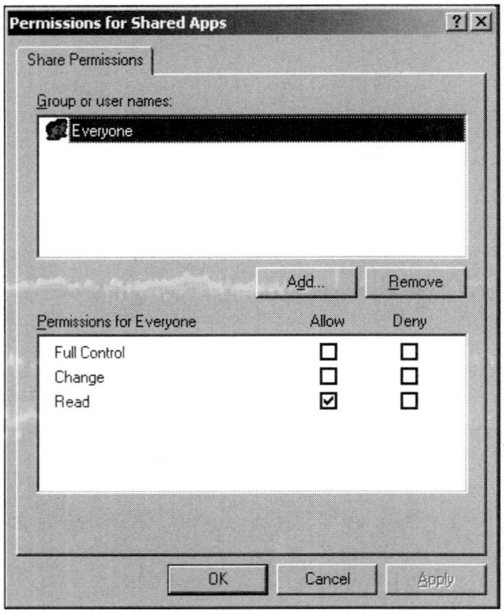

Figure 5-8 Viewing the DACL of the Apps shared folder

It is important to remember that share permissions only apply to users that connect to a shared folder over the network; they do not apply to a user logged on to the local machine where the shared folder is defined. Windows Server 2003 supports three different share permissions, as explained in Table 5-1.

Table 5-1 Share permissions in Windows Server 2003

Windows Server 2003 Permission	Permissions Granted
Read	Allows the user to browse the file and folder names (including subfolders) read the data in a file, and execute programs
Change	Includes the read permission, plus permission to add and delete files and subfolders, and change the data in the files
Full Control	Includes the Read and Change permission, plus the rights (on NTFS partitions) to change permissions or take ownership of a folder or file

Notice that Windows Server 2003 does not include a No Access share permission as Windows NT did in the past. Instead, to deny a user or group access to a shared folder, an administrator must explicitly deny the user that particular permission, as shown in Figure 5-9.

As discussed previously, when a new share is created, the default permission on the shared folder gives the Everyone group read access. One of the first steps an administrator should perform after creating a share is to substitute the Everyone group for one that includes authenticated domain users. In many companies, the Domain Users group is given the Full Control shared folder permission, while resources are made more secure through the use of NTFS permissions.

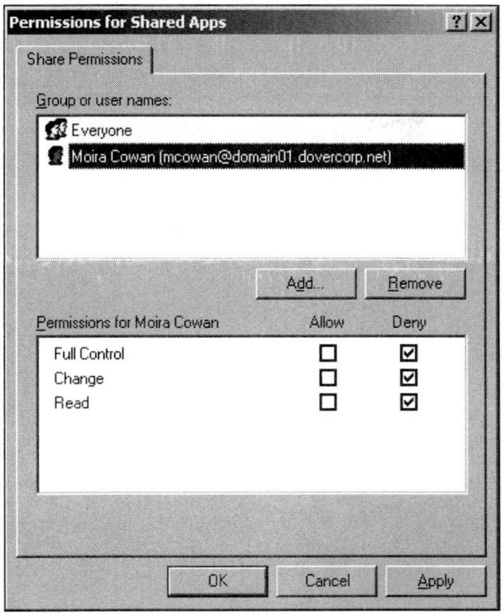

Figure 5-9 Denying Full Control to the Apps shared folder

Note: The Everyone group includes all users who have access to the network, regardless of whether they have been authenticated in the domain.

When a share is created and a user is assigned permission to that share, the user also has the same level of permissions to all subfolders and files inside that share. In other words, the permissions configured on the shared folder are inherited by all of the objects that it contains. In Activity 5-4, you configure and test the effects of different shared folder permissions.

Activity 5-4: Implementing shared folder Permissions

Time Required: 15 minutes

Objective: Control access to resources using shared folder permissions.

Description: The IT manager at Dover Leasing is very concerned with ensuring that all network resources are properly secured so that only authorized network users can access shared folders and their contents. He has asked you to ensure that only members of the Domain Admins group have Full Control permission for the Marketingdocs shared folder, while members of the Marketing Users group are granted Change permission. All other users should not be granted access to the folder. In this activity, you configure permissions on the Marketingdocs shared folder to implement the requirements outlined by the IT manager.

1. Open **My Computer** and access the properties of the D:\mktgdocs folder.
2. Click the **Sharing** tab, and then click the **Permissions** button. The Permissions for Marketingdocs dialog box opens.
3. In the Group or user names list box, ensure that **Everyone** is selected and click the **Remove** button.
4. Click **Add**. The Select Users, Computers, or Groups dialog box opens.
5. In the Enter the object names to select text box, type **Domain Admins** and click **OK**. Domain Admins should be added to the Group or user names list of the Permissions dialog box, with the configured permission of Allow Read.
6. In the Allow column, check the **Full Control** check box.

7. Click **Add**. In the Enter the object names to select text box, type **Marketing Users** and click **OK**.
8. Ensure that the Marketing Users group is selected in the Group or user names list box. In the Allow column, check the **Change** check box, and then click **OK**.
9. Close all open windows.
10. At the **Run** command, type **\\server*XX*\marketingdocs** and click **OK**. The Marketingdocs window opens.
11. Right-click an area of white space in the window, select **New**, and then click **Folder**. Rename the folder **July Documents** and then close the window.
12. Log off, and log on again using the **mcowan** account with the password **Password01**.
13. At the **Run** command, type **\\server*XX*\marketingdocs** and click **OK**. The Marketingdocs window opens.
14. Attempt to create a new folder called **August Documents** in the Marketingdocs folder. This will be possible because all members of the Marketing Users group have the Change permission to the shared folder.
15. Close all open windows and log off.
16. Log on as user **mmanore** with the password **Password01**.
17. At the **Run** command, type **\\server*XX*\marketingdocs** and click **OK**. The mmanore account is not able to access the folder because it lacks sufficient permissions.
18. Close all open windows and log off. Log on using your **Admin*XX*** account.

Shared folder permissions are cumulative. All the permissions assigned to a user, and any group of which the user is a member, are combined and the combination of all the permissions applies. For example, imagine if the user Moira Cowan is a member of both the Marketing and Managers groups. If the Marketing group is assigned the Read permission to a share and the Managers group is assigned Change, Moira's effective permission would be a combination of both, equivalent to Change. A single but important exception to this rule applies: when a user (or a group of which a user is a member) is denied a permission, the denied entry always overrides any permissions that are allowed. So, if the Marketing group was ultimately denied Full Control to the shared folder, Moira would not have access because this permission would override the fact that she is granted the Change permission as a member of the Marketing group. In Activity 5-5, you explore how the cumulative nature of shared folder permissions can impact user access.

Activity 5-5: Testing Cumulative shared folder Permissions

Hands-on Project

Time Required: 10 minutes

Objective: Test the effect of cumulative permissions on user access to a shared folder.

Description: The IT manager at Dover Leasing has asked you to test the impact of cumulative shared folder permissions by creating a new shared folder and then assigning the Read permission to the Moira Cowan user account, while assigning the Marketing Users group the Change permission. He has also asked you to test the impact of denying permissions to users to be sure that this can be used as a technique to quickly deny access to problem users. In this activity, you create a new folder and then test the impact of having multiple different permissions apply to a user account.

1. Open **My Computer** and, on drive **D:**, create a new folder called **test**.
2. Access the properties of the new test folder and click the **Sharing** tab. Share the folder using the same name, and then access its permissions.
3. Remove the **Everyone** group from the Group or user names list box to ensure that only the required users have access to the folder.

4. Add the user **Moira Cowan** to the Group or user names list with the **Allow Read** permission only.
5. Add the **Marketing Users** group to the Group or user names list with the **Allow Read** and **Allow Change** permissions only.
6. Close all open windows and log off. Log on using the **mcowan** user account with the password **Password01**.
7. At the **Run** command, type **\\server*XX*\test** and click **OK**. The test window opens.
8. Attempt to create a new folder within the folder called **moiratest**. This operation will be successful because the Moira Cowan user account has the effective permission of Change as a result of also being a member of the Marketing Users group.
9. Close all open windows and log off. Log on using your **Admin*XX*** account.
10. Right-click the **D:\test** folder, and click **Properties**. Click the **Sharing** tab, and click the **Permissions** button.
11. In the Group or user names list box, click the **Moira Cowan** user account to highlight it. In the Deny column, check the **Full Control** check box and click **OK**. Click **Yes** in the Security dialog box.
12. Close all open windows and log off. Log on using the **mcowan** user account with the password **Password01**.
13. At the **Run** command, type **\\server*XX*\test** and click **OK**. When the message appears specifying that the folder \\server*XX*\test is not accessible, click **OK**. The user Moira Cowan can no longer access the shared folder because the Deny Full Control permission overrides any other permissions that apply to her account.
14. Log off and then log on again using your **Admin*XX*** account.

Note: Windows Server 2003 also includes the ability to share folders for HTTP and FTP access using a feature called a **Web folder**. Because the use of Web folders requires **Internet Information Services (IIS)** to be properly installed and configured, we look at this feature in detail in Chapter 7.

INTEGRATING SHARED FOLDERS WITH NTFS PERMISSIONS

When permissions are set on a shared folder, the permissions determine what restrictions apply to the folder when it is accessed from another computer across a network connection. These restrictions do not apply if the user were to log on locally to the computer. This is where NTFS file and directory permissions can assist in your security plan. NTFS permissions are applied whenever a file or folder is accessed, regardless of whether the person is logged on to the computer where the file is located or the person is accessing the file across a network connection. To assist in troubleshooting file access problems, it is essential to understand how NTFS file and directory permissions protect resources and how these permissions work when combined with share-level permissions. The next section discusses NTFS file and directory permissions in greater detail.

NTFS File and Directory Permissions Concepts and Rules

It is important to understand the different NTFS file and directory permissions, as well as how they are applied. Remember that NTFS permissions can only be applied to files and folders that exist on partitions formatted with the NTFS file system. As such, NTFS permissions cannot be applied to files or folders that reside on partitions formatted using the FAT or FAT32 file systems.

- NTFS permissions are configured via the Security tab, which is accessed by right-clicking any file or folder and clicking Properties.

- NTFS permissions are cumulative. If a user is a member of multiple groups that have different permissions, the final permission is the sum of all permissions.
- Permissions that are explicitly denied always override those that are allowed. For example, if the Mark Manore user account is explicitly denied Full Control on a folder through an individual or group permission assignment, this overrides any permissions that Mark may have been allowed via other group memberships.
- NTFS folder permissions are inherited by child folders and files, unless otherwise specified. Clearing the Allow inheritable permissions from the parent to propagate to this object and all child objects check box in the Advanced section of the Security property sheet can prevent the inheritance of NTFS permissions.
- NTFS permissions can be set at a file level, as well as at a folder level.
- When a new access control entry is added to an NTFS file or folder, the default permissions allow the user or group both the Read and the Read and Execute permissions for files, along with the List Folder Contents permission for folders.
- Windows Server 2003 has a set of standard NTFS permissions, as well as special permissions.

Table 5-2 lists the standard NTFS permissions.

Table 5-2 Standard NTFS permissions

Windows Server 2003 Permissions	Permissions Granted
Full Control	Allow the user to make any changes to the file or folder; details of the Full Control permission are listed in Table 5-3
Modify	Gives full permissions except the permission to delete subfolders and files, change permissions, and take ownership
Read And Execute	Gives permissions to traverse folders, list folders, read attributes and extended attributes, read permissions, and synchronize; these permissions are inherited by both files and folders
List Folder Contents	Same as Read and Execute permissions, except that the permissions are inherited only by folders and not by files; visible only on folders
Read	Same as Read and Execute, except without the permission to traverse folder; inherited by files and folders
Write	Gives permissions to create files and folders, write attributes and extended attributes, read permissions, and synchronize
Special Permissions	Used to designate that a user has been allowed or denied one or more of the more granular special permissions configured in the Advanced section of the security settings; Special permissions are detailed in Table 5-3

Activity 5-6: Implementing NTFS Permissions

Time Required: 20 minutes

Objective: Configure and test NTFS permissions on a local folder.

Description: While the IT manager at Dover Leasing is certainly concerned about controlling access to shared folders on network servers, he is equally concerned about controlling access to local files and folders as well. In this activity, you have been asked to implement standard NTFS permission on a folder to review not only the default permissions but also the behavior of permission inheritance.

1. Open **My Computer** and access the properties of the D:\test folder created in the previous activity.

2. Click the **Security** tab to view the NTFS permissions assigned to users and groups by default. Click each individual entry in the Group or user names list box to view the properties associated with these accounts. Note that although each group is assigned different permissions to the folder, assigned permissions appear within a gray box and cannot be changed. This is because the permissions have been inherited from a parent folder, in this case the NTFS permissions assigned to drive D.
3. Access the properties of drive **D:** and click the **Security** tab. Notice that the same NTFS permissions that applied on the test folder also apply on the D: drive. The difference is that these permissions were assigned directly to the D: drive by default when the partition was created and can be changed.
4. Add the user account **Moira Cowan** to the Group or user names list with the **Allow Read** permission only and click **OK**. When the Security dialog box appears, click **Yes**.
5. Open the **Security** tab of the test folder to confirm that the Moira Cowan user account now appears in the list of Group or user names. Click the **Moira Cowan** account to confirm that it has inherited the permissions assigned in the previous step.
6. Click **Add** to add the **Marketing Users** group to the Group or user names list on the **Security** tab. Note that the group is assigned the allow Read and Execute, List Folder Contents, and Read permissions on the folder by default. Click **OK**.
7. Open the **D:\test** folder. Right-click an area of white space, select **New**, and then click **Text Document**. Name the file **ntfstest.txt**.
8. Right-click the **ntfstest.txt** file and click **Properties**.
9. Click the **Security** tab to view the NTFS permissions associated with this file. Note that the permissions configured for this file have been inherited from the D:\test folder.
10. In the Group or user names list box, click **Users** and then click **Remove**. Read the Security dialog box that appears, outlining the fact that the group Users cannot be removed because its settings are inherited from a parent folder. Click **OK**.
11. Click the **Advanced** button. The Advanced Security Settings for test dialog box opens.
12. Uncheck the **Allow inheritable permissions from the parent to propagate to this object and all child objects** check box.
13. When the Security dialog box opens, read its message, click **Copy**, and then click **OK**.
14. Click each user or group in the Group or user names section to view the associated NTFS permissions. Note that permissions are now directly applied to users and groups rather than being inherited. This is a result of clicking the Copy button in the previous step.
15. In the Group or user names list box, click **Users** and then click **Remove**. Notice that this time, the Users group is removed without issue. Close all open windows.
16. Log off and then log on again using the **mcowan** user account.
17. Open **My Computer** and attempt to create a new text file in the D:\test folder. Notice that this action is denied because the Moira Cowan user account does not have sufficient permissions for the D:\test folder as a member of the Marketing Users group.
18. Close all open windows and log off. Log on again using your **Admin*XX*** account.

Special NTFS Permissions

Windows Server 2003 provides access to 14 individual NTFS permissions that can be used to specify an even more granular level of access to a file or folder. Occasionally, one of the standard permissions may not provide enough control or, conversely, may provide a slightly higher level of access than a user requires.

To access the special permissions, click the Advanced button in the Security dialog box on the Properties tab for the folder or file. The resulting Access Control Settings dialog box allows you to assign special permissions to user or group accounts. To view the special NTFS permissions assigned to a user or group, click the user or group and then click the Edit button. The Permission Entry dialog box opens, as shown in Figure 5-10.

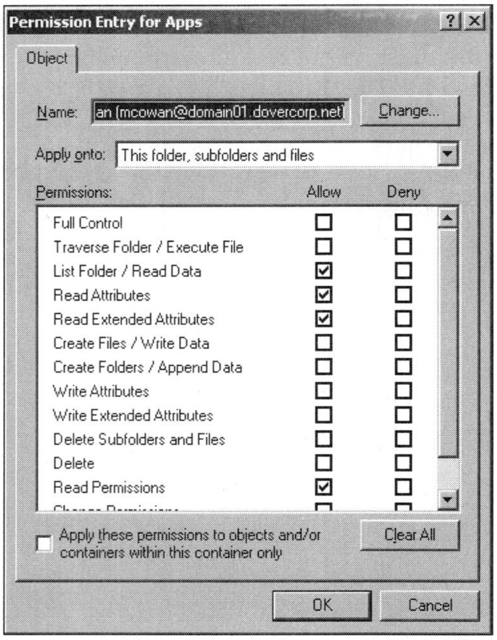

Figure 5-10 Viewing advanced NTFS permissions

The Permission Entry dialog box enables you to assign special NTFS permissions, while also providing a way to control permission inheritance settings. Special permissions can be applied in the following ways:

- This folder only
- This folder, subfolders, and files (default)
- This folder and subfolders
- This folder and files
- Subfolders and files only
- Subfolders only
- Files only

Table 5-3 shows the special access permissions that you can apply and their function.

Table 5-3 Special access permissions

Special Permission	Function
Full Control	Provides the same level of access as the standard Full Control permission
Traverse Folder/Execute File	Controls whether a user can pass through folders that they do not have explicit permission to enter to get to an intended folder; for example, a user may not have permission to read the Salesdata folder, but may have Read permission to JuneSales.doc in the Salesdata folder. If the user has traverse folder permissions, the user would be able to open the JuneSales.doc file
List Folder/Read Data	Controls whether a user can view the contents of folders and read data files with a folder

Table 5-3 Special access permissions (continued)

Special Permission	Function
Read Attributes	Controls the ability to view the attributes of a file or folder
Read Extended Attributes	Controls the ability to view the extended attributes of a file or folder; extended attributes are additional information attached to a file, as defined by an application
Create Files/Write Data	Controls the ability to create files within a folder (applies to folders only), while also controlling the ability to make changes to files and overwriting existing content (applies to files only)
Create Folders/Append Data	Controls the ability to create additional folders within a folder (applies to folders only), while controlling the ability to make changes to the end of the file but not change, delete, or overwrite existing data (applies to files only)
Write Attributes	Controls the ability to change the attributes of a file or folder, such as read-only or hidden; attributes are defined by NTFS
Write Extended Attributes	Controls the ability to change the extended attributes of a file or folder; extended attributes are defined by programs and can vary
Delete Subfolders and Files	Controls the ability to delete subfolders and files, even if the standard delete permission has not been granted on the subfolder or file
Delete	Controls the ability to delete a file or folder
Read Permissions	Controls the ability to read the security permissions of a file or folder
Change Permissions	Controls the ability to change the security permissions of a file or folder
Take Ownership	Controls the ability to take ownership of a file or folder

5

Hands-on Project

Activity 5-7: Viewing and Implementing Special NTFS Permissions

Time Required: 15 minutes

Objective: View, configure, and test special NTFS permissions.

Description: Having now used standard NTFS permissions to configure and test file and folder access, you have been asked by the IT manager to test the ability to control resource access using the special NTFS permissions. In this activity, you attempt to deny Marketing users the ability to read the NTFS permissions associated with a file or folder.

1. Open **My Computer** and create a new folder on drive **D:** called **Special Permissions**.
2. Open the properties of the Special Permissions folder and click the **Security** tab.
3. Add the **Marketing Users** group to the Group or user names list, granting it the default permissions only. Close all open windows.
4. Log off and then log on again using the **mcowan** user account.
5. Right-click the **D:\Special Permissions** folder, then click **Properties**. Click the **Security** tab to view the permission settings configured for different accounts. Note that while the permissions can be read by the mcowan user account, they cannot be changed. Close all open windows.
6. Log off and then log on again using your **Admin*XX*** account.
7. Right-click the **D:\Special Permissions** folder, then click **Properties**. Click the **Security** tab, and then click **Advanced**. The Advanced Security Settings for Special Permissions dialog box opens.
8. In the Permission entries list box, click the entry for the **Marketing Users** group and then click **Edit**.
9. In the Permissions section, click the **Read Permissions** check box in the Deny column to specifically disable the ability to read the NTFS permissions associated with this folder. Click

OK to close the Permission Entry for Special Permissions dialog box, and then click **OK** to close the Advanced Security Settings for Special Permissions dialog box. Click **Yes** in the Security dialog box.

10. In the Group or user names list box, click the **Marketing Users** group account to view its configured security settings. Notice that the Special Permissions Deny column now includes a check mark. Close all open windows.
11. Log off and then log on again using the **mcowan** user account.
12. Attempt to access the **Security** tab in the Properties dialog box for the D:\Special Permissions folder. This tab is no longer available because, as a member of the Marketing Users group, Moira Cowan has been denied the ability to view permission settings.
13. Close all open windows and log off. Log on again using your **Admin*XX*** account.

To easily determine the effective NTFS permissions that apply to a user or group, Windows Server 2003 includes the Effective Permissions tab in the Advanced Security Settings dialog box for a file or folder, shown in Figure 5-11. In Activity 5-8, you use the Effective Permissions tab to determine the effective NTFS permissions that apply to a user and group for a specific folder.

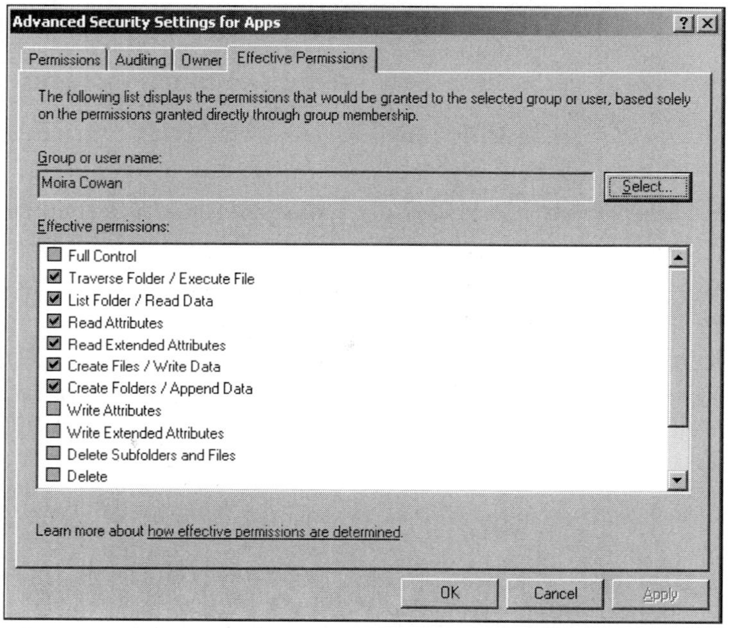

Figure 5-11 Viewing a user's effective permissions

Activity 5-8: Viewing Effective Permissions

Hands-on Project

Time Required: 5 minutes

Objective: View effective permissions for a user on an NTFS folder.

Description: Although the IT manager is now convinced of the benefits that NTFS security will provide for Dover Leasing, he is still worried that the application of permissions to many different users and groups may result in mistakes being made with respect to the effective level of permissions assigned to users. In this activity, you use the Effective Permissions tab in the Advanced Security Settings of a folder to view the effective NTFS permissions that apply to both a user and group.

1. Open **My Computer** and right-click the **D:\test** folder. Click **Properties** from the shortcut menu, then click the **Security** tab.
2. Click the **Advanced** button to access the Advanced Security Settings dialog box for test dialog box.

3. Click the **Effective Permissions** tab.
4. Click the **Select** button.
5. In the Enter the object name to select text box, type **Moira** and click **OK**. Review the effective NTFS permissions that apply to the Moira Cowan user account.
6. Click the **Select** button again and, this time, add the **Marketing Users** group. Review the effective NTFS permissions that apply to this group.
7. Close all open windows.

Combining Share and NTFS Permissions

NTFS permissions are often combined with share permissions to provide a strong combination of local and remote security for files and directories. When share and NTFS permissions are combined, the following rules apply:

- When a user is accessing a share across a network and both NTFS and share permissions apply, the most restrictive permission of the two becomes the effective combined permission. For example, if the effective shared folder permission is Full Control, but the effective NTFS permission is Read, then the user will be granted the Read permission to the resource.
- When a user accesses a file locally, only NTFS permissions apply.

In Activity 5-9, you test the impact of configuring both NTFS and shared folder permissions.

Activity 5-9: Combining and Testing NTFS and shared folder Permissions

Time Required: 10 minutes

Objective: Determine the impact of combining shared folder and NTFS permissions.

Description: Although you understand how both shared folder and NTFS permissions combine, you are worried that the new junior administrators will have difficulty with properly configuring these permissions to allow the correct level of user access. You have decided to test the impact of different permission combinations to develop a set procedure that can be used by new junior administrators at Dover Leasing. In this activity, you test the impact of combining both shared folder and NTFS permissions for both local and network resource access.

1. Open **My Computer** and create a new folder on drive **D:** called **Combined**. Share this folder using the default name.
2. Click the **Security** tab, and then click the **Advanced** button. Uncheck the **Allow inheritable permissions from the parent to propagate to this object and all child objects** check box. When the Security dialog box opens, click **Remove**, and then click **OK**.
3. In the Security dialog box that opens, read the message and then click **Yes**.
4. Add the **Domain Users** group to the Group or user names list, granting the group the **Allow Modify** permission.
5. Click the **Sharing** tab, and then click the **Permissions** button. Remove the **Everyone** group from the list, and then add the **Domain Users** group with the **Allow Read** permission. Click **OK**, and then click **OK** again to exit the properties of the Combined folder.
6. Attempt to create a new folder called **Documents** in the **D:\Combined** folder. This operation should complete successfully because the Domain Users group has the NTFS Modify permission on the folder. Close My Computer.
7. Open the **Run** command, type **\\server*XX*\combined**, and then press **Enter**. The Combined window should open.

8. Right-click an area of white space in the window and then attempt to create a new folder. When the Unable to create folder dialog box opens, read the message and then click **OK**. You are unable to create a new folder because the share permission is Read, and when the folder is accessed over the network, this is the effective permission that applies because it is more restrictive.
9. Right-click the **D:\Combined** folder and click **Properties**. Click the **Sharing** tab, click **Permissions** and change the permissions for the Domain Users group to **Allow Full Control**. Click **OK** to exit, and then click **OK** to close the Combined Properties dialog box.
10. Open the **Run** command again, type **\\serverXX\combined**, then click **OK**. The Combined window should open.
11. Attempt to create a new folder in this window called **Documents2**. The operation should complete successfully because the combination of the Full Control share permission and the Modify NTFS permission make Modify the effective permission on the folder. Close all open windows.

Configuring File Encryption

Another method to secure files and folders is to use encryption. The ability to encrypt files adds another level of protection on top of setting share or NTFS permissions. The **encrypting file system (EFS)** uses public key cryptography to transparently encrypt folders and files.

Note: Encryption is only available on partitions formatted with NTFS version 5.0 or later.

File and folder encryption is implemented using two main types of encryption keys. When data is marked to be encrypted, the EFS encrypts the data using a special session key known as a **file encryption key (FEK)**. The FEK is added to a header attached to the encrypted data known as the **data decryption field (DDF)**. The DDF is subsequently encrypted using the user's public key, so only they can decrypt it using their corresponding private key.

The main challenge associated with using encryption to secure file resources is that if a user were to leave the company, all data that had been encrypted with their public key would be inaccessible by other user accounts. One exception to this is when an administrator renames the user account to which the private key is associated. In this case, the new user would be able to access data encrypted by the private key because only the username associated with the account has changed. For data recovery purposes, Windows Server 2003 includes a special role known as a **data recovery agent**. In the event that a user encrypts data and then leaves the company or loses their private key, the user designated as the recovery agent can recover the encrypted data. When data is encrypted using EFS, the FEK of the data recovery agent is also stored in a second header called the **data recovery field (DRF)**. This key is encrypted using the data recovery agent's public key, thus making the data recovery agent capable of decrypting or recovering EFS-encrypted files and folders. By default, the local administrator of a stand-alone workstation or member server is designated as the recovery agent. In a domain environment, the domain administrator account is configured as the only data recovery agent by default, though additional recovery agents can be designated using Certificate Services and Group Policy.

EFS encryption for a file or folder is configured using advanced attributes in Windows Explorer. The advanced attribute settings for a folder are shown in Figure 5-12.

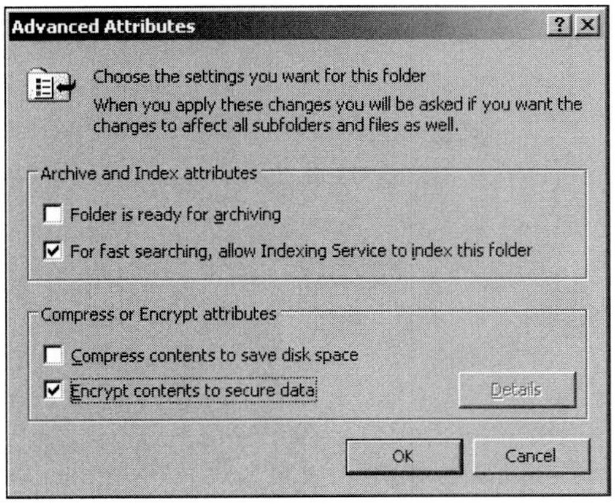

Figure 5-12 Setting the encryption attribute

Before using EFS to encrypt data, keep the following points in mind:

- If you set the encryption attribute on a folder, the folder itself is not actually encrypted, only the contents of the folder.
- Once a folder's encryption attribute is set, any data saved in the folder, or copied or moved into the folder, is encrypted.
- If an encrypted file is copied or moved into a folder that is not encrypted, the file retains its encryption attribute as long as the file system is NTFS; encrypted files moved to a FAT partition are automatically decrypted.
- Encryption and compression are mutually exclusive; you cannot encrypt and compress data at the same time.

In Activity 5-10 you configure a folder to encrypt files using EFS and then attempt to access an encrypted file using different user accounts.

Activity 5-10: Encrypting Files and Folders Using EFS

Time Required: 15 minutes

Objective: Implement and test file encryption security using EFS.

Description: Dover Leasing is interested in having its laptop users use EFS to better protect corporate data on these machines should they be lost or stolen. In this activity, you configure a folder to use EFS encryption and then attempt to access files within the folder using different user accounts.

1. Open **My Computer** and create a new folder on drive **D:** named **Encrypted**.
2. Right-click the **Encrypted** folder and click **Properties**.
3. On the **General** tab, click the **Advanced** button to open the folder's Advanced Attributes settings.
4. Check the **Compress contents to save disk space** check box, and then check the **Encrypt contents to secure data** check box. Notice that only one of these two options can be selected at any time.
5. Click **OK** to exit the Advanced Attributes window, and then click **OK** again to exit the properties of the Encrypted folder. Notice that the text in the name of the Encrypted folder changes to the color green. This is to help easily identify encrypted folders and files.
6. Open the **Encrypted** folder and create a new text file within it called **encrypted.txt**. In the encrypted.txt file, type **this is an encrypted file**, then save your changes and close the file. Access the **Advanced Attributes** of this file to ensure that the **Encrypt contents to secure data** check box is checked. Close the Advanced Attributes dialog box.

7. Close all open windows and then log off. Log on as the user **mmanore** with the password **Password01**.
8. Open **My Computer** and attempt to open the **D:\Encrypted** folder. Remember that although EFS will mark a folder with the encryption attribute, the folder itself is not encrypted. As such, it opens without issue.
9. Attempt to open the **encrypted.txt** file by double-clicking on it. Notice that access is denied because Mark Manore does not have the private key necessary to decrypt the file. Close all open windows.
10. Log off and then log on again as **Administrator** with the password **Password01**.
11. Open the **D:\Encrypted** folder and attempt to open the file **encrypted.txt**. Notice that the file opens because the domain Administrator account is the default recovery agent. Close all open windows.
12. Log off and then log on again using your **Admin*XX*** account.

Note: Windows Server 2003 also includes the cipher.exe command-line utility to perform bulk encryption and decryption of files and folders. For more information on cipher.exe, see the Windows Server 2003 Help and Support Center.

Monitoring Access to Shared Folders

To assist in maintaining network security and statistics, you may need to periodically monitor shared folder and open-file access. Keeping track of the number of users connected to a specific network share can help you plan for future capacity requirements and fine-tuning of performance levels. In Windows Server 2003, you are able to see how many people are connected to a share, who they are, and what files they have open at any given time.You can also disconnect users from a specific share or send network messages alerting users of pending changes to the server's status, such as a planned reboot.

This Computer Management utility is the tool used to perform shared folder monitoring and management tasks on a Windows Server 2003 network. As with most MMC-based tools, the Computer Management console facilitates the management of both local and remote computers on the network. To monitor computers in a domain environment, you need to be logged on as a member of the Administrators or Server Operators groups.

The Sessions node in Computer Management provides information about the users that are currently connected to a server, as illustrated in Figure 5-13.

Tip: To manage a different computer, right-click Computer Management (Local), select Connect to another computer, and then provide the name of the server you wish to manage.

The Open Files node in Computer Management provides information about all of the files that users currently have open. This information can be used to troubleshoot file-access problems, such as when two users attempt to access the same file but one of the users is granted read-access only.

If you want to disconnect an open file connection or session, simply right-click the entry in the details pane, and click Close Open File or Close Session on the shortcut menu. This can assist you in situations where you have changed permissions on a folder or file and you want the new permissions to take effect immediately.

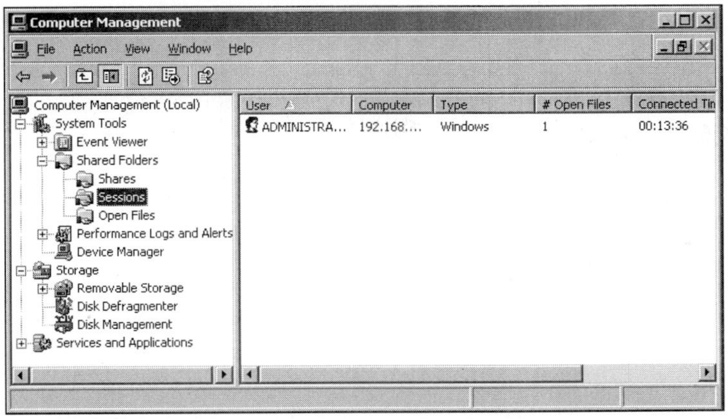

Figure 5-13 Monitoring the number of sessions connected to the local computer

To help prevent data loss, it is always a best practice to send users a warning message before disconnecting sessions or shutting down a server. The Computer Management tool facilitates this by allowing you to send a console message to all users connected to the server. Illustrated in Figure 5-14, the Send Console Message feature allows you to supply a custom warning message that appears as a dialog box on the user's screen. In Activity 5-11, you monitor access to shared folders and send console messages to connected users.

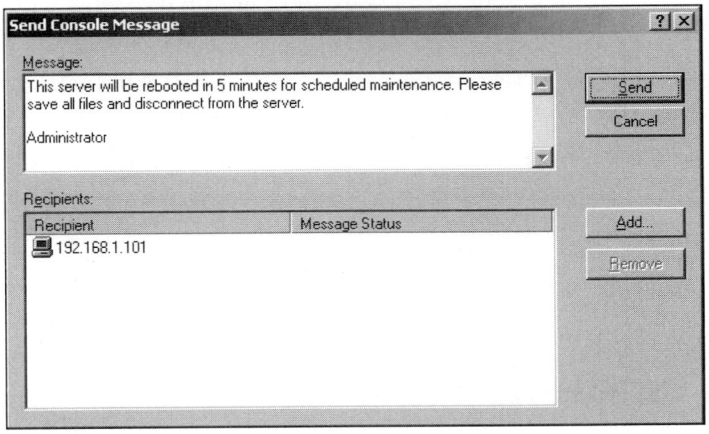

Figure 5-14 Sending a console message to connected users

Activity 5-11: Monitoring Access to Shared Folders and Sending Console Messages

Time Required: 10 minutes

Objective: Monitor access to shared folders and send messages to connected users.

Description: The IT manager at Dover Leasing has asked you to identify ways in which help desk and network support staff can monitor user connections to corporate servers, as well as send out warning messages when a server is about to be brought offline for scheduled maintenance. In this activity, you explore the feature and functions of the Shared Folder node of Computer Management to better understand the monitoring and messaging features of the tool.

1. Open the **Run** command, type **compmgmt.msc**, and then click **OK**. The Computer Management tool opens when this executable file is specified.
2. Click the **plus sign (+)** next to the Shared Folders node to expand it, if necessary.

3. Click the **Sessions** node to view all current network sessions active on your server.
4. If no user sessions appear on this list, open the **Run** command and type **\\server*XX*\combined** and click **OK**. Once it appears, leave the Combined window open.
5. Switch back to the Computer Management tool, and press **F5** to refresh the display. Your Admin*XX* account should now appear in the details pane, along with your connection time.
6. Click the **Open Files** node to view its details. Notice that your Admin*XX* account is also listed here and that D:\Combined is listed as an Open File.
7. Right-click the **D:\Combined** Open File entry and click **Close Open File**. Click **Yes** in the Shared Folders dialog box. Notice that even though the Open File entry is removed from the list, the Combined window is still open on your machine.
8. Close the **Combined** window. Open the **Run** command and type **\\server*XX*\combined** and click **OK**.
9. Switch back to the **Computer Management** window again, and press **F5**. The Open File entry should now appear in the list again.
10. Because the Messenger service is disabled by default in Windows Server 2003, you will need to enable it in order to send console messages to connected users. Click **Start**, select **Administrative Tools**, and click **Services**. Right-click on the **Messenger Service** and click **Properties**. In the Startup type drop down box, click **Automatic**, and then click the **Apply** button. In the Service status section, click Start. Click **OK** to close the Messenger Properties window, and then close the Services window.
11. Right-click the **Shared Folders** node in Computer Management, click **All Tasks**, and then click **Send Console Message**. The Send Console Message dialog box opens.
12. In the Message text box, type **The server will be shut down in five minutes. Please save and close all open files**. Click the **Send** button.
13. Read the message when it appears on your screen, and then click **OK** to close it.
14. Close all open windows.

CONFIGURING AND MANAGING A DISTRIBUTED FILE SYSTEM

The DFS allows administrators to simplify access to multiple shared-file resources by making it appear as though multiple shared-file resources are stored in a single hierarchical structure. For example, if the network has eight Windows Server 2003 systems that provide a variety of shared folders to network users, DFS can be set up so that users do not have to know which specific server offers which shared folder. All of the folders can be set up to appear as though they are on one server and under a single folder structure. This eliminates the need for users to have to browse the network looking for shared resources. DFS also makes managing folder access easier for server administrators.

> **Note:** To access Windows Server 2003 DFS resources, clients must be running DFS client software. Although new Windows versions such as Windows 2000 and XP include this ability by default, older versions such as Windows 98 or NT 4.0 must have the **Active Directory client extensions** installed to access resources through DFS. You can download the Active Directory client extensions from the Microsoft Web site.

DFS is configured using the Distributed File System console in the Administrative Tools menu or by using the Distributed File System MMC snap-in.

A DFS share resembles a tree structure and consists of a root and DFS links. When configuring DFS, the root is configured first, then the DFS links. The DFS root is at the top of the tree structure and is the container for DFS links. The DFS links point to shared folders throughout the network, as illustrated in Figure 5-15.

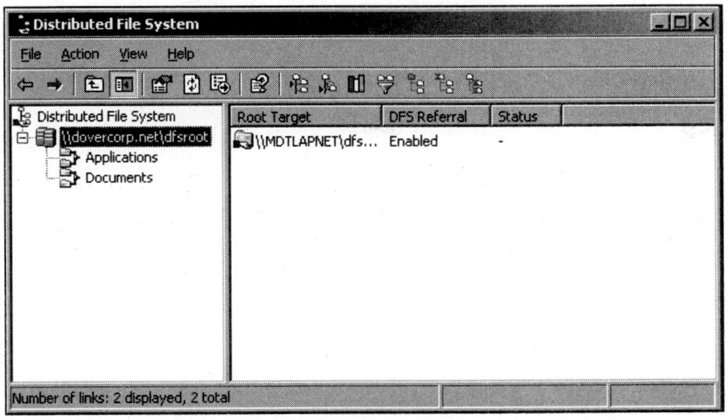

Figure 5-15 Viewing a DFS root and links

DFS Models

There are two models for implementing DFS: the stand-alone model and the domain-based model. The stand-alone DFS model offers limited capabilities compared to the domain-based model. Table 5-6 summarizes the difference between the two models.

Table 5-4 Difference between Stand-alone DFS and Domain-based DFS

DFS Model	Description
Stand-alone DFS	DFS information is stored on the local server where DFS is configured. This model offers no fault tolerance.
Domain-based DFS	DFS information is stored within Active Directory. Links can be configured to point to multiple copies of a share for fault tolerance. DFS root must be on an NTFS partition.

The hierarchical structure of DFS in the domain-based model is called the DFS topology or logical structure. There are three elements to the DFS topology:

- The DFS root
- The DFS links
- Servers on which the DFS shared folders are replicated as replica sets

A **DFS root** is a main container that holds links to shared folders that can be accessed from the root. The server that hosts the DFS root is called the host server. When a network client views the shared folders under the DFS root, all of the folders appear as though they were physically located in one main folder on the DFS root computer, even though the folders may actually reside on many different computers in the domain.

A **DFS link** is a pointer to the physical location of shared folders that are defined in the root. DFS links can also be made to another DFS root on a different computer or to an entire shared volume on a server.

A **replica set** is a set of shared folders that is replicated or copied to one or more servers in a domain. Configuring a replication set includes establishing links to each server that participates in the replication, as well as setting up synchronization so that replication takes place among all servers at a specified interval, such as every 15 minutes.

The first step in creating a DFS is to configure a DFS root of either the stand-alone or domain-based variety. Once the root is configured, you can create DFS links that point to the actual physical location of the shared files and folders. In Activity 5-12, you create a new domain-based DFS root along with multiple DFS links.

Activity 5-12: Implementing Domain-Based DFS and Creating Links

Time Required: 15 minutes

Objective: Create a new domain-based DFS root and add DFS links.

Description: The IT manager at Dover Leasing has recognized that based on the large number of servers that the company plans to implement, users may have difficulty finding the resources that they will most commonly need access to. Because of this, he has asked you to investigate whether or not the distributed file system will help to make resource access easier for users. In this activity, you create a new domain-based DFS root and then add DFS links for shared folders on multiple servers.

1. Click **Start**, select **Administrative Tools**, and then click **Distributed File System**.
2. Right-click the **Distributed File System** icon and then click **New Root**. The Welcome to the New Root Wizard appears. Click **Next**.
3. At the Root Type screen, ensure that the **Domain root** radio button is selected and click **Next**.
4. At the Host Domain screen, ensure that your domain is selected on the **Trusting domains list** and then click **Next**.
5. At the Host Server screen, click the **Browse** button. In the Find Computers screen, select your server and then click **OK**. Click **Next** to continue.
6. At the Root Name screen, type **dfsroot** in the Root name text box and click **Next**.
7. At the Root Share screen, type **d:\dfsroot** in the Folder to share text box and click **Next**. When asked whether you want to create the folder, click **Yes**.
8. Click **Finish** to close the New Root Wizard.
9. Right-click your new **DFS root** and then click **New Link**.
10. In the New Link dialog box, type **Marketing Applications** in the Link name text box.
11. In the Path to target text box, type **\\server*XX*\applications** where *XX* is your student number, and then click **OK**. The new link appears under your DFS root.
12. Open **My Computer**, and create a new shared folder on your **D:** drive called **partner**. Ensure that the shared folder permissions on this folder are set to allow the Everyone group the Read permission at a minimum.
13. In the Distributed File System window, add another **DFS link** named **Partner**, specifying the path to the **partner** folder on your partner's server in the Path to target text box.
14. To test whether the DFS root functions correctly, open the **Run** command, type **\\domain*XX*.dovercorp.net\dfsroot**, and click **OK**. Ensure that both the Marketing Applications and Partner folders appear beneath as the contents of the dfsroot folder.
15. Right-click the **Partner** folder in the dfsroot window and click **Properties**. Notice the Location path specified on the General tab.
16. Click the **DFS** tab. Notice that the actual path to the shared folder on your partner's server is listed in the Referral list.
17. Close all open windows.

Managing DFS

After a new DFS root system is set up, there are several tasks involved in managing the root, which can include:

- Deleting a DFS root
- Removing a DFS link

- Adding root and link replica sets
- Checking the status of a root or link

Each of these tasks is described in the following sections.

After a DFS root is created, it is possible to delete it—when you want to configure it differently, for example. To delete a DFS root, open the Distributed File System console, and right-click the root you want to delete. You can then click Delete Root on the shortcut menu.

To remove a link from the DFS root, right-click the link in the details pane on the right and then click Delete Link on the shortcut menu.

One of the features of a domain-based DFS is that an entire DFS root or specific DFS links in a root can be replicated on servers other than the one that contains the master folder. The replication capability is what enables you to provide fault tolerance as well as load balancing of requests between servers. On a network in which there are multiple servers, replication can prove to be a vital service to provide uninterrupted access for users, in case the computer with the master folder is inaccessible. Load balancing also is vital as a way to provide users with faster service and better network performance by enabling users to access the nearest server containing the DFS shared folders. DFS takes advantage of Active Directory sites by ensuring that users are forwarded to a replica within their own site, if one exists.

Note: You can configure replication to occur manually or automatically. If you choose to use automatic replication, ensure that the File Replication Service is started and set to start automatically because automatic DFS replication relies on this service.

The most common problem associated with DFS shared folders is that one or more DFS links are inaccessible because a particular server is disconnected from the network, shut down, or has failed. You can quickly check the status of a DFS root, link, or replica by right-clicking it in the right pane of the Distributed File System management tool, and then clicking Check Status. A DFS root, link, or replica that is working and fully connected has a green check mark in a white circle through its folder icon. One that is disconnected has a white "x" in a red circle through its folder icon.

CHAPTER SUMMARY

- To create a shared folder, you are required to have the appropriate rights. A domain administrator or server operator has the default rights to create shared folders within a domain.
- Windows Server 2003 supports three share permissions: Read, Change, and Full Control. Share permissions are cumulative. If a user is a member of multiple groups that have different permissions, the final permission is the sum of all permissions.
- NTFS permissions are cumulative. If a user is a member of multiple groups that have different permissions, the final permission is the sum of all permissions.
- When a shared folder and NTFS permissions are combined, the most restrictive permission applies.
- A denied permission overrides an allowed permission.
- Files and folders can be encrypted using the encrypted file system.
- DFS can be used to logically group network resources in a single tree structure.

Key Terms

access control entry (ACE) — An entry in an object's discretionary access control list (DACL) that grants permissions to a user or group. An ACE is also an entry in an object's system access control list (SACL) that specifies the security events to be audited for a user or group.

Active Directory client extensions — These allow legacy operating systems to perform searches in Active Directory; they also provide site awareness and access to Windows Server 2003 distributed file systems.

Computer Management console — A predefined Microsoft Management Console (MMC) application that allows you to administer a variety of computer-related tasks on the local computer or a remote computer.

data decryption field (DDF) — The header field in an EFS-encrypted file that is used to store the file encryption key (FEK) encrypted by the user's public key.

data recovery agent — Individual responsible for recovering encrypted data in the event a user's private key is lost or otherwise unavailable.

data recovery field (DRF) — The header field in an EFS-encrypted file that is used to store the file encryption key (FEK) encrypted by the recovery agent's public key.

DFS link — A pointer to the physical location of a share on the network.

DFS root — The top level of a DFS tree structure that contains links to the shared folders on the network.

DFS topology — The logical structure of a distributed file system, which includes the DFS root and DFS link.

discretionary access control list (DACL) — A part of the security descriptor of an object that contains a list of user or group references that have been allowed or denied permissions to the resource.

distributed file system (DFS) — A file system that organizes shared folders located throughout a local or wide-area network into a single logical tree structure.

encrypting file system (EFS) — Windows Server 2003 enables you to encrypt files and folders on NTFS volumes for security purposes.

file encryption key (FEK) — The encryption key used to encrypt a file using EFS.

replica set — A set of shared folders that is replicated or copied to one or more servers in a domain.

shared folder — A data resource container that has been made available over the network to authorized network clients.

Review Questions

1. Which of the following is not a shared folder permission in Windows Server 2003?
   a. Read
   b. Full Control
   c. Modify
   d. Change
2. By default, NTFS permissions set on a folder are inherited by files stored within the folder. True or False?
3. Which user account or group is used as the default data recovery agent in a Windows Server 2003 domain?
   a. Domain Admins
   b. Enterprise Admins
   c. Recovery Agent
   d. Administrator

4. If an administrator cannot remove standard NTFS permissions on a folder because the necessary boxes are grayed out, what is most likely the cause of the problem?
   a. data corruption
   b. incorrect effective permissions
   c. inheritance settings
   d. encryption settings
5. By default, the Everyone group is assigned the Full Control permission to shared folders on Windows Server 2003 computers. True or False?

6. What are the default permissions assigned to a group when it is added to the Security tab of an NTFS folder? (Choose all that apply.)
   a. Read
   b. Write
   c. List Folder Contents
   d. Read and Execute
7. What term is used to describe individual entries in a Discretionary Access Control List (DACL)?
   a. access entries
   b. access control entries
   c. access list entries
   d. access principal entries
8. Which of the following is not a standard NTFS folder permission?
   a. Read
   b. Read and Write
   c. Modify
   d. List Folder Contents
9. When a file is encrypted using EFS, what is used to encrypt the file?
   a. the user's public key
   b. the user's private key
   c. a file encryption key
   d. a data decryption key
10. Which two of the following allow you to create a shared folder? (Choose two answers.)
    a. Active Directory Users and Computers
    b. Windows Explorer
    c. Computer Management console
    d. Performance Monitor
11. How can you create a shared folder but make it hidden so it is not visible through My Network Place or Network Neighborhood?
    a. Right-click the shared folder, and click the Hide Share option.
    b. Place a $ at the end of the share name.
    c. Place a $ at the beginning of the share name.
    d. A shared folder cannot be hidden.

12. Bob is a member of the following groups that have been assigned different shared permissions for the Accounting Docs folder:

Accountants	Change
Managers	Full Control
Users	Read

What is Bob's effective permission to the Accounting Docs folder?

a. Change

b. Full Control

c. Read

d. No Access

13. Robert is a member of the Sales group and the Managers group. Each group has been assigned the following share permissions and NTFS permissions to the Accounting Docs folder:

Group	Share permission	NTFS permission
Managers	Full Control	Modify
Sales	Read	Write

What is Robert's effective permission for the Accounting Docs folder when he accesses it from across the network?

a. Full Control

b. Modify

c. Read

d. Write

14. Using the example in Question 13, what is Robert's effective permission when he accesses the Accounting Docs folder locally?

a. Full Control

b. Modify

c. Read

d. Write

15. What utility allows you to create a new share on a domain controller from your workstation running Windows XP Professional?

a. Windows Explorer

b. Active Directory Users and Computers

c. Server Manager

d. Computer Management

16. When a user has been assigned multiple share permissions through group membership, the user's effective permission is the most restrictive. True or False?

17. You set permissions on your shared resources stored on your file server. Some of the information is high security. You are concerned about the possibility of someone taking the drive and being able to access the files. What technology can you implement to add another level of file and folder security?

a. compression

b. encrypting file system

c. distributed file system

d. file protection system

18. You can either enable the compression attribute or the encryption attribute for a folder or file, but not both. True or False?
19. The file encryption key is encrypted with the user's private key when EFS is used. True or False?
20. Which of the following groups can share a folder on a Windows Server 2003 computer? (Choose the two best answers.)

a. Administrators

b. Account Operators

c. Server Operators

d. Backup Operators

Case Projects

Case Project 5-1

This case project involves configuring share and NTFS permissions. Dover Leasing is in the process of reviewing their current structure and practices. There has been talk of minor security breaches occurring in which users are able to gain access to information they should not be permitted to view. Management would like you to make some recommendations as to how permissions can be changed on specific folders.

1. Two network servers maintain confidential information pertaining to financial data and employee data. Users access the folders both locally and on the network. Only members of the Managers group, Human Resources group, and Accountants group should have access to these folders. Explain how permissions can be implemented, including a short description of how share permissions and NTFS permission work together.
2. Dover Leasing has recently hired a new server administrator to assist you. He has worked with Windows NT 4.0 in the past and is unfamiliar with Windows Server 2003. Prepare a brief explanation for the new administrator about how to configure share and NTFS permissions.

Case Project 5-2

A new junior administrator at Dover Leasing has just configured a variety of NTFS permissions on a shared folder named Marketing on a newly installed server. After completing his configuration, he notices that some of the Marketing users are having trouble accessing the server with the correct level of access, if at all. What are some of the possible permission-related reasons that users might be having trouble connecting?

Case Project 5-3

To understand how NTFS and share permissions work together, consider the following example and answer the accompanying questions.

Table 5-5 Permissions example

Users	Group Membership
User1	Sales, Marketing, domain users
User2	Managers, domain users

Directory Structure	Share Permissions	NTFS Permissions
SalesData	Sales - Full Control	Sales - Modify
	Managers - Read	Marketing - Full Control
CompanyData	domain users - Change	default
HRData	Managers - deny Full Control	default

1. What permissions would User1 have to the SalesData folder if the user were accessing the folder across a network connection?
2. What permissions would User1 have to the SalesData folder if the user were logged on to the computer where the folder was located?
3. What permissions would User2 have to the CompanyData folder if accessing the folder across the network?
4. What permissions would User2 have to the HRData folder if accessing the folder across the network?
5. What permissions would User2 have to the HRData folder if accessing the folder on the computer on which it is located?

Case Project 5-4

Dover Leasing has decided to implement DFS but is debating whether to use a domain-based or stand-alone root. What are some of the advantages that a domain-based DFS root provides over a stand-alone root?

CHAPTER

6

MANAGING PRINTERS, PUBLISHING, AUDITING, AND DISK RESOURCES

After reading this chapter and completing the exercises, you will be able to:

- Create and modify shared printer resources
- Set up and manage published resources in Active Directory
- Audit access to shared resources
- Manage data storage

The concept of sharing resources among many different users is a primary reason why almost all companies implement networks today. Networks have evolved from simple peer-to-peer arrangements where users would share files from their local workstations to large and complex entities that may include hundreds, if not thousands, of interconnected and shared resources. This evolution means that an administrator is not only responsible for ensuring that shared resources are available to users but also that these resources are managed and monitored effectively.

Although sharing file resources is still the most common reason to implement a network, sharing access to print devices is probably a close second. Windows Server 2003 includes the ability to act as a **print server**, allowing both locally attached and network-interface print devices to be installed and shared amongst network users. In this chapter, you will learn how to install and share print resources, how to configure permissions to control **printer** access, and about some of the more advanced configuration features of print devices in a Windows Server 2003 environment.

Once you have created and shared file and print resources on your network, users may need a simple and effective way to search for these objects. Publishing resources into Active Directory allows any Active Directory-aware client to perform a simple search on the network. This chapter illustrates how to configure resource publishing and perform Active Directory searches.

Although sharing resources and configuring appropriate permissions is critical, it is equally important to regularly monitor these resources for security purposes. Windows Server 2003 provides the ability to monitor resource access through its auditing capabilities. Additional tasks that a network administrator will likely need to perform in a Windows Server 2003 environment are related to proper disk management and maintenance. Examples of these tasks include configuring volumes, controlling the amount of disk space that a person may use to store data on a shared network location, or enabling compression. The final sections of this chapter help you understand how to configure and monitor security settings and manage disk resources.

Creating and Modifying Shared Printer Resources

Managing a Windows Server 2003 network includes configuring and maintaining an efficient network of shared printers. You need to know how to install and configure these printers to ensure that users have an appropriate level of access when needed. One of the most common troubleshooting tasks for any network administrator is ensuring the continued availability of the shared network printers.

To successfully configure and troubleshoot Windows Server 2003 printing, you should be aware of very specific terms used to define the components of the printing system. The following list defines these terms:

- *Print device*—The actual hardware device that produces the printed document; there are two main types of print devices: a local **print device** and a network print device. Local print devices are connected directly to a port on the print server or workstation. A network print device connects to a print server through its own network adapter and connection to the network.
- *Printer*—A configuration object in Windows Server 2003 that controls the connection to the print device.
- *Print driver*—Files that contain information that Windows Server 2003 uses to convert raw print commands to a language that the printer understands; a specific **print driver** is needed for each print device model used and for each type of operating system in place.
- *Print server*—The computer in which the printers and print drivers are located; this is usually where you set up and configure the shared printing system.

To set up an efficient printing environment, it is also important to make sure that your network meets the following hardware requirements:

- *One or more computers to act as print servers*—Although both Windows Server 2003 and Windows XP Professional can be used as print servers, Windows XP Professional only supports a maximum of 10 simultaneous client connections. This makes XP an inappropriate choice as a print server in all but the smallest network environments.
- *Sufficient space on the hard drive for the print server*—This is very important because Windows Server 2003 uses space on the hard drive to queue and buffer documents as they are being directed to the print device.
- *Sufficient RAM beyond that of the minimum Windows Server 2003 requirements*—This is critical if you expect to have a large number of print jobs and still require acceptable performance.

Adding a Printer as a Local Print Device

Smaller networks may have workstations or servers that share print devices connected directly to a local port on the computer. To add and share a local print device, you need to have administrator privileges on the computer that will act as the print server. Use the Add Printer Wizard to install and configure printers on systems running Windows Server 2003. Access this tool from the Printers and Faxes program on the Start menu, as illustrated in Figure 6-1.

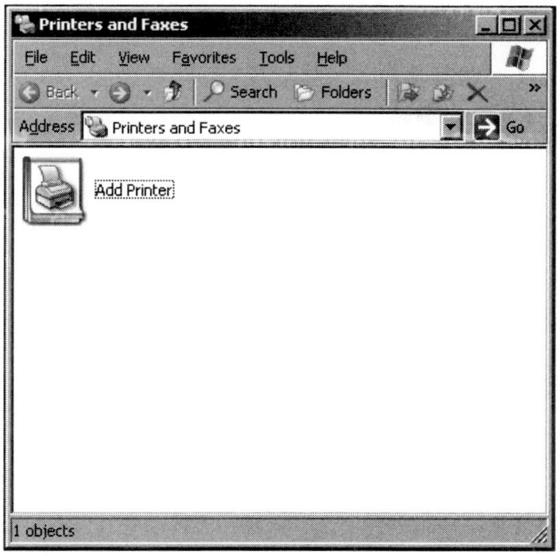

Figure 6-1 Viewing the Printers and Faxes folder

The Add Printer Wizard provides access to all of the necessary configuration options to get a local printer up and running (you will install a local printer using this Wizard in Activity 6-1). As with Windows 2000, the Windows Server 2003 Add Printer Wizard lets you detect printers via Plug and Play, as shown in Figure 6-2. Conversely, the Wizard also allows you to manually configure printers by make and model, allowing you to add a manufacturer's driver from a supplied disk if necessary.

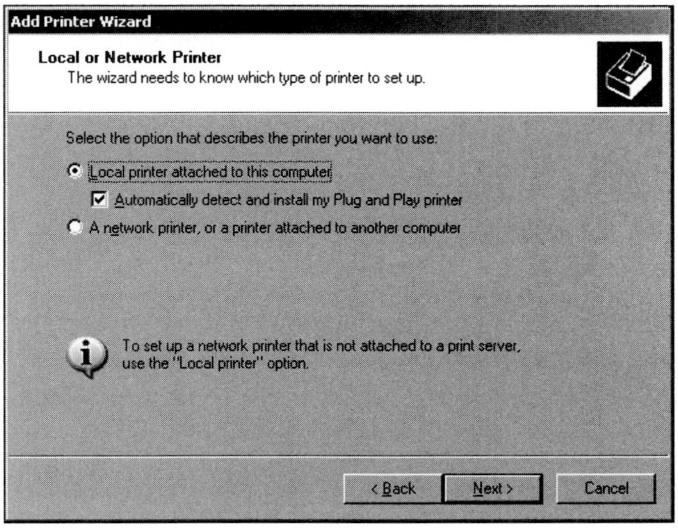

Figure 6-2 Adding a local printer

Additional configuration options specified during the local printer installation process include the port that the print device connects to, as illustrated in Figure 6-3. The Add Printer Wizard also allows you to specify if the device will serve as the Windows default printer and whether the printer should be shared to provide network access (you will share a local printer for network access in Activity 6-2). More advanced options, such as configuring printer permissions, priorities, and features such as print pooling, are handled once the printer is already installed by accessing its properties. Configuring additional printer settings will be looked at later in this section.

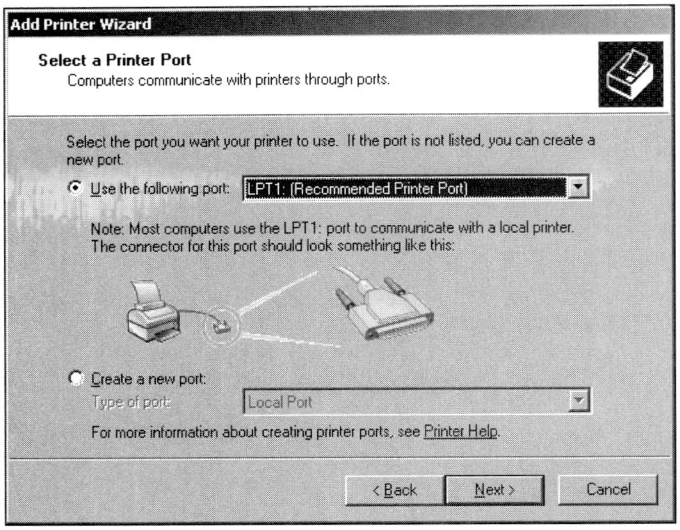

Figure 6-3 Configuring the local port

Activity 6-1: Installing a Local Printer

Time Required: 10 minutes

Objective: Use the Add Printer Wizard to install a local printer.

Description: The IT manager at Dover Leasing is interested in migrating all corporate printers from various platforms to Windows Server 2003-based print servers. He has asked you to begin the testing process by installing and configuring a locally connected print device that will eventually be shared for access by network users. In this activity, you will install and configure a new local printer using the Add Printer Wizard from the Printers and Faxes tool.

1. Click **Start**, and then click **Printers and Faxes**.
2. In the Printers and Faxes window, double-click the **Add Printer** icon to start the Add Printer Wizard. Click **Next** at the Welcome screen.
3. At the Local or Network Printer screen, ensure that the **Local printer attached to this computer** radio button is selected. Uncheck the **Automatically detect and install my Plug and Play printer** check box. Click **Next**.
4. At the Select a Printer Port screen, ensure that **LPT1** is selected in the Use the following port list box and click **Next**.
5. At the Install Printer Software screen, click **HP** in the Manufacturer list. In the Printers list, click **HP LaserJet 6P** and click **Next**.
6. At the Name Your Printer screen, type **HPLaserJet-Server*XX*** in the Printer name text box, where *XX* is your assigned student number. Click **Next**.
7. At the Printer Sharing screen, select the **Do not share this printer** radio button and click **Next**.
8. At the Print Test Page screen, select the **No** radio button and click **Next**.
9. At the Completing the Add Printer Wizard screen, review the stated configuration information and then click **Finish**.
10. Verify that the new printer appears in the Printers and Faxes windows with a checkmark icon specifying that it is the default printer. Close the Printers and Faxes window.

Activity 6-2: Sharing a Local Printer for Network Access

Time Required: 5 minutes

Objective: Share an installed printer to allow network access.

Description: Having created a local printer in the previous activity, you now decide to share this printer to allow network clients to print to it. In this activity, you will access the properties of the printer to configure sharing.

1. Click **Start**, and then click **Printers and Faxes**.
2. Right-click the **HPLaserJet-Server*XX*** icon and then click **Properties**.
3. On the General tab, type **Marketing Laser Printer** in the Comment text box
4. Click the **Sharing** tab, and then click the **Share this printer** radio button. In the Share name text box, type **MarketingLaser** and then click **OK**.
5. When the Printer Properties dialog box opens, read the message about access from MS-DOS workstations and then click **Yes**. Notice that a hand icon appears under the printer in the Printers and Faxes windows, designating it as a shared resource.
6. Click **Start**, and then click **Run**. In the Open text box, type **\\Server*XX***, where *XX* is your assigned student number, and then click **OK**.
7. When the \\Server*XX* window opens, look for the MarketingLaser printer icon. Notice that it also includes the description specified in Step 3.
8. Close all open windows.

Adding a Printer as a Network Print Device

Many corporate print devices have integrated network interface cards that do not require a direct connection to the computer acting as the print server via a parallel port or USB connection. These network print devices use TCP/IP or other protocols to allow communication over the network.

You can also use the Add Printer Wizard to add network print devices to your network (you will install a network printer in Activity 6-3). The main difference is that instead of choosing to configure the device using a local port, you need to create a new TCP/IP port to facilitate communication directly over the network. To create this new TCP/IP port, click the Create a new port radio button on the Select a Printer Port screen, and then click the Standard TCP/IP port option. Ultimately, doing this opens the Add Standard TCP/IP Printer Port Wizard, as illustrated in Figure 6-4. Once the configuration of the TCP/IP port is complete, the Add Printer Wizard continues as it does for any local printer.

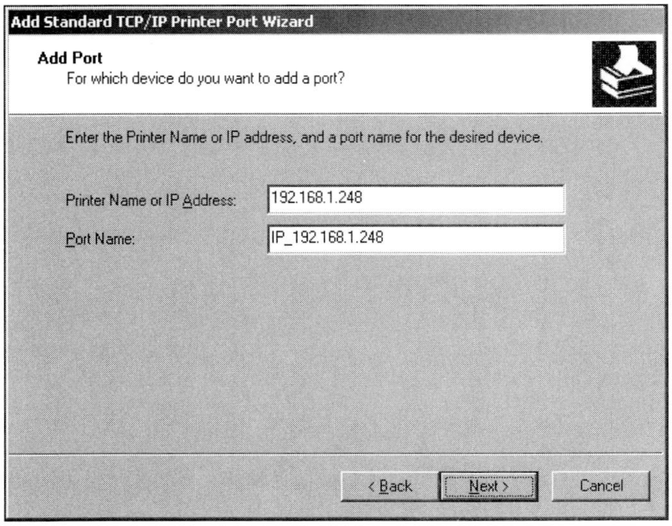

Figure 6-4 Configuring a network printer

Activity 6-3: Installing a Network Printer

Time Required: 10 minutes

Objective: Install a network printer using the Add Printer Wizard and by browsing the network.

Description: After successfully sharing a printer over the network, you decided to explore some of the methods used to install network printers. In this activity, you will install a network printer connected to your partner's server using both the Add Printer Wizard and by browsing the network.

1. Click **Start**, and then click **Printers and Faxes**.
2. Double-click the **Add Printer** icon to open the Add Printer Wizard. At the Welcome screen, click **Next**.
3. At the Local or Network Printer screen, click the **A network printer, or a printer attached to another computer** radio button, and click **Next**.
4. At the Specify a Printer screen, click the **Connect to this printer** radio button and then type **\\serverXX\MarketingLaser** in the Name text box, where XX is your partner's student number. Click **Next**. Select the **No** radio button on the Default Printer screen, then click **Next**.
5. Click **Finish** to close the Add Printer Wizard.
6. Verify that the new network printer appears in the Printers and Faxes window. Notice that the icon used to represent a network printer is different from the one used to represent a local printer.
7. In the Printers and Faxes window, right-click your partner's network printer and click **Delete**. When the Printers dialog box opens, click **Yes**.
8. Open the **Run** command. In the Open text box type **\\Server*XX*** where *XX* is your partner's student number, and then click **OK**.
9. In the list of shared resources that appears, right-click the **MarketingLaser** icon and then click **Connect**. This will install the printer on your computer.
10. Verify that the MarketingLaser printer installed in the previous step appears in the Printers and Faxes window.
11. Close all open windows.

Configuring an Existing Printer

Once you have a printer installed, you may want to modify some of the configuration options such as sharing, permissions, and other advanced settings. To modify these options, right-click the printer icon and click Properties to access the properties of the printer (you will explore printer properties in Activity 6-4). Figure 6-5 illustrates some of the configuration options and tabs available in the properties of a printer.

Activity 6-4: Exploring Printer Properties

Time Required: 15 minutes

Objective: Explore the configurable properties for an installed printer.

Description: The IT manager at Dover Leasing has given you the responsibility of configuring the properties of all printers to be installed on the network. Because of this, you decide to explore the property settings associated with a printer to better prepare yourself. In this activity, you will open and explore the properties of the printer originally installed in Activity 6-1.

1. Click **Start**, and then click **Printers and Faxes**.
2. Right click the **HPLaserJet-Server*XX*** icon where *XX* is your assigned student number, and then click **Properties**.

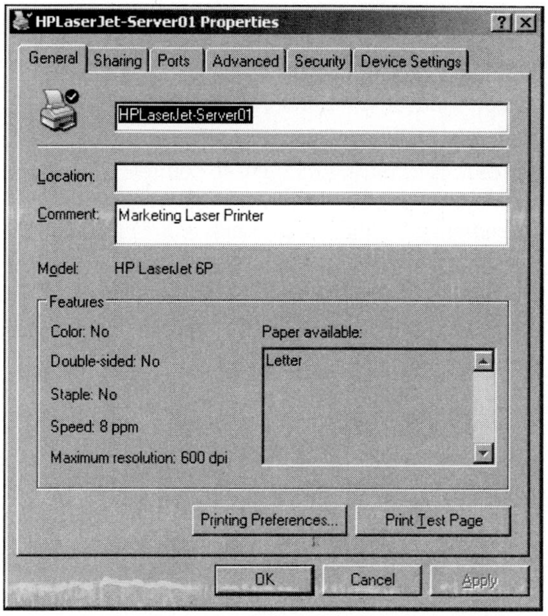

Figure 6-5 Modifying printer properties

3. On the General tab, click the **Printing Preferences** button. This opens the Printing Preferences dialog box for the printer, allowing you to configure settings such as paper layout and quality settings. Browse through the configurable settings and then click **OK**.
4. Click the **Sharing** tab. Notice that this tab is used to configure sharing settings, as well as whether this printer will be listed in the directory. Click the **Additional Drivers** button, noting that this dialog box shows you which drivers are currently installed, while also allowing you to install additional drivers. Click **Cancel** to close the Additional Drivers dialog box.
5. Click the **Ports** tab. Notice that this tab is used to configure printer port settings, as well as enable settings like printer pooling.
6. Click the **Advanced** tab. Notice that this tab allows you to configure settings such as the availability of the printer as well as the printer spooling options. Click the **Separator Page** button, and then click the **Browse** button. This allows you to configure a separator page that will be printed before a user's print job. Click **Cancel** twice to return to the printer properties dialog box.
7. Click the **Security** tab. Notice that this tab allows you to configure security settings for the printer.
8. Click the **Device Settings** tab. Notice that this tab allows you to configure properties specific to the printer model, such as the types of paper used in various trays and the amount of physical memory installed in the print device.
9. Click **Cancel** to close the printer properties dialog box, and then close the Printers and Faxes window.

Two of the most important configuration options for printers are the Sharing and Security tabs. The Sharing tab allows you to enable or disable printer sharing and Active Directory publishing, as well as install additional drivers for other operating systems that may need to use the printer. The Security tab allows you to control printer permissions, in much the same way that this tab is used to control NTFS permissions for files and folders. There are three main levels of print permissions, as well as the ability to configure more granular special permissions. Print permissions are illustrated in Table 6-1. You will configure printer security permissions in Activity 6-5.

Table 6-1 Printer permissions

Permission	Description
Print	Allows users to connect to a printer, print documents, and edit the user's own print jobs; by default, the Everyone group has this permission.
Manage Documents	Allows all of the Print permissions except users having the right to control document print jobs of all users; by default, the Creator Owner special group has Permission to control document print jobs of all users.
Manage Printers	Allows all of the Print and Manage Documents permissions and also allows the user to share, modify, or delete printers and their properties; by default, administrators, print operators, and server operators have this permission.
Special Permissions	Much like NTFS special permissions, these provide a more granular level of control over printer security. The additional special printer permissions include the ability to control whether users can take ownership of a printer, view printer permissions, or change printer permissions.

Note: Just like NTFS and shared-folder permissions, printer permissions are cumulative.

Activity 6-5: Configuring Printer Permissions

Time Required: 15 minutes

Objective: Configure printer security permissions.

Description: Dover Leasing has a number of different printers scattered through a variety of departments and business units. Because each department is responsible for paying for maintenance costs associated with their printers, the department heads want to ensure that only users within their departments have the ability to print to these printers. The IT manager at Dover Leasing has asked you to ensure that all printers are properly secured according to this requirement. However, he also wants to ensure that members of the Help Desk group have the ability to manage printers, while all domain administrators are granted the Manage Printers permission. In this activity, you will configure permissions on the Marketing Department's laser printer.

1. Click **Start**, and then click **Printers and Faxes**.
2. Right-click the **HPLaserJet-Server*XX*** icon, where *XX* is your assigned student number, and click **Properties**.
3. Click the **Security** tab.
4. In the Group or user names list, click the **Everyone** group, and then click **Remove**.
5. Click the **Add** button. In the Select Users, Computers, or Groups dialog box, type **Marketing Users** in the Enter the object names to select text box, and then click **OK**. Notice that once added, the Marketing Users group is granted the Allow Print permission by default.
6. Click the **Add** button. In the Select Users, Computers, or Groups dialog box, type **Help Desk Users** in the Enter the object names to select text box, and then click **OK**. In addition to the Allow Print permission, grant the Help Desk Users group the **Manage Documents** permission.
7. Click the **Add** button. In the Select Users, Computers, or Groups dialog box, type **Domain Admins** in the Enter the object names to select text box, and then click **OK**. In addition to the Allow Print permission, grant the Domain Admins group the **Manage Printers** permission.
8. Click **OK** to close the Properties dialog box.
9. Open the **Run** command and in the Open text box type **notepad.exe** and press **Enter**. This will open Notepad. In the Notepad window, type **testing**. Click **File** on the menu bar, and then click **Print**.

10. In the Print dialog box, ensure that the default printer is selected and then click **Print**. Click **Print** in the Print dialog box. Close Notepad.
11. In the Printers and Faxes window, double-click the **HPLaserJet-Server*XX*** icon, where *XX* is your assigned student number. This displays the print queue for the HPLaserjet-Server*XX* printer, including the print job that you just sent. Close the HPLaserjet-Server*XX* window.
12. Log off and then log back on as the user **cmedved** with the password **Password01**.
13. Open **Notepad**, type some text, and then attempt to print the document to the **HPLaserJet-Server*XX*** printer. Notice that it doesn't appear in the list of available printers because the Chris Medved user account is not a member of a group with sufficient permissions to print to the device.
14. Close all open windows and log off. Log on using your **Admin*XX*** account.

Tip: Windows Server 2003 also lets you determine a user's effective printer permissions via the Effective Permissions tab in the Advanced Security Settings of a printer.

Printer Pools and Priorities

Some advanced features of Windows Server 2003 printing include setting up printer pools and configuring printer priorities.

A **printer pool** consists of a single printer that is connected to a number of print devices. The advantage of a printer pool is that it allows many physical print devices to function as a single logical printer, thus providing better document distribution in high-volume environments while reducing the time that users must wait for documents to print. One cautionary note is that all print devices configured to be part of the same printer pool must be capable of using the same print driver, or output problems will almost certainly occur. A printer pool is configured by clicking the Ports tab and then placing a check mark in the box next to the Enable printer pooling command, as shown in Figure 6-6.

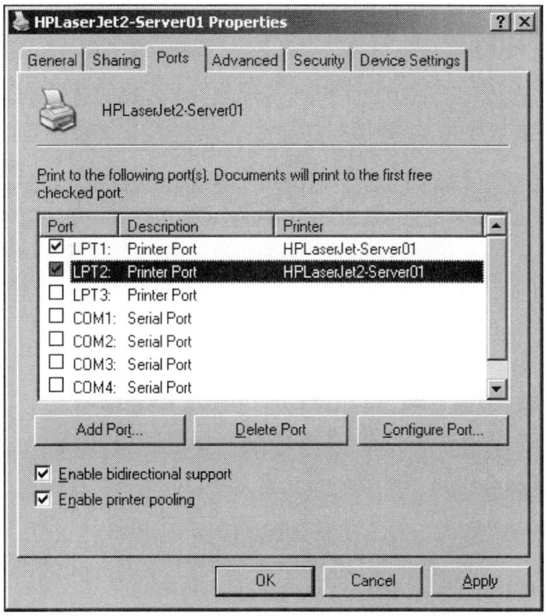

Figure 6-6 Enabling the printer pooling feature

There may be times that you need to set **printer priorities** for different groups of users (you will explore this in Activity 6-6). For example, you may want to configure your print environment to give precedence to any printouts from the CEO of the company, even if there are other documents already ahead of it in the print queue.

Print priorities are especially useful in cases where you want different groups of users to have different levels of priority to a limited number of print devices. To configure printer priorities, install two printers on the print server and connect them both to the same print device. Configure the priority of each printer by clicking the Advanced tab and then adjusting the Priority to a number between 1 and 99, with 1 being the lowest priority and 99 being the highest priority, as shown in Figure 6-7. Again, higher priority printers print first.

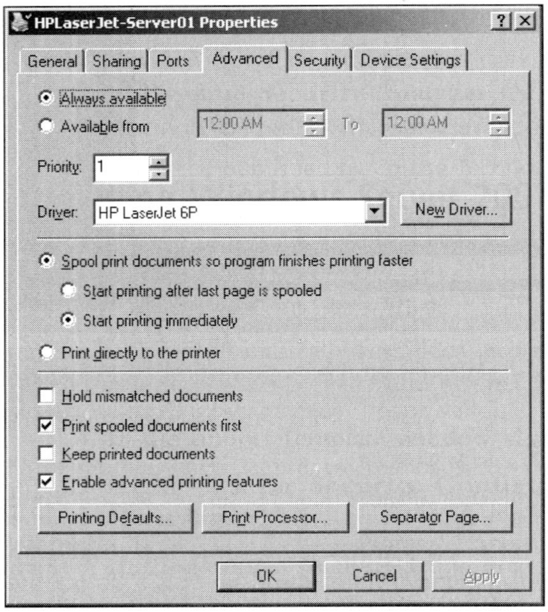

Figure 6-7 Configuring printer priority

The next step in configuring print priorities is to only allow specific users to print to a specific printer. For example, if you want the CEO to always have first priority at printing, only allow the CEO to print to the printer with the higher priority setting. All other users print to the printer with the lower priority setting. To do this, configure the printer security settings, as discussed earlier in this section.

Activity 6-6: Configuring Printer Priorities

Time Required: 10 minutes

Objective: Configure two printers to use the printer pooling feature in Windows Server 2003.

Description: The Marketing Department creates the largest volume of documents on a regular basis at Dover Leasing. Although the department is planning to upgrade all print devices later in the year, they currently have a number of spare HP LaserJet 6P units that they would like to better utilize. Because you are aware of the fact that Windows Server 2003 provides the printer pooling feature, you decide to configure printer pooling for two units in the Marketing Department. In this activity, you will first install an additional HP LaserJet 6P printer and then configure printer pooling with the original printer installed in the Activity 6-1.

1. Click **Start**, and then click **Printers and Faxes**.
2. In the Printers and Faxes window, double-click the **Add Printer** icon to start the Add Printer Wizard. Click **Next** at the Welcome screen.
3. At the Local or Network Printer screen, ensure that the **Local printer attached to this computer** radio button is selected. Uncheck the **Automatically detect and install my Plug and Play printer** check box if necessary. Click **Next**.
4. At the Select a Printer Port screen, select **LPT2** in the Use the following port list box and click **Next**.

5. At the Install Printer Software screen, ensure that **HP** is selected in the Manufacturer list, and that **HP LaserJet 6P** is selected in the Printers list. Click **Next**.
6. At the Use Existing Driver screen, ensure that **keep existing driver** is selected, then click **Next**.
7. At the Name Your Printer screen, type **HPLaserJet2-Server*XX*** in the Printer name text box, where *XX* is your assigned student number. In the Do you want to you use this printer as the default printer section, click the **Yes** radio button and click **Next**.
8. At the Printer Sharing screen, ensure that the **Do not share this printer** radio button is selected and click **Next**.
9. At the Print Test Page screen, ensure that the **No** radio button is selected and click **Next**.
10. At the Completing the Add Printer Wizard screen, review the stated configuration information and then click **Finish**.
11. Right-click the **HPLaserJet2-Server*XX*** icon and then click **Properties**.
12. Click the **Ports** tab. Click the **Enable printer pooling** check box in the lower left of the window, If necessary, click the checkbox next to **LPT2** in the ports column. Check the checkbox next to **LPT1**, then click **OK**. This will allow documents sent to the HPLaserJet2-Server*XX* printer to print from both printers as availability dictates.
13. Close all open windows.

Setting Up and Updating Client Computers

Once the printer is added and configured, you must next set up the client computers to be able to print to the print server. If there is a mix of client operating systems throughout the network, a different version of the print driver is needed for each operating system that is connected to the print server.

Any client computers that run Windows 2000, Windows Server 2003, or Windows XP automatically download the print driver when they initially connect to the printer. Windows 95, Windows 98, Windows ME, and Windows NT 4.0 clients also automatically download the print driver, but only if there is a copy of the appropriate driver on the print server. Install additional print drivers by accessing the Additional Drivers dialog box from the Sharing tab, as shown in Figure 6-8.

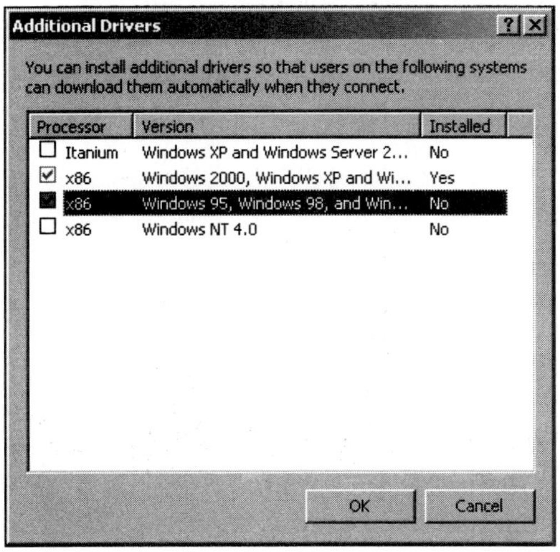

Figure 6-8 Installing additional print drivers

If you have any older Windows clients on your network such as Windows 3.x, or non-Microsoft clients such as Macintosh or UNIX clients, you must manually install the necessary print driver. Non-Microsoft clients may also require additional print services such as Print Services for Macintosh or UNIX to be installed on the print server.

Note: To add, remove, and update additional print drivers, click Server Properties on the File menu of the Printers and Faxes folder. The Drivers tab lists all installed printer drivers, as shown in Figure 6-9. In Activity 6-7, you will install additional print drivers for Windows 98.

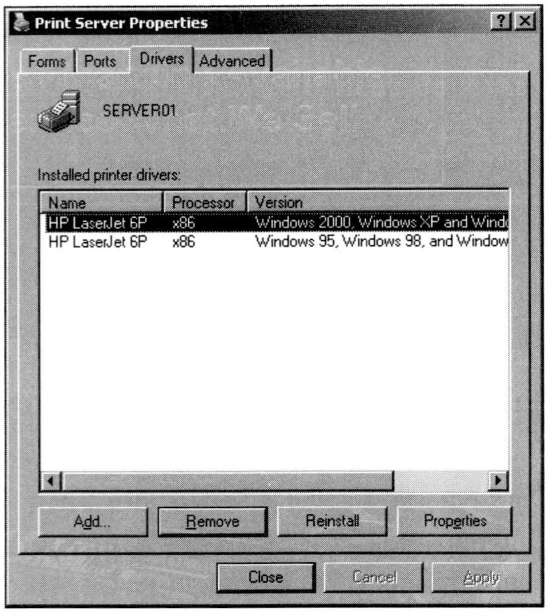

Figure 6-9 Viewing the installed printer drivers

Activity 6-7: Installing Additional Print Drivers

Time Required: 5 minutes

Objective: Install additional print drivers for the Windows 98 operating system.

Description: Although Dover Leasing has almost fully migrated all of their existing workstations to Windows XP, a number of Windows 98 clients continue to exist and will for the foreseeable future. The IT manager at Dover Leasing has asked you to ensure that the appropriate drivers for Windows 98 are installed on the server in addition to the default drivers. In this activity, you will install additional drivers for Windows 98 in the properties of the HPLaserJet2-Server*XX* printer.

1. Click **Start**, and then click **Printers and Faxes**.
2. Right-click the **HPLaserJet2-Server*XX*** icon, where *XX* is your assigned student number, and then click **Properties**.
3. Click the **Sharing** tab, and then click the **Additional Drivers** button.
4. In the Additional Drivers dialog box, click the check box next to **x86 for Windows 95, Windows 98, and Windows Millennium Edition** and then click **OK**.
5. When prompted for the location of the driver files, type the path **D:\source\i386** in the Copy files from text box and then click **OK**.
6. Click **Close** to close to properties of the printer.
7. Close all open windows.

Troubleshooting Printers

The two most common printing problems that you are likely to encounter are:

- *Print jobs that become stuck in the print queue*—Some documents may appear in the print queue, but they do not print, and they cannot be deleted. To fix this problem, on the print server, open the Services console on the Administrative Tools menu, right-click the Print Spooler service, and then click Restart. Note that any print jobs that are in the queue are deleted. You will explore the spooler service in Activity 6-8.

- *Failure of a print device*—A print device may fail because of a paper jam, hardware failure, or a stuck print job. Any documents that are behind the current document in the queue can be redirected to a new print device. To redirect the print jobs, access the properties of the printer that is connected to the failed print device. Click the Ports tab, and then click the port to another printer assigned on the print server. If you need to redirect to another print server, click the Add Port button to add a local port that is directed to the IP address and share name of the other print server.

Hands-on Project

Activity 6-8: Configuring the Spooler Service

Time Required: 10 minutes

Objective: View and configure properties of the spooler service.

Description: Dover Leasing's IT manager informs you that in the past printers have stopped printing due to the Print Spooler service hanging. Because of this, he has asked you to familiarize yourself with stopping and restarting the spooler service. In this activity, you will use the Services node in the Computer Management console to view Print Spooler service settings and restart the service.

1. Click **Start**, right-click **My Computer**, and then click **Manage**.
2. In the Computer Management window, click the **plus sign (+)** next to the Services and Applications node to expand it.
3. Click the **Services** node to view it contents.
4. Scroll through the list of services until you find the Print Spooler service.
5. Double-click **Print Spooler** to view its properties. Notice that the service is configured to start automatically when Windows Server 2003 starts.
6. Click the **Log On** tab. Notice that the Print Spooler service is enabled as part of the only existing hardware profile.
7. Click the **Recovery** tab. Notice that when the service fails, it is configured to restart automatically.
8. Click the **Dependencies** tab. Notice the services upon which the Print Spooler service depends in order to function correctly. In this case, if the Remote Procedure Call is not running, the Print Spooler service cannot function.
9. Click **OK** to close the properties window of the Print Spooler service.
10. Right-click the **Print Spooler** service in the list of services and then click **Restart**. Notice the dialog box indicating that the service is restarting.
11. Close all open windows.

Publishing Resources in Active Directory

Windows Server 2003 Active Directory provides a mechanism that can assist network clients in effectively searching for frequently accessed network resources such as shared folders and printers. A shared resource can be **published** into Active Directory, which means that Active Directory contains an object that represents a link or direct information on how to use or connect to the shared resource. Network users can then query Active Directory to find these published resources. To publish resources into Active Directory, you must be logged in with administrative rights.

To query the Active Directory database, client computers must be running either Windows 2000 or Windows XP Professional. Windows 9x- and NT-based computers (often referred to as *down-level* operating systems) must have the **Active Directory client** installed to connect to and query Active Directory. Additionally, the Active Directory client software allows down-level operating systems to access domain DFS resources and use NTLMv2 for authentication, and makes them aware of Active Directory sites.

> Note
>
> You can download the client extensions by accessing *www.microsoft.com* and performing a search for Active Directory client extensions.

Publishing Shared Folders into Active Directory

In the past, whenever a user required access to a shared folder, they needed to have knowledge of the server on which the share resided. Administrators attempted to fix this problem by creating scripts that mapped the required shares to the user account during logon. Logon scripts that map folder shares to drive letters are quite effective but may not map to every share that a client needs to regularly access. You can waste an extensive amount of time searching for files, especially if there are a number of file servers in the organization.

In an attempt to solve this problem, Windows Server 2003 allows administrators to define what are known as published folders. A **published folder** is an Active Directory object that points to an associated folder share on a file server. Clients can then search the directory for the folder by its share name or by specifying preconfigured keywords.

Publishing a shared folder into Active Directory does not actually create a physical share on the file server. You must configure a shared folder before attempting to publish the resource into Active Directory. Refer back to Chapter 5 for more information on creating and configuring shared folders. Once you have created a shared folder, you can publish a link to the shared folder in the directory. The benefit of this model is that the physical location of a shared folder can be changed, and if the properties of the published folder are edited to reflect the change, users might never be aware that the change took place.

You publish shared folders using the Active Directory Users and Computers tool. Like all other objects that can be created in Active Directory, an administrator can specify the container in which the new shared folder will be published. Figure 6-10 illustrates the New Object - Shared Folder dialog box for a shared folder object that will be created in the root of the *DomainXX.Dovercorp.net* domain.

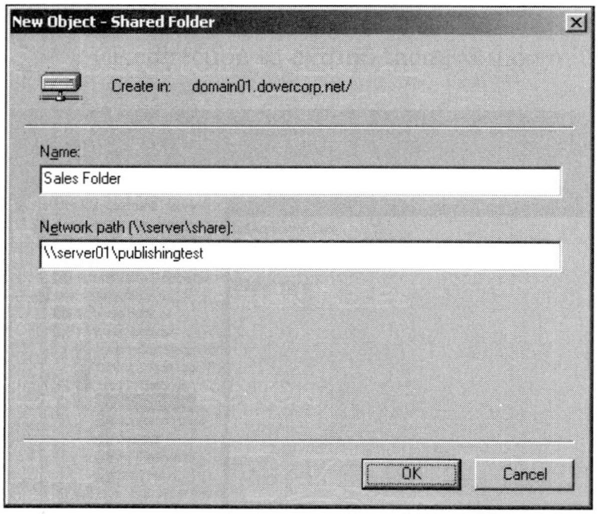

Figure 6-10 Configuring a published folder in Active Directory

After you have created the published shared folder object, it appears in the corresponding container as shown in Figure 6-11.

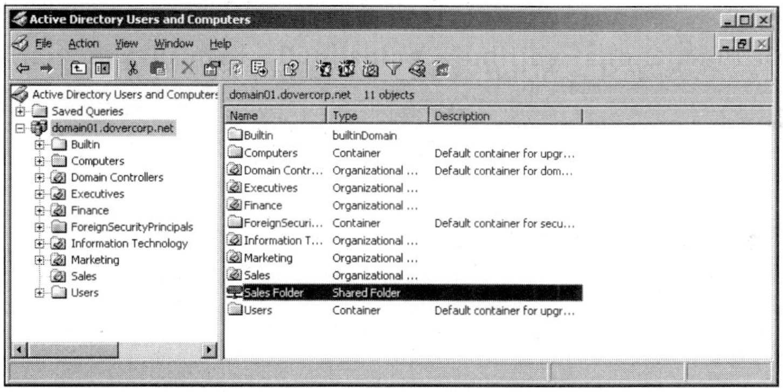

Figure 6-11 Viewing a published folder in Active Directory

In Activity 6-9, you will publish an existing shared folder into Active Directory using the Active Directory Users and Computers tool.

Activity 6-9: Publishing and Accessing Folders in Active Directory

Time Required: 10 minutes

Objective: Publish and access a shared folder in Active Directory.

Description: Although Dover Leasing has never used them in the past, the IT manager is very interested in training administrators on how to find published folders in Active Directory. He believes that publishing shared folders will make it much easier for administrators to find and maintain the folders they are responsible for. In this activity, you will create and publish a new shared folder in Active Directory and then attempt to find it using Active Directory Users and Computers.

1. Open **My Computer** and create a new shared folder on your **D:** drive called **publishingtest**. Close My Computer.
2. Open **Active Directory Users and Computers**.
3. Click the **Sales** OU to view its contents.
4. Right-click the **Sales** OU, select **New**, and then click **Shared Folder**. The New Object – Shared Folder dialog box opens.
5. In the Name text box, type **Sales**. In the Network path text box, type **\\Server*XX*\publishingtest**, where *XX* is your assigned student number, and then click **OK**.
6. Notice the new Sales shared folder icon that appears in the Sales OU. Right-click the **Sales** published folder and click **Properties**.
7. In the Description text box, type **Public Sales Documents** and then click **OK**.
8. Click the icon for your domain, click **Action** on the menu bar, and then click **Find**.
9. In the Find Users, Contacts, and Groups dialog box, click **Shared Folders** in the **Find** list box.
10. Click the **Advanced** tab. Click the **Field** list arrow and then click **Description**.
11. If necessary, click **Starts with** in the Condition field list box. In the Value field text box, type **Public Sales**. Click the **Add** button, and then click the **Find Now** button.
12. Notice that the Sales published folder appears in the Search results field.
13. Close the Find Shared Folders dialog box, and then close Active Directory Users and Computers.

To assist users in searching for published folders, an administrator can add a number of keywords that represent or describe the contents of the folder object. For example, if you have published a folder called

Applications, you might want to associate keywords such as "programs," "software," "Microsoft," or "Excel" with it. The keywords can be any common words or phrases that a user might use to search for the resource.

To add keywords to a published shared folder object, access its properties and then click the Keywords button, as shown in Figure 6-12.

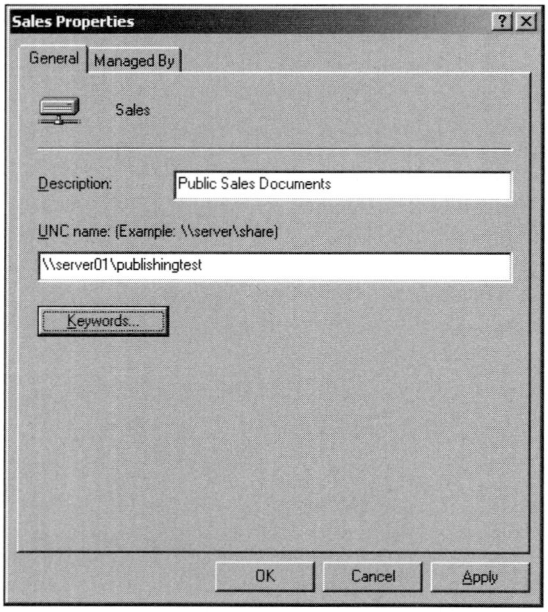

Figure 6-12 The published shared folder properties dialog box

After clicking the Keywords button, an administrator can add the required keywords or phrases for the folder, as shown in Figure 6-13.

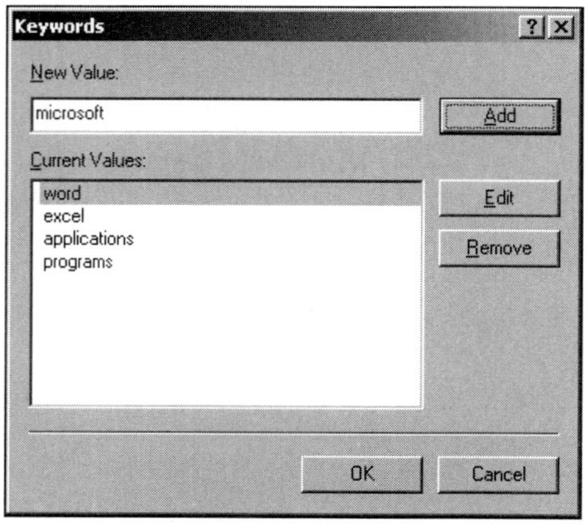

Figure 6-13 Configuring key words for a published folder share

Publishing Printers into Active Directory

To help users find network printer resources, you can also publish shared printers into Active Directory (see Activity 6-10). In fact, any Windows Server 2003- or Windows 2000-compatible printer that is installed on a domain print server is automatically published into Active Directory during installation. By default, published printer objects are hidden in the Active Directory Users and Computers interface.

To view the published printers in Active Directory Users and Computers, click View on the menu bar, and click Users, Groups, and Computers as containers. This option modifies the view to show objects that are associated with a user, group, or a computer object. Printer objects are associated with the computer object that acts as its print server. When the container in which the print server is located is expanded, computer objects can also be expanded to view the printer objects associated with them, as shown in Figure 6-14.

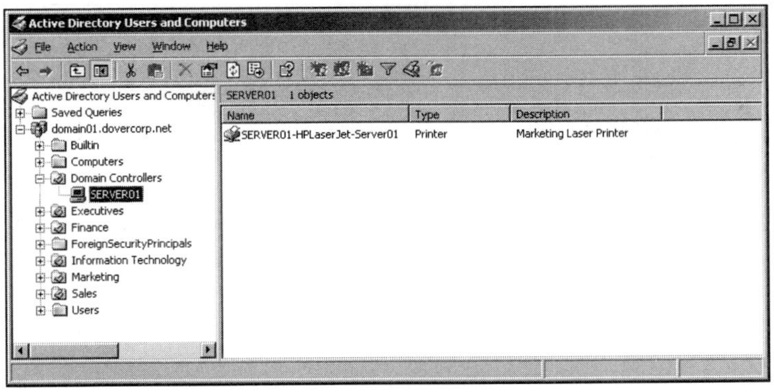

Figure 6-14 Viewing a published printer object in Active Directory

Printer shares that are created on pre-Windows 2000 print servers are not published into Active Directory by default. However, these printers can be added manually to the directory by creating new published printer objects in Active Directory Users and Computers. Like shared folder objects, these printers can be published in whichever container makes the most sense, based on your environment and administrative goals. The New Object – Printer dialog box is illustrated in Figure 6-15.

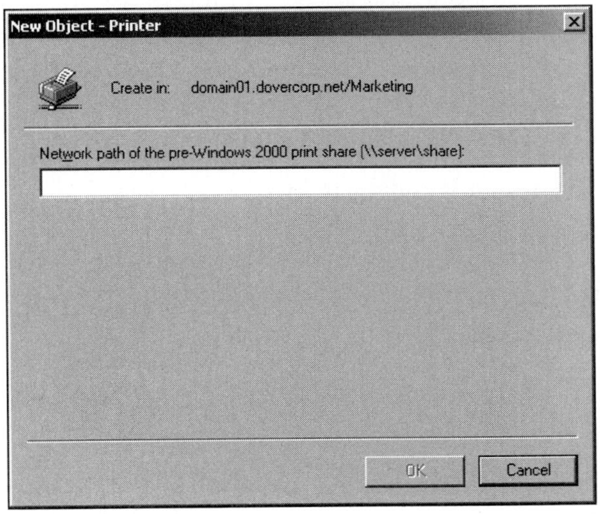

Figure 6-15 Configuring a pre-Windows 2000 published printer share

Note: Publishing printers into Active Directory manually can involve a great deal of administrative effort in large environments. To help ease this burden, a script called "pubprn.vbs" in the %systemroot%\System32 directory can be used to help automate the process. View the header of the pubprn.vbs script for more information on its configuration.

Activity 6-10: Publishing Printers in Active Directory

Time Required: 10 minutes

Objective: Configure printer publishing settings and publish printers manually in Active Directory.

Description: Because Dover Leasing's network includes such a wide variety of printers connected to different operating systems, the IT manager has asked you to explore how printers can be made easier to find in Active Directory. Although he wants most printers to be published in the directory, he is also concerned with users finding and attempting to access the printers belonging to the Marketing Department. In this activity, you will browse existing published printers, manually publish a fictitious printer object in Active Directory, and then manually disable the publishing of printers belonging to the Marketing Department.

1. Open **Active Directory Users and Computers**.
2. Click **View** on the menu bar, and then click **Users, Groups, and Computers as containers.**
3. Click the **plus sign(+)** next to the Domain Controllers OU to expand its contents.
4. Click the **Server*XX*** icon to view the new objects that are now visible. Notice that the shared printer created earlier in the chapter is now visible as a published object in Active Directory.
5. Right-click the **SERVER*XX*-HPLaserJet-Server*XX*** printer icon listed and click **Properties**. Notice that searchable features of the printer including its description and ability to print in color are configurable from this interface.
6. Click the **Color** check box and then click **OK**.
7. Click **Start**, and then click **Search**.
8. In the Search Companion window, click **Other search options**, click **Printers, computers, or people** and then click **A printer on the network**.
9. In the Find Printers window, ensure that your domain is selected in the **In** list box. Click the **Features** tab, check the **Can print color** check box, and then click the **Find Now** button. The HPLaserJet-Server*XX* printer configured in Step 5 should appear in the Search results pane.
10. Right-click **HPLaserJet-Server*XX*** listed in the Search results pane to view the available options. Notice that a user can install a printer from this interface.
11. Close the Find Printers window and the Search Results window.
12. Click **Start**, and then click **Printers and Faxes**.
13. Right-click the **HPLaserJet-Server*XX*** icon, and then click **Properties**.
14. Click the **Sharing** tab, uncheck the **List in the directory** check box, and then click **OK**.
15. Open the **Search** program from the **Start** menu and then attempt to search for a printer that is capable of printing in color again. Note that the HPLaserJet-Server*XX* printer is not found because it is no longer published in Active Directory.
16. Close all open windows.

Managing Published Printers

When a print server is removed from the network, its Active Directory object is automatically removed from the database. This prevents users from trying to connect to print servers that are not actually running. Active Directory removes the orphaned printer objects when the computer acting as its print server does not respond to requests. This process serves to verify that all printer objects are still valid in Active Directory. Although the pruning process can be enabled or disabled via Group Policy settings, a print server will automatically republish a pruned printer once it is again connected to the network and online.

There may be some printers that you do not want to have published in Active Directory for different reasons, such as cost and security. For example, you may only want specific users to be able to find and print to an expensive, color laser printer. By the same token, you might not want regular users to be able to search for the printer used by the Accounting group. The publishing settings of a printer are controlled via a check box on the Sharing tab of a printer's properties, as shown in Figure 6-16.

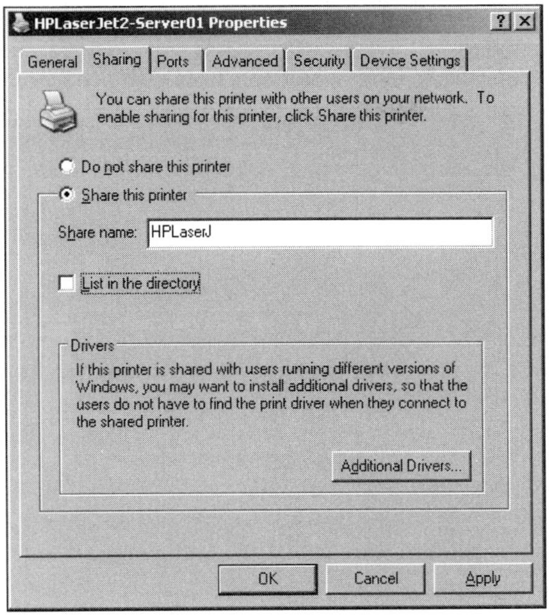

Figure 6-16 Turning off printer publishing

Searching for Objects in Active Directory

Once objects are published in Active Directory, users can easily perform searches to find the objects using the Search or Find tool (depending on the client operating system) from their Start menu. However, the ability to search the directory is often much more important for administrators because they may be responsible for managing thousands of objects or more. To facilitate this requirement, the Active Directory Users and Computers tools provide two main features in the form of the Find command and the Saved Queries folder.

The Active Directory Users and Computers Find command, which was also available in Windows 2000, allows an administrator to search for objects by name, configured attributes, and location in Active Directory, as illustrated in Figure 6-17.

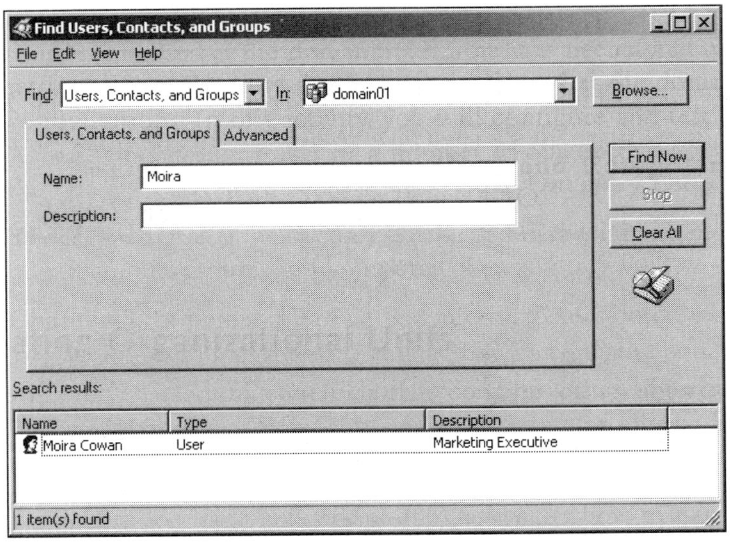

Figure 6-17 Searching Active Directory

The Active Directory Users and Computers Saved Queries feature is new in Windows Server 2003 and allows an administrator to define queries that can be quickly run as often as necessary. For example, administrators might create a query that allows them to quickly identify all of the user accounts within a domain that have been disabled, as illustrated in Figure 6-18. Then, when administrators need to identify all of the accounts that match the criteria specified, they simply need to click the query in the Saved Queries folder. You'll create saved queries in Activity 6-11.

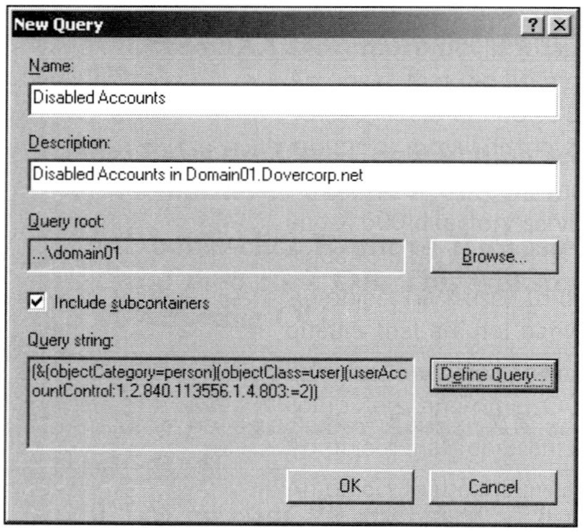

Figure 6-18 Viewing the properties of a saved query

Activity 6-11: Creating Saved Queries in Active Directory Users and Computers

Hands-on Project

Time Required: 10 minutes

Objective: Create saved queries to find objects in Active Directory.

Description: After using the Find command in Active Directory Users and Computers extensively, you decide that it would save a great deal of time if you created and saved common queries instead. In this activity, you will create a saved query that automatically displays a list of all disabled accounts.

1. Open **Active Directory Users and Computers**.
2. Browse to the **Information Technology** OU and then access the properties of the **Mark Manore** user account.
3. Click the **Account** tab. In the Account options section, check the **Account is disabled** check box, and then click **OK**.
4. Right-click the **Saved Queries** folder, select **New**, and then click **Query**.
5. In the New Query dialog box, type **All Disabled Accounts** in the Name text box. In the Description text box, type **query to list all disabled user accounts in the domain**.
6. Click the **Define Query** button. In the Find Common Queries dialog box, click the **Disabled accounts** check box and then click **OK**.
7. Click **OK** to close the New Query dialog box.
8. Click the **plus sign (+)** next to Saved Queries. Click **All Disabled Accounts** to view the results of the query. Notice that a number of accounts, including that of Mark Manore, are displayed as being disabled.
9. In the **Information Technology** OU, right-click the **Mark Manore** user account, and click **Enable Account**. Click **OK** in the Active Directory dialog box.
10. Press **F5** to refresh the screen. Notice that the Mark Manore user account no longer appears in this list.
11. Close Active Directory Users and Computers.

AUDITING ACCESS TO SHARED RESOURCES

Monitoring network events is an increasingly critical and important facet of any network security strategy. Monitoring helps detect potential threats, increases user accountability, and provides evidence of security breaches if or when they occur. Monitoring can also be used for resource planning. Auditing specific resources, such as printer and file shares, can tell you how often they are being accessed by users. For example, if you determine through auditing that a specific share is heavily used by users on the network, you may need to create another instance of the share on another server, or physically move it to a system that is more capable of handling the required workload.

Auditing in Windows Server 2003 is used to monitor and track activities on a network. You can specify which events to monitor based on your security or resource planning requirements. When an audited event does occur, a record of it is written to the **security log**. The audit entry in the security log provides you with information such as the user who performed the action, the specific action that was performed (e.g., a logon attempt), and whether it was a success or failure. **Event Viewer** is used to view the audit entries stored in the security log.

Before you can begin auditing security events or the access of network resources, you must first set up an audit policy. An **audit policy** defines the events on a network that Windows Server 2003 records in the security log as they occur. For example, if you choose to monitor failed logon attempts, when a user attempts to log on with an invalid username and/or password, an event is written to the security log. Keep in mind that an event is not written to the security log on the local computer; rather, the event is written to the security log on the domain controller that attempted to validate the user. In other words, events are stored in the security log of the computer on which the event transpires.

When implementing an audit policy, you need to determine those events you wish to track, along with whether you want to track the successes and/or failures. The audit policy settings available in Windows Server 2003 are illustrated in Figure 6-19. You'll explore these settings in Activity 6-12.

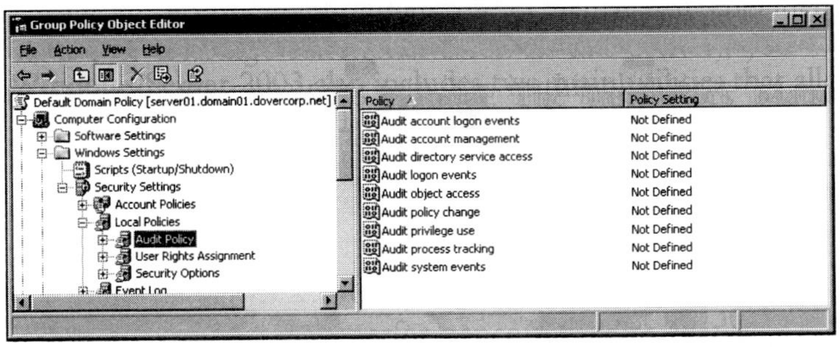

Figure 6-19 Viewing Windows Server 2003 Audit policies

Activity 6-12: Exploring Default Auditing Settings

Time Required: 10 minutes

Objective: Explore the default audit settings configured on a Windows Server 2003 domain controller.

Description: Having read about Windows NT 4.0 in the past, you understand that by default, no auditing settings were configured on these servers. To verify whether this is still the case with Windows Server 2003, you decide to explore the default auditing settings configured on your domain controller. In this activity, you will explore the properties of the default domain controller Group Policy object to view its default settings.

1. Open **Active Directory Users and Computers**.
2. Right-click the **Domain Controllers** OU and click **Properties**.
3. Click the **Group Policy** tab. Ensure that Default Domain Controllers Policy is selected on the Group Policy Object Links list, and then click the **Edit** button.
4. In the Computer Configuration section, click the **plus signs (+)** next to Windows Settings, Security Settings, and Local Policies to expand them.
5. Click the **Audit Policy** node to view its contents. Notice the nine policy settings and their configured default values in the Policy Setting column.
6. Double-click the **Audit account logon events** icon to view its configured settings. Notice that the policy setting is enabled but that only success events are being audited by default.
7. Browse through additional policy settings as time permits, but make no changes.
8. Close all open windows.

Table 6-2 outlines the different types of events that can be monitored in a Windows Server 2003 environment.

Table 6-2 Events that can be monitored

Event Category	Explanation of Event
Audit account logon events	Activated when a user logs onto a computer; logon accounts are generated where the account is located (such as on the local computer or a domain controller), whereas logon events are generated where the logon event occurs.
Audit account management	Activated whenever a user or group is created, deleted, or modified; this category also tracks successful or unsuccessful password changes.
Audit directory service access	Activated when an Active Directory object is accessed; the specific Active Directory object that is to be audited must also have auditing enabled.
Audit logon events	Activated when a user logs on or off a local computer or Active Directory; audits logon failures to find out if password hacking is taking place.
Audit object access	Activated when an object such as a folder or printer is accessed; the administrator must also configure the specific object for audit successes and failures.
Audit policy change	Activated when a policy that affects security, user rights, or auditing is changed.
Audit privilege use	Activated whenever a user uses an assigned right, such as changing the system time, or taking ownership of a file.
Audit process tracking	Activated any time an application process takes place; can assist developers in discovering which files or registry settings an application accesses when executing a command.
Audit system events	Activated when a system event takes place, such as the computer restarting.

Configuring Auditing

Once you have determined the events that need to be audited based on the security requirements of your network, you are ready to configure an audit policy. The following section outlines the requirements of which you should be aware, the steps in configuring an audit policy, and some general guidelines.

> **Note:** How you configure an audit policy is determined by the role of the computer on the network. If the computer is a member server or workstation in a domain, an audit policy can be implemented using Group Policy objects assigned to the domain or different OUs. For domain controllers, audit policy settings are implemented via the Default Domain Controllers Policy applied to the Domain Controllers OU. For nondomain stand-alone workstations and servers, audit settings can be defined by using the Local Security Policy tool on a system-by-system basis.

Requirements

The following requirements must be met to configure an audit policy:

- You must be a member of the Administrators group or be assigned the Manage auditing and security log user right.
- If you are auditing files and folders, they must reside on an NTFS volume (auditing is not available on FAT volumes).

Setting Up an Audit Policy

To set up an audit policy (as in Activity 6-13), you must first choose the events you wish to monitor and then decide whether to monitor the successes and/or failures of these events, as illustrated in Figure 6-20. However, if you are auditing access to files, folders, printers, and Active Directory objects, you also need to configure auditing settings on the specific resources for which you want to monitor access. Configuring object access auditing settings will be looked at later in this section.

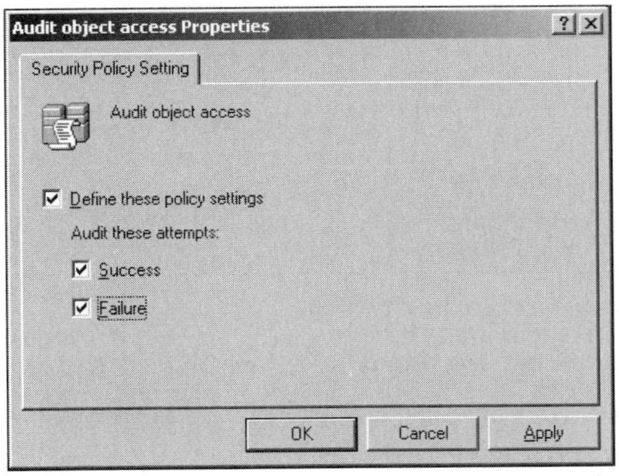

Figure 6-20 Configuring an audit policy

Activity 6-13: Configuring and Testing New Audit Policy Settings

Time Required: 10 minutes

Objective: Configure and test new audit policy settings.

Description: The IT manager at Dover Leasing has informed you that he wants to implement a new corporate security policy that not only logs all failed domain logon attempts, but that will also provide the capability to log different types of object access events. In this activity, you will make changes to the default auditing policy such that all unsuccessful logon attempt are audited and the ability to audit object access is enabled.

1. Use Active Directory Users and Computers to open and view the settings of the **Default Domain Controllers Policy** Group Policy object auditing settings, as described in Activity 6-12.
2. Double-click the **Audit account logon events** icon to view its properties.
3. In the Audit these attempts section, click the **Failure** check box and click **OK**.

4. Double-click the **Audit object access** icon to view its properties.
5. In the Audit these attempts section, click both the **Success** and **Failure** check boxes and click **OK**.
6. Close the Group Policy Object Editor window, the Domain Controllers Properties dialog box, as well as Active Directory Users and Computers.
7. Click **Start**, then click **Run**. Type **gpupdate.exe**, then press **Enter**.
8. Log off.
9. Attempt to log on as the user **Admin*XX*** with the password **pass**. This logon attempt will fail.
10. Log on as the user **Admin*XX*** with your correct password.
11. Click **Start**, select **Administrative Tools**, and click **Computer Management**. Click the **plus sign (+)** next to Event Viewer to view its contents.
12. Click the **Security** icon to view the contents of the security log.
13. Search through the security log for a Failure event in category **Account Logon** that uses the event ID number **675**. Double-click this Failure event to open it and view its details.
14. Read through the information provided by the event and then close all open windows.

Windows Server 2003 will automatically refresh audit policy settings every 90 minutes on a workstation or server and every 5 minutes on a domain controller as per normal Group Policy processing. If no changes occur, these settings are also refreshed every 16 hours by default. If you want to apply the changes immediately, you can do one of the following:

- Restart the computer.
- At the command prompt, issue the gpupdate.exe command.

Note: Remember that Group Policy settings are applied in the order Local, Site, Domain, and Organizational Unit. As such, auditing settings configured at one level may be overridden by settings configured at another. Refer back to Chapter 4 for an overview of Group Policy processing settings.

Auditing Object Access

If your files and folders reside on an NTFS volume, you can set up auditing to monitor user access (such as in Activity 6-14). For example, some information such as employee records or financial data may be confidential. To maintain a high level of security for this information, you need to enable auditing to detect any attempted or successful security breaches. This is especially useful if you want to track which users are attempting to access files or folders that contain sensitive data.

To configure auditing settings for specific files or folders, access the Advanced Security Settings on the particular resource. Figure 6-21 illustrates the Auditing Entry dialog box for a folder called Accounting. Notice that the interface allows you to configure different types of access attempts, including whether these attempts were successful or failed.

Tip: When configuring auditing of object access, you should generally audit access by the Everyone group to ensure that all access attempts, including those by unauthenticated users, are recorded.

Auditing can also be configured for objects that are stored within Active Directory. The process is very similar in that the audit policy is first configured, then auditing is enabled for individual objects within Active Directory such as computers, users, groups, and OUs.

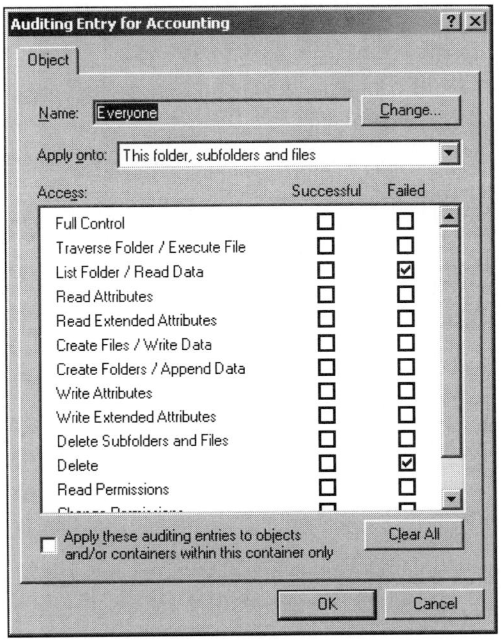

Figure 6-21 Configuring auditing on a shared folder

Activity 6-14: Configuring Auditing on an NTFS Folder

Time Required: 10 minutes

Objective: Audit attempted and successful access to an NTFS folder.

Description: Although Dover Leasing has decided to implement NTFS security on all files and folders stored on corporate servers, the IT manager is still very interested in gathering information about which users are attempting to access restricted resources. In this activity, you will configure object access auditing settings to track attempted access to a secured folder.

1. Open **My Computer** and create a new folder on drive **D:** called **Accounting**. Secure this folder with NTFS permissions such that only the Domain Admins account has Full Control of the folder for the time being. Leave the properties dialog box of the folder open once complete.
2. On the **Security** tab, click the **Advanced** button, and then click the **Auditing** tab.
3. Click the **Add** button. In the Select User, Computer, or Group dialog box, type **Everyone** in the Enter the object name to select text box and click **OK**.
4. In the Auditing Entry for Accounting dialog box, click the **Failed** check box next to List Folder / Read Data along with the **Failed** checkbox next to Delete and then click **OK**.
5. Click **OK** to exit the Advanced Security Settings for Accounting dialog box, and then click **OK** again to close the properties dialog box of the Accounting folder.
6. Log off and then log back on using the **mcowan** user account with the password **password**.
7. Open **My Computer**, browse to drive **D:**, and then attempt to open the **Accounting** folder. Access should be denied according to the NTFS permissions you configured in Step 1.
8. Right-click the **Accounting** folder and click **Delete**. When asked if you're sure you want to delete the folder, click **Yes**.
9. When the Error Deleting File or Folder message appears, click **OK**.
10. Log off and then log back on using your **AdminXX** account.

11. Open **Computer Management** and then access the **Security** log. Search for Failure events that use the event ID **560**.
12. Double-click any event using ID **560** to view its contents. View additional **560** events as time permits.
13. Close all open windows.

Best Practices

To implement an audit policy that effectively meets your security requirements, it is a good idea to take some time to properly plan the implementation. Planning includes determining the computers for which auditing should be configured, what objects need to be audited, the type of events to audit, and whether to audit the successes, failures, or both. An audit policy can quickly become unmanageable and provide you with information that is of no use. By the same token, excessive auditing can seriously degrade the performance of network servers and workstations. Only choose to audit those events that are going to provide you with valuable information about your network. Here are some general guidelines that you should follow when you are planning your audit policy:

- Only enable auditing for those events that can provide you with useful information. Auditing unnecessary events increases overhead and fills up the security log with information that is not useful.
- Review the audit entries in the security log on a regular basis so you are aware of any security issues.
- Enable auditing for sensitive and confidential information.
- Audit the Everyone group instead of the Users group because the Everyone group includes unauthenticated users.
- Audit the use of user rights assignment so that administrative users are more accountable for their actions.
- Always audit the Administrators group so you can track changes made by users who are members of this group.

Analyzing Security Logs

Once an audit policy has been created, an entry is written to the security log each time an event occurs that is defined within the policy. For example, if you enable auditing for object access and then audit all successful and failed read attempts on a folder called Accounting Docs, when a user opens the folder or attempts to open it, an entry would be written to the security log. You can then use Event Viewer to examine the contents of the log. All information that is written to the log is a result of the audit policy that you configure.

Tip: For security purposes, only administrators and those users assigned the Manage Auditing and Security Log user right can view the contents of the security log.

To open Event Viewer and view the contents of the security log, access Event Viewer from the Administrative Tools menu. The contents of the security log are displayed in the details pane, providing a summary of each audit entry, including the date and time that the event occurred and the user who performed the action, as shown in Figure 6-22. A key icon represents successful events, and unsuccessful events (failures to perform a specific action) are represented by a lock icon. Double-click an audit to provide detailed information about the specific event, as illustrated in Figure 6-23.

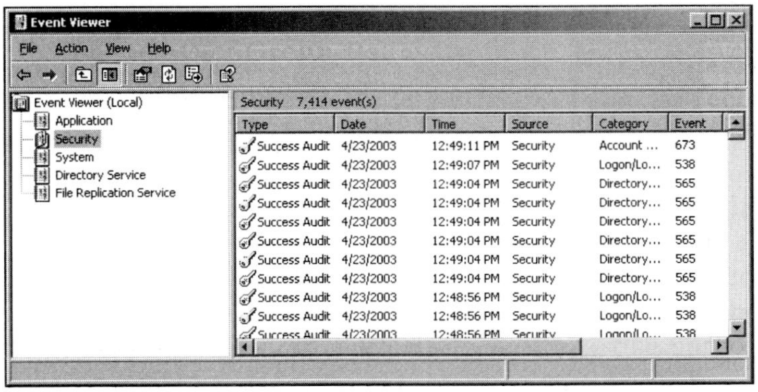

Figure 6-22 The Event Viewer Security log

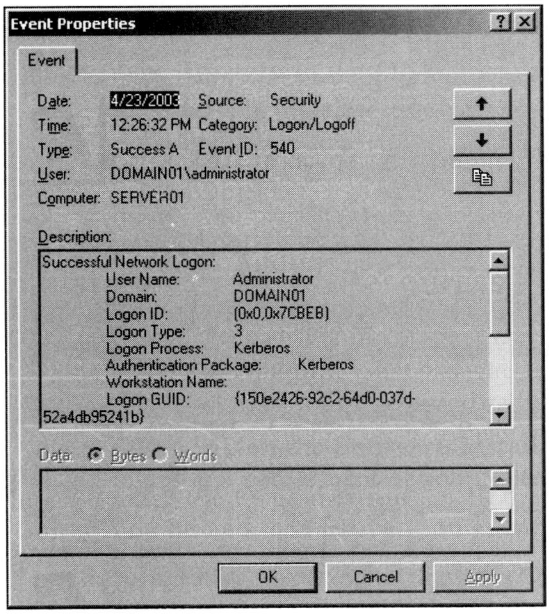

Figure 6-23 The details of a security log event

Tip

By default, the security log shows events that occurred on the local computer. You can also use Event Viewer to view the security log on a remote computer by right-clicking Event Viewer (Local), and then clicking Connect to another computer.

Depending on the number and type of events you choose to audit, the security log can quickly grow in size, making it difficult to pick out certain events. Fortunately, Event Viewer has a Find option that allows you to search through the security log to locate specific events. You can search for specific event types such as successful events or unsuccessful events, but you can also do a more detailed search by providing an event ID, category of event, or even a user logon name. To use the Find option, click the Security Log within the Event Viewer console, click View on the menu bar, and click the Find option. The Find in local System dialog box opens, as shown in Figure 6-24.

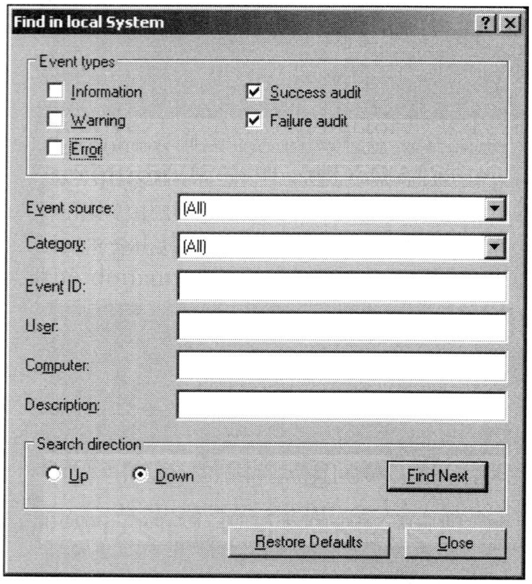

Figure 6-24 Finding information in the security log

Events in the security log can also be filtered so only those events matching your criteria are displayed in the details pane. This is useful if you have a large number of audit entries in the log and want to view entries based on event type or entries that occurred during a specific date and time. Similar to the Find option, you can also filter events based on event ID, category, user logon name, and computer name. To use the filter command, click the security log within the Event Viewer console, and click the Filter option located on the View menu. The Filter tab is shown in Figure 6-25. You will use both of these options to configure Event Viewer log properties in Activity 6-15.

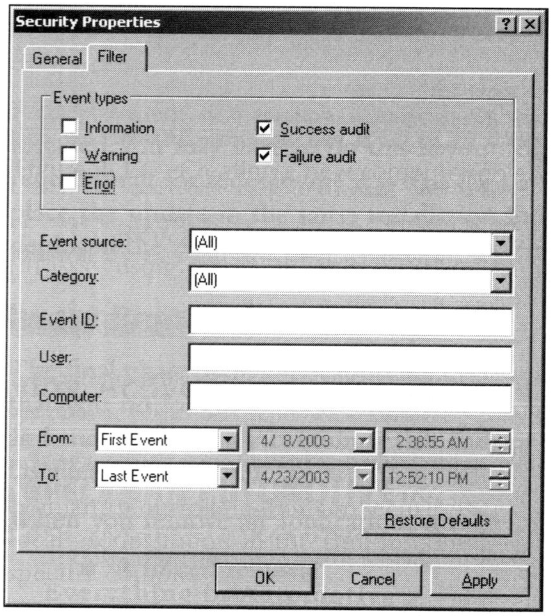

Figure 6-25 Filtering information in the security log

Note: You may have noticed a number of other logs available within Event Viewer. The application and system logs are found on all computers running on Windows Server 2003. The application log contains information such as warnings and error messages generated by any program. The system log contains information such as warnings and error messages that are generated by the operating system. Other logs, such as directory service, DNS service, and file replication service logs are only displayed in Event Viewer if the server is running their associated services. For example, all DNS servers include the DNS service log to track DNS-specific error and information messages.

Activity 6-15: Configuring Event Viewer Log Properties

Hands-on Project

Time Required: 10 minutes

Objective: Configure properties for log files in Event Viewer.

Description: After viewing the extremely large number of events that are found in the security log with only a very basic audit policy applied, you decide to look into alternative methods to quickly search for and find events. In this activity, you will use both the find and filter features in Event Viewer to sort through log files entries.

1. Click **Start**, select **Administrative Tools**, and then click **Computer Management**.
2. Click the **plus sign (+)** next to Event Viewer to expand its contents, and then click the **Security** log to view all events. Click the first event in the list to highlight it.
3. Right-click the **Security** log, select **View**, and then click **Find**.
4. In the Event source list box, click **Security**.
5. In the Category list box, click **Logon/Logoff**. Uncheck both the **Information** and **Success Audit** checkboxes.
6. In the User text box, type **AdminXX**, and then click the **Find Next** button a number of times. Notice that the event highlighted in the background continues to change as the Find command moves through the list of events in the log that meet the criteria specified.
7. Click the **Close** button.
8. Right-click the **Security** log icon, select **View**, and then click **Filter**. The properties dialog box of the Security log opens to the Filter tab.
9. Repeats Steps 4 to 7 above to provide the information that should be used to filter the log. Click **OK** once complete.
10. Notice that the security log is now filtered to display only those events that have met the specified criteria.
11. Double-click any of the events listed to view its properties. Notice that the source, category, and user sections meet the criteria that you specified in Step 9.
12. Right-click the **Security** log, select **View**, and then click **All Records**. Notice that all events now appear in the security log once again.
13. Close all open windows.

Configuring the Event Viewer

In the past, one of the problems with auditing a large number of events was that the security log becomes full very quickly. By default, the security log of a Windows 2000 server was set to a maximum default size of 512 KB and once it reached this size, logging stopped. This has been changed in Windows Server 2003, where the default initial security log size is 16 MB. However, this should not be used as an excuse to not check the security log regularly because events may be overwritten once the maximum log file size is reached depending on configured settings. One way to avoid this problem, which was already mentioned, is to audit only those events that are essential. Another way is to change the default settings or properties of the security log. Better still, make a point of reviewing and archiving the security log files on a regular basis.

To configure the properties of the security log, right-click the Security log and click Properties. The Security Properties dialog box opens, as illustrated in Figure 6-26. On the General tab you can configure the properties of the log, which you will do in Activity 6-16. Table 6-3 summarizes the configuration options available.

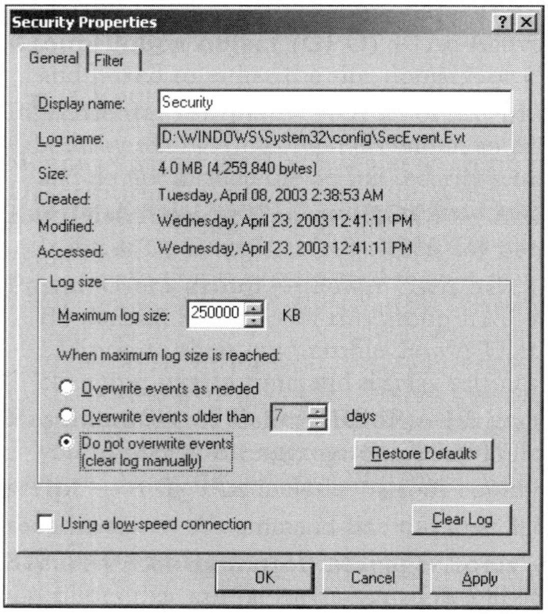

Figure 6-26 Configuring log properties

Table 6-3 Security log configuration options

Option	Description
Display name	Allows you to change the name of the log view; this is useful for distinguishing between different views of the same log or for distinguishing between logs on different computers.
Log name	Allows you to change the name and location of the log.
Size	Specifies the size of the log file; the default is 16 MB.
Overwrite events as needed	If you choose this option, all new events overwrite the oldest events when the log file becomes full; if you plan to use this option, check the log file at regular intervals.
Overwrite events older than *X* days	Allows you to set the number of days before a log is overwritten (between 1 and 365).
Do not overwrite events (clear log manually)	Events in the log are not overwritten and new events are discarded when the log becomes full and until the log is manually cleared.
Using a low connection speed	Specifies whether the log is located on another computer and whether you are connected using a low-speed device (such as a modem).

Hands-on Project

Activity 6-16: Editing Security Log Settings and Saving Events

Time Required: 10 minutes

Objective: Edit security log settings and save events for archiving purposes.

Description: The IT manager at Dover Leasing has asked you to implement a process to ensure that security log settings are never overwritten. Based on the large number of servers that will ultimately need to be managed at Dover, he has asked you to configure the security log settings to a maximum size of approximately 200 MB. Because log files must be emptied manually to ensure that events are not overwritten, he has also asked you to save the security log files using a date-related format. In this activity, you will configure the properties of the security log to meet the requirements outlined by the IT manager.

1. Open **Computer Management** and click the **plus sign (+)** next to Event Viewer to expand it, if necessary.
2. Right-click the **Security** log and then click **Properties**.
3. In the Log size section, type **250000** in the Maximum log size text box.
4. In the When maximum log size is reached section, click the **Do not overwrite events (clear log manually)** radio button and then click **OK**.
5. A message appears telling you that the log file size must be an increment of 64K. Click **OK** to continue.
6. Click **Action** on the menu bar, and then click **Save Log File As**.
7. In the File name text box, type **seclog-MM-DD-YY** using today's date for the filename variables.
8. Click the **Save as type** list arrow to view the different formats in which a log file can be saved. On this list, click **Event Log (*.evt)**, and then click the **Save** button.
9. Note that the security log events are not cleared as part of a save operation. It's worth noting that you are prompted to save events when you attempt to clear an event log, however.
10. Right-click the **Security** node and click **Clear all Events**. When prompted with whether you want to save the security log, click **No**. This will empty the security log with the exception of any new events.
11. Right-click the **Security** node and click **Open Log File**. Click the log file saved in Step 7 and then click **Security** in the Log type list box. Click **Open**. Notice that the contents of the saved log now appear in the security log.
12. Close all open windows.

MANAGING DATA STORAGE

Windows Server 2003 provides a number features for managing data storage. One of the features, known as a **dynamic disk**, overcomes many of the limitations and restrictions imposed by the traditional **basic disk**. **Disk quotas** are also supported in Windows Server 2003 to provide administrators with a way to track and limit the amount of disk space available to users. Both of these management features are discussed in the following section.

Basic versus Dynamic Disks

Windows Server 2003 supports two types of disks for storage: basic and dynamic. Basic disks are the traditional storage type and use primary partitions, extended partitions, and logical drives. Dynamic disks are a storage type originally introduced in Windows 2000 that include a variety of enhancements over basic disks, as illustrated in the following section.

You can configure a computer with both basic and dynamic disks at the same time, but if a volume, such as a mirrored volume, contains partitions from multiple physical disks, you must initialize all disks as the same type. As such, a mirrored volume could not span areas on both a basic and dynamic disk.

Basic Disks

A basic disk is divided into primary and extended partitions where each partition acts as a separate storage unit. You can configure a basic disk with a maximum of four primary partitions, or three primary partitions and one extended partition.

Primary partitions are used by default when Windows Server 2003 is installed on a new server. You can format each primary partition with either FAT, FAT32, or NTFS, and assign a drive letter. Of the primary partitions that are configured, you must mark one (and only one) as the active partition. Also known as the system partition, this is the partition that contains the files required to start the operating system. On Windows operating systems, the System partition is almost always drive C:.

> **Note** The boot partition is where the operating system files are installed. In a Windows Server 2003 installation, this is the partition where the %systemroot% (or Windows) folder resides. Unlike the system partition, the boot partition can be located on a primary or an extended partition.

To overcome the limitation of only being able to create four primary partitions on a basic disk, you also have the option of creating up to three primary and one extended partitions. You can create an extended partition using free hard-disk space. Extended partitions are not formatted or assigned a drive letter. Instead, the space within an extended partition is further divided into logical drives. Each logical drive within the extended partition is formatted and assigned a drive letter.

When you install Windows Server 2003, all disks are automatically initialized as basic. You can convert disks from basic to dynamic after the installation, or they can remain as basic.

Dynamic Disks

A dynamic disk does not use traditional partitioning, thus making it possible to set up a large number of volumes on one disk while providing the ability to extend volumes on to additional physical disks. Some of the reasons why you may opt to implement dynamic disks include the following:

- Volumes can be extended.
- RAID volumes can be configured.
- Missing or offline disks can be reactivated.
- Changes to disks can be made without having to restart the computer.
- Mirrored and RAID-5 volumes can be applied.

Dynamic disks do not contain primary and extended partitions but are instead configured with volumes. The different types of volumes that can be configured on a dynamic disk are discussed later in this section.

Configuring Volumes

The Disk Management snap-in is the tool used to centrally configure and manage volumes (you'll use this tool in Activity 6-17). Although you can add it to a new or existing MMC, Disk Management is also available as a node from within the Computer Management tool. When you click the Disk Management node in Computer Management, the details pane displays a graphical view of the physical drives and volumes on the system, as shown in Figure 6-27.

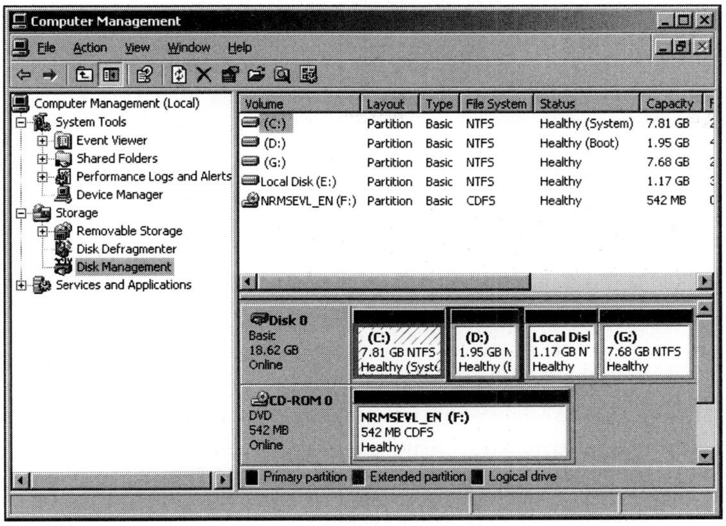

Figure 6-27 Graphical view within Disk Management

Before you can create any volumes on a Windows Server 2003 system, you must first convert disks from basic to dynamic; otherwise, the only options available will be to create traditional partitions. You can convert a basic disk to dynamic using the Disk Management snap-in; right-click the disk you want to convert and then click Convert to Dynamic Disk, as illustrated in Figure 6-28.

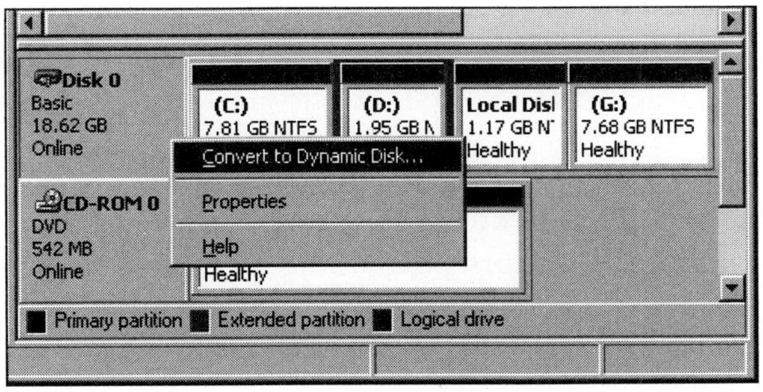

Figure 6-28 Converting to a Dynamic Disk

Keep the following key points in mind before you upgrade a disk from basic to dynamic:

- You must have administrative privileges to perform the upgrade.
- The disk must contain at least 1 MB of free space for the upgrade to succeed.
- No data is lost when you upgrade from basic to dynamic. To revert back to a basic disk, however, all volumes must first be deleted. You can then restore data from backup once the disk has been reverted to basic.
- Once upgraded, the disk can only be locally accessed by operating systems that support dynamic disks such as Windows 2000, Windows XP, or Windows Server 2003. Converting to a dynamic disk does not affect network access to shared resources on the disk.
- Once upgraded, primary and extended partitions become simple volumes.

Note

To create any new fault-tolerant volumes in Windows Server 2003, such as a mirrored or RAID-5 volume, disks must first be converted to dynamic.

Once you have converted to dynamic, you can create any of the following Windows Server 2003 volumes, depending on the number of physical disks in your computer:

- Simple volume
- Spanned volume
- Striped volume
- RAID 5 volume
- Mirrored volume

You create a simple volume from free space on a single disk. It can consist of a single area of free space or multiple areas of free space on the same disk. You can extend a simple volume to include an area of free space on the same disk or another physical disk. Once you extend a simple volume to include free space from another physical disk, it becomes a spanned volume. You create a simple volume within Disk Management by right-clicking an area of free space on the disk where the volume is to reside and clicking Create Volume.

A spanned volume consists of free space from multiple physical disks. It can include space from up to a maximum of 32 disks. When data is written to a spanned volume, it is first written to the free space on the first disk (filling all available space), and then written to the free space on the next physical disk. A spanned volume does not offer any fault tolerance. If any disk within the spanned volume fails, data within the entire volume is lost and must be restored from backup. You can create a spanned volume by right-clicking an area of free space and clicking the Create Volume option.

Note: The areas of free space included in a spanned volume do not have to be the same size.

You can add free space to a simple or spanned volume as long as it is formatted with the NTFS file system and does not contain the system or boot volume. You can extend a volume by selecting a volume in Disk Management and choosing the Extend Volume option. Of course, extending a volume requires that free disk space be available on at least one drive.

A striped volume writes data across two or more physical disks (up to 32) and is sometimes referred to as RAID-0. Data is written evenly across all disks in the volume in 64-KB blocks. For example, if you save a 320-KB file to a striped volume, the first 64 KB is written to disk one, the next 64 KB is written to disk two, and so on. Striped volumes offer high performance but no fault tolerance.

A RAID-5 volume is very similar to a striped volume, with the exception that it offers fault tolerance. RAID-5 requires a minimum of three physical disks to implement and can include space from up to 32 disks. Data is also written evenly across the disks in 64-KB blocks. The main difference with a RAID-5 volume is that parity information is also striped across the disks for use in reconstructing data in the event that a single physical disk in the volume should fail. Because of the parity information that is stored in a RAID-5 volume, the amount of overall disk space available on the volume is reduced. For example, in a RAID-5 implementation using four physical disks, 25% of the available storage space would be allocated to parity information.

A mirrored volume offers fault tolerance by duplicating data from one physical disk onto another one. Should one of the physical disks fail, data is still available from the mirrored copy. In terms of performance, a mirrored volume is slower in read performance than a RAID-5 volume but provides faster write performance.

Note: In some literature, you may see a mirrored volume described using the term *disk duplexing*. Disk duplexing refers to a mirrored volume configuration where each disk is connected to its own controller card.

Activity 6-17: Creating an Extended Partition and Logical Drives using Disk Management

Hands-on Project

Time Required: 10 minutes

Objective: Create an extended partition and a logical drive using the Disk Management tool.

Description: In the past, the IT staff at Dover Leasing has relied upon the DOS FDISK utility to create and manage partitions on Windows 98 workstations. Because the company has recently moved to using a combination of Windows XP Professional and Windows Server 2003 on most computers, the IT manager at Dover Leasing has asked you to test the Disk Management tool before evaluating any third-party disk-management utilities. In this activity, you will use the free space available on your hard drive to create a new extended partition and then define a new logical drive within that partition.

1. Open the **Computer Management** tool.
2. Click the **plus sign (+)** next to the Storage icon to view its contents if necessary, and then click **Disk Management**.
3. Review the current disk properties, including its size, its type (basic disk), and the fact that both existing partitions are primary partitions according to the legend at the bottom of the window.
4. Right-click an area of unallocated space at the end of Disk 0 and click **New Partition**.
5. Click **Next** at the New Partition Wizard welcome screen.
6. At the Select Partition Type screen, click the **Extended partition** radio button and read the Description section. Notice that the option to create a logical drive is not currently available because an extended partition doesn't currently exist. Click **Next**.
7. At the Specify Partition Size screen, ensure that the Partition size in MB text box matches the value found in the Maximum disk space in megabytes (MB) section and then click **Next**.
8. At the Completing the New Partition Wizard screen, click **Finish**.
9. In the Disk Management window, notice the new extended partition that is visible on Disk 0. Note also that because this is an extended partition, it is not formatted and does not have a drive letter assigned.
10. Right-click within the new extended partition and click **New Logical Drive**. When the New Partition Wizard welcome screen opens, click **Next**.
11. At the Select Partition Type screen, notice that the only available option is to create a logical drive. Click **Next**.
12. At the Specify Partition Size screen, ensure that the Partition size in MB text box matches the value found in the Maximum disk space in megabytes (MB) section and then click **Next**.
13. At the Assign Drive Letter or Path screen, accept the default value in the **Assign the following drive letter** list box and then click **Next**.
14. At the Format Partition screen, ensure that the **Format this partition with the following settings** radio button is selected. In the Volume label text box, type **Logical Drive** and then click **Next**.
15. At the Completing the New Partition Wizard screen, review the summary information provided in the You selected the following settings section and then click **Finish**.
16. After returning to the Disk Management details screen, notice that the Status column of the partition in the upper pane is set to Formatting and provides information as to the percentage of the format operation currently complete.
17. Once the format operation completes and the new partition's status is set to Healthy, close Computer Management.
18. Open **My Computer** and verify that the new logical drive is now accessible.
19. Close all open windows.

Disk Quotas

In all server environments, available disk space eventually becomes an issue. This is often a result of users storing large data files or archiving e-mail messages (which may include attachments) in their home directories. Depending on the number of users on the network and the amount of data they are storing, disk space can easily become scarce and needs to be managed.

Windows Server 2003 uses disk quotas as a means of monitoring and controlling the amount of disk space available to users. Administrators can use disk quotas as a capacity-planning tool or as a way of managing data storage.

Using disk quotas has the following advantages:

- Prevents users from consuming all available disk space
- Encourages users to delete old files as they reach their disk quota
- Allows an administrator to track disk usage for future planning
- Allows administrators to track when users are reaching their available limits

You can enable disk quotas on any NTFS volume, but they are disabled by default. By enabling disk quotas on a volume, you can see the amount of disk space that is being consumed by users, allowing you to use them as a capacity-planning tool. To use disk quotas as a management tool, you can set default quotas that specify the maximum amount of space allocated to network users. This is particularly useful for volumes hosting home folders, which tend to consume a lot of disk space. For example, many organizations establish a default quota of 10 to 100 MB per user on home folder volumes. The default quota prevents a few users from occupying disk space that is needed for all users, while also encouraging users to save only essential information and delete files and folders that are no longer needed.

Tip: Disk quotas can be implemented only on NTFS volumes, and they are set on a per-user/per-volume basis.

To configure disk quotas, access the properties of a volume and click the Quota tab, as shown in Figure 6-29. You will configure disk quotas as part of Activity 6-18.

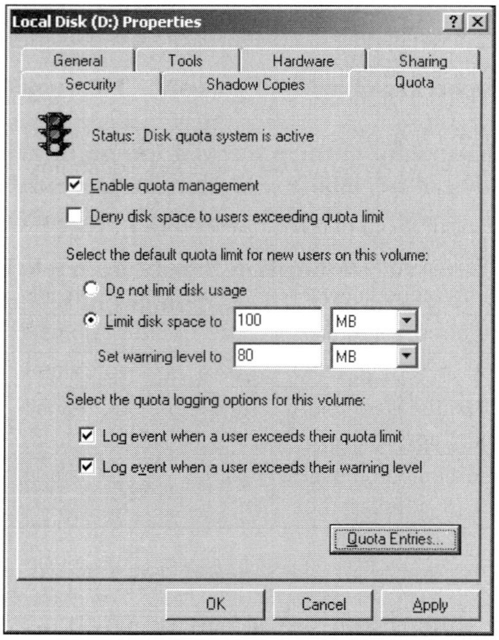

Figure 6-29 Configuring disk quotas

Table 6-4 summarizes the options available on the Quotas tab of an NTFS volume.

Table 6-4 Disk quota configuration parameters

Parameter	Description
Enable quota management	Tracks disk space on the volume and allows for the configuration of disk quotas
Deny disk space to users exceeding quota limit	Once users reach their quota limit, they are denied any more disk space
Do not limit disk usage	Tracks disk usage, but does not limit disk space to users
Limit disk space to	Sets the default amount of disk space that is available to users
Set warning level to	Sets the default amount of disk space that a user can consume before a warning message is sent to the user stating the quota is being reached
Log event when a user exceeds their quota limit	Causes an event to be entered in the system log to notify the administrator that the user has reached their quota
Log event when a user exceeds their warning level	Causes an event to be entered in the system log to notify the administrator that the user is approaching their quota

Exceptions can be created for users who require more disk space than others. You can set disk quotas for specific user accounts by clicking the Quota Entries button on the Quota tab, and then clicking New Quota Entry on the Quota menu. This allows you to choose the user account for which you want to establish a quota and configure appropriate quota limits for that user. This updates the Quota Entries dialog box to reflect the quota for that user account, as shown in Figure 6-30.

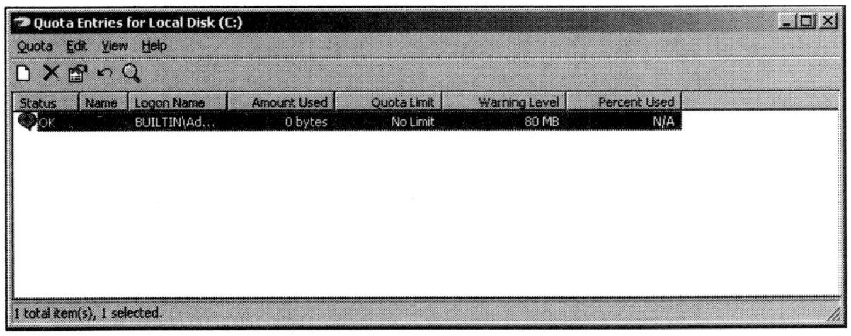

Figure 6-30 Configuring individual disk quota entries

It is important to keep in mind that the amount of disk space a user is currently occupying changes when ownership of files transfers from one user account to another. For example, imagine if Moira creates a database called Clients.mdb that occupies 1022 KB on a volume with disk quotas enabled. After Moira creates and saves the database, her available disk space is decreased by 1022 KB. If Moira later changes job roles within the company and John takes ownership of the database, Moira's available disk space would increase by 1022 KB, while John's would be decreased by the same amount.

Note: At any time, you can click the Quota Entries button to view both the disk quota limit and warning level configured for any account, as well as the amount of disk space currently being used by an account.

Activity 6-18: Configuring and Managing Disk Quotas

Time Required: 10 minutes

Objective: Enable and manage disk quotas settings.

Description: The IT manager at Dover Leasing is very concerned about the amount of disk space that users are allocated to store their personal files. In the past, users were told that they could use a maximum of 40 MB of disk space in their home folder, but a third-party quota-management system was never implemented. As such, many users simply ignored the directive, and available disk space is constantly an issue on Dover's servers. Understanding that Windows Server 2003 allows you to configure disk quotas for users on a partition-by-partition basis, the IT manager has asked you to test the implementation of quotas to determine whether or not they will meet Dover's needs.

1. Open **My Computer**.
2. Right-click drive **D:** and then click **Properties**.
3. Click the **Quota** tab. Notice that the status notice and icon both point out that disk quotas are currently disabled for the partition.
4. Click the **Enable quota management** check box.
5. Click the **Limit disk space to** radio button and type **100 MB** in the text boxes to its right.
6. In the Set warning level to text boxes, type **80 MB**.
7. Click the **Log event when a user exceeds their quota limit** check box.
8. Click the **Log event when a user exceeds their warning level** check box.
9. Review all of the choices selected. Notice that although quota information is tracked for this volume, the option to Deny disk space to users exceeding quota limit was not selected. As such, these quotas settings would be considered "soft" because they do not actually deny disk space to users and would instead be used for monitoring purposes. Click **OK**.
10. When the Disk Quota dialog box opens, read the message and then click **OK**. Allow a few minutes for the disk to be rescanned and quota information gathered if necessary.
11. Open the **Properties** of drive **D:** and click the **Quota** tab. Notice that the Disk quota system is now active and that the quota icon has changed.
12. Click the **Quota Entries** button.
13. In the Quota Entries dialog box, double-click the entry that appears for the user **Moira Cowan** to view its properties. Note the quota used and quota remaining information provided.
14. Change the quota entry for Moira Cowan such that her quota limit and warning level are both set to **1 KB**. Click **OK**. Notice that the icon next to the quota entry changes to a warning because this user is now over their quota limit.
15. Close all open Windows.

Managing File and Folder Compression

On volumes that are formatted with NTFS, you can enable data **compression** to reduce the amount of disk space that folders and files take up (as you will in Activity 6-19), thus allowing more data to ultimately be stored on the volume. Once a volume, folder, or file is compressed, you do not need any additional utilities to uncompress it. When a user accesses the file, it is automatically uncompressed in a manner completely transparent to the user.

Configuring compression is as simple as enabling or disabling the compression attribute of a file or folder within Windows Explorer. Enable compression by checking the Compress contents to save disk space check box, as illustrated in Figure 6-31.

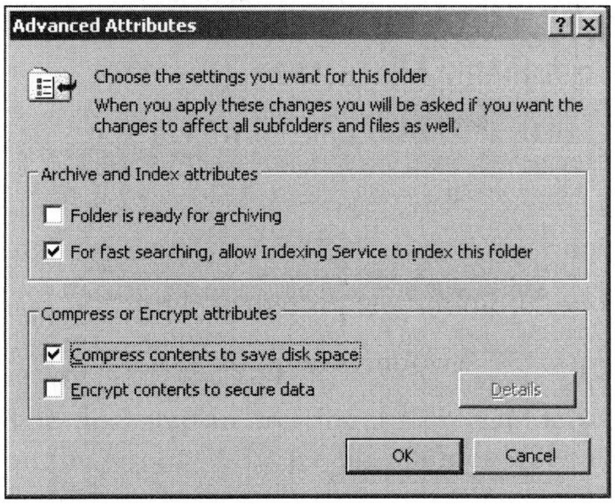

Figure 6-31 Setting the compression attribute

Note: Remember that compression and encryption are mutually exclusive. That is, even though it appears as though both can be selected simultaneously, only one of the two attributes can be configured at any point in time.

After a folder or file has been compressed, it is displayed in a different color within Windows Explorer (making it easy for an administrator to identify what is and what isn't compressed). Compressed folders and files are displayed in blue by default, though you can change this option from within the folder's options.

As with permissions and encryption, the compression attribute can be affected when copying and moving files. Keep the following points in mind when using the compression attribute:

- If a file is *copied* to another folder within the same NTFS volume, it automatically inherits the compression attribute of the destination folder.
- If a file or folder is *moved* within the same NTFS volume, it retains its compression attribute.
- If a file or folder is *copied* between NTFS volumes, the file or folder inherits the compression attribute of the destination folder.
- If a file or folder is *moved* between NTFS volumes, the file or folder inherits the compression attribute of the destination folder.

Note: Because compression is only available on NTFS volumes, if a folder or file is copied or moved to a FAT volume, the compression attribute is not retained.

Activity 6-19: Configuring Folder Compression

Time Required: 5 minutes

Objective: Configure a folder to compress its contents.

Description: Both the Legal and Marketing Departments at Dover Leasing generate enormous quantities of data over the course of a year. Although much of the old marketing data can be deleted after this time, all files belonging to the Legal Department must be archived indefinitely. Because of the large amount of disk space that this data occupies, the IT manager has asked you to evaluate ways in which the amount of disk space used by these files can be reduced. In this activity, you will test the impact of using the NTFS compression attribute to save disk space.

1. Open **My Computer**, and then browse to drive **D:**. Create a new folder called **Compress** and then copy the **setup.bmp** file from the C:\WINDOWS\System32 folder into this new folder.

2. Right click the **Compress** folder and click **Properties**. Note both the Size and Size on disk information provided on the **General** tab.
3. Click the **Advanced** button to open the Advanced Attributes dialog box.
4. In the Compress or Encrypt attributes section, click the **Compress contents to save disk space** check box and then click **OK**.
5. Click **OK** to exit the properties of the Compress folder.
6. When the Confirm Attribute Changes dialog box opens, ensure that the **Apply changes to this folder, subfolders and files** radio button is selected and then click **OK**.
7. In the My Computer interface, notice that the Compress folder is now listed in blue text, which designates it as having its compression attribute set.
8. Right-click the **Compress** folder and then click **Properties**. Notice that while the Size value has not changed, the Size on disk value is now significantly reduced from its original value.
9. Close all open windows.

Chapter Summary

- Two kinds of printer devices can be shared: a local print device, which is a print device connected to a port on a print server, or a network print device, in which the print device has its own network connection and IP address.
- You can publish both printer and folder shares into Active Directory to make it easy for clients to find the shared resources.
- You can use Auditing in Windows Server 2003 to monitor and track activities on a network. You can specify which events to monitor based on your security requirements. When an event does occur, a record of it is written to the security log.
- Windows Server 2003 supports both basic and dynamic disks.
- You can convert basic disks to dynamic disks without losing any data. To revert back to a basic disk, you must delete all volumes and restore data from backup.
- Depending on the number of users on the network and the amount of data they are storing, disk space can soon become scarce. Windows Server 2003 uses disk quotas as a way of managing data storage. You can configure disk quotas on a per-user/per-volume basis.
- You can use compression to save disk space on server volumes and partitions.

Key Terms

Active Directory client — This software allows legacy operating systems to perform searches in Active Directory; it also provides site awareness, the ability to use NTLMv2 authentication, and access to domain DFS resources.

audit policy — Defines the events on the network that Windows Server 2003 records in the security log as they occur.

auditing — The process that tracks the activities of users by recording selected types of events in the security log of a server or a workstation.

basic disk — The traditional storage type that divides physical disk space into primary partitions, extended partitions, and logical drives.

compression — Data is stored in a format that takes up less disk space, enabling you to store more data.

disk quotas — A Windows Server 2003 feature that is used as a means of monitoring and controlling the amount of disk space available to users.

dynamic disk — A new storage system supported by Windows Server 2003 that divides physical disk space into volumes.

Event Viewer — A component you can use to view and manage event logs, gather information about hardware and software problems, and monitor security events. Event Viewer maintains logs about program, security, and system events.

print device — The actual hardware device that produces the printed document. A local print device connects directly to a port on the print server. A network print device connects to a print server through its own network adapter and connection to the network.

print driver — Files that contain information that Windows Server 2003 uses to convert raw print commands to a language that the printer understands.

print server — The computer in which the printers and print drivers are located. This is usually where you set up and configure the shared printing system.

printer — A configuration object in Windows Server 2003 that controls the connection to the print device.

printer pool — Consists of a single printer that is connected to a number of print devices.

printer priorities — Configuring multiple printers to print to the same print device. One printer is then configured to print before any of the other printers by adjusting the priority setting from 1 (lowest priority) to 99 (highest priority).

published — An Active Directory object that represents a link or direct information on how to use or connect to the shared resource.

published folder — An Active Directory object that points to a related shared folder on a file server.

security log — A Windows Server 2003 event log used to record security events such as auditing information.

Review Questions

1. Your organization requires that all users be limited to 100 MB of disk storage space on each volume in which they store data, including the volume hosting home folders. How should you proceed?
   a. Configure a disk quota of 100 MB for each disk.
   b. Configure a warning level of 100 MB.
   c. Configure a disk quota of 100 MB for each volume.
   d. Limiting disk space is not possible in Windows Server 2003.
2. By default, disk quotas are enabled for each NTFS volume. True or False?
3. Mike and Jason both have a disk quota of 4 MB. Jason creates an employee database that is 600 KB in size. A change in job roles later requires Mike to take ownership of the database. How does this affect their available storage space?
   a. Both users' available storage space is decreased by 600 KB.
   b. Jason's available space remains the same. Mike's is decreased by 600 KB.
   c. Both users' available storage space is increased by 600 KB.
   d. Jason's available space is increased by 600 KB. Mike's is decreased by 600 KB.
4. The hard drive on a server is partitioned into four separate volumes. Users store data on volumes E, F, and G. Volume E is formatted with FAT32, and volumes F and G are both NTFS volumes. You attempt to enable disk quotas on volume E through the properties of the volume but cannot find the quota tab. What is the problem?
   a. The volume is currently in use.
   b. The volume must be formatted with NTFS.
   c. Disk quotas are enabled through Active Directory Users and Computers.
   d. You must use the Quotas command at the command prompt to enable disk quotas.

5. By default, auditing on all domain controllers is turned on. True or False?
6. Your company decides to audit access to confidential folders and files stored on all domain controllers. You are responsible for implementing the required audit policy. Through Windows Explorer, you attempt to configure the auditing settings on the Accounting Docs folder using the Auditing tab, but your access attempts are not successfully logged. What must you do first?
   a. Format the volume hosting the Accounting Docs folder with NTFS.
   b. Enable auditing for object access in the Default Domain Controllers Policy.
   c. Enable auditing for object access through the local security policy.
   d. Publish the share in Active Directory.
7. Which tool can be used to view the audit entries within the security log?
   a. Security Viewer
   b. Performance Monitor
   c. Event Monitor
   d. Event Viewer
8. The security log on your server is checked every other day for any new audit entries. How can you ensure that no entries are overwritten until they are checked by a member of the Administrators group or by a user with the appropriate user rights?
   a. Under the properties for the security log, click the option to "Overwrite events as needed."
   b. Under the properties for the security log, click the option "Overwrite events older than *X* days," and set the value to 2.
   c. Under the properties of the security log, set the default log size to 1 MB.
   d. Under the properties for the security log, click the option "Do not overwrite events (clear the log manually)."
9. What two ways can you give a user the right to view the security log? (Choose two answers.)
   a. Add them to the Administrators group.
   b. Add them to the Security group.
   c. Assign them the right to view the security log.
   d. Assign them the right to manage auditing and the security log.
10. Which Windows Server 2003 advanced printer configuration setting allows you to use multiple print devices as a single logical printer?
    a. Print Spooler
    b. printer pooling
    c. printer priority
    d. printer permissions
11. What is the default printer permissions assigned to users when they are added to the Security tab of a printer's properties?
    a. Print
    b. Manage Printers
    c. Manage Documents
    d. Full Control
12. An administrator at Dover Leasing wants to be able to search for user accounts that meet certain criteria on a regular basis. How is this most easily accomplished?
    a. by using the Find command in Active Directory Users and Computers
    b. by using the Search command on the Start menu

c. by writing a custom script

d. by using the Saved Queries feature in Active Directory Users and Computers

13. How often are Group Policy auditing settings refreshed on a Windows Server 2003 domain controller?

    a. every 10 minutes

    b. every 90 minutes

    c. every 5 minutes

    d. every 60 seconds

14. A compressed file that is moved to a different folder on the same NTFS partition retains its compression attribute. True or False?

15. A maximum of four primary partitions and one extended partition can be configured on a Windows Server 2003 basic disk. True or False?

16. Your Windows Server 2003 has an HP Laser Jet printer attached to it and is acting as a print server. A new driver has recently been released for Windows XP Professional clients. What must you do to distribute the updated drivers to the clients?

    a. Install the updated driver on the printer server, and manually update the driver on the Windows XP clients.

    b. Install the updated driver on the print server, and nothing more.

    c. Install the updated driver on the print server, and instruct users to manually download the new driver.

    d. Install the updated driver on the client workstations only.

17. You recently installed a new printer on your print server. Users are now reporting that their documents are not printing, and they cannot delete their documents from the print queue. You open up the print queue, see the documents listed, and discover that you cannot delete the entries. What is likely causing the problem?

    a. The Print Spooler service is stalled.

    b. The incorrect driver is installed.

    c. There is not sufficient space on the hard disk for spooling.

    d. Users do not have the correct protocol installed.

18. Which of the following offer fault tolerance? (Choose all that apply.)

    a. spanned volumes

    b. mirrored volumes

    c. striped volumes

    d. RAID-5 volumes

19. You want to configure an audit policy that will track when users attempt to delete a folder. Which of the following options should you enable in your audit policy?

    a. audit object access

    b. audit directory service access

    c. audit account management

    d. audit privilege use

20. You attempt to create a mirrored volume using Disk Management but are not given the option. You have not made any configuration changes since installing Windows Server 2003. What must you do?
    a. Format the partitions with NTFS.
    b. Convert the disks to basic.
    c. Convert the disks to dynamic.
    d. Reinstall Windows 2000.

Case Projects

Case Project 6-1

This case project involves configuring auditing and disk quotas. Dover Leasing is in the process of reviewing their current structure and practices. Management would like to know if there is a way to track user access so that if a security breach does occur, there is a record of it. Management has also expressed a concern over the amount of disk space users are consuming, and you need to come up with a solution to address this.

1. Once the appropriate permissions have been established, you want to be able to track user access to various folders. Explain how you can use auditing and the general steps that you need to complete to implement an audit policy.
2. Management has expressed a concern over disk usage because of the number of support calls indicating that server volumes are full. To date, all you have been doing is sending out memos asking users to delete any temporary or old files. Discuss how Dover Leasing can use disk quotas to limit usage and plan for future storage capacity requirements.

Case Project 6-2

Dover Leasing is in the process of adding two new print devices on the network. One is for the Managers group and the other is for the Sales and Accountants groups. Both printers are identical and are connected to two separate servers. You have been asked to advise the Help Desk users about how to set up the printers.

1. How should the new print devices be configured to ensure that network users can connect to them?
2. What permissions should be assigned to those users responsible for managing the printers?
3. Explain how printer permissions are configured so the appropriate groups have access to the printers.

Case Project 6-3

Dover Leasing is interested in implementing a disk-management strategy that will allow them to use the fault-tolerance features of Windows Server 2003. Outline each of the fault-tolerant disk methods available on Windows Server 2003, how they work, and the requirements for implementation.

Case Project 6-4

To understand how printer permissions work, consider the following example and answer the questions below.

Table 6-5 Permissions example

Users:	Group Membership:
User1	Sales Users, Marketing Users, Managers, Domain Users
User2	Help Desk Users, Managers, Domain Users, Domain Admins
User3	Accounting Users, Domain Users, Project Planners

Table 6-5 Permissions example (continued)

Printer	Printer Permissions
LaserJetA	Sales Users – Print
	Managers – Manager Documents
	Domain Users – Print
	Everyone – Print
	Domain Admins – Manage Printers
LaserJetB	Domain Users – Manage Documents
	Domain Admins – Manage Printers
	Help Desk Users – Print
LaserJetC	Accounting Users – Print
	Project Planners – Print
	Everyone – Deny Print
	Help Desk Users – Manage Documents

1. What permissions would User1 have to the LaserJetA printer?
2. What permissions would User2 have to the LaserJetC printer?
3. What permissions would User3 have to the LaserJetB printer?
4. What permissions would User1 have to the LaserJetB printer?
5. What permissions would User2 have to the LaserJetA printer?
6. What permissions would User3 have to the LaserJetC printer?

CHAPTER

7

ADMINISTERING WEB RESOURCES IN WINDOWS SERVER 2003

After reading this chapter and completing the exercises, you will be able to:

- Install and configure Internet Information Services (IIS)
- Create and configure Web-site virtual servers and virtual directories
- Configure Web-site authentication
- Configure and maintain FTP virtual servers
- Update and maintain security for an IIS server
- Create and modify Web folders
- Install and use the Remote Administration (HTML) tools
- Troubleshoot Web client-browser connectivity

Windows Server 2003 includes a variety of Internet-related services that can assist a company in developing an effective online Internet or intranet presence. Companies are beginning to realize the potential and importance of Web-based services to provide employees and customers efficient and alternative ways of interacting with the organization.

To help develop and host these services, Microsoft has included an application called **Internet Information Services (IIS)** within Windows Server 2003. IIS provides the foundation for the Web-related services that an organization needs to create an effective and secure Internet or intranet presence. In this chapter, you learn how to install, configure, maintain, and secure a Windows Server 2003 IIS server. You also learn how to configure each of the components that IIS has to offer an organization, such as Web and FTP services. The final section of this chapter discusses client connectivity troubleshooting issues that you may face as users attempt to access the Internet or your internal intranet.

Installing and Configuring Internet Information Services

Internet Information Services (IIS) 6.0 is a Windows Server 2003 application that provides Web-related services to an organization. IIS consists of four main components:

- *World Wide Web (HTTP) services*—Provides the capability of hosting multiple Web sites accessible from the Internet or an intranet
- *File Transfer Protocol (FTP) services*—Can be installed and configured to have the ability to copy files between the server and a remote location
- *Network News Transfer Protocol (NNTP) services*—Used to provide a means of maintaining a list of topics and threaded conversations between users, such as a corporate discussion newsgroup in which employees can post messages and read replies related to various company matters
- *Simple Mail Transfer Protocol (SMTP) services*—Included in IIS to provide e-mail capabilities to the other services, such as HTTP or NNTP; for example, you might create a Web form that requires the response to be e-mailed to another location

These services can be implemented to host a corporate intranet or Internet presence. An organization that hosts a corporate intranet can provide employees with the following:

- Interactive online company resources, such as employee handbook information, employee news, or department meeting minutes
- Team collaboration using various applications, such as Office XP
- Web-based applications to assist employees in filling out forms or other internal business processes

An Internet presence for an organization can provide customers with the following:

- Additional customer service, such as online manuals or frequently asked questions about products or services
- The ability to order products online and track shipping progress
- Dynamic company information and news bulletins

To make these services available to your employees and customers, it is important that you understand how to configure, maintain, and secure IIS. These concepts are discussed in the sections that follow.

Installing Internet Information Services

Unlike previous versions in Microsoft server platforms, IIS 6.0 is not installed by default during a standard installation of Windows Server 2003. Instead, you can manually install individual IIS components via the Add or Remove Programs applet in Control Panel.

Table 7-1 lists and explains each of the individual components you can install as part of IIS.

Table 7-1 Internet Information Services components

IIS Component	Purpose
Background Intelligent Transfer Service (BITS) server extension	Allows clients to use spare bandwidth for data transfers and resume transfers in the event that a session disconnects or a computer restarts
Common Files	The required IIS program files
File Transfer Protocol (FTP) Service	Used to install and create FTP sites, which allow you to upload and download files to and from the server
FrontPage 2002 Server Extensions	Enables creating, developing, and maintaining Web sites with Microsoft FrontPage and Visual InterDev
Internet Information Services Manager	Installs the Internet Information Services MMC snap-in to allow IIS server management

Table 7-1 Internet Information Services components (continued)

IIS Component	Purpose
Internet Printing	Enables Web-based printer management and allows printing to a shared printer via the HTTP protocol
NNTP Service	Enables an IIS server to function as a NNTP server to distribute, receive, and post Usenet articles
SMTP Service	Enables an IIS server to function as a SMTP Server, which gives the ability to provide support for e-mail on a network or the Internet
World Wide Web Service	Enables an IIS server to function as a Web server on an intranet or the Internet

In Activity 7-1, you will install IIS components on your server.

Activity 7-1: Installing Internet Information Services

Time Required: 20 minutes

Objective: Install Internet Information Services components.

Description: Dover Leasing has hosted their Web site on an Apache-based Linux server for the past four years. Although this Web site has met their needs, the IT manager has decided that the entire site should be moved over to a Windows Server 2003 system running IIS to eventually take advantage of advanced features such as ASP.NET. In this activity, you will install IIS 6.0 on your server for testing purposes.

1. Click **Start**, select **Control Panel**, and then click **Add or Remove Programs**.
2. In the Add or Remove Programs dialog box, click the **Add/Remove Windows Components** button to open the Windows Components Wizard.
3. On the Windows Components screen of the Windows Components Wizard, as shown in Figure 7-1, click **Application Server** in the Components list box and then click the **Details** button.

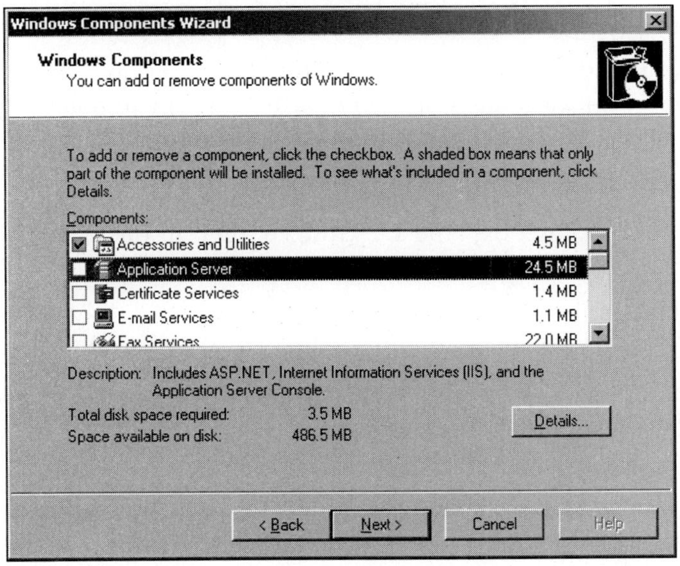

Figure 7-1 Installing Internet Information Services using the Windows Components Wizard

4. In the Application Server dialog box, click **Internet Information Services (IIS)** in the Subcomponents of Application Server list box and then click the **Details** button.

5. In the Internet Information Services (IIS) dialog box, shown in Figure 7-2, click each individual component listed in the Subcomponents of Internet Information Services (IIS) list box to read its description.

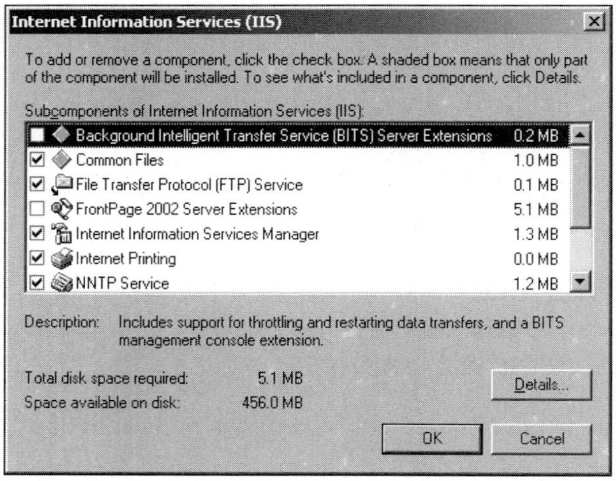

Figure 7-2 Viewing additional IIS applications and components

6. Ensure that the ckeckboxes next to the following services are checked:
   - Common Files
   - File Transfer Protocol (FTP) Service
   - Internet Information Services Manager
   - Internet Printing
   - NNTP Service
   - SMTP Service
   - World Wide Web Service

   Once these boxes are checked, click **OK**.
7. On the Application Server screen, notice that the Internet Information Services check box is checked but slightly grayed out. This means that only some of the IIS subcomponents were selected. Click **OK**.
8. At the Windows Components screen, click **Next**.
9. If prompted with the Files Needed dialog box, type **D:\Source\i386** in the text box and click **OK**.
10. Once all components have installed, click the **Finish** button, and then close the Add or Remove Programs dialog box.

After a successful installation of IIS, you notice a number of changes on the server. Some of these changes include additional folders on the hard drive, additional user objects in Active Directory, and additional services installed within the operating system.

It is important to understand the location and purpose of the folders that are created by IIS during installation. By default, it is in these folders that the IIS system files and the physical files for your Default Web or FTP site are located. Table 7-2 explains these folders in greater detail.

Installing IIS also adds two new user accounts and one new group account to Active Directory Users and Computers. The first user object is ISUSR_*servername,* which is an account that IIS uses to provide **Anonymous access** to the server. The second user object is IWAM_*servername,* which is an account used to allow IIS to start out-of-process applications. The IIS_WPG group is the IIS 6.0 worker process group that serves individual namespaces like *www.dovercorp.net* configured on the server. Individual user accounts should not be added to the IIS_WPG group.

Note When IIS is installed on a domain controller, these user and group accounts are added to the Active Directory database. When installed on a member server, the accounts are added to that server's local accounts database.

Figure 7-3 highlights the new accounts created in Active Directory after IIS is successfully installed.

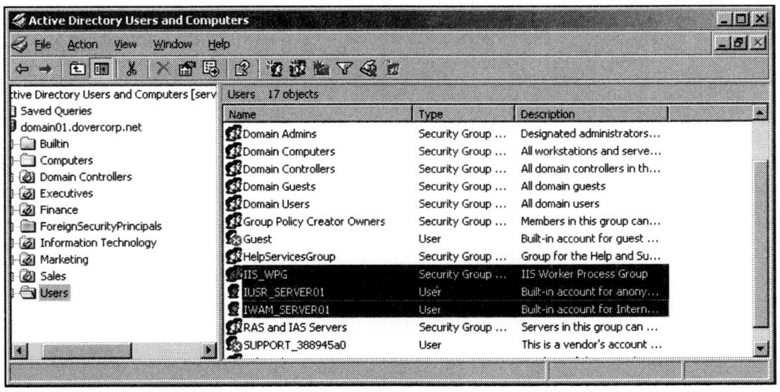

Figure 7-3 Viewing the IIS user and group accounts

Table 7-2 IIS folder structure

Folder	Contents
%systemroot%\system32\inetsrv	Contains all of the program files and dll files needed for IIS to function
C:\Inetpub	Contains various sub-folders, such as ftproot, wwwroot, nntproot, and mailroot, which store all of the source content for the FTP, Web, NNTP, and SMTP services provided by the server
C:\WINDOWS\Help\iishelp	Contains the IIS documentation

Installing IIS also adds several operating-system services to Windows Server 2003, which you can view and control from the Services console on the Administrative Tools menu. The new services available after an IIS installation include:

- *FTP Publishing Service*—Provides an FTP Server service (daemon) that enables FTP clients to upload and download files to and from the FTP Server
- *IIS Admin Service*—Provides the programmatic interface for managing IIS and its components; it is also the parent process for all IIS services, which means that to stop this service, all other IIS services must be stopped
- *Network News Transfer Protocol (NNTP)*—Provides an NNTP Server that enables newsreader clients to post and read messages, and enables IIS to exchange NNTP messages with other NNTP servers in your organization and on the Internet
- *Simple Mail Transfer Protocol (SMTP)*—Provides an SMTP Server that enables the sending and receiving of SMTP e-mail messages
- *World Wide Web Publishing Service*—Provides a Web Server that can host one or more Web Sites

Figure 7-4 shows the Services console open with the FTP Publishing Service highlighted.

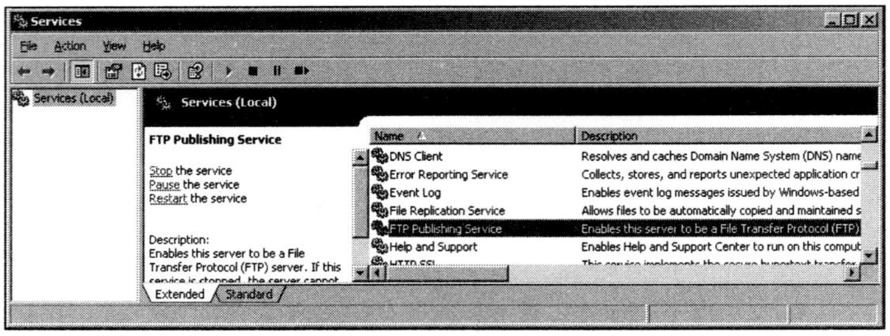

Figure 7-4 Viewing the IIS Services

Additionally, installing IIS also allows you to use the Web sharing feature to make files and folders available to network clients via the HTTP protocol. We'll explore Web sharing in more detail later in this chapter. In Activity 7-2, you will explore the system changes that occur as a result of installing IIS.

Activity 7-2: Viewing System Changes after Installing IIS

Time Required: 10 minutes

Objective: View changes made to Windows Server 2003 after installing IIS.

Description: Because you will be responsible for the configuration and security of Dover Leasing's Web servers once implemented, you want to better understand the changes that IIS makes to a Windows Server 2003 system once installed. In this activity, you will browse through user, group, directory, and service changes to obtain a picture of how an IIS installation will impact your servers.

1. Open **Active Directory Users and Computers**.
2. Click on your domain to expand it, if necessary, and then click the **Users** container to view its contents.
3. Browse for the **IIS_WPG**, **IUSR_*servername*** and **IWAM_*servername*** accounts to read the description associated with each. Open the properties of each to view the groups of which these objects are members.
4. Close Active Directory Users and Computers.
5. Open **My Computer** and browse to the **C:** drive.
6. Double-click the **Inetpub** folder to view its contents. This is where the various 'root' folders are located for different IIS services.
7. Open the **wwwroot** folder, and then double-click the file **iisstart.htm** to open it. The file will open in Internet Explorer and will display the "under construction" message.
8. In the Internet Explorer address bar, type **http://localhost** and press **Enter**. Notice that your Web server opens the page viewed in Step 7.
9. Close Internet Explorer.
10. In the My Computer window, browse to the **C:\WINDOWS\system32\inetsrv** folder to view the files and folders required by IIS to function.
11. Close My Computer.
12. Click **Start**, select **Administrative Tools**, and then click **Services**.

13. In the Services window, browse for the following services, making note of their current status and startup types:
    - FTP Publishing Service
    - IIS Admin Service
    - Network News Transfer Protocol (NNTP)
    - Simple Mail Transfer Protocol (SMTP)
    - World Wide Web Publishing Service
14. Double-click the **Network News Transfer Protocol (NNTP)** icon to view its properties.
15. On the **General** tab, click the **Stop** button to stop the service, click **Manual** in the Startup type list box, and then click **OK**. This will prevent the NNTP service from starting automatically the next time your server reboots.
16. Close all open windows.

Architectural Changes in IIS 6.0

Although IIS version 6.0 is in many ways similar to the 5.0 version included with Windows 2000, a number of architectural changes have been introduced. Most of these changes relate to how processes are managed and maintained by IIS, although the central storage location for IIS configuration information, known as the **metabase**, has also changed. In previous IIS versions, the metabase was stored as a single binary file named Metabase.bin. Although this file served its function well, its binary nature made it difficult to read the file directly and make changes to it. In IIS 6.0, the metabase is now stored in two standard Extensible Markup Language (XML) files, known as MetaBase.xml and MBSchema.xml. The purpose of each of these files is outlined as follows:

- MetaBase.xml—This file contains the actual configuration settings for IIS 6.0
- MBSchema.xml—This file contains the XML schema that provides the default values of the various metabase properties

One advantage of the metabase configuration being stored in XML format is the ability to easily read and diagnose issues, because the files are stored in a human-readable format that can be viewed with any text editor. Secondly, the XML files provide better read performance than the old Metabase.bin file, resulting in faster service startup. Finally, the metabase being stored in XML format provides an industry-standard data representation method that can easily be programmed to.

Tip

Both the MetaBase.xml and MBSchema.xml files can be found in the %systemroot%\system32\inetsrv directory.

A number of process management and administration features have also been introduced with IIS 6.0. These features are designed to help ensure a more robust environment that provides better overall system stability, performance, and administrative capabilities. Table 7-3 outlines some of these new features and their intended purpose.

Table 7-3 IIS 6.0 Process management and administration features

New Feature	Purpose
HTTP.SYS	A kernel-mode driver that now accepts and manages all incoming HTTP requests. All HTTP responses are cached in kernel mode, eliminating the need to switch to user mode and thus delivering better performance.
IIS 5.0 Isolation Mode	An application mode that ensures compatibility for applications designed to run on IIS 5.0.

Table 7-3 IIS 6.0 Process management and administration features (continued)

New Feature	Purpose
Worker Process Isolation Mode	An application mode that puts different applications into their own application pool. Each pool has its own worker processes and remains independent of other pools, thus providing a higher level of system reliability, given that one pool will not crash another.
Remote Administration (HTML) tool	IIS 6.0 provides the Remote Administration (HTML) tool to allow administrators to manage an IIS server from any Web browser.

For more information on the new architectural and management features of IIS 6.0, see the Internet Information Services 6.0 Administrator Guide — %systemroot%\Help\iis.chm.

Configuring Web Server Properties

After installing the IIS components, the IIS MMC snap-in is the primary tool used for configuration purposes. This tool is available on the Administrative Tools menu, and is shown in Figure 7-5.

Note: Windows Server 2003 also includes a number of Visual Basic scripts that allow you to configure individual sites and their elements from the command line. Many of these scripts will be explored in activities later in this chapter.

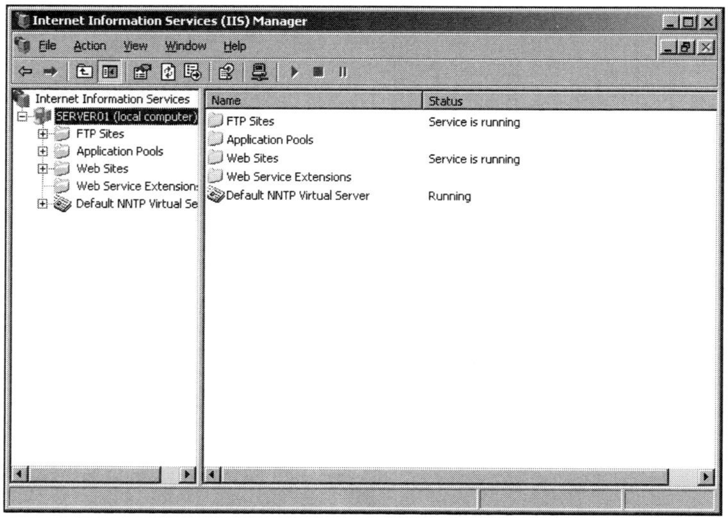

Figure 7-5 The Internet Information Services console

As illustrated in Figure 7-5, the IIS console displays the default sites and services that are initially installed. As more Web sites and FTP servers are added to the server, they appear as individual nodes in the interface that can be independently started, stopped, and configured. The default sites and services are described as follows:

- *FTP Sites*—This folder holds all configured FTP sites, including the **Default FTP Site** that responds to TCP port 21 on all of the server's configured IP addresses that are not assigned to another FTP site.
- *Application Pools*—This folder holds applications that are assigned to one or more Web sites, which isolates their processes from other Web sites.
- *Web Sites*—This folder holds all configured Web sites, including the **Default Web Site** that responds to TCP port 80 on all unassigned IP addresses of the server. This Web site is initially empty except for the "under construction" page placed in the wwwroot directory by default and may be used to create a custom Web site for your organization.

- *Web Service Extensions*—By default, IIS disables all request handlers designed to process dynamic content such as Active Server Pages or CGI extensions. This folder allows you to control the status of existing extensions and add new ones.
- *Default SMTP Virtual Server*—This e-mail component server responds to port 25 on all of the server's IP addresses that have not been assigned to another SMTP site.
- *Default NNTP Virtual Server*—This newsgroup server responds to port 119 on all of the server's configured IP addresses that have not been assigned to another NNTP site.

As you create new Web or FTP sites, each has its own icon listed in appropriate folder in the details pane of the console. Creating new Web and FTP sites is discussed in greater detail later in the chapter. In Activity 7-3, you will explore the interface of the IIS MMC snap-in.

Activity 7-3: Exploring the Internet Information Services MMC Snap-in

Hands-on Project

Time Required: 5 minutes

Objective: Explore the IIS MMC snap-in.

Description: Although it has been decided that you will ultimately be responsible for managing all IIS servers at Dover Leasing, a number of users in the Web groups will be responsible for the day-to-day administration of individual servers. The IT manager at Dover Leasing is worried that these users will not properly understand the impact of any changes that they make and has asked you to develop a short training class that will teach them how to use the IIS MMC console. In this activity, you will explore the basic console layout and navigation.

1. Click **Start**, select **Administrative Tools**, and then click **Internet Information Services (IIS) Manager**.
2. If necessary, click the **plus sign (+)** next to your server to expand its contents. Click the **FTP Sites** node to view its contents. Notice that the Default FTP Site is listed, along with its status.
3. Click the **plus sign (+)** next to Application Pools to view its contents. By default, only a single Application Pool known as the DefaultAppPool exists.
4. Click the **plus sign (+)** next to Web Sites to view its contents. Notice that only the Default Web Site exists because no additional Web sites have been defined.
5. Click **Web Service Extensions** to view its contents. Notice the default status' of the built-in extensions, as shown in Figure 7-6.

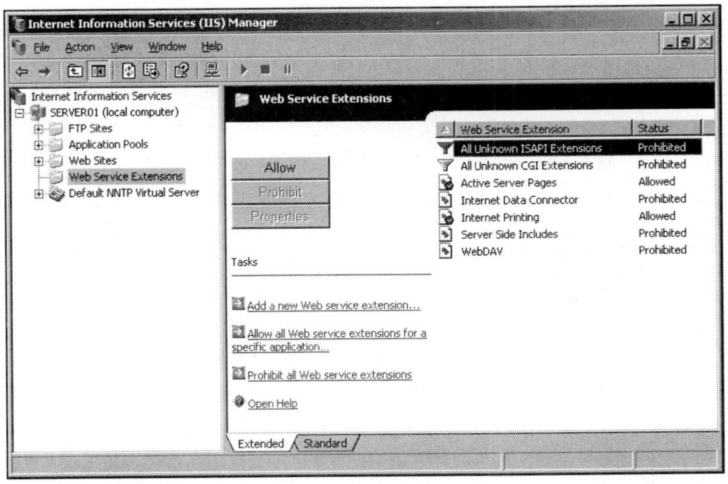

Figure 7-6 Viewing Web Service Extensions in the IIS Console

6. Click **Default SMTP Virtual Server** to view its contents.
7. Click **Default NNTP Virtual Server** to view its contents. Also notice that the icon associated with the service identifies it as being stopped, a result of stopping the service in the previous activity.
8. Leave the Internet Information Services window open.

Caution

To increase security, it is recommended to stop any IIS site or service that you are not using in your organization.

The first step in configuring IIS is to understand how configuration settings can be implemented on a server-wide basis. By accessing the properties of the Web Sites or FTP Sites folder in the Internet Information Services tool, **master properties** can be configured for all Web and FTP sites hosted on the server, as shown in Figure 7-7. Master properties are IIS parameters that are configured at the site-folder level and are inheritable by all Web or FTP sites hosted on the server. If your IIS server hosts a large number of sites, this feature is convenient because you can quickly set various common configurations, such as security and performance tuning, on all Web or FTP sites at once rather than configuring all settings on each site individually.

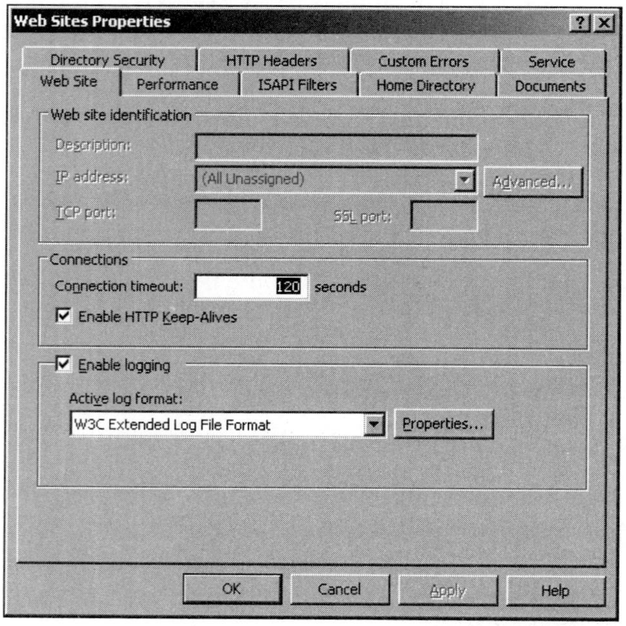

Figure 7-7 Configuring the master properties of an IIS Web site

Any property that is not specific to an individual site can be set at the site-folder level. For example, you cannot set the TCP port at the site-folder level because each Web site might be using different port numbers. However, if you want to limit all Web sites on your server to a specific number of connections, you are able to configure this as a site-folder property and have it be inherited by all sites on the server.

If an individual site has its own configuration settings, and you decide to change the master properties, IIS gives you the option of whether or not to apply the changes to the preconfigured site. For example, if you configure the Default Web Site to only allow 500 connections and then set the master properties on the Web Sites folder to allow 700 connections, you will be prompted with the Inheritance Overrides dialog box asking which existing sites should inherit the new settings. This is illustrated in Figure 7-8.

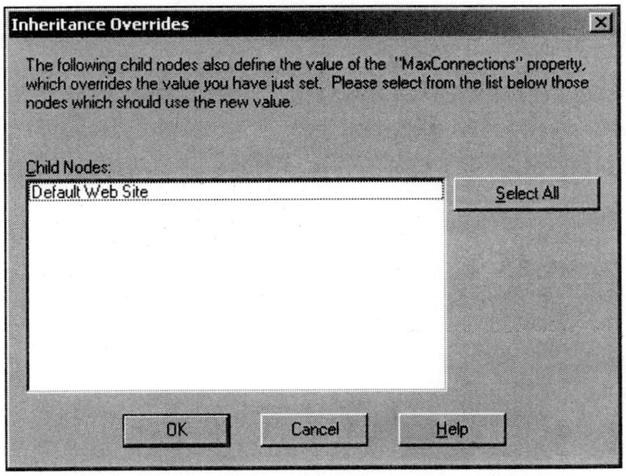

Figure 7-8 Configuring Inheritance Overrides

Any configuration settings that are changed at the site, folder, or file level override the Master Properties and allow you to determine how inheritance takes place for any objects below the level that you are modifying. In Activity 7-4, you will configure the master properties of the WWW service on your server.

Activity 7-4: Viewing and Configuring the Master Properties of the WWW Service

Time Required: 10 minutes

Objective: Configure the master properties of the WWW service.

Description: Although Dover Leasing currently has only one public Web site, the company is looking to move more of their internal processes to Web-based platforms in the future. Ultimately, this could lead to each Web server at Dover having 10 or more Web sites installed. Although changing the properties of these Web sites individually might be possible, you would rather avoid it based on your growing workload. In this activity, you will explore and configure settings on the master property sheets of a Web server.

1. In the Internet Information Services window, right-click the **Web Sites** folder and click **Properties**.
2. On the **Web Site** tab, click the **Properties** button in the Enable logging section.
3. In the Logging Properties dialog box, click the **Weekly** radio button in the New log schedule section. Notice the location and naming convention for the log file as listed on the lower portion of the screen. Click **OK**.
4. Click the **Performance** tab. In the Web site connections section, click the **Connections limited to** radio button, and in the corresponding spin box type **700**.
5. Click **OK** to exit the Web Sites Properties dialog box.
6. To test whether the master properties configuration settings were inherited, click the **plus sign (+)** next to the Web Sites folder to expand it if necessary, right-click **Default Web Site**, and then click **Properties**.
7. Click the **Properties** button in the Enable logging section to verify that Weekly is specified in the New log schedule section. Click **OK**.
8. Click the **Performance** tab to verify that the Default Web Site now has a Connections limited to value of 700. Click **OK** to close the Default Web Site Properties dialog box.
9. Leave the Internet Information Services window open.

Creating and Configuring Web-Site Virtual Servers

IIS has the ability to host a large number of Web sites or **virtual servers** on a single server. A virtual server is simply a unique Web site that behaves as if it were on its own dedicated server. To make sure that no configuration conflicts take place between sites, you should consider the following details about each site before beginning the configuration process:

- Identify the IP address to which the Web site responds.
- Identify the TCP port to which the Web site responds.
- If you have multiple virtual servers responding to the same IP address, identify the **host header** name to which your new Web site responds.

Each Web site on your server must have a way of being uniquely identified. There are three ways that you can be sure that each Web site is unique:

- Use a separate IP address to distinguish each Web site. This requires you to configure multiple IP addresses on the server's network interface(s).
- Use a single IP address with a specific port number for each Web site. For example, you might have a Web site at 192.168.1.100 with a host name of *www.dovercorp.net* that uses the default port 80, and another Web site using the same IP address, but with the host name *www.sevenacres.com*, which uses port 8000. The client connecting to *www.sevenacres.com* would then have to append a colon and the port number to the IP address or fully qualified domain name (FQDN) to access the second site, as in 192.168.1.100:8000 or *www.sevenacres.com:8000.*
- Use a single IP address with multiple host headers representing each Web site. A host header is usually the fully qualified DNS name that clients type in to their browser to a Web site. For example, if you host two Web sites on your server, you may create *www.dovercorp.net* and *www.sevenacres.com* as host headers for the single IP address 192.168.1.100.

Note: To enable the use of host names or FQDNs, you must configure proper DNS entries for each of the preceding points. DNS resolves host names and FQDNs to IP addresses. For example, you could type *www.dovercorp.net* instead of having to remember the IP address associated with the Web site. More information on DNS is discussed in Chapter 9.

In Activity 7-5, you will configure a new Web site to accept requests on TCP port 8080.

Activity 7-5: Creating a New Web Site Using the Web Site Creation Wizard

Time Required: 20 minutes

Objective: Create a new Web site using the Web Site Creation Wizard.

Description: After you showed the IT manager your basic configuration of the Default Web Site, he has asked you to create a new and dedicated site for the *Dovercorp.net* domain. This site will initially be used for testing purposes as the Web designers at Dover work on designing and testing the use of various dynamic-content programming features. Because your server only has one IP address currently assigned, you decide to change the port number of the existing site so that the designers can access the new site using the default HTTP port. In this activity, you will first change and test the port number assigned to the Default Web Site and then create a new site to be used by the designers at *Dovercorp.net*.

1. In the Internet Information Services window, click the **plus sign (+)** next to the Web Sites folder to expand it, if necessary. Right-click the **Default Web Site** and click **Properties**.
2. On the **Web Site** tab, type **8080** in the TCP port text box, and then click **OK**.

3. Right-click the **Default Web Site** icon and click **Stop**. Once the site is listed as stopped in the State section of the details pane, right-click the **Default Web Site** again, and click **Start**.
4. To test whether the Default Web Site is still responding on TCP port 80, open **Internet Explorer** and type **http://localhost** in the address bar and press **Enter**. A message stating that the page cannot be displayed will appear because the Default Web Site is now listening for requests on TCP port 8080.
5. In the Internet Explorer address bar, type **http://localhost:8080**, and press **Enter**. The "Under Construction" message should now appear.
6. Open **My Computer**, and create a new folder on your **D:** drive called **Dovercorpwebsite**. Close My Computer.
7. In the Internet Information Services window, right-click the **Web Sites** folder, select **New**, and then click **Web Site**.
8. At the Web Site Creation Wizard welcome screen, click **Next**.
9. At the Web Site Description screen, type **Dovercorp.net** in the Description text box and click **Next**.
10. At the IP Address and Port Settings screen, illustrated in Figure 7-9, accept the default values and click **Next**.

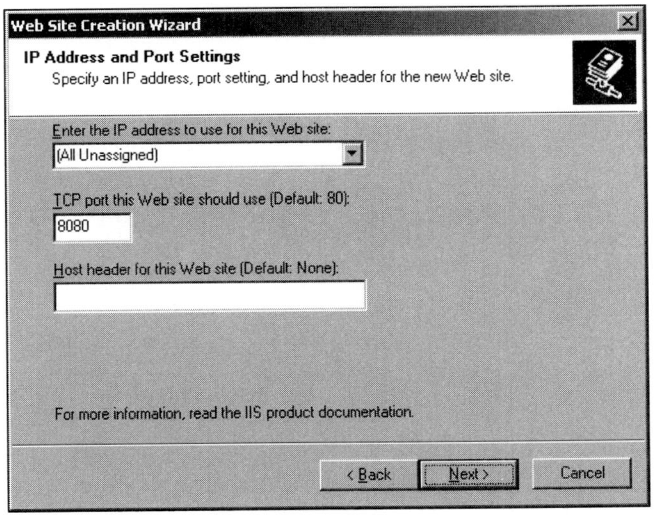

Figure 7-9 Assigning an IP Address and port number to a new Web site

11. At the Web Site Home Directory screen, type **D:\dovercorpwebsite** in the Path text box and click **Next**.
12. At the Web Site Access Permissions screen, as illustrated in Figure 7-10, click the **Browse** check box and then click **Next**.
13. Click **Finish** to complete the Web Site Creation Wizard.
14. Verify that the new *Dovercorp.net* Web site appears under the Web Sites folder.
15. Leave the Internet Information Services window open.
16. Open **My Computer** and browse to the **D:\Dovercorpwebsite** folder.
17. Create a new text file in the folder called **index.txt**, and then open the file.

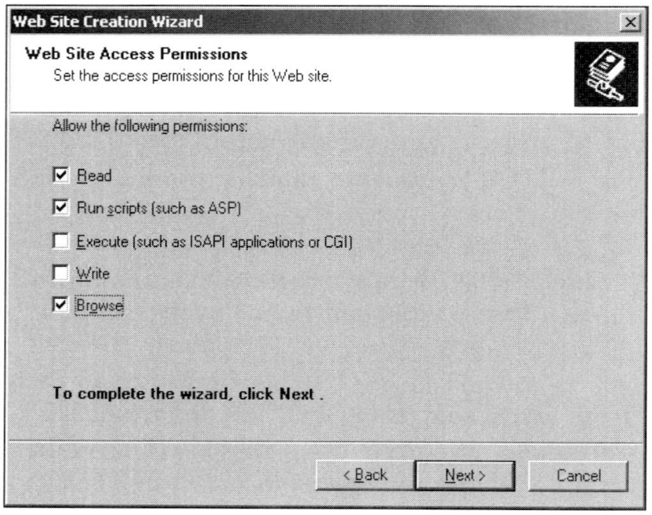

Figure 7-10 Configuring Web site access permissions

18. Type the following HTML code into the file:

```
<html>
<head>
<title>Dovercorp.net Web Page</title>
</head>
<body>
<h1>Dovercorp.net Web Site Test</h1>
</body>
</html>
```

    Save and close the file, and then rename it **index.htm**. At the Rename warning message, click **Yes**.

19. In Internet Explorer, attempt to open the page **http://localhost**. The HTML page created in Step 18 will appear.
20. Close all open windows.

The Web Site Creation Wizard provides a simple, step-by-step method of creating and initially configuring Web sites. However, administrators are often required to create many different Web sites on different servers throughout an organization. To help facilitate and automate this process, Microsoft provides a variety of VB scripts that an administrator can use to automate IIS configuration tasks. An example of such a script is iisweb.vbs, which can be used to create new Web sites from the Windows Server 2003 command line. In Activity 7-6, you will create a new Web site from the command line using the iisweb.vbs script.

Activity 7-6: Creating a New Web Site Using the iisweb.vbs Script

Time Required: 10 minutes

Objective: Create a new Web site using a script instead of the Internet Information Services tool.

Description: While exploring the Windows Server 2003 Help and Support Center documentation, you learn that you can also create Web sites using VB scripts provided when IIS was installed. In this activity, you will create a new Web site for testing purposes using the iisweb.vbs script.

1. Click **Start**, click **Run**, and then type **cmd** in the **Open** text box. Click **OK**.
2. Type **mkdir d:\testsite** at the command prompt and press **Enter**. This directory will be used as the home directory for the new Web site. Type c:\windows\system32 and press Enter.

3. Type **cscript iisweb.vbs /create d:\testsite "New Web Site Test" /b 8100 /dontstart** at the command prompt and press **Enter**. This command will create a new website called New Web Site Test that uses TCP port 8100 for connections and is not started by default.
4. The results of the iisweb command will be displayed, as shown in Figure 7-11.

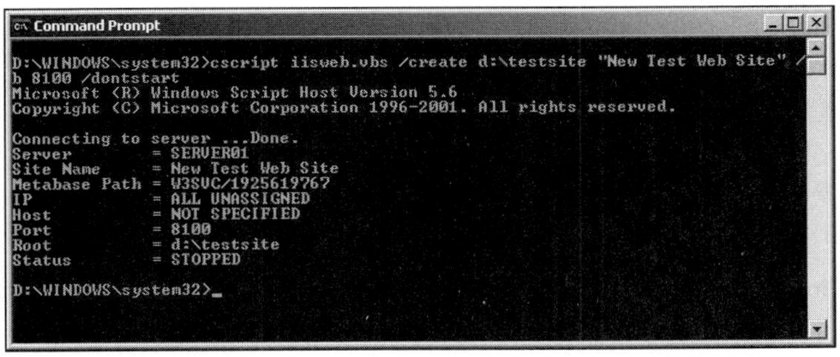

Figure 7-11 Creating a Web site using the Iisweb.vbs script

5. Close the command prompt, and then open the **Internet Information Services** tool.
6. If necessary, expand **ServerXX** (where XX is your assigned student number). Click the **plus sign (+)** next to the Web Sites folder to expand it, if necessary. The new Web site with the name New Web Site Test should appear, with its state set to Stopped, as shown in Figure 7-12.

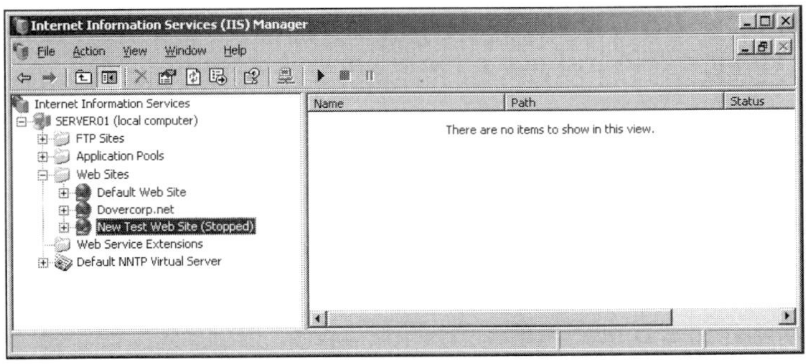

Figure 7-12 Viewing the new Web site

7. Right-click **New Web Site Test** and then click **Properties** to confirm that it is configured to use TCP port 8100 for connections.
8. Close all open windows.

> **Note:** Windows Server 2003 includes a variety of VB scripts for the purpose of configuring and managing Internet Information Services. See the Help and Support Center for more information.

Modifying Web-Site Properties

Once the Web Site Creation Wizard or a script like iisweb.vbs has been used to create your Web site, you can then modify a number of properties to fine-tune some of the parameters of the site. Configuring the properties pages for a specific Web site affects only that site and no others. The Default Web Site Properties dialog box is shown in Figure 7-13.

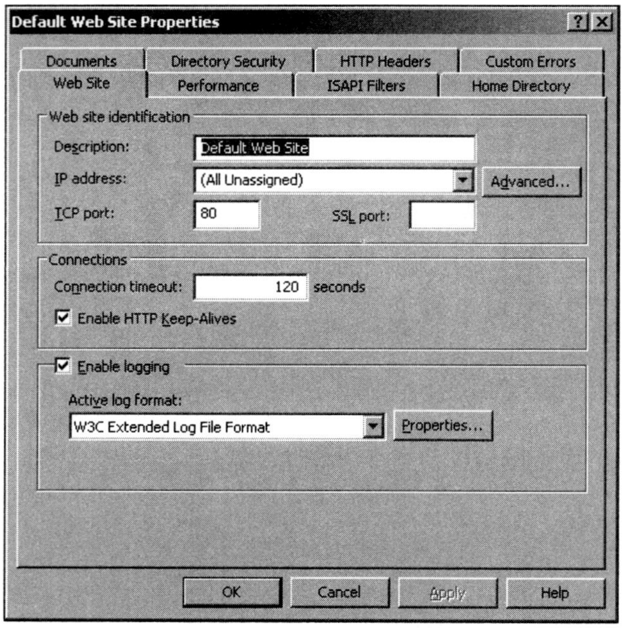

Figure 7-13 Configuring the Default Web Site properties

You may have noticed that the Properties dialog box is very similar to the master properties dialog box discussed earlier in the chapter. It is important to remember that any parameters configured at the Web-site level override the master properties that may have been set at the server level.

Table 7-4 explains each of the tabs on the Properties dialog box.

Table 7-4 Web site properties tabs

Properties Tab	Purpose
Web Site	Used to configure the IP address, TCP port, number of connections, and logging
Performance	Used to modify performance-based parameters such as **bandwidth throttling** and maximum Web-site connections
ISAPI Filters	Used to set up Internet Server Application Programming Interface (ISAPI) filters that respond to events that occur on the server during the processing of an HTTP request
Home Directory	Used to control where the Web site looks for Web content and to set security on that specific folder
Documents	Used to define a default Web page search order for the Web site and enable a common footer to be placed at the bottom of each Web page
Directory Security	Used to configure security for the Web site, such as authentication control, IP address or domain name restrictions, and SSL certificate configurations
HTTP Headers	Used to configure expiration dates on Web-site content, custom HTTP headers, and content ratings; content expiration is effective when you want to control the amount of time that your Web-site material is to be cached in a client's Web browser cache folder
Custom Errors	Used to customize common Web browser error messages that may be displayed to users who experience an error

In Activity 7-7, you will configure the properties of the *Dovercorp.net* Web site.

Activity 7-7: Configuring Web-Site Properties

Time Required: 15 minutes

Objective: Configure properties for an individual Web site.

Description: The IT manager at Dover Leasing is very interested in the ability to configure Web sites with different properties based on their individual requirements. Although many of Dover's Web sites will use common security settings, he wants you to become familiar with the individual property settings and how these can be used to control the way in which users will ultimately interact with the *Dovercorp.net* site to begin with. In this activity, you will explore and configure individual property settings of the *Dovercorp.net* Web site.

1. Open the **Internet Information Services** tool.
2. If necessary, expand **ServerXX** (where XX is your assigned student number). Click the **plus sign (+)** next to the Web Sites folder to expand it, if necessary. Right-click the **Dovercorp.net** Web site and then click **Properties**.
3. Click the **Performance** tab. In the Web site connections section, type **500** in the Connections limited to spin box.
4. Click the **Documents** tab, and then click the **Add** button. In the Add Content Page dialog box, type **index.html** in the text box and then click **OK**.
5. Click the **Move Up** button until index.html appears at the top of the list content pages.
6. Click **OK** to save the properties configured thus far.
7. Open **My Computer** and create a new text file in the **D:\Dovercorpwebsite** folder. Open the new file in Notepad and type the following:

   ```
   <html>
   <body>
   <p>This is a test document footer</p>
   </body>
   </html>
   ```

   Save the file and rename it **footer.html**. Click **Yes** in the Rename warning box.
8. In the Internet Information Services tool, right-click the **Dovercorp.net** Web site, click **Properties**, and then click the **Documents** tab.
9. Click the **Enable document footer** check box. Click the **Browse** button, then click **D:\Dovercorpwebsite\footer.html,** and click **Open**.
10. Click the **Directory Security** tab. Click the **Edit** button in the Authenticated and access control section. Notice that the Web site is configured to use Integrated Windows authentication and that Anonymous access is enabled using the IUSR_*servername* account. Click **OK**.
11. Click the **HTTP Headers** tab and click the **Enable content expiration** check box. This will set the content to expire after 1 day.
12. Click the **Edit Ratings** button in the Content rating section.
13. Click the **Enable ratings for this content** check box. Click each individual RSACi rating category to view its default configuration, and then click **OK**.
14. Click the **Custom Errors** tab. In the list of HTTP errors, click the entry for error **404**, as shown in Figure 7-14, and then click the **Edit** button. Note the File path listed. Click **Cancel**.
15. Click **OK** to close the Dovercorp.net Properties dialog box.
16. In the My Computer window, browse to the **C:\WINDOWS\Help\iisHelp\common** folder. Right-click the file **404b.htm**, select **Open With**, and then click **Notepad**.
17. Edit the line **<h1->The page cannot be found</h1>** to read **<h1> The page cannot be found on the Dovercorp.net Web site</h1>**. Close the file, saving your changes.
18. Open **Internet Explorer**, type **http://localhost** in the address bar, and press **Enter**.

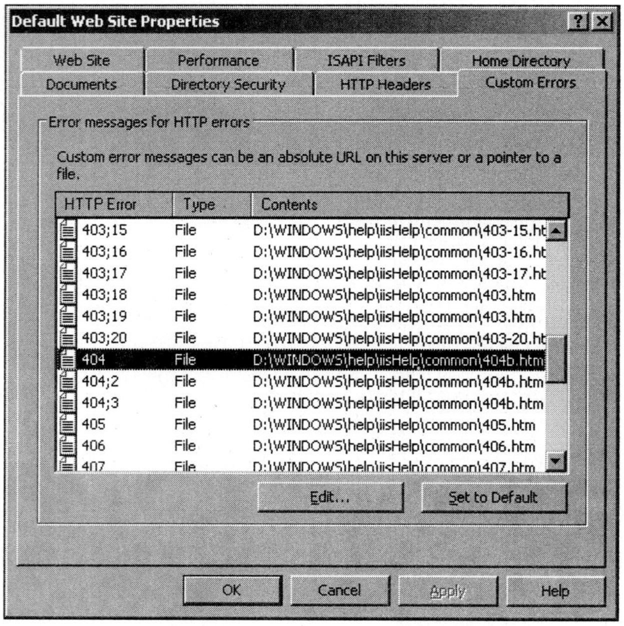

Figure 7-14 Defining custom error messages for a Web site

19. Notice that the *Dovercorp.net* Web page opens, but that this time it includes the footer configured in Step 9.
20. Type **http://localhost/unknown** in the Internet Explorer address bar and press **Enter**.
21. Notice that the custom 404 error message configured in Step 17 now appears when a page cannot be found.
22. Close all open windows.

Creating Virtual Directories

You may have information that is stored on multiple servers throughout your organization. If you want any of this information to be included in your Web site, you can create a **virtual directory** that specifically points to the shared folder that stores the data. Clients would then access the information by appending the **alias** name of the virtual directory to the Web-site host name. An alias can be used to hide the real directory name and to simplify the path that the server should use to access the information. For example, Dover Leasing may have a shared folder called Company Customers. For your intranet site, you might create a virtual directory that has an alias name of Customers. Employees would then type "www.dovercorp.net/customers" to access the virtual directory. The employees will not be able to tell that the information has come from a different server and folder. In Activity 7-8, you will configure a virtual directory that points to a shared folder on your partner's server.

Activity 7-8: Creating and Configuring a Virtual Directory

Hands-on Project

Time Required: 15 minutes

Objective: Create and configure a virtual directory.

Description: The Legal and Marketing Departments at Dover Leasing create large volumes of documents over the course of a year. Although many of these documents are contracts stored in paper form, the staff often needs access to electronic versions for revision or review purposes. One issue that makes this difficult is the fact that these documents are often spread across different directories on different servers, which can make individual documents difficult to find. Eventually, the IT manager at Dover Leasing would like the network to be configured such that all Marketing and Legal users will have access to their required documents via a browser interface. In this activity, you will create and configure a virtual directory on the *Dovercorp.net* Web site that points to a folder on a different server.

1. Open **My Computer**. Create a new folder called **D:\virtualdirectory**. Share the folder with the same name. Configure the folder such that the **Everyone** group also has the **Allow Read** shared folder and NTFS permissions.
2. Create a new text file in the **D:\virtualdirectory** folder. Open the file in Notepad and type the following:

```
<html>
<body>
<H1>This is a virtual directory on ServerXX</H1>
</body>
</html>
```

   The *XX* in this code should be replaced with your server number. Save the file, and then rename it **index.htm**. Close My Computer.

3. Open the **Internet Information Services** tool. Click the **plus sign (+)** next to your server name and then click the **plus sign (+)** next to Web Sites.
4. Right-click the **Dovercorp.net** Web site, select **New**, and then click **Virtual Directory**. The Virtual Directory Creation Wizard opens. Click **Next**.
5. At the Virtual Directory Alias screen, type **customers** in the Alias text box, and then click **Next**.
6. At the Web Site Content Directory screen, type **\\server*XX*\virtualdirectory** in the Path text box, where ***XX*** is your partner's student number. Click **Next**.
7. On the Security Credentials screen, ensure that the **Always use the authenticated user's credentials when validating access to the network directory** check box is selected, then click **Next**.
8. At the Virtual Directory Access Permissions screen, accept the default values by clicking **Next**.
9. Click **Finish** to complete creating the virtual directory.
10. Ensure that the **customers** virtual directory is visible, as illustrated in Figure 7-15.

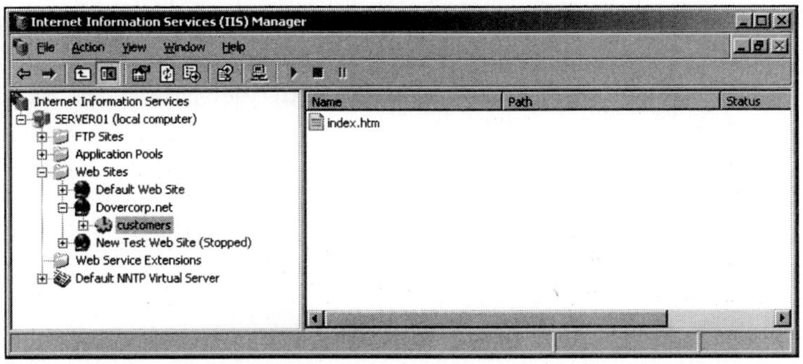

Figure 7-15 Viewing the customers virtual directory

11. Right-click the **customers** virtual directory and click **Properties**.
12. The customers Properties dialog box will open listing the network directory acting as the source for the virtual directory, as illustrated in Figure 7-16. Click **Cancel**.

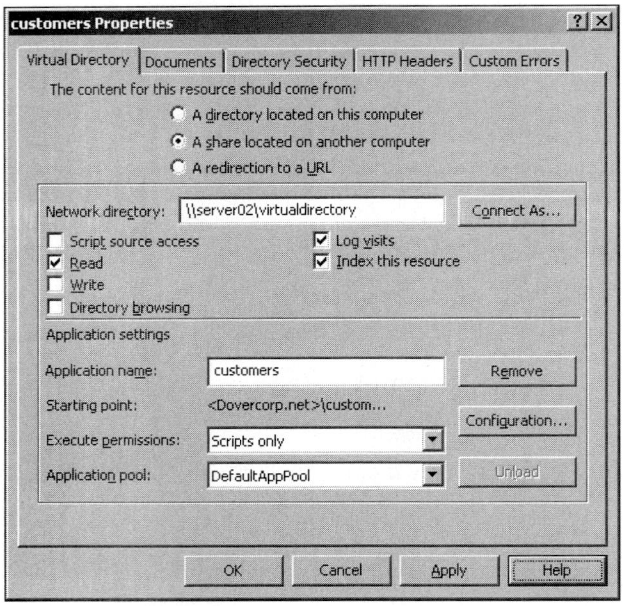

Figure 7-16 Viewing the properties of a virtual directory

13. Open **Internet Explorer** and type **http://localhost/customers** in the address bar. Press **Enter**. The Web page with the message This is a virtual directory on Server*XX* will appear, where *XX* is your partner's student number.
14. Close all open windows.

Tip: You can also create a virtual directory by using the Windows Server 2003 Web Sharing feature, which you will explore later in this chapter.

CONFIGURING AUTHENTICATION FOR WEB SITES

All Windows Server 2003 servers require that any user who tries to access the server be authenticated to a valid user account. **Authentication** refers to determining whether or not a user has a valid user account with the proper permissions to access a resource, such as a shared folder or Web site. After a user account has been validated, it is given access to all resources to which it has the proper permissions. Windows Server 2003 Web servers are no exception to this rule. Proper authentication and permissions have to be in place before a client can access a Web site on the server.

IIS provides five levels of authentication that can be used to validate users that are trying to access a Web site stored on the server:

- Anonymous access
- Basic authentication
- Digest authentication
- Integrated Windows authentication
- .NET Passport authentication

Authentication settings are configured from within the properties of a Web site in the Authentication and access control section of the Directory Security tab. The Authentication Methods dialog box is shown in Figure 7-17.

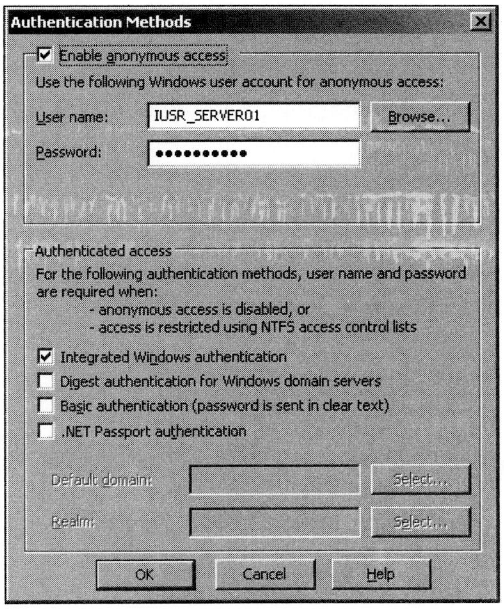

Figure 7-17 Configuring Web site authentication options

Anonymous Access

Anonymous access allows users to access a Web site without having to provide a user name and password. When a user attempts to access your Web site, IIS uses the IUSR_*servername* user account to provide the required authentication credentials. This user account is a member of the Domain Users (on a domain controller) and Guests groups by default. Alternatively, you can change these credentials by specifying the user name and password of a different user account.

Basic Authentication

Basic authentication prompts users for a user name and password to be able to access the Web resource. The user needs to have a valid Windows Server 2003 user account to be able to gain access to the Web site. One problem with Basic authentication is that the user name and password are transmitted using Base64 encoding (not encryption) and can easily be captured and read by hackers.

Digest Authentication

This authentication method was originally introduced in Windows 2000 with IIS 5.0. **Digest authentication** works the same way as Basic authentication except that the user name and password are hashed using the MD5 algorithm to prevent hackers from obtaining the information. To use Digest authentication users must be running Internet Explorer 5.0 or higher and have an account in Active Directory or a trusted domain. An IIS server using Digest authentication must also be part of an Active Directory domain and must be running HTTP 1.1 and WebDAV.

Integrated Windows Authentication

Integrated Windows authentication does not ask the user for a password but rather uses the client's currently logged-on credentials to supply a challenge/response to the Web server. This option is primarily used on internal intranets. Once this choice has been enabled, it can only be used if Anonymous access is disabled on the Web site and Windows file permissions have been set, requiring users to provide authentication to access the resources.

.NET Passport Authentication

IIS 6.0 supports a new authentication method not found in previous versions. **.NET Passport authentication** is a configurable option that allows a Web site to use the functionality of the .NET Passport service to authenticate user identities. Although this feature is a configurable option in the Authentication Methods dialog box, this is only for testing purposes. Ultimately, the ability to authenticate users with a .NET Passport will rely on a company carrying out a variety of preproduction tests with Microsoft, as well as a registration process.

Note

For more information about .NET Passport authentication, see the Microsoft .NET Passport Business Services Web site at *http://www.microsoft.com/net/services/passport/business.asp*.

Note that if multiple authentication methods are configured, the following rules apply:

- If Anonymous authentication and one other method are selected, the other method only applies if Anonymous authentication fails.
- FTP sites cannot use Digest, Integrated Windows, or .NET Passport authentication.
- Both Digest and Integrated Windows authentication take precedence over Basic authentication.

In Activity 7-9, you will configure and test Web-site authentication options.

Hands-on Project

Activity 7-9: Configuring and Testing Web-Site Authentication Options

Time Required: 10 minutes

Objective: Configure different Web-site authentication options.

Description: Although the *Dovercorp.net* Web site will ultimately allow access to anonymous public Internet users, the IT manager would like to have the ability to require authenticated access to various Dovercorp Leasing Web sites that may be created in the future. To better understand some of the different authentication options available, you decide to change the authentication settings of the *Dovercorp.net* Web site for testing purposes. In this activity, you will configure and then test the impact of both Anonymous access and Basic authentication.

1. Open the **Internet Information Services** tool. Click the **plus sign (+)** next to your server name and then click the **plus sign (+)** next to Web Sites.
2. Right-click the **Dovercorp.net** Web site and click **Properties**.
3. Click the **Directory Security** tab.
4. In the Authentication and access control section, click the **Edit** button.
5. Note that both Anonymous and Integrated Windows authentication are currently configured for the *Dovercorp.net* Web site.
6. Open **Internet Explorer**, and in the address bar type **http://localhost**, and press **Enter**. Because Anonymous access is allowed, you are not required to authenticate to access the site. Close Internet Explorer.
7. Right-click the **Dovercorp.net** Web site and click **Properties** again, if necessary. In the Authentication Methods window, click the **Enable anonymous access** and **Integrated Windows authentication** check boxes to uncheck them.
8. Click the **Basic authentication** check box. When the IIS Manager dialog box opens, read the message it presents, as shown in Figure 7-18, and then click **Yes**. Click **OK** to close the Authentication Methods dialog box.
9. Click **OK** to close the Dovercorp.net Web site properties dialog box.

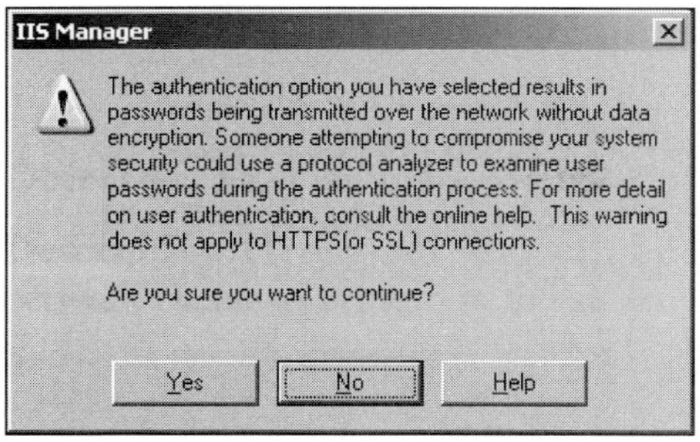

Figure 7-18 Authentication option warning message

10. Open **Internet Explorer**. In the address bar, type **http://localhost**, and press **Enter**. When the Connect to localhost authentication dialog box opens, type **mcowan** in the User name text box and **Password01** in the Password text box. Click **OK**.
11. The *Dovercorp.net* Web site homepage opens once authentication is complete.
12. Configure the *Dovercorp.net* Web site back to its original authentication settings.
13. Close all open windows.

Configuring Server Certificates and Secure Sockets Layer

The Directory Security tab also allows you to configure secure Web communication by implementing **Secure Sockets Layer (SSL)** protocol. This protocol is used to encrypt Web traffic between a client and the Web server. Clients can access a secure server using SSL by using URLs that begin with https:// instead of the common http:// prefix. HTTPS communication is established by default over TCP port 443.

The first step in using SSL on a Web server is to obtain and install a server certificate from a certificate authority (CA) such as Verisign, Inc., or you can install certificate services on a server in your organization and create your own for internal purposes. Until a certificate is installed on the server, IIS is not capable of providing secure connections to clients using SSL. Certificates are installed and configured from the Directory Security tab of a Web site's Properties dialog box, as shown in Figure 7-19.

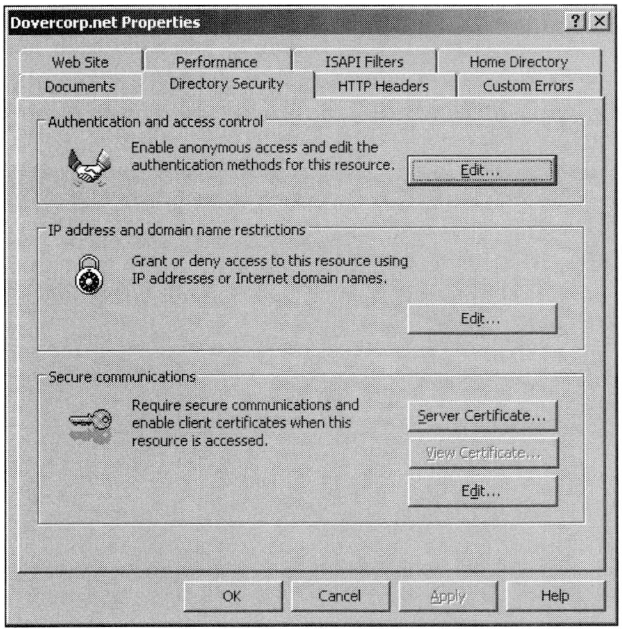

Figure 7-19 Viewing the Directory Security tab of a Web site

For Internet Web sites that will be made accessible to the general public, you should obtain a proper certificate from a recognized CA to ensure a path of trust. Once you obtain a certificate, you can install it using the IIS Certificate Wizard, as shown in Figure 7-20.

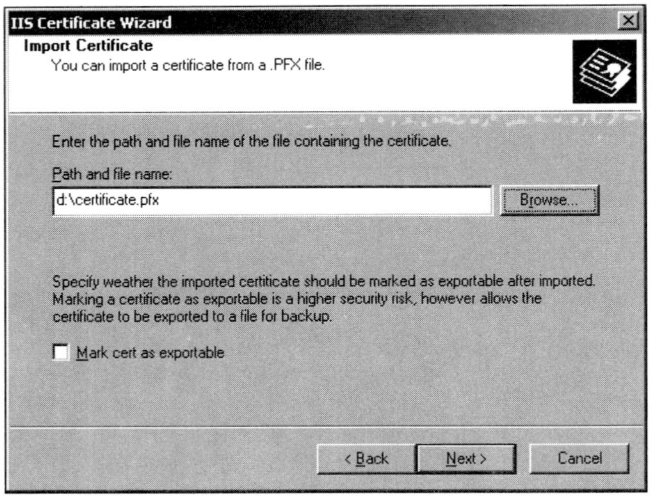

Figure 7-20 Importing a certificate using the IIS Certificate Wizard

Once you install a certificate, you must enable a Web site for SSL as shown in Figure 7-21. TCP port 443 is the default HTTPS port and must be used unless users explicitly state the port number when they connect.

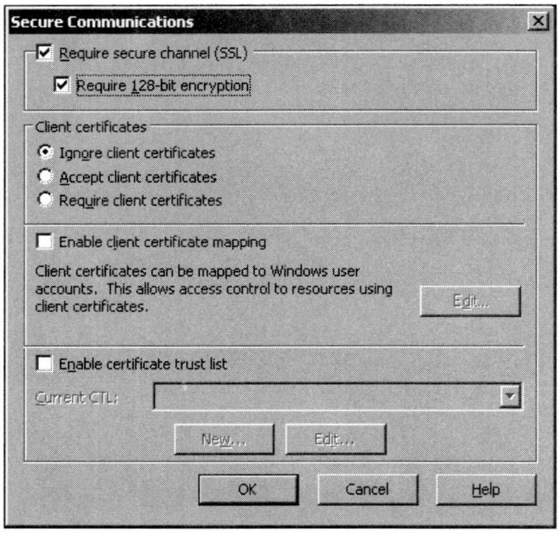

Figure 7-21 Requiring a Web site to use secure communications

Configuring FTP Virtual Servers

File Transfer Protocol (FTP) is used to transfer files between two computers that are both running TCP/IP. The FTP service included with IIS 6.0 enables users to transfer files to and from it using FTP client software such as the command-line ftp utility or a Web browser. The following section looks at some of the basic concepts behind FTP, how to configure the FTP properties, as well as how to create and manage an FTP site.

File Transfer Protocol

FTP is an industry-standard method of transferring files between two hosts running TCP/IP. Although HTTP has replaced FTP for many download functions, it is still a useful protocol for file transfers and is still widely used on both private networks and the Internet today. Unlike HTTP, which only uses a single port for connections during a single session, FTP uses two ports, TCP ports 20 and 21. TCP port 21 is usually used to initiate the connection and for diagnostic functions, while data is usually ultimately passed over TCP port 20.

FTP uses the **Transmission Control Protocol (TCP)** for file transfers. TCP is a connection-based protocol, which means a session is established between the two hosts before any data is transferred.

Some of the important features of TCP include the following:

- The sending computer sends a number of packets to a recipient at once but then waits for an acknowledgment that data was received before sending any more packets. If the sending computer does not receive an acknowledgement, it retransmits the original data.
- All packets at the sending computer are assigned a sequence number so their data can be reorganized at the receiving computer.
- Each packet also contains a checksum for ensuring the integrity of the data.

To use FTP to transfer files between two computers, one machine must be running FTP client software and the other FTP server software. For example, the server might be running FTP server software such as IIS 6.0, while the client could be using the FTP command-line utility included with Windows Server 2003.

Tip

There are a number of easy-to-use, graphical FTP utilities that you can download from the Internet as shareware and freeware. Perform a search for FTP using your favorite search engine to find a list of available downloads.

Configuring FTP Properties

Like the WWW service, you can configure multiple FTP sites running on a single IIS 6.0 server. Each site behaves and operates independently and, to a client, it appears as though they are running on separate FTP servers. Each site has its own set of property sheets allowing you to customize settings on a site-by-site basis. There are five tabs available from the site properties, as shown in Figure 7-22 and summarized in Table 7-5.

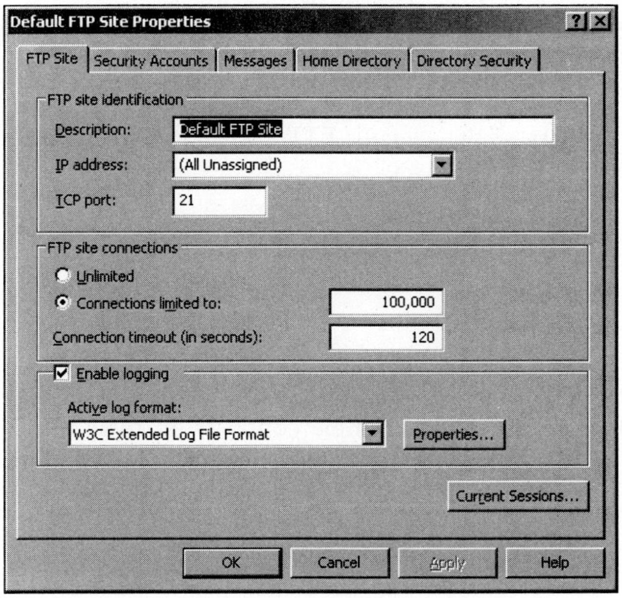

Figure 7-22 The Default FTP Site properties

Table 7-5 FTP site property tabs

Tab	Description
FTP Site	Used to configure site identification, configure connection limits, and enable FTP logging.
Security Accounts	Allows you to configure which account is used for Anonymous access to the FTP site; you can also disable Anonymous access, requiring all users to have a user account and password to access the site.
Messages	Allows you to configure both the welcome and exit messages that are displayed to users that connect to and disconnect from the FTP site
Home Directory	Where the files published through your FTP site are stored; using this tab, you can change the default home directory location to another directory on the server or to a directory located on another server. You can also set the type of access allowed to the folder (read and/or write). The directory style listing lets you select the folder style listing that is displayed to FTP users.
Directory Security	Allows you to grant or deny access to the FTP site based on IP addresses, as shown in Figure 7-23; you can grant access to all computers except those listed in the exception box, or you can deny access to all computers except the ones listed. You can configure access based on individual IP addresses, network addresses, or fully qualified domain names.

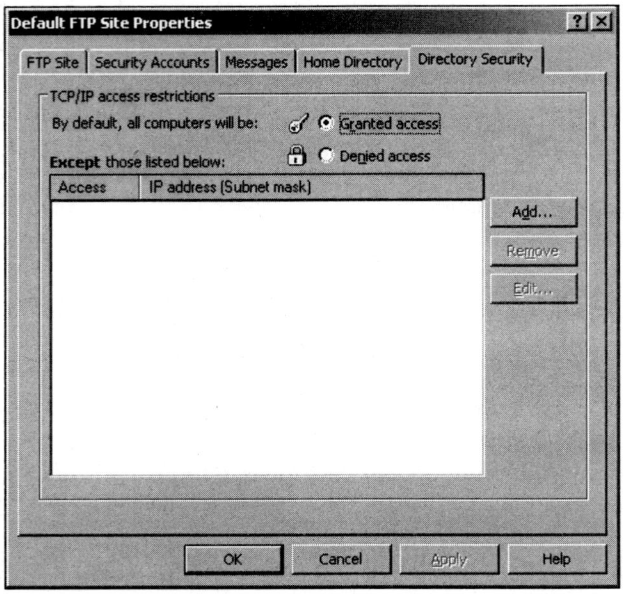

Figure 7-23 Viewing the Directory Security tab

In Activity 7-10, you will configure the properties of the Default FTP site and connect to it for testing purposes.

Activity 7-10: Configuring and Testing the Default FTP Site

Time Required: 15 minutes

Objective: Configure and test the Default FTP site.

Description: Dover Leasing has always provided customers with access to various sample contracts via a fax-back service. Although the company plans to place many sample contracts on their new Web site in the future, the IT manager has asked you to explore the possibility of providing access to contracts via FTP as well. In this activity, you will configure the properties of the Default FTP site and then test it to ensure that anonymous users can connect without issue.

1. Open the **Internet Information Services** tool.
2. Click the **plus sign (+)** next to your server name and then click the **plus sign (+)** next to the FTP Sites folder to expand it.

3. Right-click the **Default FTP Site** and click **Properties**.
4. On **FTP** tab, browse the information provided, noting that the port number is set to the default value of 21. Click the **Current Sessions** button.
5. Because no users are currently connected via FTP, there should be no users listed in the FTP User Sessions section. Click **Close**.
6. Click the **Security Accounts** tab. Notice that the FTP service allows Anonymous access by default. If this option is de-selected, basic authentication is required.
7. Click the **Messages** tab.
8. In the Banner text box, type **Dovercorp.net FTP server**.
9. In the Welcome text box, type **Thank you for logging on to the Dovercorp.net FTP Server**.
10. In the Exit text box, type **Thanks for stopping by – goodbye!**
11. Click the **Home Directory** tab. In the FTP site directory section, click the **Write** check box. This will allow users to upload files to this FTP server.
12. Click **OK** to close the Default FTP Site Properties dialog box.
13. Click **Start**, click **Run**, and in the Open text box type **cmd** and press **OK**. At the command prompt, type **ftp localhost** and press **Enter**. Notice the banner message that appears.
14. At the User prompt, type **anonymous** and press **Enter**.
15. At the Password prompt, type the e-mail address **user@dovercorp.net**. This is required when logging on using the anonymous user account. Press **Enter**. Notice the Welcome message that appears, as shown in Figure 7-24.

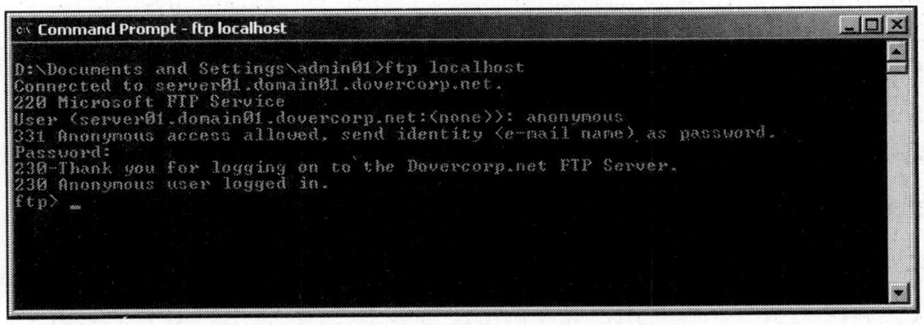

Figure 7-24 Logging into an FTP server as an anonymous user

16. In the Internet Information Services window, right-click the **Default FTP Site**, click **Properties**, and then click the **Current Sessions** button. The currently logged-on user will appear in the list.
17. At the command prompt, type **bye** and press **Enter** to close the FTP session. Notice the Exit message that appears.
18. Close all open windows.

Now that you are familiar with the different configuration settings associated with an FTP site, let's look at how to create a new FTP virtual server using the Internet Services Manager.

Creating an FTP Site Virtual Server

Much like virtual Web servers, you can create new FTP sites using either the Internet Information Services tool or by scripting. These FTP sites also follow the same principles as Web sites in that they allow you to create virtual directories that can be both local and remote to the IIS server. In Activity 7-11, you will create a new FTP site as well as an FTP virtual directory.

Activity 7-11: Creating and Testing a New FTP Site and Configuring a Virtual Directory

Time Required: 20 minutes

Objective: Creating a new FTP site and virtual directory.

Description: After viewing the FTP server that you configured in Activity 7-10, the IT manager at Dover Leasing has asked you to configure an additional FTP site for the purpose of testing multiple sites, as well as FTP virtual directories. Ultimately, the IT manager thinks that it may be possible to use FTP to enable various customer service representatives who work from home to quickly and easily gain access to various documents found on different servers. In this activity, you will create and test a new FTP site that includes a virtual directory located on a different server.

1. Open **My Computer** and create two new folders on your **D:** drive named **ftpsite** and **ftpvirdir**, respectively. Grant the Everyone group the **Allow Full Control** NTFS permissions to both folders. Share the **ftpvirdir** folder and grant the Everyone group the **Allow Full Control** shared folder permission.
2. Create a new text file in the **D:\ftpvirdir** folder called **customers.txt**. Edit this file to include the text **Customer readme file from ServerXX** (where ServerXX is your assigned student number) and then save it.
3. Close My Computer.
4. Click **Start**, select **Control Panel**, select **Network Connections**, and then click **Local Area Connection**. Click the **Properties** button.
5. Click **Internet Protocol (TCP/IP)** and then click **Properties**.
6. On the **General** tab, click the **Advanced** button.
7. In the IP addresses section, click the **Add** button. In the TCP/IP Address dialog box, type **192.168.100.*XX*** in the IP address text box (where *XX* is your assigned student number) and **255.255.255.0** in the Subnet mask text box. Click **Add**.
8. Click **OK** twice, and then click **Close**. Close the Local Area Connection Status dialog box.
9. Open the **Internet Information Services** tool.
10. Click the **plus sign (+)** next to your server name, and then right-click the **FTP Sites** folder, select **New**, and click **FTP Site**. The FTP Site Creation Wizard opens. Click **Next**.
11. At the FTP Site Description screen, type **FTP site for clients** in the Description text box and click **Next**.
12. At the IP Address and Port Settings screen, click the IP address configured in Step 7 in the **Enter the IP address to use for this FTP site** list box. Click **Next**.
13. At the FTP User Isolation screen, click **Next**.
14. At the FTP Site Home Directory screen, type **D:\ftpsite** in the text box, and click **Next**.
15. At the FTP Site Access Permissions screen, click the **Write** check box, as shown in Figure 7-25, and click **Next**.
16. Click **Finish** to create the new FTP site.
17. Test the new FTP site by opening a **command prompt** and typing **ftp 192.168.100.*XX*** (where XX is your assigned student number) and pressing **Enter**. When prompted for a user name and password, use the user name **anonymous** and the password **user@dovercorp.net**. Once connected, type **bye** to close the connection.

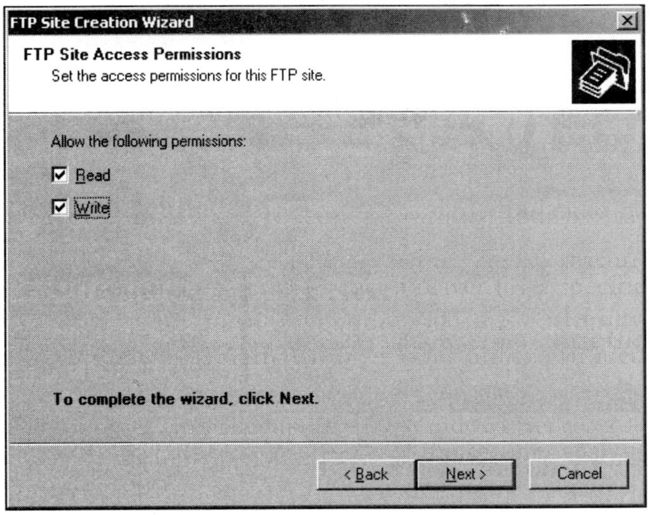

Figure 7-25 Configuring FTP Access Permissions

7

18. In the Internet Information Services window, right-click **FTP site for clients**, select **New**, and then click **Virtual Directory**.
19. At the Virtual Directory Creation Wizard welcome screen, click **Next**.
20. At the Virtual Directory Alias screen, type **customers** in the Alias text box and click **Next**.
21. At the FTP Site Content Directory screen, type **\\\\Server*XX*\ftpvirdir** where *XX* is your partner's student number in the text box, and click **Next**.
22. At the Security Credentials screen, ensure that the **Always use the authenticated user's credentials when validating access to the network directory** check box is checked and click **Next**.
23. At the Virtual Directory Access Permissions screen, click **Next**, and then click **Finish**.
24. At the command prompt, type the command **d:** and then press **Enter** to change the focus of the command prompt to the root of your D: drive. At the command prompt, type **ftp 192.168.100.*XX***, where *XX* is your student number and press **Enter**.
25. Log on with a user name of **anonymous** and a password of **user@dovercorp.net**.
26. At the ftp> prompt, type **cd customers** and press **Enter**. This will move you into the customers virtual directory.
27. At the prompt, type **ls** and press **Enter** to view a listing of all files. Note that a file named **customers.txt** appears in the list.
28. At the command prompt, type **get customers.txt** and press **Enter**. This transfers the customers.txt file to your server. Type **bye** at the command prompt and press **Enter**.
29. Open **My Computer** and verify that the file customers.txt exists in the root of your D: drive. Open the file to verify that it came from your partner's server.
30. Close all open windows.

Updating and Maintaining Security for an IIS Server

Whenever information is published to users on the Internet, the topic of security arises. You want to be able to provide users access to certain information on your Web servers while restricting access to all other information and the rest of the network. There are several ways an administrator can secure access to information on a Web server. These alternatives are discussed in the following section.

As with any other type of server, once it is installed and configured, an IIS server still needs to be maintained and updated. This usually includes performing regular backups, stopping and starting IIS-related services, and applying updates. These topics are discussed in the next few sections.

Resource Permissions

One of the first ways to control access to information is to set permissions specifying the types of access users are granted. When securing Web content, there are two types of permissions that you can apply to secure resources: NTFS permissions and IIS permissions. To provide the most security for your Web content, you should take advantage of both Windows Server 2003 NTFS security as well as IIS security.

NTFS Permissions

You can control access to Web-server resources stored on an NTFS volume by using NTFS permissions. You should apply NTFS permissions to any Web pages and virtual directories published to your Web server to obtain the highest degree of security possible.

Note

One of the differences between NTFS permissions and IIS permissions is that different NTFS permissions can be assigned to users and groups, whereas IIS permissions are global.

IIS Permissions

Combining NTFS permissions and IIS permissions provides the most security for your Web content. IIS permissions can be configured for any of the following:

- Web sites and FTP virtual servers
- Virtual directories
- Physical directories
- Files

When restricting access to virtual directories, physical directories, and files, there are two primary types of permissions that can be set: the Read permission and/or Write permission. The Read permission allows users to view the contents and the Write permission allows users to add content to virtual directories and folders, as well as change the contents of a file.

If a Web site or virtual directory contains any scripts or executables, you can also configure the Execute permission by choosing None, Scripts, or Scripts and Executables from the Home Directory or Virtual Directory tab.

Note

When combining NTFS permissions and IIS permissions, the most restrictive permission is the effective permission.

In Activity 7-12, you will restrict access to a Web site using both IIS and NTFS permissions.

Hands-on Project

Activity 7-12: Configuring IIS and NTFS Permissions

Time Required: 10 minutes

Objective: Protect Web-site resources using both IIS and NTFS permissions.

Description: As part of your role at Dover Leasing, you are responsible for the overall security of network resources. Because the *Dovercorp.net* Web site will be accessible by the general public once completed, you are worried about resources being properly secured. Having read that the highest degree of security in IIS is provided when both IIS and NTFS permissions are applied, you decide to test their impact to be sure that they work correctly. In this activity, you will test denying Read permission to the *Dovercorp.net* customers virtual directory using both IIS and NTFS permissions.

1. Open the **Internet Information Services** tool.
2. Click the **plus sign (+)** next to your server name to expand it. Click the **plus signs (+)** next to the Web Sites folder and then the Dovercorp.net Web site to expand them. Right-click the **customers** virtual directory and then click **Properties**.
3. On the **Virtual Directory** tab, click the **Read** check box to uncheck it and then click **OK**.
4. Open **Internet Explorer**. In the address bar, type **http://localhost** and press **Enter**. The *Dovercorp.net* Web site will open.
5. In the address bar, type **http://localhost/customers** and press **Enter**. The page is not displayed because IIS Read access was disabled. Note that the HTTP error code listed on the page is 403.2, which means that Read access is denied. Close Internet Explorer.
6. In the Internet Information Services tool, access the properties of the customers virtual directory and click the Read check box to re-enable the permission. Click **OK** to close the customers Properties dialog box.
7. Open **My Computer**, and access the properties of your **D:\virtualdirectory** folder. This is the folder that your partner's server connects to as the customers virtual directory.
8. Click the **Security** tab and set the **Deny Read** permission for all listed groups. Click **OK** to close the virtualdirectory Properties dialog box. Ensure that your partner has completed this step before moving on to Step 9.
9. Open **Internet Explorer**, type **http://localhost/customers** in the address bar, and press **Enter**. Notice that the Connect to serverXX.DomainXX.Dovercorp.net authentication dialog box opens. This is because all users have been explicitly denied the NTFS Read permission to the folder.
10. Close all open windows.

IP Address and Domain Name Security

You can secure Web content by granting or denying access to users based on their IP address or domain name. You can grant or deny access to an individual IP address or to a particular address range.

An example of how an administrator might use IP address and domain name security is when your company provides Web content to another business such as a business partner or a client. The administrator could deny access to all IP addresses except those on the business partner's or client's network. In Activity 7-13, you will restrict access to the *Dovercorp.net* Web site using IP address restrictions.

Hands-on Project

Activity 7-13: Testing IP Address Restrictions

Time Required: 10 minutes

Objective: Test the ability to control Web-site access by IP address.

Description: The current Dover Leasing Web server has been the target of attack by three different hackers. Although you were not able to determine the identities of these users by viewing the security logs, you were able to determine their IP addresses. Based on these previous experiences, you decide to test the ability to block access to Web sites based on a user's configured IP address. In this activity, you will block access to the *Dovercorp.net* Web site from your server's configured IP address for testing purposes.

1. Open the **Internet Information Services** tool.
2. Click the **plus sign (+)** next to your server name to expand it. Click the **plus sign (+)** next to the Web Sites folder to expand it, and then right-click the **Dovercorp.net** Web site and click **Properties**.
3. Click the **Directory Security** tab. In the IP address and domain name restrictions section, click the **Edit** button.

4. In the IP Address and Domain Name Restrictions dialog box, click the **Add** button.
5. In the Deny Access dialog box, as shown in Figure 7-26, type **127.0.0.1** in the IP address text box to deny access to this Web site for your computer. Click **OK**. Click **OK** to close the Dovercorp.net Properties dialog box.

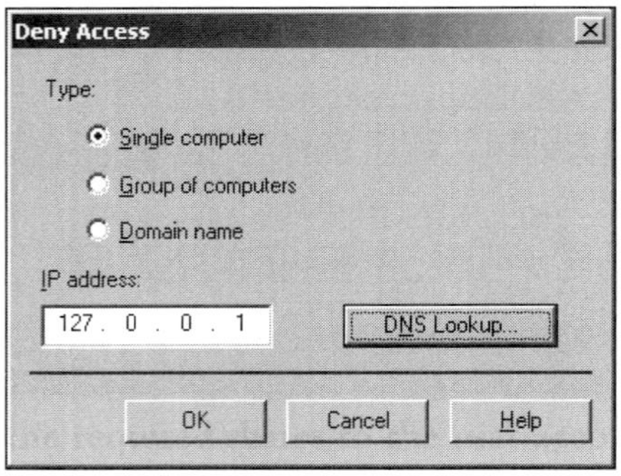

Figure 7-26 Denying access to the Web site

6. Open **Internet Explorer**, type **http://localhost** in the address bar, and press **Enter**. The page does not display because your IP address has been rejected. Notice that the error code listed on the page is a 403.6 forbidden error.
7. In the Internet Information Services window, right-click the **Dovercorp.net** Web site and click **Properties**.
8. Click the **Directory Security** tab. In the IP address and domain name restrictions section, click the **Edit** button.
9. In the IP Address and Domain Name Restrictions dialog box, click the entry for 127.0.0.1 and click the **Remove** button. Click **OK**.
10. Click **OK** to close the Dovercorp.net Properties window.
11. Close all open windows.

Starting and Stopping Services

At some point, for administrative purposes, you may need to stop and restart services related to IIS. IIS 6.0 makes it simple to stop and restart services by allowing services, along with individual sites, to be stopped and restarted through the Internet Information Services console.

Backing Up the IIS Configuration

It is generally a good idea to periodically back up the configuration settings of your IIS Server. IIS 6.0 stores its configuration settings in a database referred to as the IIS metabase that can be backed up separately. This is useful in the event that you have to restore your IIS Server settings.

The default location for backups is the %systemroot%\system32\inetsrv\Metaback directory. The metabase can be backed up using one of five methods:

- Use the backup utility in the IIS console to back up the database.
- Copy the contents of the backup directory to another folder to provide redundancy after an initial backup has been performed.
- Use the metabase editor tool to export the contents of the database to a text file.
- Use the iisback.vbs script.
- Use the Windows Server 2003 Backup utility or a third party utility and choose to backup System State data.

The easiest way to back up the metabase is to use the Internet Information Services tool. In Activity 7-14, you will back up and restore the IIS configuration of your server.

Activity 7-14: Backing Up the IIS Configuration

Time Required: 10 minutes

Objective: Back up and restore the configuration of an IIS server.

Description: The IT manager at Dover Leasing is concerned about all server data being backed up on a regular basis. He is also worried about the *Dovercorp.net* Web site being down for extended periods due to lost data or server problems, seeing as this has happened in the past. To help ensure that you can quickly respond to events in the future, he has asked you to test the backup and restore features found within the Internet Information Services console. In this activity, you will use the backup and restore facilities of IIS to backup, verify, and then restore your server's configuration.

1. Open the **Internet Information Services** tool.
2. Right-click the **Server*XX* (local computer)** icon, select **All Tasks**, and then click **Backup/Restore Configuration**.
3. In the Configuration Backup/Restore dialog box, click the **Create Backup** button, as shown in Figure 7-27.

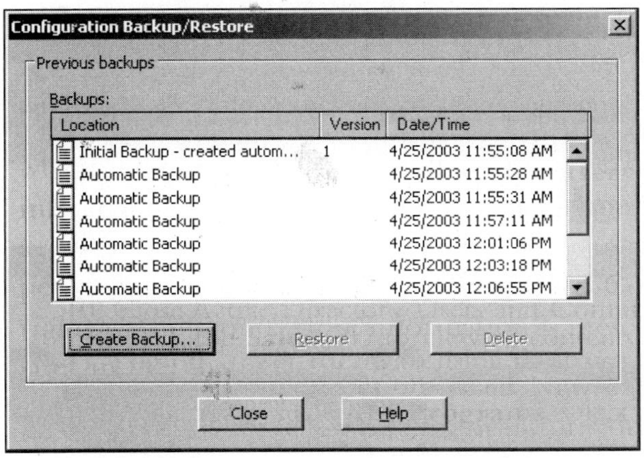

Figure 7-27 Backing up and restoring the IIS configuration

4. In the Configuration Backup dialog box, type **test IIS backup** in the Configuration backup name text box and click **OK**.
5. Notice that your new backup appears at the top of the Backups list box in the Configuration Backup/Restore dialog box. Click the **Close** button.
6. Open **My Computer** and browse to the **C:\WINDOWS\system32\inetsrv\Metaback** folder. Confirm that two files that begin with the name "test IIS backup" are stored in this folder.
7. Close **My Computer**.
8. In the Internet Information Services window, right-click your server, select **All Tasks**, and then click **Backup/Restore Configuration**.
9. In the Configuration Backup/Restore dialog box, click **test IIS backup**, and then click **Restore**.
10. Read the message that appears in the IIS Manager dialog box, and then click **Yes**.
11. When the IIS Manager dialog box opens specifying that the operation completed successfully, click **OK**.
12. Close all open windows.

Tip

You can also export the IIS 6.0 metabase configuration using the iiscnfg.vbs script. Exporting the configuration of the metabase is useful in cases where you want to import your configuration to another computer running Windows Server 2003. For more information on importing or exporting the IIS metabase, see the Internet Information Services 6.0 Administrator Guide or the Help and Support Center.

IIS 6.0 also introduces a new history feature that tracks changes to the MetaBase.xml and MBSchema.xml files. Whenever changes are made to these files via system configuration tasks (or by directly editing them), copies of the changed files are written to the %systemroot% \system32\inetsrv\History folder on the server. You can subsequently use these files if the metabase ever needs to be rolled back to a previous configuration.

Updating IIS 6.0

As with most software that you install on your server, updates are regularly released to fix any known bugs and security issues that are reported. The two common types of updates that you apply to your IIS Server are service packs and hot fixes. Hot fixes are usually released to fix a certain component and are usually released between service packs. They are small software fixes designed to solve a known security issue. Service packs are usually an accumulation of software patches and fixes that fix bugs that have been discovered. Service packs are more significant upgrades than hot fixes.

Note

Before you apply any patch, hot fix, or service pack, make sure you perform a full backup of your server.

Security is one of the most important aspects of running a Web server. Often, hot fixes and patches are released to fix a known security issue. Therefore, it's crucial that network administrators know which hot fixes have been applied to a Web server and, more importantly, which hot fixes haven't been applied. One of the tools you can use to determine what hot fixes and service packs need to be installed on a server is the Microsoft Baseline Security Analyzer, originally discussed in Chapter 2. You can use this tool to determine which IIS hot fixes are currently installed on your Web server.

Note

Microsoft provided a utility known as the IIS Lockdown Tool to secure previous versions of IIS. In Windows Server 2003, the ability to further secure Web services is provided via the Web Service Extensions node in the IIS console.

Creating and Modifying Web Folders

Once you have IIS installed on servers, your organization may have data that they want to be shared via HTTP or FTP access by clients. For example, your company may want its yearly financial reports to be publicly available on the Internet.

Windows Server 2003 also includes a feature that allows you to create and share files on a Web server using a **Web folder**. A Web folder is designed to be accessed from the Internet or an intranet using the HTTP or FTP protocols. Once IIS is properly installed and Web folders are configured, many common applications such as Office XP are capable of opening and saving files to the Web folder just like any standard Windows shared folder.

Configuring a folder to be shared over the Web is similar to regular folder sharing except you use the Web Sharing tab to configure folder properties. If the IIS Web server is configured properly, you can choose the specific Web site from which you want this folder to be available. Figure 7-28 shows the Web Sharing tab for a folder named Apps.

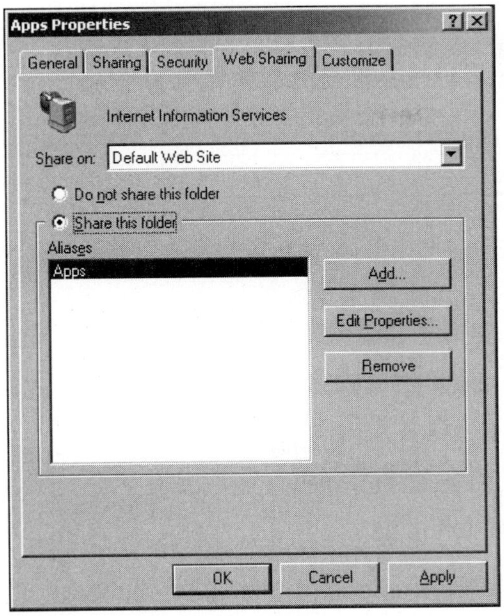

Figure 7-28 Sharing a folder using the Web Sharing tab

Shared Web folders do not have to use the actual folder name to be referenced. Web folders can instead use an alias name to which you want your Web clients to refer when accessing the shared resource. Figure 7-29 illustrates the Edit Alias dialog box.

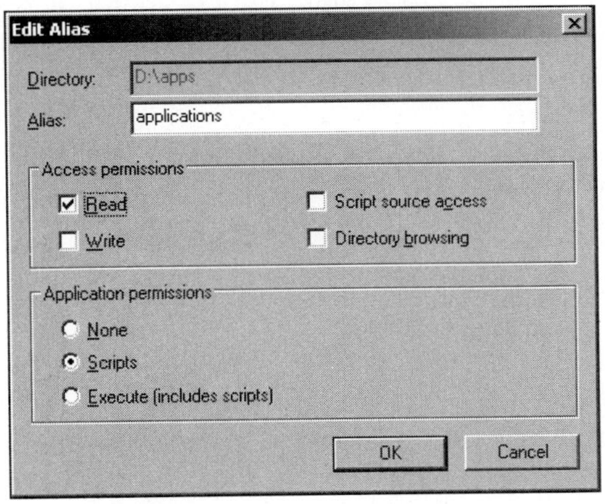

Figure 7-29 Creating an alias for a Web Shared folder

In the Edit Alias dialog box, you should also configure the access permissions and application permissions that you would like Web clients to have for the data within the shared resource. Tables 7-6 and 7-7 explain the various Web folder access permissions.

Table 7-6 Web folder access permissions

Access Permission	Description
Read	Allows users to read and display Web-based information
Write	Allows users to modify the contents of the shared Web folder
Script source access	Allows users to view the contents of Web-based scripts
Directory browsing	Allows users to browse the actual folder structure of the shared resource

Table 7-7 Application permissions

Application Permission	Description
None	Provides no permissions to execute script or application commands
Scripts	Allows the user to run scripts to perform Web-based functions
Execute (includes scripts)	Allows users to run scripts or applications over the Web-based connection

Network clients can open a Web-based file share using one of three main methods:

- *Internet Explorer*—To open a Web folder using Internet Explorer, click the File menu, and then click Open. Type the URL of the folder share (*http://webserver/share*) in the Open text box, and then click the check box next to Open as a Web Folder.
- *My Network Places*—Open My Network Places, and double-click the Add Network Place Wizard. You can then type the URL of the Web folder in the form of *http://webserver/share*.
- *Microsoft Office XP*—In a Microsoft Office application, click File, click Open, and then type the URL of the Web folder in the File name text box.

In Activity 7-15, you will configure and access a folder using Web Sharing.

Activity 7-15: Configuring Web Folders and Exploring Access Methods

Time Required: 10 minutes

Objective: Configure and access a Web shared folder.

Description: Although users at Dover Leasing still use mapped network drives as their primary method of accessing file server resources, the IT manager has asked you to explore the possibility of also providing browser-based access to files and folders. In this activity, you will use the Web Sharing feature of Windows Server 2003 to create and test access to a new virtual directory.

1. Open **My Computer**.
2. Create a new folder on your **D:** drive called **websharing**. Create a new text document in the folder called **test.txt**, and edit the file to include the text **Web sharing test**.
3. Right-click the new **websharing** folder and click **Properties**.
4. Click the **Web Sharing** tab.
5. In the Share on list box, click the **Dovercorp.net** Web site.
6. Click the **Share this folder** radio button.
7. When the Edit Alias dialog box opens, accept all default values and click **OK**. Click **OK** again to close the websharing folder properties dialog box.
8. Open the **Internet Information Services** tool. Verify that a new virtual directory called "websharing" now appears under the Dovercorp.net Web site.
9. Open **Internet Explorer**, type **http://localhost/websharing**, and press **Enter**.
10. Notice that a directory listing appears for this folder because directory browsing is enabled for Web Sharing folders by default and because a default document page was not found in the folder.
11. Click the **test.txt** file to view its contents. Because text files can be viewed in Internet Explorer, it appears within the browser window.
12. Close all open windows.

Installing and Using Remote Administration (HTML) tools

As discussed earlier in this chapter, IIS 6.0 provides the ability to manage IIS servers remotely via the Remote Administration (HTML) tools. Once installed, use these tools to manage not only IIS 6.0 servers, but also a variety of system elements including network settings, disk quotas, and more via a standard Web browser. This allows an administrator to easily configure system settings from any computer on the network.

The Remote Administration (HTML) tools are not installed on Windows Server 2003 by default, and must be added manually via the Add/Remove Windows Components feature of Add or Remove Programs in Control Panel. In Activity 7-16, you will first install and then explore the Remote Administration (HTML) tools using Internet Explorer.

Activity 7-16: Install and Explore the Remote Administration (HTML) Tools

Time Required: 15 minutes

Objective: Install and then explore the Remote Administration (HTML) tools to manage your server.

Description: Although the IT manager intends to have administrative staff use the Internet Information Services MMC to manage IIS servers normally, he has asked you to install the Remote Administration (HTML) tools for evaluation purposes. In this activity, you will first install these tools and then explore various settings from Internet Explorer.

1. Click **Start**, select **Control Panel**, and then click **Add or Remove Programs**.
2. Click **Add/Remove Windows Components**.
3. In the Components text box, click **Application Server** and then click the **Details** button.
4. In the Application Server window, click **Internet Information Services (IIS)** and then click the **Details** button.
5. In the Internet Information Services (IIS) window, click **World Wide Web Service** and then click the **Details** button.
6. In the World Wide Web Service window, click the check box next to **Remote Administration (HTML)** as shown in Figure 7-30. Click **OK**.

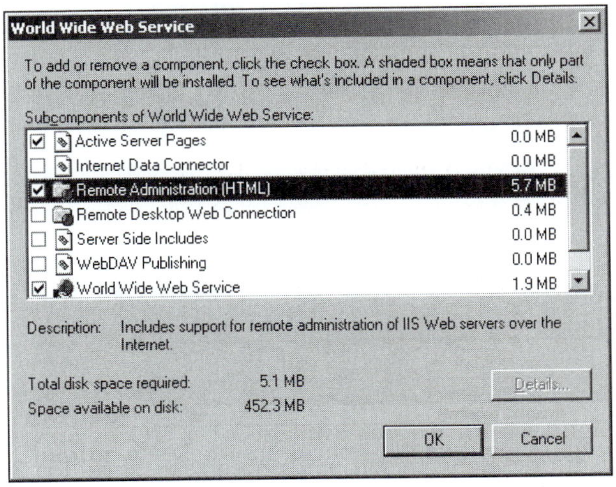

Figure 7-30 Adding the Remote Administration (HTML) tools

7. Click **OK** to close the Internet Information Services (IIS) window, click **OK** to close the Application Server window, and then click **Next**.
8. Click **Finish**.

9. Click the **Close** button to close the Add or Remove Programs window.
10. Click **Start**, select **All Programs**, and then click **Internet Explorer**. To add a site to the Trusted Sites list, click **Tools**, then click **Internet Options**. Click the **Security** tab, and select **Trusted sites** in the zones list. Click the **Sites** button. In the Trusted sites dialog box, type **127.0.0.1**. Click **Add**, and then click **Close**.
11. In the Internet Explorer address bar, type **https://127.0.0.1:8098** and press **Enter**. This connects you to the Remote Administration Web site using a secure connection.
12. When the first Security Alert window appears, click **OK**. When the second Security Alert window appears, click **Yes**.
13. In the User name text box, type **Admin*XX***. Type your password in the Password text box, and then click **OK**. The Server Administration Web site opens, as shown in Figure 7-31.

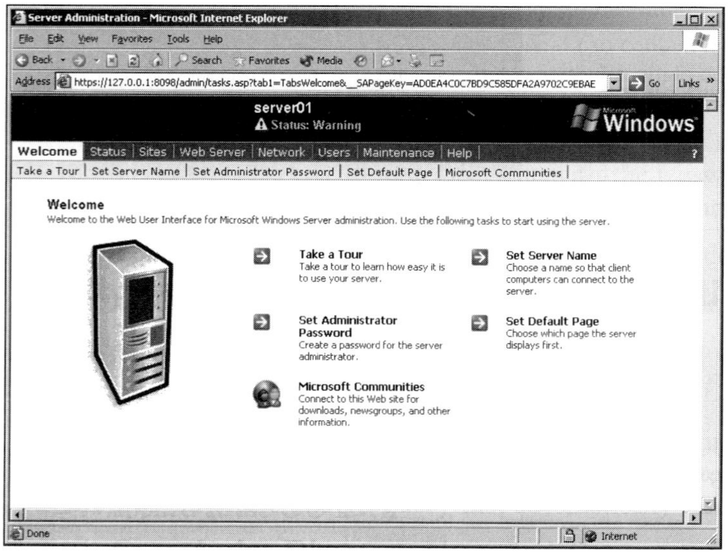

Figure 7-31 Accessing the Server Administration Web site

14. Click on the **Sites** link in the blue menu bar. This opens the Web Site Configuration page, which allows site properties to be changed or new sites to be created.
15. Click on the **Web Server** link in the blue menu bar. This opens the Web Server administration page, allowing you to change different server settings.
16. Click on the **Web Master Settings** link. In the Maximum connections section, type **1000** in the Limited to text box and click **OK**.
17. Click on the **Network** link in the blue menu bar, and then click on the **Interfaces** link. This page allows you to change the configuration settings of the server's network adapters.
18. Click on the **Maintenance** link in the blue menu bar. Browse through available settings as time permits.
19. Close Internet Explorer.

TROUBLESHOOTING WEB CLIENT CONNECTIVITY PROBLEMS

A major part of any administrator's job is troubleshooting network problems. One of the most common problems that may occur when running an IIS server is clients not being able to access one of the sites. The following section looks at some of the common client connectivity problems that can occur and how you can troubleshoot the various problems.

> **Note:** Client connectivity problems usually occur because of access or authentication problems.

Client Access Problems

If users are unable to gain access to an IIS Server, there are several configuration settings that you can verify to troubleshoot the problem.

- Verify the TCP/IP configuration settings that have been configured on the client. Use the IPCONFIG command on Windows NT, 2000, or XP machines to verify that the correct IP settings have been assigned. You can use WINIPCFG to verify IP settings on Windows 9x machines. Use the PING command to verify connectivity with remote computers.
- Check the proxy settings that have been configured through the client's Web browser. To be able to access intranet Web sites, be sure to click Bypass proxy server for local addresses in the proxy server configuration settings of your Web browser.
- Check for obvious problems such as whether the proxy server is available and online and whether the client is connected to the network.
- Enable or disable the Show friendly HTTP error messages options in the properties of Internet Explorer. If enabled, full details of connection errors are shown.
- Use a protocol analyzer to capture packets moving between the client and the Web server to determine where communications errors may be taking place.

If users complain that they are unable to gain access to a Web site or FTP site configured on an IIS server, check any one of the following:

- Check the permissions assigned to the site. Make sure that the Users group has been assigned the NTFS Read permission to the directory. Make sure the IIS Read permission has been assigned to the site's home directory.
- Check to see which authentication method has been configured for the site.
- Check to see what IP address and domain name restrictions have been applied to the site.
- If there is a connection limit set for the site, make sure this limit has not been exceeded.
- If the service has been configured to use a port other than the default, make sure the client is specifying the correct port number.
- If you have not enabled Anonymous access, make sure the client has a valid user account.
- Client computers may contain invalid cached DNS information about a specific Internet location. From the command prompt, type "ipconfig /flushdns" to clear the DNS cache.

Chapter Summary

- Internet Information Services includes four main components that include the World Wide Web (HTTP) services, File Transfer Protocol (FTP) services, Network News Transfer Protocol (NNTP) services, and Simple Mail Transfer Protocol (SMTP) services.
- The first step to configuring IIS is to understand how the master properties affect the overall Web server. The master properties are IIS parameters that can be configured on the server and are inheritable by all Web and FTP sites hosted on the server. If an individual site has its own configuration settings and you decide to change the Master Properties, IIS gives you the option of whether or not to apply the changes to the preconfigured site.
- Multiple Web sites can be distinguished on a single Web server by either configuring individual IP addresses for each site, configuring individual port numbers for each site, or by configuring a host header for each site.
- A virtual directory can be used to include information that may be stored on a different server from the one on which the Web site home directory is located.
- By default, Anonymous access is used to allow public access to a Web site.
- Five main authentication methods used in IIS are Anonymous, Basic, Digest, .NET Passport, and Integrated Windows authentication.
- Regular IIS maintenance tasks include backing up the IIS configuration, starting or stopping services, and installing of hot fixes or service packs.

Key Terms

alias — The name of a virtual directory, or name used to hide the real name of a directory and to simplify the directory name that would be used to access the information.

Anonymous access — Allows users to access a Web site without having to provide a user name and password.

authentication — Refers to determining whether a user has a valid user account with the proper permissions to access a resource such as a shared folder or Web site.

bandwidth throttling — Allows you to limit the network bandwidth that is available for Web and FTP connections to the server.

Basic authentication — Prompts users for a user name and password to be able to access the Web resource. The user name and password are then transmitted using Base64 encoding.

Default FTP site — An FTP server that responds to TCP/IP port 21 on all of the server's configured IP addresses that are not assigned to another site.

Default NNTP virtual server — A newsgroup server that responds to port 119 on all of the server's configured IP addresses that have not been assigned to another site.

Default SMTP virtual server — An e-mail component server that responds to port 25 on all of the server's IP addresses that have not been assigned to another site.

Default Web site — A Web site configured with FrontPage extensions that responds to TCP/IP port 80 on all unassigned IP addresses of the server. This Web site is initially empty and may be used to create a custom Web site for your organization.

Digest authentication — Prompts users for a user name and password to be able to access the Web resource. The user name and password are hashed to prevent hackers from obtaining the information.

File Transfer Protocol (FTP) — Used to transfer files between two computers that are both running TCP/IP.

host header — The fully qualified DNS name that is used to access a Web site on an IIS Server.

Integrated Windows authentication — Does not ask the user for a password but rather uses the client's currently logged-on credentials to supply a challenge/response to the Web server.

Internet Information Services (IIS) — A Windows Server 2003 component that provides Web-related services to an organization.

master properties — IIS parameters that are configured on the server and are inheritable by all Web and FTP sites hosted on the server.

metabase — IIS 6.0 stores its configuration settings in a database referred to as the IIS metabase.

.NET Passport authentication — An IIS authentication method that utilizes .NET Password user names and passwords.

Secure Sockets Layer (SSL) — This protocol is used to encrypt Web traffic between a client and the Web server.

Transmission Control Protocol (TCP) — A connection-based protocol, which means a session is established between the two hosts before any data is transferred.

virtual directory — A mapping to a physical directory containing content to be included on a Web site.

virtual servers — A unique Web or FTP site that behaves as if it were on its own dedicated server.

Web folder — A folder designed to be accessed from the Internet or an intranet using the HTTP or FTP protocols.

7

Review Questions

1. You are planning to install a Web-enabled e-mail package in your organization. Which IIS service is used to enable the sending of e-mail messages?
   a. NNTP
   b. SMTP
   c. HTTP
   d. FTP
2. IIS is automatically installed during a standard installation of Windows Server 2003. True or False?
3. Which of the following are the two user accounts automatically created during an installation of IIS? (Choose two.)
   a. IWAM_*servername*
   b. Anonymous_*user*
   c. WEBUser_*servername*
   d. IUSR_*servername*
4. Master properties can be configured to set the IP address and TCP port for all sites located on the server. True or False?
5. Individual site properties override master properties by default. True or False?
6. You are a network administrator responsible for maintaining your company's Web servers. There have recently been several hot fixes released for IIS 6.0. What tool can you use to determine the hot fixes currently installed on your Web servers?
   a. Add or Remove Windows Components
   b. Device Manager
   c. MBSA
   d. System Information

7. A client is reporting that he is unable to connect to your server running IIS. Which of the following could be causing the problem? (Choose all that apply.)
   a. permissions assigned to the Web and FTP sites
   b. TCP/IP parameters assigned to the client
   c. any IP address and domain name restrictions applied
   d. whether or not Anonymous access has been disabled
8. Which of the following IIS permissions can be assigned to a virtual directory? (Choose all that apply.)
   a. Full Control
   b. Read
   c. Write
   d. Delete
9. You have configured a new FTP site on your Web server. The site has been configured to only allow Read access. You have also enabled Anonymous access using the IUSR_Server1 account. In addition, you also notice that the following NTFS permissions are in place.

   Users: Full Control

   IUSR_Server1: Change

   Guests: Change

   What type of permission do users have to your new FTP site?
   a. Full Control
   b. Change
   c. Read
   d. No Access
10. You are the administrator of your company's Web server. You changed the FTP port from 21 to 1223. Clients report that they are not able to access the FTP server. What is most likely causing the problem?
    a. You have configured clients with incorrect permissions.
    b. There are IP address restrictions in place.
    c. Clients are connecting to the default port.
    d. There are domain name restrictions in place.
11. Directory security can be configured using which of the following? (Choose all that apply.)
    a. IP address
    b. Network address
    c. Username
    d. Domain name
12. You are configuring directory security for your FTP site. You select the granted access option and add the following IP network group address: 129.10.0.0. You also add the following single computer IP address: 135.15.121.10. Which of the following statements are true?
    a. All computers on the129.10.0.0 network are granted access to your FTP site.
    b. The IP address 135.15.121.10 is not granted access to your FTP site.
    c. All computers on the129.10.0.0 network are not granted access to your FTP site.
    d. The IP address 135.15.121.10 is granted access to your FTP site.

13. What protocol does FTP use to establish a session?
    a. TCP
    b. HTTP
    c. UDP
    d. POP3
14. When you are creating a virtual directory, which of the following are possible options for the location of the directory? (Choose all that apply.)
    a. a directory other than the home directory
    b. a URL
    c. a directory in a remote computer
    d. none of the above

15. Which of the following options can be used to back up the configuration settings of your IIS Server? (Choose all that apply.)
    a. Use the backup program included with Windows.
    b. The Iisback.vbs script
    c. Use the backup program within the IIS console.
    d. Use third-party backup software.
16. Which TCP port number does HTTP use by default?
    a. 21
    b. 80
    c. 443
    d. 119
17. What TCP port number does HTTPS use by default?
    a. 400
    b. 433
    c. 443
    d. 8080
18. You are configuring authentication for your IIS server. You want all users to provide their Windows Server 2003 user name and password before gaining access to the Web resources. You also do not want the user names and passwords sent in clear text. Which authentication method should you configure?
    a. Anonymous authentication
    b. Basic authentication
    c. Digest authentication
    d. Integrated Windows authentication
19. You want to configure a maximum connection limit for all sites configured on your Web server. At what level should you make the configuration change?
    a. master
    b. site
    c. folder
    d. file
20. All Web content published through your IIS server must be stored locally. True or False?

CASE PROJECTS

Case Project 7-1

Dover Leasing is planning to install a Web server on their corporate network. In a planning session, managers and representatives from each department raise several concerns. You have been asked to address these concerns in the next planning session.

1. Managers are unsure of the different authentication methods available. List the various methods of authentication and the differences between them.
2. Each department will have their own Web site and wants to control whether users from other departments will be able to access their site. List the various ways in which access to these sites could be controlled.
3. If the Web server will host multiple sites, what methods can be used to uniquely identify each one?

Case Project 7-2

You are configuring a new FTP site for Dover Leasing's Web server. The managers would prefer the information to be physically stored on another server. The site will be used to provide access to some of your company's Web content to network users and an external customer. Your managers are concerned about security because no other external clients or business partners should be allowed to access this content. You have been asked to create a document addressing some of the issues and concerns.

1. Outline each of the steps in creating and configuring the new FTP site.
2. Security is a major issue and has been emphasized by your managers. Include in your document the various options you will use to secure the new FTP site so that only the appropriate users have access.
3. Include in your document how NTFS and IIS permissions can be used together to provide the most security.
4. Your managers are also concerned with the security of IIS 6.0 and want to make sure that the latest service packs and hot fixes are always applied. How will you track what hot fixes and patches need to be installed on your server?

Case Project 7-3

A friend who owns an ISP has come to you for advice about offering services based on the Windows Server 2003 version of Internet Information Services. Mainly he is concerned about the large number of Web sites that he will need to create and the amount of time this will take. Secondly, he has security concerns about implementing services he doesn't require such as NNTP and FTP. What can you suggest that would help to alleviate his concerns?

Case Project 7-4

One of the managers of the Marketing Department at Dover Leasing has come to you with a question. Although the department will have their own Web server and a person responsible for the Web site, she would rather not have this person be responsible for installing virtual directories via the IIS console. What alternative would you suggest to allow virtual directories to be easily created without using the IIS console or scripting?

CHAPTER

8

ADMINISTERING TCP/IP

After reading this chapter and completing the exercises, you will be able to:

- Understand basic concepts about TCP/IP
- Configure TCP/IP on Windows Server 2003
- Troubleshoot TCP/IP and network connectivity using various utilities
- Administer Dynamic Host Configuration Protocol (DHCP) in Windows Server 2003

Administering Windows Server 2003 includes the implementation and management of a variety of networking protocols and services. Windows Server 2003 has been designed so that many of its main features, such as Active Directory, require the use of TCP/IP. This is a vital component that all network administrators need to understand and master to successfully manage and troubleshoot a Windows Server 2003 network environment. The first few sections of this chapter introduce you to TCP/IP concepts, as well as the methods used to configure TCP/IP on Windows Server 2003 systems. Utilities used to validate and troubleshoot local computer configurations and network connectivity are also discussed.

TCP/IP works with services such as the **Dynamic Host Configuration Protocol (DHCP)** to facilitate the dynamic assignment of IP addresses and related settings to network systems. In this chapter, you will learn how DHCP works, along with the procedures involved in configuring, managing, and troubleshooting DHCP on the network.

Although the Domain Name System (DNS) and related services are looked at in more detail in Chapter 9, the ability to integrate DHCP with DNS is also looked at later in this chapter.

UNDERSTANDING TCP/IP

Transmission Control Protocol/Internet Protocol (TCP/IP) consists of a suite of protocols and utilities that are used for network communication and troubleshooting on local networks and the Internet. Over the past 10 years, TCP/IP has become the most popular network protocol in use. The main reason for this is that TCP/IP is the protocol suite used for Internet-based communications. As the Internet continues to grow in popularity and becomes the basis for many corporate communication services, companies have little choice but to implement TCP/IP as their primary network protocol. Another advantage of TCP/IP is that it is an open-standard, vendor-independent protocol. It can be used to provide network communication between computers running different operating systems throughout not only an organization but also the world.

In Windows Server 2003 environments, Active Directory depends on TCP/IP and related services to function. This requires that you as a network administrator understand the various components included with TCP/IP, along with their purpose. The following topics are reviewed in later sections to assist you in understanding the fundamentals of TCP/IP.

- TCP/IP architecture
- TCP/IP protocol stack
- TCP/IP installation

TCP/IP Architecture

TCP/IP maps to a four-layer conceptual model described in Table 8-1.

Table 8-1 The four layers of the TCP/IP model

Layer	Description
Application	Identifies which applications use TCP/IP and how they interact with the lower-level protocols
Transport / Host-to-host	Provides communication sessions between hosts
Internet	Responsible for addressing packets and determining the routing of packets on the network
Network Interface	Determines how data is transmitted on the physical network medium

The TCP/IP Protocol Stack

TCP/IP is a suite of protocols, each operating at one of the four layers described in Table 8-1 and each providing a specific function. The following protocols are discussed in this section:

- Transmission Control Protocol
- User Datagram Protocol
- Address Resolution Protocol
- Internet Control Message Protocol
- Internet Group Management Protocol
- Internet Protocol

Transmission Control Protocol

The **Transmission Control Protocol (TCP)** operates at the transport layer and is responsible for the reliable transmission of data on a TCP/IP network. TCP is a connection-based protocol, which means all packets sent using TCP are verified and ultimately assembled at the destination host in the correct order.

TCP is also responsible for breaking up large blocks of data into smaller units called segments, and then reassembling those segments when they arrive at the destination. The segments are assigned sequence numbers that tell the destination host how to reassemble them. TCP also provides reliable delivery using acknowledgements; if a sender does not receive confirmation that data sent using TCP arrived at the destination, it will ultimately resend the required data.

User Datagram Protocol

The **User Datagram Protocol (UDP)** is another protocol that functions at the transport layer. Unlike TCP, UDP is a connectionless protocol and provides no guarantee of packet delivery, but it does provide speed advantages in the form of lower overhead. No acknowledgements, sequencing, or session establishments occur between hosts using UDP. Instead, UDP relies upon higher-layer applications to provide any required reliability features.

Address Resolution Protocol

The **Address Resolution Protocol (ARP)** works at the Internet layer and is responsible for mapping IP addresses to hardware media access control (MAC) addresses. A network card's MAC address is typically assigned to the card as part of its manufacturing process. When a host running TCP/IP is connected to an Ethernet network and needs to communicate with another host or router on the same network, it must resolve the destination host's IP address to its MAC address. This is usually accomplished via an ARP broadcast sent to hosts on the same segment, requesting the MAC address associated with the IP address in question. Ultimately, computers store this information in their ARP cache for a variable length of time to reduce the total amount of bandwidth consumed by ARP broadcasts.

Every Windows Server 2003 computer has an ARP cache that stores recently resolved mappings of IP addresses to MAC addresses, as well as any static entries that have been configured manually.

The ARP cache can contain both dynamic and static entries. Dynamic entries are stored in the ARP cache for two minutes by default. However, if the entry is used within those two minutes, then the entry is stored for 10 minutes before being removed. In Activity 8-1, you will use the arp command to view, add, and delete entries in your server's ARP cache.

Note: The IP addresses, subnet masks, and default gateway values specified in this chapter may be different than those used on your network. Be sure to reconfirm the appropriate network setting values with your instructor prior to starting the activities.

Activity 8-1: Viewing and Configuring ARP Cache Entries

Time Required: 10 minutes

Objective: View, add, and delete ARP cache entries.

Description: The IT manager at Dover Leasing is very concerned about reducing all network traffic that may not be necessary. Because he knows that ARP traffic is broadcast based, he has asked you to explore how ARP entries are cached on Windows Server 2003 systems, as well as whether it would be feasible to move to a process where all ARP cache entries are made static rather than dynamic. In this activity, you will view and configure ARP cache entries on your server.

1. Click **Start**, click **Run**, and in the Open text box type **cmd**. Press **Enter**.
2. At the command prompt, type **arp /?** and press **Enter** to view the switches associated with the ARP command. Take some time to read each of the different switches and their purpose.
3. To view current entries stored in the ARP cache, type **arp –a** and press **Enter**. Depending upon your recent network activities, there may be many entries found in the ARP cache, or none at all.
4. Type **ping *<ip address>***, where *<ip address>* is the IP address of your partner's server, and press **Enter**.

5. To view the new ARP cache entry, type **arp –a** and press **Enter**. Notice that a dynamic entry is now in the ARP cache, mapping your partner's IP address to the MAC address of your partner's network adapter card, as illustrated in Figure 8-1.

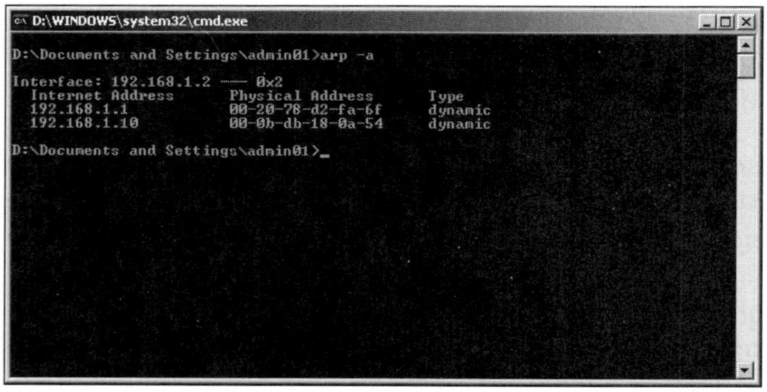

Figure 8-1 Viewing the results of the arp –a command

6. Type **ipconfig** and press **Enter**. Note the IP address assigned to your default gateway.
7. Type **arp –s <default gateway ip address> 00-00-00-00-00-01**, where <default gateway ip address> is the address of your assigned gateway, and press **Enter**. This will add an incorrect static entry into your ARP cache.
8. Type **arp –a** to view all ARP cache entries, including the static entry added in Step 7.
9. Type **ping <default gateway ip address>**, where <default gateway ip address> is the address of your assigned gateway, and press **Enter**. Notice that the command results in four Request timed out messages because the MAC address associated with the default gateway is incorrect and cannot be contacted.
10. Type **arp –d <default gateway ip address>**, where <default gateway ip address> is the address of your assigned gateway, and press **Enter**. This deletes the static ARP cache entry belonging to the default gateway IP address.
11. Type **arp –a** and press **Enter**. Verify that the static entry has been removed from the ARP cache.
12. Type **ping <default gateway ip address>** and press **Enter**. Notice that four reply messages are received because ARP is again occurring dynamically.
13. Type **arp –a** and press **Enter**. Notice that a dynamic entry now appears for the default gateway IP address.
14. Close the command prompt window.

Internet Control Message Protocol

The **Internet Control Message Protocol (ICMP)** operates at the network layer and is used to exchange network status and error information between two hosts. For example, the **ping** command uses ICMP to test for basic IP connectivity between systems running TCP/IP. Both the **pathping** and the **tracert** utilities also use ICMP packets to check for network connectivity. If the two hosts can communicate, you receive a successful reply; if there is a problem with TCP/IP connectivity on or between the hosts, you receive a destination host unreachable message. Although ICMP is primarily used for testing and diagnostic functions, it is also capable of changing the configuration of hosts in certain situations. For example, a router might inform a host of a better route to use to reach a destination network, or it might ask a sending host to transmit at a lower speed during periods of network congestion. ICMP utilities such as ping, pathping, and tracert are looked at in more detail later in this chapter.

Internet Group Management Protocol

The **Internet Group Management Protocol (IGMP)** operates at the network layer and is used to manage network and host information when a network application requires the use of multicasts to communicate. IGMP informs routers and multicast devices of the multicast group membership.

Internet Protocol

Internet Protocol (IP) is the Internet-layer protocol responsible for addressing and routing packets so that they are delivered to the correct host on the local network or across routers to a host on another subnet or network. IP is a connectionless protocol, which means that it does not guarantee the delivery of the packets. Ensuring that the packets arrive is the responsibility of the higher-level protocols like TCP.

The current version of IP is known as IPv4 and uses a 32-bit addressing scheme. IP addresses are generally represented using dotted-decimal notation, such as 192.168.1.1. A subnet mask is used to determine which portion of an address represents the network and which portion represents a unique host on that network. For example, the IP address 192.168.1.1 using a subnet mask of 255.255.255.0 would indicate that the host is part of network 192.168.1.0, with a host ID of 1.

When the current version of the IP was originally developed, little thought was put into the fact that the Internet would grow to the size it is today. As such, much of the IP address space is depleted or tightly controlled by governing bodies. To help account for this and to allow for continued growth, two different strategies evolved. The first was the creation of a new version of IP that supports a much larger address space, known as IPv6. The second strategy involved designating some of the IPv4 address ranges as private or for internal network use only. These address ranges include:

- 10.0.0.0–10.255.255.255
- 172.16.0.0–172.31.255.255
- 192.168.0.0–192.168.255.255

Although companies can use these address ranges at will, at least one public IP address is always required to connect to the Internet.

Now that you are familiar with the protocols that make up the TCP/IP protocol suite, you need to know how to install and configure TCP/IP.

Installing TCP/IP

If your network adapter is automatically detected during the installation of Windows Server 2003, TCP/IP is installed by default. If TCP/IP is not installed during setup, it can be added afterward. In Activity 8-2, you will explore the current network settings assigned to your server.

Activity 8-2: Exploring Windows Server 2003 Network Settings

Time Required: 10 minutes

Objective: Browse Windows Server 2003 network settings.

Description: As part of your job as a junior network administrator at Dover Leasing, you are responsible for creating structured troubleshooting documents for help desk staff. Although you are familiar with configuring network settings on Windows 2000 and Windows XP, you decide that a new step-by-step document should be created for the help desk staff. In this activity, you will access and browse through the network settings in Windows Server 2003.

1. Click **Start**, select **Control Panel**, and then double-click **Network Connections**.
2. In the Network Connections window, right-click **Local Area Connection** and click **Properties**.

3. In the Local Area Connection Properties dialog box, click the **Install** button, as shown in Figure 8-2.

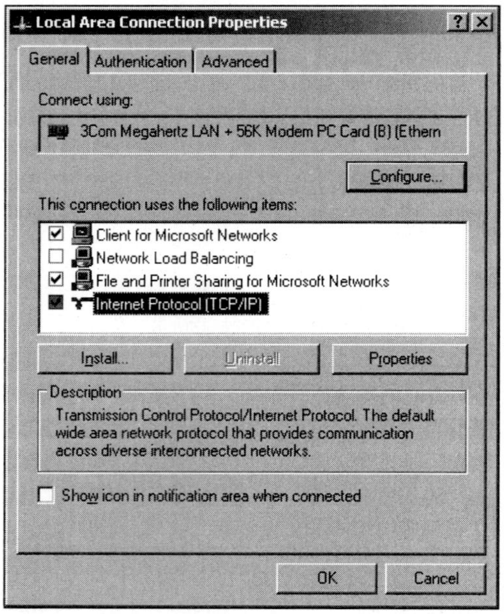

Figure 8-2 Local Area Connection properties

4. In the Select Network Component Type dialog box, ensure that **Client** is selected and then click **Add**. Note that only one additional option, Client Service for Netware, exists. Click **Cancel**.
5. In the Select Network Component Type dialog box click **Protocol**, and then click **Add**. Note the various network protocols available on Windows Server 2003, as shown in Figure 8-3. Click **Cancel**.

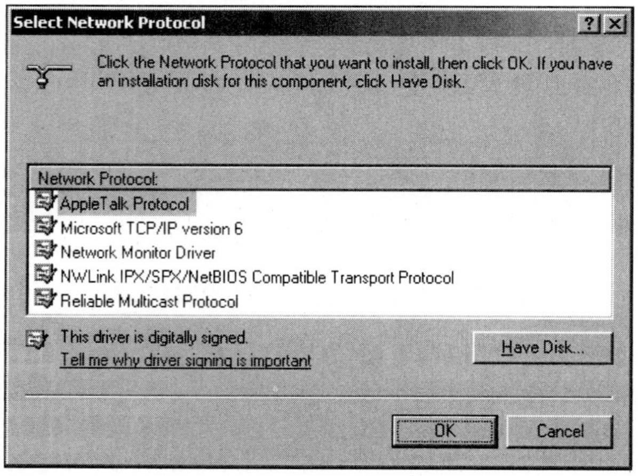

Figure 8-3 Installing network protocols

6. Click **Cancel** to close the Select Network Component Type dialog box.
7. In the Local Area Connection Properties dialog box, click **Internet Protocol (TCP/IP)** in the This connection uses the following items list box, and then click **Properties**.
8. Review the TCP/IP configuration settings applied to your server, and then click the **Advanced** button.

9. On the **IP Settings** tab, note the IP addresses and default gateway address assigned to your server. This screen allows you to configure additional IP addresses for the network interface, or additional default gateway addresses.
10. Click the **DNS** tab, and review the various options and configuration settings found on this screen.
11. Click the **WINS** tab, and review the various options and configuration settings found on this screen.
12. Click the **Options** tab, and then click the **Properties** button. This opens the TCP/IP Filtering dialog box, as illustrated in Figure 8-4. Here you can configure the TCP, UDP, and IP protocol ports to which Windows Server 2003 will accept or reject connections.

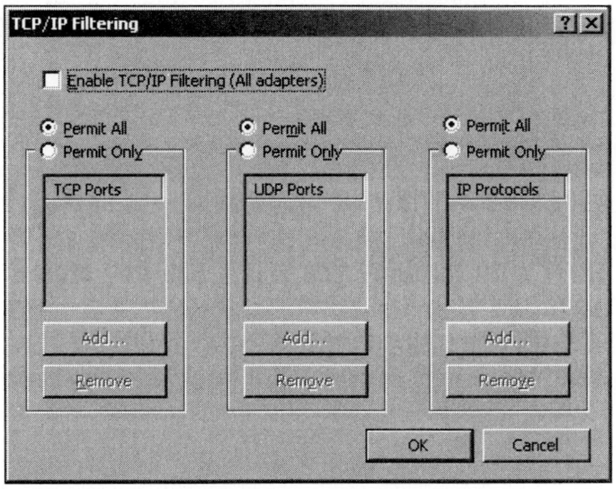

Figure 8-4 TCP/IP filtering settings

13. Click **Cancel** to close the TCP/IP Filtering dialog box, click **Cancel** to close the Advanced TCP/IP Settings dialog box, and then click **Cancel** again to close the Internet Protocol (TCP/IP) Properties dialog box.
14. Click **OK** to close the Local Area Connection Properties dialog box, and then close the Network Connections window.

Once TCP/IP has been installed, you can either manually configure addressing parameters or you can implement dynamic addressing using DHCP. Configuring TCP/IP using both methods is discussed in the next section.

Configuring TCP/IP on Windows Server 2003 Computers

All hosts on a TCP/IP network require an **IP address** and a **subnet mask** at a minimum. Depending on the complexity of the network, other IP parameters may also need to be assigned, such as a **default gateway** or the IP addresses of DNS name servers.

Note: See Table 8-2 for a description of each of these options.

You have two options when determining how to configure IP addresses on workstations and servers. You can configure each one manually with a static IP address, meaning an IP address that is permanently assigned to the computer until it is manually changed, or you can configure the computers to obtain an IP address automatically. This requires a DHCP server on the network, which is discussed later in the chapter.

Configuring Static IP Addresses

The decision on whether to use a static or dynamic IP-addressing method is often a function of the size of your network. For example, a small network that consists of only a few hosts may be a good candidate for manual addressing, whereas a network consisting of hundreds or thousands of hosts probably would not be. However, even in an environment that does use DHCP for automatic IP address assignment, there may be hosts that require a static IP address, either as a function of the services they offer or for reference purposes. For example, a DHCP server always requires a static IP address. Similarly, most companies will configure all servers with static IP addresses, if only for tracking and diagnostic purposes. In these cases, IP address settings must be configured manually.

Note: By default, Windows Server 2003 is configured to obtain an IP address automatically via DHCP, but you can still manually assign one by modifying the server's TCP/IP properties.

For each network card configured to use TCP/IP, you need to configure an IP address and a subnet mask. These settings are configured via the TCP/IP Properties dialog box, as shown in Figure 8-5. Table 8-2 outlines each of the configuration options found on this screen and its purpose.

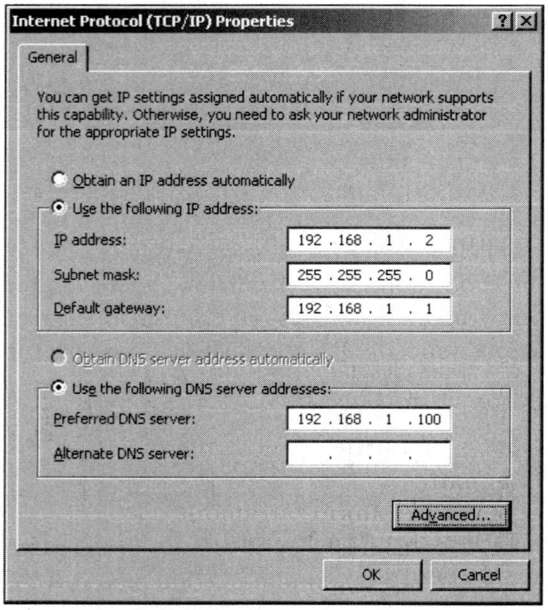

Figure 8-5 Manually configuring TCP/IP properties

Table 8-2 TCP/IP options

Option	Description
IP address	A 32-bit number represented in dotted-decimal notation that uniquely identifies a host; each host on a given network requires a unique IP address, such as 192.168.1.1
Subnet mask	A 32-bit number represented in dotted-decimal notation that is used in conjunction with the IP address to identify the network to which the host belongs, such as 255.255.255.0
Default gateway	A 32-bit number represented in dotted-decimal notation that uniquely identifies the IP address of the router to which packets destined for other networks should be forwarded

In Activity 8-3, you will manually configure your server's TCP/IP settings.

Activity 8-3: Configuring TCP/IP Settings Manually

Time Required: 10 minutes

Objective: Configure static IP address settings on Windows Server 2003.

Description: As part of creating the help desk troubleshooting and configuration document, you decide to list the steps to configure TCP/IP settings manually because this method will be used for all servers at Dover Leasing. In this activity, you will first configure TCP/IP settings on your server manually and then confirm the settings using the ipconfig utility.

1. Click **Start**, select **Control Panel**, and then double-click **Network Connections**.
2. In the Network Connections window, right-click **Local Area Connection** and click **Properties**.
3. In the This connection uses the following items list box, click **Internet Protocol (TCP/IP)**, and then click the **Properties** button.
4. In the Internet Protocol (TCP/IP) Properties dialog box, click the **Obtain an IP address automatically** radio button to clear all current TCP/IP settings.
5. Click the **Use the following IP address** radio button to allow IP settings to be configured manually.
6. In the IP address text box, type **192.168.1.*X***, where *X* is your assigned student number. Press the **Tab** key.
7. In the Subnet mask text box, notice that the value 255.255.255.0 is filled in automatically and press the **Tab** key.
8. In the Default gateway text box, type **192.168.1.100**.
9. In the Preferred DNS server text box, type **192.168.1.100**. Click **OK**.
10. Click **OK** to close the Local Area Connection Properties dialog box, and then close the Network Connections window.
11. Click **Start**, click **Run**, and in the Open text box type **cmd** and press **Enter**.
12. At the command prompt, type **ipconfig** and press **Enter**. Verify that the output of this command matches the settings configured in the previous steps, and then close the command prompt window.

Configuring IP Addresses Dynamically

If there is a server on the network running DHCP, you can configure computers on the network to receive IP addresses dynamically. Dynamic IP addressing can eliminate some of the administrative problems associated with configuring static IP addresses, such as the chance of human error (incorrectly typing an IP address) or IP address duplication, which occurs when a single IP address is assigned to multiple hosts. Both of these problems typically cause IP communication to fail on the affected systems.

A DHCP server is configured with a range of IP addresses that will be assigned to clients on the network, ensuring no duplicate addresses exist and that clients receive the correct configuration settings. The clients on the network are then configured to obtain an IP address automatically. This option was shown in Figure 7-2.

Automatic Private IP Addressing

Consider the following scenario: You install DHCP on one of your servers on the network and configure all clients to obtain an IP address automatically. Then, for some reason, the DHCP server goes offline, and clients are unable to lease an IP address.

Windows Server 2003 implements a technology known as **automatic private IP addressing (APIPA)** that allows DHCP-enabled clients to assign themselves an IP address and subnet mask in the event that a

DHCP server is unavailable. The client generates an IP address in the range of 169.254.0.0 to 169.254.255.255 with the subnet mask 255.255.0.0. (The Internet Assigned Numbers Authority has reserved the range of IP addresses for this purpose.)

Once the client generates an IP address within this range, it sends out a broadcast on the network to make sure the address isn't already being used. The client continues to use this IP address until it detects an online DHCP server.

Keep in mind that automatic IP addressing provides a client with limited functionality on the network. The only parameters that are assigned are an IP address and a subnet mask. The client is only able to communicate with those computers also using this range of IP addresses and is only able to communicate with computers on the same network or subnet. As a best practice, it is often worthwhile to assign an address from this range as a secondary address to servers that exist on the same subnet as client computers. Then, even if the DHCP server were to go offline, a client could still connect to and use local servers.

Hands-on Project

Activity 8-4: Testing Automatic Private IP Addressing

Time Required: 10 minutes

Objective: Test the impact of Automatic Private IP Addressing.

Description: The majority of the client workstations at Dover Leasing will ultimately be using DHCP to obtain their TCP/IP settings. Before implementing DHCP, you decide to test the impact on clients when a DHCP server is unavailable. In this activity, you will configure your server to act as a DHCP client to test whether it will be allocated an address in the APIPA range when a DHCP server is unavailable.

1. Click **Start**, select **Control Panel**, and then double-click **Network Connections**.
2. In the Network Connections window, right-click **Local Area Connection** and click **Properties**.
3. In the This connection uses the following items list box, click **Internet Protocol (TCP/IP)**, and then click the **Properties** button.
4. In the Internet Protocol (TCP/IP) Properties dialog box, click the **Obtain an IP address automatically** radio button to clear all current TCP/IP settings, as illustrated in Figure 8-6.

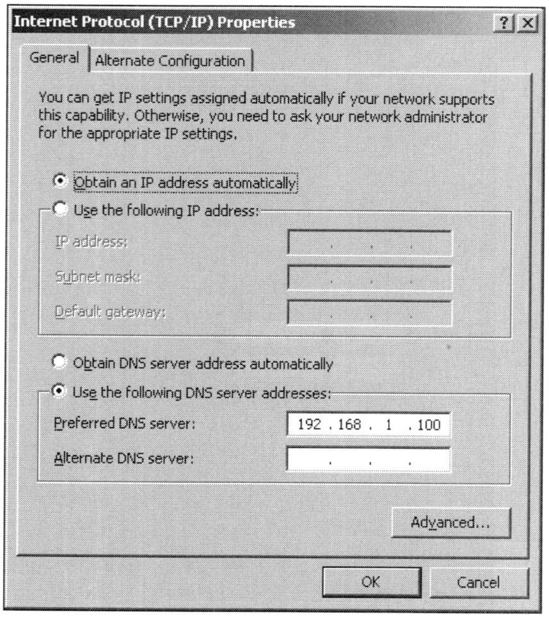

Figure 8-6 Configuring TCP/IP properties dynamically using DHCP

5. Click **OK**, and then click **OK** again to close the Local Area Connection Properties dialog box.
6. Click **Start**, click **Run**, and in the **Open** text box type **cmd** and press **Enter**.
7. At the command prompt, type **ipconfig /renew** and press **Enter**. After the error message appears, type **ipconfig** and press **Enter**. Verify that the output of this command now shows that your server has an IP address in the 169.254.0.0 APIPA range, as illustrated in Figure 8-7.

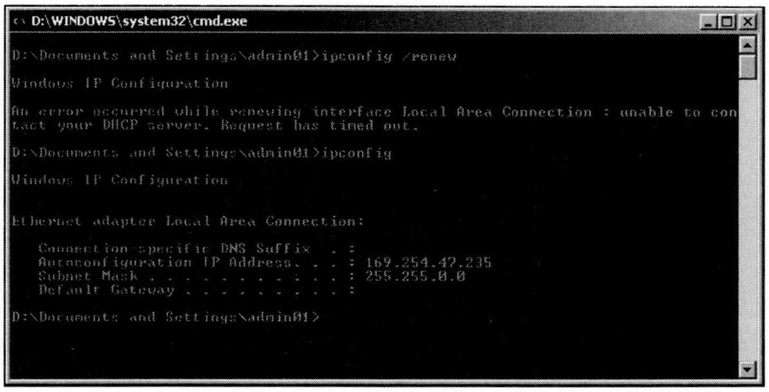

Figure 8-7 Viewing APIPA settings using ipconfig

8. Type **ping 192.168.1.1** and press **Enter**. Notice that replies are not received because your IP address is now in a different address range than the one normally used on the LAN.
9. Right click the **Local Area Connection** icon in the Network Connections window and click **Properties**.
10. In the This connection uses the following items list box, click **Internet Protocol (TCP/IP)**, and then click the **Properties** button.
11. Configure the following TCP/IP settings, where *X* is your assigned student number:
    - IP address: 192.168.1.*X*
    - Subnet mask: 255.255.255.0
    - Default gateway: 192.168.1.*X*, where *X* is the last digit of the IP address for the classroom default gateway

    Click **OK** to close the Internet Protocol (TCP/IP) Properties dialog box, and then click **OK** to close the Local Area Connection Properties dialog box.
12. In the command prompt window, type **ipconfig** and press **Enter**. Notice that your server now has its TCP/IP settings configured correctly once again.
13. Close all open windows.

8

Troubleshooting TCP/IP and Network Connectivity

Once TCP/IP is installed and configured, it is a good idea to test connectivity to make sure that computers can properly communicate over the network. There may also be times when you have to troubleshoot network connectivity problems between computers. TCP/IP comes with several command-line utilities that can be used to verify and troubleshoot network connectivity.

Verifying TCP/IP Configurations

The first step in troubleshooting network connectivity is to verify the TCP/IP configuration settings on the computer with the problem. On computers running Windows Server 2003, you can use the **ipconfig** command to verify the addressing parameters assigned to a host. There are several parameters that can be used with this command, as summarized in Table 8-3.

Table 8-3 Ipconfig parameters

Parameter	Description
/all	Displays the full TCP/IP parameters assigned to all network adapters
/release	Sends a message to the DHCP server to release the IP address that has been assigned to the network adapter
/renew	Renews the IP configuration information from a DHCP server
/flushdns	Used to purge the DNS resolver cache; this switch can be used in an attempt to troubleshoot DNS name resolution problems
/registerdns	Used to renew all DHCP leases and to reregister dynamic DNS information
/displaydns	Displays the contents of the DNS resolver cache on the server
/showclassid	Displays the DHCP class IDs assigned to an adapter
/setclassid	Configures the DHCP class ID for an adapter

Note: Windows 9x machines primarily use the **winipcfg** command to display the TCP/IP configuration settings. This command is very similar to the ipconfig utility used in Windows NT/2000/XP and Windows Server 2003.

The information that is displayed using ipconfig or winipcfg can assist you in determining if the computer is using a correct IP address, subnet mask, or default gateway configuration. If local configuration settings are correct, then the next step is to test network connectivity using tools described in the section that follows. In Activity 8-5, you will explore the capabilities of the ipconfig utility.

Activity 8-5: Exploring the Ipconfig Utility

Hands-on Project

Time Required: 10 minutes

Objective: Explore the capabilities of the ipconfig command.

Description: As part of developing a set of troubleshooting and testing procedures for the help desk staff at Dover Leasing, you decide that it will be necessary for you to be familiar with the various options available with different network diagnostic commands. In this activity, you will use the ipconfig utility to gather information about your local server and explore some of the different switches that the command offers.

1. Click **Start**, click **Run**, in the Open text box type **cmd**, and press **Enter**.
2. Type **ipconfig /?** and press **Enter**. Read through the various switches that can be used with the ipconfig command.
3. Type **ipconfig** and press **Enter**. Notice that without any switches, the ipconfig command will only display information about your server's IP address, subnet mask, and default gateway, as shown in Figure 8-8.

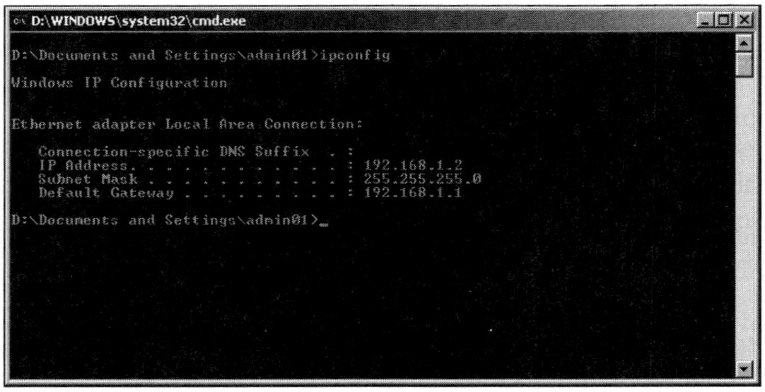

Figure 8-8 Viewing TCP/IP settings using the ipconfig command

4. Type **ipconfig /all** and press **Enter**. Notice that the /all switch displays all TCP/IP configuration information for your server, as illustrated in Figure 8-9.

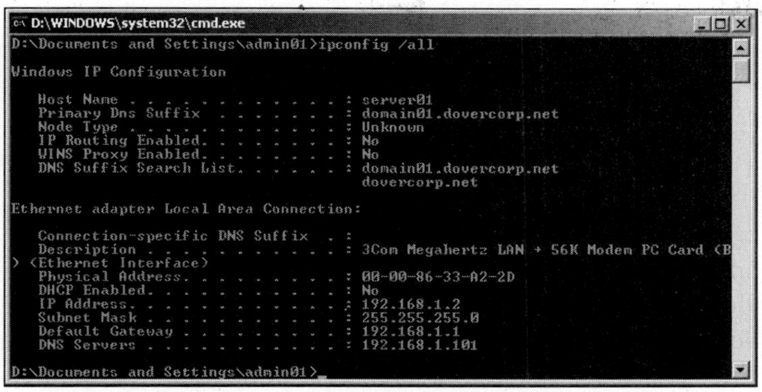

Figure 8-9 Viewing results of the ipconfig /all command

5. Type **ipconfig /release** and press **Enter**. Notice that this command is not permitted because your server is currently not enabled for DHCP.
6. Type **ping www.course.com** and press **Enter**.
7. Type **ipconfig /displaydns** and press **Enter**. This command shows the contents of the DNS resolver cache on your server, including the entry for *www.course.com*, as shown in Figure 8-10.

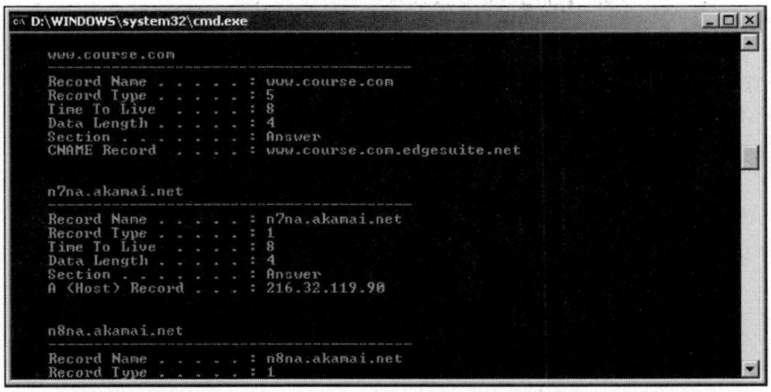

Figure 8-10 Viewing results of the ipconfig /displaydns command

8. Close the command prompt window.

Verifying Network Connectivity

As an administrator, you may have to troubleshoot a loss of client network connectivity from time to time. As discussed in the previous section, one of the first things you need to do is verify that the system's local IP settings are correct to eliminate this as the source of the problem. Next you can look at network configuration settings to determine where any loss of connectivity is occurring.

Windows Server 2003 provides a variety of TCP/IP utilities to troubleshoot connectivity problems, including the following:

- Ping
- Tracert
- Pathping
- Arp

- Route
- Netdiag

Once you've verified the addressing parameters assigned to the computer, you can use the ping command to test for network connectivity. The ping command tests network connectivity with other hosts on the network by sending ICMP packets to a remote computer and then listening for an echo reply from the remote host.

> **Tip:** If you can successfully ping the IP address of a host on a different subnet or network, this is a good indication that TCP/IP is correctly installed and configured.

Some of the more common switches that can be used with the ping command are described in Table 8-4.

Table 8-4 Ping parameters

Parameter	Description
-t	Ping the specified host until stopped; to stop the ping, press Ctrl+C; to pause and view statistics, press Ctrl+Break
-a	Resolves the IP Address to a host name
-n *<count>*	Specifies the number of echo requests to send (e.g., ping –n 10 *<target IP address>*)
-l *<size>*	Specifies the size of echo requests to send, in bytes

In Activity 8-6, you will use the ping utility to test for TCP/IP network connectivity.

Activity 8-6: Testing Network Connectivity Using the Ping Command

Time Required: 10 minutes

Objective: Use the ping command to test for network connectivity.

Description: Although you already understand the basic purpose of the ping command, you decide to explore some of the utility's advanced switches and settings. In this activity, you will issue the ping command along with various switches to test network connectivity with other hosts.

1. Click **Start**, click **Run**, in the Open text box type **cmd**, and then press **Enter**.
2. Type **ping /?** and press **Enter**. Review all of the switches that can be used with the ping command, as illustrated in Figure 8-11.

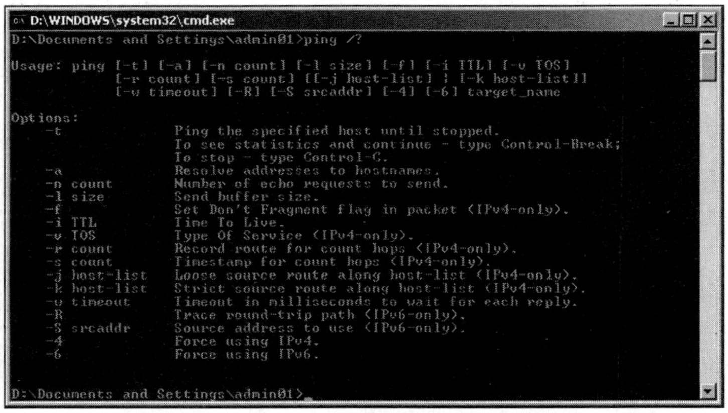

Figure 8-11 Viewing switches for the ping command

3. Type **ping 192.168.1.100** and press **Enter**. This command sends four ICMP echo requests to the instructor server and results in four received echo replies. Notice that by default, each of the ping requests is 32 bytes in length, as shown in Figure 8-12.

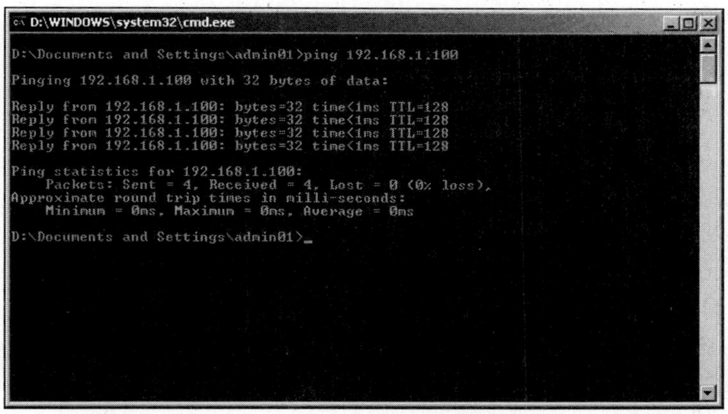

Figure 8-12 Testing connectivity using the ping command

4. Type **ping –t 192.168.1.100** and press **Enter**. This command sends a continuous ping to the instructor server, rather than just the standard four requests.
5. Hold down the **Ctrl** key and then press the **Break** key. Notice that a list of the current statistics occurs but that the ping command continues uninterrupted.
6. Press **Ctrl+C** to stop the continuous ping.
7. Type **ping –n 8 192.168.1.100** and press **Enter**. The ping command now sends eight echo requests rather than the standard four.
8. Type **ping –l 1000 192.168.1.100** and press **Enter**. Notice that the size of the echo request packets are now 1000 rather than 32 bytes in length.
9. Type **ping 127.0.0.1** and press **Enter**. This command is used to ping the loopback interface on your server.
10. Type **ping –a 127.0.0.1** and press **Enter**. While this command pings your server's loopback interface, notice that it also resolves the IP address to the hostname loopback, as illustrated in Figure 8-13.

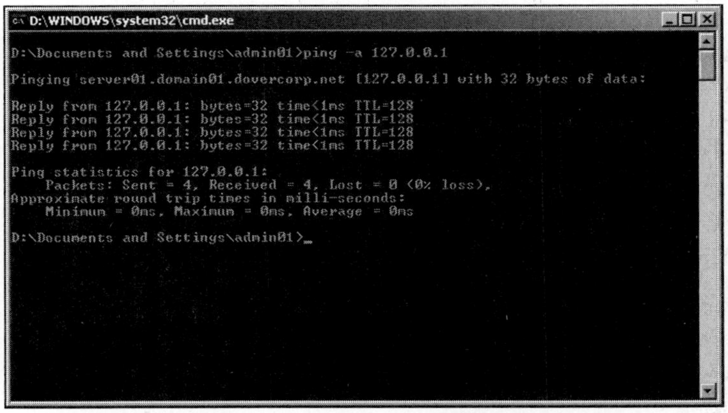

Figure 8-13 Resolving addresses to hostnames using ping -a

11. Close the command prompt window.

> **Note:** The IP address range 127.0.0.1 to 127.255.255.254 is reserved for loopback diagnostic functions. If you ping an address in this range and receive a reply, it indicates that TCP/IP is initialized on your system.

If you can ping the default gateway, but cannot ping the IP address of a remote host, you need to verify that the routers between the local host and the remote host are operational. This can be done using the tracert command. This TCP/IP utility traces the route a packet takes to reach a destination host. It displays all the routers a packet must pass through in the journey to the remote host. If packets are unable to reach the remote host via the ping command, it may indicate that the remote host is unavailable. However, it may also indicate that a network problem exists on the path between you and the remote host. Using tracert helps a network administrator to better understand the true nature of a TCP/IP network communication issue.

Some of the more common switches that can be used with the tracert command are described in Table 8-5.

Table 8-5 Tracert parameters

Parameter	Description
-h	Maximum number of hops used to search for the client
-w <timeout>	The amount of time in milliseconds to wait before timing out

In Activity 8-7, you will use the tracert command to determine the network path used to reach different Internet hosts.

Activity 8-7: Testing Network Connectivity Using the Tracert Command

Time Required: 10 minutes

Objective: Test network connectivity using the tracert command.

Description: In the past, the help desk staff have used only the ping utility as their primary source of network troubleshooting information. Although ping provides basic information about network connectivity, it does not help if a problem exists on the path between the source and destination hosts. As such, you also want all help desk staff to use the tracert utility to test connectivity in the future. In this activity you will use the tracert utility to test for connectivity to a remote host on the Internet.

1. Click **Start**, click **Run**, in the Open text box type **cmd**, and then press **Enter**.
2. Type **tracert /?** and press **Enter**. Review the list of switches that can be used with the tracert command, as shown in Figure 8-14.

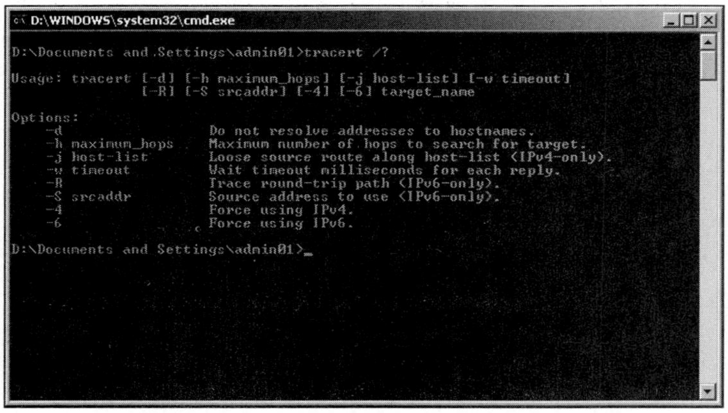

Figure 8-14 Viewing switches for the tracert command

3. Type **tracert www.course.com** and press **Enter**. This command will trace the path taken to reach the *www.course.com* Web server from your location, similar to the output illustrated in Figure 8-15.

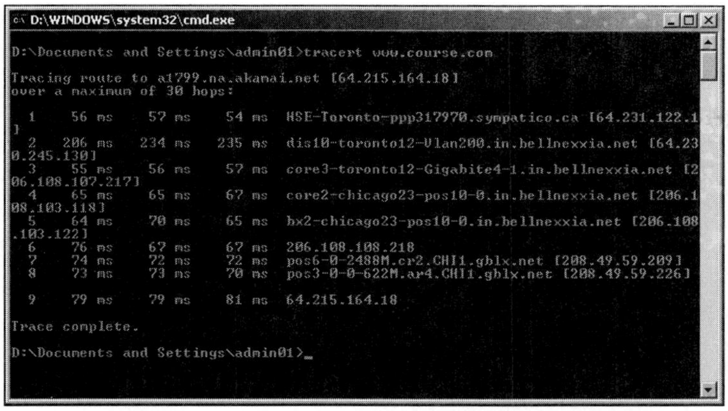

Figure 8-15 Testing network connectivity using the tracert command

4. Review the output of the tracert command, noting the different time measurements associated with reaching different routers in the path to the destination. Note the total number of hops required for you to reach the site, and compare your output to the path listed in Figure 8-15.
5. Type **tracert –w 50 www.yahoo.com** and press **Enter**. This specifies that tracert should only wait 50 milliseconds for any given reply. Notice the differences and similarities between the paths to reach *www.yahoo.com* and *www.course.com*.
6. Type **tracert –h 3 www.yahoo.com** and press **Enter**. This specifies that a maximum of three hops can be used to search for the destination host. Notice that the command completes after three hops, and that *www.yahoo.com* was not reached.
7. Close the command prompt.

Another utility that can be used to troubleshoot routing problems is pathping, which combines the functions of both the ping and tracert commands. The pathping command sends echo request messages to each router between a source and destination host. Once complete, it computes results based on the packets returned from each router, displaying the degree of packet loss at each router. This can help you determine which routers are experiencing network problems or congestion.

Table 8-6 lists some of the parameters that can be used with the pathping command.

Table 8-6 Pathping parameters

Parameter	Description
-n	Prevents the command from resolving IP addresses of routers to their host names
-h	Specifies the maximum number of hops required to search for the destination host (the default is 30)
-p	Specifies the number of milliseconds to wait between consecutive pings
-w	Specifies the number of milliseconds to wait for each reply
TargetName	Specifies the destination host either by IP address or host name

Activity 8-8: Testing Network Connectivity Using the Pathping Command

Time Required: 15 minutes

Objective: Use the pathping utility to test network connectivity between hosts.

Description: Although the tracert utility provides information about the time it takes to reach each router in the path between a source and destination host, you decide that the help desk staff will need a better picture of the degree of packet loss at each router a packet traverses. In this activity, you will use the pathping utility to determine the path between a source and destination host, as well as the degree of packet loss at each router.

1. Click **Start**, click **Run**, in the Open text box type **cmd**, and then press **Enter**.

2. Type **pathping /?** and press **Enter** to view the switches available for use with the pathping command, as illustrated in Figure 8-16.

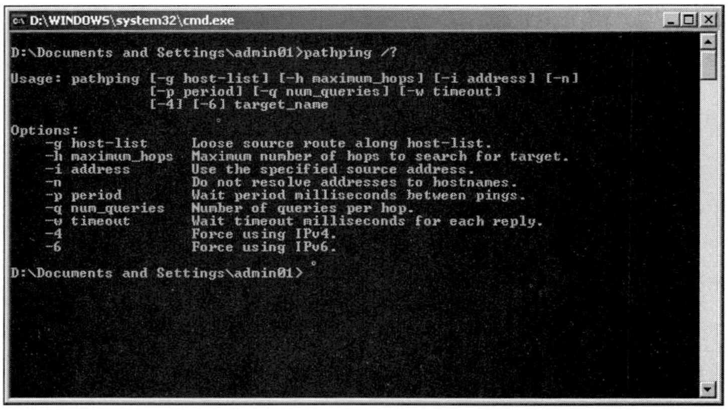

Figure 8-16 Viewing switches for the pathping command

3. Type **pathping www.course.com** and press **Enter**. This command first displays output similar to the tracert command and then computes the degree of packet loss at each router hop. Note that the calculation process takes 300 seconds, as illustrated in Figure 8-17.

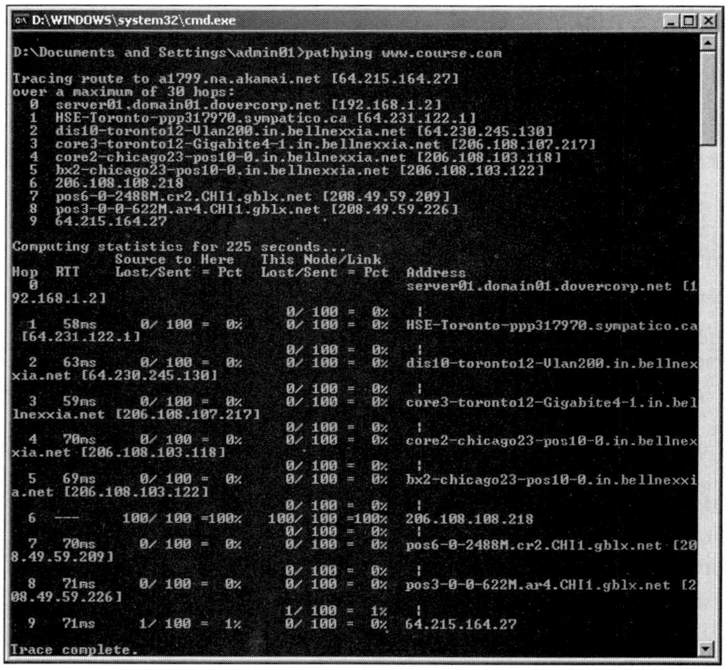

Figure 8-17 Viewing results of the pathping command

4. Type **pathping www.yahoo.com** and press **Enter**. Note the similarities and differences between the output provided for both *www.course.com* and *www.yahoo.com*.

5. Close the command prompt.

As discussed previously, ARP is used to resolve IP addresses to the physical MAC address of a network adapter. Your computer contains an ARP cache of the most recently resolved entries. Although ARP is usually a dynamic process that ensures only correct mappings exist in the ARP cache, problems can arise when the IP address of a host is switched to another computer or when a network card is changed. Similarly, an incorrect permanent ARP cache entry can also be the cause of network communication issues, as originally seen in Activity 8-1.

If a client is having connectivity problems with a remote host, you can also use the route command to verify that the correct route to a destination network exists in the host's routing table. The route command is used to view or modify the contents of a system's local routing table. Each entry in the routing table consists of a network ID, a forwarding address, the interface used to forward packets to a destination, and a metric. The entry tells the local computer where to forward packets to reach the destination host. In most cases, a company will not explicitly configure host-routing table entries but will rely on a single default route instead. On a Windows Server 2003 computer, the default route is specified in the routing table using the destination network address 0.0.0.0. If you look closely, you'll also notice that the default route is configured to forward packets to the address specified as the default gateway. In other words, the host will always forward packets to the default gateway address, assuming that one exists and that another specific route to a destination network has not been configured in the routing table.

Table 8-7 illustrates some of the more common parameters that can be used with the route command.

Table 8-7 Route parameters

Command	Description
add	Adds a route to the routing table
change	Modifies an existing entry
delete	Deletes an existing route
print	Prints the route or routes

Hands-on Project

Activity 8-9: Testing Network Connectivity Using the Route Command

Time Required: 10 minutes

Objective: Use the route command to view and change host-routing table information.

Description: In the past, Dover Leasing has always relied on the configuration of a default gateway address on client workstations to reach hosts on different subnets. Although this approach worked well when the network was small and simple, the configuration of multiple new subnets has made the paths used often less than optimal. Because of this, you decide to explore the route command, which could be used to explicitly define routes to certain networks, even with the configuration of a default gateway address. In this activity, you will use the route command to view and change routing table information on your server.

1. Click **Start**, click **Run**, in the Open text box type **cmd**, and then press **Enter**.
2. Type **route print** and press **Enter**. The routing table on your server is displayed, as illustrated in Figure 8-18. Notice that the first entry is for the default route, 0.0.0.0, and uses your server's configured default gateway address as its gateway.
3. Type **route delete 0.0.0.0** and press **Enter**. This command removes the default route from your server.
4. To confirm that the default route has been removed, type **route print** and press **Enter**.
5. To view the impact of removing the default route, type **ipconfig** and press **Enter**. Notice that your server no longer has a default gateway address assigned.
6. Type **route add 0.0.0.0 mask 0.0.0.0 192.168.1.101** and press **Enter**. This adds a new and incorrect default route to your server, pointing at the instructor server.
7. Type **route print** and press **Enter** to view the current routing table. Notice that the gateway address for the default route now points to address 192.168.1.101.

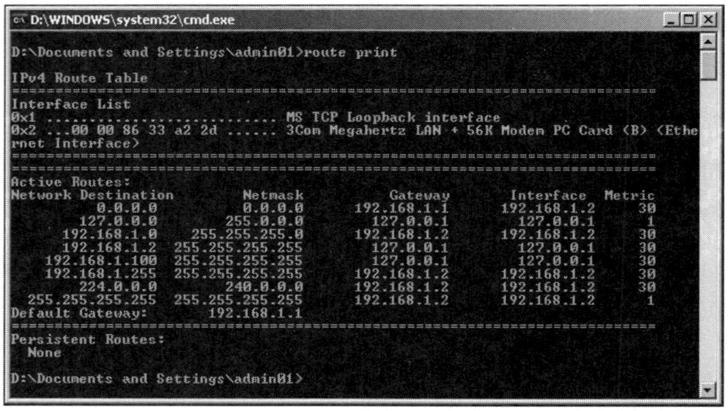

Figure 8-18 Viewing results of the route print command

8. To test the impact of the new routing table entry, open **Internet Explorer**, type **www.course.com** in the Address bar, and then press **Enter**. The page is not displayed, because a route to *www.course.com* cannot be found.
9. At the command prompt, type **route delete 0.0.0.0** and press **Enter** to remove the incorrect default route.
10. Type **route add 0.0.0.0 mask 0.0.0.0 192.168.1.*X*** (where *X* is the correct last digit for the classroom default gateway) and press **Enter** to reinstate the correct default route.
11. Use Internet Explorer to attempt to access **www.course.com**. The page is now displayed without issue.
12. Close all open windows.

The last primary utility that you can use to troubleshoot IP configuration and network connectivity is the netdiag command (see Activity 8-10). This utility can be used to diagnose and troubleshoot a variety of network connectivity problems. Some of the useful information that netdiag will provide includes a list of installed hotfixes, IP address and DNS settings, domain configuration information, and more.

Table 8-8 lists some of the more popular switches that can be used with the netdiag utility.

Table 8-8 Common netdiag parameters

Command	Description
/v	Verbose mode
/q	Quiet output; only errors will be reported
/l	Log output to Netdiag.log
/fix	Fix trivial problems
/test:<*testname*>	Performs only the netdiag tests specified
/skip:<*testname*>	Skips the netdiag tests specified

Note: Activity 8-10 requires that the Windows Server 2003 Support Tools are installed on your server. If the Netdiag command is no longer available, follow the steps originally outlined in Activity 1-9 in Chapter 1 to install them.

Activity 8-10: Testing Network Connectivity Using the Netdiag Command

Time Required: 10 minutes

Objective: Use the netdiag command to view network diagnostic information.

Description: Although the help desk staff at Dover Leasing is mainly concerned with troubleshooting basic connectivity problems, the network support group has to be concerned with many additional network configuration and communication parameters. In this activity, you will use the netdiag command to test the network configuration parameters of your server.

1. Click **Start**, click **Run**, in the Open text box type **cmd**, and then press **Enter**.
2. Type **netdiag /?** and press **Enter**. Review the available netdiag switches, as illustrated in Figure 8-19.

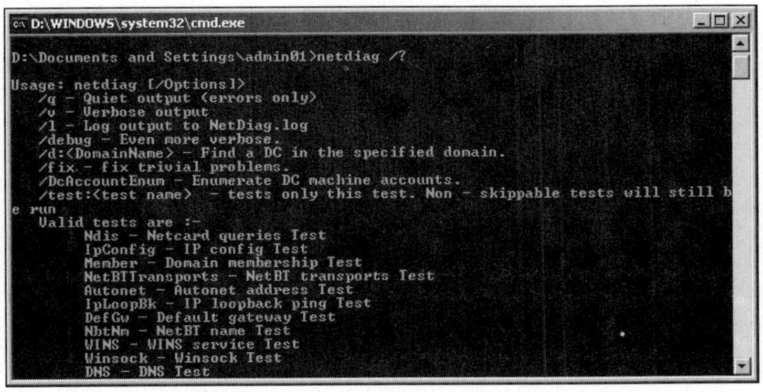

Figure 8-19 Viewing switches for the netdiag command

3. Type **netdiag** and press **Enter**. This will perform all netdiag tests on your server. Take some time to review all of the information provided by the command's output, as illustrated in Figure 8-20.

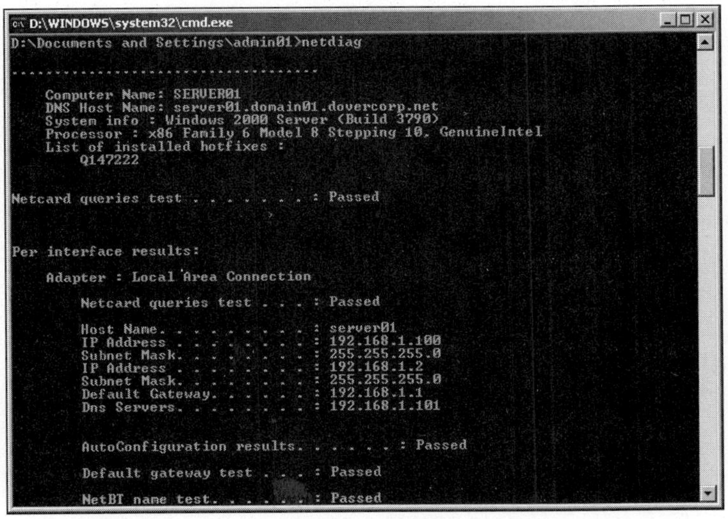

Figure 8-20 Viewing results for the netdiag command

4. Type **netdiag /l** and press **Enter**. This command will also perform all netdiag tests, but it will also output the results to a file named NetDiag.log.
5. Close the command prompt.
6. Click **Start**, and then click **My Computer**.
7. Browse to the **C:\Documents and Settings\Admin*XX*** folder. In this folder, double-click the file **NetDiag.log** to open it in Notepad. Notice that it contains the complete output of the netdiag command issued in Step 4.
8. Close all open windows.

You should now be familiar with how to install, configure, and verify TCP/IP connectivity. If you choose to implement dynamic IP addressing on your network, you will also need to know how to install and configure a DHCP server, which is discussed in the following section.

Administering DHCP in Windows Server 2003

To implement automatic IP addressing for network systems, a DHCP service has to be installed on at least one server on your network. The Dynamic Host Configuration Protocol (DHCP) is used to centralize the administration of IP addresses and various options and to eliminate the administrative overhead of statically assigning the information to each network host.

After the DHCP service is installed, it needs to be configured with a range of IP addresses and related settings to lease to clients. This range is called a DHCP **scope**. When a client is configured to use DHCP, it receives an IP address and a subnet mask, plus any options that may have been configured for the scope. The options that a DHCP server can assign to clients include IP addresses for a default gateway, a WINS server, a DNS server, and more.

An IP address that is assigned to a client from a DHCP server is known as a DHCP lease. The client essentially leases the address from the DHCP server for a period of time before it expires, which is eight days by default. A DHCP client attempts to lease an IP address in one of the following situations:

- TCP/IP is installed and started for the first time.
- The client releases its IP address and attempts to renew another one.
- The client attempts to release a specific IP address and is denied.

Note: An IP address can be released using the ipconfig /release command and a new IP address can be leased using the ipconfig /renew command.

The following process occurs when a DHCP client attempts to lease an IP address from a DHCP Server:

1. The DHCP client begins by broadcasting a DHCPDISCOVER message to locate the DHCP servers on the network. Because the client does not yet have an IP address, it uses the source address of 0.0.0.0 and a destination address of 255.255.255.255. The broadcast also includes the client's computer name and MAC address.
2. All DHCP servers on the network that receive the DHCPDISCOVER message respond with a DCHPOFFER message. If there is more than one DHCP server on the network, the client accepts the first offer it receives. The offer contains the IP address being offered, a subnet mask, the duration of the lease, and the IP address of the DHCP server offering the IP address.
3. Once the client has received a DHCPOFFER message, it broadcasts a DHCPREQUEST to all DHCP servers informing them that it has received an IP address and the IP address of the server from which it has leased the address. All other DHCP servers retract their offer making the IP addresses available for other clients on the network.

4. During the final step of the lease process, the DHCP server sends a DHCPACK message to the client indicating the lease process was successful. If optional components are configured on the DHCP server (such as the IP address of the gateway), this information is included in the DHCPACK message.

A DHCP client periodically attempts to renew its lease to ensure that it has the most up-to-date configuration settings for the network. When 50% of the configured lease duration expires, the DHCP client sends a DHCPREQUEST message to the original DHCP server that offered the address. If the server is available, the IP address is renewed with a new lease duration and an update of any changed configuration settings. If the original DHCP server is unavailable, the client continues to use its current IP configuration until 87.5% of the lease duration expires. At this point, the client sends out a DHCPDISCOVER message to any DHCP server that is available on the network.

Note

If you restart a DHCP client, it automatically attempts to renew the IP address that it had when it shut down. If it cannot contact the original DHCP server, the client computer attempts to contact its default gateway. If the default gateway responds, and there is still time left on the lease, it continues to use the same IP configurations. If the client cannot find the DHCP server or the default gateway, it stops using its leased IP address and assigns itself an address from the APIPA 169.254.0.0 to 169.254.255.255 range. The client computer then attempts to contact a DHCP server every five minutes in an attempt to obtain valid IP configurations.

Now that you are familiar with how a DHCP server provides DHCP clients with IP addressing information, you need to know how to install, configure, and administer the DHCP service on a network.

Installing a DHCP server includes the following steps, each of which are discussed in their respective sections:

- Install the DHCP service.
- Configure the DHCP server with at least one scope.
- Activate the new scope.
- Authorize the DHCP server.

Installing a DHCP Server

Installing the DHCP service is a relatively simple process. Because the DHCP server cannot be a DHCP client, make sure it has been assigned a static IP address, subnet mask, and default gateway (if required on the network) before installing the service. In Activity 8-11, you will install the DHCP service on your server.

Activity 8-11: Installing the DHCP Service

Hands-on Project

Time Required: 15 minutes

Objective: Install the Windows Server 2003 DHCP service.

Description: The IT manager at Dover Leasing has decided that DHCP will ultimately be deployed for the purpose of allocating IP addressing information to most client workstations. Although this has already been decided, you have been asked to install and test the Windows Server 2003 version of DHCP before deployment. In this activity, you will install the DHCP service on your server.

1. Click **Start**, select **Control Panel**, and then click **Add or Remove Programs**.
2. Click the **Add/Remove Windows Components** button.
3. At the Windows Components Wizard screen, click **Networking Services** in the Components list and then click **Details**.
4. In the Networking Services dialog box, click the check box next to **Dynamic Host Configuration Protocol (DHCP)**, as illustrated in Figure 8-21.

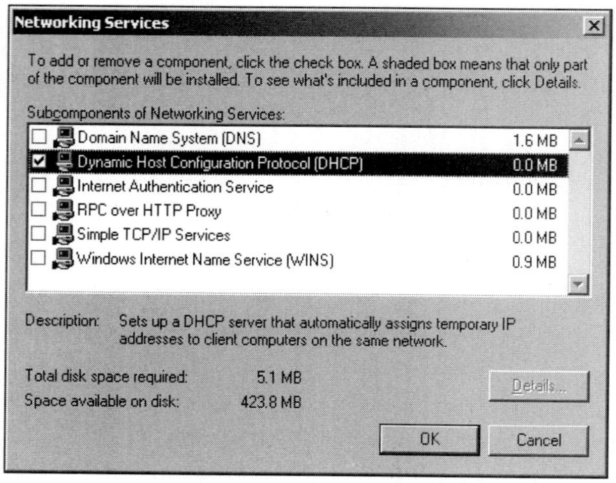

Figure 8-21 Installing the DHCP service

5. Click **OK**, and then click **Next**.
6. When the Windows Components Wizard is completed, click **Finish**.
7. Click the **Close** button to exit the Add or Remove Programs window.
8. Click **Start** and select **Administrative Tools** to verify that the DHCP tool menu item is now available.
9. Close any open windows.

Configuring DHCP Scopes

Once the DHCP service is installed, the DHCP server needs to be configured with at least one scope to provide any useful functions to network clients. As defined earlier, a scope is a range of IP addresses and associated settings that can be handed out to network clients configured to use automatic addressing. When creating a DHCP scope, keep the following points in mind:

- Each DHCP scope should include only unique addresses to avoid duplicate IP addresses being handed out on the network. DHCP servers do not share information with one another, so any address overlap between scopes or servers can cause client connectivity problems.
- Any IP addresses that have been statically assigned to clients should be excluded from a scope to avoid duplication.
- DHCP servers can be configured with multiple scopes to assign IP addresses to hosts on different subnets.

If you have multiple DHCP servers on your network, it is essential that you plan your scopes completely before implementation. DHCP servers do not inform each other about what IP addresses they have assigned to clients and, if you configure two DHCP servers with the same scope, there is a good chance that there will be duplicate IP addresses on the network. Therefore, when configuring the scopes, make sure that the IP addresses between DHCP servers do not overlap. Although DHCP servers do not explicitly share IP address information with one another, it is possible to have a Windows Server 2003 DHCP server test to ensure that an IP address is not in use, as you'll see in Activity 8-12.

DHCP scopes are configured using the DHCP MMC. In Activity 8-12, you will use the New Scope Wizard to configure a new DHCP scope on your server.

Hands-on Project

Activity 8-12: Configuring and Activating a DHCP Scope

Time Required: 20 minutes

Objective: Configure and activate a DHCP scope.

Description: Having worked with DHCP on Windows NT 4.0 in the past, you are familiar with the basic idea of a scope and how it allocates IP addressing information to clients. However, based on the many additions and changes in the Windows Server 2003 DHCP service, you decide that it will be necessary to walk through the configuration of a DHCP scope and its associated properties. In this activity, you will configure and activate a new DHCP scope, as well as configure settings to help avoid IP address conflicts once multiple DHCP servers are installed.

1. Click **Start**, select **Administrative Tools**, and then click **DHCP**. This opens the DHCP MMC snap-in, as illustrated in Figure 8-22.

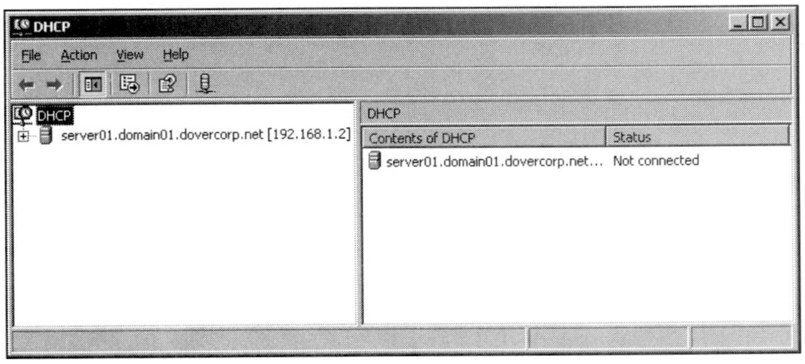

Figure 8-22 The DHCP MMC snap-in

2. Right-click the server icon and click **New Scope**.
3. At the New Scope Wizard screen, click **Next**.
4. At the Scope Name screen, type **Test Scope** in the Name text box and **Test Scope for Head Office** in the Description text box. Click **Next**.
5. At the IP Address Range screen enter the following, as illustrated in Figure 8-23:
   - Start IP address: **192.168.2.1**
   - End IP address: **192.168.2.30**
   - Subnet mask: **255.255.255.0**

   Click **Next**.
6. At the Add Exclusions screen, type **192.168.2.3** in both the Start IP address and End IP address text box and click **Add**. This will exclude the address 192.168.2.3 from being allocated to clients by the scope. Click **Next**.
7. At the Lease Duration screen, accept the default value of 8 days, as illustrated in Figure 8-24, and click **Next**.
8. At the Configure DHCP Options screen, click the **No, I will configure these options later** radio button and click **Next**.
9. Read the information provided on the Completing the New Scope Wizard screen, and then click **Finish**.

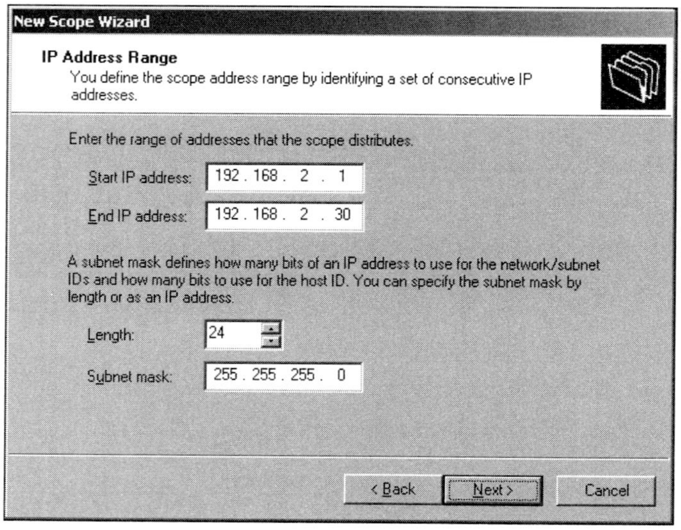

Figure 8-23 Configuring DHCP scope address range and subnet mask

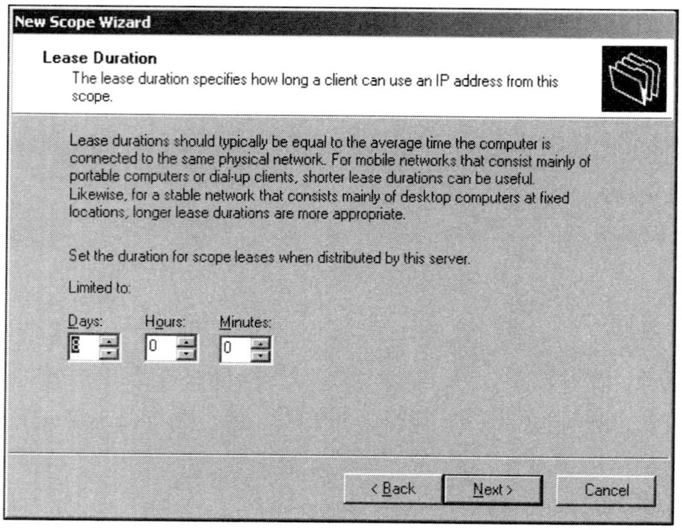

Figure 8-24 Specifying the DHCP lease duration period

10. If necessary, click the **plus sign (+)** next to your server in the DHCP tool to view its contents, and then click the **plus sign (+)** next to the new scope. Notice that the new scope appears in the interface, but it is still not activated as illustrated by the red arrow on the scope icon shown in Figure 8-25.

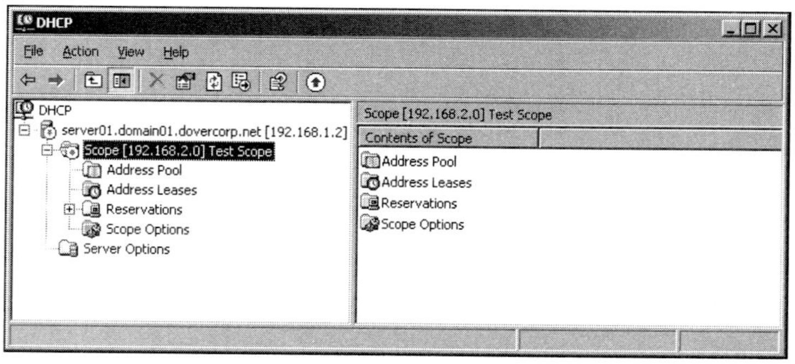

Figure 8-25 DHCP scope elements

11. Click the **Address Pool** icon to view its contents. Notice that both the range of addresses in the scope as well as the excluded address are listed.
12. Click the **Address Leases** icon. The details window will be blank because the scope is not activated and hasn't leased any addresses to clients.
13. Click the **Reservations** icon, and read through the information provided about the purpose of a reservation.
14. Click the **Scope Options** icon, and read the information about why scope options are used.
15. Right-click the **Scope [192.168.2.0] Test Scope** icon and click **Properties**. Notice that the General tab allows you to configure basic scope parameters including the IP address range and lease duration, as shown in Figure 8-26. Click **OK**.

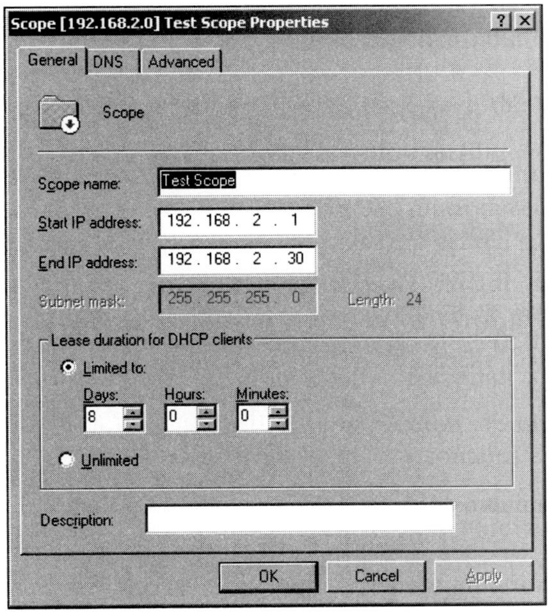

Figure 8-26 DHCP scope properties

16. Right-click your server icon and click **Properties**.
17. Click the **Advanced** tab. In the Conflict detection attempts spin box, select **2**, as shown in Figure 8-27. Click **OK**. This will ensure that the DHCP server will attempt to detect a potential IP addressing conflict twice before leasing an IP address to a client.
18. Right-click the **Scope [192.168.2.0] Test Scope** icon and click **Activate**. Although the scope is now activated, the server will still not hand out IP addresses to clients until authorized in Active Directory.
19. Leave the DHCP window open.

If you need to configure scope options such as default gateway or DNS server addresses, make sure you do this prior to activating the scope. You can configure these settings either during the New Scope Wizard, or after the scope has been created. Later in this chapter, you will configure DHCP options at both the scope and server levels.

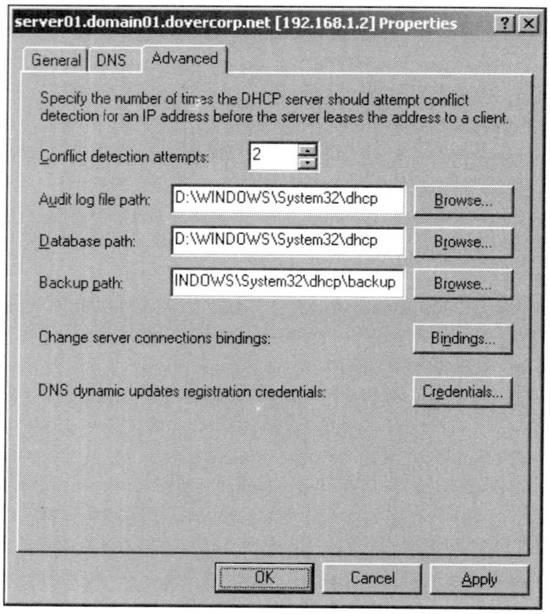

Figure 8-27 Configuring DHCP server conflict detection settings

Client Reservations

There may be instances where a client on the network requires the same IP address to be assigned at all times. You can assign static IP addresses to the clients or you can configure them to be DHCP clients and create client reservations. A client reservation reserves an IP address within the scope for a particular client so it is always reassigned the same address. The DHCP server uses a client's MAC address to determine if it has an IP address reserved and which IP address should be assigned to it. In Activity 8-13, you will create a reservation in your DHCP scope.

Activity 8-13: Creating a DHCP Client Reservation

Time Required: 5 minutes

Objective: Configure a DHCP client reservation.

Description: Although most client workstations at Dover Leasing will be configured using DHCP, a few workstations use special applications that will require them to always use the same IP address. Instead of configuring these systems manually, you decide to configure DHCP client reservations instead. In this activity, you will create a client reservation for one address allocated to the DHCP scope created in Activity 8-12.

1. In the DHCP window, click the **plus sign (+)** next to Scope [192.168.2.0] Test Scope to expand it, if necessary.
2. Right-click the **Reservations** icon and click **New Reservation**.
3. In the New Reservation dialog box, type the following, as illustrated in Figure 8-28:
   - Reservation name: **Moira's PC**
   - IP address: **192.168.2.20**
   - MAC address: **00-00-00-00-00-01**
   - Description: **Reservation for Moira's PC**

   Click **Add**, and then click **Close**.
4. Notice that the reservation for Moira's PC now appears in the Reservations section of the scope, as shown in Figure 8-29.
5. Leave the DHCP window open.

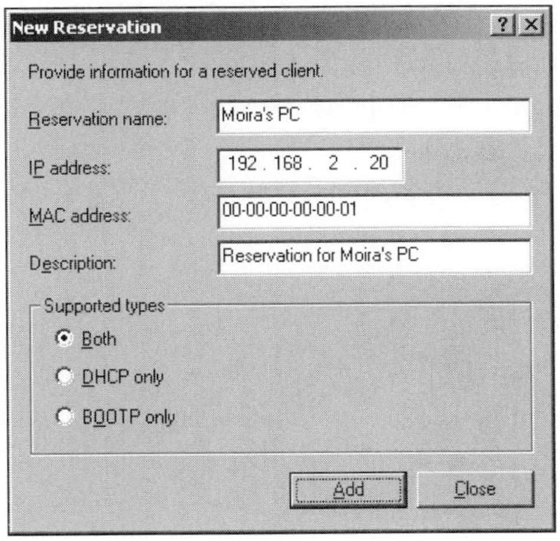

Figure 8-28 DHCP client reservation settings

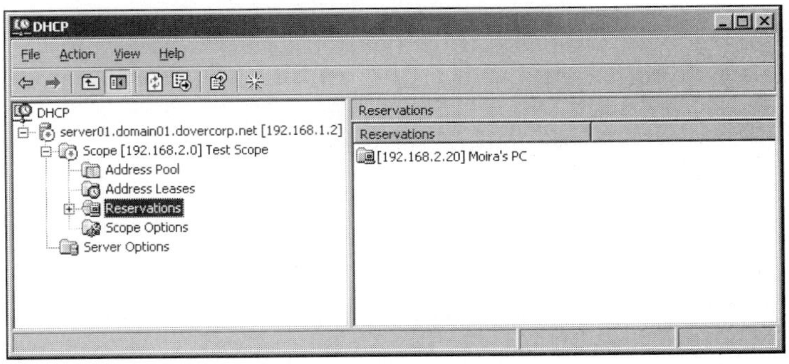

Figure 8-29 Viewing all DHCP client reservations

Superscopes

Many networks today consist of multiple subnets (or segments) either for security purposes or to better optimize the flow of network traffic. Each of the segments has its own network address that uniquely identifies it.

A **superscope** is a grouping of scopes created for multiple subnets on a physical network. Superscopes are usually created to make the administration of multiple scopes easier. For example, consider a business spanning multiple floors within a building that has a single Ethernet network configured. Each floor could have its own logical IP address range, but all floors are part of the same physical Ethernet network. For administration purposes, you could create a scope for each floor and group the scopes in a single superscope. When multiple logical IP subnets are part of the same physical network, this configuration is often referred to as multinetting. When a host in one logical subnet wants to communicate with a host in another logical subnet, a router must still be involved, even when the hosts are part of the same physical segment. As such, router interfaces connected to a multinetted physical segment should be configured with multiple IP addresses, one for each logical subnet it needs to communicate with.

In Activity 8-14, you will create a new DHCP scope and then combine it with an existing scope to create a superscope.

Activity 8-14: Creating a DHCP Superscope

Hands-on Project

Time Required: 20 minutes

Objective: Create a DHCP superscope.

Description: The Dover Leasing network consists of over 50 subnets, each of which maps to a dedicated Ethernet network. Although this one-to-one mapping exists today, the IT manager is worried that based on the growth of certain subnets, it may be necessary to multinet the network in the future. Because of this, he has asked you to explore the concept of superscopes and test their configuration in the DHCP console. In this activity, you will create a new scope and then use it and the scope created in Activity 8-12 to define a superscope.

1. In the DHCP window, right-click the **server** icon and click **New Scope**.
2. At the New Scope Wizard screen, click **Next**.
3. At the Scope Name screen, type **Second Test Scope** in the Name text box and **Test Scope for New Logical Subnet** in the Description text box. Click **Next**.
4. At the IP Address Range screen, enter the following:
   - Start IP address: **192.168.3.1**
   - End IP address: **192.168.3.30**
   - Subnet mask: **255.255.255.0**

   Click **Next**.
5. At the Add Exclusions screen, click **Next**.
6. At the Lease Duration screen, accept the default value of 8 days, and click **Next**.
7. At the Configure DHCP Options screen, click the **No, I will configure these options later** radio button and click **Next**.
8. Read the information provided on the Completing the New Scope Wizard screen, and then click **Finish**.
9. In the DHCP window, right-click the **Scope [192.168.3.0] Second Test Scope** icon and click **Activate**.
10. Right-click your server icon and then click **New Supercope**.
11. At the New Superscope Wizard welcome screen, click **Next**.
12. At the Superscope Name screen, type **Dovercorp** in the Name text box and click **Next**.
13. At the Select Scopes screen, highlight both of the available scopes (to highlight both scopes, hold down the **CTRL** key while selecting them.), as illustrated in Figure 8-30, and click **Next**.

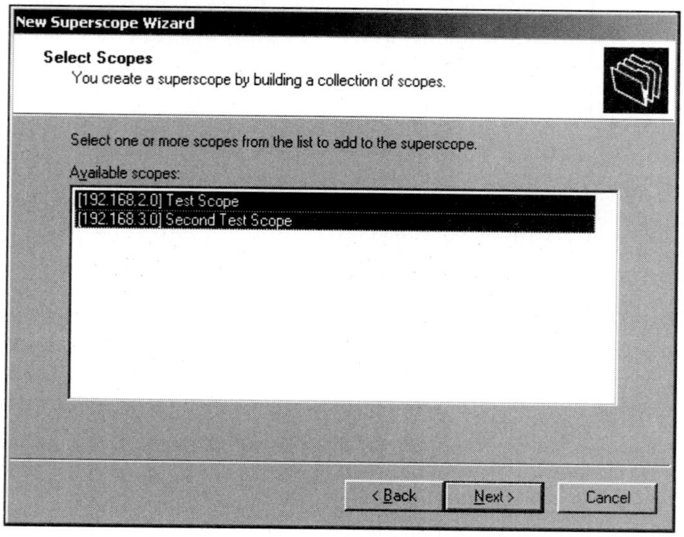

Figure 8-30 Adding DHCP scopes to a superscope

14. Click **Finish** to create the new superscope.

15. Click the **plus sign (+)** next to Superscope Dovercorp to expand it. Notice that both scopes are now part of the new superscope.
16. Right-click the **Superscope Dovercorp** icon and then click **Delete**.
17. When the DHCP dialog box opens, read the message and then click **Yes**. Notice that although the superscope has been deleted, both original scopes still exist.
18. Leave the DHCP window open.

Multicast Scopes

Before looking at multicast scopes in DHCP, it is important to have a concept of what **multicasting** is. Multicasting is sending a message to a group of clients, but not all clients, using a single destination address. It is not the same as a broadcast message that is sent to every host on a network. With multicasting, the message is intended for a specific group of recipients. Multicasting uses a special range of IP addresses to provide this functionality. Also known as the Class D address range, the IP addresses 224.0.0.0 through 224.239.255.255 are reserved for multicast addressing.

DHCP servers in Windows Server 2003 can assign multicast addresses to clients as well as traditional unicast addresses. DHCP clients are assigned a multicast address if they join a multicast group (such as a group of users conferencing using Microsoft NetMeeting) and a multicast scope has been defined. Clients that are configured with static IP addresses can also receive multicast configuration information from a DHCP server. Multicast scopes are configured with class D IP addresses and provide users with multicast addresses, thus making the administration and configuration of multicast groups simpler.

Authorizing a DHCP Server

Once the DHCP service is installed and scopes are configured and activated, the last step is to authorize a DHCP server in Active Directory. This feature is designed to increase security and stability on a network by attempting to eliminate the possibility of the DHCP service being mistakenly or maliciously installed on a server and leasing IP addresses to clients. Although only those Windows Server 2003 and Windows 2000 DHCP servers that have been authorized by an administrator are permitted to lease IP addresses, this functionality does nothing to prevent Windows NT or third-party DHCP servers from allocating IP addresses to clients.

Whenever the DHCP service is installed with Windows Server 2003, it sends out a DHCPINFORM broadcast to all other DHCP servers. Any other Windows 2000 or Windows Server 2003 DHCP servers on the network reply with a DHCPACK message that contains information about Active Directory and the location of the domain controllers. The server that is attempting to start its DHCP services queries Active Directory to see if it is on the list of authorized servers. If the server is on the list, the DHCP service starts as usual. If the server is not found on the list, the DHCP service starts, logs an error in the event log, but does not answer client requests. It's worth noting that only a member of the Enterprise Admins group in an Active Directory forest has the ability to authorize a DHCP server. In Activity 8-15, you will authorize your DHCP server in Active Directory to respond to client requests.

Activity 8-15: Authorizing a DHCP Server

Hands-on Project

Time Required: 10 minutes

Objective: Authorize a DHCP server.

Description: The IT manager at Dover Leasing is very concerned about the potential impact of network administrators accidentally implementing DHCP servers on the network without prior consent because this may cause serious configuration issues. Because of this, he has asked you to explore the authorization process for a DHCP server in a Windows Server 2003 domain environment. In this activity, you will authorize your DHCP server and explore the different ways in which DHCP server authorization can be controlled.

1. In the DHCP MMC window, right-click the **server** icon and click **Authorize**, as shown in Figure 8-31. The DHCP server is now authorized.

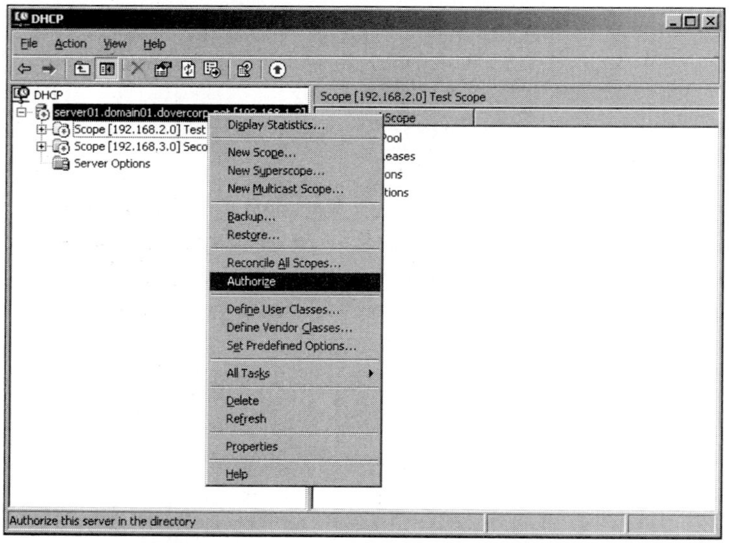

Figure 8-31 Authorizing a DHCP server

2. To verify that the server is authorized, right-click the **DHCP** icon and click **Manage authorized servers**.
3. Verify that your server appears in the list of Authorized DHCP servers, as shown in Figure 8-32.

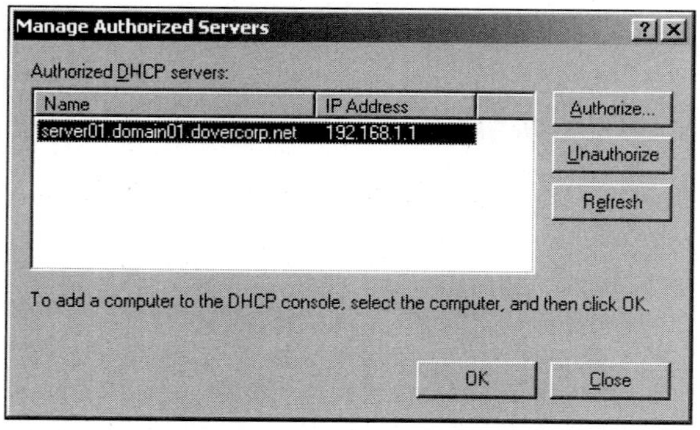

Figure 8-32 Managing authorized DHCP servers

4. Click the **Authorize** button. This provides an alternate method of authorizing DHCP servers. Click **Cancel**.
5. To unauthorize your DHCP server, click your server's name in the Authorized DHCP servers list box, and then click the **Unauthorize** button. Note that your server no longer appears in the list box. Click **Close**.
6. Authorize your server again, using one of the two methods learned in this activity.
7. Leave the DHCP window open.

Note

To be able to authorize servers on a Windows Server 2003 network, you must belong to the Enterprise Admins group located in the forest root domain.

Using DHCP Options

As mentioned previously, configuring a DHCP scope requires that a range of IP addresses and a subnet mask be supplied at a minimum. However, a range of different options can also be assigned to clients. Table 8-9 summarizes the most commonly used DHCP options.

Table 8-9 Commonly used DHCP options

Option	Description
003 Router	The default gateway
006 DNS Server	List of IP addresses for DNS name servers
015 DNS Domain Name	DNS domain name, such as *Dovercorp.net*
044 WINS/NBNS Servers	List of IP addresses for NETBIOS name servers
046 WINS/NBT Node Type	The type of NetBIOS name resolution clients use; the following options are available: 1=B-node (broadcast), 2=P-node (peer), 4=M-node (mixed), and 8=H-node (hybrid)

8

There are different levels at which scope options can be configured. For example, you may want some options to apply to all clients on the network, while other options, such as the default gateway, may be specific to a certain scope. The level at which you create the DHCP options determines which scopes or clients are affected. The three levels of scope options that can be configured are server, scope, and client.

- *Server options*—Server options apply to all scopes configured on the DHCP server. Server options are used when all clients require the same configuration information regardless of the subnet they are on. Options related to DNS and WINS are often defined at the server level.
- *Scope options*—Scope options only apply to a specific scope and the clients that lease an IP address from that scope. For example, if there are different scopes configured for different subnets, the appropriate default gateway can be configured for each scope. Options set at the scope level override any conflicting settings from the server level.
- *Client options*—Client options apply to the specified client reservation. Any conflicting options applied at the client level override options configured at the server or scope level.

Hands-on Project

Activity 8-16: Configuring DHCP Options

Time Required: 10 minutes

Objective: Configure DHCP server and scope options.

Description: In addition to basic IP address and subnet mask settings, the IT manager at Dover Leasing wants additional information, such as a default gateway address and DNS settings, to be assigned to clients via DHCP. Because a large number of scopes will need to be configured for all of the various subnets currently in use at Dover Leasing, you decide to explore using both server and scope options to reduce the required amount of administrative effort. In this activity, you will configure DNS settings at the server-option level and router information at the scope-option level.

1. In the DHCP MMC window, click the **plus sign (+)** next to Scope [192.168.2.0] Test Scope to expand it.
2. Right-click the **Scope Options** icon and then click **Configure Options**. The Scope Options dialog box opens, as illustrated in Figure 8-33.
3. On the **General** tab, scroll through the **Available Options** list box to get an idea of the various options that can be configured for DHCP clients. As time permits, click some options (without checking their associated check boxes) to understand the different types of values they support.

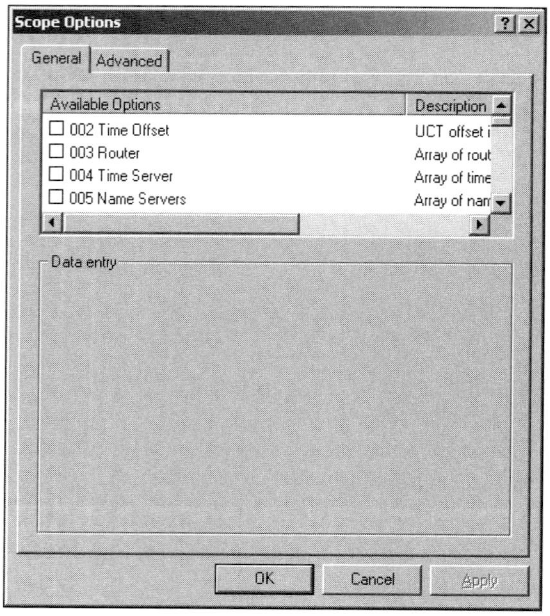

Figure 8-33 Viewing DHCP scope options

4. In the Available Options list box, click the check box next to **003 Router**.
5. In the Data entry section, type **192.168.2.1** in the IP address text box and then click **Add**, as illustrated in Figure 8-34.

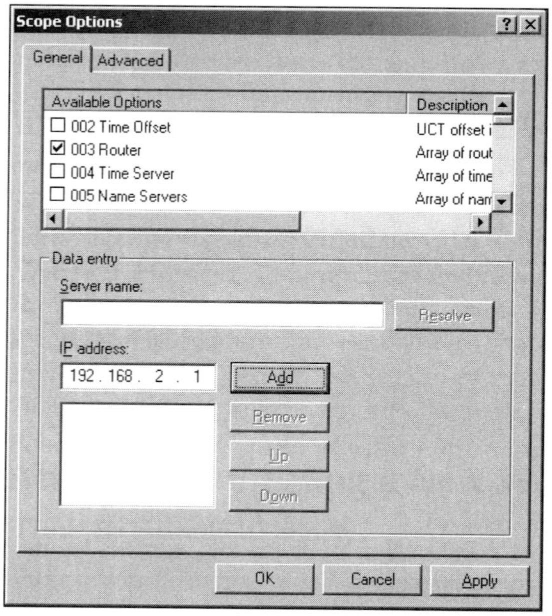

Figure 8-34 Configuring the 003 Router scope option

6. Click **OK** to close the Scope Options dialog box.
7. In the DHCP window, click the **Scope Options** folder to view the new entry. If it hasn't yet appeared, press **F5** to refresh the screen.
8. Right-click the **Server Options** icon and then click **Configure Options**.

9. In the Server Options dialog box, scroll down until you reach the 006 DNS Servers option. Click the check box next to 006 DNS Servers.
10. In the Data entry section, type **192.168.2.100** in the IP address text box. Click **Add**.
11. In the Available Options section, scroll down until you reach the 015 DNS Domain Name option. click the check box next to 015 DNS Domain Name.
12. In the Data entry section, type **dovercorp.net** in the String value text box.
13. Click **OK** to close the Server Options dialog box.
14. If necessary, click the **Server Options** icon to view all of the server options now assigned to your DHCP server, as illustrated in Figure 8-35. The DHCP server will provide these options for all scopes configured on the server.

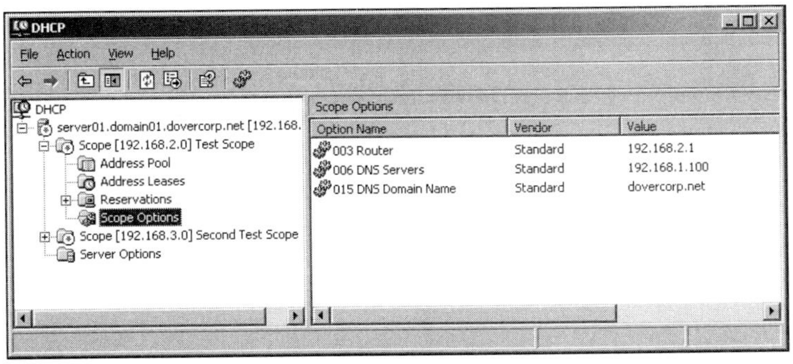

Figure 8-35 Viewing DHCP server options

15. Close all open windows.

Configuring DHCP in a Routed Network

If your network contains multiple subnets connected via routers, you need to spend some time planning your DHCP implementation. When a client attempts to lease an IP address, the client sends out a broadcast message to locate the DHCP servers on the network. The problem in a subnetted environment is that, by default, routers do not pass broadcast traffic to other networks. One of the reasons why networks are subnetted is to cut down on the propagation of broadcast traffic.

In a routed network, you have three options for implementing DHCP. Your first option is to install and configure a DHCP server on each subnet. If you have a small number of subnets, this may be feasible, but in large networks the resources may not be available for the number of DHCP servers that might be required. A second option is to configure network routers to forward DHCP broadcast traffic. In a smaller network, this may be a suitable option, but in larger networks it increases network traffic because the broadcasts are then forwarded to all subnets on the network. A third option is to configure a DHCP relay agent on each of the subnets.

The DHCP relay agent included with Windows Server 2003 relays DHCP broadcast messages between DHCP clients and DHCP servers across a routed network. For example, imagine a subnet with a DHCP relay agent, but no DHCP server configured. When a client broadcasts an IP address request, the message is heard by the DHCP relay agent, who then forwards it directly to a configured DHCP server. Because the DHCP server sends the message to the DHCP server as a unicast instead of a broadcast, it has no trouble reaching the server across network routers.

Note

A server that is running the DHCP service cannot be configured as a DHCP relay agent.

DHCP relay agents are configured using the Routing and Remote Access tool on Windows Server 2003 servers. In Activity 8-17, you will first disable the DHCP Service on your server and then configure it as a DHCP relay agent.

Activity 8-17: Configuring a DHCP Relay Agent

Time Required: 10 minutes

Objective: Install and configure a DHCP relay agent.

Description: Based on the large subnets that will need to be supported by DHCP at Dover Leasing, the IT manager has decided that four DHCP servers should ultimately be implemented. Because each subnet will not have its own DHCP server, you have been asked to test the installation and configuration of a DHCP relay agent. In this activity, you will install and configure a DHCP relay agent using the Routing and Remote Access console.

1. Click **Start**, select **Administrative Tools**, and then click **Services**.
2. In the Services window, right-click the **DHCP Server** icon, and then click **Properties**.
3. In the DHCP Server Properties dialog box, click **Disabled** in the **Startup type** list box, as illustrated in Figure 8-36, and then click OK.

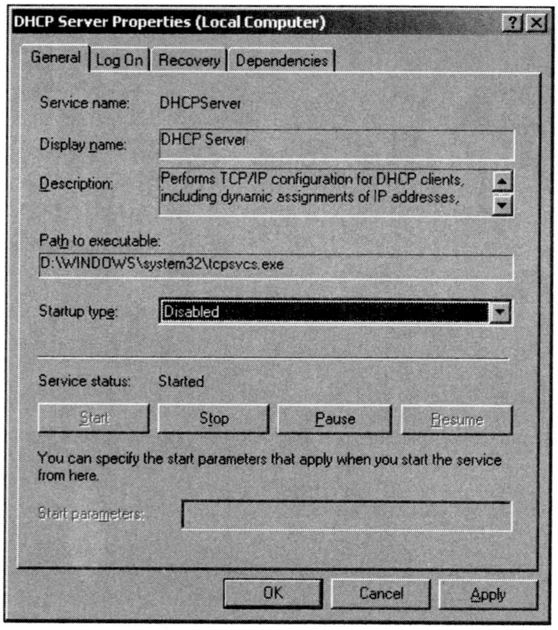

Figure 8-36 DHCP Server service startup properties

4. Close the Services window.
5. Click **Start**, select **Administrative Tools**, and then click **Routing and Remote Access**. The Routing and Remote Access tool opens, as illustrated in Figure 8-37.
6. Right-click your server icon and click **Configure and Enable Routing and Remote Access**.
7. At the Routing and Remote Access Server Setup Wizard welcome screen, click **Next**.
8. At the Configuration screen, click the **Custom configuration** radio button, and then click **Next**.
9. At the Custom Configuration screen, click the **LAN routing** check box, click **Next**, and then click **Finish**.

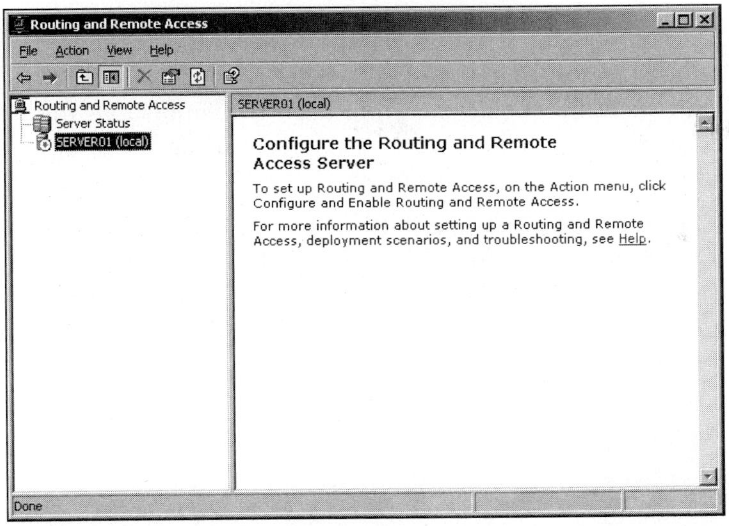

Figure 8-37 The Routing and Remote Access console

10. When prompted as to whether you want to start the Routing and Remote Access service, click **Yes**. Notice that once the service is started, the icon for your server includes an upward-pointing green arrow.
11. If necessary, click the **plus sign (+)** next to your server icon to expand it.
12. If necessary, click the **plus sign (+)** next to IP Routing to expand it.
13. Right-click the **General** icon, and click **New Routing Protocol**.
14. In the New Routing Protocol dialog box, ensure that **DHCP Relay Agent** is selected in the Routing protocols list box, as shown in Figure 8-38. Click **OK**.

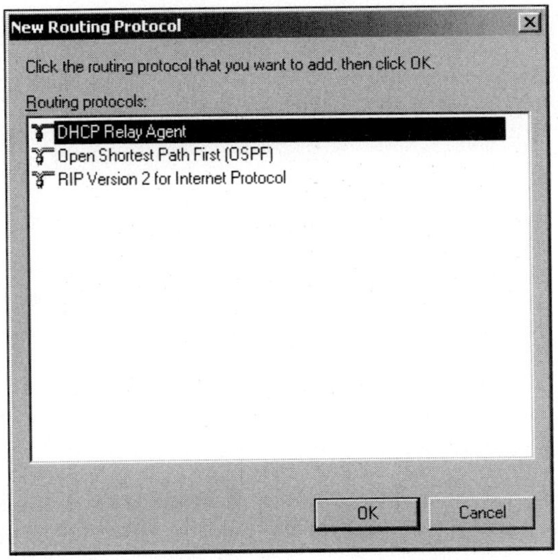

Figure 8-38 Installing a DHCP relay agent

15. Right-click the new **DHCP Relay Agent** icon and click **New Interface**.
16. In the New Interface for DHCP Relay Agent dialog box, click **Local Area Connection** and click **OK**.
17. At the DHCP Relay – Local Area Connection Properties screen, click **OK**.
18. Close the Routing and Remote Access tool.

DHCP and DNS Integration

One important feature of Windows Server 2003 is the integration of DHCP and DNS. Dynamic DNS (DDNS) allows name servers and clients to automatically update the DNS database, eliminating the need for an administrator to have to manually update the zone file each time a change is made (such as a client leasing a new IP address). DNS is discussed in greater detail in Chapter 9.

By default, the Windows Server 2003 DHCP service automatically registers any PTR (reverse host) records with the DNS server and allows the DHCP clients to register their own A (host) records. DNS PTR records map a host's IP address to its domain name, whereas an A record maps it hostname to an IP address. Although this is the default behavior of DHCP service in Windows Server 2003, a number of different DNS registration possibilities exist, as shown in Figure 8-39.

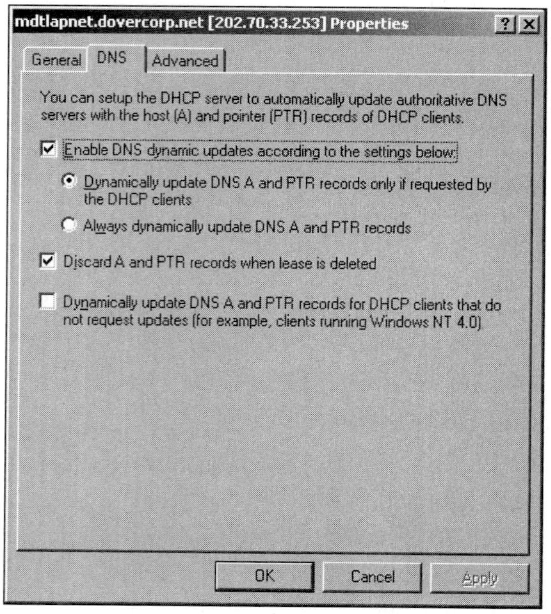

Figure 8-39 DHCP and DNS integration properties

The following options are available on the DNS tab:

- *Dynamically update DNS A and PTR records only if requested by the DHCP clients*—This option is selected by default. If requested by the client, the DHCP server updates both the A record and PTR record with the DNS server. Windows 2000 and XP clients, however, are capable of updating their own records with a DNS server, so in an environment with only Windows 2000 or XP clients, this option is sufficient.
- *Always dynamically update DNS A and PTR records*—This option forces the DHCP server to always update records on behalf of the client.
- *Discard A and PTR records when lease is deleted*—This option is enabled by default. This option forces the DHCP server to send a request to the DNS server to remove a client's record when their IP address lease expires.
- *Dynamically update DNS A and PTR records for DHCP clients that do not request updates*—This option forces the DHCP server to update the DNS zone file for clients that do not support dynamic DNS (such as non-Microsoft clients or older Microsoft clients).

Note

Make sure that the DHCP server's TCP/IP client settings include the IP address of the DNS server to which it will be sending DNS updates.

Maintaining DHCP Services

You should monitor DHCP servers to discover or prevent future problems with the DHCP service. There are two primary ways that you can monitor DHCP servers:

- Periodically look at the Event Viewer system log for any DHCP-related events.
- Use DHCP audit logging. Enabled by default in the DHCP MMC snap-in, this forces the DHCP server to place detailed event logs in the DHCP database directory (%systemroot%\system32\dhcp). The file name takes the form of DhcpSrvLog-*xxx.log* (where *xxx* represents the first three letters of the day of the week).

Figure 8-40 illustrates a DHCP audit log file.

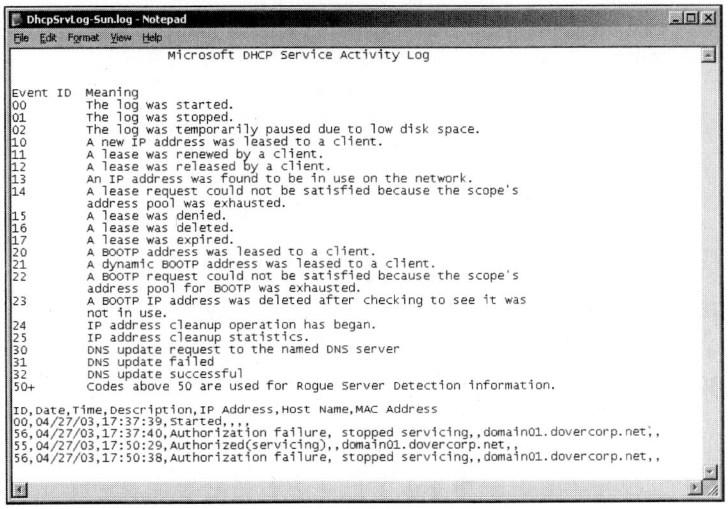


```
                    Microsoft DHCP Service Activity Log


Event ID  Meaning
00        The log was started.
01        The log was stopped.
02        The log was temporarily paused due to low disk space.
10        A new IP address was leased to a client.
11        A lease was renewed by a client.
12        A lease was released by a client.
13        An IP address was found to be in use on the network.
14        A lease request could not be satisfied because the scope's
          address pool was exhausted.
15        A lease was denied.
16        A lease was deleted.
17        A lease was expired.
20        A BOOTP address was leased to a client.
21        A dynamic BOOTP address was leased to a client.
22        A BOOTP request could not be satisfied because the scope's
          address pool for BOOTP was exhausted.
23        A BOOTP IP address was deleted after checking to see it was
          not in use.
24        IP address cleanup operation has began.
25        IP address cleanup statistics.
30        DNS update request to the named DNS server
31        DNS update failed
32        DNS update successful
50+       Codes above 50 are used for Rogue Server Detection information.

ID,Date,Time,Description,IP Address,Host Name,MAC Address
00,04/27/03,17:37:39,Started,,,,
56,04/27/03,17:37:40,Authorization failure, stopped servicing,,domain01.dovercorp.net,,
55,04/27/03,17:50:29,Authorized(servicing),,domain01.dovercorp.net,,
56,04/27/03,17:50:38,Authorization failure, stopped servicing,,domain01.dovercorp.net,,
```

Figure 8-40 DHCP service activity log

8

Chapter Summary

- TCP/IP consists of a suite of protocols that you can use to configure, manage, and troubleshoot network connectivity. Some of these protocols include TCP, UDP, ARP, and IP.
- All hosts on a TCP/IP network require an IP address and a subnet mask. A default gateway is needed to communicate outside of the local subnet. You can assign IP addresses statically to a host computer or dynamically by using a DHCP server.
- There are several utilities, such as ipconfig and ping, that you can use to verify and troubleshoot TCP/IP.
- Once the DHCP service is installed, you must create and activate a unique scope and authorize the DHCP server in Active Directory. You can also add various scope options, such as the IP address of the default gateway.
- Windows 2000 and XP DHCP clients automatically update resource records with the DNS server. You can configure the DHCP server to perform all updates and perform updates on behalf of legacy clients.

Key Terms

Address Resolution Protocol (ARP) — Works at the Internet layer and is responsible for mapping IP addresses to MAC addresses assigned to the network interface adapter. These can be either dynamic or static entries. Dynamic entries are stored in the ARP cache for 2 to 10 minutes. Static entries stay in the cache until the computer is restarted.

automatic private IP addressing (APIPA) — An IP addressing technique that is used to temporarily assign an IP address in the range 169.254.0.0 through 169.254.255.255 in the event that a client cannot obtain an address from a DHCP server.

default gateway — This is the 32-bit number of the router on the local network, which is used to communicate with hosts outside of the local subnet.

Dynamic Host Configuration Protocol (DHCP) — Used to centralize the administration of IP addresses and various options, and eliminate the administrative overhead of statically assigning the information to each network host.

Internet Control Message Protocol (ICMP) — Operates at the network layer and is used to exchange status and error information between two hosts.

Internet Group Management Protocol (IGMP) — Operates at the network layer and is used to manage network and host information when multicasting is used.

Internet Protocol (IP) — The Internet-layer protocol responsible for addressing and routing packets so that they are delivered to the correct host on the local network or across routers to a host on another subnet.

IP address — The 32-bit number that uniquely identifies a host on a TCP/IP network.

ipconfig — A command used to verify the addressing parameters assigned to a computer.

ipconfig/all — The ipconfig command plus the all parameter is used to produce a full display of assigned parameters.

multicasting — Sending a message to multiple clients or a group of clients.

pathping — A command that combines the functions of the ping and tracert commands. The pathping command checks network connectivity by sending echo request messages to each router between a source and destination host and then computing the result based on packets returned from each router.

ping — A command used to test for connectivity between hosts on the network by sending ICMP packets to a remote computer and listening for an echo reply from the remote host.

scope — A range of IP addresses configured on a DHCP server that can be handed out to network clients.

subnet mask — The 32-bit number that identifies the network to which a TCP/IP host belongs.

superscope — A grouping of scopes created for multiple subnets on a physical network.

tracert — A command used to determine the route taken to a destination by sending ICMP echo packets with varying time-to-live (TTL) values to the destination.

Transmission Control Protocol (TCP) — Operates at the transport layer and is responsible for reliably transmitting data on a TCP/IP network.

Transmission Control Protocol/Internet Protocol (TCP/IP) — Consists of a suite of protocols and utilities that are used for network communication and troubleshooting on local networks and the Internet.

User Datagram Protocol (UDP) — A connectionless protocol that functions at the transport layer and provides no guarantee of delivery.

winipcfg — A command used on Windows 9x machines to display the TCP/IP configuration settings.

Review Questions

1. Your network consists of many subnets, and managing the DHCP scopes has become difficult. What feature of Windows Server 2003 DHCP can you use to make the administration of multiple scopes more manageable?

   a. multicast scopes

   b. client reservations

   c. superscopes

   d. dynamic DNS

2. Your network consists of multiple subnets and multiple gateways connecting the different segments. When configuring the 003 Router scope option, at which level should the option be configured?
   a. server
   b. DHCP
   c. client
   d. scope
3. Options configured at the server level override options configured at the scope and client levels. True or False?
4. You install the DHCP service on one of your network servers. You configure an IP scope and some additional scope options, and activate the scope. You soon discover that clients on the network are not receiving IP addresses. What is likely causing the problem?
   a. You must configure a minimum of two scopes.
   b. Clients are configured with static IP addresses.
   c. The DHCP service is not started.
   d. The DHCP server must be authorized in Active Directory.
5. Your network consists of two subnets. You create two scopes on your DHCP server. Scope1 (for subnet 1) has a range of 192.168.2.10 to 192.168.2.30. Scope2 (for subnet 2) has a range of 192.168.3.10 to 192.168.3.20. The subnets are connected via a single router. You configure the 003 router option at the server level and type the IP address of 192.168.2.31. Users on subnet 1 now report that they can access resources on their own subnet but cannot access resources on subnet 2. What is likely causing the problem?
   a. The router is not operational.
   b. The 003 router option should be configured at the scope level.
   c. The DHCP server is offline.
   d. Clients on subnet 1 are not receiving IP addresses.
6. Which of the following TCP/IP commands can be used to verify the IP addressing parameters assigned to a computer?
   a. arp
   b. ping
   c. tracert
   d. ipconfig
7. Which of the following TCP/IP commands can be used to verify network connectivity with a host on another subnet? (Choose all that apply.)
   a. ping
   b. ipconfig
   c. tracert
   d. arp
8. A DHCP Relay Agent is configured via the Routing and Remote Access console. True or False?
9. Your network consists of several IP subnets connected by routers. One of your goals is to minimize the number of broadcasts on the network. Clients on each subnet are configured for dynamic IP addressing. You install the DHCP service on one of the Windows Server 2003 servers. What else must you do so clients on each subnet can obtain IP addressing information?
   a. Install the DHCP relay agent on the DHCP server.
   b. Install the DHCP relay agent on one server on each subnet.
   c. Install the DHCP relay agent on all client workstations.
   d. Configure the routers to forward DHCP broadcasts.
10. The DHCP relay agent can be installed on the DHCP Server. True or False?

11. What type of DHCP message is sent out by a new client when attempting to obtain an IP address from a DHCP server?
    a. DHCPDISCOVER
    b. DHCPACK
    c. DHCPREQUEST
    d. DHCPINFORM
12. Which command can be used to view the entries stored in a client's local DNS resolver cache?
    a. ipconfig /registerdns
    b. ipconfig /flushdns
    c. ipconfig /displaydns
    d. ipconfig /viewdns
13. What technique should be used to ensure that a DHCP client always receives the same IP address?
    a. APIPA
    b. manual configuration
    c. server reservation
    d. client reservation
14. What switch should be used with the ping command to resolve the IP address supplied to a hostname?
    a. -s
    b. -a
    c. -p
    d. -r
15. Which of the following commands can be used to view the route taken to reach a destination host? (Choose all that apply.)
    a. ping
    b. netdiag
    c. tracert
    d. pathping
16. A client will always forward packets destined for other networks to its configured default gateway. True or False?
17. What technique can be used to help reduce the possibility of multiple DHCP servers allocating the same IP address to more than one client on a Windows Server 2003 network?
    a. conflict detection
    b. manual IP address configuration
    c. APIPA
    d. superscopes
18. IP addresses handed out by APIPA fall into the range 192.168.1.1 to 192.168.255.254. True or False?
19. Which of the following are considered private ranges of IP addresses? (Choose all that apply.)
    a. 10.0.0.1 – 10.255.255.254
    b. 172.16.0.1 – 173.47.255.254
    c. 192.168.0.1 – 192.168.255.254
    d. 168.254.0.1 – 168.254.255.254
20. To authorize a DHCP server, you must be a member of the Enterprise Admins group. True or False?

Case Projects

Case Project 8-1

Your network currently implements static IP addressing. With the rapid increase in network growth and the implementation of multiple IP subnets, you are proposing a switch from static IP addressing to dynamic addressing.

1. In your proposal, include a description as to why it is a good idea that your network implements DHCP.
2. List the steps involved in installing and configuring a DHCP server.
3. The network consists of six different subnets that are connected with routers. Each of the subnets has a different gateway. How will you configure the scope options on the DHCP server? The network also has a DNS server and a WINS server.
4. The DHCP server will be placed on one of the subnets. Describe the three options you have for ensuring that clients on other subnets can still get IP addresses from a DHCP server on another subnet.

Case Project 8-2

The Dover Leasing network currently has a number of different network protocols in use including TCP/IP, IPX/SPX, and NetBEUI. Outline three reasons why a company might consider moving to TCP/IP as their only network protocol, as well as a reason why a company may need to continue running other protocols as well.

Case Project 8-3

The IT manager at Dover Leasing has asked you to prepare a document that outlines some of the advantages of using DHCP to configure client IP settings instead of static addressing. List some of the challenges associated with static IP addressing along with some of the reasons why a company should consider using DHCP instead.

CHAPTER

9

ADMINISTERING DNS

After reading this chapter and completing the exercises, you will be able to:

- Understand the fundamentals of the Domain Name System (DNS)
- Install the DNS service on Windows Server 2003
- Create and configure both standard and Active Directory–integrated DNS zones
- Understand the purpose of name resolution files in Windows Server 2003
- Troubleshoot name resolution problems in Windows Server 2003

Administering a Windows Server 2003 network that uses Active Directory requires a network administrator to have a thorough understanding of the **Domain Name System (DNS)**. Although Windows operating systems have traditionally relied upon the NetBIOS protocol for domain communication functions, a network that uses Active Directory requires DNS to be installed and configured in order to function correctly.

Before implementing Active Directory on any network, it is essential for administrators to have a solid understanding of the purpose of DNS and how its various components interact with one another. The first section of this chapter outlines the concept of resolving host names to IP addresses, along with an overview of how the domain name system is structured and functions.

Once the fundamentals of DNS are covered, this chapter continues with a look at how to configure the DNS services on Windows Server 2003. This includes a look at how to install the DNS service, the different types of DNS zones that you can configure, and the various resource records that allow DNS to provide useful services on an IP-based network.

This chapter concludes with a look at the methods and tools used to troubleshoot Windows Server 2003 name resolution problems, as well as specific utilities used to gather information and troubleshoot problems with DNS.

DNS Fundamentals

DNS is one of the most important network services that a network based on TCP/IP and Active Directory uses. Windows Server 2003 uses DNS for two essential tasks: resolving host and domain names to IP addresses and locating network services in an Active Directory environment. For example, DNS is the service used to resolve host names such as Server1 to an IP address such as 192.168.1.100. Similarly, DNS is also used in Active Directory domains to help client computers find network services such as the domain controllers used to authenticate user logons. This section discusses the basics of DNS, as well as the name resolution process.

Basics of DNS

DNS is a distributed database that was originally developed for the purpose of resolving host names to IP addresses on the Internet. Before the implementation of DNS, the entire Internet namespace was essentially flat; that is, a host on the Internet could have a name that identified it, such as Server1. However, only a single server on the Internet could have that name. Host names and their corresponding IP addresses were stored in a simple text file named HOSTS.TXT. Although this method worked well when the Internet was small and limited in scope, managing a single file for name resolution purposes quickly became unmanageable and, ultimately, a choke point for the Internet. Unlike the flat namespace that HOSTS.TXT employs, DNS uses a hierarchical structure. Instead of relying on just a host name, DNS introduced the concept of a domain name, such as *microsoft.com*. DNS enables users to access servers using a user-friendly name, such as *www.microsoft.com*. When resolved by a DNS server, this name is converted to its associated IP address, thus facilitating communication over an IP-based network. Users do not have to remember the IP address of a host on the Internet because the DNS server converts the name to the proper IP address as required.

To understand DNS, it is important to understand its three main components:

- *Domain namespace*—The DNS hierarchical structure of domains
- *DNS zones*—One or more DNS domains grouped together for administrative purposes
- *Name servers*—A DNS server that holds all of the host records for a specific zone

At the top of the DNS hierarchical structure is the root domain, which is often represented by a period, or ".". Below the root domain are the first-level domains. On the Internet, specific organizational types, such as *.com* or *.org*, or geographic representations such as .mn, which represents Mongolia, represent the first-level domains.

Below the first-level domains are second-level domains. Second-level domains usually represent an organization's name, such as Microsoft or Dovercorp. Companies register these names explicitly beneath a first-level domain, creating a corporate domain name such as *microsoft.com*. Because second-level domains need to be registered, only one company can have a second-level domain name beneath any first-level domain. Beneath the second-level domains, there may be a number of subdomains that divide a second-level domain into logical separations. For example, Dover Leasing may want to divide their domain into two subdomains: sales and marketing. Subdomains beneath second-level domains do not need to be explicitly registered with the Internet authorities. Companies can create these subdomains at will, as long as their DNS servers are correctly configured to resolve subdomain names.

Within a specific domain, there are a number of **host** computers. A host is any computer that is a member of a specific DNS domain within the network structure. A host is referred to by its **fully qualified domain name (FQDN)**, which describes the location of the host in relation to the DNS namespace. For example, a computer with the host name "www" in the marketing domain of *Dovercorp.net* would have an FQDN of *www.marketing.Dovercorp.net*. Figure 9-1 illustrates a portion of the domain namespace of DNS.

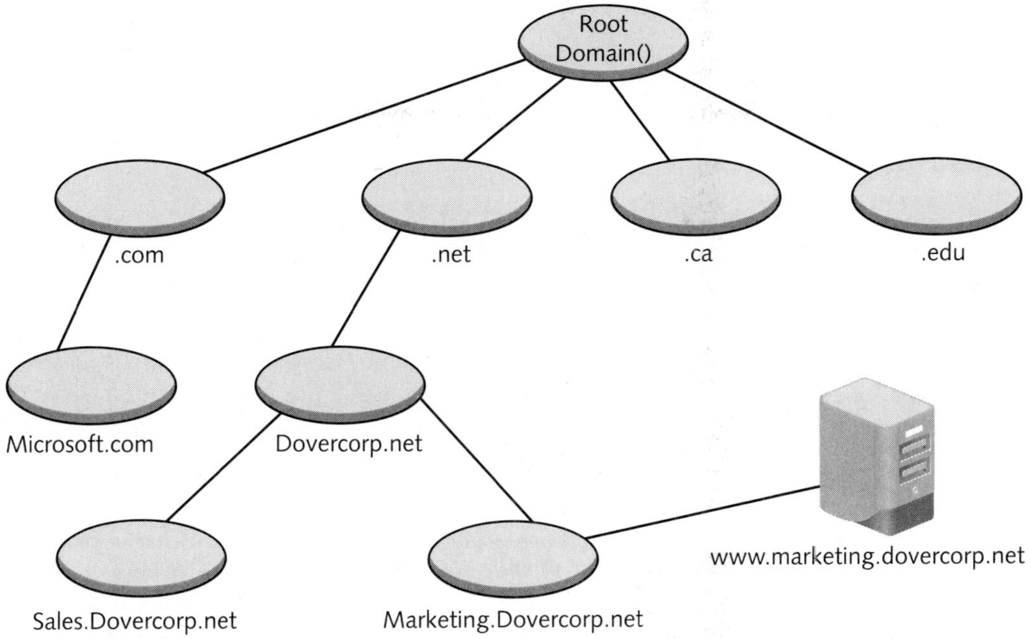

Figure 9-1 The DNS namespace

9

DNS zones are one or more domains that are grouped together for administrative purposes. For example, Dover Leasing can create two zones to enable different administrators to manage the *marketing.Dovercorp.net* and *sales.Dovercorp.net* domains separately. Conversely, a single zone can also be created that would include all three domains of Dover Leasing: *Dovercorp.net*, *marketing.Dovercorp.net*, and *sales.Dovercorp.net*. The only requirement is that domains included within the same zone fall into a contiguous namespace. For example, the domains *sevenacres.com* and *Dovercorp.net* could not be part of the same DNS zone.

There are two types of zones that can be configured on DNS servers: **forward lookup zones** and **reverse lookup zones**. A forward lookup zone is the most common type of zone, which is used to perform standard host name-to-IP address forward lookup queries. For example, a DNS query for *www.microsoft.com* would be processed by a forward lookup zone, which would return the associated IP address to the client. A reverse lookup zone is a special type of zone that performs reverse DNS queries, or those looking for the FQDN or host name associated with a known IP address. For example, a mail server might be configured to conduct reverse DNS lookups for all e-mail received to confirm that the message originated at the domain name specified in the e-mail's "from" address field. To keep the number of required DNS servers to a minimum, multiple forward and reverse lookup zones can be configured on a single DNS server.

The information that is used to resolve computer names to IP addresses is stored in what is known as a zone database file on a DNS server. The main DNS name server that contains all of the records for a specific DNS zone is called the **primary DNS server**. The primary DNS server is said to be **authoritative** for a zone, meaning that it is the final source of information for any queries about a given host that is part of one of the domains configured in its zone file. For example, Dover Leasing might have an authoritative DNS server for a zone that includes the DNS domain called *Dovercorp.net*. This **zone file** would hold all of the resource records for the *Dovercorp.net* domain, such as individual host records, mail exchanger records, and service records. If a client needed to resolve the IP address for any computer or service in the *Dovercorp.net* domain, the primary DNS server at Dover Leasing would be the definitive source for this information.

To assist in providing redundancy and load balancing, primary DNS servers can also be associated to one or more secondary DNS servers. A **secondary DNS server** contains zone information that is copied from a primary DNS server or other secondary servers. Unlike a primary DNS server, the copies of any zone files stored on a secondary DNS server are read-only versions. Secondary servers can be used as a backup in case the primary server fails or to help load-balance DNS client requests.

To ensure that both the primary server and the secondary server have the same information, zone information must be transferred between the two. Copying DNS database information between primary and secondary name servers is referred to as a **zone transfer**.

The Name Resolution Process

When a client needs to communicate with a computer on a local network or the Internet, the host name or FQDN is usually supplied. Each client is configured to contact a specific DNS name server whenever it needs to resolve an FQDN to an IP address. The following steps illustrate an example of an Internet client wanting to connect to *www.Dovercorp.net*:

1. The client computer generates a request to resolve *www.Dovercorp.net* to an IP address and sends a **recursive query** to its locally configured DNS name server. A recursive query is a command that specifies the return of a complete and full answer to the query, not a pointer to another DNS server.
2. The DNS server that receives the recursive query checks its zone database files to see whether it holds zone information for the *Dovercorp.net* domain. Because it is not responsible or authoritative for the *Dovercorp.net* domain, the DNS server sends an **iterative query** to a DNS server that is authoritative for the root domain. Thirteen root servers currently exist on the Internet to form the backbone of the DNS namespace. An iterative query means that if the DNS server cannot resolve the name, it gives the requester a pointer to another DNS server that is authoritative for the next level of the FQDN supplied.
3. Because an entry for *www.Dovercorp.net* is not listed in the root domain, the DNS root server sends a reply to the querying client's DNS server with the IP addresses of servers authoritative for the *.net* domain.
4. The client's DNS server then sends an iterative query to a DNS server that is authoritative for the *.net* domain.
5. The DNS server that is authoritative for the *.net* domain does not have an entry for the client *www.Dovercorp.net* but does send the DNS server the IP address of a different name server that is authoritative for the *Dovercorp.net* domain.
6. Again, the client's DNS server sends an iterative query, this time to the DNS server that is authoritative for the *Dovercorp.net* domain.
7. The DNS server that is authoritative for the *Dovercorp.net* domain finds the record that represents *www.Dovercorp.net* and then sends the IP address back to the client's DNS server.
8. The client's DNS server now has the information that is needed and completes the client's original recursive query by supplying the correct IP address for *www.Dovercorp.net*.

When the client's local DNS server successfully resolves the query, the information is cached by the client system. The query also remains in the DNS server cache for a period defined by the *Dovercorp.net* DNS administrator, usually at least an hour. This helps to save both time and bandwidth in the event that another client of the DNS server also needs to resolve the same name in this time period. By the same token, the DNS server will also cache information about the location of the *.net* and *Dovercorp.net* DNS servers, making subsequent name resolution requests to these domains faster.

Installing DNS

The DNS service is not installed by default during the Windows Server 2003 installation process. Although the DNS service can be installed and configured automatically as part of promoting a server to be an Active Directory domain controller, it can also be added as a separate service similar to DHCP. In Activity 9-1, you will install the Windows Server 2003 DNS service.

Activity 9-1: Installing the DNS Service

Time Required: 10 minutes

Objective: Install the Windows Server 2003 DNS service.

Description: Although the DNS service has already been configured on one server in the *Dovercorp.net* forest, the IT manager is interested in installing DNS on alternate servers both to support additional domains and to load-balance requests among future servers. In this activity, you will install the DNS service on your server.

1. Click **Start**, select **Control Panel**, and then click **Add or Remove Programs**.
2. In the Add or Remove Programs dialog box, click the **Add/Remove Windows Components** button to open the Windows Components Wizard.
3. At the Windows Components screen, double-click **Networking Services**.
4. At the Networking Services screen, click the check box next to **Domain Name System (DNS)**, as shown in the Figure 9-2. Click **OK**.

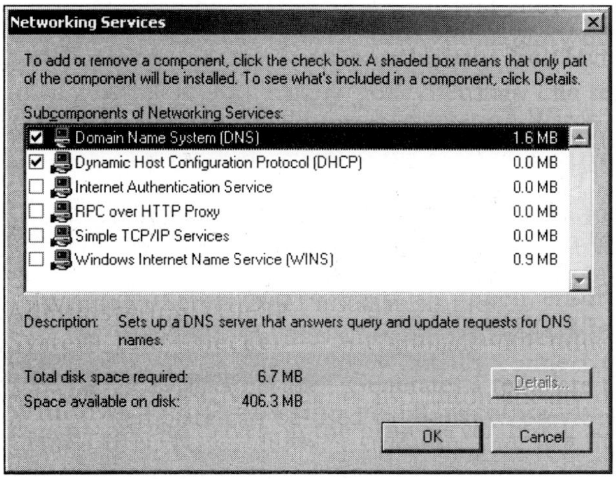

Figure 9-2 Adding the DNS service

5. Click **Next**.
6. At the Completing the Windows Components Wizard screen, click **Finish**.
7. Click **Close** to close the Add or Remove Programs dialog box.
8. Click **Start**, select **Administrative Tools**, and verify that the DNS tool is available.

Note: If a valid DNS server is not detected during the process of promoting a Windows Server 2003 system to a domain controller, the Active Directory Installation Wizard offers to automatically install and configure DNS as part of the process.

Once installed, a DNS server is managed via the DNS MMC. By default, no zones or related information exist on a DNS server until explicitly configured. However, a DNS server without configured zone files can still serve an important function, known as a **caching-only server**. A DNS caching-only server is not authoritative for any DNS zones but is still capable of forwarding DNS queries to other DNS servers and caching the results. Many companies implement caching-only DNS servers to help speed up the name resolution process in branch offices and remote locations.

A number of properties can be configured for a new DNS server regardless of whether or not it stores zone information. Table 9-1 outlines the purpose of the various tabs found in the properties of a DNS server, as illustrated in Figure 9-3.

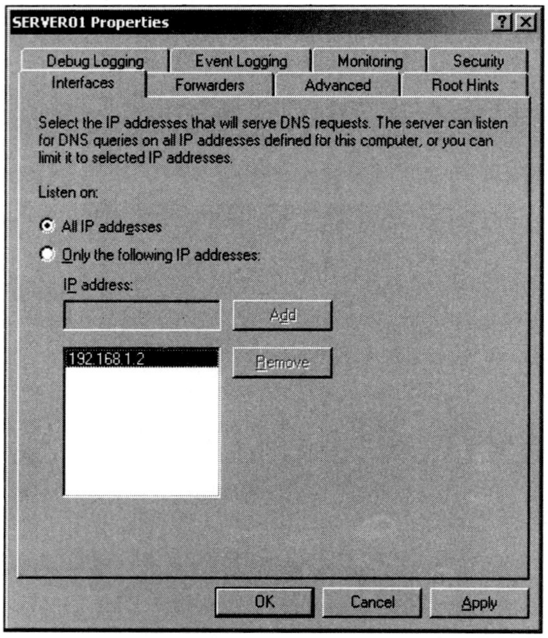

Figure 9-3 Properties dialog box for a DNS server

Table 9-1 DNS server properties

DNS Server Property Sheet	Purpose
Interfaces	Used to specify whether all of the server's interfaces will reply to DNS requests or only specified interfaces.
Forwarders	Used to configure the IP addresses of other DNS servers to which queries should be forwarded when they cannot be resolved by the local DNS server; Windows .NET Server 2003 DNS allows different DNS servers to be specified as forwarders depending on the domain name the server is attempting to resolve.
Advanced	Used to configure DNS server options as well as the data types supported by DNS and the location of the service startup files
Root Hints	Lists the Internet DNS root servers, as gathered from the CACHE.DNS file
Debug Logging	Used to enable DNS debug logging; when enabled, results are logged to the dns.log file looked at earlier.
Event Logging	Used to specify the level of events that should be logged into the DNS event log; all events all logged by default.
Monitoring	Allows tests to be carried out to determine that a DNS server is functioning correctly
Security	Used to configure security settings related to DNS.

In Activity 9-2, you will explore the various tabs in your DNS server properties dialog box in the DNS MMC.

Activity 9-2: Exploring DNS Server Properties

Time Required: 10 minutes

Objective: Review the various properties of a Windows Server 2003 DNS server using the DNS console.

Description: After installing the Windows Server 2003 DNS service, you decide to take some time to familiarize yourself with the various properties that can be configured at the server level. In this activity, you will explore the various settings available in the properties of your DNS server.

1. Click **Start**, select **Administrative Tools**, and then click **DNS**.
2. In the DNS window, click the **plus sign (+)** next to your server name to expand its contents, as illustrated in Figure 9-4.

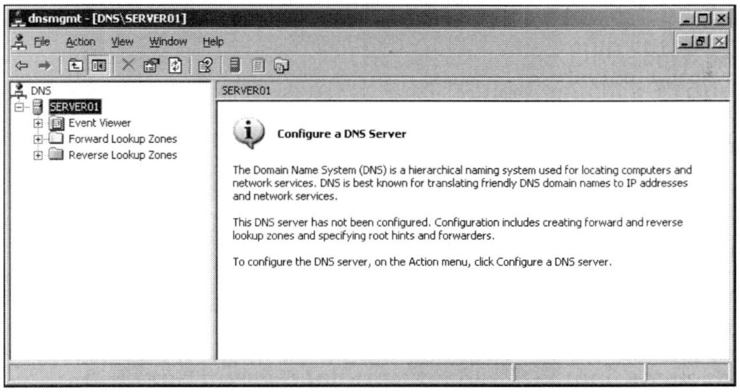

Figure 9-4 The DNS console window

3. Click the **Forward Lookup Zones** node to view its contents. No zones appear in the details window until explicitly configured.
4. Right-click your server's **icon** and then click **Configure a DNS Server**.
5. At the Configure a DNS Server Wizard screen, click the **DNS Checklists** button. This opens the Microsoft Management Console help file and provides access to check lists designed to help you install and configure the DNS service.
6. Close the Microsoft Management Console help window, and then click **Cancel**.
7. Right-click your server's **icon** and click **Properties**.
8. Read through the information provided on the Interfaces tab, noting its configuration elements.
9. Click the **Forwarders** tab, noting that it allows you to configure various forwarding options for your DNS server.
10. Click the **Advanced** tab. This screen allows you to configure advanced DNS server properties, such as whether recursion and DNS round robin are enabled or disabled, as illustrated in Figure 9-5.
11. Click the **Root Hints** tab. This tab displays a list of the DNS root servers, as illustrated in Figure 9-6.

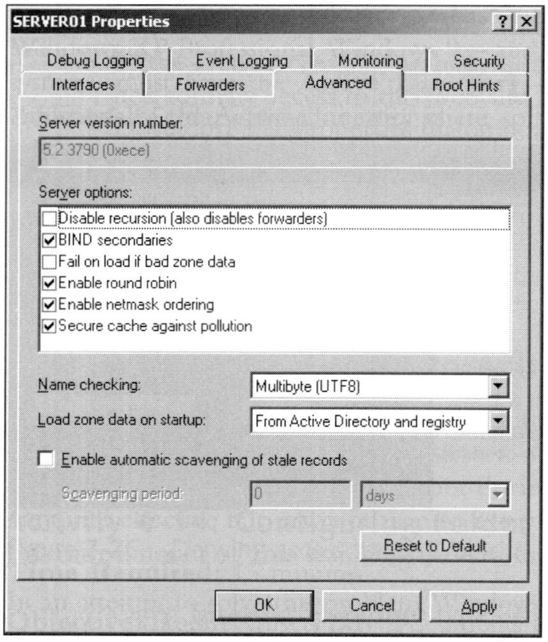

Figure 9-5 The Advanced tab in a DNS server properties dialog box

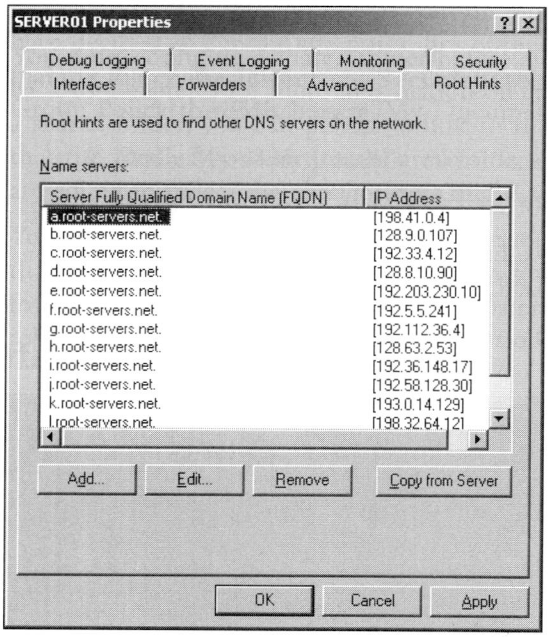

Figure 9-6 The Root Hints tab of the DNS server properties dialog box

12. Click the **Debug Logging** tab. Settings on this tab allow you to configure debugging options that will be written to the dns.log file once enabled.
13. Click the **Event Logging** tab. Settings on this tab allow you to configure the level of logging for DNS events. By default, all DNS events are logged, as shown in Figure 9-7.
14. Click the **Monitoring** tab. This tab allows you to test DNS resolution settings for your server.
15. Click the **Security** tab. This tab allows you to control the level of access that users and groups have to DNS server configuration settings.

16. Click **Cancel** to close the properties dialog box for your DNS server. Leave the DNS window open.

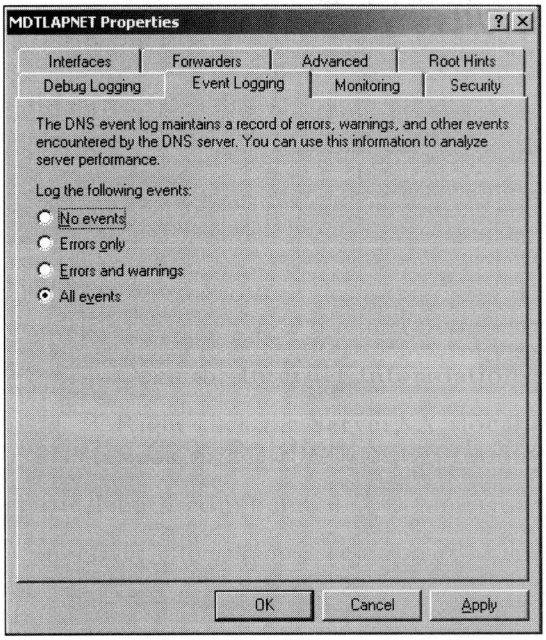

Figure 9-7 The Event Logging tab of the DNS server properties dialog box

Creating and Configuring DNS Zones

To create and configure a forward or reverse lookup zone, you must be a member of the local Administrators group on the server. If the server is a domain controller, you need to be a member of at least one of the following global groups: Domain Admins, Enterprise Admins, or DNS Admins.

Windows Server 2003 supports two main types of DNS zones—standard zones and **Active Directory–integrated zones**. Both zone types, including their similarities and differences, are discussed in detail in the following sections.

Standard DNS Zones

A standard DNS zone is the traditional zone type used by most implementations of DNS. Unlike an Active Directory–integrated zone that stores zone information within the Active Directory database, a standard zone simply places DNS zone information into a text file stored in the %systemroot%\system32\dns folder on the server. When a standard DNS zone is implemented, the following files can be found within this folder:

- *CACHE.DNS*—This file contains records for all 13 of the Internet root servers. If the number of root servers increases or changes, this file can be replaced on all DNS servers.
- *dns.log*—This file gathers DNS information when DNS Debug Logging is explicitly enabled in the DNS console.
- *domainname.dns*—This file acts as the storage location for a given zone and holds all applicable resource records. An example of this file is shown in the *sevenacres.com.dns* file illustrated in Figure 9-8.

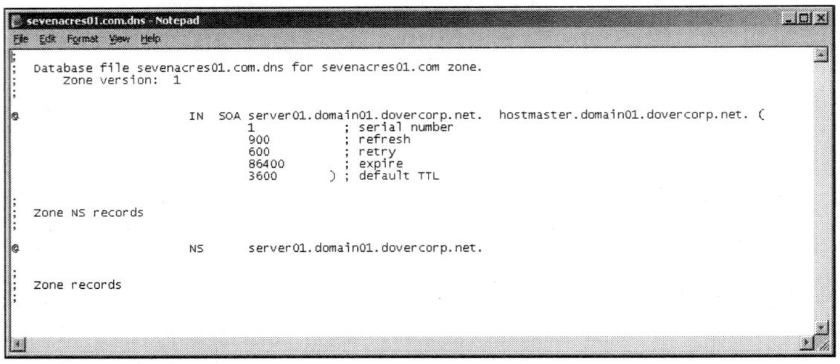

```
sevenacres01.com.dns - Notepad
File Edit Format View Help
;
;  Database file sevenacres01.com.dns for sevenacres01.com zone.
;      Zone version:  1
;

@                       IN  SOA server01.domain01.dovercorp.net.  hostmaster.domain01.dovercorp.net. (
                            1            ; serial number
                            900          ; refresh
                            600          ; retry
                            86400        ; expire
                            3600       ) ; default TTL

;
;  Zone NS records
;

@                       NS      server01.domain01.dovercorp.net.

;
;  Zone records
;
```

Figure 9-8 The *sevenacres01.com.dns* zone database file

Two main types of standard DNS zones exist—**standard primary zones** and **standard secondary zones**. A standard primary zone is authoritative for one or more domains and represents the only writable copy of the zone file. Standard secondary zones are created on a different DNS server after the standard primary zone and are used for load balancing and redundancy of DNS. Although one standard primary and one standard secondary zone is recommended by the DNS specification, administrators can create as many secondary zones as they wish to meet the needs of their environment.

The most common type of standard DNS zone is a forward lookup zone. This type of zone contains information used by DNS clients to resolve known host names and FQDNs to IP addresses. In Activity 9-4, you will implement a new standard primary zone on your DNS server.

Activity 9-4: Configuring a DNS Standard Primary Zone and Exploring Zone Properties

Time Required: 10 minutes

Objective: Configure a standard primary DNS zone and explore zone-related properties.

Description: To test the new installation of DNS on your server, the IT manager at Dover Leasing has asked you to configure a standard primary forward lookup zone on your server for the *sevenacres.com* domain. You decide that after configuring the new zone it will be important to be familiar with the various zone properties that can be configured on individual zones. In this activity you will first create a new zone for the *sevenacres.com* domain and then explore the various properties of the newly created zone.

1. In the DNS console window, right-click the **Forward Lookup Zones** icon and click **New Zone**.
2. At the New Zone Wizard welcome screen, click **Next**.
3. At the Zone Type screen, ensure that the **Primary zone** radio button is selected. Uncheck the check box next to **Store the zone in Active Directory**, as illustrated in Figure 9-9. This will stop the zone from becoming Active Directory integrated. Click **Next**.

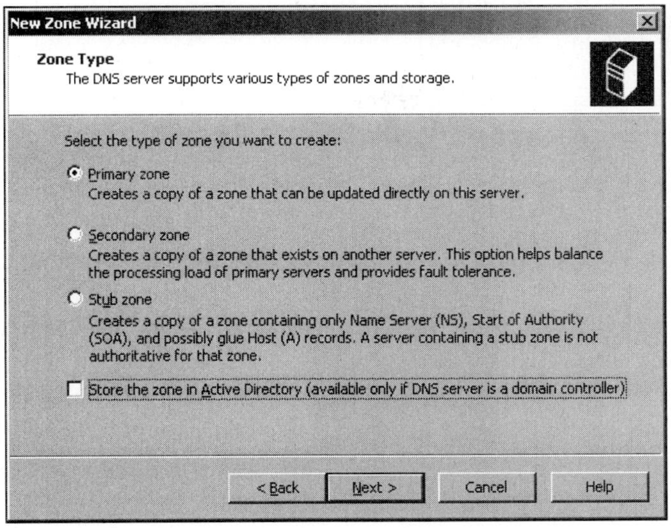

Figure 9-9 Configuring a new standard primary zone using the New Zone Wizard

4. At the Zone Name screen, type **sevenacres*XX*.com** in the Zone name text box, where *XX* is your assigned student number. Click **Next**.
5. At the Zone File screen, review the default settings and click **Next**.
6. At the Dynamic Update screen, review the default settings, as shown in Figure 9-10. Click **Next**.

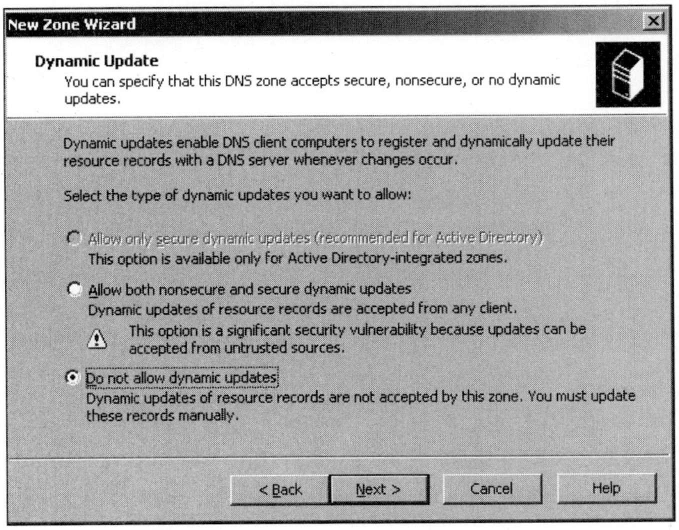

Figure 9-10 DNS dynamic update settings in New Zone Wizard

7. Click **Finish** to complete the creation of the new zone. Verify that a new folder with the name *sevenacres*XX.*com* appears beneath the Forward Lookup Zones folder in the DNS console.
8. Click the **sevenacres*XX*.com** folder to verify that two resource records now appear in the zone, as illustrated in Figure 9-11.

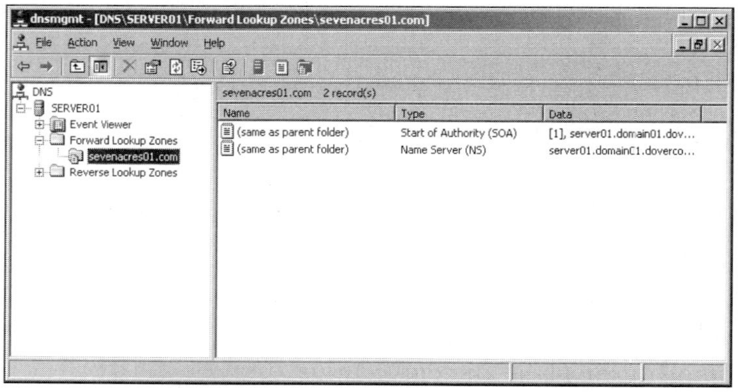

Figure 9-11 Resource records in the *sevenacresXX.com* zone

9. Right-click the **sevenacresXX.com** folder and click **Properties**. The *sevenacresXX.com* Properties dialog box opens, as shown in Figure 9-12.

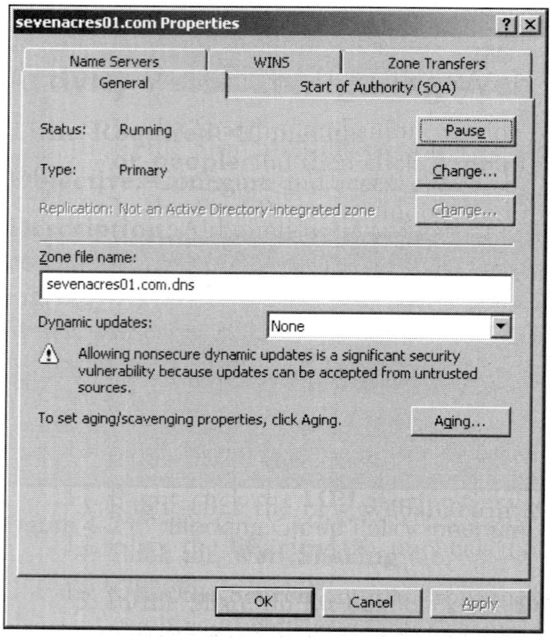

Figure 9-12 Properties dialog box of the *sevenacresXX.com* zone

10. Notice that the General tab allows you to pause a zone, identifies the zone type, and allows you to configure the zone for dynamic updates.
11. Click the **Start of Authority (SOA)** tab. This screen allows you to configure the SOA record for the *sevenacres*XX*.com* zone, as shown in Figure 9-13.
12. Click the **Name Servers** tab. This tab displays a list of the DNS servers responsible for the *sevenacres*XX*.com* zone.
13. Click the **WINS** tab. This tab allows you to enable WINS lookup and configure the IP addresses of WINS servers that should be consulted for unresolved name resolution requests.
14. Click the **Zone Transfers** tab. This allows you configure how your primary server will interact with secondary servers for the purpose of zone transfers.

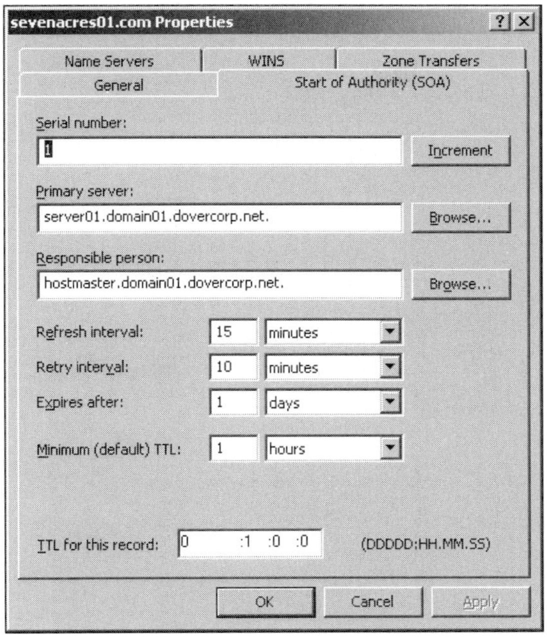

Figure 9-13 The Start of Authority (SOA) settings for the *sevenacresXX.com* zone

15. Click **Cancel** to close the *sevenacresXX.com* Properties dialog box, but leave the DNS console window open.

Although many companies neglect to create them, reverse lookup zones should always be created after an associated forward lookup zone has been implemented. A reverse lookup zone is used to resolve a known IP address to its associated host name or FQDN. Once created, a standard reverse lookup zone adds an additional file to the %systemroot%\system32\dns directory, in a format similar to *1.168.192.in-addr.arpa.dns*. The numeric part of the filename represents the IP network ID associated with the zone in reverse order, whereas the domain name *in-addr.arpa* designates the zone as being a reverse zone. In Activity 9-5, you will create a new standard reverse lookup zone associated with the standard forward lookup zone created in Activity 9-4.

Activity 9-5: Configuring a DNS Standard Reverse Lookup Zone

Time Required: 10 minutes

Objective: Configure a standard primary reverse lookup zone.

Description: After creating the standard primary forward lookup zone for *sevenacresXX.com*, you decide that it would be a wise move to also configure an associated reverse lookup zone as a best practice. In this activity, you will create a standard primary reverse lookup zone for the *sevenacresXX.com* domain.

1. In the DNS console window, right-click the **Reverse Lookup Zones** icon and click **New Zone**.
2. At the New Zone Wizard welcome screen, click **Next**.
3. At the Zone Type screen, ensure that the **Primary zone** radio button is selected. Uncheck the check box next to **Store the zone in Active Directory**, and click **Next**.
4. At the Reverse Lookup Zone Name screen, type **192.168.1** (or the appropriate network ID for your network as per your instructor's instructions) in the Network ID text box, as shown in Figure 9-14. Notice that the Reverse lookup zone name text box is automatically populated with the new reverse zone name. Click **Next**.
5. At the Zone File screen, review the information provided and click **Next**.
6. At the Dynamic Update screen, click **Next**.

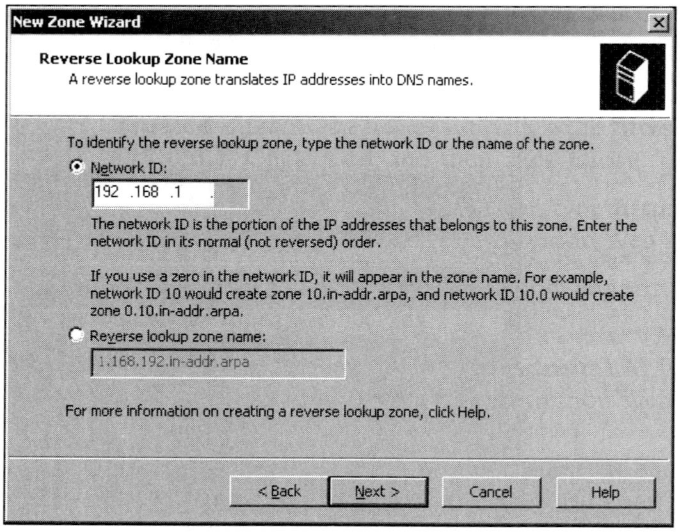

Figure 9-14 Configuring a reverse lookup zone

7. Click **Finish** to complete the New Zone Wizard.
8. Click the new reverse zone folder named **192.168.1.x Subnet** to view its contents. Notice that the new reverse zone also contains two resource records, as illustrated in Figure 9-15.

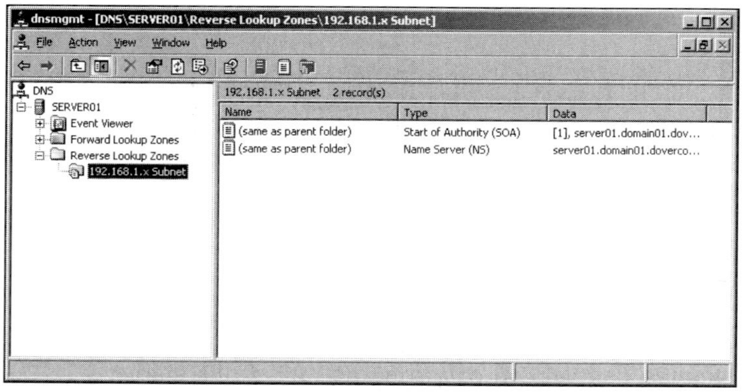

Figure 9-15 Resource records in the 192.168.1.x Subnet reverse zone

9. Leave the DNS console window open.

After both the forward lookup and reverse standard primary zones have been created, it is highly recommended that at least one secondary zone be configured on an alternate server for the purpose of fault tolerance and load balancing. In Activity 9-6, you will implement standard secondary zones that will support the standard primary zones created on your partner's server in Activities 9-4 and 9-5.

Activity 9-6: Configuring DNS Standard Secondary Zones

Time Required: 10 minutes

Objective: Configure standard secondary forward and reverse lookup zones.

Description: Although you have successfully implemented standard primary forward and reverse lookup zones on your server, the IT manager at Dover Leasing has asked you to configure your server as a secondary server to two primary zones configured on a test server. In this activity, you will create two standard secondary zones that will use your partner's DNS server as their primaries. Secondary zones for both your partner's forward and reverse lookup zones will be created.

1. In the DNS console window, right-click the **Forward Lookup Zones** icon and click **New Zone**.
2. At the New Zone Wizard welcome screen, click **Next**.
3. At the Zone Type screen, click the **Secondary zone** radio button, as illustrated in Figure 9-16. Click **Next**.

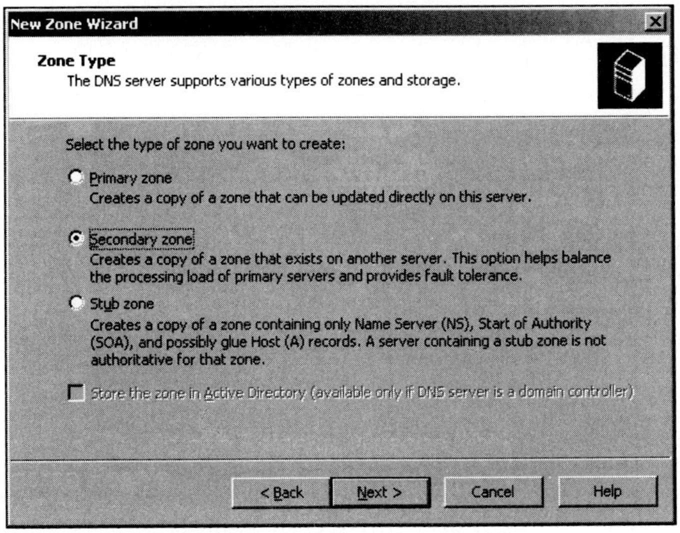

Figure 9-16 Creating a secondary zone

4. At the Zone Name screen, type **sevenacresXX.com** in the Zone name text box, where *XX* is your partner's student number. Click **Next**.
5. At the Master DNS Servers screen, type your partner's IP address in the IP address text box, as illustrated in Figure 9-17. Click **Add**, and then click **Next**.

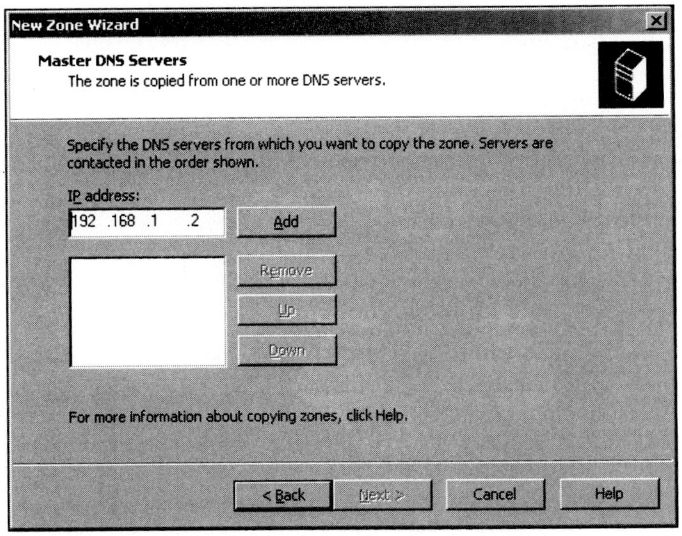

Figure 9-17 Configuring a master DNS server for a secondary server

6. Click **Finish** to complete the New Zone Wizard.
7. In the DNS console interface, click the **Forward Lookup Zones** icon if necessary. Verify that your partner's *sevenacres*XX*.com* zone is listed as a secondary zone.

8. Click the **sevenacres*XX*.com** folder, where *XX* is your partner's student number, to verify that your server now includes records for your partner's zone.
9. Leave the DNS console window open.

Active Directory–Integrated DNS Zones

Although the implementation of standard primary and secondary zones on only two servers is rather straight forward, configuring multiple secondary zones and associated zone transfer settings can be extremely time consuming in large DNS implementations. By the same token, a standard DNS zone supports only unsecured dynamic updates by client computers. That is, any computer with access to the DNS server could add its own resource record to the zone database file, assuming that it understands the dynamic update process and that the DNS server has been configured to allow dynamic updates.

Starting in Windows 2000, Microsoft introduced the concept of Active Directory–integrated DNS zones, mainly to take advantage of the security and replication features of Active Directory. Instead of storing zone information in text files in the %systemroot%\system32\dns directory, zones that are configured as Active Directory integrated instead store zone information within the Active Directory database. One immediate advantage of this technique is that DNS zone information is automatically replicated to all domain controllers specified in the Active Directory environment. For example, an administrator might choose to have DNS zone information replicated to all domain controllers within a specific domain, or alternatively, all domain controllers within the Active Directory forest. This automatic replication helps to eliminate the need to configure zone transfer and maintain DNS zone transfer settings.

Furthermore, Active Directory–integrated DNS zones also provide an additional layer of security if dynamic DNS updates are enabled through a feature called secure dynamic updates. When secure dynamic updates are configured for a DNS zone, only computers that are properly authenticated and listed in the zone's access control list (ACL) are able to add their resource records to the DNS zone file.

In Activity 9-7, you will create a new Active Directory–integrated zone on your server.

Activity 9-7: Configuring an Active Directory–Integrated Zone

Hands-on Project

Time Required: 10 minutes

Objective: Create an Active Directory–integrated zone.

Description: Although Dover Leasing has always used UNIX-based DNS servers in the past, the IT manager is intrigued by the security and administrative benefits provided by Active Directory–integrated DNS zones. As such, he has asked you to create an Active Directory–integrated forward lookup zone on your DNS server for testing purposes. In this activity, you will create a new Active Directory–integrated zone on your DNS server.

1. In the DNS console window, right-click the **Forward Lookup Zones** icon and click **New Zone**.
2. At the New Zone Wizard welcome window, click **Next**.
3. At the Zone Type screen, ensure that the **Primary zone** radio button is selected and that the **Store the zone in Active Directory** check box is checked, as shown in Figure 9-18. Click **Next**.
4. At the Active Directory Zone Replication Scope screen, click the **To all DNS servers in the Active Directory forest Dovercorp.net** radio button, as shown in Figure 9-19. Click **Next**.

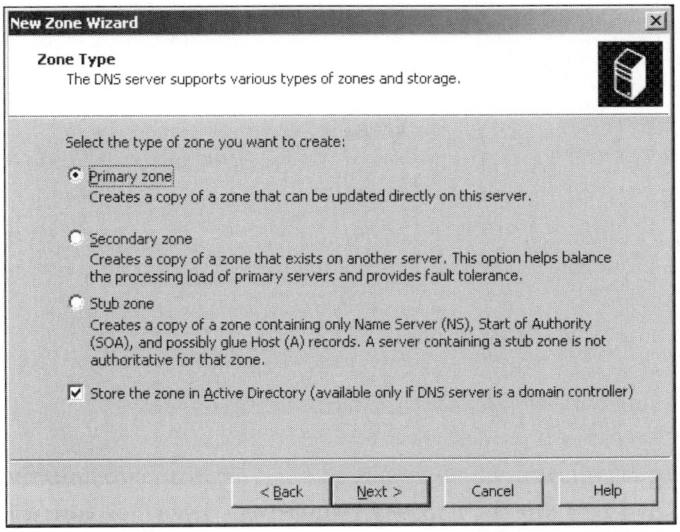

Figure 9-18 Creating an Active Directory–integrated zone

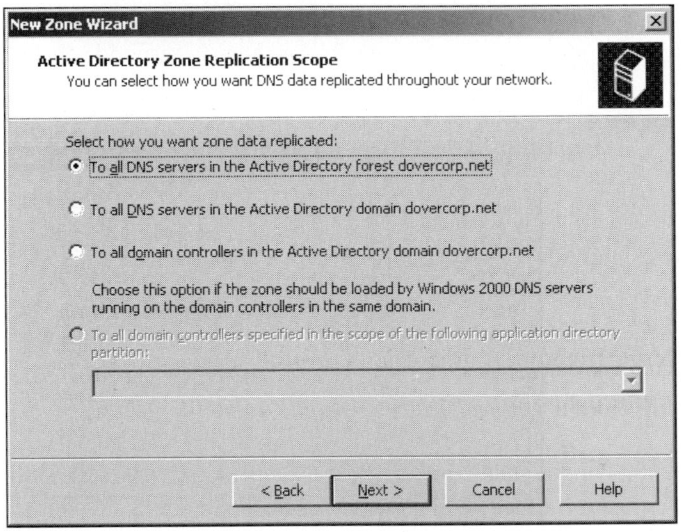

Figure 9-19 Configuring the replication scope of an Active Directory–integrated zone

5. At the Zone Name screen, type **adzone*XX*.com** in the Zone name text box, where *XX* is your assigned student number. Click **Next**.
6. At the Dynamic Update screen, ensure that **Allow only secure dynamic updates** is selected, as shown in Figure 9-20. Click **Next**.
7. Click **Finish** to create the new zone.
8. If necessary, click the **Forward Lookup Zones** icon to verify that the new zone has been added to your server as an Active Directory–integrated zone.
9. Click the **adzone*XX*.com** folder to view the resource records created by default for your new zone.
10. Leave the DNS console window open.

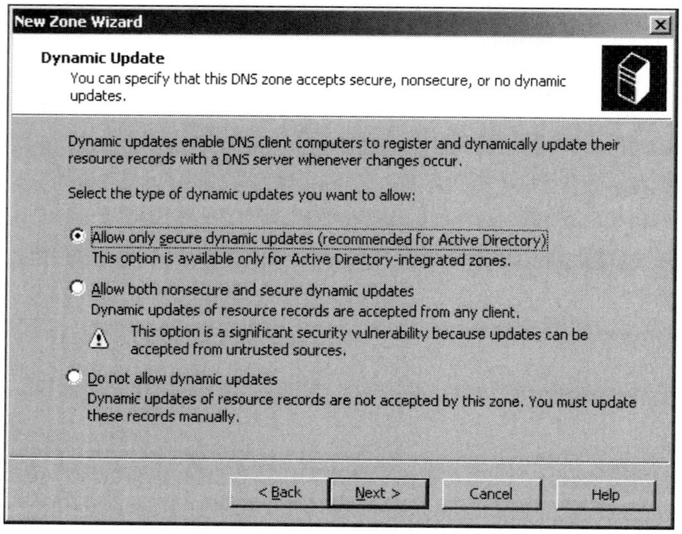

Figure 9-20 Configuring an Active Directory–integrated zone for secure dynamic updates

Note: Although using Active Directory–integrated zones will replicate DNS information to all domain controllers, the DNS service must still be installed on these servers for them to respond to client DNS requests.

DNS Resource Records

Once a new DNS zone is created and defined, resource records must be added to the server for it to respond to DNS client requests. Although clients can automatically add their own host records to a zone if dynamic updates are enabled, resource records can also be added to a zone file manually. Two resource records are created by default and added to a new zone once created. The Start of Authority (SOA) record designates a server as being authoritative for a zone and stores additional information such as the zone file serial number, time-to-live (TTL) intervals, and more. A second entry, known as a Name Server (NS) record, specifies the FQDN of a name server that is authoritative for the zone.

Note: Remember that only Windows 2000, Windows XP, and Windows Server 2003 DNS clients are capable of using the DNS dynamic update feature. Other clients' operating systems will require the assistance of the DNS dynamic update settings found in DHCP.

There are a number of DNS resource record types, the most common of which are explained in Table 9-2.

Table 9-2 DNS resource record types

Resource Record Type	Purpose
SOA (Start of Authority)	Indicates the authoritative name server for the zone as well administrative information, such as the serial number, zone transfer intervals, and TTL (Time to Live for indicating how long information should be cached)
A (Address or Host)	Indicates the IP address for a specific host name
NS (Name Server)	Defines the name servers responsible or authoritative for a specific zone
CNAME (Canonical Name or Alias)	Allows you to specify additional names or aliases for computers that have host names
MX (Mail Exchanger)	Specifies a server to which e-mail applications can send mail
PTR (Pointer)	Used in reverse lookup zones to provide IP-to–domain name resolution; these records can be created automatically as part of configuring new A records
SRV (Service Locator)	Registered automatically by Windows .NET Server and Windows 2000 services so that clients can find a service by querying DNS; you can also manually add these records to support such services as Exchange 2000 Instant Messaging

In Activity 9-8, you will manually configure a variety of different resource records in your DNS server's zone.

Activity 9-8: Configuring DNS Resource Records

Time Required: 10 minutes

Objective: Configure DNS resource records.

Description: After completing the initial configuration of every different type of zone file, you decide that the time has come to begin creating various resource records. Although Windows Server 2003 DNS supports dynamic updates, the IT manager at Dover Leasing has already let you know that a number of records will need to be defined for the UNIX servers still acting at Dover Leasing's mail and Web servers. In this activity, you will create resource record entries in both the forward and reverse lookup zones for your *sevenacresXX.com* domain.

1. In the DNS console window, click the **sevenacres*XX*.com** folder (where *XX* is your assigned student number) under Forward Lookup Zones to view its contents.
2. Right-click the **sevenacres*XX*.com** folder and click **New Host (A)**.
3. The New Host dialog box opens. In the Name text box, type **server1**. In the IP address text box, type **192.168.1.253**, as shown in Figure 9-21. Click the **Add Host** button.

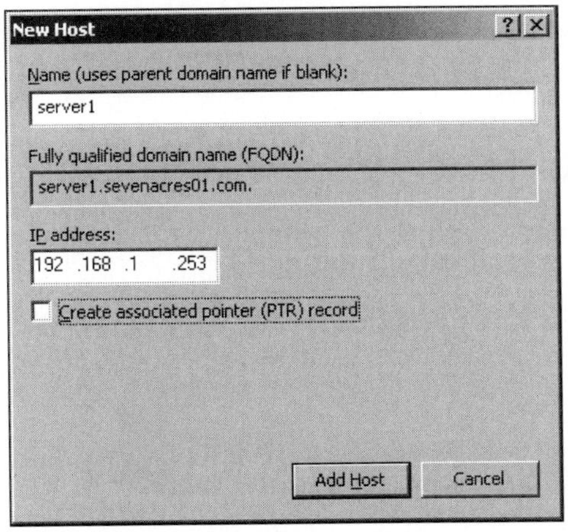

Figure 9-21 Creating a new host resource record

4. In the DNS dialog box, read the message that appears, and then click **OK**. Click **Done** to close the New Host dialog box. Notice that a new Host record appears in the contents of the *sevenacresXX.com* zone.
5. Right-click the **sevenacres*XX*.com** folder (where *XX* is your assigned student number) and again click **New Host (A)**.
6. In the Name text box, type **server2**. In the IP address text box, type **192.168.1.254**. Click the check box next to **Create associated pointer PTR record** and click **Add Host**. This will create not only a new A record in the *sevenacresXX.com* forward lookup zone but also a PTR record in the associated reverse lookup zone.
7. In the DNS dialog box, click **OK**. Click **Done** to close the New Host dialog box.
8. In the DNS console window, click the **plus sign (+)** next to the Reverse Lookup Zones icon to expand it, if necessary.
9. Click the **192.168.1.x Subnet** folder to view the contents of the reverse zone. Press **F5** to refresh the contents of the zone file, if necessary. Notice that a new Pointer (PTR) record appears for server 192.168.1.254.

10. Double-click the **192.168.1.254** resource record. This will open the properties dialog box of the resource record, as shown in Figure 9-22.

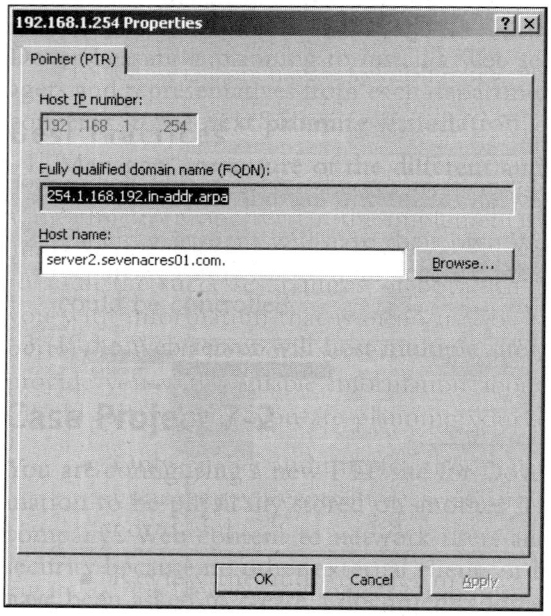

Figure 9-22 The properties dialog box of a PTR resource record

11. Click **Cancel** to close the properties dialog box of the 192.168.1.254 resource record.
12. Right-click the **sevenacres*XX*.com** folder (where *XX* is your assigned student number) and click **New Alias (CNAME)**.
13. In the New Resource Record dialog box, type **www** in the Alias name text box, and type **server1.sevenacres*XX*.com** (where *XX* is your assigned student number) in the Fully qualified domain name (FQDN) for target host text box. Click **OK**.
14. Click the **sevenacres*XX*.com** folder (where *XX* is your assigned student number) to confirm that the new Alias (CNAME) record has been created. This record allows the host *server1.sevenacresXX.com* to also be accessed by the alias www.
15. Right-click the **sevenacres*XX*.com** folder (where *XX* is your assigned student number) and click **New Mail Exchanger (MX)**.
16. In the Fully qualified domain name (FQDN) of mail server text box, type **server2.sevenacres*XX*.com** (where *XX* is your assigned student number) and click **OK**. This will create an MX resource record that will ultimately be used to locate the *sevenacresXX.com* mail server.
17. Leave the DNS console window open.

As learned earlier in this section, Active Directory–integrated DNS zones do not require that you explicitly configure zone transfer settings because zone information is replicated to other domain controllers automatically. However, when you configure standard primary and secondary DNS servers, the secondary server must obtain zone information from the primary server or another secondary server via a zone transfer. The source of a zone transfer for a secondary server is known as a **master server**.

Windows Server 2003 supports two different zone transfer methods between primary and secondary DNS servers, as follows:

- *Full zone transfer (AXFR)*—A full zone transfer will transfer the entire contents of the DNS zone database from a standard primary server to a standard secondary server. This type of zone transfer is used when a new secondary server initially requests the zone database file from the primary server.

- *Incremental zone transfer (IXFR)*—Once a secondary server has received a full zone transfer from a primary server, it will subsequently only request any changes to the zone database file not currently present in its version of the DNS zone database.

A secondary DNS server always initiates the zone transfer process. Some of the different scenarios under which a zone transfer would occur include the following:

- The refresh interval for the zone has expired.
- The primary server notifies the secondary servers that changes to the zone file exist.
- The DNS service is restarted on the secondary server.
- The zone transfer process is manually initiated from the DNS console of the secondary server.

Because the zone transfer process will occur automatically whenever the refresh interval for the zone expires, explicitly configuring zone transfer settings is not required. However, Windows Server 2003 DNS also supports the use of DNS Notify, a feature that allows a primary DNS server to notify any secondary servers of when changes to the DNS zone database have occurred. This is accomplished by configuring the Notify properties of a DNS zone with the IP addresses of all standard primary servers, as shown in Figure 9-23.

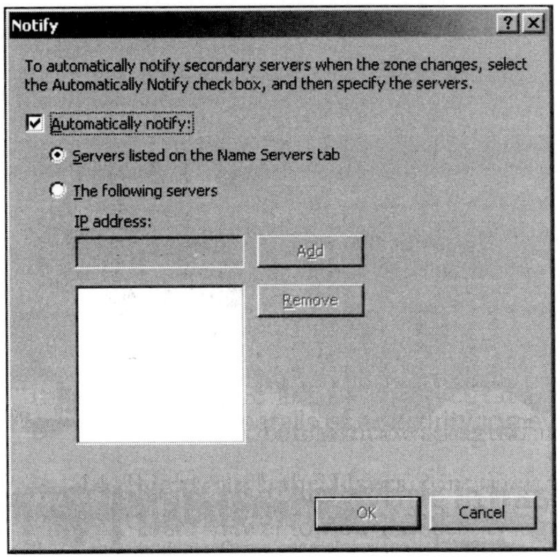

Figure 9-23 Configuring the notify properties for a primary zone

In Activity 9-9, you will configure zone transfer settings for your server's standard zone.

Activity 9-9: Configuring Zone Transfer Settings

Time Required: 5 minutes

Objective: Configure DNS zone transfer settings.

Description: Although you have already confirmed that your secondary servers have initiated the zone transfer process with your partner's primary server, you decide to configure notify properties so that your primary server will immediately let any of its configured secondary servers know when a change to the zone database takes place. In this activity, you will configure zone transfer settings for your standard primary zone.

1. In the DNS console window, right-click your **sevenacres*XX*.com** folder (where *XX* is your assigned student number) and click **Properties**.

2. Click the **Zone Transfers** tab. This displays the zone transfer settings for the zone, as illustrated in Figure 9-24.

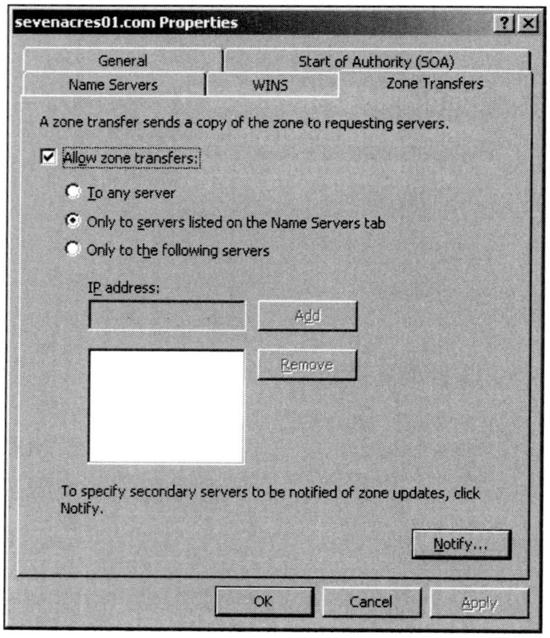

Figure 9-24 The Zone Transfers tab of a DNS zone's properties dialog box

3. Click the **Only to the following servers** radio button. In the IP address text box, enter your partner's IP address, and click **Add**.
4. Click the **Notify** button.
5. Click **The following servers** radio button. In the IP address text box, type the IP address of your partner's computer and click **Add**. Click **OK**. Your server will now automatically notify its configured secondary server when a change occurs to its zone file.
6. Click **OK** to close the properties dialog box of the *sevenacres*XX*.com* zone.
7. Leave the DNS console window open.

DNS Forwarders

When a new standard primary or Active Directory–integrated DNS zone is configured on a Windows Server 2003 server, that zone is considered to be authoritative for the domains that it contains. Normally, if a DNS server cannot answer a query that it receives, it will send an iterative query to another up-level server in the DNS hierarchy, such as a server authoritative for the *.com* or root domain. Although this system works, performing queries in this manner is not always the most efficient method. For example, a company may have many internal DNS servers used to support servers on their networks. If each of these servers were to query other Internet DNS servers for every query they could not resolve, considerable traffic and bandwidth might be wasted.

As an alternative, a company might consider the use of **DNS forwarders** to speed up the name resolution process. When DNS forwarders are used, a DNS server that cannot resolve a query will first forward that query to its configured DNS forwarder, to see whether it possibly can. Because busier DNS servers tend to have more name resolution information cached, it often makes sense to configure your local DNS servers to use your ISP's DNS servers as a forwarder. In that way, you can potentially eliminate much of the name resolution traffic that would have to travel to other more distant DNS servers.

In Activity 9-10, you will configure your DNS server to use the instructor server as a DNS forwarder.

Activity 9-10: Configuring DNS Forwarders

Time Required: 10 minutes

Objective: Configure a DNS server to use a DNS forwarder.

Description: You are aware that your DNS server will forward queries to an up-level DNS server such as a root server in the event that it cannot locally resolve a request. However, you also know that the main DNS server at Dover Leasing currently handles much more query traffic than your current test server and thus will likely have more information cached. In this activity, you will configure your DNS server to use the instructor DNS server as a DNS forwarder.

1. In the DNS console window, right-click your server icon and click **Properties**.
2. Click the **Forwarders** tab, and then click the **New** button.
3. In the New Forwarder dialog box, type **course.com** in the DNS domain text box, as illustrated in Figure 9-25. This will allow you to forward all DNS queries for the *course.com* domain to the DNS server of your choice. Click **OK**.

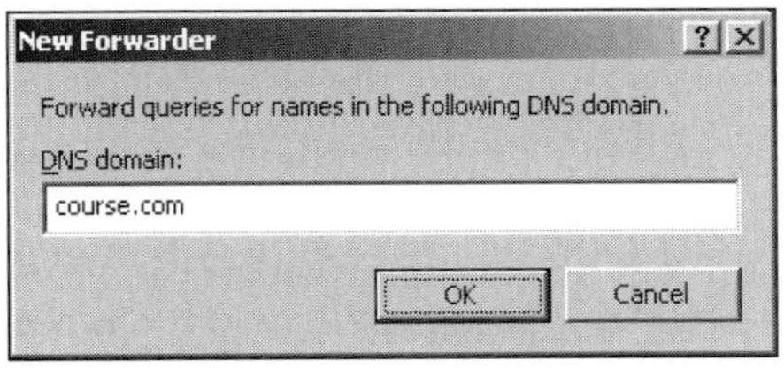

Figure 9-25 Configuring a new forwarder for a specific DNS domain

4. In the Selected domain's forwarder IP address list text box, type your partner's IP address and then click **Add**. This will forward all queries for the *course.com* domain to your partner's DNS server.
5. Click **All other DNS domains** in the DNS domain list box. Notice that no forwarders are yet configured for all other DNS domains, as illustrated in Figure 9-26.

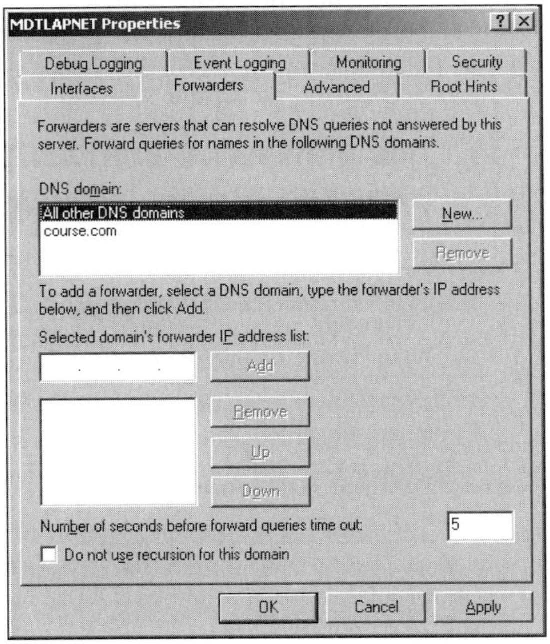

Figure 9-26 Configuring DNS forwarder settings

6. In the Selected domain's forwarder IP address list text box, type **192.168.1.100** (or the IP address for your instructor's computer) and click **Add**. This will configure your DNS server to forward all queries for other domains, except *course.com*, to the DNS service on the Instructor server.
7. Click **OK** to close the properties dialog box of your DNS server.
8. Leave the DNS console window open.

Configuring Dynamic DNS Updates

As you learned earlier, Windows Server 2003 DNS supports the dynamic updating of resource records. An administrator no longer has to manually update the resource records in a zone file because clients and name servers on the network can automatically update the zone database on their own. For example, when a client leases a new IP address from the DHCP server, it can automatically update the mapping of its name to its IP address in the zone file.

When a client receives an acknowledgement from a DHCP server that it has successfully leased an IP address, the client then sends a DNS update request to the DNS server to update its A record in the zone file. The DHCP server then sends an update to the DNS server on behalf of the client to update the client's PTR record by default.

Note: If there are legacy clients on the network, you must configure DHCP to update the A records and the PTR records with the DNS server on behalf of the clients.

Before you can use dynamic updates, you must first configure the DNS service to allow them. Dynamic updates are configured on a zone-by-zone basis in the properties of the zone for which you wish to enable them. There are three available options for configuring dynamic updates, as follows:

- *No*—Dynamic updates are disabled for the zone.
- *Yes*—Dynamic updates are enabled for the zone.
- *Only secure updates*—Dynamic updates are enabled but are only accepted from computers that have a computer account within Active Directory. Using this option means that only users that are authorized can update the zone file providing more security. The Only secure updates option is only available on DNS servers that are also domain controllers and have Active Directory–integrated zones.

Tip: One important consideration with dynamic updates is whether or not your DNS implementation supports Active Directory. If it does, you must configure dynamic updates for domain controllers to properly register their service records.

In Activity 9-11, you will configure DNS dynamic update settings for zones on your DNS server.

Activity 9-11: Configuring a DNS Zone for Dynamic Updates

Time Required: 10 minutes

Objective: Configure a DNS zone to support dynamic updates.

Description: Although your DNS server currently appears to be functioning correctly, none of its zones are configured to support dynamic updates by default. In this activity, you will explore and configure the DNS dynamic update settings for both your standard primary forward lookup zone, as well as your Active Directory–integrated zone.

1. In the DNS console window, right click the **sevenacres*XX*.com** folder (where *XX* is your assigned student number) and click **Properties**.

2. On the **General** tab, click the **Dynamic updates** list arrow, as shown in Figure 9-27. Note that because the zone is a standard primary zone, the only options available are Nonsecure and secure.

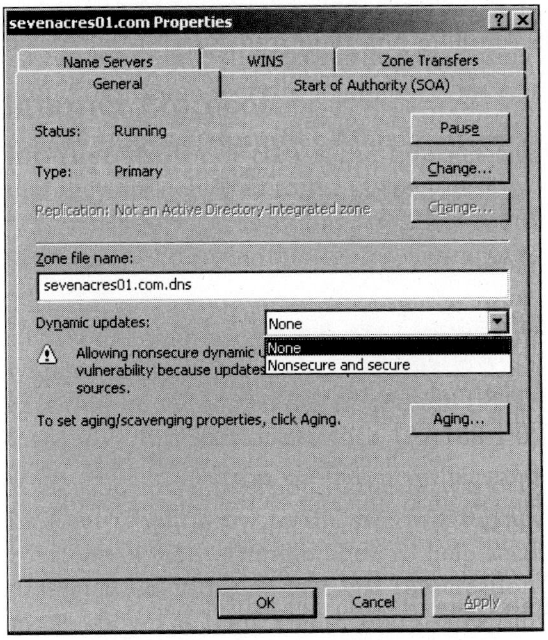

Figure 9-27 Configuring DNS dynamic updates

3. Click **Nonsecure and secure** in the Dynamic updates list box and click **OK**.
4. Right-click the **adzone*XX*.com** folder (where *XX* is your assigned student number) and click **Properties**.
5. On the General tab, click the **Dynamic updates** list arrow. Notice that because the zone is Active Directory integrated, an additional option, Secure only, is also available.
6. Do not change the dynamic update settings of the *adzone*XX*.com* zone, and click **OK** to close its properties dialog box.
7. Close the DNS console window.

Configuring DNS Client Settings

For a client computer to properly resolve FQDNs to IP addresses and vice versa, you must configure it with the IP address of a DNS server in its TCP/IP properties. Although configuring client TCP/IP settings was originally looked at in Chapter 7, that discussion was limited to the configuration of a DNS server IP address and not advanced properties.

The DNS tab of the Advanced properties of a client's TCP/IP settings allows you to configure additional DNS-related settings that will impact how a client interacts with a DNS server. This tab is illustrated in Figure 9-28.

The first portion of the DNS tab allows you to add or remove the IP addresses of DNS servers that the client will use, as well as control the order in which the servers are contacted. By default, this section is populated with the IP addresses of servers added when the client's basic TCP/IP properties were configured. However, this section allows you to add additional DNS servers for the client to use, beyond the normal use of a primary and secondary DNS server address only. The arrow buttons to the right can be used to control the order in which these DNS servers are queried.

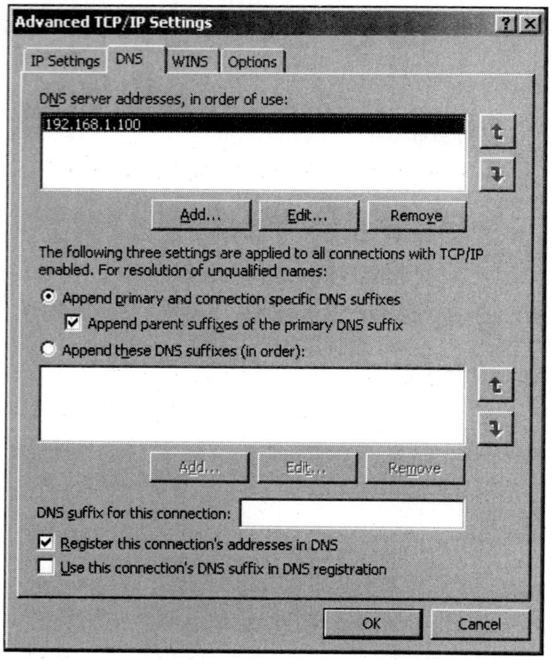

Figure 9-28 Client DNS settings in the Advanced TCP/IP Settings dialog box

The middle section of the DNS tab allows you to control how the client will handle name resolution requests that are not fully qualified—in other words, those that specify only a host name rather than an FQDN. Windows Server is capable of handling this situation using the following three configuration options:

- *Append primary and connection specific DNS suffixes*—This option, which is selected by default, tells the client to append it's primary DNS suffix when only a host name is provided and to also use the connection-specific suffix if one is configured.
- *Append parent suffixes of the primary DNS suffix*—This option tells the client to also append any parent suffixes to the DNS request in situations where the previous setting does not resolve the name. For example, after attempting to query DNS for the host *server1.marketing.Dovercorp.net*, a client would then attempt to query DNS using the parent suffix, for example *server1.Dovercorp.net*.
- *Append these DNS suffixes (in order)*—This option allows an administrator to specify the exact list of suffixes that should be appended to the host name, along with an associated order. For example, if this list contained the DNS suffixes *sevenacres.com* and then *Dovercorp.net*, a query for the host server1 would first result in a DNS query for *server1.sevenacres.com*, and then a query for *server1.Dovercorp.net* if it were not found.

By changing the way that DNS deals with unqualified host names, an administrator has a more granular level of control over the name resolution process.

Lastly, the DNS tab allows you to configure DNS settings specific to a particular network connection. For example, you might have a server that has multiple network cards. In this scenario, you might want one network card to register a specific FQDN in DNS, while the other uses completely different parameters. The last two check boxes on the DNS tab allow you to control whether the client will attempt to dynamically update DNS and which domain suffix it will use. All three settings in this section are outlined as follows:

- *DNS suffix for this connection*—This option allows a DNS suffix to be specified for the connection other than the default domain associated with the computer.
- *Register this connection's addresses in DNS*—This option allows clients to register their computer name and IP address with the DNS server.

- *Use this connection's DNS suffix in DNS registration*—This option allows the client to register the computer name along with the DNS suffix. Use this option only if the DNS suffix is different from the domain name.

In Activity 9-12, you will configure client DNS settings for your server.

Activity 9-12: Configuring Client DNS Settings

Time Required: 10 minutes

Objective: Configure client DNS settings.

Description: Having focused on server-based DNS configuration settings up to this point, the IT manager has asked you to explore the various DNS client settings available on Windows Server 2003 and how they might be optimized to provide for better client performance. In this activity, you will explore and test changes to the default DNS client settings on your server.

1. Click **Start**, select **Control Panel**, select **Network Connections**, and then right-click **Local Area Connection** and click **Properties**.
2. On the General tab, double-click **Internet Protocol (TCP/IP)** to access its properties.
3. In the Use the following DNS server addresses section, type your server's IP address in the Preferred DNS server text box.
4. Click the **Advanced** button, and then click the **DNS** tab. Notice that the DNS server configured in Step 3 appears in the list of DNS servers for this client to use.
5. Click the **Append these DNS suffixes (in order)** radio button.
6. Click **Add**.
7. In the TCP/IP Domain Suffix dialog box, type the FQDN of your partner's domain, similar to what is illustrated in Figure 9-29. Click **Add**.

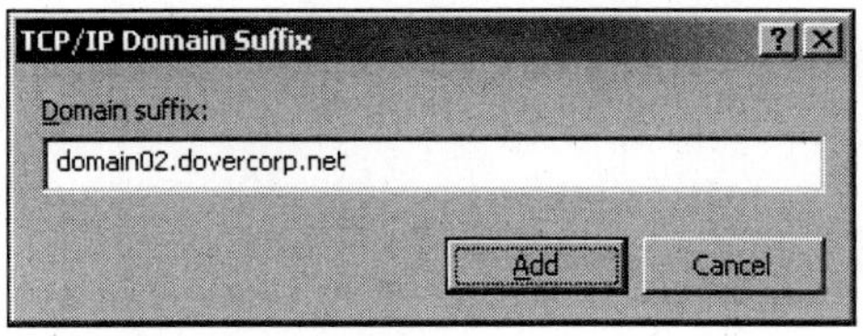

Figure 9-29 Adding a domain suffix to a DNS client

8. Click **Add** again, then type **sevenacres*XX*.com** (where *XX* is your assigned student number) in the Domain suffix text box and click **Add**.
9. Notice that both your partner's domain and the *sevenacresXX.com* domain now appear in the list of DNS suffixes to be used, as shown in Figure 9-30. In this case, all name resolution requests that do not supply an FQDN will have these two domain names appended in the order in which they appear in this list.
10. Click **OK** to close the Advanced TCP/IP Settings dialog box, and click **OK** to close the Internet Protocol (TCP/IP) Properties dialog box.
11. Click **OK** to close the Local Area Connection properties dialog box.
12. Click **Start**, click **Run**, then type **cmd** and press **Enter**.
13. At the command line, type **ping www** and press **Enter**. Because of the manner in which unqualified names are now handled, the server first attempted to find a host named www in your partner's domain and, after this failed, managed to find a record for www in the *sevenacresXX.com* domain, which it used to perform the ping. Note that the ping still fails because a host with the IP address 192.168.1.253 does not exist on the network.

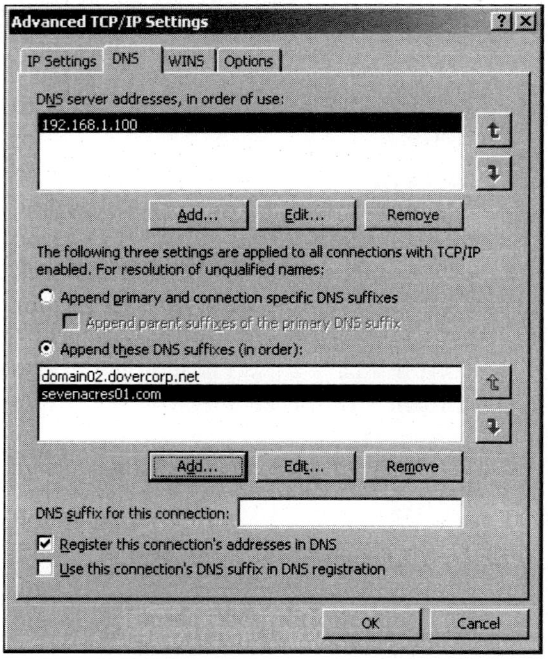

Figure 9-30 Configuring resolution for unqualified names

14. Close the command prompt window.

Testing the DNS Server

After your DNS server has been installed and configured, you may want to test the server to ensure that lookup queries and resource records are properly configured. There are two utilities that you can use to perform these tests:

- *DNS Monitor*—Found on the Monitoring tab of a DNS server's properties, this tool allows you to perform both simple and recursive DNS queries. A simple query is a test where the DNS server queries itself to verify correct configuration. You can also test the DNS server by forwarding a recursive query to another configured DNS server. The results of both tests provide simple pass/fail information.
- *Nslookup*—This utility is installed with TCP/IP and is the classic diagnostic command-line utility used with DNS. You can use Nslookup to view resource records and perform queries on any DNS server.

In Activity 9-13, you will use both the DNS Monitor and Nslookup tools to test the configuration of your DNS server.

Activity 9-13: Testing the DNS Service Using DNS Monitor and Nslookup

Time Required: 10 minutes

Objective: Test the DNS service using the DNS Monitor and Nslookup tools.

Description: You have been informed that Windows Server 2003 includes two primary utilities for the purpose of testing basic DNS functionality for clients. In this activity, you will use both the DNS Monitor and Nslookup utilities to test whether your DNS server is capable of resolving queries correctly. When this is complete, you will return your server to its original DNS client settings.

1. Click **Start** and then click **Run**. In the Open text box, type **cmd** and then press **Enter**.
2. At the command prompt, type **nslookup /?** and press **Enter**. The options available for the nslookup command appear, as illustrated in Figure 9-31.

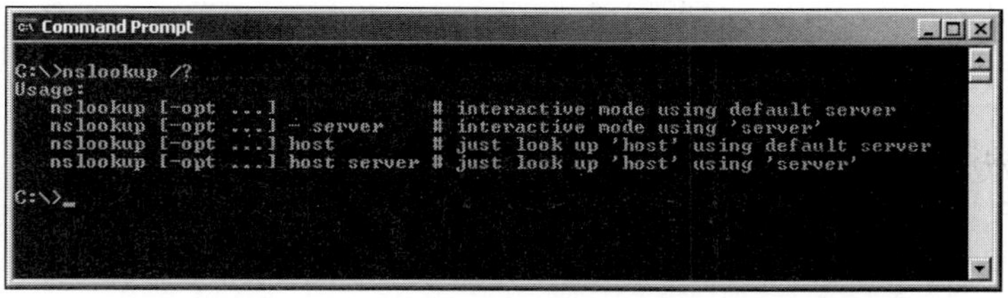

Figure 9-31 Viewing options available with the Nslookup command

3. Type **nslookup www.sevenacres*XX*.com** where *XX* is your assigned student number, and press **Enter**. A result should be returned by your server, as shown in Figure 9-32.

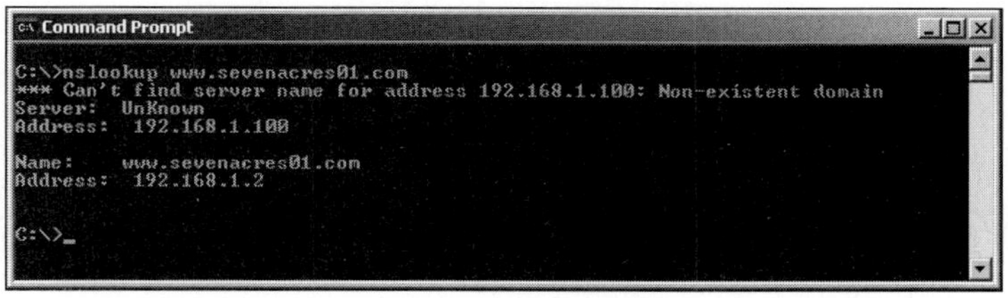

Figure 9-32 Testing DNS settings using the Nslookup command

4. Close the command prompt window.
5. Click **Start**, select **Administrative Tools**, and then click **DNS**.
6. Right-click your server icon, and then click **Properties**.
7. Click the **Monitoring** tab. Click the check boxes next to both **A simple query against this DNS server** and **A recursive query to other DNS servers**, as shown in Figure 9-33.

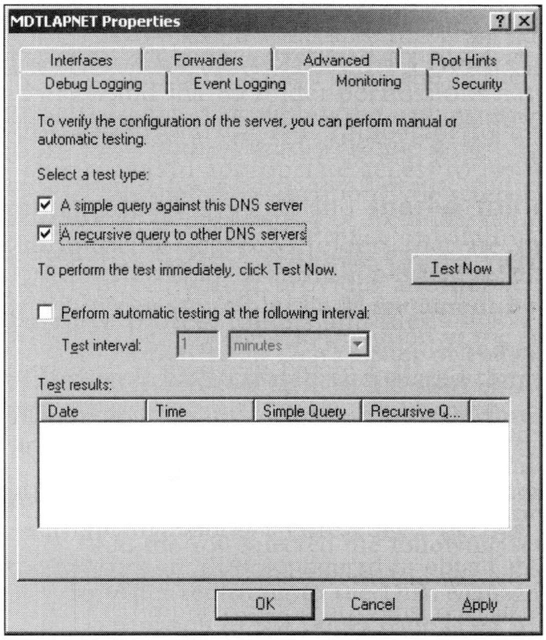

Figure 9-33 Testing a DNS server via the Monitoring tab

8. Click the **Test Now** button. If both tests complete successfully, the word Pass will appear in the Test results window.
9. Close the DNS server properties dialog box, and then close the DNS console window.
10. Click **Start**, select **Control Panel**, select **Network Connections**, and then right-click **Local Area Connection** and click **Properties**.
11. Double-click **Internet Protocol (TCP/IP)** to access its properties.
12. In the Use the following DNS server addresses section, type **192.168.1.100** (or the IP address of your instructor's computer) in the Preferred DNS server text box.
13. Click the **Advanced** button, and then click the **DNS** tab.
14. Click the **Append primary and connection specific DNS suffixes** radio button. Click the **Append parent suffixes of the primary DNS suffix** check box.
15. Click **OK** to close the Advanced TCP/IP Settings dialog box, and click **OK** to close the Internet Protocol (TCP/IP) Properties dialog box.
16. Click **OK** to close the properties dialog box of Local Area Connection.

Name Resolution Files

Although Windows Server 2003 relies on the DNS service for name resolution and service location functions associated with Active Directory, it is still capable of using static text files for the purpose of resolving names to IP addresses. One such file, known simply as HOSTS, can be configured locally on client systems for the purpose of providing services for resolving host names and FQDNs to IP addresses. A second file, known as LMHOSTS, exists for the purpose of mapping NetBIOS names to IP addresses. Both files are looked at in the following sections.

The HOSTS File

Windows Server 2003 stores a file named HOSTS in the %systemroot%\system32\drivers\etc directory. By default, this file consists of a single host name to IP address mapping—the localhost entry, with an IP address of 127.0.0.1. It is because of this entry that an attempt to ping the host name localhost results in a ping being sent to the loopback address.

Although this file is not normally configured on a widespread basis due to the administrative effort and potential for errors that it would introduce, the HOSTS file is an important part of the name resolution process on Windows Server 2003 servers, as will be looked at later in this chapter. The HOSTS file is still commonly used for testing purposes, especially in cases where host name or FQDN resolution is required, but DNS has yet to be configured. For example, if a new website were being created at *web1.Dovercorp.net*, an administrator could test functionality by placing an appropriate entry in the local computer's HOSTS file before configuring DNS. This would allow name resolution to occur normally until DNS is ultimately configured.

One important consideration with entries in the HOSTS file is the problems that they can create in environments that do use DNS. When a client attempts to use a host name or FQDN to connect to a server, the HOSTS file is always checked before DNS. As such, an incorrect entry in this file can lead to network connectivity problems.

In Activity 9-14, you will configure and test settings in your server's local HOSTS file.

Activity 9-14: Configuring and Testing Name Resolution with HOSTS files

Time Required: 10 minutes

Objective: Configure and test name resolution using the HOSTS file.

Description: Although Dover Leasing will rely upon DNS for almost all name resolution requirements, there are often cases when members of the IT department need to test settings related to new servers. In these cases, they would like to use a name resolution method that doesn't rely upon the IT manager approving additions to the DNS database. Because of this, you have decided to test whether using a local HOSTS file will better meet their needs. In this activity, you will configure the local HOSTS file on your server to see whether it will properly resolve name resolution requests.

1. Click **Start**, and then click **My Computer**.
2. Browse to the **C:\WINDOWS\system32\drivers\etc** folder.
3. Right-click the file **HOSTS**, and then click **Open**. If necessary, in the Windows dialog box, click the **Select the program from a list** radio button, then click **OK.**
4. When the Open With window opens, click **Notepad** on the list of available programs, and then click **OK.** The HOSTS file opens in Notepad, as shown in Figure 9-34.

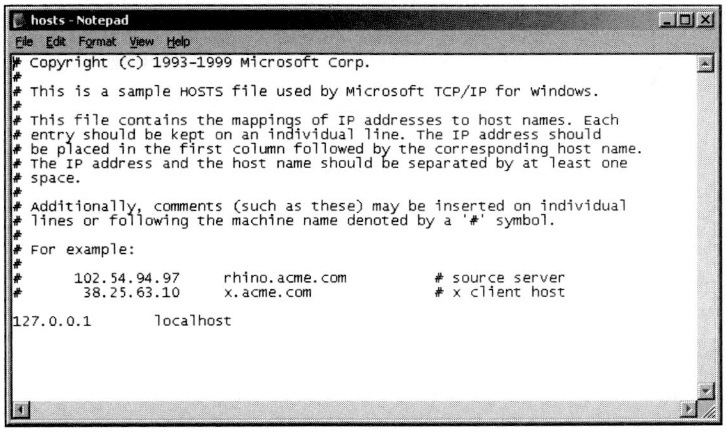

Figure 9-34 The default configuration of the HOSTS file

5. Notice that by default, the HOSTS file contains only a single entry, mapping the host name localhost to the loopback IP address, 127.0.0.1.
6. On the line directly beneath the localhost entry, type **127.0.0.1**, press the **Tab** key, and then type **myserver**.
7. Click **File**, and then click **Save**. Leave the HOSTS file open.
8. Click **Start** and then click **Run**. In the Open text box, type **cmd** and then press **Enter**.
9. At the command line, type **ping localhost** and press **Enter**. Notice that four replies are received and that the name localhost was resolved to the IP address 127.0.0.1, as shown in Figure 9-35.

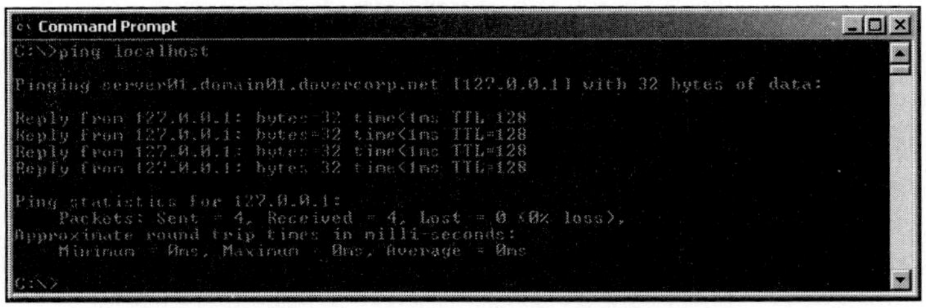

Figure 9-35 Resolving a host name using a HOSTS file entry

10. Type **ping myserver** and press **Enter**. Notice that the host name myserver is also resolved to the IP address 127.0.0.1 because of the entry in the HOSTS file.
11. On the line directly below the myserver entry in the HOSTS file, type **1.1.1.1**, press the **Tab** key twice, and then type **www.yahoo.com**.
12. Click **File**, and then click **Save**. Leave the HOSTS file open.
13. On the command line, type **ping www.yahoo.com** and press **Enter**. Notice that the server now attempts to ping the IP address 1.1.1.1 rather than attempting to resolve the *www.yahoo.com* FQDN using DNS.
14. Remove the entry for **www.yahoo.com** from the HOSTS file and save your changes. Close the command prompt and the HOSTS file. Leave the My Computer window open.

The LMHOSTS File

Another important file used in the name resolution process on a Windows Server 2003 system is the LMHOSTS file. This file also exists in the %systemroot%\system32\drivers\etc directory, but includes the extension .SAM (for sample) by default. The sample file includes information about the configuration of LMHOSTS, including different settings that can be defined within the file. Once configured and saved, the LMHOSTS file should not include a file extension.

Although the two files appear similar in many ways, there is one important difference between a HOSTS and an LMHOSTS file. While a HOSTS file is used to resolve host names and FQDNs to IP addresses, an LMHOSTS file exists for the purpose of mapping NetBIOS names to IP addresses. While Windows 2000, XP, and Server 2003 all tend to rely on host names for most domain functions, older clients, such as those running Windows 98 or Windows NT still use NetBIOS for domain functions such as authentication and connecting to servers.

If configured, an LMHOSTS file definitely has an impact on how names are resolved on a Windows Server 2003 network. However, a Windows Server 2003 system can also be configured to disable LMHOSTS processing if required. In Activity 9-15, you will configure and test settings in your server's LMHOSTS.SAM file, and then disable processing of the LMHOSTS file.

Activity 9-15: Viewing and Disabling Processing of LMHOSTS files

Time Required: 10 minutes

Objective: View and disable processing of LMHOSTS files.

Description: After learning about the name resolution process on Windows Server 2003, you have decided that disabling processing of the LMHOSTS file would probably be the best idea at Dover Leasing. Before doing so, however, you decide to review the LMHOSTS.SAM file because you feel that it may eventually come in handy in cases where NetBIOS name resolution is an issue. In this activity, you will first view the LMHOSTS.SAM file on your computer and then disable processing of the LMHOSTS file.

1. In the My Computer window, right-click the **LMHOSTS.SAM** file and click **Open**. If necessary, in the Windows dialog box, click the **Select the program from a list** radio button, then click **OK**.
2. In the Open With window, click **Notepad**, and then click **OK**.
3. The LMHOSTS.SAM file opens in Notepad, as shown in Figure 9-36.
4. Read through the instructions included in the LMHOSTS.SAM file, and then close the file.
5. Close the My Computer window.
6. Click **Start**, select **Control Panel**, select **Network Connections**, and then right-click **Local Area Connection** and click **Properties**.
7. Double-click **Internet Protocol (TCP/IP)** to view its properties.

8. Click the **Advanced** button, and then click the **WINS** tab, as illustrated in Figure 9-37.

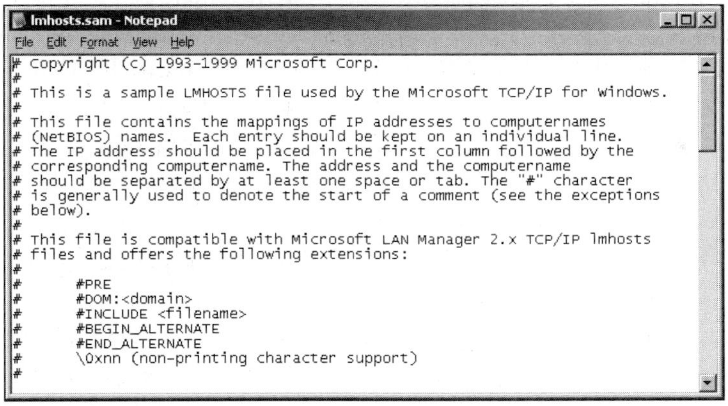

Figure 9-36 The sample LMHOSTS file

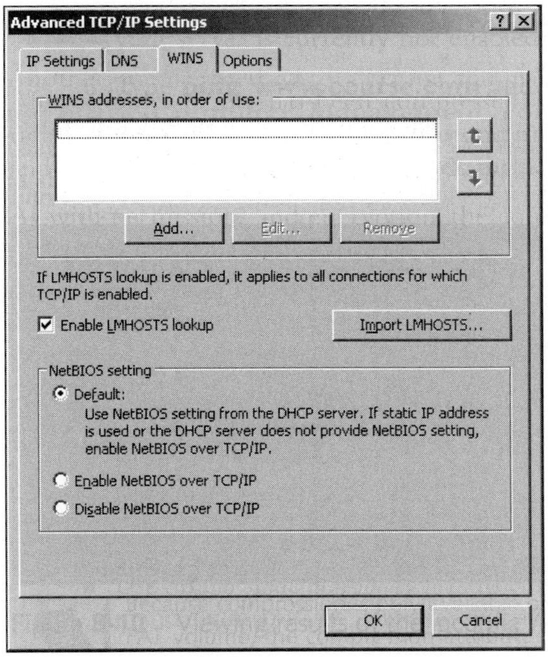

Figure 9-37 The WINS tab of Advanced TCP/IP Settings dialog box

9. Uncheck the check box next to **Enable LMHOSTS lookup**. This disables all processing of the LMHOSTS file on your server.
10. Click **OK** to close the Advanced TCP/IP Settings dialog box, and then click **OK** to close the Internet Protocol (TCP/IP) Properties dialog box.
11. Click **OK** to close the Local Area Connection Properties dialog box.

TROUBLESHOOTING NAME RESOLUTION PROBLEMS

Troubleshooting name resolution issues on a Windows Server 2003 network can be a tricky affair. Because Microsoft operating systems have traditionally supported the NetBIOS method of naming, name resolution becomes more complex because both host names and NetBIOS names must be considered. Just as DNS is the primary method used to resolve host names to IP addresses, there is also a method to resolve

NetBIOS names to IP addresses. Windows Server 2003 can use a service called the **Windows Internet Name Service (WINS)** to assist in resolving NetBIOS names to IP addresses. A WINS server is very similar to a DNS server except that it maintains a list of IP addresses and NetBIOS names. In addition to name resolution, it is used to assist pre-Windows 2000 clients in finding network resources such as domain controllers. Like DNS, you can also install the WINS service via the Add or Remove Programs applet in Control Panel.

When a WINS server has been implemented, and a client needs to resolve a NetBIOS name such as \\server1, Windows Server 2003 follows a specific process in the attempt to discover the IP address. Being familiar with this process can help you diagnose name resolution problems on the network. The following steps outline the process that a client uses to resolve a NetBIOS name to an IP address:

1. The client attempts to communicate with another computer using a NetBIOS utility such as net use. Because the network uses TCP/IP, this name must be resolved to an IP address. The first place that is checked is the NetBIOS name cache. The NetBIOS name cache contains the most recently used NetBIOS names, as well as any that were preloaded using the #PRE tag in an LMHOSTS file. You can view the NetBIOS name cache by typing "nbtstat -c" at the command prompt.
2. If the name is not in the cache, a WINS server is queried, assuming one is configured.
3. If a WINS server is not available or does not have an entry for the NetBIOS name requested, a network broadcast takes place to find out if the target computer can be reached. Name resolution may still fail at this point because routers are generally configured not to pass broadcast traffic.
4. The next step in the name resolution process involves checking the client's LMHOSTS file for an associated entry. Note that only nonlocal computers are listed in an LMHOSTS file because a broadcast would find any local computers before this step.
5. If name resolution fails up to this point, the client will actually attempt to read its local HOSTS file. Although this file does not contain entries for NetBIOS names, a computer's NetBIOS name and host name are the same by default on a Windows Server 2003 computer.
6. The final method of resolution is to check a configured DNS server to see if a DNS name is the same as the NetBIOS name. If resolution does not take place after this step, the client receives an error message.

Tip

Remember that even though both files are used in the name resolution process, the HOSTS file is used to map host names and FQDNs to IP addresses, whereas LMHOSTS maps NetBIOS names to IP addresses.

If you are attempting to troubleshoot a host name problem, host name resolution also follows a process similar to NetBIOS name resolution:

1. When a client attempts to contact another computer using its host name or FQDN, the first step the computer takes is to check to make sure that the target name is not its own.
2. Next, the computer will check its local HOSTS file, looking for a matching entry.
3. If a match is not found in the HOSTS file, the "final" step in the process is to query a DNS server. However, if the DNS server is configured to allow WINS lookups, name resolution may continue to a WINS server.
4. If the WINS server fails to provide a resolution, a local broadcast takes place in an attempt to find the target computer.
5. If the broadcast fails to resolve the host name, the final step taken by the client is to check its LMHOSTS file for an entry. If name resolution does not take place after this step, the client receives an error message.

DNS Troubleshooting Utilities

Both the Nslookup and DNS Monitoring utilities provide a quick and effective way to test whether or not a DNS server is functioning as it should be. However, a variety of different tools can provide much more detailed information about why a server is not behaving as it should when it appears to be experiencing problems. The following sections outline some of the more advanced DNS troubleshooting utilities that a Windows Server 2003 administrator should be familiar with.

The DNSCMD.EXE Utility

The Dnscmd.exe utility included with Windows Server 2003 is a command-line tool used to manage Microsoft DNS servers. Not only a troubleshooting tool, Dnscmd.exe allows a network administrator to add, delete, view, and configure DNS settings from the command line. To use the utility, a user must be a member of the Administrators or Server Operators group on the target computer.

The Dnscmd.exe utility allows an administrator to control a wide variety of DNS functions, as well as view DNS information. Some of the more common switches used with the Dnscmd.exe utility for troubleshooting purposes are listed in Table 9-3.

Table 9-3 Dnscmd.exe switches

Dnscmd.exe Switch	Purpose
/info	Provides general information about the DNS server
/statistics	Provides detailed statistical information about the DNS server
/clearcache	Clears the DNS server cache
/zoneinfo	Provides information about the configuration of zone properties
/zonepause	Pauses a zone
/zoneresume	Resumes a zone
/zoneprint	Displays all resource records for a zone
/zonerefresh	Forces a refresh of a secondary zone from its master

Note

For a complete list of all the available switches for the Dnscmd.exe utility, type Dnscmd /? at the command line.

In Activity 9-16, you will use the Dnscmd.exe utility to view information about your DNS server.

Hands-on Project

Activity 9-16: Using the Dnscmd.exe Utility

Time Required: 10 minutes

Objective: View DNS configuration settings using the Dnscmd.exe utility.

Description: Although almost all administrative tasks at Dover Leasing are handled using the Windows graphical user interface, there are times when configuration via a telnet connection is required. In this activity, you will use the command-line Dnscmd.exe utility to obtain information about your DNS server for future reference.

1. Click **Start** and then click **Run**. In the Open text box, type **cmd** and then press **Enter**.
2. At the command line, type **dnscmd /?** and press **Enter**. A list of available switches for the dnscmd.exe utility appears, as shown in Figure 9-38.

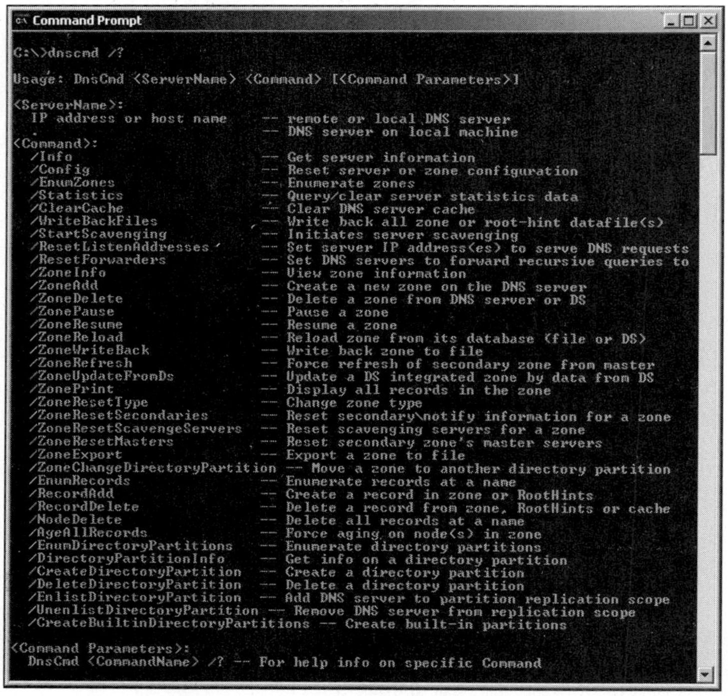

Figure 9-38 Switches available with the dnscmd command

3. Type **dnscmd /info** and press **Enter**. General information about the local DNS server is provided. Review the information provided by the command.

4. Type **dnscmd /statistics** and press **Enter**. Notice the large volume of detailed information provided by this command.

5. Type **dnscmd /zoneinfo sevenacres*XX*.com allowupdate** (where *XX* is your assigned student number) and press **Enter**. This command will return information about whether the specified zone allows dynamic updates, as shown in Figure 9-39. In this case, the returned value is equal to 1, meaning the zone does allow dynamic updates.

Figure 9-39 Using the dnscmd utility to determine whether a zone supports dynamic updates

6. As time permits, explore some of the other dnscmd switches listed in Table 9-3, and then close the command prompt window.

Event Viewer DNS Events Log

Once the DNS service is installed on a Windows Server 2003 computer, an additional Event Viewer log file is added strictly for the purpose of logging DNS server messages. The DNS Events log file can be accessed via the Event Viewer MMC, or additionally from the DNS MMC. Like all Event Viewer log files, information, error, and warning events are stored in the log. However, the events that are listed in the log are strictly related to the DNS server service. It's worth noting that messages relating to DNS client issues are still logged in the system log.

A variety of message types may appear in the DNS log over time. However, some of the more common messages that you're likely to encounter are listed in Table 9-4.

Table 9-4 DNS Events log event IDs

Event ID	Meaning
2	The DNS service has started correctly.
3	The DNS service has shut down.
408	The DNS server could not open a socket on port 53, the default port used by DNS. This may indicate an incorrectly configured IP address or that another application is using port 53 on the server.
414	The DNS server currently has no primary domain suffix configured.
708	There are no zones configured on the DNS server, so it is currently functioning as a DNS caching-only server.
6527	The secondary zone expired before the server could obtain a zone transfer from its master server.

In Activity 9-17, you will review entries found in your server's DNS Events log.

Activity 9-17: Viewing the DNS Events Log

Time Required: 10 minutes

Objective: View entries in the DNS Events log.

Description: The IT manager at Dover Leasing is very concerned about properly monitoring all DNS servers once implemented. Because of this, he has asked you to explore the DNS event-logging functions in Windows Server 2003. In this activity, you will explore various log file entries in the DNS Events log.

1. Click **Start**, select **Administrative Tools**, and then click **DNS**.
2. In the DNS console window, click the **Event Viewer** icon to view its contents.
3. In the details pane, double-click the **DNS Events** icon to view DNS log file entries, as shown in Figure 9-40.

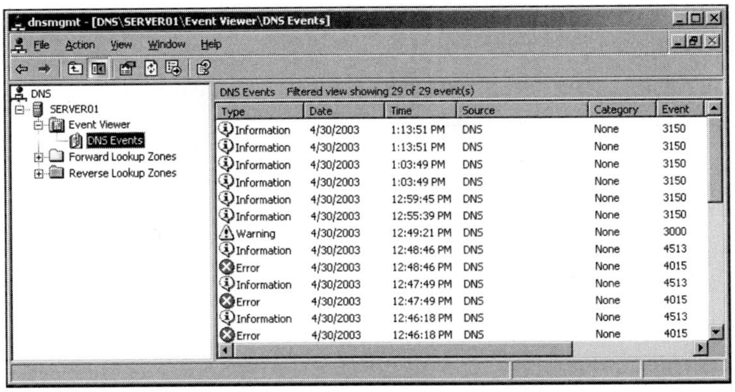

Figure 9-40 The DNS Events log

4. Scroll through the event log entries until you reach an event with an Event ID number of 2. Double-click this entry to view its properties, as shown in Figure 9-41. Click **OK** to close the Event Properties dialog box.
5. As time permits, scroll through the DNS Events log to view additional entries associated with the Event ID numbers listed in Table 9-4, and then close the DNS console.

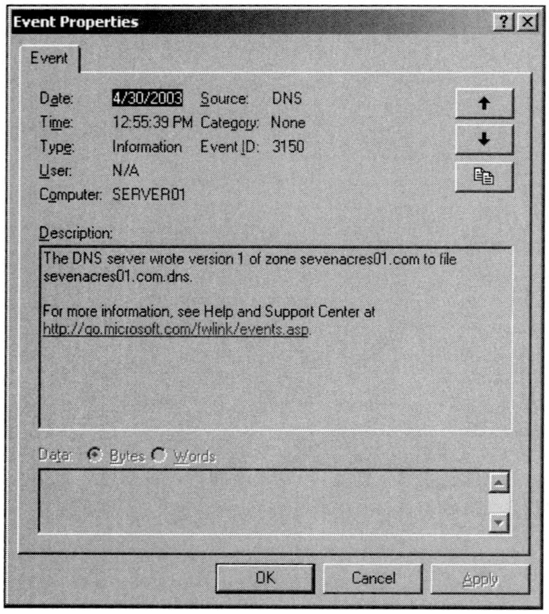

Figure 9-41 A DNS Event log entry

Other DNS Troubleshooting Utilities

Windows Server 2003 includes a variety of utilities that are not exclusively for the purpose of troubleshooting DNS but do provide useful DNS-related troubleshooting information. These include the following:

- *Netdiag.exe*—This network connectivity testing tool provides the ability to test DNS connectivity when used with the /test:DNS switch.
- *Netsh.exe*—This command allows you to perform tests on a wide variety of network services, including DNS.
- *Netstat.exe*—This command allows you to view the status on TCP and UDP ports on the local computer when used in conjunction with the –an switch.
- *Portqry.exe*—This port-querying utility allows you to query a particular port on a network server to find out its status. For example, the command portqry.exe –n 10.0.0.1 –e 53 –p both would query host 10.0.0.1 to see whether or not its TCP and UDP ports 53 were in a listening mode.

For more information about the Netdiag, Netsh, Netstat, and Portqry tools, see the Windows Server 2003 Help and Support Center.

Chapter Summary

- DNS is a Windows Server 2003 service used to resolve host names and FQDNs to IP addresses and to locate network services.
- There are three types of DNS zones: standard primary, standard secondary, and Active Directory integrated. Primary servers are authoritative for a zone and the secondary servers act as a backup, maintaining a copy of the zone file. An Active Directory–integrated zone stores the zone information in Active Directory. Zone information stored in an Active Directory–integrated zone is replicated to other domain controllers.
- A forward lookup zone file contains resource records that map host names to IP addresses, while a reverse lookup file is used to map IP addresses to host names.
- When a DNS server is not configured with any zone-related information, it acts as a DNS caching-only server.

- DNS client configuration settings impact the way in which a client will be registered in DNS, as well as the way in which it will query a DNS server.
- When configuring a DNS server, you can choose whether or not to allow dynamic updates. You can also choose to only allow those computers with accounts in Active Directory to perform updates.
- The Nslookup and DNS Monitor utilities both provide methods to test the functionality of a DNS server.
- The HOSTS file is a text file used to map host names and FQDNs to IP addresses. The LMHOSTS file maps NetBIOS names to IP addresses. Both may impact the name resolution process.
- The Dnscmd.exe utility and the DNS Event log file are two of the primary methods that can be used to troubleshoot DNS-related name resolution problems.

Key Terms

Active Directory–integrated zone — The zone data is stored in the Active Directory database rather than in a zone file.

authoritative — The primary DNS server that acts as the final source of information for any queries about a given host that is part of one of the domains configured in its zone file.

caching-only server — A DNS server with no zone files configured that only caches information.

DNS forwarder — The server to which unresolved DNS queries can be forwarded if configured.

DNS zone — One or more DNS domains grouped together for administrative purposes.

Domain Name System (DNS) — Used for two essential tasks: resolving host names to IP addresses and for the location of network services, such as domain controllers that provide user authentication.

forward lookup zone — Used to perform the standard forward lookup queries for host name to IP address.

fully qualified domain name (FQDN) — Describes the location of the host in relation to the DNS namespace. For example, a computer named "webserver" in the marketing domain of *Bayside.com* would have the FQDN of *webserver.marketing.bayside.com*.

host — Any computer that is a member of a specific DNS domain within the network structure.

iterative query — If the DNS server cannot resolve a name, it gives the requestor a pointer to another DNS server that is authoritative for the next level of the FQDN supplied.

master server — The source of zone updates for a DNS secondary server.

primary DNS server — A DNS server that is authoritative for a zone, meaning that it is the final source of information for any queries about a given host that is part of one of the domains configured in its zone file.

recursive query — A command that specifies the return of a complete and full answer to the query, not a pointer to another DNS server.

reverse lookup zone — A specific type of zone that performs reverse queries to resolve IP addresses to host names.

secondary DNS server — A DNS server that contains zone information that is copied from a primary DNS server or other secondary servers.

standard primary zone — The DNS zone file is stored as a regular read/write text file in the %systemroot%\system32\dns folder.

standard secondary zone — A read-only zone file is copied from a configured standard primary zone.

Windows Internet Name Service (WINS) — A Windows Server 2003 service that is used to resolve NetBIOS names to IP addresses.

zone file — A DNS configuration file that holds all of the resource records for the domain, such as computer name records, mail exchanger records, and service records.

zone transfer — Copying the DNS database information between the primary and secondary zones.

Review Questions

1. What term is used to describe a Windows Server 2003 DNS server without any zones configured?
   a. DNS forwarder
   b. Caching-only
   c. Standard Primary
   d. Active Directory integrated
2. On what port does a DNS server typically function by default?
   a. 21
   b. 52
   c. 53
   d. 54
3. An entry configured in a local HOSTS file can interfere with proper DNS name resolution. True or False?
4. Which of the following commands can be used to test proper DNS name resolution? (Choose all that apply.)
   a. Nslookup
   b. Ipconfig
   c. DNS Monitor
   d. Portqry
5. Which of the following clients are not capable of automatically registering themselves with a dynamic DNS server? (Choose all that apply.)
   a. Windows 2000
   b. Windows XP
   c. Windows NT
   d. Windows 98
6. Which of the following would be the name of the database file associated with the reverse lookup zone for network 131.107.0.0?
   a. 131.107.in-addr.arpa
   b. 107.131.in-addr.arpa
   c. 131.107.in_addr.arpa
   d. 107.131.in_addr.arpa
7. Where in the Windows Server 2003 file system does the file HOSTS reside?
   a. C:\windows
   b. C:\windows\system32
   c. %systemroot%\system32\dns
   d. %systemroot%\system32\drivers\etc
8. When an A record is created for a host in a forward lookup zone, which resource record type can be created automatically in the corresponding reverse lookup zone?
   a. MX
   b. CNAME
   c. PTR
   d. NS

9. Which resource record designates a DNS server as being authoritative for a zone?
   a. A
   b. SOA
   c. NS
   d. PTR
10. A DNS server cannot be a standard primary server and standard secondary server for different zones at the same time. True or False?
11. You are planning to install the DNS service. You want the zone file to be replicated to all domain controllers. What type of zone will you configure?
   a. primary zone
   b. replicated zone
   c. Active Directory–integrated zone
   d. standard secondary zone
12. Which zone transfer method is used to transfer the entire zone file from a primary to a secondary server?
   a. AXFR
   b. OXFR
   c. IXFR
   d. FXFR
13. What technique can be used so that a primary name server informs all secondaries immediately once a change occurs in the zone database?
   a. DNS Notify
   b. Caching-only server
   c. DNS Forwarder
   d. Active Directory–integrated zone
14. What designation is used to represent the DNS root domain?
   a. *in-addr.arpa*
   b. *.com*
   c. *.net*
   d. .
15. You are a network administrator for a medium-size network. All clients have been upgraded to Windows 2000. All servers that are running Windows NT 4.0 are to be upgraded to a Windows 2000 Server in the near future. Clients are configured for dynamic DNS, but the entries are not appearing in the zone file. What is causing the problem?
   a. DHCP needs to be configured to perform updates.
   b. DNS needs to be configured to allow updates.
   c. Clients are not configured correctly.
   d. Servers need to be upgraded to Windows 2000.
16. A DNS zone can be configured to only accept updates from computers that have accounts in Active Directory. True or False?

17. Which of the following records represents an alias for a configured DNS host?
    a. CNAME
    b. A
    c. MX
    d. SRV
18. Which type of zone is recommended if you are installing DNS on a domain controller?
    a. primary
    b. standard secondary
    c. Active Directory–integrated
    d. domain
19. What resource record represents a host acting as a mail server?
    a. MX
    b. CNAME
    c. PTR
    d. SRV
20. What does Windows Server 2003 support so that DNS records can be dynamically updated?
    a. automatic IP updates
    b. dynamic IP updates
    c. automatic DNS
    d. dynamic DNS

CASE PROJECTS

Case Project 9-1

The IT manager at Dover Leasing is very concerned with name resolution problems that might arise as the company upgrades clients and servers that have relied upon NetBIOS names to access network resources. List all of the different elements that might impact how a client computer resolves names on a network.

Case Project 9-2

As a network administrator at Dover Leasing, you have been asked to participate in the rollout of Windows Server 2003 and Windows XP Professional at one of the company's smaller business units. Their infrastructure consists of three separate companies, each of which will be configured as their own domain (including their own DNS domain so each can maintain control). You have been specifically asked to implement the DNS structure.

1. What type of DNS servers will you implement for each of the separate companies? How will redundancy be implemented? Explain your answer.
2. How will you configure the DNS servers between the domains so users can resolve host names outside of their local domain?
3. Administration of zone files should be minimal. How can dynamic DNS be implemented to reduce administration? How will it be configured on the network? Will the DHCP servers be required to perform updates on behalf of the clients?

Case Project 9-3

Dover Leasing has traditionally implemented both a standard primary and standard secondary DNS server at their head office location only. Having recently implemented Active Directory, users at various remote office locations are complaining that DNS resolution requests seem to be taking excessive amounts of time. Outline at least two different methods that could be used to speed up name resolution requests in these remote offices.

Case Project 9-4

The IT manager at Dover Leasing has decided to implement four new DNS domains to support various new Web sites and business units over the course of the next year. He has asked you to specify how many new DNS servers will be required to support the new domain. Outline the most efficient way to implement these four new domains at Dover Leasing.

CHAPTER

10

MONITORING AND TROUBLESHOOTING WINDOWS SERVER 2003

After reading this chapter and completing the exercises, you will be able to:

- Monitor Windows Server 2003 health and performance
- Troubleshoot Windows Server 2003 startup procedures
- Use advanced startup options and other tools used in operating system recovery
- Use the Windows Server 2003 backup utility

Many businesses today rely heavily on their servers for day-to-day operations. Expectations are set for network server availability and performance. When a server goes down or starts to perform poorly, many routine functions are affected and the complaints soon filter in. This means that as a network administrator, you need to ensure that a server is capable of meeting performance expectations and that server downtime is minimal.

This chapter begins by looking at server performance and why it is important to monitor the health of your server. You are introduced to tools, such as the Windows Server 2003 System Monitor and the Performance Log and Alert components, that can be used to monitor the performance of a server. You are also shown how the information you gather can alert you to server problems so that you can diagnose them.

This chapter also discusses the troubleshooting of system startup procedures. You should be familiar with the tools and options that are available with Windows Server 2003 to troubleshoot an operating system that fails to start. The more familiar you are with the tools, the faster you can troubleshoot the problem, and the sooner you can get the server back online.

Monitoring Windows Server 2003 Health and Performance

Maintaining your server is similar to maintaining an automobile. When you purchase a new automobile, it must be serviced on a regular basis to ensure its performance over time. Many of the new cars and trucks today also come with tools that can alert you to problems when they occur. Server maintenance is similar. Often, administrators configure servers for network use, while not realizing that over time, server performance can deteriorate for a number of reasons.

One of the more important reasons for monitoring the health of your server is that it can help alert you to problems before they occur or become more serious. Over time, networks change; the demands placed on a server can vary or increase. Monitoring server performance can help you determine what normal behavior is for your server under the current demands and alert you to any performance issues that may be occurring if the normal behavior changes. This normal behavior is known as **baseline** performance.

Windows Server 2003 comes with several built-in tools that can be used to monitor server health and performance, including:

- System Monitor
- Performance Logs and Alerts
- Event Viewer
- Task Manager

The following sections introduce you to these tools, providing you with a description of how they can be used to monitor your server and how to use them.

System Monitor

System Monitor is one of the most useful tools for collecting data on real-time server performance. As part of the Windows Server 2003 Performance MMC, this tool allows you to track how system resources are being used and how they are behaving under the current workload. System Monitor collects data that you can use for the following tasks:

- *Server performance*—If you use System Monitor on a regular basis, it can help you understand how the server performs under the current workload.
- *Problem diagnosis*—You can use the data that is collected to diagnose server components that may not be performing optimally, causing a bottleneck within the server.
- *Capacity planning*—You can use the information to see how server usage is changing over time and plan ahead for future upgrades.
- *Testing*—If configuration changes are made, you can use the data to observe the impact that the changes have on the server.

Note: System Monitor is similar to the Performance Monitor tool included in Windows NT Server 4.0.

Using System Monitor, you can define the components you want to monitor and the type of data you want to collect. You choose the **performance objects** you want to monitor, such as memory, and the specific type of **performance counters** or data associated with the object for which you want to gather data. You can further customize the data you want to capture by specifying the source or computer you want to monitor. You can use System Monitor to gather data from the local computer or from a network computer for which you have appropriate permissions. Although the System Monitor tool includes a number of performance objects and associated counters to monitor by default, additional objects and counters are added when various services and applications are added to a server, such as DNS or Microsoft SQL Server.

Using System Monitor

When you first open the Performance tool, System Monitor automatically begins displaying performance data. By default, the tool displays data related to the memory, processor, and physical disk objects for the local computer, as displayed in Figure 10-1.

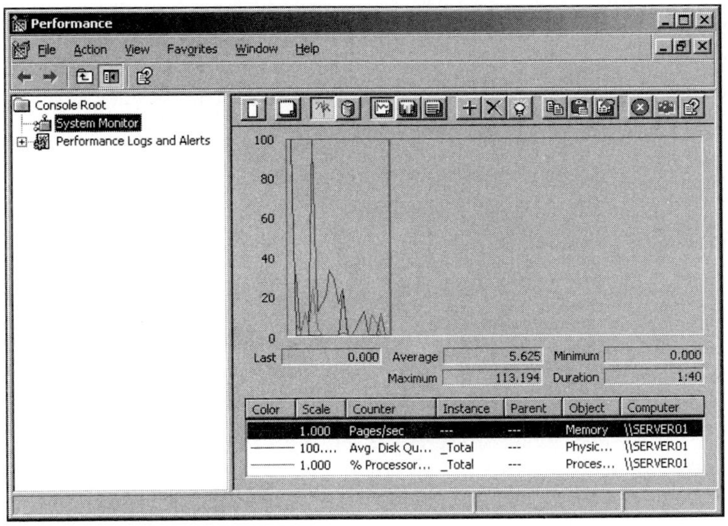

Figure 10-1 System Monitor counters in graph view

The information that System Monitor captures can be displayed in one of three views:

- *Graph*—Displays counter information as a continuous graph updated onscreen in real time
- *Histogram*—Displays counter information as a histogram, with information updated onscreen in real time
- *Report*—Displays a text-based report view of counters, with information updated onscreen in real time

The System Monitor interface provides a number of options for viewing performance data, including the ability to add additional performance counters as required, switch between display views, highlight a selected counter, copy and paste selected information, and freeze the display for analysis purposes. The System Monitor toolbar, found at the top of the details pane in System Monitor, allows you to easily control these functions. In Activity 10-1, you will explore the various settings of the System Monitor tool.

Activity 10-1: Exploring System Monitor Settings

Hands-on Project

Time Required: 10 minutes

Objective: Explore Windows Server 2003 System Monitor settings.

Description: The IT manager at Dover Leasing has informed you that all corporate servers will eventually be monitored for performance purposes using the Windows Server 2003 System Monitor utility. He has asked you to become familiar with the tool and explore its various features because all networking-related staff will eventually need to be trained on this tool. In this activity, you will explore the various features of System Monitor.

1. Click **Start**, select **Administrative Tools**, and click **Performance**. The Performance console opens and System Monitor begins running automatically using the three default counters.
2. Click the **View Histogram** button on the toolbar at the top of the System Monitor details pane, as shown in Figure 10-2. This illustrates the same counter information as a histogram.

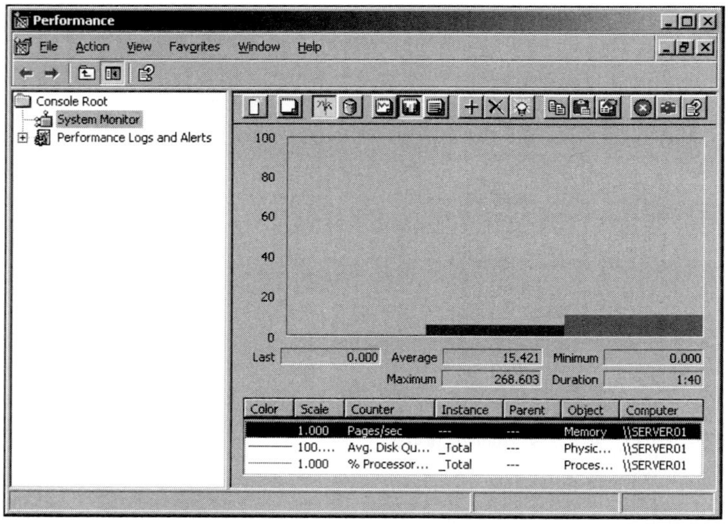

Figure 10-2 System Monitor counters in histogram view

3. Click the **View Report** button on the System Monitor toolbar, as illustrated in Figure 10-3. This shows the same counter information using the report view.

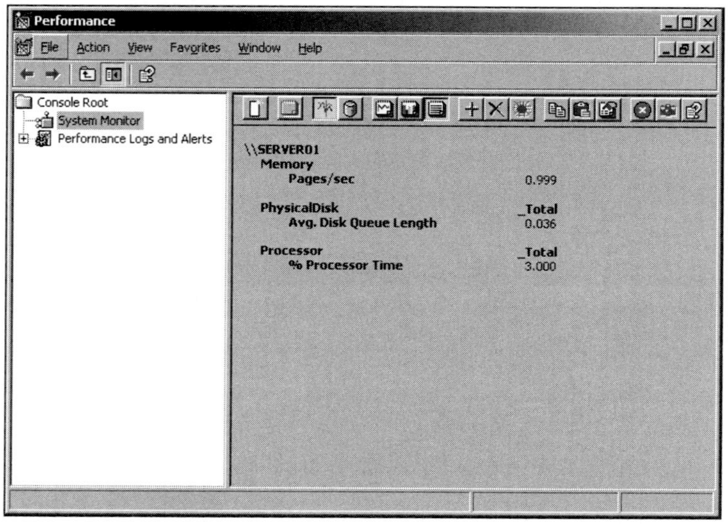

Figure 10-3 System Monitor counters in report view

4. Click the **View Graph** button to return to the original graph view.
5. Click the **% Processor Time** counter at the bottom in the details screen, and then click the **Highlight** button. Notice that the % Processor Time counter in the graph now appears as a thick white line to make it easier to distinguish from the other counters. Click the **Highlight** button again to remove highlighting from the counter.
6. Right click on any area within the counter listing at the bottom of the details pane and click **Properties**, as shown in Figure 10-4.
7. In the System Monitor Properties dialog box, click **\Processor(_Total)\% Processor Time** if necessary, and then click on the largest line thickness in the Width list box, as shown in Figure 10-5. Click **OK**. The % Processor Time counter now appears as a thick red line on the graph.
8. Click the **Freeze Display** button on the System Monitor toolbar. This pauses the System Monitor view until the button is pressed again.

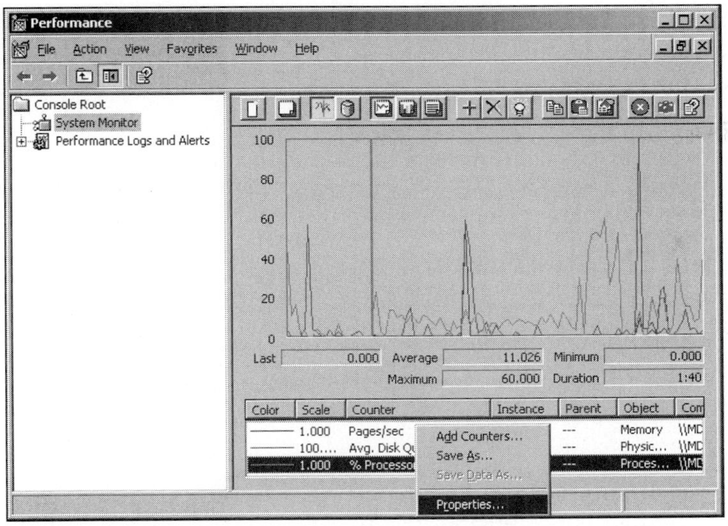

Figure 10-4 Accessing System Monitor counter properties

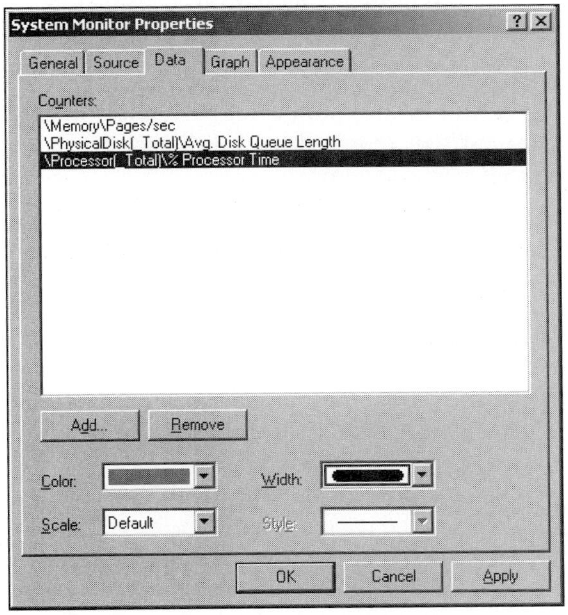

Figure 10-5 Changing the properties of a System Monitor counter

9. Click the **Update Data** button four or five times to allow the graph to move forward. This button allows you to update the onscreen data manually.
10. Click the **Freeze Display** button again to allow data to be gathered.
11. Click the **Clear Display** button on the System Monitor toolbar to clear and restart all onscreen counters.
12. Leave the Performance console window open.

Performance Objects and Counters

Monitoring performance on your server should be a regular maintenance task. The information you gather can help to establish a baseline of server performance and identify what is considered normal server performance under typical operating conditions. As you continue to monitor your server over time, you can compare the data against the baseline to identify how performance is changing as the network changes and workloads increase. Doing so allows you to pinpoint bottlenecks, such as components that may be hindering server performance, before they become a serious problem.

Note: Any time you upgrade or add a component to a system, whether it is a hardware or software component, you should run System Monitor to determine the effect the change has on server performance.

When monitoring server performance, there are a few performance objects that should be included, as well as specific performance counters associated with each one.

- *% Processor Time*—This processor counter measures the percentage of time that the processor is executing a nonidle thread. If the value is continually at or over 80%, a CPU upgrade may be required.
- *% Interrupt Time*—This processor counter measures hardware interrupts. If you experience a combination of Processor Time exceeding 90% and % Interrupt Time exceeding 15%, check for malfunctioning hardware or device drivers.
- *Pages/Second*—This memory counter measures the number of pages read in or out to disk to resolve hard page faults. If this number exceeds 20 or more page faults per second, add more RAM to the computer.
- *Page Faults/Second*—This memory counter measures the number of hard and soft page faults per second. A hard page fault refers to a request that required hard disk access, whereas a soft page fault refers to a request found in another part of memory.
- *% Disk Time*—This physical and logical disk counter measures the percentage of elapsed time that the selected disk drive is busy. If above 90%, try moving the page file to another physical drive or upgrade the hard drive.
- *Average Disk Queue Length*—This physical and logical disk counter measures the average number of requests currently outstanding for a volume or partition. If averaging over two, then drive access may be a bottleneck. You may want to upgrade the drive or hard drive controller. Implementing a Stripe Set with multiple drives may also fix this problem.

Note: In Windows NT, all disk counters were turned off by default. In Windows 2000, the physical disk object is turned on by default and the logical disk object is turned off by default. In Windows Server 2003, all disk counters are enabled by default.

In Activity 10-2 you will add various counters to the System Monitor interface.

Hands-on Project

Activity 10-2: Adding Counters to System Monitor

Time Required: 10 minutes

Objective: Add object counters to the System Monitor tool.

Description: After exploring the various features of the System Monitor interface, you decide to add various counters to the tool to get a better sense of server performance and the purpose of the various counters. In this activity, you will add counters to the System Monitor interface, explore the Explain feature for counter objects, and view the counter results using the graph, histogram, and report views.

1. In the Performance console, click the **New Counter Set** button on the System Monitor toolbar. Notice that all counters are removed from the System Monitor details pane.
2. Click the **Add** button on the System Monitor toolbar. The Add Counters dialog box opens, as shown in Figure 10-6.

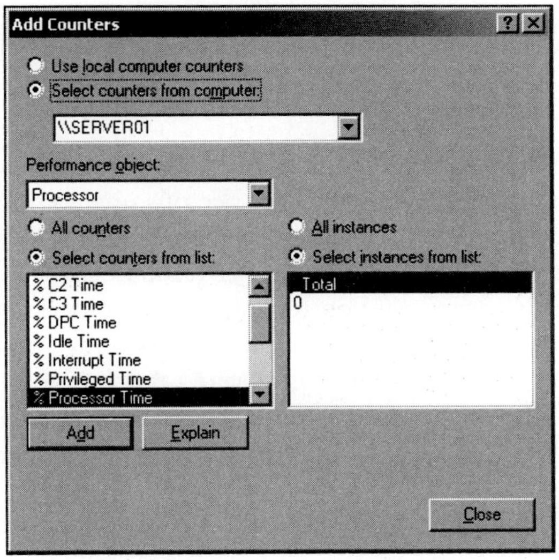

Figure 10-6 Adding counters to System Monitor

3. In the Performance object list box, click **PhysicalDisk**.
4. In the Select counters from list list box, click **% Disk Read Time**. In the Select instances from list list box, click the first entry under _Total, and then click **Add**.
5. In the Performance object list box, click **Memory**.
6. In the Select counters from list list box, click **Available MBytes**. In the Select instances from list list box, click **_Total** if possible.
7. Click the **Explain** button. This opens a window that explains the purpose of the selected counter, as shown in Figure 10-7.

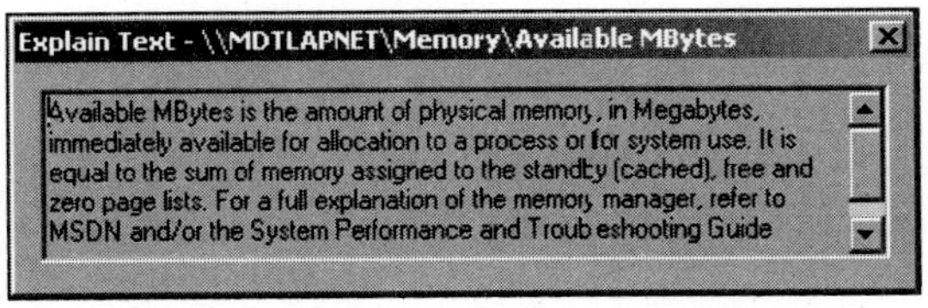

Figure 10-7 Viewing an explanation of a System Monitor counter

8. Close the Explain Text window.
9. Click the **Add** button to add the counter to System Monitor.
10. In the Performance object list box, click **Network Interface**.
11. Click the **All counters** radio button, and then click **Add**. This will add all of the performance counters for the Network Interface object to the graph.
12. Click **Close**.
13. Notice that the number of counters now available on the graph has increased dramatically. Click the **View Histogram** button to view the counter data using that method, and then click the **View Report** button.
14. Click the **New Counter Set** button to clear all counters from System Monitor.
15. Close the Performance console window.

Tip: There are many performance counters available in System Monitor, and it is very difficult to know what each one does. Use the Explain button in the Add Counters window to view the description of each counter associated with an object.

Gathering the data is the easy part. The difficult part is interpreting the information to determine what component is affecting performance. The difficulty lies in the fact that the performance of some components can affect other components. It may appear from the data that one component is performing poorly when this can be the result of another component performing poorly, or even too well. For example, if you determine that your processor is running over 80%, your first instinct may tell you to upgrade the processor or install multiple processors if the motherboard supports it. Through further analysis, however, you may find a lack of memory is the bottleneck that is causing excess paging. You would have discovered this by monitoring the Pages/Second Memory counter. Thus, monitoring multiple components on a regular basis should give you an idea of how they perform together and make troubleshooting server performance that much easier.

The System Monitor tool provides a number of alternatives in terms of saving or viewing historical performance data. One particularly interesting feature is the ability to save System Monitor data to an HTML file. This allows an administrator to post performance data on a Web server, such that it could subsequently be easily viewed and retrieved. When System Monitor data is saved in this format, many of the control functions of the tool are still available through the Web interface. In other words, the data presented in not a simple graphics file, but rather an interactive interface.

The System Monitor tool is also capable of displaying older data that may have been saved to a log file or database using the **Performance Logs and Alerts** tool. This tool will be looked at in more detail in the next section.

In Activity 10-3, you will use the System Monitor tool to save and view a System Monitor graph.

Activity 10-3: Saving and Viewing System Monitor Data

Time Required: 10 minutes

Objective: Explore options for saving System Monitor data.

Description: Although the IT manager at Dover Leasing is aware of the fact that multiple servers can be monitored on a single System Monitor graph, he has asked you to explore the possibility of making counter data available via a Web browser for those users who will not have access to the MMC. In this activity, you will save the output of various System Monitor counters to an HTML file and then access that HTML file using Internet Explorer to monitor your server.

1. Click **Start**, select **Administrative Tools**, and then click **Performance**.
2. Allow the System Monitor graph to gather information until the end right side of the window is almost reached, and then click the **Freeze Display** button.
3. Right-click on an area within the graph and click **Save As**.
4. In the Save As dialog box, click the **D:** drive in the Save in list box.
5. In the File name text box, type **sysmon**, and then click the **Save** button.
6. Open **My Computer**. Browse to the **D:** drive, and then double-click the file **sysmon.htm**.
7. The sysmon.htm file will open in Internet Explorer and will display the System Monitor details pane, as shown in Figure 10-8.
8. In the Internet Explorer window, click the **Avg. Disk Queue Length** counter at the bottom of the window, and then click the **Highlight** button. Notice that even though the System Monitor information is displayed in a Web browser, some of its ordinary functions are still available.
9. Click the **View Histogram** button, and then click the **View Report** button. Notice that both of these functions are also supported from the Web browser interface.

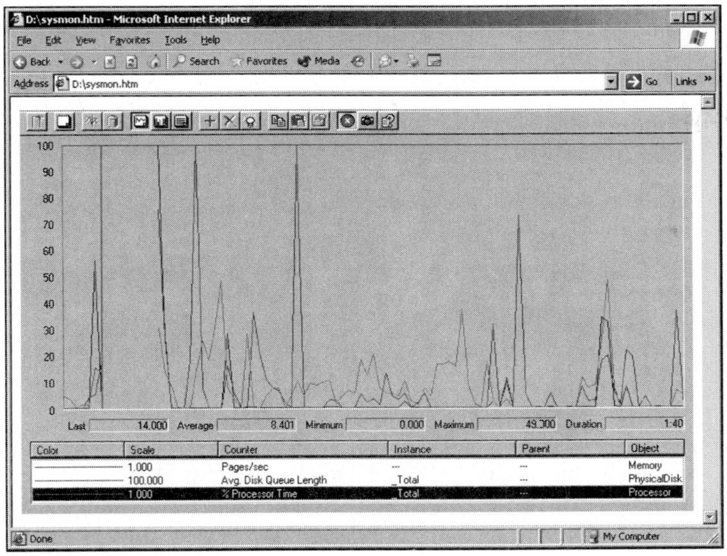

Figure 10-8 Viewing System Monitor data using Internet Explorer

10. Click the **Freeze Display** button in the Internet Explorer window to deselect it. When the System Monitor Control dialog box opens, click **Yes**. Notice that the Web page automatically begins updating counter data again.
11. Close Internet Explorer.
12. Click the **New Counter Set** button to clear all counters from System Monitor.
13. Close the Performance console window, and close all open windows.

Performance Logs and Alerts

Another tool available within the Performance console is Performance Logs and Alerts. This tool allows you to automatically collect data on the local computer or from another computer on the network, and then view it using System Monitor or another program such as Microsoft Excel or a relational database such as Microsoft SQL Server.

Performance Logs and Alerts allows you to perform the following tasks:

- Collect data in a binary, comma-separated, or tab-separated format. The binary versions of the log files can be read with System Monitor, but comma- and tab-separated data can easily be imported into another program for analysis.
- View data both while it is being collected and after it has been collected.
- Configure parameters such as start and stop times for log generation, file names, and file size.
- Configure and manage multiple logging sessions from a single console window.
- Set up **alerts** so a message is sent, a program is run, or a log file is started when a specific counter exceeds or drops below a configured value.

You can access Performance Logs and Alerts through the Performance console. There are three options available under Performance Logs and Alerts, as shown in Figure 10-9: **Counter Logs**, **Trace Logs**, and Alerts.

Counter logs take the information that you view using System Monitor and save it to a log file. One of the main advantages of using counter logs is that you can configure logging to start and stop at different intervals. Trace logs are similar to counter logs but are triggered to start when an event occurs. You can use alerts to configure an event to occur when a counter meets a predefined value. For example, you might choose to run a specific program or utility automatically when a certain threshold is reached, or send a message to a network administrator.

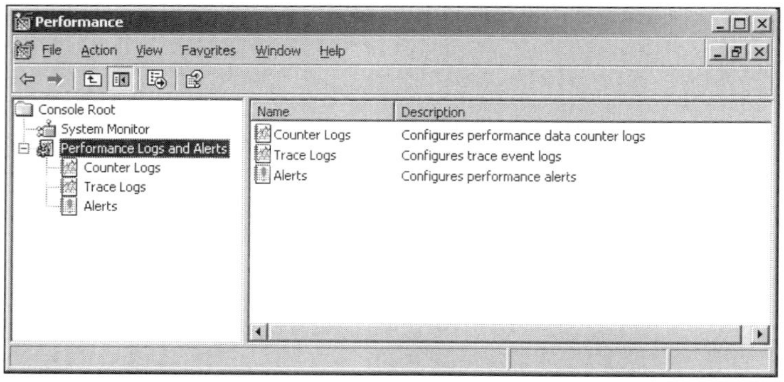

Figure 10-9 The Performance Logs and Alerts tool

Configuring Alerts

Logging does increase overhead on a server, so it is not something you want to have running all the time. It is essential that you set up a regular schedule for collecting data and ensure that the data is reviewed to make sure no problems are developing or occurring. Because logging should not be running all the time, alerts can be set up to notify you of a potential problem. For example, you can configure an alert to monitor the processor usage and notify you if it exceeds 80%.

Table 10-1 summarizes the available options on the Action tab, as illustrated in Figure 10-10.

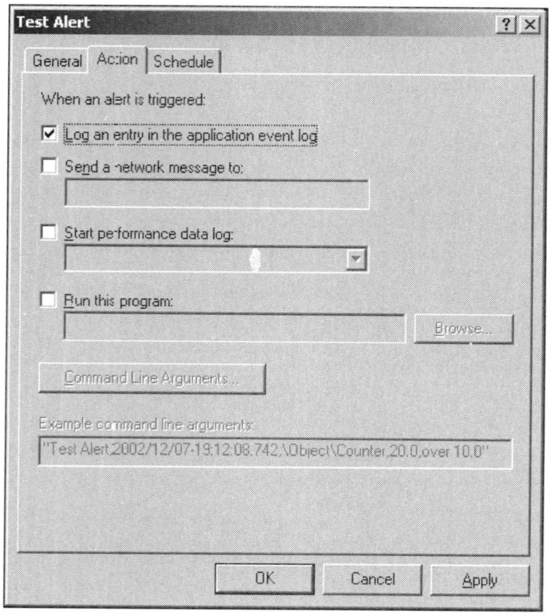

Figure 10-10 Associating actions with a configured alert

Table 10-1 Actions that can be taken when an alert is triggered

Option	Description
Log an entry in the application event log	An entry is added to the **application log** when the event is triggered.
Send a network message to	Messenger service sends a message to the specified computer when the alert is triggered.
Start performance data log	Counter log is run when the alert is triggered.
Run this program	Specified program is run when the alert is triggered.
Command Line Arguments	Specified command line arguments are copied when the Run this program option is used.

In Activity 10-4, you will configure Performance Logs and Alerts settings on your Windows Server 2003 computer.

Activity 10-4: Configuring Performance Logs and Alerts

Hands-on Project

Time Required: 15 minutes

Objective: Configure performance logging and alerts.

Description: Although the servers at Dover Leasing are monitored regularly during business hours, the company still does not have staff on hand outside of business hours to monitor system performance. Because of this, the IT manager has asked you to look into features of the Performance console that will allow data to be gathered after hours. Similarly, he would also like to have alerts configured such that an administrator would receive an onscreen message in the event that a critical server threshold is reached. In this activity, you will explore and configure various logging options as well as configure alerts using Performance Logs and Alerts.

1. Click **Start**, select **Administrative Tools**, and then click **Performance**.
2. Click the **plus sign (+)** next to Performance Logs and Alerts to expand its contents.
3. Click the **Counter Logs** icon to view its contents. Notice that a single sample log exists by default with the name System Overview.
4. Double-click the **System Overview** icon to view its properties. The System Overview Properties dialog box opens, as shown in Figure 10-11.

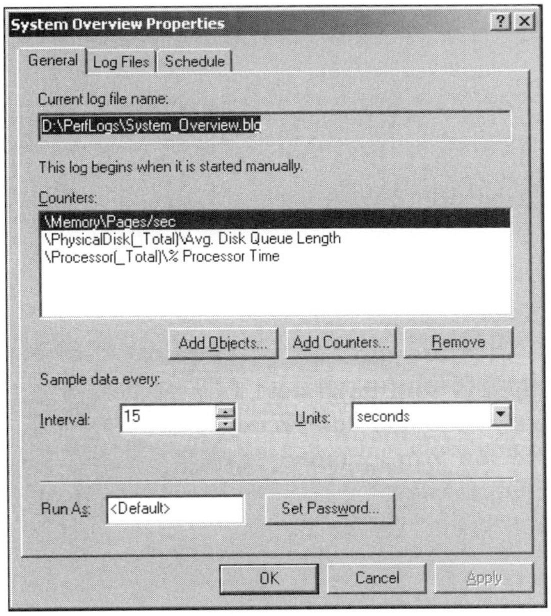

Figure 10-11 Configuring logging properties

5. Notice the log file name associated with the log, the counters that the log includes, and the interval at which data is being gathered.
6. Click the **Log Files** tab.
7. Click the **Log file type** list arrow to view all of the different log type options available, as illustrated in Figure 10-12.

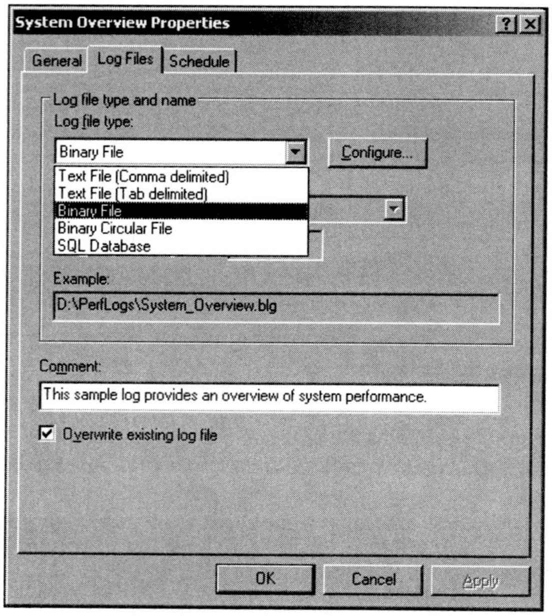

Figure 10-12 Specifying a log file format

8. Click the **Schedule** tab. This tab allows you to schedule stop and start times for the log if necessary.
9. Click **Cancel**.
10. Right-click the **System Overview** icon and click **Start**. Notice that the icon turns from red to green.
11. Wait approximately two minutes, and then right-click the **System Overview** icon and click **Stop**.
12. Click the **System Monitor** icon. On the System Monitor tool bar, click the **View Log Data** button.
13. When the System Monitor Properties dialog box opens, click the **Log files** radio button, and then click **Add**.
14. In the Select Log File dialog box, browse to **C:\PerfLogs**, click the **System_Overview.blg** file to select it, click **Open**, and then click **OK**. This loads the data stored in the System_Overview.blg log file into the System Monitor window.
15. Under Performance Logs and Alerts, click the **Alerts** icon to view its contents. There are no alerts configured by default.
16. Click **Start**, select **Administrative Tools**, and then click **Services**.
17. Right-click the **Alerter** service icon and click **Properties**.
18. In the Startup type list box, click **Automatic**. Click **OK**.
19. Right-click the **Alerter** service and click **Start**.
20. Right-click the **Messenger** service icon and click **Properties**.
21. In the Startup type list box, click **Automatic**. Click **OK**.
22. Right-click the **Messenger** service and click **Start**.
23. In the Performance window, right-click **Alerts** and click **New Alert Settings**.
24. In the New Alert Settings dialog box, type **CPU Utilization** in the Name text box and click **OK**.
25. On the General tab of the CPU Utilization dialog box, click the **Add** button.

26. In the Add Counters dialog box, click the **Add** button to add the % Processor Time counter, and then click **Close**.

27. Type **30** in the Limit text box to have the alert triggered when CPU utilization reaches a value over 30%, as illustrated in Figure 10-13.

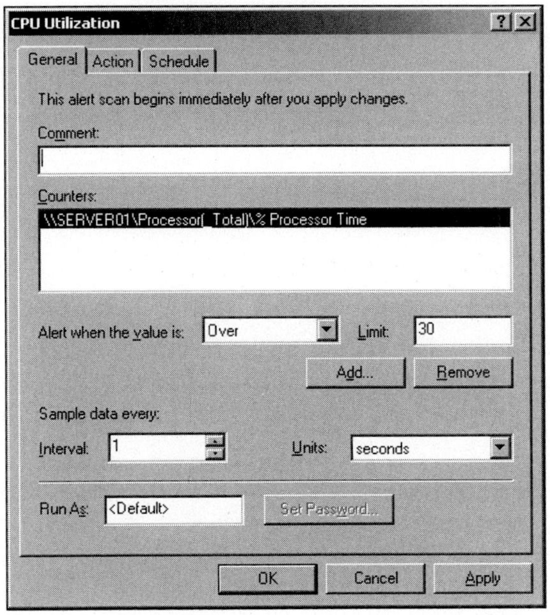

Figure 10-13 Configuring alert threshold values and sample intervals

28. In the Interval spin box, type **1**.

29. Click the **Action** tab. Click the check box next to **Send a network message to** and then type **localhost** in the associated text box. Click **OK**.

30. Click **Start**, click **Run**, and type **wmplayer.exe** in the Open text box. Click **OK**. The Windows Media Player opens, which will usually increase the CPU utilization for brief periods.

31. When the Messenger Service dialog box opens onscreen, as illustrated in Figure 10-14, read its contents and click **OK**.

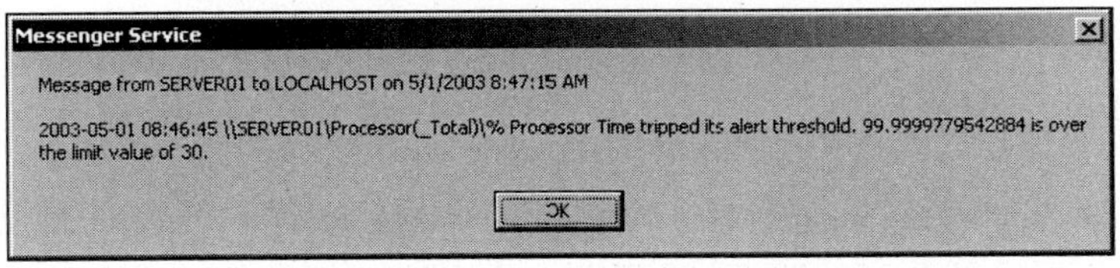

Figure 10-14 A network message sent when an alert is triggered

32. Close all open windows.

Event Viewer

Perhaps the most common and effective monitoring and troubleshooting tool in Windows Server 2003 is **Event Viewer**. You can use Event Viewer to gather information and troubleshoot software, hardware, and system problems.

Events that occur on a system are tracked and recorded in different log files. You can use Event Viewer to view the contents of the log files. For example, you can use Event Viewer to view the contents of the **System log** to determine when, and possibly why, a specific service failed to start.

Whenever you are troubleshooting a problem with a server, one of the first places to look to gather information about the cause is Event Viewer. Entries in the log files can alert you to warnings and errors that are occurring, the component or application that is generating the message, and possibly why the problem is happening. Most entries also include an event ID that you can research on Microsoft's Web site (or the vendor's Web site in the case of third-party counters) to gather more detailed information on the problem and find a possible solution.

Note: You can use both the *support.microsoft.com* Web site and the Windows Server 2003 Help and Support tool to research event ID messages.

Events are typically written to one of three log files:

- *Application log*—Information, warnings, and errors generated by programs installed on the system are written to the application log.
- *Security log*—Events pertaining to the audit policy are written to the **Security log**. For example, if the audit policy is tracking failed logon attempts, an event is written to the security log each time a user is unsuccessful in logging on. By default, security logging is disabled until an audit policy is configured.
- *System log*—Information, warnings, and errors generated by Windows Server 2003 system components, such as drivers and services, are written to the system log.

Note: A domain controller has two additional logs: the directory service log, which records events logged by Active Directory, and the file replication service log, which logs file replication events. A server installed with the DNS service also includes the DNS server log, which records events related to the DNS server service.

By default, any user can view the contents of the application and system log. Only administrators can view the security log, as well as those users who have been assigned the Manage Auditing and Security Log right.

The system and application logs display the following types of events:

- *Information*—When a component or application successfully performs an operation; information events are identified by an "I" icon.
- *Warning*—When an event occurs that may not be a problem at the current time, but may become a problem in the future; an exclamation point icon indicates warnings.
- *Error*—When a significant event has occurred, such as a service failing to start or a device driver failing to load; an "x" icon indicates errors.

Note: There are two other types of events that are logged. These are successes and failures of actions that are performed on the network based on the configuration of an audit policy. Refer to Chapter 5 for the configuration of security audit policies.

Interpreting Events

When you click a log file within Event Viewer, the details pane lists all the events that have occurred and provides general information about each one, such as:

- Type of event (information, warning, or error)
- The date and time that the event occurred
- The source of the event (the component or application that logged the event)
- The category and event ID
- The computer on which the event occurred

An example of an event message is shown in Figure 10-15.

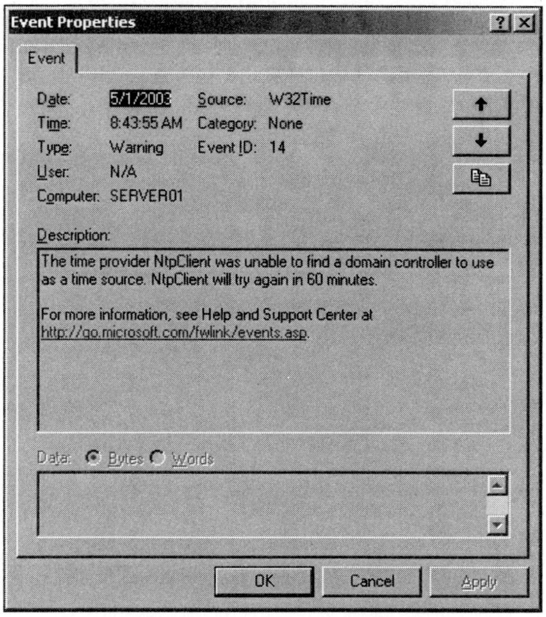

Figure 10-15 Details of an event log entry

The header for an event provides the same information listed above. The event description provides an administrator with a description of what occurred and why the event is significant, which is usually the most useful information.

> **Note**
> The data field of an event displays information that is generated by the program or component. It contains binary data that can be used to support technicians to troubleshoot the problem.

In Activity 10-5, you will explore events in your server's system and application logs.

Activity 10-5: Viewing Event Viewer System and Application Log Events

Time Required: 10 minutes

Objective: View events in the Event Viewer system and application logs.

Description: The IT manager at Dover Leasing has decided that all IT staff will need to be familiar with using the Windows Server 2003 Event Viewer tool to monitor system and application events on corporate servers. In this activity, you will explore events in both the Event Viewer system and application logs.

1. Click **Start**, select **Administrative Tools**, and then click **Event Viewer**. Event Viewer opens, as shown in Figure 10-16.
2. Click the **Application** icon to view the contents of the application log.
3. Double-click the first **Information** event found in the list to view its properties. The Event Properties dialog box will open, similar to the one shown in Figure 10-17.
4. Read the information contained in the event header and Description fields, and then click the **down arrow** button. The next event in the application log is displayed.
5. Click the **Cancel** button.
6. Click the **System** icon to view the contents of the system log.

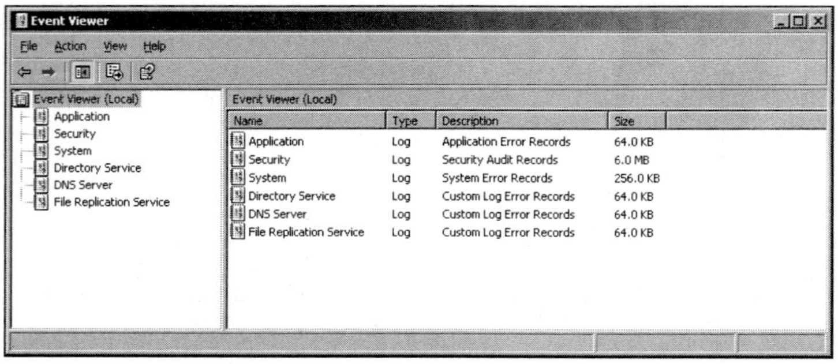

Figure 10-16 The Event Viewer tool

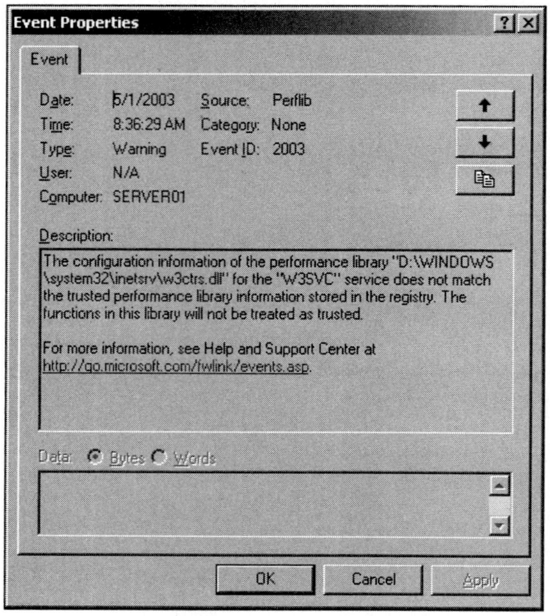

Figure 10-17 Viewing the properties of an Application log event

7. Double-click the first **Error** event found in the list to view its properties. Read through the details of the event header and Description fields.
8. Scroll to the bottom of the description field if necessary and then click the hyperlink at the bottom of the section to visit the Microsoft events Web site. Click **Yes** in the Event Viewer dialog box. The site will open in Internet Explorer automatically.
9. Close all open windows.

Task Manager

Another tool that you can use to monitor server health and performance is **Task Manager**. This tool provides one of the fastest ways to check server performance and determine what processes are running on the system.

The Task Manager tool consists of five different tabs: Applications, Processes, Performance, Networking, and Users, as shown in Figure 10-18.

The Applications tab displays the interactive programs that are currently running and what their status is (running or not responding). This tab is most useful for ending a program that is frozen or has stopped responding.

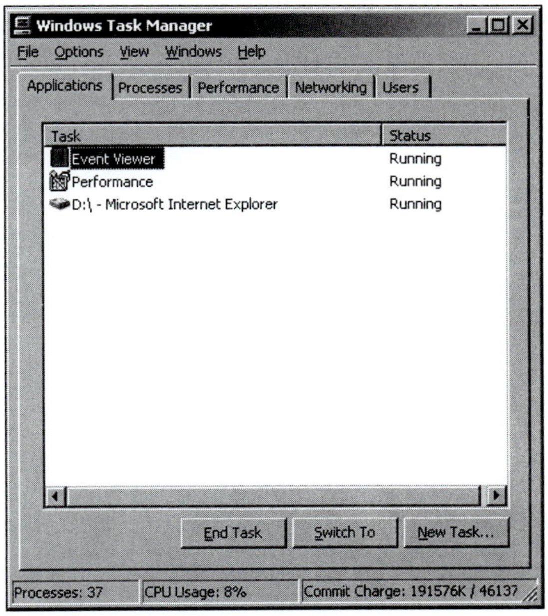

Figure 10-18 The Windows Task Manager tool

The Processes tab displays information about the processes currently running on a Windows Server 2003 system. By default, it displays information such as the name of the process, the percentage of CPU time being used by the process, and the amount of memory each process is consuming.

The Performance tab provides a quick view of a system's current performance. It is not meant to provide detailed performance information but is a quick way of checking performance to determine if there is a problem. You can then use another tool such as System Monitor for further investigation. Table 10-2 summarizes the information that is provided on the Performance tab.

Table 10-2 The Performance tab

Component	Description
CPU Usage/CPU Usage History	Shows the percentage of CPU being used and graphs both current and historical CPU usage
Mem Usage/Mem Usage History	Shows the amount of memory currently in use
Totals	Displays the total number of handles, threads, and processes
Physical Memory	Displays the total amount of memory, how much is available, and the amount of memory used for the system cache
Commit Charge	Displays the amount of memory that has been committed to all applications currently running
Kernel Memory	Displays the amount of memory that has been allocated to kernel functions, the amount of memory that could be paged to disk, and the amount of nonpaged memory

The Networking tab provides a graphical representation of the current network utilization for a given network connection. This includes information about the status of a network connection, the speed at which it is connected, and the level of network utilization in both a percentage and graphical format.

Note

Windows Server 2003 also includes a fifth tab named Users in the Task Manager interface. This tab allows you to disconnect, logoff, or send messages to other users who may be connected to the server via technologies such as Remote Desktop or Terminal Services.

In Activity 10-6, you will explore the Windows Server 2003 Task Manager tool.

Activity 10-6: Using Task Manager

Time Required: 10 minutes

Objective: Use Task Manager to control applications and processes and gather basic system performance data.

Description: Although System Monitor provides detailed system performance information, it can be time consuming to configure and interpret in cases where only a basic snapshot of system information is required. In this activity, you will review how you can use Task Manager to control applications and processes, as well as gather basic information about the performance and network utilization of your server.

1. Click **Start**, and then click **My Computer**.
2. Press **Ctrl+Alt+Delete** to access the Windows Security program.
3. Click the **Task Manager** button. The Applications tab will list the My Computer program as running, along with any other applications that you may have open.
4. Ensure that the entry for My Computer is selected, and then click the **Switch To** button. The My Computer window moves to the foreground.
5. On the Task Manager Applications tab, click the **End Task** button. The My Computer window will close.
6. Click the **Processes** tab. This tab lists all currently running processes including their current CPU and memory usage, as shown in Figure 10-19.

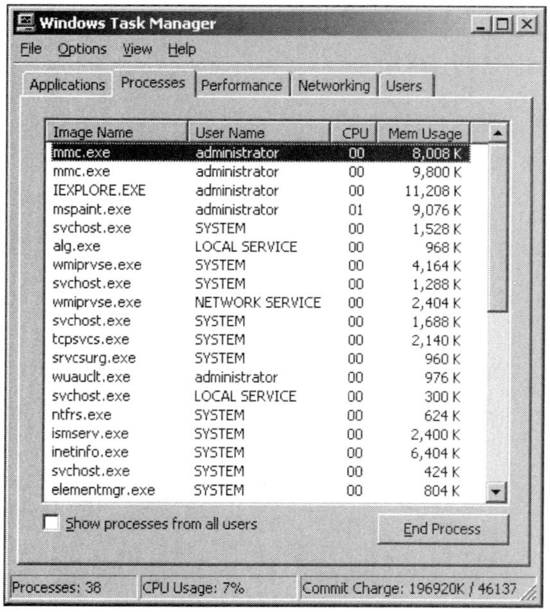

Figure 10-19 The Task Manager Processes tab

7. Click the **dns.exe** entry and click the **End Process** button. This stops the DNS process on your server. Click **Yes** in the Task Manager Warning dialog box.
8. Right-click the **taskmgr.exe** entry, select **Set Priority**, and then click **AboveNormal.** This will give the taskmgr.exe process higher priority to the system processor. When the warning message appears onscreen, read it and then click **Yes**.
9. Click the **Performance** tab, as shown in Figure 10-20. Review the performance data for your server, noting that this tab displays information about the memory and CPU usage of your PC.

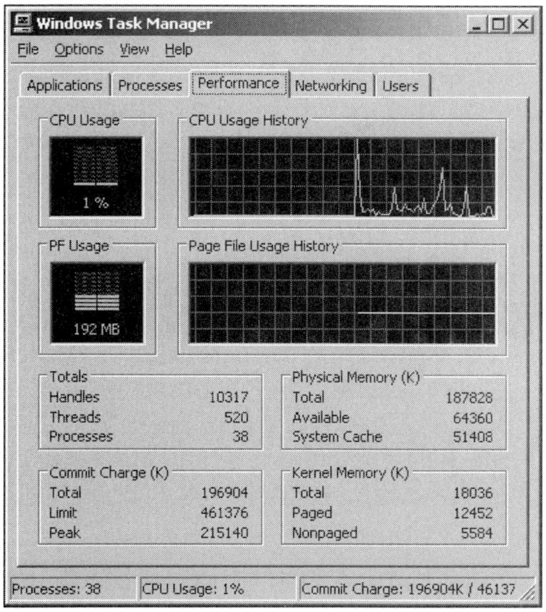

Figure 10-20 The Task Manager Performance tab

10. Click **View** on the menu bar, and then click **Show Kernel Times**. Notice that a new red line is added to both the CPU Usage and CPU Usage History graphs. This red line indicates the percentages of processor usage attributed to kernel rather than user processes.
11. Click the **Networking** tab. This tab displays a graph of network activity, as shown in Figure 10-21.

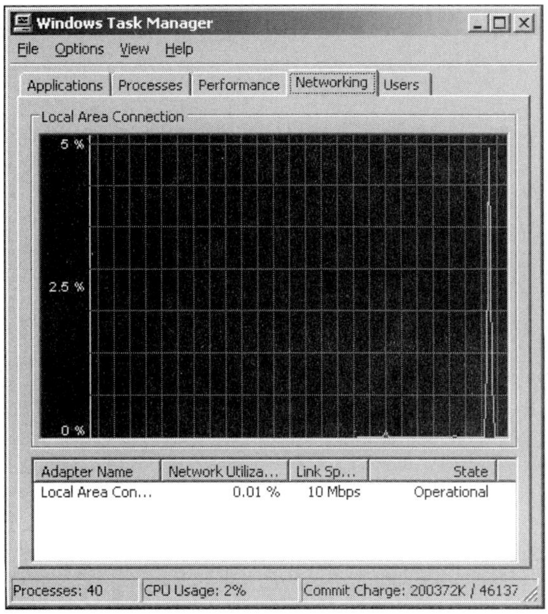

Figure 10-21 The Task Manager Networking tab

12. Click **Start**, click **Run**, and type **cmd** in the Open text box. Click **OK**.
13. On the command line, type **ping -t -1 1000 192.168.1.10** (or the IP address of your instructor's computer, if different) and press **Enter**. Switch back to Task Manager to view the graph on the networking tab.
14. Close all open windows.

Identify and Disable Unnecessary Services

When it comes to optimizing and securing your server, one of the first things you can do is disable any unnecessary components, such as services. When a service is unnecessarily installed during setup or is no longer used, it should be disabled. Running unnecessary services consumes additional system resources such as memory and CPU, thus adding overhead to a system. For example, if you have installed Internet Information Services on a server for test purposes and then no longer require it, the service should be uninstalled, or disabled via the Services MMC. If not, it will continue to run in the background and will consume resources, even though it may not be performing any valuable system function.

The services that you disable depend on the role the server plays on the network. For example, a Web server requires different services than a print server. The other thing you need to consider are service dependencies. Before you stop or disable a service, check to see if there are any other services running that depend on the service. Use the Dependencies tab of a service to view which other services it depends upon to function correctly. Use this tab in the properties of a service to view the other services that are dependant upon the one you are disabling. Figure 10-22 illustrates the Dependencies tab of the DHCP Server service.

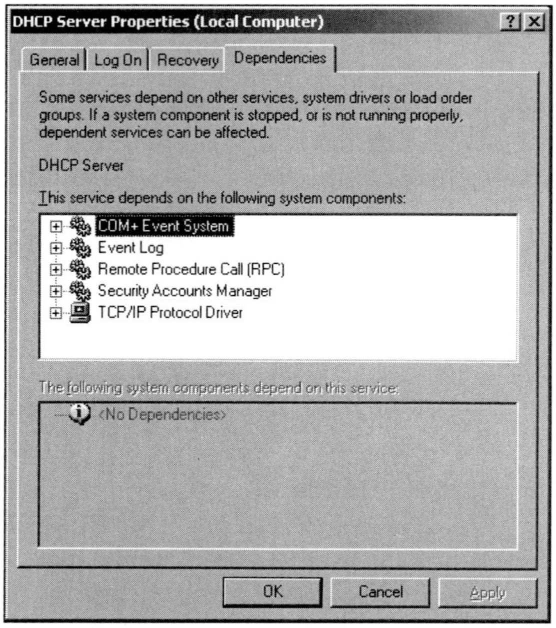

Figure 10-22 Viewing the dependencies of the DHCP Server service

The Services MMC allows you to configure a variety of settings related to how services function and respond to potential problems on a Windows Server 2003 system. The properties of a service include four different configuration tabs, as follows:

- *General*—Displays a service's name, description, the path to the executable file, service startup parameters, and buttons allowing you to start, stop, pause, and resume a service
- *Log On*—Allows you to specify the user name that a service will run as, along with the hardware profiles for which the service will be enabled
- *Recovery*—Allows you to configure the computer's response when a service fails, including different actions depending on the number of failures; also allows you to specify a program that should be run when a service failure occurs
- *Dependencies*—Specifies the services that a service depends upon to function correctly, as well as the services that depend on this service to function.

In Activity 10-7, you will configure the properties of various services on your server.

Hands-on Project

Activity 10-7: Configuring Windows Server 2003 Services

Time Required: 10 minutes

Objective: Configure the startup properties and settings of Windows Server 2003 services.

Description: The IT manager at Dover Leasing is very concerned about the levels of resource utilization of corporate servers, including the impact that this ultimately has on performance for users. He is also concerned about the security risks associated with having unnecessary services running on various servers throughout the organization. In this activity, you will configure service startup settings, as well as other configuration options, such as how a service reacts to a failure.

1. Click **Start**, select **Administrative Tools**, and then click **Services**. The Services MMC opens, as illustrated in Figure 10-23.

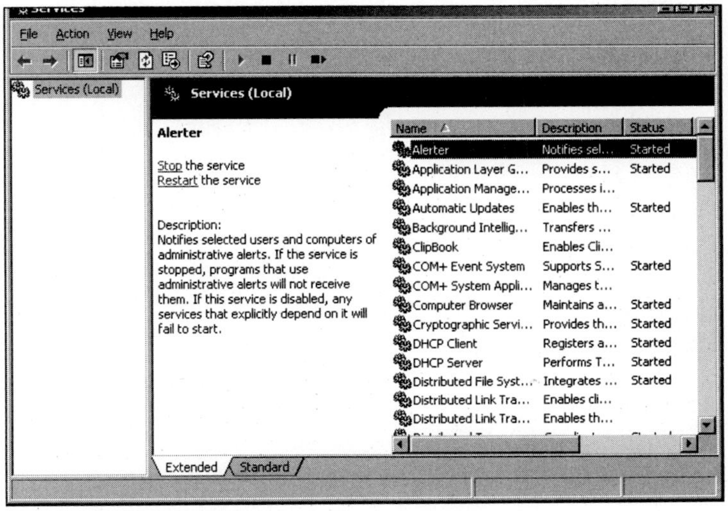

Figure 10-23 The Services MMC console

2. Right-click the **Remote Desktop Help Session Manager** service icon, and then click **Properties**. The Remote Desktop Help Session Manager Properties dialog box opens, as shown in the Figure 10-24.

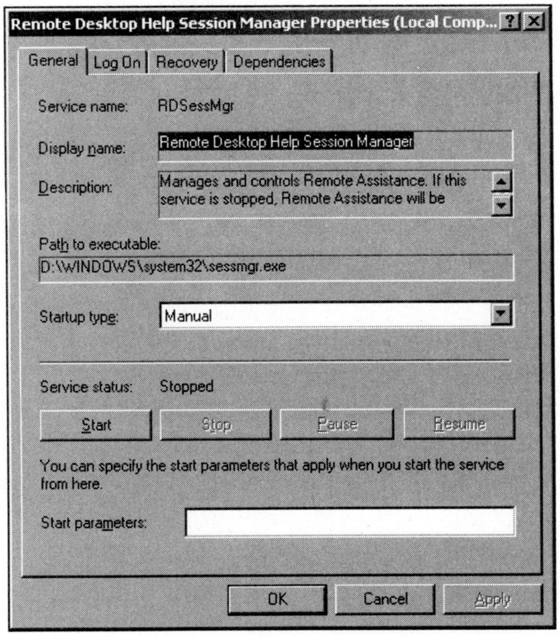

Figure 10-24 Viewing the properties of the Remote Desktop Help Session Manager service

3. In the Startup type list box, click **Automatic**. This sets the Remote Desktop Help Session Manager service to start automatically the next time the computer restarts.
4. Click the **Apply** button, and then click the **Start** button. This manually starts the Remote Desktop Help Session Manager service.
5. Click the **Log On** tab. This displays the properties of the account under which the Remote Desktop Help Session Manager service will run, as shown in Figure 10-25.

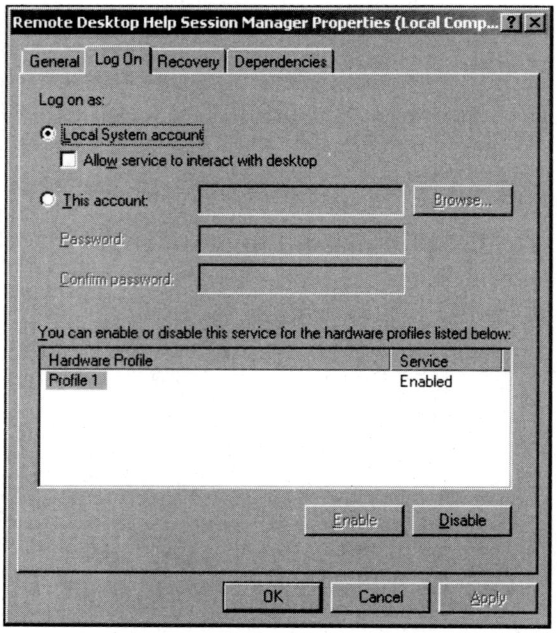

Figure 10-25 Configuring service log on settings

6. Click the **Recovery** tab.
7. In the First failure list box, click **Restart the Service**.
8. In the Second failure list box, click **Run a Program**, as shown in Figure 10-26.

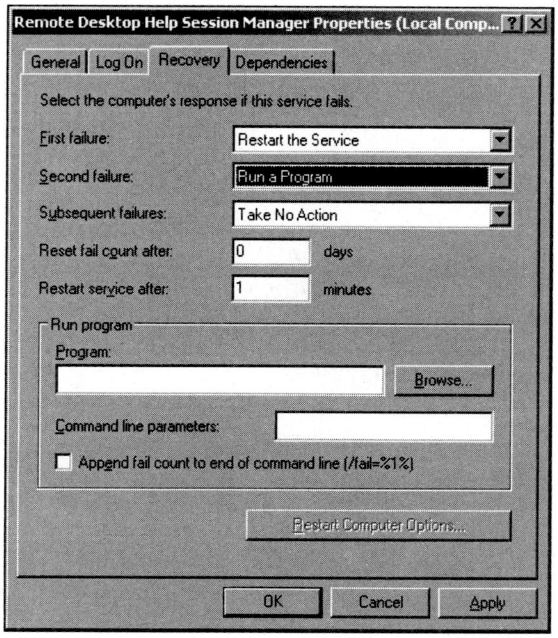

Figure 10-26 Configuring service recovery settings

9. In the Program text box, type **cmd.exe**. This will cause the Command Prompt program to start in the event that the Remote Desktop Help Session Manager service fails for a second time.
10. Click the **Dependencies** tab. Review the list of services that the Remote Desktop Help Session Manager service depends upon. Click **OK**.
11. Right-click the **FTP Publishing Service** icon and click **Properties**.
12. In the Startup type list box, click **Disabled**. This will prevent the FTP service from starting the next time the computer reboots. Click **OK**.
13. Close all open windows.

Monitoring your server's health and performance and using this information to optimize it is only part of your job as a network administrator. Another important task that comes with the job is ensuring server availability and minimizing downtime. The following section provides information on troubleshooting Windows Server 2003 startup procedures and introduces you to the tools available to troubleshoot related problems.

TROUBLESHOOTING WINDOWS SERVER 2003 STARTUP PROCEDURES

System startup problems can occur for a variety of reasons, including missing files, corrupt files, and configuration errors. To successfully troubleshoot problems related to startup, it is essential that you have an understanding of the Windows Server 2003 startup process.

One of the most common reasons for experiencing startup problems is because of missing or corrupted files. For a system running Windows Server 2003 to boot successfully, it requires certain files to be located on the system and boot partitions.

Note

The system partition on a Windows Server 2003 system is almost always drive C:, whereas the boot partition is the partition in which the WINDOWS folder resides and operating system files are stored.

Windows Server 2003 requires the following files to be located on the system partition to start up successfully:

- *Ntldr*—This file loads the operating system.
- *Boot.ini*—This file is used by Ntldr to create the Boot Loader Operating System Selection menu.
- *Ntdetect.com*—This file is used to gather a list of hardware components installed on the system and passes the information back to Ntldr.
- *Ntbootdd.sys*—This file is used only for those systems booting from a SCSI disk with the BIOS disabled.

Windows Server 2003 also requires the following files be located on the boot partition to start up:

- *Ntoskrnl.exe*—This is the Windows Server 2003 kernel file that is located in the %systemroot% \system32 folder.
- *System*—This file contains configuration settings and is responsible for controlling the device drivers and services loaded during initialization.
- *Device drivers*—These files are required for different device drivers.
- *Hal.dll*—This is the interface between the Windows Server 2003 kernel and the system hardware.

In Activity 10-8, you will explore the various files used in the Windows Server 2003 boot process.

Activity 10-8: Exploring the Windows Server 2003 Startup Files

Time Required: 5 minutes

Objective: Explore the Windows Server 2003 startup files.

Description: Having learned about the files involved in the Windows Server 2003 startup process, you decide to browse through the file system to determine the location of these files, as well as their attributes. In this activity, you will use My Computer to view the location and properties of some of the files used in the Windows Server 2003 startup process.

1. Click **Start**, and then click **My Computer**.
2. Double-click drive **C:** to view its contents. Search for the files **NTDETECT.COM**, **ntldr**, and **boot.ini** in the root of drive C:.
3. Click **View** on the menu bar, and ensure that Details is selected.
4. In the Attributes column, notice that the NTDETECT.COM, ntldr, and boot.ini files all have their read-only, hidden, and system attributes set.
5. Double-click the **WINDOWS** folder, and then the **system32** folder. Search for the files **hal.dll** and **ntoskrnl.exe**.
6. Double-click the **drivers** folder to open it. Review the list of driver files stored in the folder, which use the file extension .sys.
7. Click the **Up** button on the My Computer toolbar to move back into the system32 directory.
8. Double-click the **config** folder and browse for the system file. This folder contains both the working and backup copies of the Windows Server 2003 Registry files.
9. Close all open windows.

The Windows Server 2003 Startup Process

As a system administrator, you will need to understand the process that occurs when a system running Windows Server 2003 boots up. The boot sequence occurs in two separate stages: the startup phase and the load phase. Having a general understanding of the process can make troubleshooting startup problems easier.

Before the startup phase, the system performs a power-on self test (POST). During the POST, the system determines the amount of physical memory and the hardware components present. A failure at this stage would indicate a hardware problem. If all the hardware components are functioning, then the boot device is located and the master boot record (MBR) is loaded into memory and executed. The MBR scans the partition table to locate the active partition. The boot sector from the active partition is loaded into memory and executed. The Ntldr is located on the active partition and initialized. At this point the startup phase begins.

The following actions occur during the startup phase:

1. NTLDR switches from real mode to a 32-bit flat memory model and starts the mini file system drivers required to load Windows Server 2003 from different file systems.
2. NTLDR accesses the boot.ini file to display the operating system selection menu.
3. If Windows Server 2003 is selected, NTLDR loads NTDETECT.COM.
4. NTDETECT.COM scans the system to determine installed hardware and passes this information to NTLDR to be added to the Registry.
5. NTLDR loads both the ntoskrnl.exe and hal.dll files.
6. NTLDR reads the registry files, selects a hardware profile, selects a control set, and then loads device drivers.

At this point the startup phase is complete, the load phase begins, and control is given to the ntoskrnl.exe file. The load phase occurs in four distinct steps: kernel load, kernel initialization, services load, and the Win32 subsystem start.

During the kernel load phase, the HAL and the System.dat are loaded. The HAL is the interface between the hardware and the operating system. The System.dat loads the drivers and services required for startup.

Next, the kernel initialization phase loads the kernel and initializes any drivers that are required. The System.dat also loads any drivers and services that need to be loaded during this phase.

During the services load phase, the remaining subsystems and any services required for Windows Server 2003 are started by the Session Manager. The registry is parsed to determine which programs are configured to run when the system is started.

The final phase occurs when the Win32 subsystem loads. The Winlogon.exe and the Local Security Authority are started and display the Ctrl+Alt+Del logon box. Keep in mind that the startup process is not considered successful until the user is able to log on.

As a Windows Server 2003 network administrator, you have little control over the majority of the files used during the startup process with the exception of where these files are placed during the installation process. However, one startup file that an administrator will commonly need to change or edit is the boot.ini file. This file can either be edited manually using a text editor such as Notepad, configured with the bootcfg.exe command, or changed using the Startup and Recovery settings found in the System program in Control Panel.

The bootcfg.exe utility is a new command-line tool included in Windows Server 2003 for the explicit purpose of configuring the boot.ini file. Table 10-3 outlines the main switches that can be used with the bootcfg.exe command.

Table 10-3 Bootcfg.exe utility switches

Bootcfg.exe Switch	Purpose
/Copy	Makes a copy of an existing boot entry in the boot.ini file
/Delete	Deletes an existing boot entry from a boot.ini file
/Query	Displays the current boot entries and settings found in a boot.ini file
/Raw	Allows any switches to be added to a boot.ini file
/Timeout	Changes the timeout value for the operating system selection screen
/Default	Changes the default boot entry in a boot.ini file
/EMS	Allows the output of the boot.ini file to be redirected to a remote computer for use with the Windows Server 2003 Emergency Management Services feature
/Debug	Specifies the port and baudrate for remote startup debugging
/Addsw	Allows predefined switches to be added to the boot.ini file
/Rmsw	Removes predefined switches from the boot.ini file
/Debug1394	Configures an IEEE 1394 port for startup debugging

Note

For more information on the Windows Server 2003 Emergency Management Services feature, see the Help and Support Center.

In Activity 10-9, you will make changes to the boot.ini file using both the System program and the bootcfg.exe utility.

Activity 10-9: Viewing and Editing the Boot.ini File

Time Required: 15 minutes

Objective: View and edit settings in the boot.ini file.

Description: Because the boot.ini file can be used to control the choices and methods available for the Windows Server 2003 boot process, you have decided to explore the file and the various settings it contains. In this activity, you will open the boot.ini file in Notepad to view its default settings and then use both the System program and the bootcfg.exe utility to make changes to the file.

1. Click **Start** and then click **My Computer**.
2. Double-click drive **C:** to view its contents.
3. Right-click the file **boot.ini** and then click **Open With**.
4. In the Open With window, ensure that Notepad is selected, and then click **OK**. The boot.ini file opens in Notepad, as shown in Figure 10-27.

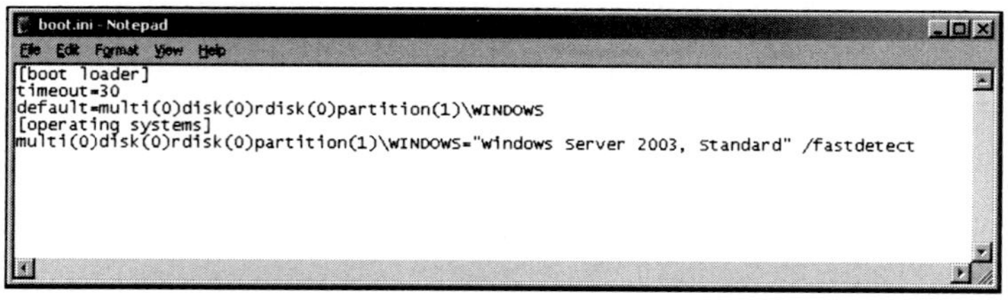

Figure 10-27 The boot.ini file

5. Review the [boot loader] section of the file. Notice that the timeout value is set to 30 by default. This means that the boot-loader screen will wait 30 seconds before loading the default operating system selection specified in the [default] section of the file.
6. Review the [operating systems] section of the file, noting that Microsoft Windows Server 2003, Enterprise Edition (or possibly Standard Edition) is the only selection available because it is the only operating system installed on your server. The path that precedes the entry is known as an ARC path and tells the operating system on which physical disk and partition the Windows folder can be found.
7. Close the boot.ini file.
8. Click **Start**, right-click the **My Computer** icon, and click **Properties**.
9. Click the **Advanced** tab.
10. In the Startup and Recovery section, click the **Settings** button. This will open the Startup and Recovery dialog box, as illustrated in Figure 10-28.
11. In the Time to display list of operating systems spin box, type **15**. Click **OK**.
12. In the Startup and Recovery section, click the **Settings** button again.
13. Click the **Edit** button. This opens the boot.ini file in a writeable format. Notice that the timeout value in the file has changed to represent the configuration change made in Step 11.
14. Close the boot.ini file, click **OK** to exit the Startup and Recovery dialog box, and then click **OK** to exit the System Properties dialog box.
15. Click **Start**, click **Run**, and then type **cmd.exe** in the Open text box. Click **OK**.
16. At the command line, type **bootcfg.exe /?** and press **Enter** to view a list of the switches available with the bootcfg.exe command.
17. Type **bootcfg.exe /query** and press **Enter**. This will display the contents of the current boot.ini file, similar to the one shown in Figure 10-29.

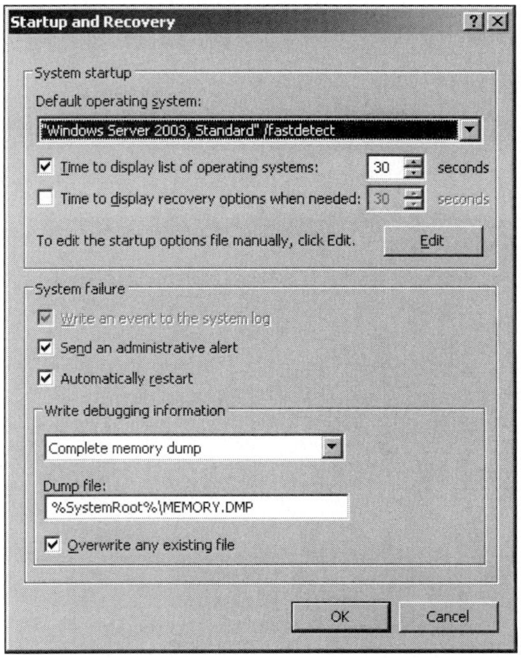

Figure 10-28 Configuring system startup properties

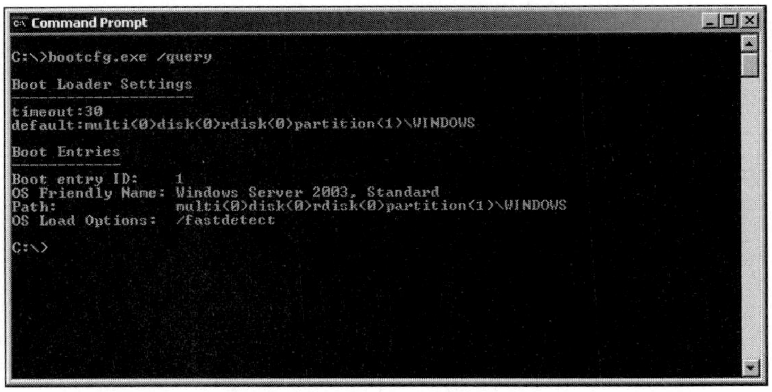

Figure 10-29 Using the bootcfg.exe utility

18. Type **bootcfg.exe /addsw /bv /id 1** and press **Enter**. This adds a switch to the boot.ini file that will force the first operating system entry listed to use only VGA drivers during the boot process.

19. In the My Computer window, right-click the **boot.ini** file and click **Open**. Notice that the first entry in the [operating systems] section of the file now includes the /basevideo switch.

20. At the command line, type **bootcfg.exe /rmsw /bv /id 1** and press **Enter**. This will remove the /basevideo switch added to the boot.ini file in Step 18.

21. Close all open windows.

Advanced Startup Options

Several things can cause a system not to start, such as the installation of new software or device drivers, or changes made to the system's configuration. If your computer fails to start, you can try using one of the advanced startup options to troubleshoot the problem. For example, you can start the computer in **safe mode**, which only loads the default Windows Server 2003 settings and the device drivers necessary to start the operating system. If you have installed new software that you think is causing the problem, you can uninstall it once in safe mode.

You can access the advanced startup options during system startup by pressing F8 while viewing the Boot Loader Operating System Selection menu. The screen that appears presents you with a list of eight advanced startup options, summarized in Table 10-4.

Table 10-4 Advanced startup options

Startup Option	Description
Safe Mode	Only the basic files and drivers required to start Windows Server 2003 are loaded. The default Windows Server 2003 settings are used. This option is useful when an application or component that is causing a problem needs to be uninstalled or disabled.
Safe Mode with Networking	This option starts the computer the same as in safe mode, but provides network connectivity. Use this option if you need access to the network to repair the problem.
Safe Mode with Command Prompt	This option starts the computer the same as in safe mode, but provides access to the Windows Server 2003 command line rather than the graphical user interface.
Enable Boot Logging	This option starts Windows Server 2003 while creating a log file that lists all the installed drivers and services that were loaded or not loaded. Use this option to determine the exact cause of startup problems. The file is called ntbtlog.txt and is stored in the %systemroot% folder.
Enable VGA Mode	This option starts Windows Server 2003 with the basic VGA driver for the video card. This is useful if you've installed a new video driver that is causing Windows Server 2003 to not start.
Last Known Good Configuration	This option starts Windows Server 2003 using registry information saved after the last successful logon. This option is useful if incorrect configuration changes have been made and you need to return to the computer's previous configuration.
Directory Services Restore Mode	This option enables you to restore the Sysvol and Active Directory Services on a domain controller. The system must be a domain controller to have this option available.
Debugging Mode	Debugging information is sent to another computer via a serial cable connection when Windows Server 2003 boots. Use this option to provide software developers with detailed debugging information about the problem.

In Activity 10-10, you will explore some of the various advanced startup options on your Windows Server 2003 system.

Hands-on Project

Activity 10-10: Viewing and Testing Advanced Startup Options

Time Required: 20 minutes

Objective: View and Test Windows Server 2003 Advanced Startup Options.

Description: Based on his experiences in troubleshooting problems in Windows 2000, the IT manager at Dover Leasing has asked you to familiarize yourself with the advanced startup options that can be used to repair a Windows Server 2003 server if necessary. In this activity, you will access the advanced startup options menu and then boot your server using the Safe Mode and Safe Mode with Command Prompt advanced options.

1. Click **Start**, and then click the **Shut Down** button. In the What do you want the computer to do? list box, click **Restart**. In the comment text box, type **testing advanced startup options**, and click **OK**.
2. At the operating system selection screen, press the **F8** key to access the Windows Advanced Options Menu.

3. Select **Safe Mode** on the list of available options, and press **Enter**.
4. If the operating system selection screen appears, select **Windows Server 2003 Enterprise Edition** (or **Standard Edition** if applicable) if necessary, and press **Enter**.
5. Log on using your **Admin*XX*** user account.
6. When the Desktop dialog box opens, read the message it provides and click **OK**.
7. Click **Start**, click **Run**, and then type **cmd.exe** in the Open text box. Click **OK**.
8. At the command line, type **ping www.course.com** and press **Enter**. Notice that the ping fails because network functionality is disabled in Safe Mode.
9. Restart your server, and access the Windows Advanced Options Menu as outlined in Step 2.
10. Click **Safe Mode with Command Prompt** on the list of available options, and press **Enter**.
11. At the operating system selection screen, select **Windows Server 2003 Enterprise Edition** (or **Standard Edition** if applicable) if necessary, and press **Enter**.
12. Log on using your **Admin*XX*** user account. Notice that the Command Prompt opens as the Windows shell environment.
13. At the command line, type **ping www.course.com**. Notice that this command also fails because Safe Mode with Command Prompt also provides no networking support.
14. Press **Ctrl+Alt+Delete** to access the Windows Security dialog box.
15. Click the **Shut Down** button, and then reboot your server normally, logging on with your **Admin*XX*** account.

Last Known Good Configuration

The **last known good configuration** allows you to recover your system from failed driver and registry changes. For example, installing a device driver that is incorrect for your hardware can cause a system to fail on startup. The last known good configuration information is stored in the registry and is updated each time the computer restarts and the user successfully logs on.

Normally when a computer is restarted, any configuration changes made before the reboot process was initiated are used. Each time you make configuration changes, these changes are copied to the default configuration that will be used the next time the computer is restarted. If these changes damage the default configuration, your computer may not be able to boot successfully. For example, the installation of new device drivers may cause the computer to stop responding and, ultimately, result in stop errors during the boot process, also known as the Blue Screen of Death (BSoD).

The last known good configuration can be thought of as a backup that can be used to restart the system in the event that the current configuration fails.

Note: Because the last known good configuration is updated each time you log on, make sure you do not log on to your server if problems are evident during the boot process. Once you do, the last known good configuration is updated with the incorrect configuration changes.

The last known good configuration is useful in situations where Windows Server 2003 configuration changes have been made that negatively impact the system. However, it cannot resolve problems such as missing or corrupt files, or if you restart and log on after the configuration changes have been made. Additional tools for system recovery are discussed later in this chapter.

In Activity 10-11, you will test the use of the last known good configuration advanced startup option on your server.

Activity 10-11: Testing Last Known Good Configuration

Time Required: 15 minutes

Objective: Test the last known good configuration advanced startup option.

Description: Because any change to a server can severely impact user productivity at Dover Leasing in the event of a failure, the IT manager has asked you to familiarize yourself with the process for using the last known good configuration feature of Windows Server 2003. In this activity, you will simulate errors by disabling both your network adapter card and DVD/CD-ROM drive, and then restore a previous server configuration by using the last known good configuration feature.

1. Click **Start**. Right-click the **My Computer** icon and click **Properties**.
2. In the System Properties dialog box, click the **Hardware** tab.
3. Click the **Device Manager** button.
4. In the Device Manager window, click the **plus sign (+)** next to the Network adapters icon to expand it.
5. Right-click your computer's network adapter, and click **Disable**. When prompted, click the **Yes** button.
6. In the Device Manager window, click the **plus sign (+)** next to the DVD/CD-ROM drives icon to expand it.
7. Right-click your computer's CD-ROM or DVD drive, and click **Disable**. When prompted, click the **Yes** button.
8. Click **Start**, and then click **Run**. In the Open text box, type **cmd** and press **Enter**.
9. At the command line, type **ping www.course.com** and press **Enter**. The ping will fail because your network adapter has been disabled.
10. Click **Start**, and then click the **Shut Down** button. In the Shut Down Windows dialog box, choose **Restart**, type **Testing LKGC** in the Comment text box, and click **OK**.
11. At the operating system selection screen, press **F8**.
12. On the Windows Advanced Options menu, select **Last Known Good Configuration** and press **Enter**.
13. At the operating system selection screen, select **Windows Server 2003 Enterprise Edition** (or **Standard Edition** if applicable) if necessary and press **Enter**.
14. When prompted, log on with your **Admin*XX*** account.
15. Click **Start**. Right-click the **My Computer** icon and click **Properties**.
16. In the System Properties dialog box, click the **Hardware** tab.
17. Click the **Device Manager** button.
18. Click the **plus signs (+)** next to both the Network adapters icon and the DVD/CD-ROM drives icon to expand them and verify that these devices are no longer disabled.
19. Close all open windows.

Recovery Console

Another tool that can be used for system recovery is the **Recovery Console**. The Recovery Console is an advanced tool for experienced administrators, allowing them to gain access to a hard drive on computers running Windows Server 2003. It can be used to perform the following tasks:

- Start and stop services
- Format drives

- Read and write data on a local hard drive
- Copy files from a floppy or CD to a local hard drive
- Perform administrative tasks

Installing the Recovery Console

You can start the Recovery Console in one of two ways. The first option is to run it from the Windows Server 2003 CD once a serious error occurs by booting from the CD. The second option is to install it on your computer permanently before you need it to resolve a problem. Once you have installed the Recovery Console, it is listed as an option from the list of available operating systems during the initial boot process. You can then start the Recovery Console by selecting it on the Boot Loader Operating System Selection menu.

If you choose not to install the Recovery Console on your system, you can start by booting your system from the Windows Server 2003 CD. Instead of choosing to reinstall the operating system, you would instead initiate the recovery process and select the option to install the Recovery Console.

> **Note:** You must be an administrator to run the Recovery Console, so accessing the console requires users to provide the correct local administrator's password for the system.

There are a variety of commands available through the Recovery Console. The following list includes some of the common commands that are used. For a complete list of commands that are available, use the Help command from within the console.

- *Copy*—Copies a file from removable media to the system folders
- *Disable*—Disables a system service or a device driver
- *Enable*—Enables or starts a system service or a device driver
- *Exit*—Closes the Recovery Console and restarts your computer
- *Fixboot*—Writes a new partition boot sector onto the system partition
- *Fixmbr*—Repairs the master boot record of the boot partition
- *Listsvc*—Lists all the services on the computer

In Activity 10-12, you will first install and then use the Windows Server 2003 Recovery Console.

Activity 10-12: Installing and Using the Recovery Console

Hands-on Project

Time Required: 20 minutes

Objective: Install and use the Recovery Console.

Description: The IT manager has mandated that the Windows Server 2003 Recovery Console should be installed on all corporate servers to provide an alternate troubleshooting and repair environment in cases where the last known good configuration feature fails to fix an issue. In this activity, you will first install and then test the Recovery Console to become familiar with the basic operation of its interface.

1. Click **Start**, and then click **Run**.
2. In the Open text box, type **D:\SOURCE\i386\winnt32.exe /cmdcons** and click **OK**.
3. In the Windows Setup dialog box, as illustrated in Figure 10-30, click **Yes**.
4. In the Windows Server 2003, Enterprise Edition Setup dialog box, click **OK**.

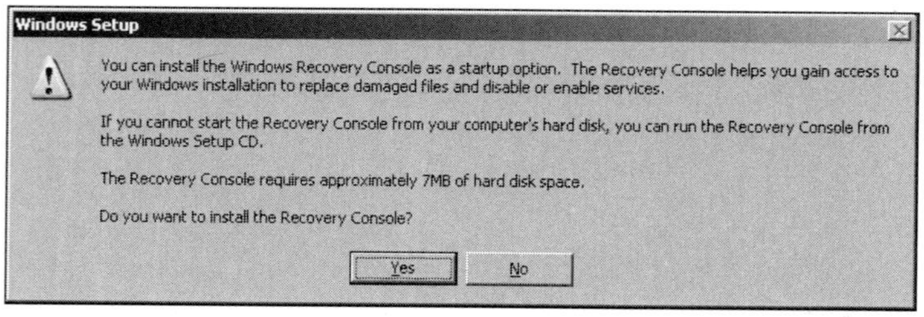

Figure 10-30 Installing the Windows Recovery Console

5. Click **Start**, and then click the **Shut Down** button. In the Shut Down Windows dialog box, click **Restart**, and then type **Recovery Console Test** in the Comment text box. Click **OK**.
6. At the operating system selection screen, select the **Microsoft Windows Recovery Console** option, and press **Enter**.
7. When the Which Windows installation would you like to log onto prompt appears, type **1** and press **Enter**.
8. At the Type the administrator password prompt, type **password** and press **Enter**. This will bring you to the C:\WINDOWS prompt.
9. Type **help** and press **Enter**. This displays a list of commands available via the Recovery Console. Press the **spacebar** to scroll though the remainder of the list and return to the command prompt.
10. Type **listsvc** and press **Enter**. This will list all of the services on the server, along with information about their status.
11. Press the **spacebar** until the HTTP service is visible onscreen. Notice that its status is set to Manual.
12. Press the **spacebar** until you return to the command prompt.
13. Type **enable http SERVICE_AUTO_START** and press **Enter**. This will configure the HTTP service to start automatically once the server reboots.
14. Type **listsvc** and press **Enter**. Press the **spacebar** under the HTTP service if visible. Notice that its status is now set to Auto.
15. Press the **ESC** key to return to the command line.
16. Type **exit** and press **Enter**. This will exit the recovery console and initiate a reboot of the server.
17. Boot your server normally, and log on using your **Admin*XX*** account.

The Automatic System Recovery Feature

Windows Server 2003 introduces a powerful new utility for the purpose of restoring system configuration information. The **Automated System Recovery (ASR)** feature allows you to restore system configuration settings in the event that a system cannot be repaired using the various safe-mode startup options or the last known good configuration feature.

ASR consists of two different elements on a Windows Server 2003 system. The first is the ASR backup, which you access from the Backup Utility. The second is a floppy disk that contains information about the backup, disk configuration information, and how the restore should be performed.

The main purpose of the ASR feature is to restore a Windows Server 2003 system to a functional state. However, ASR is only used to back up and restore system configuration information and not data files. You should back up any user data files separately before initiating ASR and then restore them once the ASR process is complete, using a tool such as the Windows Server 2003 Backup utility. Information about backing up and restoring files with the Backup utility is provided later in this chapter.

Tip: You should create a new ASR backup any time the system configuration of a server running Windows Server 2003 is changed.

If an ASR backup exists, you can restore system configuration settings by booting from the Windows Server 2003 CD and then selecting the Repair option. The information stored on the ASR floppy disk and in the ASR backup is then used to restore appropriate settings.

You create an ASR backup set using the Automated System Recovery Wizard, which you access from the Windows Server 2003 Backup Utility, as illustrated in Figure 10-31.

Note: Both Windows NT Server 4.0 and Windows 2000 included a system-restore feature known as an Emergency Repair Disk (ERD). ASR replaces the ERD feature on Windows Server 2003 systems.

THE WINDOWS SERVER 2003 BACKUP UTILITY

Windows Server 2003 includes a backup utility that allows you to restore an operating system or data in the event of a total hardware or storage media failure. The Windows Server 2003 Backup Utility builds on the backup utility originally introduced in Windows 2000 and represents a significant improvement over backup utilities included with previous versions of Windows. Using the Windows Server 2003 Backup Utility, you can perform a variety of tasks, including:

- Back up and restore files and folders
- Schedule a backup
- Back up Windows 2003 System State data
- Restore all or a portion of the Active Directory database
- Create an ASR backup

The Windows Server 2003 Backup Utility supports a wide variety of storage devices and media, such as tape drives, recordable CD-ROM drives, logical drives, and removable disks.

Backing Up and Restoring Files and Folders

The most common use of the Windows Server 2003 Backup Utility is to back up critical data and operating system files to ensure a quick recovery in the event that files are accidentally deleted or a disaster occurs.

Like most major backup programs, the Windows Server 2003 Backup Utility supports a variety of backup types, as outlined in Table 10-5.

Table 10-5 Supported backup types in Windows Server 2003

Backup Type	Description
Copy	Backs up all selected files, but does not clear the archive attribute of files backed up; is useful when you want to make an additional backup without affecting your normal backup routine
Daily	Backs up all selected files that have been changed on the day the backup is performed; does not clear the archive attribute of the files
Differential	Backs up all selected files that have been created or changed since the last normal or incremental backup; does not clear the archive attribute of the files
Incremental	Backs up all selected files that have been created or changed since the last normal or incremental backup; clears the archive attribute of these files
Normal	Backs up all selected files and clears the archive attribute of these files

Note When a backup utility clears the archive attribute of a file or folder, that effectively marks it as having been backed up. When a file is changed or a new file is created, its archive attribute is set rather than cleared.

In Activity 10-13, you will use the Windows Server 2003 Backup Utility to back up and restore selected files and folders.

Activity 10-13: Backing Up and Restoring Files and Folders

Time Required: 15 minutes

Objective: Back up and restore files using the Windows Server 2003 Backup Utility.

Description: The IT manager at Dover Leasing is currently considering many different applications as a backup solution for the company's many servers. You have been asked to test the backup and restore capabilities of the Windows Server 2003 Backup Utility as part of this analysis. In this activity, you will first back up files and then restore them to an alternate location to get a basic idea of what the program is capable of.

1. Click **Start**, select **All Programs**, select **Accessories**, select **System Tools**, and then click **Backup**.
2. In the Backup or Restore Wizard dialog box that opens, click the **Advanced Mode** link to access the complete functionality of the Backup Utility program. The Backup Utility window appears, as shown in Figure 10-31.

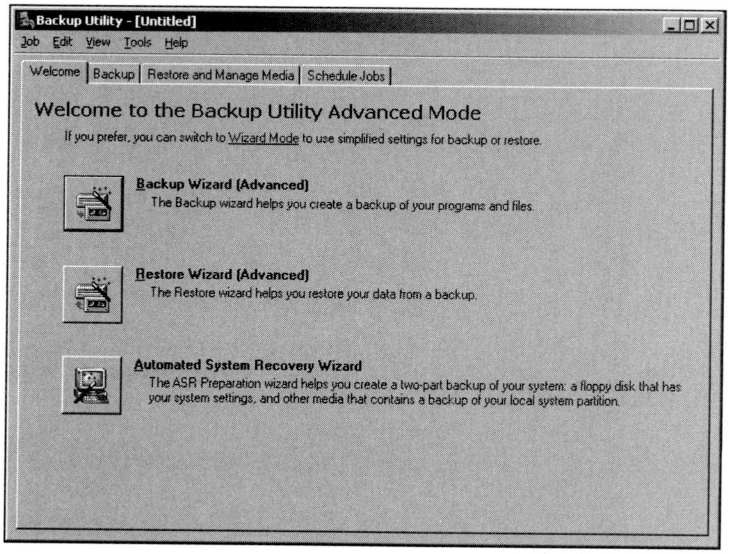

Figure 10-31 Using the Backup Utility in Advanced Mode

3. Click the **Backup** tab.
4. Click the **plus sign (+)** next to Local Disk (C:) to expand its contents.
5. Click the **plus sign (+)** next to WINDOWS to expand its contents.
6. Click the **plus sign (+)** next to system32 to expand its contents.
7. Click the **dhcp** folder to view its contents. Click the check box next to **dhcp** to select the entire folder for backup, as illustrated in Figure 10-32.
8. In the Backup media or file name text box, type **d:\backup-dhcp.bkf**, and then click the **Start Backup** button.
9. In the Backup Job Information dialog box, review the details provided as illustrated in Figure 10-33, and then click the **Start Backup** button.

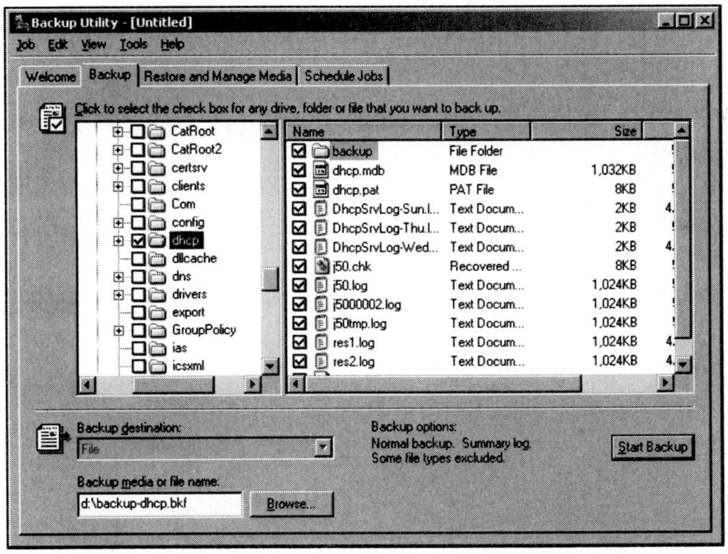

Figure 10-32 Backing up individual files and folders

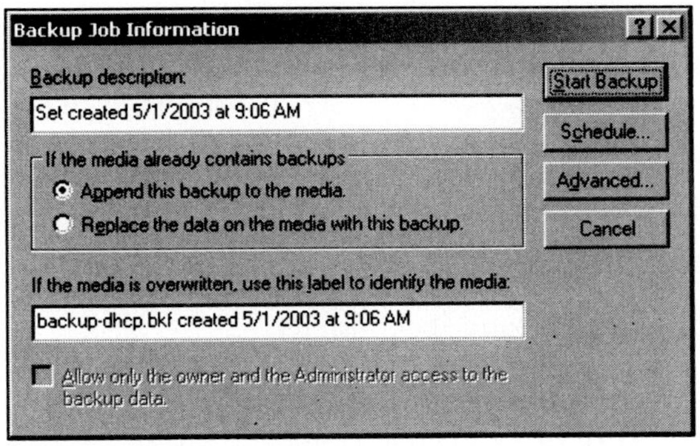

Figure 10-33 Configuring backup job settings

10. Once the backup is complete, the Backup Progress window appears. Once the backup is complete, click the **Report** button to view its contents, as shown in Figure 10-34.

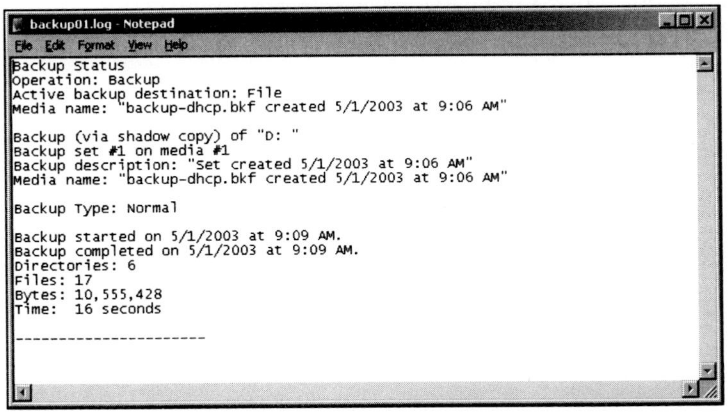

Figure 10-34 Viewing the backup status log file

11. Close the backup01.log window (the number following the name of your log file may be different).

12. Close the Backup Progress window.

13. Click the **Restore and Manage Media** tab. The backup job just created is listed, as shown in Figure 10-35.

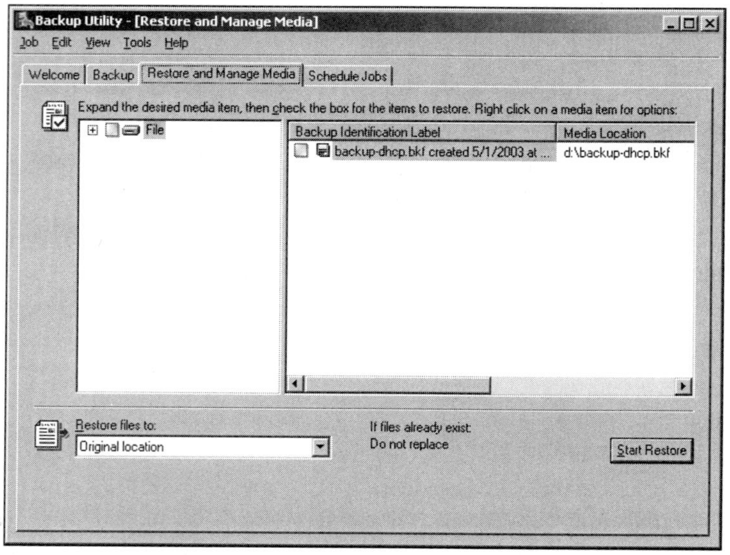

Figure 10-35 Using the restore feature of the Backup Utility

14. Click the **plus sign (+)** next to the File icon to expand its contents.
15. Click the **plus sign (+)** next to backup-dhcp.bkf to expand its contents.
16. Click the **plus sign (+)** next to D: to expand its contents.
17. Click the **plus sign (+)** next to WINDOWS to expand its contents.
18. Click the **plus sign (+)** next to system32 to expand its contents.
19. Click the **dhcp** folder to view the contents of the backup file. Click the check box next to the **dhcp** folder.
20. In the Restore files to list box, click **Alternate location**.
21. In the Alternate location text box, type **D:\dhcpbackup** and click the **Start Restore** button.
22. In the Confirm Restore dialog box, click **OK**.
23. After the Restore process is complete, click the **Close** button in the Restore Progress screen.
24. Close the Backup Utility window.
25. Click **Start**, and then click **My Computer**. Browse to the **D:** drive, and then double-click the **dhcpbackup** folder.
26. Double-click the **WINDOWS**, **system32**, and **dhcp** folders to view their contents, confirming that the contents of the backup file were restored to an alternate location.
27. Close all open windows.

Backing Up the System State

Besides the ability to back up normal data files and folders, the Windows Server 2003 Backup Utility also provides the ability to back up what is referred to as **System State** data. Backing up the System State data on a Windows Server 2003 system includes the following elements:

- Registry (always)
- COM+ Class Registration database (always)

- Boot files (always)
- Certificate Services database (if Certificate Services is installed)
- Active Directory (only on domain controllers)
- SYSVOL directory (only on domain controllers)
- Cluster service (if the server is part of a cluster)
- IIS Metadirectory (if IIS is installed)
- System files (always)

You should also back up these components regularly with your standard backup schedule. In the event of an Active Directory or system startup failure, the most common solution is to restore the System State data.

Note: One limitation to the Windows Server 2003 Backup utility is that you cannot back up individual components of the System State data. Third-party backup applications, like Veritas Backup Exec, often allow individual component backups.

If you are restoring the System State because of a corrupt Active Directory database, you must restart the computer and choose the Directory Services Restore Mode advanced startup option. You can then use the backup utility to restore the latest System State data from backup. After you restart the computer and Windows Server 2003 starts normally, Active Directory is automatically reindexed and updates Active Directory and the file replication service.

10

In the event that you are attempting to restore a portion of the Active Directory tree, a few additional steps may be required. For example, if an OU was inadvertently deleted by an administrator, you can still use the Windows Server 2003 Backup Utility to restore the System State in an attempt to restore the deleted OU. One problem with this scenario is that when an Active Directory object is restored from backup, the other domain controllers still think that the object should be deleted. When replication takes place with the other domain controllers, the newly restored object is again deleted.

This problem can be overcome by performing an **authoritative restore**. An authoritative restore marks specific objects in the Active Directory as the master copy and forces the other domain controllers to receive the change.

To perform an authoritative restore, restart the computer in directory service restore mode, restore the most recent System State from backup, and then run the Ntdsutil utility at a command prompt in authoritative restore mode.

Note: For more information about the Ntdsutil utility and its syntax, see the Windows Server 2003 Help and Support Center.

In Activity 10-14, you will use the Windows Server 2003 Backup Utility to back up System State data on your server.

Hands-on Project

Activity 10-14: Backing Up System State Data

Time Required: 15 minutes

Objective: Back up the System State data on a Windows Server 2003 domain controller.

Description: Because your server is also a domain controller, the IT manager at Dover Leasing has asked you to explore the capabilities of the Backup Utility in terms of backing up System State data including individual components. Ultimately, this will be an important criteria in whether the IT manager decides to rely on the Backup Utility or a third-party alternative. In this activity, you will back up the System State data for your server.

1. Click **Start**, click **Run**, and in the Open text box type **ntbackup** and press **Enter**. Click the **Advanced Mode** link in the Backup or Restore Wizard screen.
2. In the Backup Utility window, click the **Backup** tab.
3. Click the **System State** icon to view its contents. Notice that the individual check boxes are grayed out because individual System State components cannot be backed up by this utility.
4. Click the check box next to the **System State** icon, as illustrated in Figure 10-36.

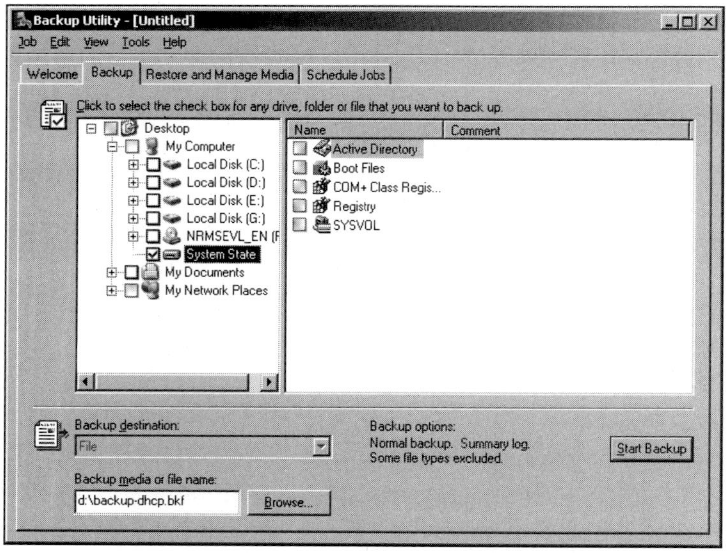

Figure 10-36 Backing up System State data

5. In the Backup media or file name text box, type **d:\systemstate.bkf** and click the **Start Backup** button.
6. In the Backup Job Information dialog box, click the **Start Backup** button.
7. After the Backup process is complete, click the **Close** button in the Backup Progress screen.
8. Close all open windows.

Chapter Summary

- The Performance console has two tools that you can use to monitor server health and performance: System Monitor and Performance Logs and Alerts.
- You can configure alerts for specific objects and counters. Once a counter exceeds or drops below the configured value, an alert is triggered. The alert can send a message, start a counter log, write an event to the application log, or run a program.
- You can use Event Viewer to view the contents of the system logs, application logs, and security logs. Processes and applications write events to the log files. Administrators can use this information to identify and troubleshoot server problems.
- Task Manager provides information on processes and applications running on a system. It also provides general information on a system's current performance.
- When optimizing the performance of your computer, use the Services icon to disable any unnecessary services to eliminate overhead.
- The Windows Server 2003 startup process occurs in two distinct phases: the startup phase and the load phase.

- Windows Server 2003 includes advanced startup options that you can use to troubleshoot and repair startup problems. You can access the advanced startup options by pressing F8 at the operating system selection screen menu.
- You can use the last known good configuration to restart your computer if the default configuration becomes damaged due to Windows Server 2003 configuration changes.
- Windows Server 2003 includes a text-mode command interpreter called the Recovery Console that allows an administrator to access the hard drive and carry out administrative tasks. You can install the Recovery Console on the computer and start it from the operating system selection menu, or you can start it directly from the Windows Server 2003 CD.
- If you are unable to recover a system using any of the Windows Server 2003 utilities, you can also use a backup created by the Automated System Recovery feature.

Key Terms

alerts — An alert performs a specified action once a counter meets the specified setting. Once an alert is triggered, a message can be sent, a program can be run, a counter log started, or an event can be written to the application log.

application log — Where applications that are written to Microsoft standards record event information. The application developer determines the type of information an application writes to the log file.

authoritative restore — Marks specific objects in the Active Directory as the master copy, and forces the other domain controllers to receive the change.

Automated System Recovery (ASR) — A new Windows Server 2003 feature that creates a floppy disk and a backup of system configuration data to repair a server using an automated process.

baseline — A performance benchmark that is used to determine what is normal server performance under a specific workload.

counter log — Performance data that is collected into a comma-separated or tab-separated format.

Event Viewer — A utility used to view the contents of the system, security, and application logs.

last known good configuration — An advanced startup option that you can use to recover a system from failed Windows 2000 configuration changes.

performance counter — A data item associated with a particular performance object used to measure a certain aspect of performance.

Performance Logs and Alerts — A tool included with Windows Server 2003 that enables you to create counter logs, trace logs, and configure alerts.

performance objects — A system component that you can monitor using System Monitor.

Recovery Console — A command-line interpreter that you can use to gain access to a local hard drive in the event that the system fails to boot.

safe mode — A method of starting Windows Server 2003 with only the basic drivers and services.

security log — Events pertaining to the audit policy are written to the security log.

system log — Where system components such as services and device drivers record information, warnings, and errors.

System Monitor — A tool that allows you to gather and view real-time performance statistics of a local or network computer.

System State — System components that are backed up as a single item within the Windows Server 2003 Backup utility. System State data includes the Registry, COM+ Class Registration database, boot files, Certificate Services database, Active Directory, the Sysvol folder, Cluster service information, the IIS Metadirectory, and system files.

Task Manager — A tool used to view the processes and applications currently running on a system. Also provides basic resource usage statistics.

trace log — Where data provider collects performance data when an event occurs.

REVIEW QUESTIONS

1. What feature of Windows Server 2003 can you use to have a message sent to your computer when a performance counter exceeds a certain value?
   a. counter logs
   b. alerts
   c. Event Viewer
   d. Task Manager
2. What tool can you use to view the contents of the system log?
   a. System Monitor
   b. Performance Console
   c. Event Viewer
   d. Task Manager
3. You are running several programs on your computer. One of them appears to have stopped responding. What tool can you use to check the status of the application?
   a. Performance Monitor
   b. System Monitor
   c. Application Manager
   d. Task Manager
4. What type of log would you create to have performance data collected and saved into a comma-separated file?
   a. trace log
   b. database log
   c. counter log
   d. system log
5. Only administrators can view the contents of the system and application logs. True or False?
6. What is the default view when System Monitor is first opened?
   a. histogram
   b. graph
   c. counter
   d. report
7. You have started to receive complaints from users on the network that the server has been performing poorly. What tool can you use to monitor and view real-time performance of the server?
   a. Event Viewer
   b. Performance Monitor
   c. Performance Logs and Alerts
   d. System Monitor
8. A service fails to start on your server. In which log file is the event recorded?
   a. application
   b. system
   c. services
   d. counter

9. What is the name of the file that contains a list of operating systems displayed at the operating system selection menu?
   a. boot.ini
   b. system.ini
   c. operatingSystems.ini
   d. mtldr.ini
10. When is the Windows Server 2003 startup process considered to be successful?
    a. after the startup phase finishes
    b. after the user logs on
    c. after the load phase
    d. after the user logs on and launches an application
11. Which of the following actions can be taken when an alert is triggered? (Choose all that apply.)
    a. A message can be sent to a computer.
    b. An event can be written to the application log.
    c. A program can be run.
    d. A counter log can be started.

10

12. You load a new device driver on your server. The server fails to boot when it is restarted. What advanced startup option can you use to recover the server?
    a. safe mode
    b. last known good configuration
    c. safe mode with networking
    d. debugging mode
13. Which of the following options can you use to start the Windows Server 2003 Recovery Console? (Choose all that apply.)
    a. Install it on the local computer and choose it from the list of available operating systems.
    b. Install and share the Recovery Console on a network server and connect to the share from the local computer using safe mode with Networking.
    c. Boot from the Windows Server 2003 CD-ROM, and choose R for recovery.
    d. Restart the computer, press F8 to access the advanced startup options, and choose the Recovery Console.
14. Which of the following files must be located on the boot partition for Windows 2000 to successfully boot? (Choose all that apply.)
    a. ntoskrnl.exe
    b. boot.ini
    c. ntbootdd.sys
    d. hal.dll
15. You can use the last known good configuration to recover from missing or corrupt files. True or False?
16. A missing file is preventing your server from starting. Which of the following options can you use to recover the system? (Choose all that apply.)
    a. safe mode
    b. Recovery Console
    c. Automatic System Recovery
    d. last known good configuration

17. You want to determine which services and drivers are and are not being loaded during startup. Which advanced startup option should you use?
    a. debugging mode
    b. safe mode
    c. Enable Boot Logging
    d. step-by-step confirmation
18. By default, any user can run the Recovery Console. True or False?
19. What tool can you use to view all processes and applications currently running on a system?
    a. App Manager
    b. System Monitor
    c. Event Viewer
    d. Task Manager
20. The Automatic System Recovery Wizard creates a bootable floppy disk as part of its process. True or False?

CASE PROJECTS

Case Project 10-1

You are responsible for the administration of three Dover Leasing servers. You have recently installed a new service on your server. The service is set to start automatically and runs continuously to service user requests. Your manager is concerned about server performance after the service is installed, and you assure him that performance should not suffer. Answer the following questions based on the scenario.

1. After you install the service, what is one of the first things you should do?
2. During peak hours, your manager stops in to see how the server is performing under the added workload. What tool can you use to quickly show your manager the current processor usage on the server?
3. You have a slight concern that the service may indeed have an impact on the amount of time the processor is utilized. The % utilization was running at times near 50% before the service was installed. You would like to be notified if the processor utilization goes above 60%. Explain how this can be done. What other actions can you configure if this occurs?
4. Because the server is working under an increased workload, you want to disable any unnecessary services to eliminate the overhead associated with running them. What should you consider before disabling any services on the server?

Case Project 10-2

A new administrator has been hired at Dover Leasing to work during evenings and weekends under your direction. One evening he decides to install a new device driver on one of the servers to enhance performance. Before checking with you or any other administrators on staff, he installs the device driver. You receive a call that upon restart the new administrator discovered that the server no longer boots successfully. The server needs to be available to users in the morning.

1. What options in Windows Server 2003 are available to recover from a failed reboot? What is each option used for?
2. What recovery tool would be appropriate for this situation?
3. You noticed after the server is recovered that the Recovery Console was not listed as an option during the operating system selection. It is company policy that this tool be installed on all servers. How can the tool be installed? If you needed to use the Recovery Console and it wasn't installed, how could you start it?

Case Project 10-3

After a serious server failure at Dover Leasing, you decide to attempt to restore the server using the Automated System Recovery (ASR) feature. Although the server now boots once more, users are calling to complain that their files are no longer accessible on the server. What is the cause of this, and what can you do to remedy the situation?

CHAPTER

11

ADMINISTERING REMOTE ACCESS SERVICES

After reading this chapter and completing the exercises, you will be able to:

- Configure remote access and virtual private network (VPN) connections
- Implement and troubleshoot remote access policies
- Configure and troubleshoot network address translation (NAT)
- Configure and troubleshoot Internet connection sharing
- Configure and manage Terminal Services

You can implement remote access services to allow users to connect to your network from any remote location. Windows Server 2003 provides many features to increase the usability and security of your remote access solutions. The Routing and Remote Access Services (RRAS) component of Windows Server 2003 enables you to configure remote access by implementing dial-up or **virtual private network (VPN)** connections to the internal network. Support for a number of authentication and encryption protocols helps to secure any communication that is established through the standard dial-up or VPN connections.

This chapter explains how to configure and troubleshoot RRAS to provide remote access and VPN connections. Remote access policies are also discussed, which can assist in controlling access to a RRAS server.

With the popularity and availability of high-speed Internet connections via cable or ADSL, a need has developed to provide shared Internet access to multiple network clients. Windows Server 2003 provides two features that can fill this need. The first feature is **network address translation (NAT)**, which is another RRAS component that can allow multiple network clients access to the Internet. The second feature is **Internet connection sharing (ICS)**, which is a similar technology but is used in smaller or home-based networks. This chapter discusses the difference between NAT and ICS, and how to configure and troubleshoot both of these services to provide shared Internet access for your network users.

This chapter also discusses how to implement and troubleshoot **Terminal Services** and **Remote Desktop** for remote access. Terminal Services is a feature available in Windows Server 2003 that can provide network clients with access to shared applications that are installed on a central server. Remote Desktop (formerly known as Terminal Services in Remote Administration mode) enables administrators to perform remote administration tasks on Windows Server 2003 and Windows XP systems.

Configuring Remote Access and Virtual Private Network Connections

One of the requirements in almost any organization is to give users remote access to the internal network. In some cases, providing this remote access may be quite simple. For example, an organization may decide to give remote access to a single network resource, such as e-mail, to only a few executives. The organization might limit the remote access even more by giving the executives access to the corporate network only from their home computer and only when they dial into the company's **remote access server**. A remote access server is a computer running Windows Server 2003 and the RRAS, which allows connections from remote users. In other cases, the requirement to provide remote access to the network can be much more complicated. A company may have a large number of users who require remote access because they spend most of their time outside the office. For example, a company may have a mobile sales force or executives who travel a great deal. These people require access to the corporate network from almost anywhere in the world. These users may be using laptops or sitting at kiosk computers in an airport. In addition to almost universal access, the users may require access to a variety of resources including e-mail, an Intranet Web server, a database server to run a client application, and files on the corporate file servers.

When a client needs to connect to a network from a remote location, you may use one of two methods to provide the connection. One method is to use standard dial-up connections. When a client uses a dial-up connection, communication is established via communication networks such as a Public Switched Telephone Network (PSTN).

A remote client typically uses a modem or an ISDN connection to dial up to the remote server and establish a connection to the internal network. To provide the remote access connection, Windows Server 2003 supports a number of remote access protocols. The most common protocol is the **Point-to-Point Protocol (PPP)**. PPP enables remote access clients and servers to communicate over a dial-up connection from any operating system that supports the PPP standards. One disadvantage to using a dial-up method is that users may have to incur long-distance charges to connect over long distances.

The second method that you can implement to provide remote access is to use a VPN. A VPN uses a LAN protocol and PPP, which are both encapsulated within a VPN protocol, to send data over a public network. This encapsulation creates an encrypted tunnel through the public network to the internal network.

Two common VPN protocols are **Point-to-Point Tunneling Protocol (PPTP)** and **Layer 2 Tunneling Protocol (L2TP)**. PPTP and L2TP are both used to establish a secure tunnel between two endpoints over an insecure network. These protocols are included with Windows Server 2003 and provide the security needed to make VPNs a common choice for remote network access. Table 11-1 explains the major differences between PPTP and L2TP.

Table 11-1 Differences between PPTP and L2TP

PPTP	L2TP
Must be used on an IP-based network	Can be used on an IP-, Frame Relay-, X.25-, or ATM-based network
Does not provide header compression	Provides header compression for better performance
Does not provide tunnel authentication	Provides tunnel authentication for increased security
Uses built-in PPP encryption	Uses IPSec to provide encryption
Can be used by most clients	Can be used by only Windows Server 2003, Windows 2000, and Windows XP computers, without downloading additional client software
Does not require clients to have a computer certificate	Requires clients to have a computer certificate or a pre-shared key configured on the client and server

One of the main advantages to using a VPN is that clients can connect to a local ISP and then connect to their internal network from anywhere in the world via the Internet.

Remote access is implemented on a Windows Server 2003 system by configuring RRAS. RRAS provides a variety of routing and remote access solutions such as dial-up and VPN connections, NAT, and more. To provide these services, there are three primary tasks that you have to complete:

- Configure RRAS with the appropriate remote access configuration.
- Configure clients to connect to the RRAS server.
- Configure user rights, security, and conditions to successfully and securely connect to the RRAS server.

You can configure Windows Server 2003 to provide remote access to clients using a number of different methods. Some of these methods include analog modems, ISDN adapters, and other broadband hardware such as DSL or cable modems. Clients can then access the server through a standard dial-up connection or through connections established via the Internet. The RRAS server can authenticate users and provide a gateway to the network resources available on the internal network.

The next several sections describe, in more detail, the methods used to create and configure dial-up and VPN connections. Various authentication and encryption protocols that you can use to help secure your remote access connections are also outlined, as well as suggestions for troubleshooting remote access connection problems. In Activity 11-1, you will enable and configure RRAS on your server.

Activity 11-1: Configuring RRAS

Hands-on Project

Time Required: 10 minutes

Objective: Configure and enable Routing and Remote Access.

Description: Over the course of the next year, Dover Leasing plans to implement a new program that will allow many of its employees to work from home to reduce costs. As part of this initiative, the IT manager has decided to explore the use of both dial-up and VPN connections as a way to facilitate user access to corporate servers. You have been asked to evaluate whether Windows Server 2003 will meet these needs. In this activity, you will configure and enable Routing and Remote Access to initially allow dial-up access to the Dover Leasing head office.

1. Click **Start**, select **Administrative Tools**, and click **Routing and Remote Access**.
2. Right-click the **Server*XX*** icon and click **Configure and Enable Routing and Remote Access**, as shown in Figure 11-1.

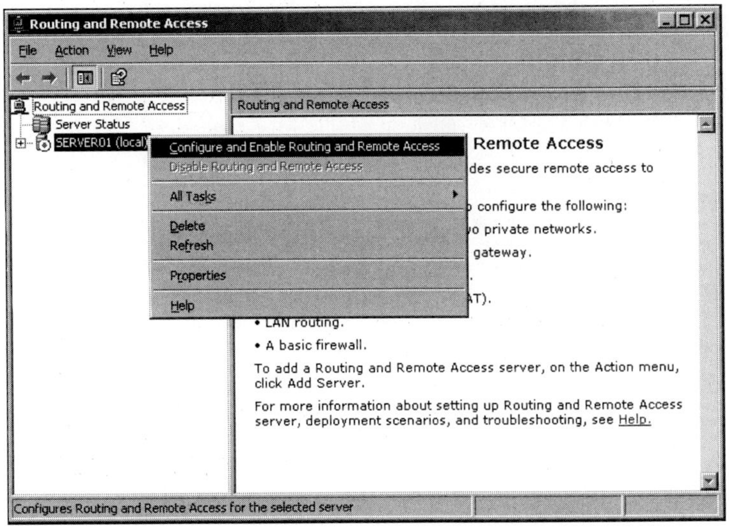

Figure 11-1 The Routing and Remote Access console

3. At the Routing and Remote Access Server Setup Wizard welcome screen, click **Next**.
4. At the Configuration screen, ensure that the **Remote access (dial-up or VPN)** radio button is selected, as shown in Figure 11-2, and click **Next**.

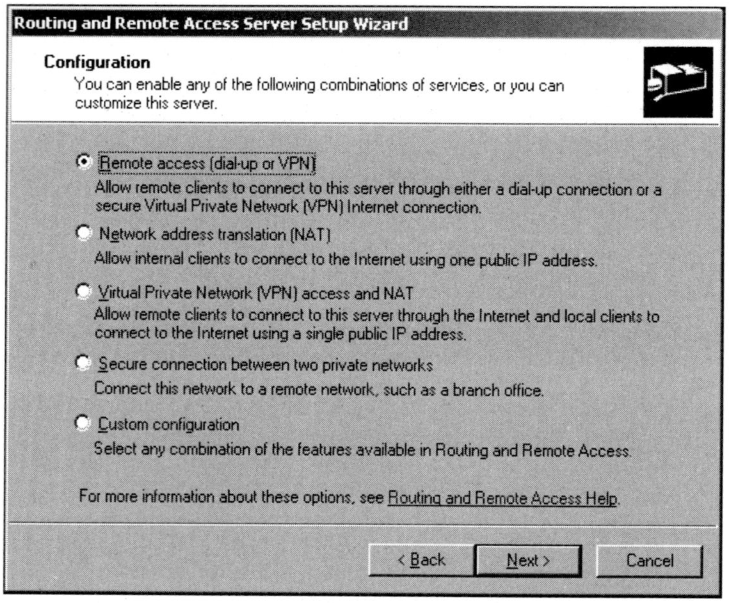

Figure 11-2 Selecting a RRAS configuration

5. At the Remote Access screen, click the **Dial-up** check box and click **Next**.
6. At the IP Address Assignment screen, read the available options and then click **Next**.
7. At the Managing Multiple Remote Access Servers screen, read the selected options, as shown in Figure 11-3, and then click **Next**.

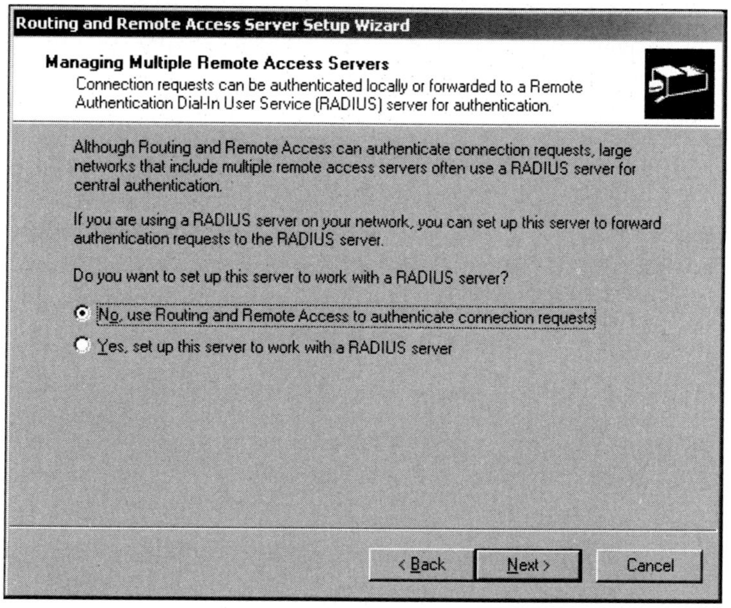

Figure 11-3 Configuring remote access authentication settings

8. Click **Finish**.

9. In the Routing and Remote Access dialog box that opens, as illustrated in Figure 11-4, click **OK**. This will ensure that clients are able to obtain addresses for a DHCP server on your network by enabling the DHCP Relay Agent.

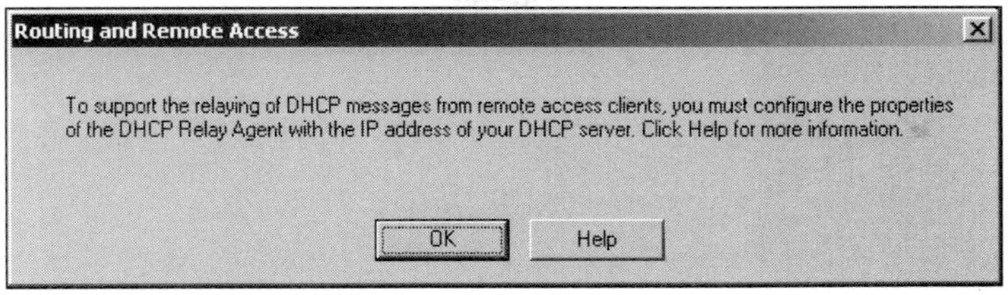

Figure 11-4 Installing a DHCP Relay Agent automatically

10. Right-click your **Server*XX*** icon and click **Properties**. The properties dialog box for your server opens, as shown in Figure 11-5. Notice that your RRAS server is now configured as a remote access server, but not as a router.

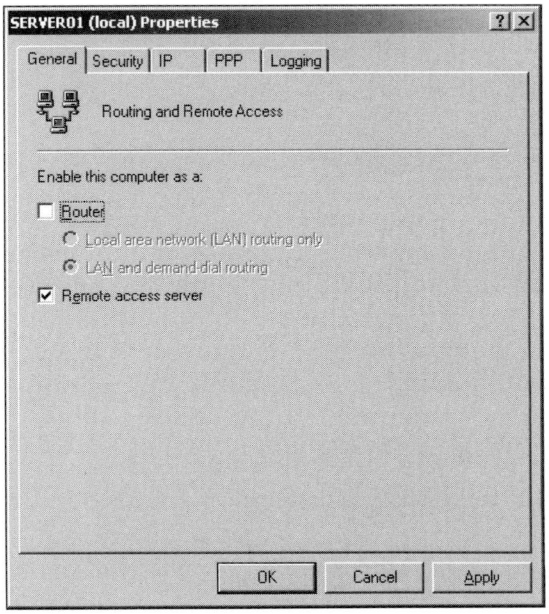

Figure 11-5 Viewing the properties of an RRAS server

11. Click the **Logging** tab, and then click the **Log additional Routing and Remote Access information** check box, as shown in Figure 11-6. This selection will ultimately save RRAS debugging information that can be useful in troubleshooting connection problems to the %windir%\tracing directory.

12. Click **OK** to close the properties dialog box of your server.

13. Click the **Ports** icon. If your server has a modem installed, it should appear in the list of available ports with a status of Inactive. If your server does not have a modem installed, a modem device will not appear.

14. Close the Routing and Remote Access window.

11

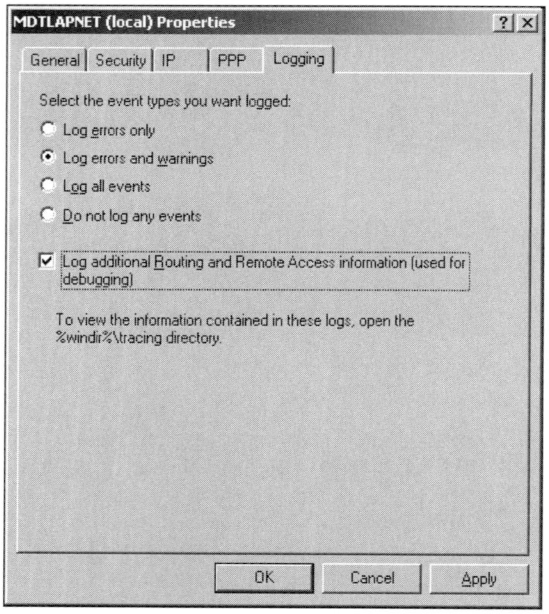

Figure 11-6 Configuring RRAS Logging settings

Configuring Dial-up Connections

Many organizations still provide dial-up remote access for users who travel extensively. Despite the fact that dial-up access is slow (with a 56-Kbps maximum connection speed using a single phone line) and often unreliable, dial-up access is often also the only option that the remote user has available. Although this is slowly changing, relatively few hotel rooms have high speed Internet connections that you can use to connect to your company network via a VPN connection; however, almost all hotel rooms have a data line that you can use to dial out using your laptop's modem. The primary advantage of dial-up access is that it is available almost anywhere.

The first step in providing remote access to clients is to configure the physical modem on the server to which the clients connect. If the users are dialing in using analog modems, you need to install and configure the modem or modems on the server. If the connection is ISDN or X.25 based, then you have to configure the hardware device for the connection. In most cases, a modem or similar device is detected by Plug and Play in Windows Server 2003 and automatically installed during the installation process or when you scan for hardware changes in Device Manager. If the modem is not detected, then use the Add New Hardware Wizard to add the correct modem. After you have added the modem(s), the next step is to configure Windows Server 2003 as a remote access server.

Now that you have installed the dial-up server, you may want to configure IP-addressing options, protocol options, and remote access clients. These three tasks are discussed next.

Configuring IP-Addressing Options for the Dial-up Server

Depending on the choice that you made during the installation, the server may or may not be using DHCP to assign IP address information to the dial-up clients. Client IP-addressing settings for an RRAS server are configured from the properties of the RRAS server, as shown in Figure 11-7.

Note

Figure 11-7 also illustrates a new RRAS feature in Windows Server 2003, namely the ability for remote access clients to resolve network names to IP addresses using broadcasts in the event that a small network does not have a WINS or DNS server. In previous Windows versions, clients would require the configuration of HOSTS or LMHOSTS files if these servers were not present.

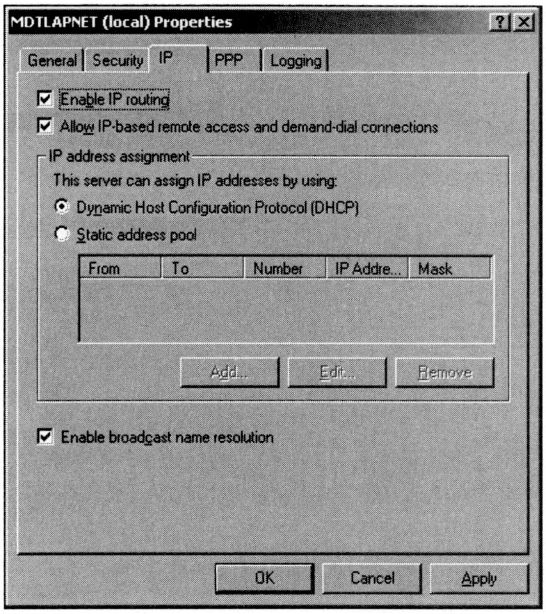

Figure 11-7 Viewing IP settings on an RRAS server

If you have enabled an RRAS server to use a DHCP server to allocate client addresses and want to change the setting, you can select to use a Static address pool. This allows you to configure a range of IP addresses that dial-up or VPN clients for this server would then receive once connected.

> **Tip:** If you are using DHCP to assign IP addresses to the dial-up clients, you must install a DHCP Relay Agent as a routing protocol or allow it to be added automatically during the Routing and Remote Access Server Setup Wizard. If not, client computers will not be able to obtain an IP address unless the RRAS server itself is running the DHCP service.

If DHCP is being used, the RRAS server initially obtains 10 IP addresses from the DHCP service. The first IP address is assigned to the RRAS server itself, and then the next nine addresses are available to be assigned to dial-up clients. If all nine addresses are allocated to remote clients, the RRAS server leases 10 more addresses from the DHCP server as necessary. In Activity 11-2, you will configure IP address settings on your RRAS server.

Activity 11-2: Configuring IP Address Settings for Remote Clients

Time Required: 10 minutes

Objective: Configure IP address settings for remote access clients.

Description: In the past, only network administrators were granted dial-in access to the Dover Leasing network to perform administrative tasks as necessary if a problem arose. The network is currently configured with a proprietary dial-in server for which remote users need a statically assigned IP address. Hoping to avoid this in the future, the IT manager has asked you to evaluate the different IP-addressing options available when Windows Server 2003 RRAS is used. In this activity, you will configure your RRAS server with a static pool of IP addresses to be allocated to remote access clients.

1. Click **Start**, select **Administrative Tools**, and then click **Routing and Remote Access**.
2. Right-click the **Server*XX*** icon, and then click **Properties**.
3. Click the **IP** tab, and then click the **Static address pool** radio button.
4. Click **Add**.

5. In the New Address Range dialog box, type **10.*X*.0.1** in the Start IP address range text box, and type **10.*X*.0.255** in the End IP address range text box, where *X* is your student number, as shown in Figure 11-8.

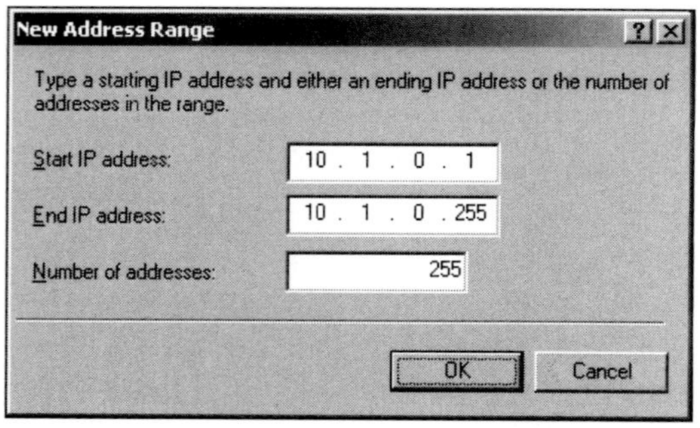

Figure 11-8 Configuring a client IP address range

6. Click **OK**. Notice that an IP address pool is now configured, as shown in Figure 11-9.

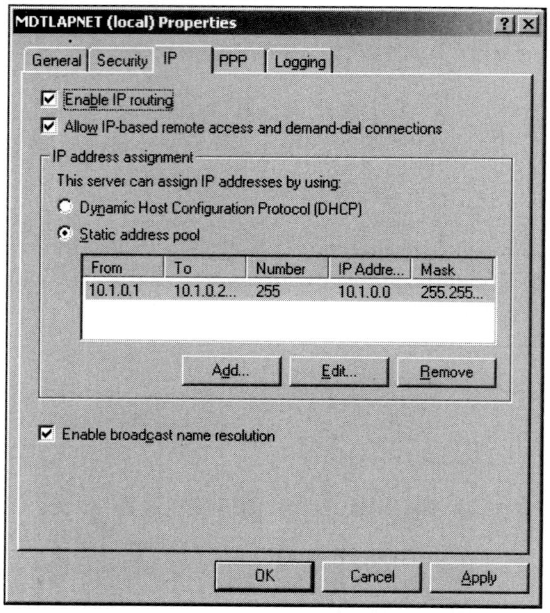

Figure 11-9 Viewing the settings of a new IP address range

7. Click **OK** to close your server's properties dialog box, and leave the Routing and Remote Access window open.

Tip

If remote clients cannot browse the network, check the IP address that has been assigned by the DHCP server. If a DHCP server is not available when the RRAS server asks for the 10 IP addresses, it then starts to hand out addresses in the 169.254.0.1 through 169.254.255.254 range. This is the APIPA range used by Windows and will probably not be routable within your network.

Multilink and Bandwidth Allocation Protocol Options

If your server has more than one physical connection that can be used for dial-up access, you can configure Windows Server 2003 to support PPP multilink or combine multiple physical connections into one connection to increase bandwidth. You can configure PPP multilink using multiple modems, ISDN, or X.25 connections. When implemented, a client can dial in to the server on multiple lines, and these lines are combined together into one logical connection.

Windows Server 2003 also uses Bandwidth Allocation Protocol (BAP) to help dynamically manage multiple links. For example, if a user is connected on both of the B channels for an ISDN connection, you can configure BAP so that when the use of one of the channels falls below a set limit for a period of time, that channel is dropped. The channel would then be available to another client. In Activity 11-3, you will explore RRAS settings relating to both PPP multilink and BAP.

Activity 11-3: Exploring PPP Multilink and BAP Options

Time Required: 5 minutes

Objective: Explore PPP multilink and BAP configuration options.

Description: Although many of Dover Leasing's employees currently have high-speed Internet access available at home, many users still rely upon traditional dial-up connections to connect to a remote location. Of these, some users have multiple phone lines and modems available that would make PPP multilink connections possible. You have been asked to explore the PPP capabilities of an RRAS dial-in server. In this activity, you will explore both the PPP multilink and BAP capabilities of your RRAS server.

1. In the Routing and Remote Access window, right click **Server*XX*** and click **Properties**.
2. Click the **PPP** tab. This displays PPP-related RRAS options, as illustrated in Figure 11-10.

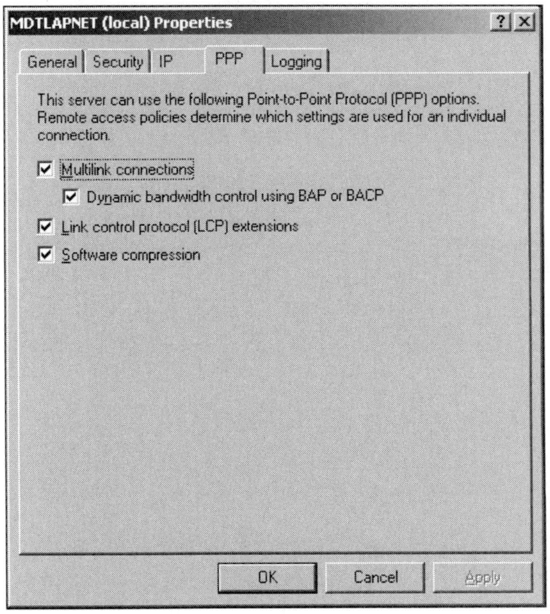

Figure 11-10 Viewing PPP settings on an RRAS server

3. In the upper right-hand corner of the properties dialog box, click the **?** button, and then click on the text **Multilink connections** to view its purpose.
4. Click the **?** button, and then click on **Dynamic bandwidth control using BAP or BAPC**.
5. Click the **?** button, and then click on **Link control protocol (LCP) extensions**.
6. Click the **?** button, and then click on **Software compression**.
7. Click **OK** to close the properties dialog box for your server, and close the Routing and Remote Access window.

Configuring Remote Access Clients

After you have prepared the RRAS server, the next step is to configure a new dial-up connection for clients. The client configuration can be completed either manually or through the Connection Manager application. In Windows Server 2003, individual connections are manually configured using the Network Connection Wizard. In Activity 11-4, you will configure a new dial-up connection on your server.

Activity 11-4: Configuring a Dial-up Client Connection

Time Required: 10 minutes

Objective: Configure a dial-up connection to connect to a private office.

Description: To connect to a Windows Server 2003 dial-in server, employees will require a new dial-up connection to be installed on their home systems or laptops. Although this process will ultimately be handled by Help Desk staff, the IT manager at Dover Leasing has asked you to create a set of instructions that can be used to define client connections. In this activity, you will use the Windows Server 2003 New Connection Wizard to define a new client connection object and explore its property settings.

1. Click **Start**, select **Control Panel**, select **Network Connections**, and then click **New Connection Wizard**.
2. At the Welcome to the New Connection Wizard screen, click **Next**.
3. At the Network Connection Type screen, click the **Connect to the network at my workplace** radio button, as shown in Figure 11-11, and click **Next**.

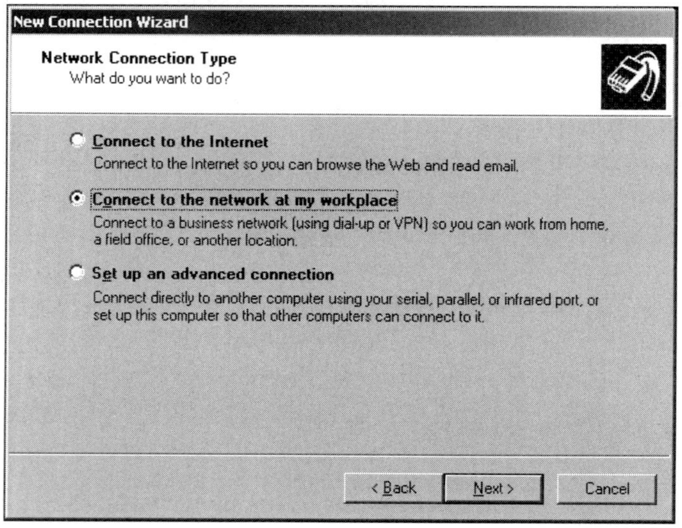

Figure 11-11 Configuring a new client connection

4. At the Network Connection screen illustrated in Figure 11-12, leave the Dial-up connection radio button selected and click **Next**.
5. At the Connection Name screen, type **Dover Leasing** in the Company Name text box and click **Next**.
6. At the Phone Number to Dial screen, type **555-5555** in the Phone number text box. Click **Next**.
7. At the Connection Availability screen, click **Next**.
8. Click **Finish**.

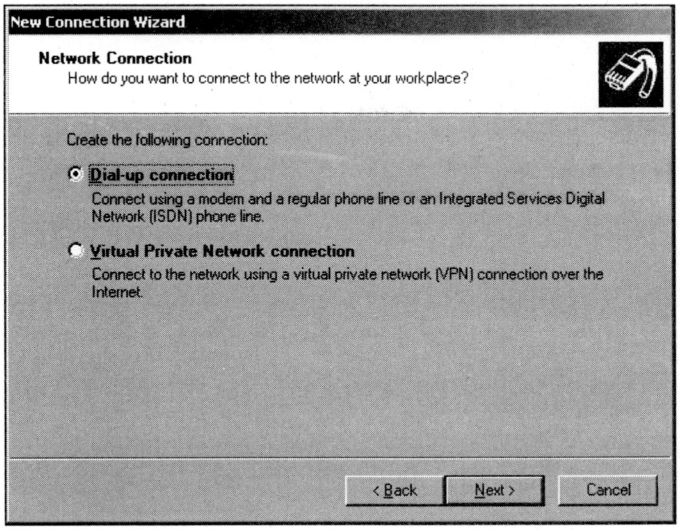

Figure 11-12 Choosing a connection type

9. Click **Start**, select **Control Panel**, and then double-click **Network Connections**. This opens the Network Connections window.
10. Right-click the **Dover Leasing** icon, and then click **Properties**. The properties dialog box of the connection opens, as illustrated in Figure 11-13.

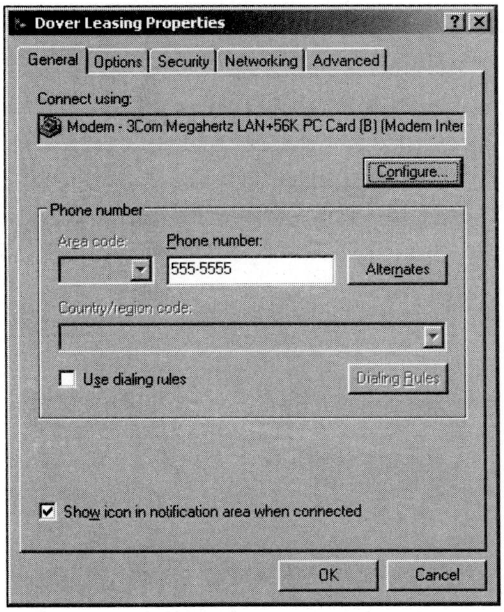

Figure 11-13 Configuring the General properties of a dial-up connection

11. Click the **Options** tab. This tab allows you to configure settings related to dialing, logging on, and redialing, as illustrated in Figure 11-14.

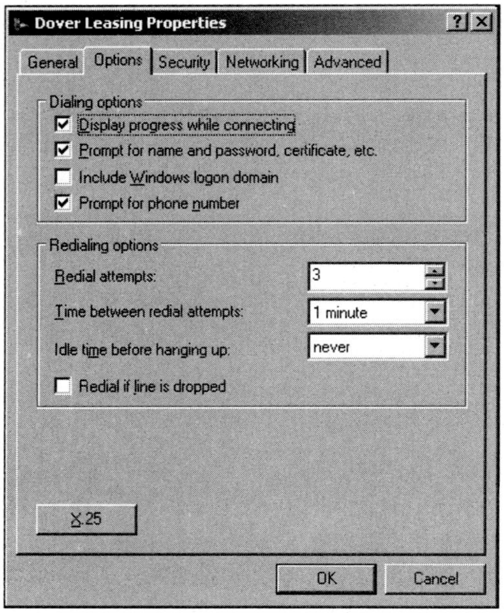

Figure 11-14 Configuring connection Options

12. Click the **Security** tab. This tab allows you to configure security and authentication options that may be required by the dial-in server, as shown in Figure 11-15.

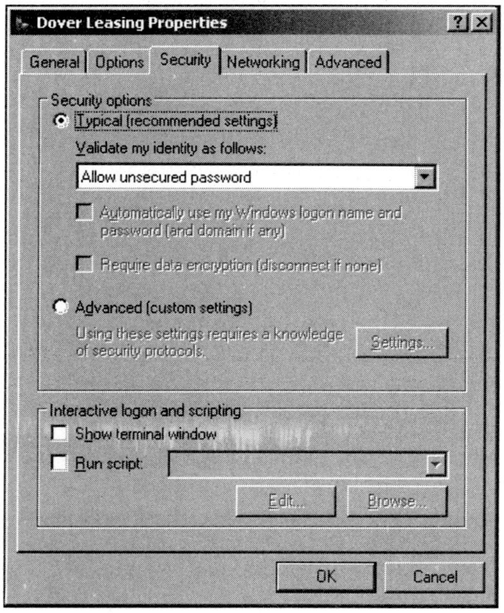

Figure 11-15 Dial-up connection Security settings

13. Click the **Networking** tab, and then double-click **Internet Protocol (TCP/IP)**. Notice that the client is configured to obtain an IP address automatically by default. Click **Cancel** in the Internet Protocol (TCP/IP) Properties dialog box.
14. Click the **Advanced** tab. This tab allows you to enable and configure settings related to the Internet Connection Firewall and Internet Connection Sharing, as shown in Figure 11-16.
15. Click **OK**, and close the Network Connections window.

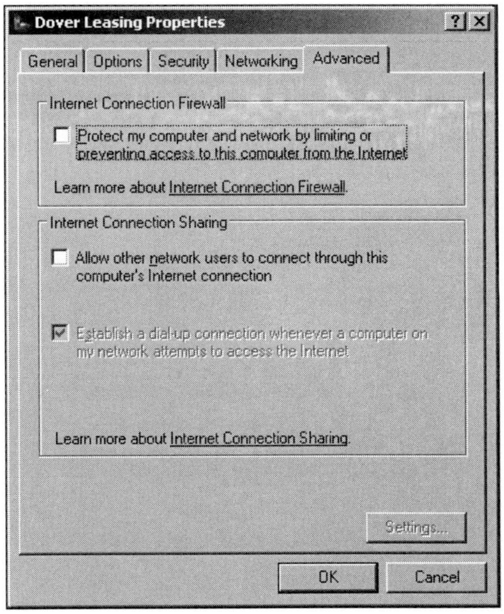

Figure 11-16 Advanced settings of a connection object

Note: The Windows Server 2003 Connection Manager Administration Kit (CMAK) is a utility that allows customized connection objects and settings to be defined for dial-up and VPN clients. For more information about CMAK, see the Help and Support Center.

Implementing Virtual Private Network Access

An increasingly popular alternative to providing the traditional dial-up remote access is to provide VPN access. A VPN is used to ensure that your data communication over a public network, such as the Internet, is secure. This is implemented by having the VPN create an encrypted tunnel between a client and a VPN server using the Internet. Alternatively, VPN connections can be created to connect two LANs, forming a type of WAN connection using the Internet as the backbone link between two locations.

To create an encrypted VPN tunnel, a dial-up client computer first establishes a connection to an Internet Service Provider (ISP), which gives the client access to the Internet. After the PPP link is established, the client negotiates a second connection to a remote access server at the corporate network that is also connected to the Internet. In this second negotiation, the client and the server agree on how the packets over the virtual connection are encapsulated and encrypted. Then, the two computers can send data across the Internet connection with the assurance that the data is secure.

You can create a VPN over any existing connection to the Internet. For example, in many parts of the world, cable modem or digital subscriber line (DSL) access to the Internet is widely available and very fast. A VPN can be created using this fast connection to the Internet, thus providing the client with secure and much faster access than traditional dial-up access to the corporate network.

Figure 11-17 illustrates how a VPN is created using a dial-up or cable modem connection to the Internet.

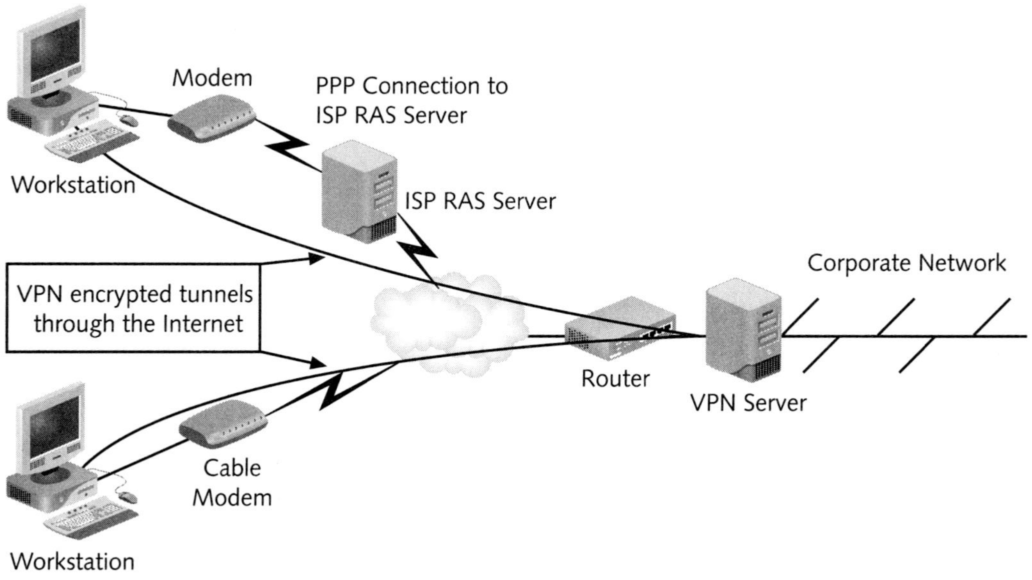

Figure 11-17 A virtual private network (VPN)

In many ways, configuring both the server and client for VPN is similar to configuring them for dial-up remote access. From the client, the VPN connection is configured as a new network connection using the New Connection Wizard. On the server side, RRAS is used to configure the VPN server.

VPN Server Configuration

As discussed, Windows Server 2003 supports two VPN protocols: PPTP and L2TP. Configuring the VPN server is similar for both protocols, with the exception that the use of L2TP/IPSec requires that a computer certificate or pre-shared key be installed or configured on client computers.

Unlike in Windows 2000, configuring L2TP/IPSec VPN connections in Windows Server 2003 can also use a pre-shared key configured on the client and server instead of requiring computer certificates to be installed.

The first step is to install two network adapters in the VPN server. One of the adapters must have a permanent connection to the Internet, and the other adapter is connected to the internal corporate network. Each of the adapters should be installed and tested before continuing. In Activity 11-5, you will enable your RRAS server to accept both PPTP and L2TP connections.

Activity 11-5: Exploring and Configuring VPN Server Settings

Time Required: 10 minutes

Objective: Explore and configure VPN-related RRAS settings.

Description: Because many of Dover Leasing's employees have high-speed DSL and cable Internet connections available at home, the IT manager is interested in providing these users with a higher-speed alternative for accessing the corporate network via a VPN connection. In this activity, you will explore and configure VPN settings on your RRAS server.

1. Click **Start**, select **Administrative Tools**, and then click **Routing and Remote Access**.
2. Click the **plus sign (+)** next to the Server*XX* icon to expand it, if necessary.
3. Right-click the **Ports** icon, and then click **Properties**. The Ports Properties dialog box opens, as shown in Figure 11-18. Notice that 128 WAN Miniports exist for PPTP and L2TP by default.

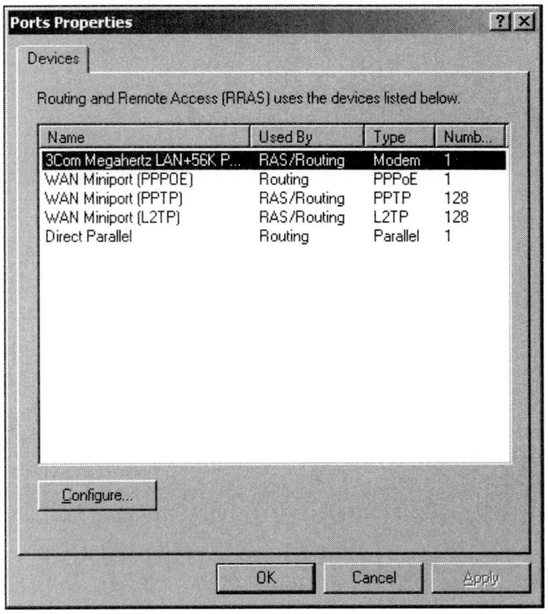

Figure 11-18 Viewing port properties

4. Click on **WAN Miniport (PPTP)** and then click the **Configure** button.
5. In the Configure Device - WAN Miniport (PPTP) dialog box, type **25** in the Maximum ports spin box, as shown in Figure 11-19. Click **OK**.

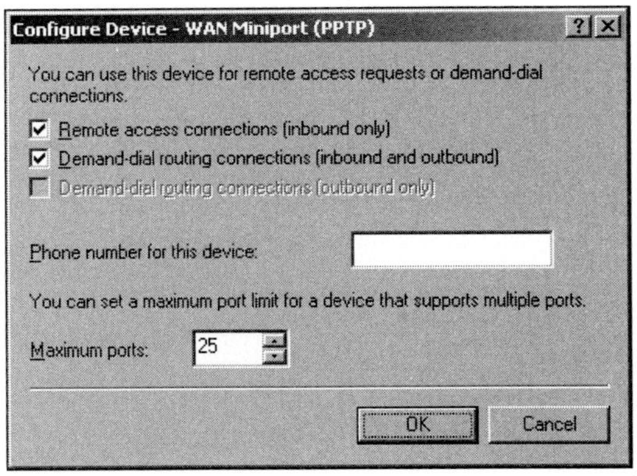

Figure 11-19 Configuring PPTP ports

6. Click **OK** to close the Ports Properties dialog box. Click on the Ports icon. Notice that 25 PPTP WAN Miniports are now available, as illustrated in Figure 11-20. This would allow 25 PPTP clients to connect to the server simultaneously.

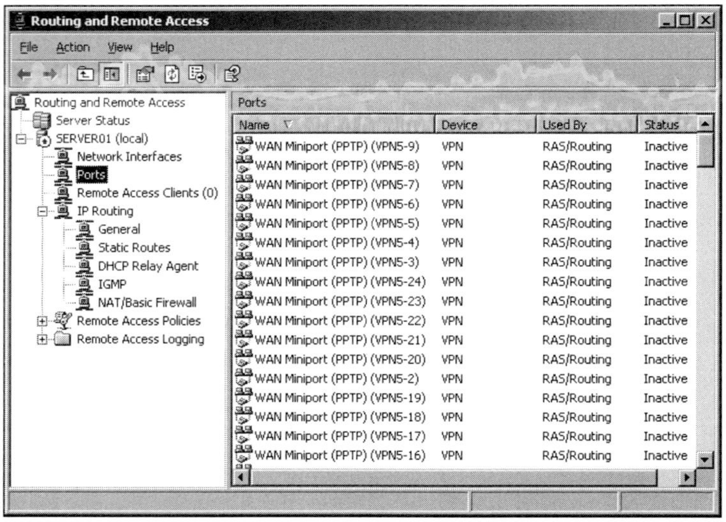

Figure 11-20 Viewing available RRAS ports

7. Right-click any one of the WAN Miniport (PPTP) ports, and then click **Status**. This displays the current status of the port, as shown in Figure 11-21. Click **Close**.

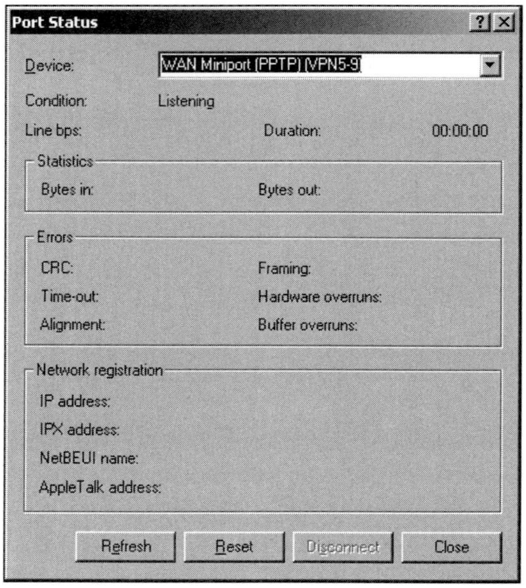

Figure 11-21 Viewing the status of a PPTP port

8. Close the Routing and Remote Access window.

VPN Client Configuration

Configuring a VPN client is also similar to configuring the dial-up client, in that you use the New Connection Wizard to create the VPN connection object. Unlike a dial-up connection, where only a phone number is specified, a VPN connection requires that an FQDN or IP address be provided instead.

If you are configuring a VPN connection for a client that connects to the Internet using a dial-up connection, the New Connection Wizard gives you the option of also specifying a dial-up connection to be dialed before the VPN connection is initiated. This allows a client to connect to a VPN server in a single step, rather than two individual steps. In cases where a dedicated connection to the Internet already exists, only the IP address or FQDN of the VPN server needs to be provided. In Activity 11-6, you will configure a client VPN connection for your server.

Activity 11-6: Configuring and Testing a VPN Client Connection

Time Required: 15 minutes

Objective: Configure and test a VPN client connection.

Description: Having worked with dial-up connections on a variety of operating systems in the past, you are interested in learning more about how to configure VPN settings using the New Connection Wizard and the properties of a connection object. In this activity, you will configure a new connection object to provide VPN access to the Dover Leasing network and then test this connection by attempting to connect to your server.

1. Click **Start**, select **Control Panel**, select **Network Connections**, and then click **New Connection Wizard**.
2. At the New Connection Wizard welcome screen, click **Next**.
3. At the Network Connection Type screen, click the **Connect to the network at my workplace** radio button. Click **Next**.
4. At the Network Connection screen, click the **Virtual Private Network connection** radio button, and click **Next**.
5. At the Connection Name screen, type **Dover Leasing VPN** in the Company Name text box and click **Next**.
6. At the Public Network screen, click the **Do not dial the initial connection** radio button, as shown in Figure 11-22. Click **Next**.

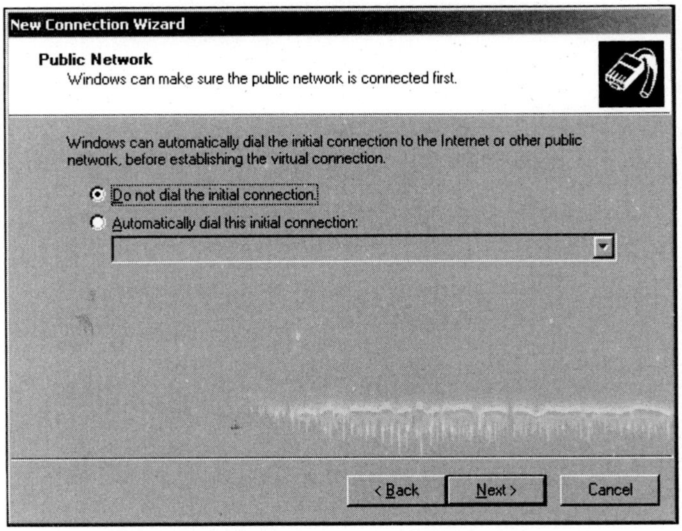

Figure 11-22 Configuring a connection to dial for a VPN connection

7. At the VPN Server Selection screen, type **192.168.1.*X*** in the Host name or IP address text box, where *X* is your student number. Click **Next**. This is illustrated in Figure 11-23.

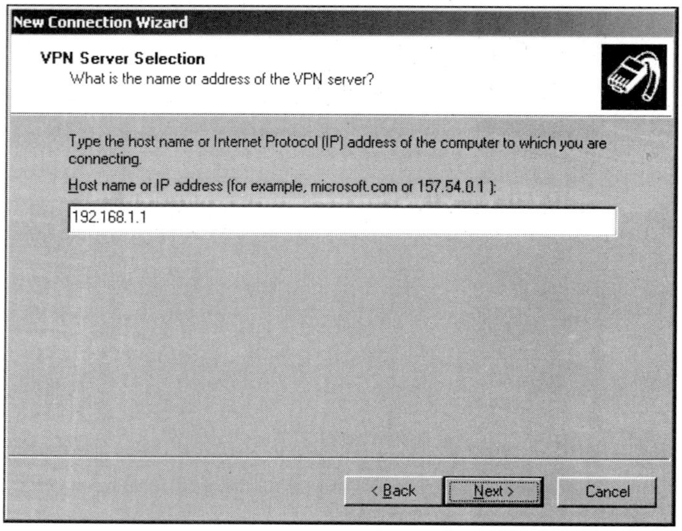

Figure 11-23 Configuring the IP address for a VPN connection

8. At the Connection Availability screen, click **Next**, and then click **Finish**.
9. At the Connect Dover Leasing VPN screen, type **Admin*XX*** in the User name text box if necessary, and your password in the Password text box, as illustrated in Figure 11-24.

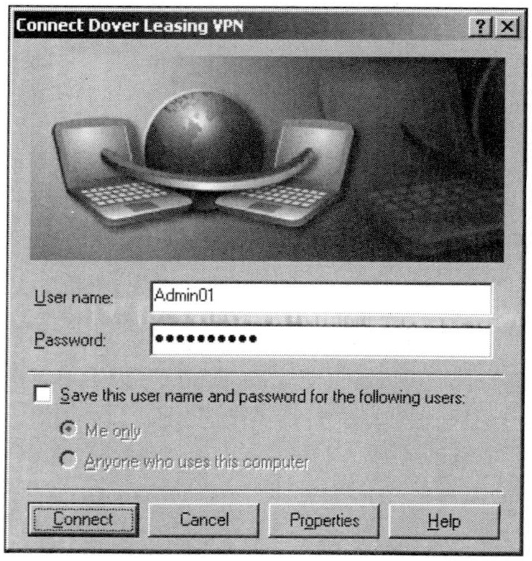

Figure 11-24 Logging on using a VPN connection

10. Click **Connect**. After a few seconds, the dialog box shown in Figure 11-25 should open because the Admin*XX* account does not have permission to access the network remotely. Click **Close**.

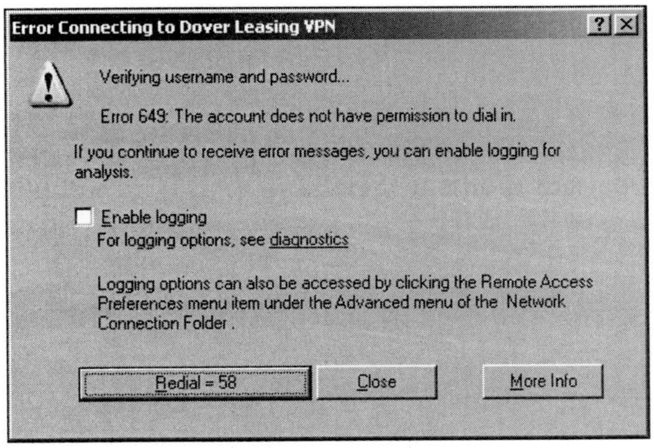

Figure 11-25 Error for user account without dial-in permission

11. Click **Start**, select **Administrative Tools**, and then click **Active Directory Users and Computers**. If necessary, click the **plus sign (+)** to expand your server.
12. Click the **Users** folder, if necessary, and then right-click the **Admin*XX*** user account and click **Properties**.
13. Click the **Dial-in** tab, and then click the **Allow access** radio button, as shown in Figure 11-26. Click **OK**, and then close Active Directory Users and Computers.

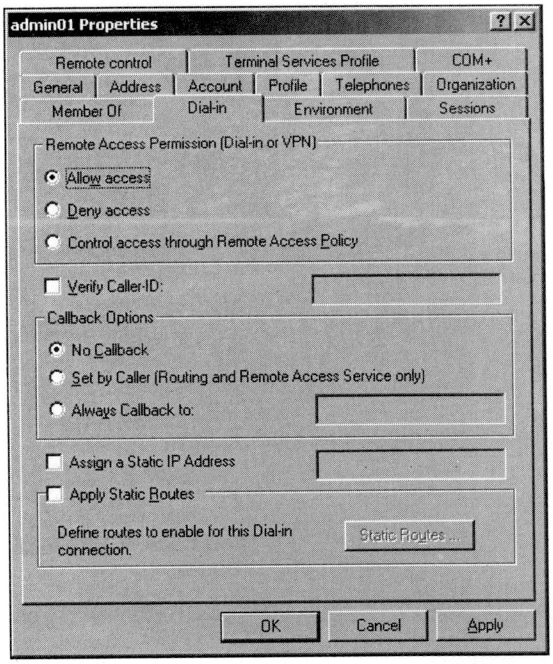

Figure 11-26 Configuring remote access permissions for a user account

14. Click **Start**, select **Control Panel**, select **Network Connections**, and then click **Dover Leasing VPN**.
15. In the Connect Dover Leasing VPN dialog box, type **Admin*XX*** in the User name text box if necessary, and your password in the Password text box. Click **Connect**.
16. Once the connection process is complete, a new network status icon will appear in your System Tray. Click this icon to open the Dover Leasing VPN Status dialog box, as shown in Figure 11-27.

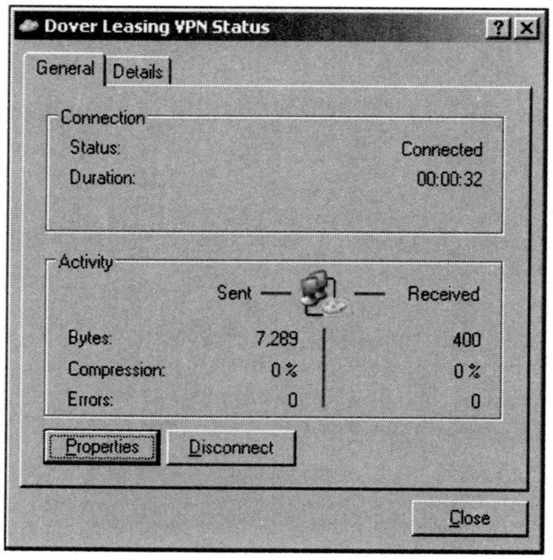

Figure 11-27 View the status of a VPN connection

17. Click the **Details** tab. This shows the current parameters of the VPN connection, as illustrated in Figure 11-28. Click **Close**.

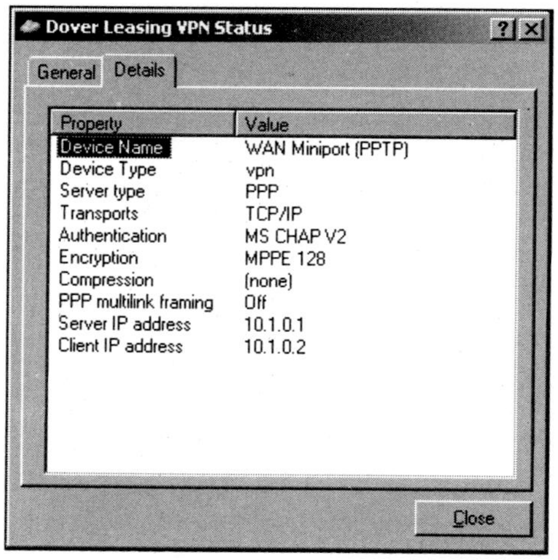

Figure 11-28 Viewing the Details of a VPN connection

18. Click **Start**, click **Run**, and in the Open text box type **cmd.exe**. Click **OK**.
19. At the command line, type **ipconfig** and press **Enter**. Notice that your server now has three IP addresses assigned, as shown in Figure 11-29. Note that one PPP adapter is for the PPTP server interface, while the other is the address assigned to the PPTP client connection.

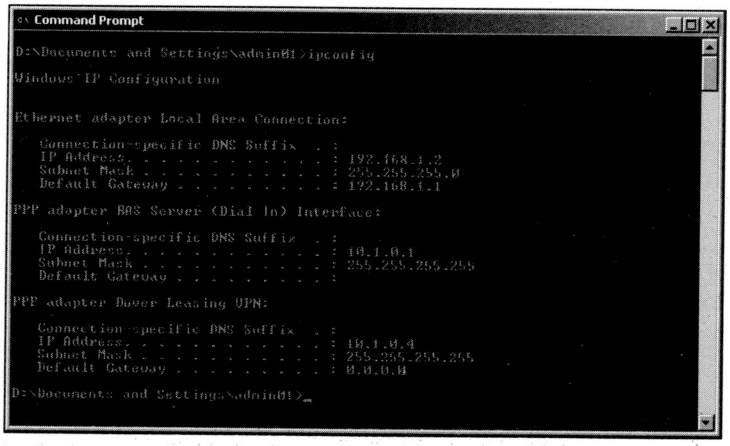

Figure 11-29 Viewing TCP/IP settings with a VPN connection

20. Click **Start**, select **Administrative Tools**, and then click **Routing and Remote Access**.
21. Click the **Remote Access Clients** icon. Notice that one active client connection now exists, as shown in Figure 11-30.

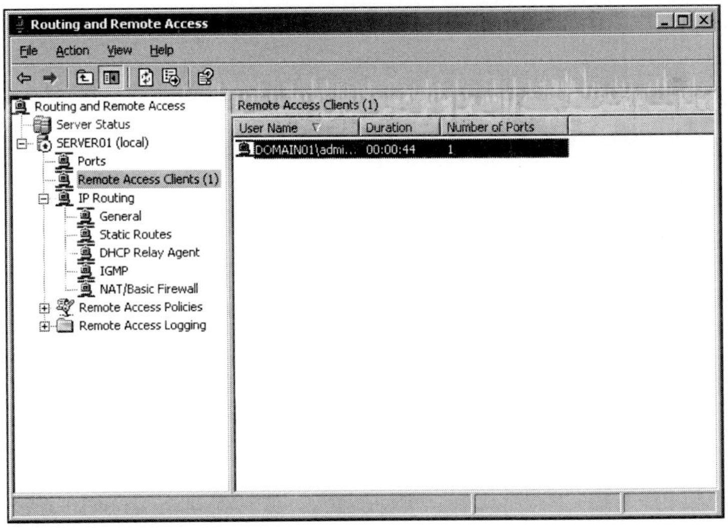

Figure 11-30 Viewing remote access client connections in the RRAS console

22. Right click on the **network status** icon for the VPN connection in the System Tray and click **Disconnect**.
23. Close all open windows.

Tip: Although the ability to control remote access connections is configured from the Dial-in tab of a user account's properties, these settings apply to both dial-in and VPN connections.

Configuring Remote Access Authentication

The first step to making remote access as secure as possible is to configure remote access authentication options. Windows Server 2003 provides several options that you can use to authenticate users who connect to a remote access server using either dial-up or VPN. The type of protocol you use depends on the level of security required and the type of clients requiring access. You also have the option of implementing unauthenticated access.

Authentication protocols for an RRAS server are configured in the Routing and Remote Access console by accessing the Security tab in the properties dialog box of a server, as illustrated in Figure 11-31. By default, Windows Authentication is used for client requests, but **remote authentication dial-in user service (RADIUS)** authentication can also be chosen in environments with a configured RADIUS server.

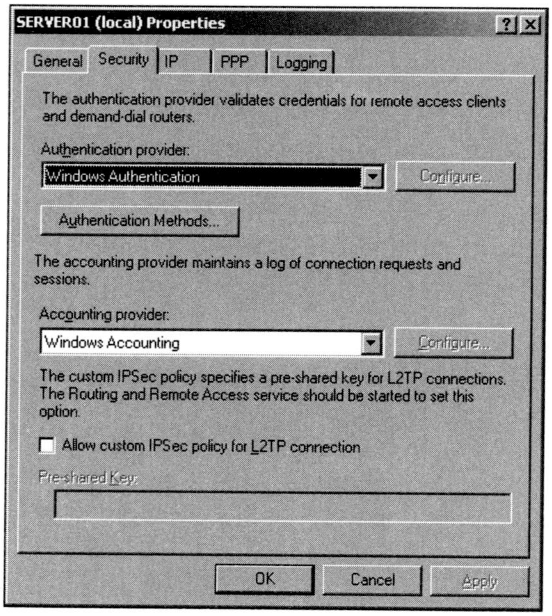

Figure 11-31 Viewing server Security settings

Windows .NET Server supports a variety of different authentication protocols. By default, the three authentication protocols that are enabled on a Windows Server 2003 RRAS system are EAP, MS-CHAP v2, and MS-CHAP, as illustrated in Figure 11-32.

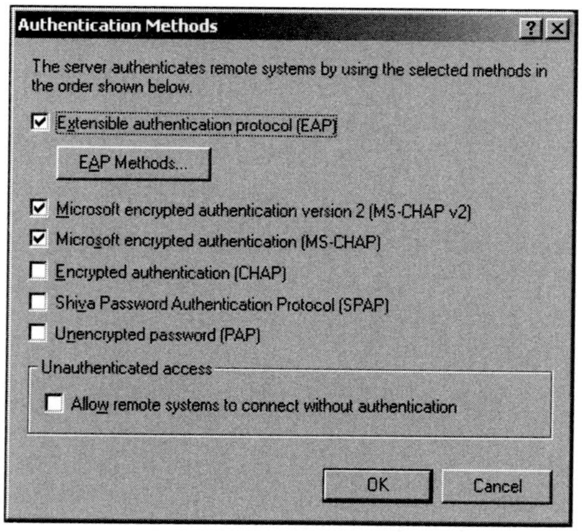

Figure 11-32 Configuring server Authentication Methods

Each of the available authentication options is discussed in the following sections.

MS-CHAP

Microsoft Challenge Authentication Protocol (MS-CHAP) uses a challenge and response handshake for authentication. To begin the authentication process, the RRAS server sends a challenge that includes a challenge string and session identifier to the client. The client responds with a user name, session identifier, password, and a nonreversible encryption of the challenge string that it received from the server. The server checks and authenticates the response if it is valid. MS-CHAP is quite secure because the password is never sent on the network in an unencrypted form.

MS-CHAP v2

MS-CHAP v2 is similar to MS-CHAP but with enhanced security options, including the following:

- LAN Manager authentication is not supported, thus improving security.
- The cryptographic key used for encrypting data is based on the user's password and the challenge string, rather than on the password only.
- Two-way authentication is supported, which means that the client can also authenticate the server.
- A different key is used to encrypt data each time a user connects, and a different key is used to send and receive data.

During MS-CHAP v2 authentication, the Remote Access Service (RAS) server sends a challenge that includes a session identifier and challenge string. The client responds with the user name and a peer challenge string that it generates. The client also sends a one-way encryption of its peer challenge string, the server challenge string, the session identifier, and the user's password. The server checks this response, and then it informs the client if authentication was successful and sends a response based on its challenge string, the peer challenge string, the client's encrypted response, and the user's password. The client must now authenticate the server's response. The client does not use the connection if unable to authenticate the server's response.

MS-CHAP (v1 or v2) is needed for password changes during logon and for using **Microsoft Point-to-Point Encryption (MPPE)** for PPP or PPTP encryption. MPPE is an encryption technique that uses encryption keys varying in length from 40 bits to 128 bits, so that packets traveling between the remote access client and the remote access or tunnel server are secure.

CHAP

Challenge Handshake Authentication Protocol (CHAP) is a challenge-response authentication protocol that uses the industry standard Message Digest 5 (MD5) hashing for encryption. It is supported by various vendors and can be implemented on a Windows Server 2003 RRAS server to enable authentication for non-Microsoft clients.

SPAP

Shiva Password Authentication Protocol (SPAP) uses a reversible encryption method employed by Shiva to encrypt a user's password, although it is not as secure as MS-CHAP or CHAP. The drawback of using this authentication method is that the password is always encrypted in the same reversible form. If you have Shiva clients connecting to your RAS server, this authentication protocol must be enabled.

PAP

Password Authentication Protocol (PAP) is the least secure authentication method because user passwords are sent in clear text. This means that anyone capable of capturing the authentication packet can read the password, which can lead to an unauthorized user gaining access to your network. This authentication method should only be used if the client does not support any of the other protocols listed previously.

EAP

Windows Server 2003 supports **Extensible Authentication Protocol (EAP)** as a remote access authentication protocol. EAP is different than the other options in that it is really a standard for designing other authentication processes. Windows Server 2003 supports two different EAP authentication options:

- *EAP-MD5*—An EAP authentication method that uses the same challenge handshake process as CHAP, but sends the requests and responses as EAP messages
- *EAP-TLS*—An EAP authentication method that is used in certificate-based security environments; used in environments that use smart cards for user logons rather than a traditional user name and password

EAP also provides an Application Programming Interface (API) that supports the creation of any device or process to perform the authentication. This means that you can use EAP when developing a new authentication process, such as a retina or fingerprint scanner, simply by designing the new process to use the EAP APIs.

Unauthenticated Access

Windows Server 2003 also supports remote access connections that do not require any authentication. This option uses the Guest account to gain access to network resources, so the account needs to be enabled and strict permissions need to be set for the account.

If you are using a Windows Server 2003 as the remote access server and Windows 95 or later Microsoft clients, you usually accept the default of supporting only EAP, MS-CHAP v1, and MS-CHAP v2 authentication. In a more secure environment, you can enforce the use of MS-CHAP v2 only. (To use MS-CHAP v2 with Windows 9x clients, you must upgrade the dial-up client.) The most secure option for remote access authentication is EAS-TLS because the user must not only know a PIN number but must also have physical possession of the smart card used during the logon process.

Another option for securing remote access is to use a random password-generating device for both the client and the server. In this case, the user is given a small device that generates a unique password every few minutes. When the user tries to access the remote access server, the user must type in the password that is currently displayed on the device. The server uses the same algorithm to generate passwords, so it has the same current password for the user and the user is authenticated. The advantage of this type of device is that it protects you in case an attacker manages to install an application on your computer that captures your keystrokes as you type in your password. Because the password is only valid for a very short time period, the attacker cannot use the password to log in again. This type of system requires dedicated third-party hardware and software to implement.

Configuring Encryption Protocols

Encryption protocols are used to encrypt the data sent between a client and an RAS server. This ensures that the data passed between a client and server is secure. Where confidentiality is required, such as for financial data, you can configure the remote access server to require encryption of all data or the connection is refused. In cases such as a VPN, encryption should always be required if data is being sent across a public network.

If you are using MS-CHAP (v1 or v2) or EAP, there are two forms of encryption that can be used: Microsoft Point-to-Point Encryption and **IP Security (IPSec)**. IPSec consists of a suite of cryptography-based protection services and protocols that provide machine-level authentication and data encryption.

The MPPE protocol encrypts data for PPP connections including PPTP. MPPE can use 40-, 56-, or 128-bit encryption schemes. For connections that use L2TP, IPSec is used for authentication and encryption of data. Before any information is sent between the two computers, IPSec negotiates the highest encryption for encrypting data and passwords. IPSec uses 56-bit Data Encryption Standard (DES) encryption or triple DES (3DES) encryption. 3DES provides the highest level of security.

Encryption protocols can be enabled through the profile of a **remote access policy**, which is covered in detail later in the chapter. Four different encryption levels are supported on an RRAS server, as outlined in Table 11-2, and illustrated in Figure 11-33.

Although you can configure different encryption settings on an RRAS server, appropriate settings must also be configured on the remote access client for the client to connect successfully. Client encryption settings are configured from the properties of a dial-up or VPN connection.

By default, a Windows Server 2003 will use encryption settings that are compatible with the default configuration of an RRAS server. In other words, the client will use an encryption setting that meets the requirements originally illustrated in Figure 11-33. However, advanced client encryption settings can be configured from the Security tab in the properties dialog box of a VPN connection object, as shown in Figure 11-34.

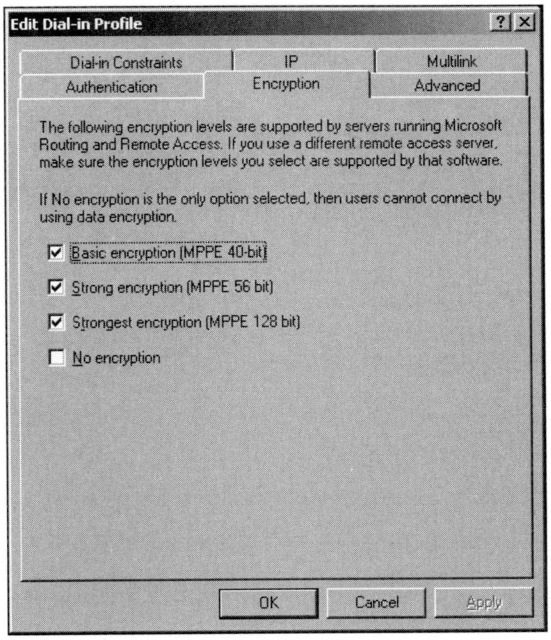

Figure 11-33 Viewing remote access profile Encryption settings

11

Table 11-2 Encryption options

Option	Description
No Encryption	Encryption is not enabled for the Remote Access policy.
Basic	MPPE 40-bit or IPSec 56-bit encryption is used.
Strong	MPPE 56-bit or IPSec 56-bit encryption is used.
Strongest	MPPE 128-bit or IPSec 3DES encryption is used.

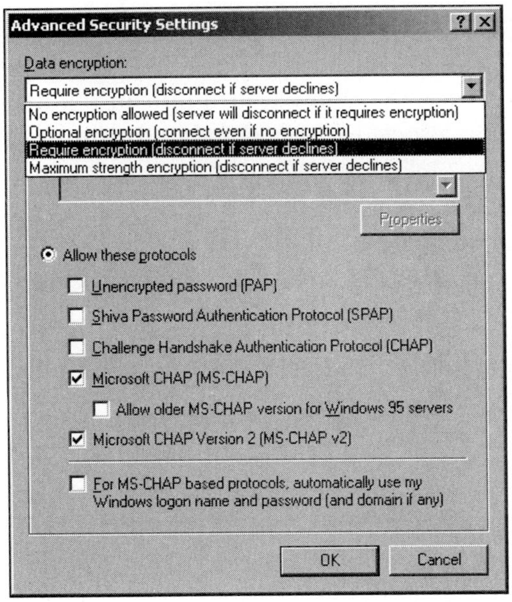

Figure 11-34 Viewing advanced security settings

Tip

Dial-up client connection objects do not use encryption by default, but encryption can also be configured if required by the dial-in server.

Troubleshooting Remote Access

If you cannot successfully connect to a dial-up or VPN-based RRAS server, check the following list of possible solutions:

- Verify that all dial-up credentials such as user name and password are correct.
- Ensure that remote access is enabled on the RRAS server.
- Check to see that ports such as PPTP or L2TP are enabled for inbound remote access connections. These ports may also be used up, which would prevent additional connections.
- If attempting to connect to a VPN server using L2TP, ensure that the client has a computer certificate properly installed.
- Ensure that the remote access server and remote access client are configured with at least one common authentication and encryption method between the two.
- Check the remote access policy to be sure that it is configured to allow access.
- Verify that there are enough addresses in the static IP address range.
- Ensure that a DHCP Relay Agent has been configured. This should be the first thing you check if clients cannot see resources inside the network. Remember that the DHCP Relay Agent provides the additional options that are needed to browse the network, such as a WINS or DNS IP address.
- Ensure that packet filters are not being used that may restrict access.
- Check to be sure that the network adapter that is connected to the Internet is configured with a static IP address.

Implementing and Troubleshooting Remote Access Policies

In earlier versions of Windows, permission to dial into an RRAS server was controlled by enabling dial-in permission directly in the properties of a user account only. One of the major drawbacks to this was that individual user accounts had to be configured, and if there were a large number of users on the network, it could dramatically increase network administration. Windows Server 2003 uses the dial-in properties of user accounts as well as remote access policies to grant users the ability to dial into an RRAS server. The combination of the two now reduces the administration associated with granting dial-in access and provides an administrator with greater flexibility for authorizing connection attempts.

By default, all user accounts in an Active Directory domain have the dial-in properties configured to the Control Access through Remote Access Policy setting. This setting allows whether or not a client will be able to connect to be determined via the settings configured in policies stored on an RRAS server.

In the following sections, you learn the elements that make up a remote access policy, the steps that you need to take to create a policy, and some troubleshooting tips that you might find useful while working with a remote access policy.

Elements of a Remote Access Policy

A remote access policy consists of the following three elements that must be evaluated before a user is allowed to dial in:

- Conditions
- Permissions
- Profile

Each element is described in turn and then the process of applying a remote access policy is outlined.

Conditions

Remote access policy conditions are attributes that are compared to a connection attempt. For example, conditions can include attributes such as the phone number from which the user is calling, the day of the week and time of day the user is permitted to dial in (or attempt a VPN connection), and the group or groups of which the user must be a member. For each user that dials in, the remote access server evaluates the conditions to make sure they match the connection attempt. The remote access server evaluates all remote access policies that are configured until it finds one that matches the connection attempt. Once the server finds a policy whose conditions are met by a connection attempt, no further conditions are considered. Because of this, the order in which remote access policies are configured can have an important impact on whether or not a user is able to connect, as well as the settings applied to them if they can connect.

Permissions

Permissions for a remote access policy are a combination of user account permissions as well as those defined in the policy. If the connection attempt matches the condition in one of the remote access policies, the remote access permissions are then evaluated. If the user is denied access under their account properties, the user is not permitted dial-in access. If the user is allowed access, the policy evaluation continues. If the dial-in permission under the properties of the user account is set to Control access through Remote Access Policy, the permissions configured in the policy are evaluated and the user is either allowed or denied access.

Note: The default remote access permission assigned on a Windows Server 2003 RRAS server is set to Deny access for all connections. Because user accounts are set to the Control Access through Remote Access Policy setting by default, users are denied access unless explicitly allowed in the properties of their user account. You can change the behavior by configuring new remote access policies and settings.

Profile

The final stage in the policy evaluation process is to match the connection attempt to the remote access policy profile. If the connection is authorized, meaning the user has been granted access either through their user account settings or through a remote access policy, the settings configured in the profile are evaluated. The profile consists of settings such as dial-in constraints, multilink properties, authentication protocols, and encryption properties. If the connection attempt matches the remote access policy profile settings, the user is granted access.

When a User Attempts a Connection

The following steps illustrate the process that occurs when a user attempts a connection:

1. The remote access policy is checked. If there is no policy, the connection attempt is rejected. If there are multiple policies, the first policy in the list is evaluated. If the conditions do not match the connection attempt, the next policy in the list is evaluated. If none of the conditions in any of the policies match the connection attempt, the attempt is denied.
2. If the conditions in one of the policies match the connection attempt, the permissions are then evaluated.
3. If the user has been denied access, the connection attempt is rejected. If the user has been granted access, the user account and remote access profile settings are evaluated. If the settings match the connection attempt, access is granted. If the settings do not match the connection attempt, access is denied.
4. If the Control access through Remote Access Policy permission is selected on the Dial-in tab of a user account, the permissions in the remote access policy are evaluated. If the Deny remote access permission is selected, access is denied. If the Grant remote access permission is selected, the user account and profile settings are evaluated. If the user account and profile settings do not match the connection attempt, access is denied. If the user account and profile settings do match the connection attempt, access is granted.

Creating a Remote Access Policy

When RRASs are installed, two default policies called Connections to Microsoft Routing and Remote Access server and Connections to other access servers are created, as illustrated in Figure 11-35. By default, this policy has one condition, which specifies that dial-in access is allowed on any date at any time, as illustrated in Figure 11-35.

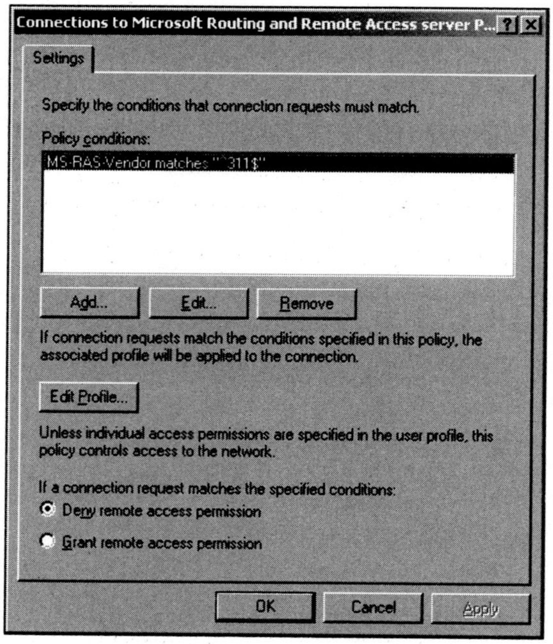

Figure 11-35 Viewing the first default remote access policy

Because this policy specifies connections to Microsoft RRAS servers, any client that attempts to connect will immediately pass the required conditions, and no further policies will be considered. However, recall that the default settings of a user account are set to the Control access through Remote Access Policy setting. The settings on this policy specifically deny access, so the user would be denied. Only if the dial-in properties of the account were set to Allow access would the profile settings of the policy be evaluated. In the default remote access policy, the number of profile restrictions is very few, limited to only the authentication settings displayed in Figure 11-36. As such, almost all clients would be able to connect if their user account settings were explicitly configured to the Allow access setting.

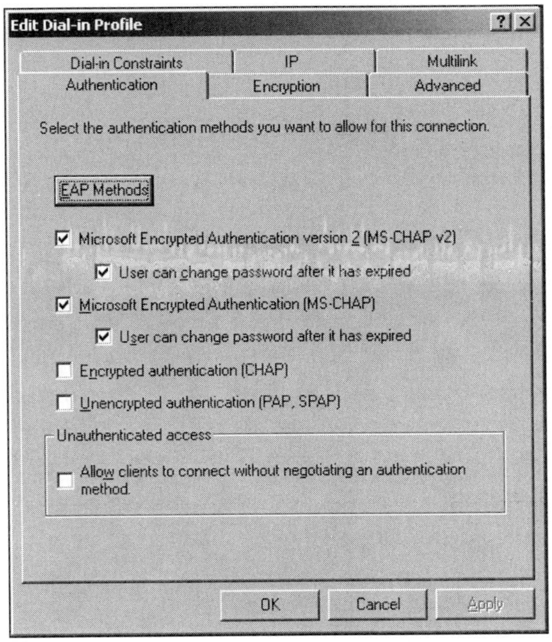

Figure 11-36 Viewing remote access policy Authentication settings

Although the default profile settings are not very restrictive, you can configure a number of additional settings to further control which clients can access the RRAS server. These are listed in Table 11-3.

Table 11-3 Editing the dial-in profile

Tab	Description
Dial-in Constraints	Configures the disconnect times, maximum idle time, day and time restrictions, whether access is restricted to a single number, and whether to restrict access based on the media used
IP	Configures how the client dialing in receives an IP address; can also be determined to restrict the protocols that a client can use
Multilink	Configures whether clients can use multilink, the number of connections they can use, and at what point a link is dropped; can also enable BAP
Authentication	Configures authentication protocols that are available for the policy
Encryption	Configures the encryption level required by clients
Advanced	Used to set RADIUS-specific attributes that can further restrict access

All remote access policies are listed under the Remote Access Policies container within the Routing and Remote Access snap-in. This interface allows you to configure the order of policy processing, as well as add, delete, or edit individual policies.

Note

If there is no policy configured, any connection attempts are denied regardless of the dial-in permissions assigned under the user account properties.

You can change the order in which the policies are evaluated by right-clicking a policy and clicking either Move Up or Move Down, depending on how you want to reorder the list. It is recommended that the policy configured for the majority of remote access users be listed first so that fewer policies have to be evaluated when a user attempts to dial in.

In Activity 11-7, you will configure and test a new remote access policy.

Activity 11-7: Configuring a Remote Access Policy

Time Required: 10 minutes

Objective: Configure a new remote access policy.

Description: As part of planning to provide remote users with access to the Dover Leasing network, the IT manager is very concerned about having a granular level of control over the security settings of all RRAS servers. Furthermore, he is interested in ensuring that the configuration of user account settings can be minimized to the greatest extent possible. In this activity, you will configure a new remote access policy that will be used to restrict connections to remote users that are part of the Domain Admins group and are connecting to the server via a VPN connection.

1. Click **Start**, select **Administrative Tools**, and then click **Routing and Remote Access**. If necessary, click the **plus sign (+)** to expand your server.
2. Click the **Remote Access Policies** node to view its contents. Notice that one policy appears by default, called Allow access if dial-in permission is enabled.
3. Right-click **Remote Access Policies** and click **New Remote Access Policy**.
4. At the New Remote Access Policy Wizard Welcome screen, click **Next**.
5. At the Policy Configuration Method screen, type **Allow Administrators VPN Access** in the Policy name text box and click **Next**.
6. At the Access Method screen, ensure the **VPN** radio button is selected, as shown in Figure 11-37, and click **Next**.

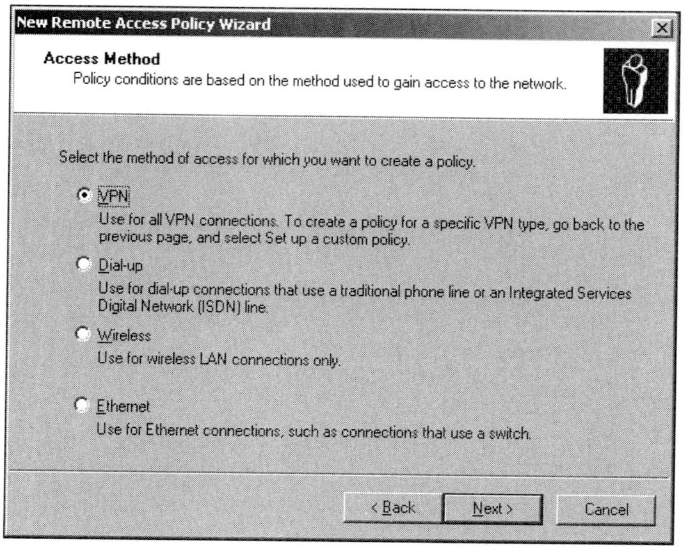

Figure 11-37 Configuring a new remote access policy for VPN users

7. At the User or Group Access screen, click **Add**. In the Enter the object names to select text box, type **DomainXX\Domain Admins** and click **OK**. Click **Next**.
8. At the Authentication Methods screen, click **Next**.
9. At the Policy Encryption Level window, click the **Basic encryption** and **Strong encryption** check boxes to uncheck them, as shown in Figure 11-38. Click **Next**.

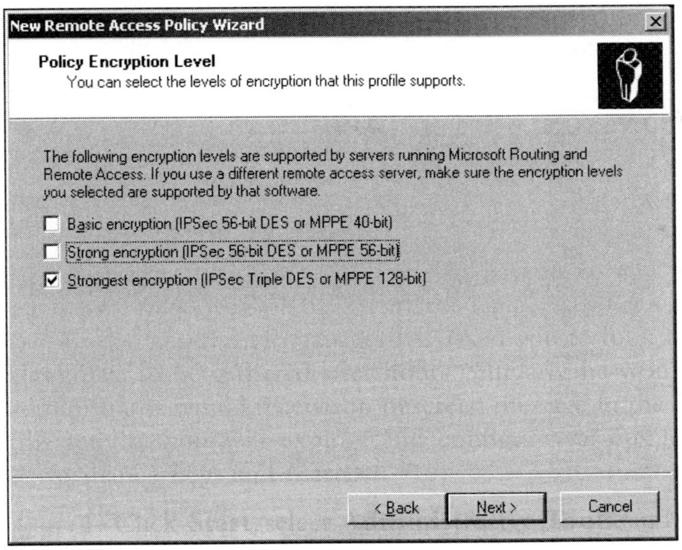

Figure 11-38 Configuring remote access policy encryption settings

10. Click **Finish**. The new remote access policy is now added as the first entry in the list.
11. Right-click the **Allow Administrators VPN Access** policy and click **Properties**.
12. Review the conditions of the new policy, as illustrated in Figure 11-39, as well as the fact that users that meet the conditions of this policy will be granted access. Click **OK**.

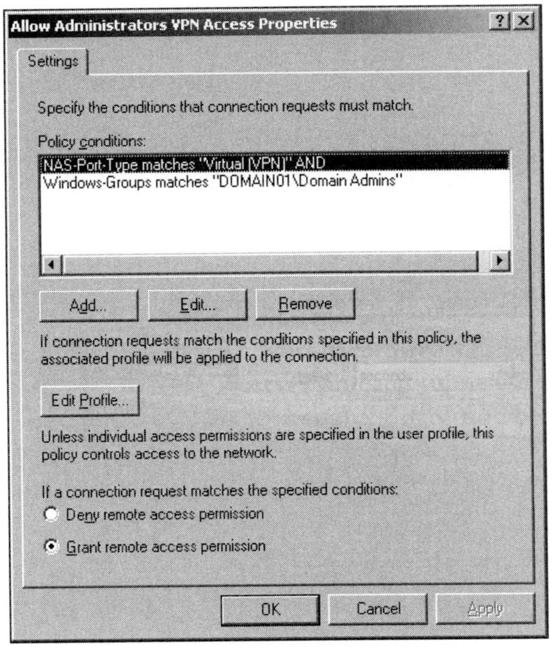

Figure 11-39 Viewing the conditions of a new remote access policy

13. Click **Start**, select **Control Panel**, select **Network Connections**, and then click **Dover Leasing VPN**.
14. Type **mcowan** in the User name text box, and type **password** in the Password text box. Click **Connect**. An error message appears because the mcowan user account does not have dial-in permission and the new policy only allows members of the Domain Admins group. Click **Close**.

15. Click **Start**, select **Administrative Tools**, and then click **Active Directory Users and Computers**. If necessary, click the **plus sign (+)** to expand your server.
16. Click the **Users** container, if necessary, to view its contents.
17. Right-click the **Admin*XX*** user account and then click **Properties**.
18. Click the **Dial-in** tab, and then click the **Control access through Remote Access Policy** radio button. Click **OK**, and then close Active Directory Users and Computers.
19. Click **Start**, select **Control Panel**, select **Network Connections**, and then click **Dover Leasing VPN**.
20. Type **Admin*XX*** In the User name text box if necessary, and type your password in the Password text box. Click **Connect**. The VPN connection is successful because this account is a member of the Domain Admins group.
21. Right-click the **VPN status** icon in the System Tray and click **Disconnect**.
22. Close all open windows.

Troubleshooting Remote Access Policies

There are several problems that can arise with remote access policies. Having a thorough understanding of how remote access policies are applied can assist you in quickly determining the source of the problem. If connection attempts to the remote access server are being rejected, check the following list of possible solutions:

- Verify that the connection attempt matches the conditions of at least one remote access policy.
- Check to be sure the user is not a member of any groups that have been denied access. Be careful of any group nesting that may be taking place, which might be configured to deny remote access.
- Ensure that the user attempting to connect has been granted permission to dial in either through a user account property or through a remote access policy.
- Check to be sure the dial-in settings configured for the user account are not conflicting with those of the remote access policy.
- Verify that the connection attempt matches all of the settings configured in the profile of the policy.

Configuring and Troubleshooting Network Address Translation

Network address translation (NAT) allows a group of computers to access the Internet using a single Internet connection and a single IP address.

If an office wanted to connect their computers to the Internet, they would have to obtain a public IP address for each computer or use a proxy server to limit the number of public addresses required. NAT provides a simple solution to this by allowing the use of private IP addresses on the internal network and mapping the private addresses to a public address when a computer requires access to the Internet. For example, a small office could assign the computers IP addresses in the range of 172.16.0.0 to 172.31.255.255 and obtain a single IP address from its ISP. When a computer on the internal network accesses the Internet, the private IP address is translated into the public IP address. The mappings of the internal client addresses and the public address are stored in a table so the server routes the request to the correct client.

A computer running NAT provides several different services, which allow multiple computers to share a single Internet connection:

- *Address translation*—The computer running NAT translates the internal IP addresses to a public address forwarding the packets between the private network and the Internet.

- *IP addressing*—The NAT computer runs a simplified version of DHCP providing IP-addressing information to clients on the internal network. The computers on the internal network are configured as DHCP clients. The NAT computer can then assign them an IP address, subnet mask, and the IP address of the default gateway (the NAT server itself).
- *Name resolution*—The NAT computer can also become a DNS proxy for internal clients. If configured, any name resolution requests that are received by the NAT server are forwarded to the appropriate DNS server on the Internet and returned to the requesting client.
- *Basic Firewall*—Windows Server 2003 includes a new NAT feature known as Basic Firewall. This allows the NAT interface connected to the Internet to act as stateful firewall, either protecting internal clients from unsolicited Internet traffic, or allowing only replies to requests that originated from this server back to the server.
- *Static Packet Filters*—The configuration of static packet filters allows an administrator to explicitly define the types of traffic that are allowed into the network without solicitation, or out of the network from internal clients.

Installing NAT

You can configure NAT by installing and enabling RRAS using the steps outlined earlier in the chapter. Make sure you select the options for Internet connection server and setting up a router with network address translation. If RRAS is already installed and configured, you can add the NAT protocol to the server manually.

After the NAT protocol is installed, you can configure it using the Routing and Remote Access snap-in. Table 11-4 summarizes the property settings associated with the NAT protocol on a Windows Server 2003 system.

Table 11-4 Configuring NAT

Tab	Description
General	Use to configure event logging; you can choose to Log errors only, Log errors and warnings, Log the maximum amount of information (use this option if you have just installed NAT and want to get an idea of what is happening), and Disable event logging.
Translation	Use to configure timeout values for translations.
Address Assignment	Use to enable the DHCP service for NAT and configure a range of IP addresses to be assigned to internal clients.
Name Resolution	Use to configure which clients the NAT server resolves IP addresses for and how name resolution is handled.

Activity 11-8: Implementing NAT

Time Required: 10 minutes

Objective: Implement NAT on a Windows Server 2003 system.

Description: In the past, all computers at Dover Leasing were assigned a static and public IP address to provide access to the Internet. Although this model once met the company's needs, growth in the number of users has meant that the company has run out of public addresses and has switched to using private IP addresses for internal clients. Although a dedicated hardware router handles the NAT function at the head office, the IT manager is interested in potentially using the Windows Server 2003 version of NAT at branch office locations. In this activity, you will install and configure NAT on your server.

1. Click **Start**, select **Administrative Tools**, and then click **Routing and Remote Access**. If necessary, click the **plus sign (+)** to expand your server.
2. Click the **plus sign (+)** next to IP Routing to expand it. Right-click the **General** icon, and then click **New Routing Protocol**.

3. In the New Routing Protocol dialog box, click **NAT/Basic Firewall** if it is not already selected, as illustrated in Figure 11-40. Click **OK**.

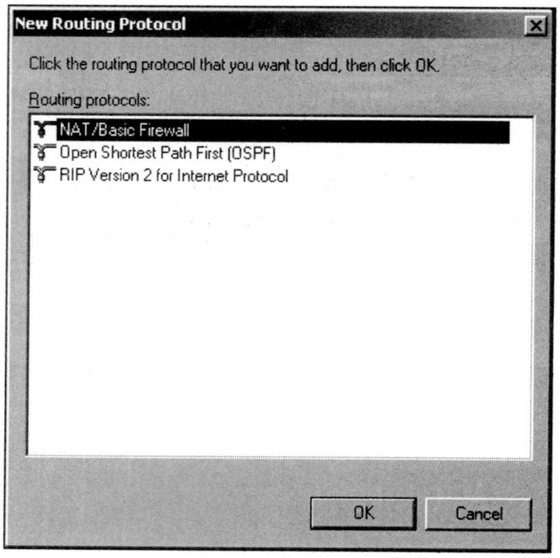

Figure 11-40 Installing NAT/Basic Firewall on an RRAS server

4. Right-click the **NAT/Basic Firewall** icon and click **Properties**. Review the options on the General tab.
5. Click the **Translation** tab to view the default timeouts associated with TCP and UDP entries.
6. Click the **Address Assignment** tab. This tab allows you to configure the NAT server to allocate IP addresses to clients automatically.
7. Click the **Name Resolution** tab, as illustrated in Figure 11-41. This tab allows you to configure the NAT server such that it will act as a DNS proxy for client requests. Click **OK**.

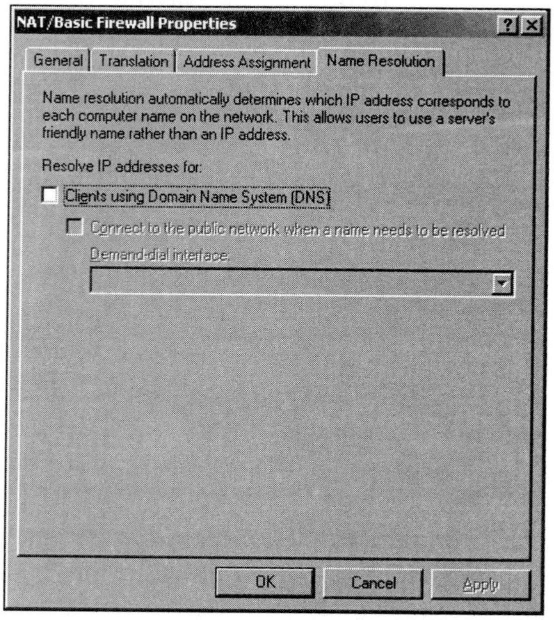

Figure 11-41 Viewing NAT Name Resolution settings

8. Right-click the **NAT/Basic Firewall** icon and click **New Interface**.

9. In the New Interface for Network Address Translation (NAT) dialog box, click **Local Area Connection** and click **OK**.
10. In the Network Address Translation Properties dialog box, click the **Public interface connected to the Internet** radio button, as illustrated in Figure 11-42.

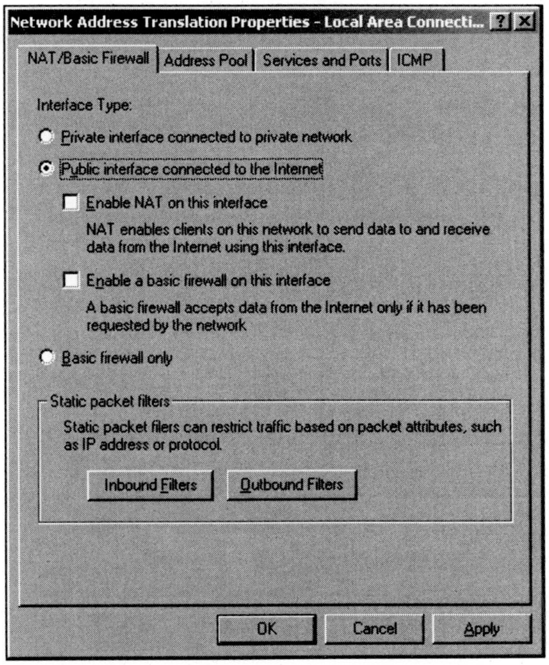

Figure 11-42 Configuring a NAT public interface

11. Click the **Enable a basic firewall on this interface** check box.
12. In the Static packet filters section, click the **Outbound Filters** button.
13. In the Outbound Filters dialog box, click the **New** button.
14. In the Add IP Filter dialog box, click the **Source network** check box. In the IP address text box, type **192.168.1.0**. In the Subnet mask text box, type **255.255.255.0**. In the Protocol list box, click **TCP**. Type **80** in the Destination port text box, as illustrated in Figure 11-43. This will stop all internal clients from accessing external Web servers configured to use TCP port 80. Click **OK**.

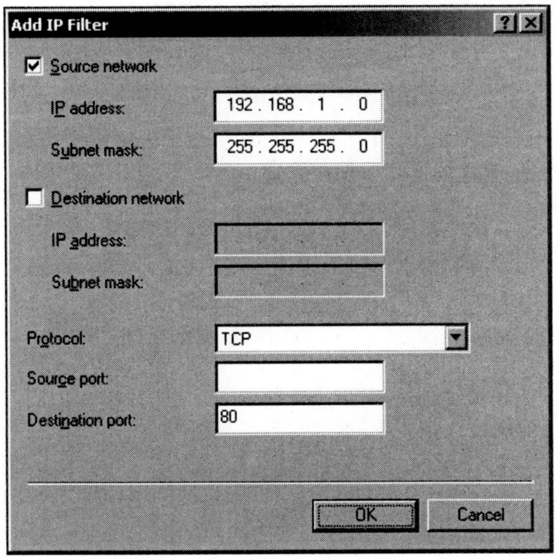

Figure 11-43 Configuring an outbound NAT filter

11

15. In the Outbound Filters dialog box, review the properties of the new filter, and click **OK**. Click **OK** to close the Network Address Translation Properties dialog box. Click **OK** in the warning dialog box.
16. Right-click the **NAT/Basic Firewall** icon and click **Delete**. When prompted to confirm, click **Yes**.
17. Right-click the **Server*XX*** icon, and then click **Disable Routing and Remote Access**. When the Routing and Remote Access dialog box opens, click **Yes**.
18. Close all open windows.

Note: NAT provides you with the option to use your own DHCP server or use the Address Assignment features built into NAT itself. This is one of the main differences between NAT and ICS. ICS does not give you the option to configure an alternate IP address range or use a different DHCP server. ICS is discussed in more detail later in the chapter.

Troubleshooting NAT

Problems with NAT can usually be attributed to incorrect configuration settings. Problems can be simple to troubleshoot if you understand how NAT works and how it is configured.

If you are experiencing a problem, work through the following:

- If clients are not receiving IP addresses from the NAT computer, verify that NAT addressing has been enabled. Also, verify that there is no other DHCP server running on the network.
- If name resolution is not working for NAT clients, check to be sure that name resolution has been enabled using the Name Resolution tab in the NAT properties dialog box. Also, check the configuration of the NAT computer using the ipconfig command to verify DNS settings.
- If packets are not being properly translated, verify that both the Internet and LAN interface have been added to the NAT protocol. Verify the range of IP addresses that has been configured on the NAT computer. Last, verify that IP packet filtering is not preventing certain Internet traffic from being sent and received.

Configuring Internet Connection Sharing

ICS provides an easy way of connecting multiple computers in a home office or small business to the Internet. Using ICS provides all computers on a LAN with complete access to Internet resources using a single public IP address.

Enabling ICS provides NAT services, IP addressing, and name resolution for computers on the internal network. Each computer can then access the Internet as if they had their own direct connection.

After installing ICS on the computer connected to the Internet, the IP address of the internal network adapter is automatically set to 192.168.0.1. A simplified version of DHCP is installed, which assigns internal clients an IP address (from the network ID of 192.168.0.0/24). A DNS proxy service is also installed to pass internal DNS requests to the DNS server that the computer running ICS is configured to use.

ICS and NAT are both used to connect a small or home office to the Internet. The differences between the two are summarized in Table 11-5.

Table 11-5 Difference between ICS and NAT

ICS	NAT
Uses a single public IP address	Can use a single public IP address or multiple public IP addresses
Assigns internal clients IP addresses from a fixed range	Can configure the range of IP addresses assigned to or used by internal clients
Provides automatic configuration once enabled	Requires some manual configuration
The DNS proxy allocator cannot be disabled	The DNS proxy allocator can be disabled
Does not provide a stateful firewall	Is capable of provided stateful firewall services as well as static inbound and outbound packet filters

Tip

The use of ICS is not limited to connecting a small office to the Internet. Connection sharing can also be enabled for a dial-up or VPN connection to a corporate office, which could then be shared amongst users at a small branch office.

Enabling ICS

ICS is relatively straightforward to enable. It does not require any configuration unless you want to change the applications and services that outside Internet users are able to access on an internal private network. In Activity 11-9, you will configure ICS and related settings for a dial-up connection on your server.

Hands-on Project

Activity 11-9: Enabling ICS on a Dial-up Client Connection

Time Required: 10 minutes

Objective: Enable ICS on a dial-up client connection.

Description: The IT manager at Dover Leasing is aware that many employees have implemented small LANs in their homes over the past few years. As part of providing employees with a remote access solution to the corporate office, he has asked you to evaluate the impact of using ICS to share access amongst a number of home computers. In this activity, you will enable ICS in the properties of a dial-up connection to view the impact that it ultimately has on a server.

1. Click **Start**, select **Connect To**, right-click **Dover Leasing**, and then click **Properties**.
2. Click the **Advanced** tab.
3. Click the **Allow other network users to connect through this computer's Internet connection** check box, as illustrated in Figure 11-44. This will automatically check the lower check box in the section, which allows the connection to be initiated whenever a client on the internal network attempts to access a resource on the remote network.
4. At the Network Connections dialog box, click **OK**.
5. Click the **Settings** button.
6. On the **Services** tab, click the **Web Server (HTTP)** check box, as shown in Figure 11-45.

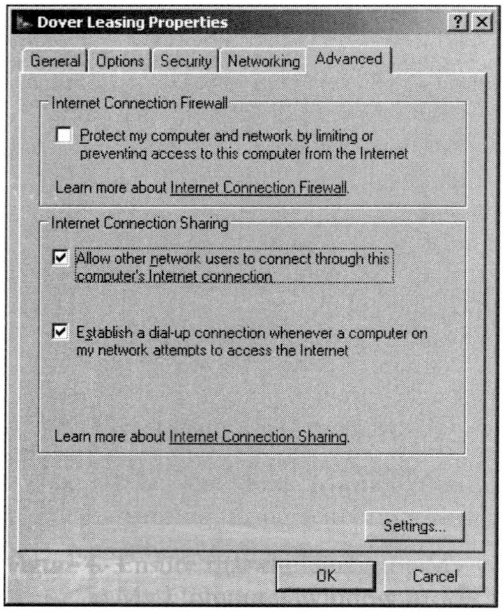

Figure 11-44 Configuring Internet Connection Sharing for a dial-up connection

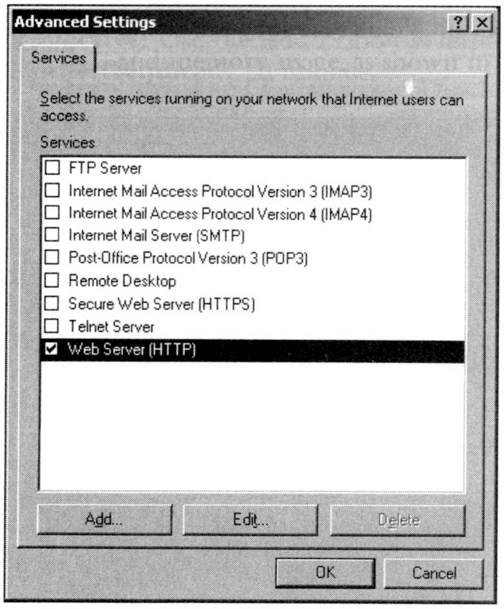

Figure 11-45 Configuring ICS to allow HTTP inbound connections

7. In the Service Settings dialog box, type **192.168.1.100** (or the IP address of the Instructor computer) in the Name or IP address of the computer hosting this service on your network text box, as illustrated in Figure 11-46. Click **OK**.
8. Click **OK** to close the Advanced Settings dialog box, and then click **OK** to close the Dover Leasing Properties dialog box.
9. When the Network Connections window illustrated in Figure 11-47 appears, read the message it provides and click **Yes**.

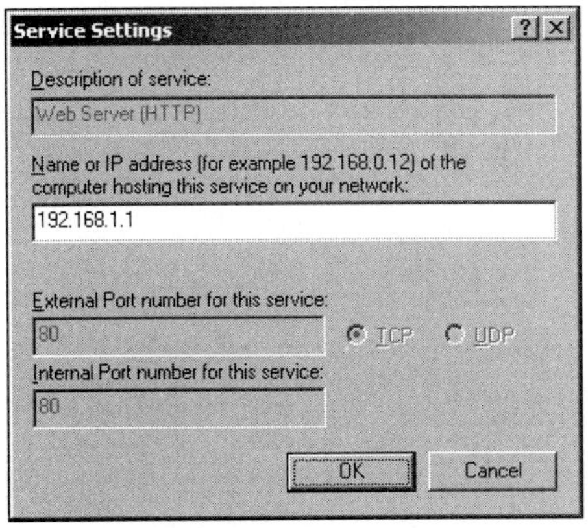

Figure 11-46 Configuring HTTP Service Settings

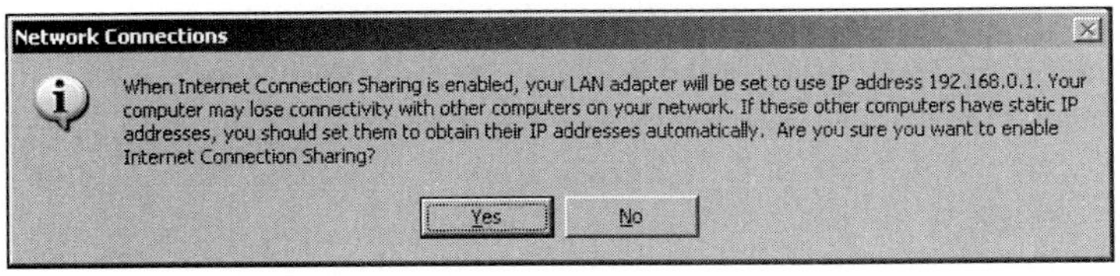

Figure 11-47 ICS changes the private network adapter's IP address

11

10. Click **Start**, click **Run**, and in the Open text box type **cmd.exe**. Click **OK**.
11. At the command prompt, type **ipconfig** and press **Enter**. Verify that the IP address of Local Area Connection is now 192.168.0.1.
12. Click **Start**, select **Connect To**, right-click **Dover Leasing**, and then click **Properties**. Click on the **Advanced** tab, and then uncheck the **Allow other network users to connect through this computer's Internet connection** check box to disable ICS. Click **OK**.
13. Close all open windows.

After ICS is installed, the computer's IP address should be set to 192.168.0.1 with a subnet mask of 255.255.255.0. Those computers that access the Internet through the computer running ICS should be configured to obtain an IP address automatically.

Note: A computer with RRAS installed and configured cannot use ICS unless RRAS is disabled.

Troubleshooting ICS

As with most other services and applications you install and configure on a computer, problems are bound to arise. Although ICS is fairly simple to use, there are some common problems that you may encounter. The following list gives some ways you can verify ICS configuration and troubleshoot common problems.

- After ICS is installed, use the ipconfig command to verify that the network adapter has been assigned the IP address of 192.168.0.1 and the subnet mask is 255.255.255.0.
- If client computers are unable to connect to the Internet, use the ipconfig command to verify that an IP address in the range of 192.168.0.2 through 192.168.0.254 has been assigned, the subnet mask is 255.255.255.0, and the default gateway is set to 192.168.0.1. Use the ping command to verify TCP/IP connectivity with the computer running ICS.

- Verify that there is no DHCP server already running on the network. This may stop the DHCP service included with ICS from functioning correctly.
- If clients are unable to access the Internet using an FQDN, verify that the IP address of a DNS server is configured in the TCP/IP properties of the connection to the Internet.
- If clients can only connect to the Internet after you manually establish a connection, verify that demand dialing is enabled on the ICS computer.

CONFIGURING TERMINAL SERVICES AND REMOTE DESKTOP FOR ADMINISTRATION

Terminal Services provides remote access to a server desktop through "thin client" software, which serves as a terminal emulator. Terminal Services transmits only the user interface of the program to the client. The client then returns keyboard and mouse clicks back to be processed by the server. Traditionally, Terminal Services has been used for two main purposes: centralized access to applications for users, and remote administration of servers. In Windows Server 2003, the ability of users to connect to a server for the purpose of running applications is properly referred to as Terminal Services. However, the ability of an administrator to connect to a server for administration purposes is now known as **Remote Desktop for Administration**. Although Remote Desktop for Administration is installed as part of Windows Server 2003, the feature is disabled by default. Terminal Services is not installed unless explicitly added to a server by an administrator.

Terminal Services can be used to centralize control of applications, allowing organizations to maintain control over specific applications such as financial applications. With Remote Desktop for Administration, a server administrator can remotely access management tools, such as Active Directory Users and Computers, the Computer Management tool, the DNS tool, and others as if physically sitting in front of that server.

In this last section of the chapter, you will learn how to install and manage both Terminal Services and Remote Desktop for Administration.

Enabling Remote Desktop for Administration

The ability to enable Remote Desktop for Administration is a rather simple process. Because it is installed by default, an administrator only needs to change a single setting in the Control Panel System program to allow connections to occur. By default, only members of the Administrators group can connect to a server using Remote Desktop for Administration. However, additional users can also be granted access via the System program. To connect to a server using Remote Desktop for Administration, users need to access the Remote Desktop Connection software from their client system. In Activity 11-10, you will enable and then connect to your server using a Remote Desktop connection.

Activity 11-10: Enabling and Testing Remote Desktop for Administration

Time Required: 10 minutes

Objective: Enable and test Remote Desktop for Administration.

Description: To help reduce administrative costs, the IT manager at Dover Leasing is interested in using the Remote Desktop for Administration feature of Windows Server 2003 to facilitate administrator access to corporate servers. In this activity, you will first enable Remote Desktop for Administration on your server and then connect to the server using the Remote Desktop Connection tool.

1. Click **Start**, select **Control Panel**, and then click **System**.
2. Click the **Remote** tab.
3. Click the **Allow users to connect remotely to this computer** check box, as shown in Figure 11-48.

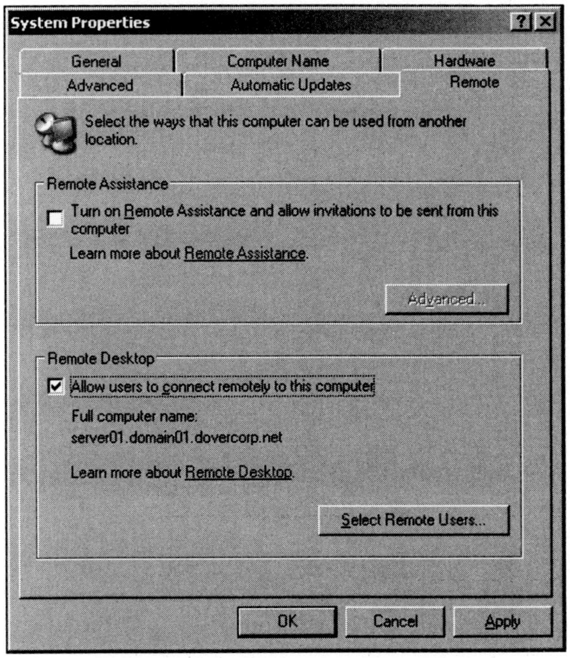

Figure 11-48 Enabling Remote Desktop for Administration

4. When the Remote Sessions dialog box opens, click **OK**.
5. Click the **Select Remote Users** button. Read the dialog box that opens, and then click **OK**.
6. Click **OK** to exit the System program.
7. Click **Start**, select **All Programs**, select **Accessories**, select **Communications**, and then click **Remote Desktop Connection**.
8. In the Remote Desktop Connection dialog box, type **192.168.1.*X*** in the Computer text box, where *X* is your assigned student number. Click the **Options** button.
9. On the General tab, type **Admin*XX*** in the User name text box if necessary, your password in the Password text box, and **Domain*XX*.Dovercorp.net** in the Domain text box, as illustrated in Figure 11-49. Click **Connect**.
10. When the Remote Desktop window opens displaying your desktop, browse through the environment as time permits. Click the **Close** button on the connection bar found at the top of the screen.
11. When the Disconnect Windows session dialog box opens, read the message and then click **Cancel**. If this method is used to close a Remote Desktop session, the session remains active on the server.
12. Click **Start**, and then click **Log Off**. Click the **Log Off** button. This closes the Remote Desktop session.

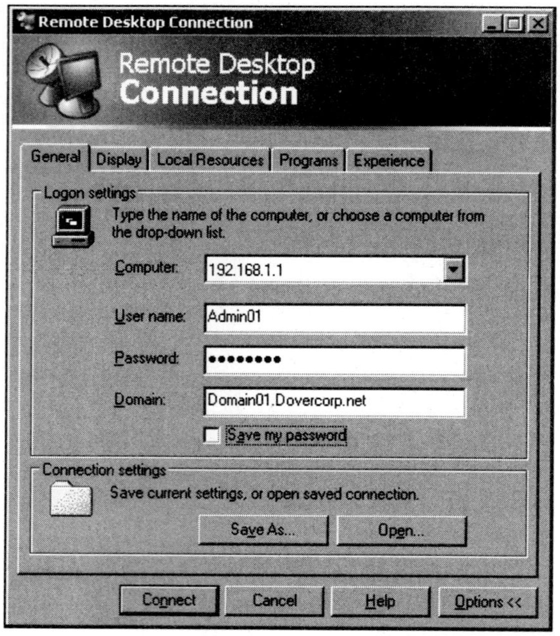

Figure 11-49 Configuring Remote Desktop Connection Logon settings

Installing Terminal Services

Terminal Services is installed from the Add/Remove Windows Components section from within the Add or Remove Programs applet found in Control Panel. Also, if you plan to set up an application server, then one Windows Server 2003 server on the network must also be configured as a Terminal Services licensing server, which would necessitate installing this option. In Activity 11-11, you will install Terminal Services on your server.

Note: Windows Server 2003 is capable of running without a license server for up to 120 days. After that period of time, clients will not be able to connect to a Terminal Server unless a license server is present on the network.

Activity 11-11: Installing Terminal Server

Time Required: 10 minutes

Objective: Install Windows Server 2003 Terminal Server.

Description: Based on the number of client applications to which Dover Leasing employees need access, related administrative tasks are taking up a disproportionate amount of time for the company's IT staff. Because of this, the IT manager at Dover Leasing is seriously considering implementing Terminal Server to centralize the install, management, and access of a number of applications. In this activity, you will install Terminal Server on your server.

1. Click **Start**, select **Control Panel**, and then click **Add or Remove Programs**.
2. Click the **Add/Remove Windows Components** button.
3. In the Windows Components Wizard window, click the check box next to **Terminal Server**. Click **Next**.
4. At the Terminal Server setup screen, read the message that appears, and click **Next**.
5. At the Terminal Server Setup screen, read the options associated with both Full Security and Relaxed Security, as illustrated in Figure 11-50. Leave the Full Security radio button selected, and click **Next**.

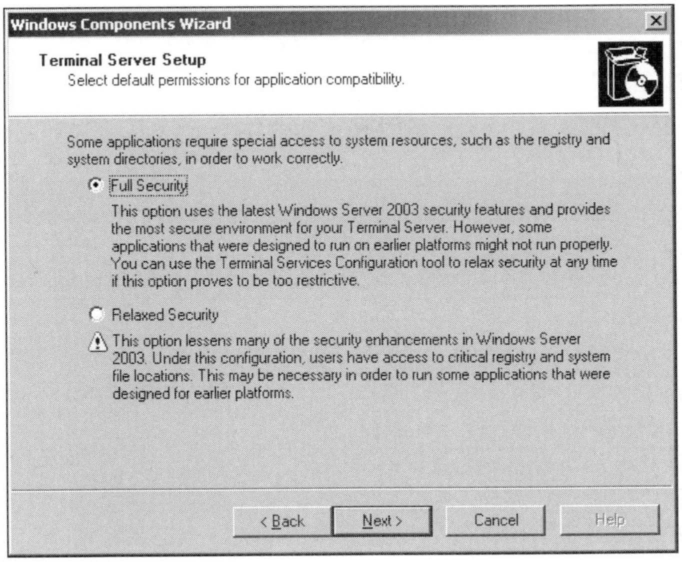

Figure 11-50 Configuring Terminal Server security settings

6. Click **Finish** to complete the installation of Terminal Server. When prompted to restart your server, click **Yes**.
7. Log on with your **Admin*XX*** user account once the reboot is complete. Close the Terminal Server Help window that appears.

Note: By default, members of the Domain Users group are added to the Remote Desktop Users group when Terminal Server is installed. The Remote Desktop Users group has the ability to log on to a Terminal Server by default.

Managing Terminal Services

There are various tools available to administer a computer running Terminal Services once it is installed. The three primary tools used for Terminal Services administration include Terminal Services Manager, Terminal Services Configuration, and Terminal Services Licensing.

Table 11-6 describes the Terminal Services administration tools.

Table 11-6 Terminal Services administrative tools

Administrative Tool	Description
Terminal Services Manager	Used to monitor and control client access to one or more terminal servers
Terminal Services Configuration	Used to configure terminal server settings and connections
Terminal Services Licensing	Used to store and track Terminal Services client access licenses

In the following sections, you learn how to configure remote connections and a Terminal Services client, how to install applications, and how to configure Terminal Services user properties. After you complete these sections, you have all the knowledge you need to create and configure a Terminal Server and provide client access to installed applications.

Configuring Remote Connection Settings

Before configuring client access to a Terminal Server, it is important that you configure the various security and connection-related settings that you require using the Terminal Services Configuration tool. This tool allows you to configure settings related to connection attempts, such as the level of encryption or authentication that is required, or the permissions assigned to various user or group accounts.

Connection settings for a Terminal Server are configured from the properties of a Terminal Server connection object. By default, one connection object exists, which allows multiple user connections to take place. Table 11-7 describes the various configuration areas found within the properties of a connection object.

Table 11-7 Property tabs for a terminal connection

Tab	Description
General	Used to configure authentication and encryption
Logon Settings	Used to configure how the user logs on, by supplying information or with preconfigured information
Sessions	Used to configure timeout settings
Environment	Used to configure a program to run automatically when a user connects
Remote Control	Used to enable remote control of a client
Client Settings	Used to configure client settings such as drive mappings and port mappings
Network Adapter	Used to configure the number of simultaneous connections
Permissions	Used to control user access based on standard permissions, such as allow or deny access

Note: Some of the settings outlined in Table 11-7 can also be configured on a user-by-user basis under the properties of a user account. Any settings configured for a connection override those configured on a user account.

One of the most important settings that you should check when configuring a Terminal Server connection is the implementation of encryption and authentication. Authentication can be set to use either no authentication or standard Windows authentication when the clients are Windows 95, 98, NT, or 2000. The encryption options available include:

- *Client Compatible*—All data sent from the client to the server is encrypted using a key based on the maximum strength supported on the client.
- *High*—Data sent from the client to the server and from the server to the client is encrypted using the highest encryption level available at the server. Clients that do not support this level will not be able to connect.

In Activity 11-12, you will explore connection settings for your Terminal Server.

Activity 11-12: Exploring Terminal Services Settings

Time Required: 10 minutes

Objective: Explore Terminal Services settings.

Description: As part of considering the implementation of Terminal Servers at Dover Leasing, the IT manager is very concerned about retaining a high degree of control over the user environment and how users connect to the server. In this activity, you will use the Terminal Services Configuration tool to configure settings related to a client connection.

1. Click **Start**, select **Administrative Tools**, and then click **Terminal Services Configuration**. The Terminal Services Configuration window opens, as illustrated in Figure 11-51.

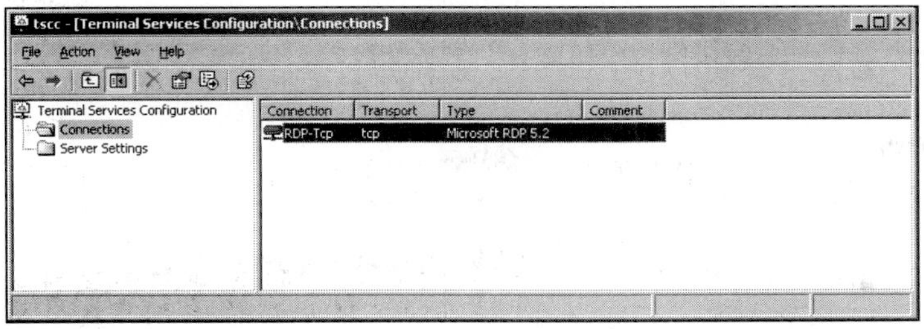

Figure 11-51 The Terminal Services Configuration console

2. Right-click the **RDP-Tcp** icon and click **Properties**.
3. On the General tab, click the **Use standard Windows authentication** check box.
4. Click the **Logon Settings** tab. Click the **Always prompt for password** check box.
5. Click the **Sessions** tab. Click the **Override user settings** check box. In the End a disconnected session list box, click **1 day**. In the Idle session limit list box, click **2 hours**, as illustrated in Figure 11-52.

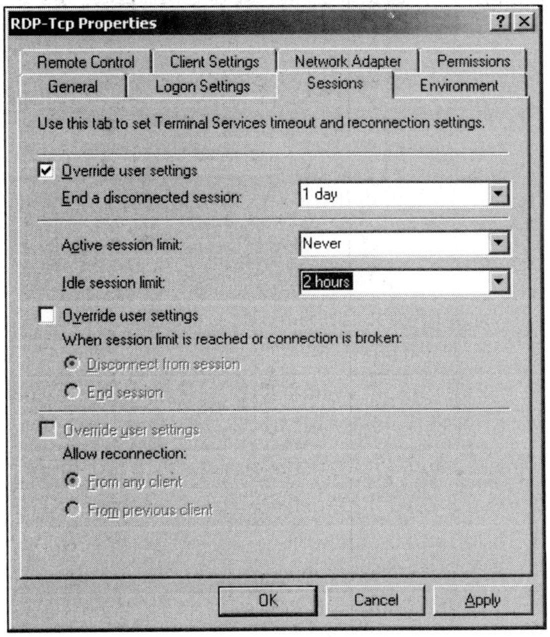

Figure 11-52 Configuring Terminal Services Sessions settings

6. Click the **Environment** tab and read through the purpose of the settings that appear.
7. Click the **Remote Control** tab and read through the purpose of the settings that appear.
8. Click the **Client Settings** tab and read through the purpose of the settings that appear, as illustrated in Figure 11-53.

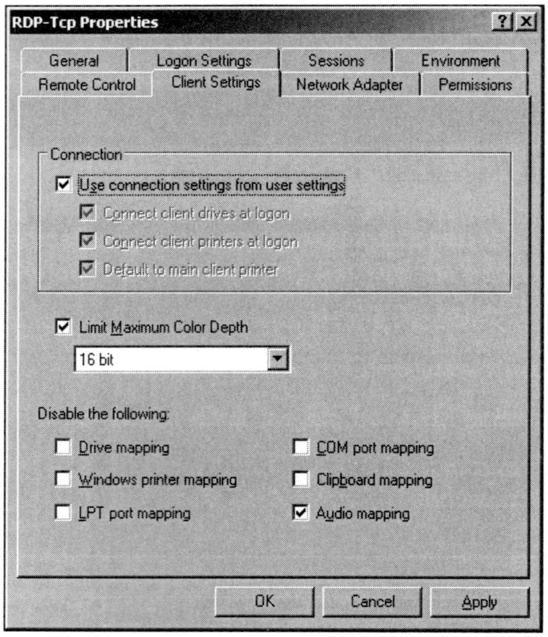

Figure 11-53 Viewing Terminal Services Client Settings

9. Click the **Network Adapter** tab and read through the purpose of the settings that appear.
10. Click the **Permissions** tab, and then click **Remote Desktop Users** in the Group or user names list box. Notice that this group has only the Allow User Access and Guest Access permissions by default, as illustrated in Figure 11-54.

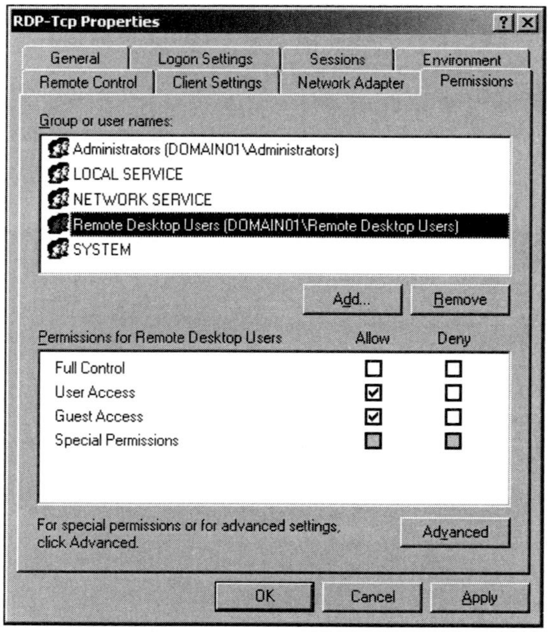

Figure 11-54 Viewing Terminal Services Permissions settings

11. Click **OK** to close the RDP-Tcp properties dialog box, and then close the Terminal Services Configuration window.

Terminal Services Client Software

Once Terminal Server is installed, client software packages are automatically added to the %Systemroot%\system32\clients\tsclient\win32 folder on the Terminal Server. This folder contains the files necessary to install the Remote Desktop Connection software that is used by clients to connect to a Windows Server 2003 Terminal Server. The client software is provided as both an MSI file (msrdpcli.msi) and as a standard Win32 executable (setup.exe). The MSI file is particularly convenient because it can be deployed using Active Directory Group Policy settings. These files can be installed on a variety of operating systems including Window 95, 98, NT 4.0, and 2000. Installation of the client files is not necessary on Windows Server 2003 or Windows XP because the Remote Desktop Connection software is already installed on these operating systems by default.

The recommended method of installing the Remote Desktop Connection software is to share the %Systemroot%\system32\clients\tsclient\win32 folder and then initiate the installation process over the network either manually or through the use of Group Policy software deployment features.

Note: Windows Server 2003 is also capable of handling client connections via a Web browser if the Remote Desktop Web Connection is installed on the server. See the Help and Support Center for more information.

Installing Applications

When you install Windows Server 2003 Terminal Server, applications need to be installed in a compatible mode for multiple users to access them simultaneously. For this reason, you may need to reinstall some applications, as indicated by the Windows Components Wizard when you install Terminal Services. The proper method of installing applications involves using the Add or Remove Programs applet in Control Panel after Terminal Server is installed. Use the same applet to uninstall and reinstall programs that were installed before setting up the server for Terminal Server.

On a terminal server, software applications should be installed only in what is known as install mode, which is automatically invoked when Add or Remove Programs in Control Panel is used. You should avoid installing programs by using the Run option or by double-clicking the installation program from Windows Explorer or My Computer. However, it is possible to place a Windows .NET Server in install mode from the command line if you choose to circumvent the Add or Remove Programs method. To do this, first issue the command change user /install. Then, after installing the application normally, issue the command change user /execute. This will ensure that the program is installed in a multi-user mode compatible with Terminal Server.

Configuring Terminal Services User Properties

When Terminal Server is installed in Windows Server 2003, it adds extra configuration options to the properties of user accounts. There are four extra tabs available when Terminal Server is installed:

- *Terminal Services Profile*—Use this tab to enable the user as a Terminal Services client, to configure a special profile used when users connect to a terminal server, and to configure a home directory.
- *Remote control*—Use this tab to configure remote control properties for the user account. You can also configure these settings under the properties for the connection and, if so, override any settings specified under the user account properties.
- *Sessions*—Use this tab to configure a maximum session time and disconnect options. You can also configure these properties under the properties for the connection and, if so, override any settings configured under the user account.
- *Environment*—Use this tab to configure a program to automatically run when the user connects to the terminal server. For example, you can use this tab to configure a special logon script to be run when a user connects to the terminal server.

Activity 11-13: Exploring Terminal Services User Account Settings

Time Required: 10 minutes

Objective: Explore Terminal Services user account settings.

Description: Although you can configure general connection and environment settings on a global basis using the Terminal Services Configuration tool, the IT manager at Dover Leasing has asked you to explore the various settings that can be configured in the properties of a user account relating to the service. In this activity, you will explore the various tabs added to the properties of a user account after Terminal Server is installed.

1. Click **Start**, select **Administrative Tools**, and click **Active Directory Users and Computers**.
2. Click the **Users** folder to display its contents, if necessary.
3. Right-click the **Admin*XX*** account and then click **Properties**.
4. Click the **Terminal Services Profile** tab, as displayed in Figure 11-55. This tab allows you to configure specific user profile settings that will be used when a user initiates a Terminal Server connection.

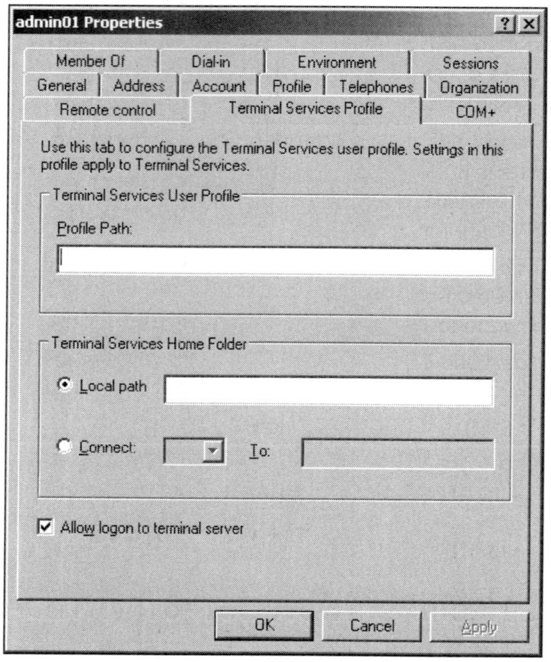

Figure 11-55 Viewing the Terminal Services Profile tab on a user account

5. Click the **Remote control** tab. This tab allows you to configure settings related to whether an administrator is allowed to connect to and control a user's Terminal Server session, as illustrated in Figure 11-56.

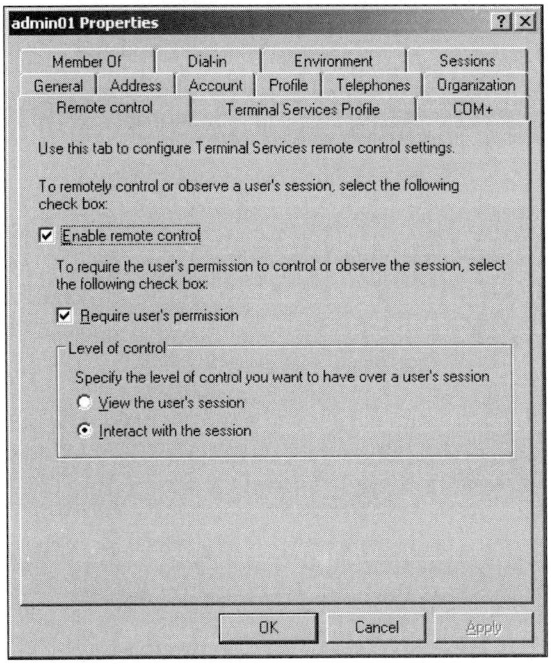

Figure 11-56 Viewing Terminal Services Remote control settings for a user account

6. Click the **Sessions** tab. This tab allows you to configure session settings for this user only.
7. Click the **Environment** tab. This tab allows you to configure settings related to the user's Terminal Server environment, such as whether a program will be run when the user logs on, as illustrated in Figure 11-57.

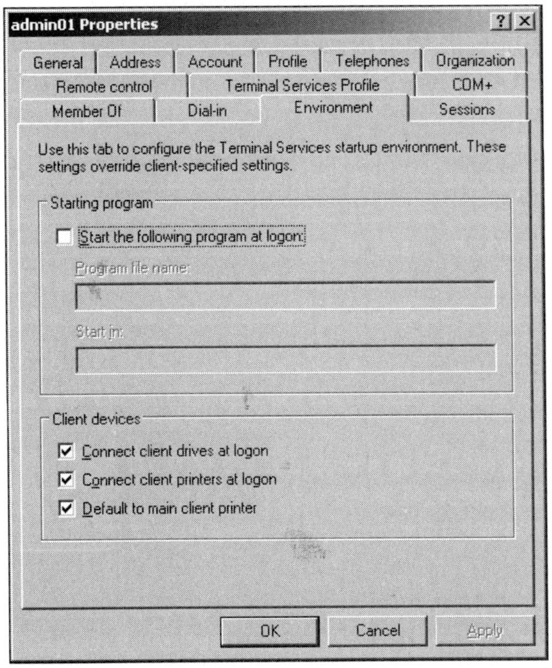

Figure 11-57 Viewing Terminal Services Environment settings for a user account

8. Close all open windows.

Chapter Summary

- A remote access server is a computer running Windows Server 2003 with Routing and Remote Access Services installed and enabled. A remote access server authenticates remote and mobile users, providing a gateway to internal network resources.
- You can implement such remote access solutions as dial-up, VPN, and NAT.
- You can configure each RAS server using the Routing and Remote Access console.
- Windows .NET Server supports two VPN protocols: PPTP and L2TP. L2TP is more secure but requires Windows Server 2003, 2000, or XP machines.
- You can use authentication and encryption protocols to secure communications between the RAS server and a dial-up client.
- Windows .NET Server supports the following authentication protocols: MS-CHAP v1 and v2, CHAP, SPAP, PAP, and EAP.
- You can control dial-in access through user account properties and through Remote Access policies. Remote Access policies consist of conditions, permissions, and profiles. Policies are evaluated in the order in which they appear under the Remote Access Policies container.
- Network address translation (NAT) and Internet connection sharing (ICS) provide a way of connecting computers in a small or home office to the Internet using a single connection.
- Terminal Server is a feature included with Windows Server 2003 that enables clients to access applications on a terminal server. Remote Desktop for Administrators gives administrators the ability to remotely administer network servers.

Key Terms

Challenge Handshake Authentication Protocol (CHAP) — A cross-platform authentication protocol designed for IP- or PPP-based exchange of passwords.

Extensible Authentication Protocol (EAP) — EAP is a standard for developing authentication methods. It allows a client and RAS server to negotiate the exact authentication scheme.

Internet connection sharing (ICS) — A feature included with Windows Server 2003 that enables a small or home office to connect to the Internet. ICS allows a single dial-up connection to be shared among multiple computers.

IP Security (IPSec) — IPSec consists of a suite of cryptography-based protection services and protocols that provide machine-level authentication and data encryption.

Layer 2 Tunneling Protocol (L2TP) — An advanced VPN protocol that is used to establish a secure tunnel between two endpoints over an insecure network. This protocol uses advanced authentication and encryption with the help of IPSec.

Microsoft Challenge Authentication Protocol (MS-CHAP) — A Microsoft-enhanced version of CHAP that can negotiate encryption levels and that uses a highly secure encryption algorithm to encrypt communications between client and host.

Microsoft Point-to-Point Encryption (MPPE) — An encryption technique that uses encryption keys varying in length from 40 bits to 128 bits so that packets traveling between the remote access client and the remote access or tunnel server are secure. Used when IP security is not available.

network address translation (NAT) — A feature included with Windows Server 2003 that enables a small or home office to connect to the Internet using a single connection. It provides address translation as well as DNS and DHCP services.

Password Authentication Protocol (PAP) — The least secure authentication protocol that sends passwords between a client and a server in clear text.

Point-to-Point Protocol (PPP) — Enables remote access clients and servers to communicate over a dial-up connection from any operating system that supports the PPP standards.

Point-to-Point Tunneling Protocol (PPTP) — A VPN protocol that is used to establish a secure tunnel between two endpoints over an insecure network.

remote access policy — A set of conditions that determines how users access the network remotely. A remote access policy consists of conditions, permissions, and profile settings.

remote access server — A computer running Windows Server 2003 and the Routing and Remote Access Service that authenticates remote or mobile users.

remote authentication dial-in user service (RADIUS) — A client/server protocol and software that enables remote access servers to communicate with a central server to authenticate dial-in users and authorize their access to the requested system or service.

Remote Desktop for Administration — A Windows Server 2003 feature that allows a server to be managed remotely using the Remote Desktop tool.

Shiva Password Authentication Protocol (SPAP) — A reversible encryption method employed by Shiva.

Terminal Services — A built-in feature of Windows Server 2003 that allows clients to access applications remotely.

virtual private network (VPN) — Uses a LAN protocol such as TCP/IP which is encapsulated within a WAN protocol to send data over a public network.

Review Questions

1. Which of the following are elements of a remote access policy? (Choose all that apply.)
   a. profile
   b. authentication
   c. permissions
   d. conditions
2. The default remote access policy grants all users permission to dial in. True or False?
3. You are configuring remote access so users can dial in. You delete the default remote access policy and configure the properties of each user account to grant dial-in access. Users report that they are receiving an access denied message when they attempt to connect. What might be the cause of the problem? (Choose all that apply.)
   a. Users who need access to dial in are not members of the correct group.
   b. There is no remote access policy configured.
   c. There is no Group Policy configured.
   d. The permission in the remote access policy is set to deny access.
4. If the permission and profile of a remote access policy do not match the connection attempt, the next policy in the list is evaluated. True or False?
5. You are configuring ICS on a network computer with a dial-up connection to the Internet. The computers on the network are currently receiving IP addresses from a DHCP server on the network. You enable ICS on the dial-up connection and connect to the Internet; however, none of the internal computers can access the Internet via the shared connection. What might be causing the problem?
   a. ICS needs to be enabled on the LAN connection.
   b. There is a DHCP server already on the network.
   c. The computers must be assigned a static IP address.
   d. The DNS option needs to be configured on the DHCP server.

6. By default, Remote Desktop for Administrators is enabled on a Windows Server 2003 system. True or False?
7. You are the server administrator for a company and are on call several evenings a week to handle problems that may occur. Unfortunately, you live about 40 minutes from work and often have to go in to work in the evenings for tasks that only take a couple of minutes. How can you make your life easier by accessing administrative programs from home?
   a. Configure NAT.
   b. Enable Remote Desktop for Administrators on the server.
   c. Configure ICS.
   d. Purchase a third-party utility because Windows Server 2003 does not provide remote access capabilities.
8. Which of the following operating systems would require the Remote Desktop Connection software to be installed in order to connect to a Windows Server 2003 Terminal Server?
   a. Windows 95
   b. Windows XP
   c. Windows 2000
   d. Windows 98
9. NAT allows you to configure the range of IP addresses to be assigned to clients on the internal network. True or False?
10. A small business is using NAT. The internal network is using the IP address range 192.168.0.0/16. The company has been assigned the external IP address of 198.10.2.25 by its ISP. To what IP address does NAT map the private IP addresses?
    a. 192.168.0.1
    b. 198.10.2.1
    c. 192.10.2.25
    d. 192.168.0.25
11. Your network is implementing smart cards for user authentication. Which of the following protocols is used for smart card authentication?
    a. PAP
    b. SPAP
    c. MS-CHAP
    d. EAP
12. If Allow access is configured on the Dial-in on the properties of a user account, remote access policies are not used. True or False?
13. Of the following authentication protocols, which one provides the highest level of security?
    a. CHAP
    b. PAP
    c. MS-CHAP v2
    d. MS-CHAP v1
14. By default, members of which group have the ability to log into a Windows Server 2003 system once Remote Desktop for Administrators is enabled?
    a. Administrators
    b. Remote Desktop Users
    c. Domain Users
    d. Guests

15. The CHAP authentication method transmits user passwords as plain text. True or False?

16. Your RAS server is configured to enable Multilink as a way to combine connections when users need more bandwidth, such as when they are using multimedia applications. However, when a user connects, the server does not seem to dynamically adjust for the amount of bandwidth needed by a user. What should you configure the RAS server to use along with multilink?

    a. PPP

    b. PPTP

    c. BAP

    d. L2TP

17. Your organization is setting up multiple RAS servers and wants to establish one set of remote access policies and one place from which to coordinate all of the VPN servers. What feature can you implement to provide centralized management of the RAS servers?

    a. NAT

    b. RADIUS

    c. VPN

    d. Terminal Services

18. Your RAS server is assigning IP addresses to dial-up clients. However, the clients are not receiving the IP addresses of the WINS and DNS servers. What step might you have omitted?

    a. Install the DHCP relay agent.

    b. Statically configure these additional parameters on clients.

    c. Configure the DHCP options on the RAS server.

    d. Disable IP forwarding.

19. Which of the following protocols can be used to establish a VPN connection? (Choose all that apply.)

    a. NAT

    b. PPTP

    c. SPAP

    d. L2TP

20. What authentication protocol should be enabled if there are non-Windows clients dialing into an RAS server?

    a. MS-CHAP

    b. PAP

    c. EAP

    d. CHAP

11

Case Projects

Case Project 11-1

The International Realtors Association is a nonprofit association of real estate companies that provides a wide range of information about the realty market worldwide. The association is located in Boston and has member groups throughout the world. One of the association's most popular services is maintaining a database of research information for all members. The database is accessed via a Windows NT 4.0 RAS server. The IT manager at Dover Leasing has asked you to set up a Windows Server 2003 RAS server where the database will eventually be located.

1. As you are creating your proposal for the International Realtors Association, include in the document the steps for installing and configuring an RAS server. Also include a brief explanation of VPN and how it may be useful for the organization.
2. Outline the different authentication and encryption protocols that can be implemented. Most of the users run Windows 98 or later on their desktops. Based on this, make a recommendation for an authentication protocol.
3. Four users are responsible for the administration of the RAS server. Provide a preliminary training paper for the administrators on the basic concepts of remote access policies and how they are applied.
4. Before implementation, you establish a test lab. After the RAS server and remote access policy is configured, you attempt to dial in as one of the members. You receive an access denied message. What are some of the things you should verify to troubleshoot the problem?

Case Project 11-2

One of the members of the International Realtors Association has approached you in regards to his own small office. He handles member services for the association, and has a small office with eight computers. Currently, each computer has its own Internet connection. You have been asked if there is a more economical way for the small office to provide Internet access for each computer.

1. What option would you recommend for the small office, and why?
2. After your proposal is reviewed, it is decided to implement ICS in the office. Your next step is to outline in a document the steps entailed in enabling and configuring ICS.
3. The small office does not require a network administrator on site but does have one they can call when problems arise. One of your tasks included in this project is to configure the server so remote administration can be performed. What Windows Server 2003 service can be implemented for remote administration? Outline the process of installing and configuring it.

Case Project 11-3

Briefly outline some of the reasons why a company might consider using Terminal Server to deploy applications rather than installing them on individual client workstations.

Glossary

access control entry (ACE) — An entry in an object's discretionary access control list (DACL) that grants permissions to a user or group. An ACE is also an entry in an object's system access control list (SACL) that specifies the security events to be audited for a user or group.

Active Directory (AD) — A directory service included with Windows Server 2003 that provides a single point of administration, authentication, and storage for user, group, and computer objects.

Active Directory client — This software allows legacy operating systems to perform searches in Active Directory; it also provides site awareness, the ability to use NTLMv2 authentication, and access to domain DFS resources.

Active Directory client extensions — These allow legacy operating systems to perform searches in Active Directory; they also provide site awareness and access to Windows Server 2003 distributed file systems.

Active Directory Domains and Trusts — An Active Directory MMC tool that allows you to configure trust relationships between domains as well as the UPN suffix for the forest.

Active Directory schema — Contains the definition of all object classes and attributes used in the Active Directory database.

Active Directory Sites and Services — An Active Directory MMC tool that allows you to configure site objects and site links, and configure replication costs and times between sites.

Active Directory Users and Computers — An Active Directory MMC tool that allows you to create various objects such as OUs, user accounts, groups, computers, and contacts.

Active Directory-integrated zone — The zone data is stored in the Active Directory database rather than in a zone file.

Add Hardware Wizard — Enables you to add hardware and troubleshoot any hardware-related problems.

Address Resolution Protocol (ARP) — Works at the Internet layer and is responsible for mapping IP addresses to MAC addresses assigned to the network interface adapter. These can be either dynamic or static entries. Dynamic entries are stored in the ARP cache for 2 to 10 minutes. Static entries stay in the cache until the computer is restarted.

alerts — An alert performs a specified action once a counter meets the specified setting. Once an alert is triggered, a message can be sent, a program can be run, a counter log started, or an event can be written to the application log.

alias — The name of a virtual directory, or name used to hide the real name of a directory and to simplify the directory name that would be used to access the information.

Anonymous access — Allows users to access a Web site without having to provide a user name and password.

application log — Where applications that are written to Microsoft standards record event information. The application developer determines the type of information an application writes to the log file.

attribute-level permissions — Define which attributes of a certain object a user or group can view or modify within Active Directory.

attributes — Used to define the characteristics of an object class within Active Directory.

audit policy — Defines the events on the network that Windows Server 2003 records in the security log as they occur.

auditing — The process that tracks the activities of users by recording selected types of events in the security log of a server or a workstation.

authentication — Refers to determining whether a user has a valid user account with the proper permissions to access a resource such as a shared folder or a Web site.

authoritative — The primary DNS server that acts as the final source of information for any queries about a given host that is part of one of the domains configured in its zone file.

authoritative restore — Marks specific objects in the Active Directory as the master copy, and forces the other domain controllers to receive the change.

Automated System Recovery (ASR) — A new Windows Server 2003 feature that creates a floppy disk and a backup of system configuration data to repair a server using an automated process.

automatic private IP addressing (APIPA) — An IP addressing technique that is used to temporarily assign an IP address in the range 169.254.0.0 through 169.254.255.255 in the event that a client cannot obtain an address from a DHCP server.

bandwidth throttling — Allows you to limit the network bandwidth that is available for Web and FTP connections to the server.

baseline — A performance benchmark that is used to determine what is normal server performance under a specific workload.

Basic authentication — Prompts users for a user name and password to be able to access the basic disk.

basic disk — The traditional storage type that divides physical disk space into primary partitions, extended partitions, and logical drives.

Basic Input/Output System (BIOS) — A program stored on a flash memory chip attached to the motherboard that establishes the initial communication between the components of the computer, such as the hard drive, CD-ROM, floppy disk, video, and memory.

caching-only server — A DNS server with no zone files configured that only caches information.

Challenge Handshake Authentication Protocol (CHAP) — A cross-platform authentication protocol designed for IP- or PPP-based exchange of passwords.

compression — Data is stored in a format that takes up less disk space, enabling you to store more data.

computer account — An Active Directory object that represents a physical computer that is a member of the domain.

Computer Management console — A predefined Microsoft Management Console (MMC) application that allows you to administer a variety of computer-related tasks on the local computer or a remote computer.

container — An object that is used to organize related objects within the Active Directory hierarchy. Container objects can consist of other child containers or leaf objects, such as OUs.

counter log — Performance data that is collected into a comma-separated or tab-separated format.

data decryption field (DDF) — The header field in an EFS-encrypted file that is used to store the file encryption key (FEK) encrypted by the user's public key.

data recovery agent — Individual responsible for recovering encrypted data in the event a user's private key is lost or otherwise unavailable.

data recovery field (DRF) — The header field in an EFS-encrypted file that is used to store the file encryption key (FEK) encrypted by the recovery agent's public key.

default domain controllers policy — The name of the default GPO that is linked to the domain controllers OU. Used primarily for configuration of policy settings that are only to be applied to the domain controllers in the domain (i.e., auditing).

default domain policy — The name of the GPO that is linked to the domain container in Active Directory; used primarily for configuration of domain-wide password policies.

Default FTP site — An FTP server that responds to TCP/IP port 21 on all of the server's configured IP addresses that are not assigned to another site.

default gateway — This is the 32-bit number of the router on the local network, which is used to communicate with hosts outside of the local subnet.

Default NNTP virtual server — A newsgroup server that responds to port 119 on all of the server's configured IP addresses that have not been assigned to another site.

Default SMTP virtual server — An e-mail component server that responds to port 25 on all of the server's IP addresses that have not been assigned to another site.

Default Web site — A Web site configured with FrontPage extensions that responds to TCP/IP port 80 on all unassigned IP addresses of the server. This Web site is initially empty and may be used to create a custom Web site for your organization.

Delegation of Control Wizard — An Active Directory MMC tool that guides you through the process of determining the permissions that you want to delegate and then configures the permissions for the object and child objects.

Device Manager — Used to view and modify hardware device properties, update device drivers, and uninstall unneeded hardware.

DFS link — A pointer to the physical location of a share on the network.

DFS root — The top level of a DFS tree structure that contains links to the shared folders on the network.

DFS topology — The logical structure of a distributed file system, which includes the DFS root and DFS link.

Digest authentication — Prompts users for a user name and password to be able to access the Web resource. The user name and password are hashed to prevent hackers from obtaining the information.

discretionary access control list (DACL) — A part of the security descriptor of an object that contains a list of user or group references that have been allowed or denied permissions to the resource.

disk quotas — A Windows Server 2003 feature that is used as a means of monitoring and controlling the amount of disk space available to users.

distinguished name (DN) — An LDAP component used to uniquely identify an object throughout the entire LDAP hierarchy by referring to the relative distinguished name, domain name, and the container holding the object.

distributed file system (DFS) — A file system that organizes shared folders located throughout a local or wide-area network into a single logical tree structure.

distribution group — A group that is only used for an e-mail distribution list.

DNS forwarder — The server to which unresolved DNS queries can be forwarded if configured.

DNS zone — One or more DNS domains grouped together for administrative purposes.

domain — A logically structured organization of objects, such as users, computers, groups, and printers, that are part of a network and share a common directory database. Domains are defined by an administrator and administered as a unit with common rules and procedures.

domain functional level — The level at which a Windows Server 2003 domain is configured, such as Windows 2000 mixed mode, Windows 2000 native mode, or Windows .NET.

domain local group — Can only be assigned permissions to a resource available in the domain in which it is created. However, group membership can come from any domain within the forest. Created on domain controllers within the domain.

Domain Name System (DNS) — A hierarchical name resolution system that resolves host names and fully qualified domain names (FQDNs) into IP addresses and vice versa. It is a method for maintaining domain naming structure and locating network resources.

driver signing — Ensures that a driver for a specific device has been verified by Microsoft and a unique digital signature has been incorporated into the driver.

dynamic disk — A new storage system supported by Windows Server 2003 that divides physical disk space into volumes.

Dynamic Host Configuration Protocol (DHCP) — Used to centralize the administration of IP addresses and various options, and eliminate the administrative overhead of statically assigning the information to each network host.

encrypting file system (EFS) — Windows Server 2003 enables you to encrypt files and folders on NTFS volumes for security purposes.

Event Viewer — A component you can use to view and manage event logs, gather information about hardware and software problems, and monitor security events. Event Viewer maintains logs about program, security, and system events.

Extensible Authentication Protocol (EAP) — EAP is a standard for developing authentication methods. It allows a client and RAS server to negotiate the exact authentication scheme.

file encryption key (FEK) — The encryption key used to encrypt a file using EFS.

File Signature Verification — This utility can identify unsigned files and give you information such as the file name, location, modification date, and version number.

File Transfer Protocol (FTP) — Used to transfer files between two computers that are both running TCP/IP.

folder redirection — A Group Policy feature that enables you to redirect the contents of the Application Data, Desktop, My Documents, My Pictures, and Start menu folders from a user's profile to a network location.

forest — A collection of Active Directory trees that do not necessarily share a contiguous DNS naming convention but do share a common global catalog and schema.

forest root domain — The first domain created within the Active Directory structure.

forward lookup zone — Used to perform the standard forward lookup queries for host name to IP address.

fully qualified domain name (FQDN) — Describes the location of the host in relation to the DNS namespace. For example, a computer named "webserver" in the marketing domain of *Bayside.com* would have the FQDN of *webserver.marketing.bayside.com*.

global catalog — An index of the objects and attributes used throughout the Active Directory structure. It contains a partial replica of every Windows Server 2003 domain within Active Directory, enabling users to find any object in the directory.

global group — A group that is mainly used for organizing other objects into administrative units. A global group can be assigned permissions to any resource in any domain within the forest. The main limitation of a global group is that it can only contain members of the same domain in which it is created.

globally unique identifier (GUID) — A unique 128-bit number assigned to the object when it is created.

Gpresult — This utility can be used to discover Group Policy-related problems and to illustrate which GPOs were applied to a user or computer. Gpresult also lists all group memberships of the user or computer being analyzed.

group — A container object that is used to organize a collection of users, computers, contacts, or other groups into a single object reference.

Group Policy — Enables the centralized management of user desktop settings, desktop and domain security, and the deployment and management of software throughout your network.

Group Policy object (GPO) — An Active Directory object that is configured to apply Group Policy and linked to either the site, domain, or OU level.

host — Any computer that is a member of a specific DNS domain within the network structure.

host header — The fully qualified DNS name that is used to access a Web site on an IIS Server.

hot fixes — Interim updates to Windows Server 2003 that are released between major service pack releases. These are used to fix operating system bugs and security issues.

incremental templates — A set of text-based security template files that you can use to apply uniform security settings on computers within an enterprise. The templates modify security settings incrementally and do not include the default security settings.

Integrated Windows authentication — Does not ask the user for a password but rather uses the client's currently logged-on credentials to supply a challenge/response to the Web server.

Internet connection sharing (ICS) — A feature included with Windows Server 2003 that enables a small or home office to connect to the Internet. ICS allows a single dial-up connection to be shared among multiple computers.

Internet Control Message Protocol (ICMP) — Operates at the network layer and is used to exchange status and error information between two hosts.

Internet Group Management Protocol (IGMP) — Operates at the network layer and is used to manage network and host information when multicasting is used.

Internet Information Services (IIS) — A Windows Server 2003 component that provides Web-related services to an organization.

Internet Protocol (IP) — The Internet-layer protocol responsible for addressing and routing packets so that they are delivered to the correct host on the local network or across routers to a host on another subnet.

interrupt request (IRQ) — A signal sent by a device to notify the processor when the device is ready to accept or send information. Each device typically has a unique IRQ number.

IP address — The 32-bit number that uniquely identifies a host on a TCP/IP network.

IP Security (IPSec) — IPSec consists of a suite of cryptography-based protection services and protocols that provide machine-level authentication and data encryption.

ipconfig — A command used to verify the addressing parameters assigned to a computer.

ipconfig/all — The ipconfig command plus the all parameter is used to produce a full display of assigned parameters.

iterative query — If the DNS server cannot resolve a name, it gives the requestor a pointer to another DNS server that is authoritative for the next level of the FQDN supplied.

Key Distribution Center (KDC) — A Kerberos version service that runs on a domain controller. It issues TGTs and service tickets for obtaining network authentication in a domain.

last known good configuration — An advanced startup option that you can use to recover a system from failed Windows 2000 configuration changes.

Layer 2 Tunneling Protocol (L2TP) — An advanced VPN protocol that is used to establish a secure tunnel between two endpoints over an insecure network. This protocol uses advanced authentication and encryption with the help of IPSec.

leaf — An object that represents resources within a selected domain. Leaf objects are stored within a container and cannot contain other objects (e.g., user or group objects).

Lightweight Directory Access Protocol (LDAP) — An access protocol that defines how users can access or update directory service objects.

local group — Can only be assigned permissions to a resource available on the local machine in which it is created.

Management Saved Console (MSC) — The filename extension of a console saved using the MMC.

master properties— IIS parameters that are configured on the server and are inheritable by all Web and FTP sites hosted on the server.

master server — The source of zone updates for a DNS secondary server.

metabase — IIS 6.0 stores its configuration settings in a database referred to as the IIS metabase.

Microsoft Baseline Security Analyzer — Analyzes the security of your server, including information about any vulnerabilities it finds.

Microsoft Challenge Authentication Protocol (MS-CHAP) — A Microsoft-enhanced version of CHAP that can negotiate encryption levels and that uses a highly secure encryption algorithm to encrypt communications between client and host.

Microsoft Hardware Compatibility List (HCL) — A list of hardware devices that have been tested by Microsoft to determine whether they can work with Windows Server 2003.

Microsoft Management Console (MMC) — A customizable management interface that can contain a number of management tools to provide a single, unified application for network administration.

Microsoft Point-to-Point Encryption (MPPE) — An encryption technique that uses encryption keys varying in length from 40 bits to 128 bits so that packets traveling between the remote access client and the remote access or tunnel server are secure. Used when IP security is not available.

Microsoft Windows installer package (MSI) — A special installation file containing all of the information needed to install an application in a variety of configurations.

Microsoft Windows Upgrade Advisor — A Windows Server 2003 utility used to check for hardware and software compatibility.

multicasting — Sending a message to multiple clients or a group of clients.

multi-master replication — A replication model in which any domain controller accepts and replicates directory changes to any other domain controller. This differs from other replication models in which one computer stores the single modifiable copy of the directory and other computers store back-up copies.

.NET Passport authentication — An IIS authentication method that utilizes .NET Password user names and passwords.

network address translation (NAT) — The process of converting between IP addresses used within an intranet or other private network (called a stub domain) and Internet IP addresses. This approach makes it possible to use a large number of addresses within the stub domain without depleting the limited number of available numeric Internet IP addresses. Also, the network is protected when NAT replaces the source internal address and ports of all outgoing packets with a single public IP address.

object — A collection of attributes that represent items within Active Directory, such as users, groups, computers, and printers.

object classes — Define which types of objects can be created within Active Directory, such as users, groups, and printers.

object-level permissions — Define which types of objects a user or group can view, create, delete, or modify within Active Directory.

organizational unit (OU) — An Active Directory logical container used to organize objects within a single domain. Objects such as users, groups, computers, and other OUs can be stored in an OU container.

originating update — The initial change to the Active Directory database performed on a specific domain controller (e.g., creating a user).

Password Authentication Protocol (PAP) — The least secure authentication protocol that sends passwords between a client and a server in clear text.

pathping — A command that combines the functions of the ping and tracert commands. The pathping command checks network connectivity by sending echo request messages to each router between a source and destination host and then computing the result based on packets returned from each router.

performance counter — A data item associated with a particular performance object used to measure a certain aspect of performance.

Performance Logs and Alerts — A tool included with Windows Server 2003 that enables you to create counter logs, trace logs, and configure alerts.

performance objects — A system component that you can monitor using System Monitor.

ping — A command used to test for connectivity between hosts on the network by sending ICMP packets to a remote computer and listening for an echo reply from the remote host.

Point-to-Point Protocol (PPP) — Enables remote access clients and servers to communicate over a dial-up connection from any operating system that supports the PPP standards.

Point-to-Point Tunneling Protocol (PPTP) — A VPN protocol that is used to establish a secure tunnel between two endpoints over an insecure network.

Power Users group — Power Users have less system access than administrators, but more than users. By default, members of this group have Read/Write permissions to other parts of the system in addition to their own profile. Power Users can perform many system-wide operations, such as changing system time and display settings, and creating user accounts and shares.

primary DNS server — A DNS server that is authoritative for a zone, meaning that it is the final source of information for any queries about a given host that is part of one of the domains configured in its zone file.

print device — The actual hardware device that produces the printed document. A local print device connects directly to a port on the print server. A network print device connects to a print server through its own network adapter and connection to the network.

print driver — Files that contain information that Windows Server 2003 uses to convert raw print commands to a language that the printer understands.

print server — The computer in which the printers and print drivers are located. This is usually where you set up and configure the shared printing system.

printer — A configuration object in Windows Server 2003 that controls the connection to the print device.

printer pool — Consists of a single printer that is connected to a number of print devices.

printer priorities — Configuring multiple printers to print to the same print device. One printer is then configured to print before any of the other printers by adjusting the priority setting from 1 (lowest priority) to 99 (highest priority).

published — An Active Directory object that represents a link or direct information on how to use or connect to the shared resource.

published folder — An Active Directory object that points to a related shared folder on a file server.

Recovery Console — A command-line interpreter that you can use to gain access to a local hard drive in the event that the system fails to boot.

recursive query — A command that specifies the return of a complete and full answer to the query, not a pointer to another DNS server.

relative distinguished name (RDN) — An LDAP component used to identify an object within the object's container.

remote access policy — A set of conditions that determines how users access the network remotely. A remote access policy consists of conditions, permissions, and profile settings.

remote access server — A computer running Windows Server 2003 and the Routing and Remote Access Service that authenticates remote or mobile users.

remote authentication dial-in user service (RADIUS) — A client/server protocol and software that enables remote access servers to communicate with a central server to authenticate dial-in users and authorize their access to the requested system or service.

Remote Desktop for Administration — A Windows Server 2003 feature that allows a server to be managed remotely using the Remote Desktop tool.

replica set — A set of shared folders that is replicated or copied to one or more servers in a domain.

replicated update — An update to the Active Directory database that has been copied from another domain controller.

replication latency — The time that it takes to replicate an Active Directory update to another domain controller.

Resultant Set of Policy (RSoP) — A graphical utility included with Windows Server 2003 that enables you to review the aggregated Group Policy settings that apply to a domain user or computer.

reverse lookup zone — A specific type of zone that performs reverse queries to resolve IP addresses to host names.

Routing and Remote Access Services (RRAS) — A Windows Server 2003 service that allows users to access a company network or access the Internet through a variety of ways such as dial-up, VPN, or NAT services.

safe mode — A method of starting Windows Server 2003 with only the basic drivers and services.

scope — A range of IP addresses configured on a DHCP server that can be handed out to network clients.

script — A file that includes various commands to automate routine operations.

secedit.exe — A command-line tool that allows you to perform security configuration and analysis.

secondary DNS server — A DNS server that contains zone information that is copied from a primary DNS server or other secondary servers.

Secure Sockets Layer (SSL) — This protocol is used to encrypt Web traffic between a client and the Web server.

security accounts manager (SAM) database — The local directory service that stores user and group information for standalone Windows NT, Windows 2000, and Windows Server 2003 computers.

Security Configuration Manager tools — A security toolset consisting of security templates and utilities that can be used to analyze and apply security configurations.

security group — A group that can be used to define permissions on a resource object.

security log — A Windows Server 2003 event log used to record security events such as auditing information.

Security Policy template — A template used to apply various security settings to an Active Directory container or object.

service packs — Periodic updates to the Windows Server 2003 operating system to fix reported bugs and security issues.

shared folder — A data resource container that has been made available over the network to authorized network clients.

Shiva Password Authentication Protocol (SPAP) — A reversible encryption method employed by Shiva.

site — A combination of one or more Internet Protocol (IP) subnets connected by a high-speed connection.

site link — A low-bandwidth or unreliable/occasional connection between sites. The site links can be adjusted for replication availability, bandwidth costs, and replication frequency. They enable control over replication and logon traffic.

slipstreaming — A process that integrates a Windows Server 2003 service pack with the original Windows Server 2003 installation files.

snap-ins — The management tools that are added to an MMC interface.

standard primary zone — The DNS zone file is stored as a regular read/write text file in the %systemroot%\system32\dns folder.

standard secondary zone — A read-only zone file is copied from a configured standard primary zone.

subnet mask — The 32-bit number that identifies the network to which a TCP/IP host belongs.

superscope — A grouping of scopes created for multiple subnets on a physical network.

System File Checker — A command-line utility that scans and verifies all of the protected system files on your computer.

system log — Where system components such as services and device drivers record information, warnings, and errors.

System Monitor — A tool that allows you to gather and view real-time performance statistics of a local or network computer.

System State — System components that are backed up as a single item within the Windows Server 2003 Backup utility. System State data includes the Registry, COM+ Class Registration database, boot files, Certificate Services database, Active Directory, the Sysvol folder, Cluster service information, the IIS Metadirectory, and system files.

Task Manager — A tool used to view the processes and applications currently running on a system. Also provides basic resource usage statistics.

taskpad — Allows you to simplify administrative procedures by providing a graphical representation of the tasks that can be performed in an MMC.

Terminal Services — A built-in feature of Windows Server 2003 that allows clients to access applications remotely.

ticket-granting ticket (TGT) — A ticket issued by the Kerberos version Key Distribution Center (KDC) for purposes of obtaining a service ticket from the ticket-granting service (TGS).

trace log — Where data provider collects performance data when an event occurs.

tracert — A command used to determine the route taken to a destination by sending ICMP echo packets with varying time-to-live (TTL) values to the destination.

transitive trust — The ability for domains or forests to trust one another, even though they do not have a direct explicit trust between them.

Transmission Control Protocol (TCP) — A connection-based protocol, which means a session is established between the two hosts before any data is transferred. Operates at the transport layer and is responsible for reliably transmitting data on a TCP/IP network.

Transmission Control Protocol/Internet Protocol (TCP/IP) — Consists of a suite of protocols and utilities that are used for network communication and troubleshooting on local networks and the Internet.

tree — A hierarchical collection of domains that share a contiguous DNS namespace.

universal group — Can be assigned permissions to any resource in any domain within the forest. Universal groups can consist of any user or group object except for local groups.

urgent replication — The immediate replication that takes place when any changes that are made to the Active Directory database are considered security-sensitive, such as account lockouts.

user account — An object that is stored in Active Directory that represents all of the information that defines a physical user who has access permissions to the network.

User Datagram Protocol (UDP) — A connectionless protocol that functions at the transport layer and provides no guarantee of delivery.

user principal name — A user-account naming convention that includes both the user name and domain name in the format user@domain.com.

virtual directory — A mapping to a physical directory containing content to be included on a Web site.

virtual private network (VPN) — Uses a LAN protocol such as TCP/IP which is encapsulated within a WAN protocol to send data over a public network.

virtual servers — A unique Web or FTP site that behaves as if it were on its own dedicated server.

Web folder — A folder designed to be accessed from the Internet or an intranet using the HTTP or FTP protocols.

Windows 2000 mixed mode — The default domain functional level consisting of Windows Server 2003 domain controllers and/or Windows NT back-up domain controllers (BDCs) and Windows 2000 domain controllers.

Windows 2000 native mode — The domain functional level consisting of Windows Server 2003 and Windows 2000 domain controllers only. No Windows NT BDCs exist in the domain.

Windows File Protection — Helps to prevent the replacement of protected Windows Server 2003 files such as .sys, .dll, .ocx, .ttf, .fon, and .exe files.

Windows installer package (MSI) — A file that contains all of the information needed to install an application in a variety of configurations.

Windows Internet Name Service (WINS) — A Windows Server 2003 service that is used to resolve NetBIOS names to IP addresses.

Windows Update — A Microsoft Web site used to automatically download and install Windows Server 2003 service packs, hot fixes, and updates.

winipcfg — A command used on Windows 9x machines to display the TCP/IP configuration settings.

ZAP file — A text file that can be used by Group Policy to deploy an application; it has a number of limitations compared to an MSI file.

zone file — A DNS configuration file that holds all of the resource records for the domain, such as computer name records, mail exchanger records, and service records.

zone transfer —Copying the DNS database information between the primary and secondary zones.

Index

$ (dollar sign), for hidden shared folder, 142

A

access. *See also* access control entry; connectivity; remote access
anonymous access, 218
Web site, 235
client access problems, 253
media access control address, 261
View Information on Remote Computer, 11–12
Web folder, 249–250
access control entry (ACE), shared folders, 146
ACE. *See* access control entry
Active Directory (AD), 1, 2. *See also* Active Directory Users and Computers; group
administration, 2–3
objects, 56
client extensions, 160
communication standards, 21–22
DN, 21
LDAP, 21
components, 17–21
domains and organizational units, 17–18
global catalog, 21
trees and forests, 19–21
computer accounts, creating, 67–68
DNS zones, 318–320
in general, 16
DNS and, 16
multi-master replication, 16
Globally Unique Identifier, 86
objects, 16
container objects, 56
delegation, 84–85
discussed, 56
distinguished name, 21
group objects, creating, 69–70, 72–73
leaf objects, 56
moving, 68–69
searching for, 16, 187–188
permissions, in general, 80–81
physical structure, 22–23
site, 22
site link, 22
publishing in
in general, 181–182
printers, 184–185
shared folders, 182–184
replication, 85–87
components and process, 86
problems identification, 86–87
schema, 17, 21
attributes, 17
object classes, 17
security, Group Policy, 3
site, 22
trees and forests, 19–21
forest root domain, 19
tree definition, 19
user account, 62–67
creating, 62–65
Active Directory Domains and Trusts, 56
Active Directory Sites and Services, 56
Active Directory Users and Computers, 55, 56
in general, 56–57
scripts, 56
GPO creation, 95–97
using, 57–59
creating saved queries, 188
security accounts manager database, 58
AD. *See* Active Directory
Add Printer Wizard, 171
Address Resolution Protocol (ARP), TCP and, 261
alert, Performance Logs and Alerts, 354, 355–359
alias, virtual directory, 232
APIPA. *See* automatic private IP addressing
application. *See also* software
assigning, 129–131
publishing, 129–131
application log, 360
viewing, 361–362
ARP. *See* Address Resolution Protocol
ASR. *See* Automated System Recovery
attributes, Active Directory schema, 17
auditing. *See also* monitoring; troubleshooting
configuring, 190–191
new audit policy settings, 191–192
on NTFS folder, 193–194
default settings, 189–190
in general, 189
object access, 192
security log analysis, 194–197
authentication. *See also* security
Web site, 234
anonymous access, 235
basic authentication, 235
configuring and testing, 236
configuring Server Certificates and Secure Sockets Layer, 237–238
digest authentication, 235
integrated Windows authentication, 235
.NET Passport authentication, 236
Automated System Recovery (ASR). *See also* recovery console
discussed, 378
automatic private IP addressing (APIPA), 267–269

B

back up. *See also* recovery console
in general, 379–382
Internet Information Services, 246–248
System State back up, 382–384
Backup Domain Controller (BDC), 71
Bandwidth Allocation Protocol (BAP), 399
PPP multilink and, 399–400
BAP. *See* Bandwidth Allocation Protocol
Basic Input/Output System (BIOS)
configuration assessment, 33–34
interrupt request, 33
BIOS. *See* Basic Input/Output System
Block Policy. *See also* Group Policy inheritance, configuring, 122–123
Blue Screen of Death (BSoD), 375
BSoD. *See* Blue Screen of Death

C

CA. *See* Certificate Authority
Certificate Authority (CA), 104, 237
Certificate Services, 156
Challenge Handshake Authentication Protocol (CHAP), 413
CHAP. *See* Challenge Handshake Authentication Protocol
class, object classes, AD schema, 17
client reservations, DHCP, 286–287
Compatws.inf template, 1 0. *See also* Security Policy template
compression
encryption and, 157
folder compression, 207–208
in general, 206–207

computer accounts. *See also* Active Directory; user account
creating, 67–68
Computer Management console
connect to another computer, 158
shared folder creation, 143–145
connectivity. *See also* access
troubleshooting
client access problems, 253
in general, 253
netdiag command, 278–280
pathping command, 275–277
ping command, 272–274
route command, 275–277
TCP/IP, 271–272
tracert command, 274–275
container. *See also* container object
built-in, distinguished from OU, 60
linking GPO to multiple containers, 121–122
container object, 56, 59, 60. *See also* object
group as, 69
Counter Logs, 355

D

DACL. *See* discretionary access control list
data decryption field (DDF), 156
data recovery agent, 156
data recovery field, 156
data storage. *See* storage
DC Security.inf template, 110
DCDIAG, replication problems, 87
DDF. *See* data decryption field
delegation, Active Directory, implementation, 84
Delegation of Control Wizard, 55
using, 84–85
desktop settings, 94
controlling, 98–99
GPO configuration, 99–100
device. *See also* Device Manager
installing and configuring, 36–38
print device, 170–172
Device Manager, 36. *See also* Hardware
exploring, 38–41
Add Hardware Wizard, 40, 41–42
DFS. *See* distributed file system
DHCP. *See* Dynamic Host Configuration Protocol
digital subscriber line (DSL), 403
discretionary access control list (DACL), 70. *See also* access
shared folder permissions, 146
as access control entry, 146
Disk Management, Creating Extended Partition and Logical Drive with Disk Management, 203
distinguished name (DN)
objects, 21
relative distinguished name, 22
distributed file system (DFS), 139. *See also* file system
in general, 160
Active Directory client extensions, 160
Implementing Domain-Based DFS and Creating Links, 162
managing, 162–163
models, 161
DFS link, 161
DFS root, 161
replica set, 161
.dll file, 45
DN. *See* distinguished name
DNS. *See* Domain Name System
DNSCMD.EXE utility, using, 337–339
domain. *See also* domain controller; domain name
Active Directory
discussed, 17–18
forest, 19
forest root domain, 19
transitive trust, 19
tree, 19
default domain policy, 94
Switching a Domain to Windows Server 2003 Functional Level, 73
domain controller
Backup Domain Controller, 71
default domain controllers policy, 94
local groups, 75
objects and, 58
domain environment, 2
domain functional level, Switching a Domain to Windows Server 2003 Functional Level, 73
domain name. *See also* Domain Name System
fully qualified domain name, 226, 304
security, 245
Domain Name System (DNS). *See also* name resolution files
Active Directory and, 16
basics, 304–306
DNS zones, 304, 305
domain namespace, 304
name servers, 304
primary DNS server, 305
secondary DNS server, 305
zone file, 305
DHCP and, 296
discussed, 3, 303
DNS client settings, configuring, 327–330
DNS forwarders
configuring, 325–326
in general, 324
DNS server, 305
testing, 330
DNS updates, configuring, 326–327
DNS zones, 304, 305
Active Directory-integrated zones, 318–320
Configuring Standard Primary Zone, 312–315
Configuring Standard Reverse Lookup Zone, 315–316
Configuring Standard Secondary Zone, 316–318
Dynamic Updates Configuration, 326–327
forward lookup zone, 305
in general, 311
reverse lookup zone, 305, 315–316
standard primary zone, 312–315
standard secondary zone, 312, 316–318
standard zone, 311–312
Zone Transfer Settings Configuration, 323–324
Events Log, 338–339
viewing, 339–340
fundamentals, 304
installation, 306–308
caching-only server, 307
name resolution process, 306
iterative query, 306
recursive query, 306
properties, 308–311
resource records
configuring, 321–323
in general, 320–321
server, testing, 330
TCP and, 259
testing, with DNS Monitor and Nslookup, 330–332
troubleshooting
DNSCMD.EXE utility, 337–339
in general, 337, 340
domain user account. *See also* user account
creating, 63–65
driver. *See also* driver signing
print driver, 170, 180
driver signing
configuring options, in general, 42–43
File Signature Verification, 44
Dsa.msc, 56, 57
DSL. *See* digital subscriber line

Dynamic Host Configuration Protocol (DHCP), 3
administration, 280–281
services maintenance, 297
client reservations, 286–287
configuration
relay agent, 294–295
in routed network, 293–294
DNS integration, 296
installation, 281–282
scopes, 280
configuration, 282–286
options, 291–293
server authorization, 289–290
superscopes, 287
creating, 287–289
TCP and, 259

E

EAP. *See* Extensible Authentication Protocol
EFS. *See* Encrypting File System
Encrypting File System (EFS), 104, 156. *See also* encryption
using, 157–158
encryption. *See also* remote access
with EFS, 157–158
encryption protocols, 414–415
IPSec, 414
remote access policy, 414
in general, 156–157
data decryption field, 156
data recovery agent, 156
data recovery field, 156
file encryption key, 156
Microsoft Point-to-Point Encryption, 413
Event Log, 104. *See also* Event Viewer
DNS, 338–339
viewing, 339–340
Event Viewer, 6. *See also* monitoring
audit entries, 189
configuring, 197–198
DNS, 338–339
in general, 359–360
interpreting events, 360–361
replication problems, 87
Viewing Shutdown Events in Event Viewer System Log, 7–8
Viewing System and Application Log Events, 361–362
.exe file, 45
Extensible Authentication Protocol (EAP), 413, 414
Extensible Markup Language (XML), 221

F

FEK. *See* file encryption key
file. *See also* file resources administration; file system; folder
file protection, testing and verifying, 47–48
protecting, Windows File Protection, 45
System File Checker, 45
system files, viewing, 46–47
file encryption key (FEK), 156
file protection, testing and verifying, 47–48
file resources administration, 3, 139
File Signature Verification, 44
using, 44–45
file system, 104
distributed file system, 139
security settings, 105–107
File Transfer Protocol (FTP), 216
default FTP site, 222
discussed, 239
publishing, 219
virtual server
configuring and testing, 240–241
creating, 241–243
in general, 238
properties configuration, 239–240
filtering. *See also* Group Policy
GPO, with security permissions, 124–125
NAT, 423
policy settings, 122–123
security log, 196
firewall, NAT, 423
folder. *See also* file; folder compression; folder redirection; shared folder; Web folder
NTFS folder, 193–194
published folder, 182
testing folder permissions, 78–80
folder compression, configuring, 207–208
folder redirection, 115, 117
configuring, with Group Policy, 118–119
forest. *See* trees
FQDN. *See* fully qualified domain name
FTP. *See* File Transfer Protocol
fully qualified domain name (FQDN), 226. *See also* domain name
DNS and, 304

G

gateway, default gateway, TCP/IP and, 265
global catalog
discussed, 21
user principle name, 21
Globally Unique Identifier (GUID), 86, 97
GPC. *See* Group Policy container
GPO. *See* Group Policy object
Gpresult.exe, 125
troubleshooting with, 126–127
GPT. *See* Group Policy template
group. *See also* Active Directory; group membership; group object; Group Policy; group scope
defined, 69
distribution group, 70
in general, 70
discretionary access control list, 70
nesting AD group, testing folder permissions, 78–80
restricted group, 104
security group, 70
managing, 78
group membership, modifying, 73–74
group object. *See also* object
creating, 70–71, 72–73
domain local and global groups, 72–73
Switching a Domain to Windows Server 2003 Functional Level, 73
Group Policy, 156. *See also* Group Policy object
Active Directory, 3, 95
application, 98
assigning login script, 116–118
folder redirection, 115, 117
configuring, 118–119
in general, 94
inheritance
Block Policy inheritance, 122–123
in general, 119–120
settings configuration, 123–124
Security Configuration Manager tools, 107
security management
configuring account lockout policy settings, 102–103
configuring account policies, 100
configuring password policy settings, 101–102
in general, 100
Kerberos policy, 103–105
password policy, 100–101
software
assigning an application, 129–131
deployment, 129
in general, 128
maintenance, 131–132
preparation, 128–129
publishing an application, 129–131
removal, 132–133
troubleshooting
in general, 125
with Gpresult.exe, 126–127
with Resultant Set of Policy tool, 127–128

Group Policy container (GPC), 97
Group Policy object (GPO), 94, 120
adding security template, 112
configuration
file system security settings, 105–107
security settings, 105
with user desktop settings, 99–100
Configuration Categories, 96
creating
with Active Directory Users and Computers, 95–97
globally unique identifier, 97
Group Policy container, 97
Group Policy template, 97
with MMC, 94–95
default domain controllers policy, 94
default domain policy, 94
deleting, 98
filtering, with security permissions, 124–125
linking, to multiple containers, 121–122
Group Policy template (GPT), 97
group scope. *See also* scope
changing, 74–75
domain local group, 70, 72–73
in general, 70
global group, 70, 72–73
local group, 70
in general, 75–77
Local Groups and their Rights, 76
modifying membership, 77
universal group, 71
GUID. *See* Globally Unique Identifier

H

hard drive. *See* storage
hardware. *See also* software
Add Hardware Wizard
discussed, 40–41
using, 41–42
BIOS assessment, 33–34
compatibility verification
Microsoft Web site, 35–36
Microsoft Windows Update Advisor, 35–36
Microsoft Windows Upgrade Advisor, 34
device installation and configuration, 36–38
Device Manager, 36, 38–41
in general, 32
Microsoft Hardware Compatibility List, 32
installation
Add Hardware Wizard, 40–42
planning, 32
HCL. *See* Microsoft Hardware Compatibility List
Hisecdc.inf template, 110
Hisecws.inf template, 110
HOSTS file
configuring, 332–334, 396
LMHOSTS file, viewing and disabling, 334–335
hot fix. *See also* service pack; troubleshooting
discussed, 31, 248
Quick Fix Engineering, 48
updates with, in general, 48–49
HTML. *See* Remote Administration tools

I

ICS. *See* Internet connection sharing
IEEE 802.11 policies, 104
IGMP. *See* Internet Group Management Protocol
IIS. *See* Internet Information Services
iisweb.vbs script, Web site creation, 228–229
incremental template, discussed, 109–110
inheritance
Group Policy
in general, 119–120
settings configuration, 123–124
permissions, 83
installation
devices, 36–38
planning, 32
Internet. *See also* Internet connection sharing
resources administration, 3
B2B resources, 3
B2C resources, 3
IIS, 3
Internet connection sharing (ICS), 4, 391
compared to NAT, 427
enabling on dial-up connection, 427–429
in general, 426–427
troubleshooting, 429–430
Internet Control Message Protocol (ICMP)
TCP and, 262
pathping command, 262
ping command, 262
tracert command, 262
Internet Group Management Protocol (IGMP), TCP and, 263
Internet Information Services (IIS), 3, 215
anonymous access, 218
architectural changes in IIS 6.0, 221–222
metabase, 221
updating, 248
backing up, 246–248
components
FTP services, 216
HTTP services, 216
NNTP services, 216
SMTP services, 216
configuring Web server properties, 222–223
installing and configuring, 216–220
viewing changes after installation, 220–221
Lockdown Tool, 248
master properties, 224
viewing and configuring, 225
MMC snap-in, 223–225
master properties, 224
permissions, configuring, 244–245
security
in general, 243–244
IP address and domain name, 245
IP address restrictions, 245–246
resource permissions, 244
starting and stopping services, 246
updating, 248
Internet Protocol (IP), 22
TCP and, 263
Internet Service Provider (ISP), 403
interrupt request (IRQ), 33–34
IP. *See* Internet Protocol
IP address
automatic private IP addressing, 267–269
configuration, 266, 396, 423
remote clients, 397–398
security, 245
restrictions, 245–246
TCP/IP and, 265
IP Security (IPSec), 414
ipconfig command, troubleshooting with, 269–271
IPSec. *See* IP Security
IRQ. *See* interrupt request
ISP. *See* Internet Service Provider

K

Kerberos policy
Group Policy, 103–105
ticket-granting ticket, 103

L

L2TP. *See* Layer 2 Tunneling Protocol
last known good configuration. *See also* monitoring; recovery console; troubleshooting
discussed, 375–376
Layer 2 Tunneling Protocol (L2TP), 392, 404
compared to PPTP, 392
LDAP. *See* Lightweight Directory Access Protocol
Lightweight Directory Access Protocol (LDAP), 21

link
Implementing Domain-Based DFS and Creating Links, 162
site link, 22
LMHOSTS file, 396
viewing and disabling, 334–335
login script. *See also* scripts
assigning with Group Policy, 116–118
logon process. *See also* startup procedures
Event Viewer, 6
global catalog, 21
Group Policy application, 98
Logging on to Windows 2003 and Changing Password, 6
Restarting Windows Server 2003, 6–7
scripts, 56
secondary logon feature, 13
using, 13–14
using from command line, 14–15
Shutdown Event Tracker, 6
user principal name, 63
user principle name, 21
Viewing Shutdown Events in Event Viewer System Log, 7–8

M

MAC. *See* media access control
Macintosh, 32
Management Saved Console (MSC), MMC, 8
MBSA. *See* Microsoft Baseline Security Analyzer
MCSA. *See* Microsoft Certified Systems Administrator
MCSE. *See* Microsoft Certified Systems Engineer
media access control (MAC) address, 261
metabase, XML, 221
Microsoft Baseline Security Analyzer (MBSA), 50
Microsoft Certified Systems Administrator (MCSA), 2
Microsoft Certified Systems Engineer (MCSE), 2
Microsoft Challenge Authentication Protocol (MS-CHAP), 416, 418
MS-CHAP v2, 413
Microsoft Hardware Compatibility List (HCL), 32
Microsoft Management Console (MMC), 5, 56
Computer Management console, 143
creating, Customized MMC, 8–11
discussed, 1, 8
Management Saved Console, 8
snap-ins, 8, 11–12, 222, 223–225
GPO creation, 94–95
scripts, Dsa.msc, 56, 57
taskpad, 11–13
using, to View Information on Remote Computer, 11–12
Microsoft Point-to-Point Encryption (MPPE), 413
Microsoft Windows installer package (MSI), 128
Microsoft Windows Update Advisor, 35–36
Microsoft Windows Upgrade Advisor, 34
MMC. *See* Microsoft Management Console
monitoring. *See also* auditing; Event Viewer; System Monitor; Task Manager; troubleshooting
discussed, 348
identify and disable unnecessary resources, 366
MPPE. *See* Microsoft Point-to-Point Encryption
MS-CHAP. *See* Microsoft Challenge Authentication Protocol
MSC. *See* Management Saved Console
MSI. *See* Microsoft Windows installer package
multicasting, scopes, 289

N

name resolution files. *See also* Domain Name System
in general, 332
HOSTS file, configuring, 332–334
troubleshooting, in general, 335–336
NAT. *See* network address translation
net command, using, 15
netdiag command. *See also* troubleshooting
troubleshooting TCP/IP, 278–280
using, 15
.NET Passport authentication, 236. *See also* authentication
network. *See also* network administration; virtual private network
Exploring Windows Server 2003 Network Settings, 263–265
routed network, DHCP configuration, 293–294
virtual private network, 4
network address translation (NAT), 4, 391
compared to ICS, 427
in general, 422–423
implementing, 423–426
installing, 423
troubleshooting, 426
network administration. *See also* Windows Server 2003
Active Directory administration, 2–3
file and print resources administration, 3
in general, 2
Routing and Remote Access Services, 2
Internet resources administration, 3
monitoring and troubleshooting, 4
network infrastructure administration, 3
operating system installation and maintenance, 2
procedures, network troubleshooting process, 4–5
RRAS administration, 4
network infrastructure
administration, 3
Domain Name System, 3
Network News Transfer Protocol (NNTP), 216, 219
NNTP. *See* Network News Transfer Protocol
Novell NetWare, 32
Nslookup, testing DNS, 330–332
NTFS file permissions, 139. *See also* NTFS folder; permissions
integrating with shared folder permissions
combining and testing, 155–156
concepts and rules, 149–150
effective permissions, 154–155
in general, 149, 155
implementation, 150–151
special NTFS permissions, 151–153
viewing and implementing, 153–155
NTFS folder. *See also* folder
auditing configuration, 193–194

O

object. *See also* object classes
access auditing, 192
Active Directory, 16
discussed, 56
moving, 68–69
searching for, 16, 187–188
Users and Computers, 60
container objects, 56, 59, 60
defined, 16
distinguished name, 21
relative distinguished name, 22
group object, creating, 70–71, 72–73
OU object, creating, 61–62
performance object, 348
site object, 19
object classes, AD schema, 17
.ocx file, 45
operating system. *See also* software
installation and maintenance, 2
organizational unit (OU), 55
Active Directory, 17–18
as container object, 60
distinguished from container object, 60

creating, 59–61
OU object, 61–62
defined, 18
diagramming, 32
OU. *See* organizational unit

P

PAP. *See* Password Authentication Protocol
password. *See also* security
Group Policy
configuring password policy settings, 101–102
policy, 100–101
Logging on to Windows 2003 and Changing Password, 6
ownership control, 63
Password Authentication Protocol, 413
Shiva Password Authentication Protocol, 413
Password Authentication Protocol (PAP), 413
performance counter, 348
adding, 352–354
performance object and, 351–352
Performance Logs and Alerts, 354
configuring, 356–359
discussed, 355–359
Counter Logs, 355
Trace Logs, 355
performance object, 348. *See also* object
performance counters and, 351–352
permissions, 1. *See also* security
exploring, 81–83
Account Operators group, 82
Domain Admins group, 82
filtering GPO with, 124–125
in general, 80–81
attribute-level permissions, 81
object-level permissions, 81
IIS
configuring, 244–245
resource permissions, 244
inheritance, 83
NTFS and shared folder permissions, 139
combining and testing, 155–156
concepts and rules, 149–150
effective permissions, 151–154
in general, 149
implementation, 150–151
special permissions, 151–154
printer
configuring, 176–177
pools and priorities, 177–178
remote access policy, 417
shared folder
in general, 146–147
implementing, 147–148
testing, 148–149
testing folder permissions, 78–80
Web folder, 249–250
ping command. *See also* troubleshooting
TCP and, 262
testing connectivity, 272–274
Point-to-Point Protocol (PPP), 392
multilink and BAP options, 399–400
Point-to-Point Tunneling Protocol (PPTP), 392, 404
compared to L2TP, 392
Power Users group, 110
PPP. *See* Point-to-Point Protocol
PPTP. *See* Point-to-Point Tunneling Protocol
print resources administration, 3
print server, 169
printer. *See also* printer priorities
access control, 169
Add Printer Wizard, 171
adding
installing additional print drivers, 180
installing local printer, 172–173
installing network printer, 174
as local print device, 170–172
as network print device, 173
setting up client computer, 179–180
sharing local printer for network access, 173–174
configuring existing printer, 174
exploring printer properties, 174–176
configuring spooler service, 181
creating and modifying printer resources, 170
print device, 170
print driver, 170, 180
permissions
configuring, 176–177
printer pools and priorities, 177–178
publishing, 184–185
managing published printer, 186
troubleshooting, 170, 180–181
printer pool, 177
printer priorities, 177
configuring, 178–179
PSTN. *See* Public Switched Telephone Network
public key policies, 104
Public Switched Telephone Network (PSTN), 392
publishing
in Active Directory
in general, 181–182
printers, 184–185
shared folders, 182–184
application, 129–131
FTP, 219
pubprn.vbs, 185. *See also* scripts

Q

QFE. *See* Quick Fix Engineering
query
creating saved queries, 188
iterative query, 306
recursive query, 306
Quick Fix Engineering (QFE), 48. *See also* hot fix

R

RADIUS. *See* remote authentication dial-in user service
recovery console. *See also* back up; troubleshooting
Automated System Recovery, 178
in general, 376–377
installing, 377–378
last known good configuration, 375–376
Registry, 104
relay agent, DHCP, 294–295
remote access. *See also* access; encryption; remote connection; Terminal Services
configuration
CHAP, 413
EAP, 413, 414
in general, 411–412
MS-CHAP, 412, 414
MS-CHAP v2, 413
PAP, 413
remote authentication dial-in user service, 411
SPAP, 413
configuring remote connection settings, 433–434
remote access policy, 414
configuring, 420–422
creating, 418–419
elements, 416–417
troubleshooting, 416, 422
unauthenticated access, 414
Remote Administration (HTML) tools. *See also* remote connection
in general, 251
installing, 251–252
remote authentication dial-in user service (RADIUS), 411
remote connection. *See also* Routing and Remote Access Services; virtual private network
configuring dial-up client connection, 400–403
dial-up connections, 396–397
View Information on Remote Computer, 11–12
Remote Desktop, 391
Remote Desktop for Administration, 430
enabling and testing, 430–432

replica set, DFS, 161
replication
  Active Directory, 85–87
    components and process, 86
    problems identification, 86–87
  controlling, site objects, 19
  multi-master replication, 16
  update
    originating update, 86
    replicated update, 86
    replication latency, 86
    urgent replication, 86
  within site, 23
Replication Monitor, replication problems, 87
resource. *See also* resource sharing
  identify and disable unnecessary resources, 366
resource sharing, discussed, 169
Resultant Set of Policy (RSoP) tool, 125
  troubleshooting with, 127–128
Rootsec.inf template, 110
route command, troubleshooting TCP/IP, 277–278
Routing and Remote Access Services (RRAS), 2. *See also* remote access; remote connection
  administration, 4, 391
    ICS, 4
    L2TP, 392
    NAT, 4, 391
    PPP, 392
    PPTP, 392
    PSTN, 392
    VPN, 4, 391
  configuring, 393–396
    dial-up client connection, 400–403
    dial-up connections, 396–397
    IP address settings, 397–398
    multilink and bandwidth allocation protocol options, 398–399
    remote access clients, 400
RRAS. *See* Routing and Remote Access Services
RSoP. *See* Resultant Set of Policy

S

SAM. *See* security accounts manager
schema
  Active Directory, 21
    discussed, 17
scope. *See also* group scope; superscope
  DHCP, 280
    configuration, 282–286
    multicast scopes, 289
    options, 291–293
scripts, 56, 94
  assigning, 115
  login script, assigning with Group Policy, 116–118
  pubprn.vbs, 185
  Visual Basic, 222
secedit.exe tool, discussed, 115
Secure Sockets Layer (SSL), configuring, 237–238
Securedc.inf template, 110
Securews.inf template, 110
security. *See also* authentication; password; permissions; security management
  Active Directory, Group Policy, 3
  Active Directory Group Policy, 3
  file system security settings, 105–107
  Group Policy object, 105
  IIS
    in general, 243–244
    IP address and domain name, 245
  IP Security, 414
  IP Security settings, 105
  Microsoft Baseline Security Analyzer, 50
security accounts manager (SAM) database, 58
Security Configuration and Analysis. *See also* security management
  in general, 112–113
  secedit.exe tool, 115
  security settings analysis, 113–115
Security Configuration Manager tools
  in general, 107
    Security Policy template, 107
security group, 70. *See also* group
  managing, 78
Security Identifier (SID), 70
security log, 360. *See also* auditing; monitoring
  analysis, 194–197
  auditing, 189
  editing and saving, 198–199
  filtering, 196
security management. *See also* security; Security Configuration and Analysis
  Group Policy
    configuring account lockout policy settings, 102–103
    configuring account policies, 100
    configuring password policy settings, 101–102
    in general, 100
    Kerberos policy, 103–105
    password policy, 100–101
Security Policy template, 107. *See also* template
  applying, 110–111
    to GPO, 112
  browsing, 108–109
  creating, 111–112
  default template, 109
  discussed, 108
  in general, 109
  incremental template, 109–110
    Compatws.inf template, 110
    DC Security.inf template, 110
    Hisecdc.inf template, 110
    Hisecws.inf template, 110
    Power Users group, 110
    Rootsec.inf template, 110
    Securedc.inf template, 110
    Securews.inf template, 110
  preconfigured, 110–111
security settings, 94
Security tab
  NTFS file permissions, 151
  printer, 175
server. *See also* virtual server
  caching-only server, 307
  DHCP server, 289–290
  DNS server, 305
  master server, 322
  name server, 304
  print server, 169
service pack. *See also* hot fix; troubleshooting; update
  discussed, 31, 248
  slipstreaming, 50
  updates with, in general, 48–49
shared folder. *See also* folder; NTFS file
  creating and managing
    with Computer Management, 143–145
    hidden folder, 142–143
    with Windows Explorer, 140–142
  hidden, creating, 142–143
  monitoring access
    in general, 158–159
    sending console messages, 159–160
  permissions, 139
    discretionary access control list, 146
    in general, 146–147
    implementing, 147–148
    integrating with NTFS permissions, 149–156
    testing, 148–149
  publishing, in Active Directory, 182–184
  shared name, 141
Sharing tab, printer, 175
Shiva Password Authentication Protocol (SPAP), 413
shutdown, Viewing Shutdown Events in Event Viewer System Log, 7–8
Shutdown Event Tracker, 6
SID. *See* Security Identifier
signing. *See* driver signing

Simple Mail Transfer Protocol (SMTP), 216, 219
site, Active Directory, 22
site link, 22
slipstreaming. *See also* service pack
service pack, 50
SMTP. *See* Simple Mail Transfer Protocol
snap-ins
MMC, 8, 11–12, 222
in IIS, 223–225
software. *See also* application; hardware; utilities
Group Policy
assigning an application, 129–131
deployment, 129
in general, 128
maintenance, 131–132
preparation, 128–129
publishing an application, 129–131
removal, 132–133
restriction policies, 105
Terminal Services client software, 137
utilities
administrator utilities, 15
net utility, 5
SPAP. *See* Shiva Password Authentication Protocol
SSL. *See* Secure Sockets Layer
startup procedures. *See also* logon process
advanced options
in general, 373–374
last known good configuration, 375–376
viewing and testing, 374–375
bootcfg.exe utility switches, 371
boot.ini file, viewing and editing, 372–373
troubleshooting, in general, 369–371
storage
basic vs. dynamic disks, 199–200
Creating Extended Partition and Logical Drive with Disk Management, 203
disk quota
configuring and managing, 206
discussed, 199, 204–205
in general, 199
volumes configuration, 200–202
subnet mask, TCP/IP and, 265
superscope. *See also* scope
DHCP, 287
creating, 287–289
Support Tools. *See also* utilities
installation, 15
.sys file, 45
System File Checker, 45
system log, 359, 360. *See also* System Monitor
viewing, 361–362
System Monitor. *See also* monitoring
adding counters, 352–354
exploring, 349–351
in general, 348
performance objects, 348
Performance Logs and Alerts tool, 354
performance objects and counters, 351–352
adding counters, 352–354
Saving and Viewing Data, 354–355
using, 349
System services, 104
System State back up. *See also* back up
discussed, 382–384

T

Task Manager. *See also* monitoring
Applications tab, 362
in general, 362–364
Networking tab, 363
Performance tab, 363
Processes tab, 363
using, 364–365
Task Scheduler, 5
using, 15
taskpad, creating, in MMC, 11–13
TCP. *See* Transmission Control Protocol
TCP/IP. *See* transmission control protocol/Internet protocol
template. *See also* Security Policy template
administrative template, 98–99
Terminal Services, 391. *See also* remote access
client software, 437
configuring, 430
user properties, 437
exploring, 434–436
user account settings, 438–439
installing, 432–433
managing, configuring remote connection settings, 433–434
TGT. *See* ticket-granting ticket
ticket-granting ticket (TGT), 103
Trace Logs, 355
tracert command
TCP and, 262
troubleshooting with, 274–275
Transmission Control Protocol/Internet Protocol (TCP/IP), 3, 260. *See also* Internet Protocol; Transmission Control Protocol
configuration
automatic private IP addressing, 267–269
dynamic configuration, 267
in general, 265
manual configuration, 267
static IP address, 266
installing, 263
troubleshooting
in general, 269
ipconfig, 269–271
netdiag command, 278–280
pathping command, 275–277
ping command, 272–274
route command, 277–278
tracert command, 274–275
verifying configurations, 269–270
verifying connectivity, 271–272, 272–274, 275–277, 277–278, 278–280
Transmission Control Protocol (TCP). *See also* File Transfer Protocol
Address Resolution Protocol
cache entries, 261–262
in general, 261
ICMP and, 262
IGMP and, 263
IP and, 263
architecture, 260
FTP and, 239
in general, 259, 260
protocol stack
Address Resolution Protocol, 261
in general, 260–261
User Datagram Protocol, 261
trees. *See also* Active Directory
forests and, 19–21
forest root domain, 19
forest, 19
transitive trust, 19
tree, 19
troubleshooting. *See also* auditing; hot fix; monitoring; recovery console; service pack
connectivity
client access problems, 253
in general, 254
DNS
DNSCMD.EXE utility, 337–339
in general, 337, 340
Group Policy, 3
in general, 125
with Gpresult.exe, 126–127
with Resultant Set of Policy tool, 127–128
ICS, 429–430
last known good configuration, 375–376
name resolution files, in general, 335–336
NAT, 426

netdiag, 15
network troubleshooting process, 4–5
define the problem, 4–5
devise a plan, 5
documentation, 5
gather information, 5
ping command, 262, 272–274
printer, 170, 180–181
remote access, 416, 422
startup procedures, in general, 269–371
TCP/IP
in general, 269
netdiag command, 278–280
pathping command, 275–277
ping command, 272–274
route command, 277–278
tracert command, 274–275
verifying configurations, 269–270
verifying connectivity, 271–272
Windows Server 2003, 4
.ttf file, 45

U

UDP. *See* User Datagram Protocol
UNIX, 32
update. *See also* upgrade
DNS updates, 326–327
with hot fix and service pack, in general, 48–49
Internet Information Services, 248
Microsoft Windows Update Advisor, 35–36
originating update, 86
Quick Fix Engineering, 48
replicated update, 86
replication latency, 86
Windows Update
Microsoft Baseline Security Analyzer, 50
using, 49–50
Web site, 45, 48
upgrade, Microsoft Windows Upgrade Advisor, 34
UPN. *See* user principle name
user account. *See also* Active Directory
attributes modification, 65–67
creating in AD, 62–63
domain user account, 63–65
defined, 62
Terminal Services settings, 438–439
user rights assignment, 104
User Datagram Protocol (UDP), TCP and, 261
user principle name (UPN), logon process, 21, 63
utilities. *See also* software
administrator utilities, 15
net command, 15
netdiag, 15
Windows Server 2003 Task Scheduler, 15
File Signature Verification, 44–45
IIS Lockdown Tool, 248
Microsoft Baseline Security Analyzer, 50
net utility, 5
Support Tools installation, 15
System File Checker, 45

V

virtual directory. *See also* virtual server; Web site
creating and configuring, 232–234, 242–243
in general, 232
alias, 232
virtual private network (VPN), 4. *See also* remote connection
configuration
client configuration, 406–411
in general, 404–406
discussed, 391, 392, 403–404
server configuration, 404
virtual server. *See also* server
creating, 226
host header, 226
FTP server
creating, 241–243
in general, 238
properties configuration, 239–240
testing default site, 240–241
Visual Basic, scripts, 222
volumes configuration, 200–202. *See also* storage
mirrored volume, 202
RAID-5 volume, 202
simple volume, 202
spanned volume, 202
striped volume, 202
VPN. *See* virtual private network

W

Web folder. *See also* folder
Access Permissions, 249–250
configuring, 250
creating and modifying, 252–254
defined, 252
Web site. *See also* virtual directory
authentication
anonymous access, 235
basic authentication, 235
configuring and testing, 236
configuring Server Certificates and Secure Sockets Layer, 237–238
digest authentication, 234
in general, 234
integrated Windows authentication, 235
.NET Passport authentication, 236
creating
with iisweb.vbs script, 228–229
with Web Site Creation Wizard, 226–228
default Web site, 222
properties
configuring, 230–232
modifying, 229–230
virtual server, creating, 226
Windows 2000
mixed mode, 71
native mode, 71
Windows Explorer, shared folder creation, 140–142
Windows File Protection, 45
Windows Internet Name Service (WINS), 336
Windows NT
BDCs, 71
disk counters, 352
Windows Server 2003. *See also* network administration
configuring, 367–369
in general, 1–2
installation planning, 32
Logging on to Windows 2003 and Changing Password, 5
management tools, 5–6
MMC, 5
monitoring and troubleshooting, 4
Restarting Windows Server 2003, 6–7
Task Scheduler, 15
WINS. *See* Windows Internet Name Service
Wireless Network (IEEE 802.11) policies, 104

X

XML. *See* Extensible Markup Language

Z

ZAP file, 128
zone file, 305
zone transfer, 306

Microsoft® Windows® Server 2003 Enterprise Edition 180-Day Evaluation

The software included in this kit is intended for evaluation and deployment planning purposes only. If you plan to install the software on your primary machine, it is recommended that you back up your existing data prior to installation.

System requirements

To use Microsoft Windows Server 2003 Enterprise Edition, you need:

- Computer with 550 MHz or higher processor clock speed recommended; 133 MHz minimum required; Intel Pentium/Celeron family, or AMD K6/Athlon/Duron family, or compatible processor (Windows Server 2003 Enterprise Edition supports up to eight CPUs on one server)
- 256 MB of RAM or higher recommended; 128 MB minimum required (maximum 32 GB of RAM)
- 1.25 to 2 GB of available hard-disk space*
- CD-ROM or DVD-ROM drive
- Super VGA (800 × 600) or higher-resolution monitor recommended; VGA or hardware that supports console redirection required
- Keyboard and Microsoft Mouse or compatible pointing device, or hardware that supports console redirection

Additional items or services required to use certain Windows Server 2003 Enterprise Edition features:

- For Internet access:
  - Some Internet functionality may require Internet access, a Microsoft Passport account, and payment of a separate fee to a service provider; local and/or long-distance telephone toll charges may apply
  - High-speed modem or broadband Internet connection
- For networking:
  - Network adapter appropriate for the type of local-area, wide-area, wireless, or home network to which you wish to connect, and access to an appropriate network infrastructure; access to third-party networks may require additional charges

Note: To ensure that your applications and hardware are Windows Server 2003–ready, be sure to visit **www.microsoft.com/windowsserver2003**.

* Actual requirements will vary based on your system configuration and the applications and features you choose to install. Additional available hard-disk space may be required if you are installing over a network. For more information, please see **www.microsoft.com/windowsserver2003**.

Uninstall instructions

This time-limited release of Microsoft Windows Server 2003 Enterprise Edition will expire 180 days after installation. If you decide to discontinue the use of this software, you will need to reinstall your original operating system. You may need to reformat your drive.

© 2003 Microsoft Corporation. All rights reserved.
Microsoft and Windows are either registered trademarks or trademarks of Microsoft Corporation in the United States and/or other countries.
0103 Part No. X09-41357

Microsoft®